THE
SCIENCE
OF MIND

The Complete Edition

JEREMY P. TARCHER/PENGUIN

a member of Penguin Group (USA) Inc.

New York

THE
SCIENCE
OF MIND

The Complete Edition

ERNEST HOLMES

FOREWORD BY KATHY HEARN

INTRODUCTION BY THE REVEREND JESSE JENNINGS

JEREMY P. TARCHER/PENGUIN
Published by the Penguin Group
Penguin Group (USA) Inc., 375 Hudson Street, New York, New York 10014, USA · Penguin Group (Canada),
90 Eglinton Avenue East, Suite 700, Toronto, Ontario M4P 2Y3, Canada (a division of Pearson Penguin Canada Inc.) ·
Penguin Books Ltd, 80 Strand, London WC2R 0RL, England · Penguin Ireland, 25 St Stephen's Green, Dublin 2, Ireland (a division of
Penguin Books Ltd) · Penguin Group (Australia), 250 Camberwell Road, Camberwell, Victoria 3124, Australia (a division of
Pearson Australia Group Pty Ltd) · Penguin Books India Pvt Ltd, 11 Community Centre, Panchsheel Park, New Delhi–110 017,
India · Penguin Group (NZ), 67 Apollo Drive, Rosedale, North Shore 0632, New Zealand (a division of Pearson New Zealand Ltd) ·
Penguin Books (South Africa) (Pty) Ltd, 24 Sturdee Avenue, Rosebank, Johannesburg 2196, South Africa

Penguin Books Ltd, Registered Offices: 80 Strand, London WC2R 0RL, England

The Science of Mind originally published in 1926
The Science of Mind revised and enlarged, copyright © 1938 by The United Church of Religious Science
First Jeremy P. Tarcher/Penguin edition of both editions in one volume 2010

Most Tarcher/Penguin books are available at special quantity discounts for bulk purchase
for sales promotions, premiums, fund-raising, and educational needs. Special books or book
excerpts also can be created to fit specific needs. For details, write Penguin Group (USA) Inc.
Special Markets, 375 Hudson Street, New York, NY 10014.

Library of Congress Cataloging-in-Publication Data

Holmes, Ernest, 1887–1960.
The science of mind: the complete edition / Ernest Holmes.
p.   cm.
"Both the 1926 and the 1938 versions of *The Science of Mind* in one complete edition"—Foreword.
ISBN 978-1-58542-842-7
1. New Thought.   I. Title.
BF639.H635   2010   2010039320
299'.93—dc22

Printed in the United States of America
1   3   5   7   9   10   8   6   4   2

Book design by Stephanie Huntwork and Nicole LaRoche

Neither the publisher nor the author is engaged in rendering professional advice or services to the individual reader. The ideas,
procedures, and suggestions contained in this book are not intended as a substitute for consulting with your physician. All matters
regarding your health require medical supervision. Neither the author nor the publisher shall be liable or responsible for any loss
or damage allegedly arising from any information or suggestion in this book.

While the author has made every effort to provide accurate telephone numbers and Internet addresses at the time of publication,
neither the publisher nor the author assumes any responsibility for errors, or for changes that occur after publication. Further, the
publisher does not have any control over and does not assume any responsibility for author or third-party websites or their content.

Contents

Foreword by Kathy Hearn — ix

Introduction by The Reverend Jesse Jennings — xi

About Ernest Holmes — xv

THE SCIENCE OF MIND *Original 1926 Text* — 1

THE SCIENCE OF MIND *1938 Edition* — 293

Index — 759

Foreword

It is a tremendous boon to have both the 1926 and the 1938 versions of *The Science of Mind* in one complete edition and available to current and future students and explorers of this life-transforming spiritual philosophy. The more familiar 1938 edition, what many affectionately call "the textbook," has been a deeply loved and cherished agent of awakening and learning for people around the world for the past seventy-two years. It was this book that first opened me to an awareness of the Allness of God, my oneness with Life, and the holiness/wholeness of my own being. It was through these pages that I learned that my thoughts are creative, that I attract what is like my thinking, and that I alone—and no one else—set the limit to my demonstrations of good or expand beyond them. It was in this book that I found a spiritual approach to the challenges of daily living, along with the realization that who I am in God, and what God is in me, are greater than anything I am going through. Here I discovered that I am on earth to walk a path of successive realizations toward full expression of the God-being I have always been. As I look at the underlining and marginal notes I made as a beginning student, I remember the amazement I felt as I read for the first time, on page after page, the articulation of what I believed about God and Life. I thought I was the only one who thought this way! It was wonderful to realize that there was an entire spiritual philosophy and practice for living these spiritual ideas. Through years of ministry, I have turned to the text for speaking and teaching themes, meditations, illustrations, readings, quotations, and metaphysical Bible interpretations. My book became so well used a number of years ago that students of mine had it re-bound for me. Through time the text stands at the center of my spiritual life and work.

Several years into my experience of Science of Mind, I learned about the 1926 edition, referred to as "the original"—or as we might call it today, "the rough, uncut version." This edition has a more personal feeling, with Ernest Holmes making "I" statements and offering the reader insight into his process and realizations. He refers to the authors and thinkers whose works influenced him and thereby gives us an expanded sense of legacy. And he occasionally offers advice to students, transmitting truth to those seeking it. The most discussed chapters contain information and ideas left out of the 1938 edition. In Lesson Six of the 1926 edition, Holmes articulates various kinds of psychic phenomena, cautions about misuse of mental powers, and distinguishes between the mystic and the psychic senses. Toward the end of the book we find special articles on the meaning of true love, the emotion of sex, sublimation and repression and the conflict of desire. What we see in the 1926 edition is material that is less ordered, formalized, and distilled. Yet it reveals the breadth of Holmes's study and the full range of his exploration of the human and divine aspects of our being. One thing we witness in comparing the two editions is his evolution from exploring the powers of mind to asserting the Power of Mind—encouraging all of us to "see through the mist to the Eternal and Changeless Reality."

The tendency for us might be to feel that we must decide on a favorite edition, choosing one over the other. But the great blessing of *The Science of Mind: The Complete Edition* is that we do not have to do this. Rather, we can read the two together and discover the unique value of each. And in doing so we may arrive at an even deeper appreciation for the man, Ernest Holmes. As we walk our own paths of realization and transformation we see how he awakened and changed, all the while seeking to give words to the great spiritual revelations that filled him and then make them relevant and practicable for daily spiritual living. How fortunate we are to be recipients and inheritors of this great work.

—*Kathy Hearn*
Community Spiritual Leader, United Centers for Spiritual Living

Introduction

Those who associate themselves with Ernest Holmes's work are called Religious Scientists, and to them this is their "textbook." Until the 1980s, many were unaware there had been an earlier edition than that of 1938, much less that it had contained plenty of eye-opening material that was edited out of the second edition. Here at last, in one volume, are both books.

The Science of Mind was originally published in November 1926, by Robert M. McBride & Company of New York, and copyrighted not by Holmes himself but by his mother, Anna. Robert McBride had an interest in spiritual matters, being the son of the president of the American Bible Union, and his publishing house had brought out Ernest Holmes's first two books, *Creative Mind* and *Creative Mind and Success*, as well as his brother Fenwicke's *The Law of Mind in Action*. The company also published adventure novelist Sax Rohmer, fantasist James Cabell, and poet laureate Louise Bogan, while McBride himself wrote popular geographies of European countries.

The Science of Mind did well enough that McBride reprinted twice in 1928 and once in 1929. Then it apparently dropped out of print. This may have been due to the economic climate of the Depression, or perhaps demand was momentarily exhausted, since at that time Holmes's work was little known anywhere but on the West Coast. In any event, it was nine years until a new printing appeared (Holmes was working on it as early as 1936), by which time it had been thoroughly revised, and was about 250 pages longer.

For the 1938 edition Holmes had a collaborator, and a highly competent one at that, Maude Allison Lathem, who for many years edited the Institute of Religious Science's monthly *Science of Mind* magazine. Lathem had just partnered with Alberta Smith on a delightful volume of inspirational articles, *I Lift My Lamp* (1937), published under the Institute's own imprint. Smith had previously worked with Holmes, too, on *Questions and Answers on the Science of Mind*. Holmes's great strengths were as speaker and teacher—in person he had enormous charisma. But his thoughts when written tended to seem formal, even stiff. So he needed a hand, and down through the years Lathem, Smith, Fenwicke Holmes, and Willis Kinnear pitched in on his projects.

The 1926 textbook version was a series of lessons, the introductions to which were then grouped together as the general introduction in the 1938 volume. Diagrams in the middle of the 1926 volume went into the appendix of the 1938 edition. Daily meditations and a glossary appeared in the same location in each. But the main change was seen in the extraction of the whole sixth lesson, on psychic phenomena. Fenwicke explains, in his biography of his brother: "When his revision omitted this, he felt no loss of personal conviction as to the authenticity of psychic phenomena but that it was developing into a separate field of research." Also removed out from the earlier edition is the section on "Repression and Sublimation" which discusses emotion, libido, and the creative urge. Were discussions of sex and spiritualism deemed so indelicate or incendiary as to pose a hindrance to wider readership? This seems unlikely. Holmes never apologized for his thoughts. As it turns out, the material edited out of the 1926 text wasn't erased altogether, or even lost in a file cabinet. It can be found intact in the "Extension Study Course on the Science of Mind," fifty-two lessons, typewritten, first issued to correspondence students in 1939, and containing a lot more interesting material besides, such as papers by an academic on the mysteries of ancient Egypt, Rome, and the Gallic druids. In effect, it was lifted out of the introductory material and put in the hands of more dedicated students who would read it in an appropriate framing context. (The same thing was later done with practitioner training material, in the form of a "Clinical Course.") But now it is all back where we can easily get our hands on it.

Ernest Holmes made a regular point throughout his career of declaring that he had received no special spiritual revelation; that, in fact, he didn't believe in special revelations, or miracles, or the supernatural. To him, everyone was a revealer of truth. A miracle is a law-abiding event even when most may be oblivious of the law behind it ("Only those things are mysterious which we do not understand," he wrote.) "Nature" encompasses the paranormal and extraordinary, the arcane as well as the mundane. Within human nature is the resting place of the Divine as it relates to humanity, and one should look within the self for whatever one seeks. If anything appears to impede the experience of the sacred, it is only one's own unhealed emotional and psychological issues getting in the way, which is better recognized than ignored, to render them accessible to be addressed and transformed from fear into faith.

Holmes's was a science of spiritual psychology. But just as it wasn't a supernatural revelation, nor was it, he said, merely his own opinion, but the condensed wisdom of all time: "We should take Truth wherever we find it, making it our very own. Borrowing knowledge of Reality from all sources, taking the best from every study, Science of Mind brings together the highest enlightenment of the ages."

When Joseph Campbell bought a copy of *The Science of Mind*, it served as his "first introduction to a version of what Aldous Huxley called the Perennial Philosophy," according to his biographers Stephen and Robin Larsen. Campbell often attended lectures by Fenwicke Holmes. At one of these he asked a question about how to achieve success, and heard it suggested that he jot down notes from his interior dialogue, to find if all his interests would point in one certain direction. As the Larsens tell us, "This would be the precise technique that would allow Campbell, at a later stage of his development, to know that it was 'mythology' that would be his subject." His enormous achievements in that field were brought into the mainstream by the 1988 Bill Moyers interviews on PBS, which were filmed mostly at Skywalker Ranch; George Lucas had been inspired from reading Campbell to capture and evoke the spirit of the mythic hero's journey in his Star Wars films.

Thus every child everywhere who swings a light saber or drones, "Luke, I am your father," unwittingly invokes the universal quest for meaning and purpose as each individual's divine inheritance. At the same time, a specific piece of modern theater is performed, resulting from a series of fortuitous encounters between certain teachers and students—or more exactly, Holmes would say, the eternal circulation of certain truths is the collective consciousness of our species, which each of us may be privileged to host.

There is a school of thought—a school to which this book in your hands has very mightily contributed—that there are no accidents, that everything happens for a reason though that reason might be larger than one's present capacity to grasp it, and that, in Emerson's words, "We are begirt with spiritual laws which execute themselves." Read on, and may that which you seek come rushing to meet you.

—The Reverend Jesse Jennings

About Ernest Holmes

He began life the youngest of nine sons of William Nelson and Anna Columbia Heath Holmes, in a mill and quarry town near Maine's Penobscot River. Eighty-five years earlier, only seventy miles downstate, had been born Phineas Quimby, arguably the originator of the metaphysical healing movement in America. Ernest Holmes would come to know Quimby's work through his brief association with that of Mary Baker Eddy, Quimby's onetime patient/student and founder of the Church of Christ, Scientist, in Boston, with its array of publishing ventures. Eddy's best-known protégée, but whom she soon fired, was Emma Curtis Hopkins, who moved to Chicago to write and teach for many years her own understanding of Christian Science. Then, not long before her death, Hopkins took rooms at the Iroquois Hotel on West Forty-fourth Street in Manhattan, and welcomed her last private student into a two-week series of conversations that changed his life and, in the long run, many people's lives.

This student was Ernest Holmes, who was advancing the newest New Thought teaching vehicle, an organization he called the Institute of Religious Science. Holmes brought roses to his meetings with Hopkins and noted that she always wore a hat. Concurrently, just up the block, Algonquin Round Table members fashioned the popular culture of the day over their daily lunches. This was 1924. Holmes had two books in print, and *The Science of Mind* would soon follow.

He had gone West originally in 1912, with his mother, to help out brother Fenwicke, a Congregationalist minister assigned to a new church in Venice, California. All three then began, or continued, studying metaphysics, primarily via a correspondence course from Christian D. Larson, and the essays and lectures of Emerson and Thomas Troward. The brothers put together a magazine called *Uplift* (now *Science of Mind*) and tried their hands at a "metaphysical sanitarium" in Long Beach, though their involvement with that lasted about a year.

When Fenwicke left his pastorate to strike out on his own, Ernest accompanied him, and they toured the country as inspirational speakers on the power of the mind to heal. After his tutorial with Hopkins, Ernest returned to Southern California and for the most part remained there, speaking to increasing numbers of people at various venues, teaching classes, writing books, and administering the Institute of Religious Science and its magazine.

The nub of Holmes's teaching was that "there is a Power for good in the universe greater than you are, and you can use It." He arrived at this conclusion by virtue of his own intuitive sense that it was true; by a survey of the faith systems of the world that bore out the existence of an inner, mystical body of knowledge overlooked by most of their adherents; and by the practical application of both sets of knowledge in the lives of the people who came to him seeking answers. He believed that prayer was an act of science, neither arbitrary nor merit-based. If you could bring yourself to believe, then the universal creative process believed with you, and your belief would demonstrate itself in tangible form as changed conditions. This was not a Christian science exclusively, although Holmes often praised Jesus as recorded history's most gifted exponent of it. But your deity could be a cloud or a stone, for all that it mattered. The key was merely believing that something happened whenever you prayed. Holmes *believed in belief*.

People by the thousands, of every religious persuasion or none at all, came to hear him. They felt his teaching brought them peace of mind, and its application bettered their lot in life, and after a while some said he should start his own religion. At this Holmes balked, being a modest individual who thought the world had enough religions and just needed to practice them. Then the prospect of carrying the teaching forward beyond his time began to pull at him. The Institute gradually shifted into a church organization, its licensed practitioners (a concept borrowed from Eddy's structure) now being joined by licensed or ordained clergy, who fanned out up and down the West Coast, and thence countrywide.

The Institute's Los Angeles–area headquarters always felt—and at intervals was—just steps away from the mass media centers of the world. Holmes and his associates acted as unofficial spiritual advisors to many of the Hollywood set for fifty years. But he never sought to capitalize on this, never parlayed his connections into great fame, or more than moderate wealth.

While his work has had an incalculable subtle influence throughout American society, relatively few people know his name.

Holmes passed on in April 1960, leaving no appointed successor, and an organization that perpetually reinvents itself to more efficiently relay the legacy of his liberating and empowering teaching, "shorn of dogmatism, freed from superstition, open at the top for greater illumination." Today there are several hundred established Science of Mind meeting-places (now known as "Centers for Spiritual Living"), where the emphasis remains on the teaching of classes and the daily application of the principle that all life is One life.

—The Reverend Jesse Jennings

THE
SCIENCE
OF MIND

Original 1926 Text

These lessons are dedicated to that Truth
which frees man from himself and sets him on the pathway
of a new experience, which enables him to see
through the mist to the Eternal and Changeless Reality,

PEACE BE UNTO THEE, STRANGER

Peace be unto thee, stranger, enter and be not afraid.

I have left the gate open and thou art welcome to my home.

There is room in my house for all.

I have swept the hearth and lighted the fire.

The room is warm and cheerful and you will find comfort and rest
within.

The table is laid and the fruits of Life are spread before thee.

The wine is here also, it sparkles in the light.

I have set a chair for you where the sunbeams dance through the
shade.

Sit and rest and refresh your soul.

Eat of the fruit and drink the wine.

All, all is yours, and you are welcome.

Foreword

In presenting these lessons on Mental Science, I do not claim to have discovered any new Truth. The Truth has been known in every age by a few; but the great mass of people has never even dreamed that we live in a mental and spiritual world. To-day, however, there is a great inquiry into the deeper meaning of life because the race has reached a state of unfoldment where a broader scope is possible.

These lessons are an attempt to put into the spoken word and into print some of those great truths known to the enlightened of all ages.

To suppose that the Creative Intelligence of the world would create man in bondage and leave him bound would be to dishonor that Creative Power which we call God. On the other hand, to suppose that God could make man as an individual, without leaving him to discover himself, would be to suppose an impossibility. Individuality must be spontaneous and can never be automatic. The seed of freedom must be hid within the shell of the human. But, like the Prodigal of old, man must make the great discovery for himself. Although the journey may at times seem hard and the burden too great to bear, man still feels within a subtle sense, a mystical presence, a divine Reality. Thus, the inherent nature of himself is forever seeking to express itself in terms of freedom. We will do well to listen to this inner voice, for it tells us of a life wonderful in its scope, of a love beyond our fondest dreams, of a freedom which the soul craves.

But the great love of the Universe must be one with the great law of Its own Being, and we must approach love through the law.

This, then, is the teaching,—Love and Law. As the love of God is perfect, so the law of God is also perfect. We must understand both, "Who hath ears to hear, let him hear."

I wish to express my appreciation to the authors whose names are mentioned following the different lessons in this course of instruction, as well as to many others whose names are not mentioned. The Truth comes to us from all sources, and our understanding of it is the result of the time, thought and effort of thousands of people who have given their lives to its study.

I wish to express special appreciation to Miss Anne Shipman, of Boston, Mass., without whose untiring efforts it is not probable that these manuscripts would have ever been gotten in shape for publication; and to my mother whose great faith in these teachings has inspired me with the hope and the belief that they may be of benefit to those who study them.

E.S.H.

Contents

Peace Be Unto Thee, Stranger   4

Foreword   5

Yourself   17

Part One

THE EVOLUTION OF MAN'S THOUGHT

19

Instinctive Man • Nature Waits on Man's Self-recognition • The First Great Discovery • The Inner Sense Awakens • The Great Question "Why" • The Greatest Discovery of All Time—MIND • The Brain Does Not Think • We Do Not See the Thinker • The Body Unconscious Without the Thinker • The Conscious and the Unconscious Thought • A New Basis of Thought • The Law of Mind • Unconscious Mind at Work • Another Great Discovery—Thought Reached Others • The Discovery of Race-Thought • A Universal Medium Which All Must Come to Believe In • Another Question Comes Up—Why Are People Poor? • Man Begins to Realize That His Conditions Are Controlled by Thought • Realizes That He Must Think Correctly

Part Two

THE LESSONS

LESSON ONE: INTRODUCTION   28

Science • How Laws Are Discovered • Proof of Mind • Where Our Thoughts Go • Suggestion Becomes Memory • Mental Medium Through All • Reading Thought • Mental Law • The Word of God as Law • Threefold Nature of God • Trinity of Being • Conscious Mind in God and Man • Unity • Worship of God • Many Gods • Belief in Duality—Its Results • Duality in Theology • Duality in Philosophy • Duality and Science • An Awakening • Philosophy Leads Man's Thought • A Deep Inquiry • The Great Difficulty • The Voice of God in Creation • The Word of God • Spirit Knows Itself • Law, Servant of the Word • Forms of Spirit or Creation • Meaning of Creation • The Word Alone Is Conscious • The Thought of God • Eternal Creation • The Universe Is Alive • Conclusion

LESSON ONE: METAPHYSICAL CHART NO. I   41

LESSON ONE: METAPHYSICAL MEANING OF WORDS USED IN UNIVERSAL CHART   42

Upper Section • Middle Section • Lowest Section

LESSON ONE: THE NATURE OF BEING   53

Spirit • Soul • Two Ways of Reasoning • Body • The Changeless • Cause and Effect • Unity and Multiplicity • Immortality • Forms • Allness of Truth • Volition • Only One Mind • Individuality

LESSON ONE: RECAPITULATION   60

LESSON TWO: INTRODUCTION   62

The World Has Learned All It Can Through Suffering • What Individuality Really Means • The Meaning of Freedom • Sin and Punishment. Righteousness and Reward • The Incarnation of Spirit • Different Viewpoints • The Lesson of Nature's Laws • The Relation of Man to the Universe of Spirit • Man's Experience • Nature Waits on Man • Mental and Spiritual Laws • God and Man • Man Reënacts the Nature of God • The Two Ways to Reason • Nothing Happens by Chance • Many Are Waking Up to the Facts • The Time Has Come to Know the Truth • A Wonderful Experiment • What Psychology Teaches About Man's Nature • The Self-knowing Mind • Man's Unity with the Whole • Man a Center of God-Consciousness • Unity with Law • The Subjective Obeys the Objective • The Body • Last

Stages of Matter • The Unity of All Body • The Formless and the Formed • Individuality Means Self-Choice • The Greatest Discovery Ever Made • A Complete Unity

LESSON TWO: METAPHYSICAL CHART NO. II-A   *75*

LESSON TWO: METAPHYSICAL CHART NO. II-B   *76*

LESSON TWO: METAPHYSICAL MEANING OF
WORDS USED IN INDIVIDUAL CHART NO. II-B   *77*
  Upper Section • Middle Section • Lowest Section

LESSON TWO: THE NATURE OF MAN   *80*
  Spirit • Soul • Body • Limitless Medium • Christ and Antichrist • Man Is Identified in Mind • Treatment • The Aim of Evolution • Methods of Treatment • Subjective Law • Thought and the Creative Medium • Each Is the Logical Result of His Own Thinking • A Law of Belief • We Are Dealing with Law • The Cycle of Necessity and Karmic Law • The Law of Action and Reaction • We Argue in Mind • Wrong Use of Mind • Subjective but Not Unconscious • How Habits Are Formed • Law Is Mind in Action • We Are Bound by Our Own Freedom • Oneness with All Law • Demonstration • Karmic Law • Thought Force • Choosing Thought • Inducing Thought • Place No Limit on Principle

LESSON TWO: RECAPITULATION   *98*

LESSON THREE: INTRODUCTION   *99*
  Healing • What We Understand About Healing • Thoughts Are Things

LESSON THREE: METAPHYSICAL CHART NO. III   *103*

LESSON THREE: METAPHYSICAL MEANING
OF WORDS USED IN CHART NO. III   *104*

LESSON THREE: MENTAL HEALING   *105*
  Individuality • Man Reënacts God • Not Limited by Principle • Mental Treatment Is Real • Man Comes Through Subjectivity • Born Perfect • Race-Suggestion • Disease Is Impersonal • How to Heal • Mind Is the Actor • Disease Is Not Always Due to Conscious Thought • We Deal with Ideas • Have No Doubts • Thinking in Treatment • Do Not Try to Go Beyond Your Understanding •

What a Practitioner Must Know • Healing Is Clear Thinking • Only One Law • No Sensation in Treatments • How to Remove Doubt • The Truth Demonstrates Itself • Disease Is Mental • The Medium of Healing • Depend on Principle • Definite Work in Healing • Repeating Treatments • Remove the Complex • Healing Pain • Headache • What Right Thought Does • How Habits Are Healed • The Seed of Thought • What Can Be Healed • Why People Get Tired • The Idea Must Take Form • Resolve Things into Thoughts • Healing Insanity • What a Practitioner Does • Back of the Appearance Is the Reality • Seeing Perfection • Healing Lung Trouble • We Do Not Send Out Thoughts • Vision • Healing Constipation • Disease Not an Entity • Throat Trouble • Congestion • Paralysis • Growths • Treating Children • Power of the Word • No Age • Memory • Guidance in Treating • How to Heal • Remove Doubt • No Fear • Psycho-analysis • Deal Only with Thoughts • Nervousness • Stammering • Argument in Treatment

LESSON THREE: RECAPITULATION   *132*

LESSON FOUR: INTRODUCTION   *134*
The Law Is Infinite • The Possibilities of the Law • Spirit and Mental Law • Demonstration, or Bringing Things to Pass • Our Part • Treatment • Medium Between Man and His Manifestation

LESSON FOUR: METAPHYSICAL CHART NO. IV   *139*

LESSON FOUR: THE CONTROL OF CONDITIONS   *140*
Law of Reflection • Attracting Friends • The Principle of Prosperity • We Deal with Absoluteness • Prayer Is Its Own Answer • If You Know • No Personal Responsibility • Helping an Inventor • Look Only at What You Want • Definite Plan • Attraction • How to Demonstrate a Home • Resist Not • Healing a Misunderstanding • Fate • Attraction of Personality • See Life Expressed • Look to the Ultimate • No Mistakes • Causes and Conditions • Perfect Action • Mental Equivalents • Treating for Activity • Receiving Information • No Failures • Opportunity • No Mistakes • Demonstration by Proof • Handling a Schoolroom • The Law of Correspondence

LESSON FOUR: RECAPITULATION   *156*

LESSON FIVE: INTRODUCTION   *158*
True Mysticism and the Psychic Sense • What the Mystics Have Taught • No Ultimate Evil • Ultimate Salvation of All • Freedom from Burden • Unity of All • Realization of Individuality • Normalcy • The Great Light • What the Mystics Have Taught About the Individual • Instinct and Intuition • Illumination and Cosmic Consciousness • The Highest Practice • The Power of Jesus • Turning Within

LESSON FIVE: METAPHYSICAL CHART NO. V   *167*

LESSON FIVE: THE PERFECT WHOLE   *168*
  Individuality • Further Evolution • The Truth Is Known • The Answer Is in Man • God—Infinite
  Personality • Unity • Hold to the Good • The Infinite Is Personal to All • The Christ • Realization •
  Meditation

LESSON SIX: THE LAW OF PSYCHIC
PHENOMENA—INTRODUCTION   *177*
  Psychic Phenomena and Immortality • No Apologies

LESSON SIX: METAPHYSICAL CHART NO. VI   *179*

LESSON SIX: METAPHYSICAL MEANING OF
WORDS USED IN CHART NO. VI   *180*

LESSON SIX: PSYCHIC PHENOMENA   *180*
  The Subjective Mind • Seat of Memory • Suggestion and Subjectivity • Subjective Communication •
  Subjective Mind and Inspiration • Mental Atmospheres • How to Create Personal Charm • The
  Atmosphere of Places • The Race-Mind • The Mind of History • Telepathy • Tuning In on
  Thought • Mental Pictures • Conditions Necessary for the Best Results • Deep Telepathic Messages •
  Reading the History of the Individual • Personal Readings • Streams of Consciousness • No
  Obstructions to Thought • Entering the Stream of Thought • The Vibration of a Book • Why Saints
  Have Seen Jesus • Many Mental Pictures • The Human Aura • Halo • Unpleasant Atmospheres •
  Habit • Mania • Obsession • Personal Influence and Obsession • Obsession of Discarnate Spirits •
  General Theory of Obsession and Mental Influence • Insanity • The Psychic Power Must Be
  Controlled • Normal State • The Aim of Evolution • The State of Trance • Normal Psychic
  Capacities • Abnormal Psychic Powers • Clairvoyance • Psychometry • Clairaudience • Independent
  Voices • Apparitions • Ghosts and Phantasms of the Dead • Ghosts Sometimes Can Speak • Projecting
  the Mentality • Crystal Gazing • Black Magic • The Modern Curse • Automatic Writing •
  Independent Writing • Hudson's Theory • Smelling Where There Is Nothing to Smell • Grasping
  Objects Without the Hand • Telekinetic Energy • Table Tipping • Rappings • Theory of Ectoplasm •
  Levitation • Interesting Thoughts • What Is the Cause? • Cause for Thought • Time Will Prove All
  Things • The Spirit of Prophecy • A Lesson in Subjectivity • Explanation • Summary

LESSON SIX: PSYCHIC PHENOMENA AND IMMORTALITY   *206*

The Meaning of Immortality • Where Did Man Come from and Why? • Man Awakes with a Body • What Is the Body? • Matter • The Ether of Science • The Resurrection Body • Conclusive Facts • In What Mental State Do We Go Out? • What Causes Psychic Manifestations? • Telepathy Does Not Explain Everything • Spirit Communication • Communication Must Be Mental • We Do Not Control Spirits • The Psychic Power Should Not Be Forced

LESSON SIX: RECAPITULATION   *213*

Immortality

Part Three

SPECIAL ARTICLES

ABSOLUTENESS AND RELATIVITY   *217*

THE PROBLEM OF EVIL   *218*

THE MEANING OF THE FALL   *219*

THE GARDEN OF EDEN   *219*

SALVATION AND GRACE   *220*

THE PERFECT UNIVERSE   *221*

IMAGINATION AND WILL   *221*

HOW TO VISUALIZE   *223*

THE SEQUENCE OF THE CREATIVE ORDER   *224*

MAN'S CREATIVE POWER MARVELOUS   *224*

CONCENTRATION   *224*

THE MIRROR OF THE SUBJECTIVE   225

PERSONALITY   227
Factors Necessary for a Dynamic Personality

REPRESSION AND SUBLIMATION   231
The Spirit of Sex • Desire • The Spirit Is Expressed • Man Reënacts the Divine Nature • Congested Emotions • Irritation, Agitation and Fear • If We Were Expressed • Emotion and Intellect • The Conflict of Desire • The Emotion of Sex • The True Meaning of Love • Sex Not Necessary to the Expression of Love • When Sex Becomes Destructive • Male and Female • The Solution • Psycho-analysis • Self-analysis • Metaphysics

THE ATONEMENT   238
Man's Whole Trouble • Careful Preparation • The Vicarious Atonement • The Givingness of Spirit • The World Has Learned All That It Should Through Suffering • Our Part in the Atonement

THE PERSONALITY OF GOD   242

JESUS AS A SAVIOUR   242

SELF-EXISTENT LIFE   243

THE SUPREME AFFIRMATION   243

CHRIST AND ANTICHRIST   244

EVOLUTION   244

Part Four

DAILY MEDITATIONS FOR SELF-HELP AND HEALING

BODILY PERFECTION   247
Come, and Let Me Heal You • He Is Mighty Within Me to Heal • I Do Not Inherit Disease •

No Congestion • No False Growth • No Weariness • Perfect Hearing • Perfect Vision • The All-seeing Eye • The Healing of the Flesh • There Is No Pain

COMPLETENESS   249

Happiness and Completion • Here and Now • Majestic Calm • No Loss • Oh, for a Tongue to Express • O Soul of Mine, Look Out and See • Seeing the Perfect • The Circle Is Complete • The Things That Are

DIVINE COMPANIONSHIP   251

A Song of Hope • Be Still and Know • Cast Aside All Doubt • Divine Companionship • His Eye Is on the Sparrow • Hope Cannot Die • I Am Not Alone • I Went into a Mountain • The Joy of the Soul

FREEDOM   253

Freedom • Freedom from Sin • Free from Sensitiveness • I Keep the Promise • Love Gleams Through the Mist • No Bondage • No Condemnation • No False Habit • No Hypnotism Nor False Suggestion • No Mistakes • There Are No Responsibilities • The Time Has Come • Within Thy Law Is Freedom

HARMONY OF LIFE   256

Beauty • Friendship of the Spirit and of Man • He Wills Me to Be • I Serve • I Shall Not Doubt Nor Fear • I Was Told to Live • Law • Love • Love Dissolves All Fear • My Affairs • My Business • My Profession • No Delays • No Misrepresentations • No Obstructions • No Over-action Nor Inaction • One with Perfect Action • Peace, Poise and Power • Stillness and Receptivity • Thanksgiving and Praise • The Divine Promises Are Kept • The Inner Light • The Night Is Filled with Peace • The Seal of Approval • The Secret Way • The Shining Path • The Things I Need Come to Me • The Way Is Made Clear Before Me

IMMANENT POWER   262

As Love Enters, Fear Departs • He Will Keep Thee • Infinite Life Within • My Feet Shall Not Falter • No Harm Shall Befall Thee • Power to Live • The Circle of Love • The Circle of Protection • The Power Within Blesses All • The Quick Answer

INSPIRATION   264

A Song of Joy • Born of Eternal Day • I Arise and Go Forth • Inspiration • The Dawn Has Come • I Am Complete in Thee

PRESENCE OF THE ALL GOOD   *266*

A Marvelous Sense • Complete Confidence • Drawing the Good • I Fear No Evil • I Have Known, Always • I Meet My Good • My Atmosphere • My Good Is Complete • My Own Shall Come to Me • My Own Shall Find Me • My Soul Reflects Thy Life • Out of the Depths of Life • Sorrow Flees from Me • Substance and Supply • The Ever and the All • The House of Love

SPIRIT OF GOD WITHIN   *269*

Arise, My Spirit • Birthless and Deathless • Command My Soul • Despair Gives Way to Joy • Free Spirit Within Me • Fulness of Light • He Who Inhabits Eternity • I Listen • Joy Has Come to Live with Me • Knowledge and Wisdom • My Thought Is in Thee • O Love Divine • Peace Steals Through the Soul • Stand Forth and Speak • Subtle Essence of Spirit Within Me • The Christ Within • The Everlasting Arms • The Mantle of Love • The Voice of Truth • The Witness of Truth • Through the Long Night Watches • Thy Strength Is Sufficient • Waiting on Thee • Whose Right It Is to Come

THE POWER OF THE WORD   *275*

I Control My Mental Household and Conquer All Fear and Doubt • My Word Comes Back to Me • My Word Shall Bear Fruit • Nothing Can Hinder • O Man, Speak Forth Thy Word • The Power of the Word • The Word of Power • The Unassailable Truth and the Irresistible Word • I Behold in Thee His Image

UNITY   *277*

I See No Evil • I Shall Never Die • Love to the World • My Life Is One with God • No Misunderstandings • The Divine Plan for Me • The Personality of God • The Radiation of Life • Unity • Within Thee Is Fulness of Life

Glossary   *281*

The Call   *291*

YOURSELF

Oh, weary heart, laden with earth's weight and care,
Oh, feet, stumbling on the way, bleeding and bare,
Oh, arms outstretched, and hands upheld in prayer,
Oh, back, which so oft has felt the lash and rod,
Oh, soul, which cries aloud for the living God,
Oh, life, struggling to free itself from the clod;
Know this: there is no power from without,
Yourself must answer every fear and meet all doubt
With some divine, indwelling power
Which you yourself, upon yourself, shall shower;
And giving, take, and taking, give
Unto that life which you, yourself, shall live.

PART ONE

THE EVOLUTION OF MAN'S THOUGHT

INSTINCTIVE MAN

If we traced man's history back into the dim past we should come to a place where he did not consciously know himself. We should come to a place where Instinctive Man alone existed; for the self-conscious man had not yet evolved.

Nothing can be more apparent than that man, as he now appears, is the result of growth and unfoldment. But in order to unfold, he had to have something from which to unfold, and since he is intelligent, he must have unfolded from an intelligent cause.

Instinctive Man, then, means that Inner Something, or Life, which we do not see but which is, of course, there. We might say that Instinctive Life is God in man, or the idea of God, working through man. But if Instinctive Man is an idea of God, why is he not perfect? The answer is that he is perfect, but that as soon as individuality is evolved he must be left alone to discover himself. Even God could not make a mechanical individuality. If man is created with the attributes of self-choice and free will, he must be let alone to make the great discovery for himself.

Nature Waits on Man's Self-recognition

We note, that from the day when Instinctive Life brought man to the point of self-choice, it let him alone, and from that day Instinctive Life has waited on man's unfoldment. It is true that during all this time it has carried on the automatic functions of the body and has even silently told man what to do; but it has let him alone in all other ways. It may, and must, hold man as a perfect being, but it also must let him discover this fact for himself. During all of this time, however, Instinctive Life, or God, must be silently waiting for the great discovery to be made and must always be ready to respond to man's advancement. We note this to be true along the line of man's progress. For instance, consider the discovery of any of nature's forces; we know that they must have always existed; but, so far as man is concerned, they exist to him only after he has discovered, and learned how to make use of them. Electricity was a reality in the universe when Moses led the Children of Israel from the land of Egypt, but neither Moses nor any of his followers knew anything about it, and so they did not receive any benefits from its use. This is true of any and all of the natural laws; they always existed, and as soon as understood may be used. In this way, Instinctive Life waits upon man's discovery of the natural laws and his discovery of himself and his relationship to the great Whole.

If this is so evidently true of all the forces in the natural world we must expect to find the same thing to be true of those inner and finer forces within man. The unfoldment of these inner and finer forces through man is what we call his evolution.

The First Great Discovery

The first great discovery that man made was that he could think. This was the day when he rose from the ground and said, "I AM." This marked the first great day of personal attainment; and from that day man became an individual and had to make all further progress himself; any compulsory evolution stopped when man became an individual, and from that day he had to work in conscious union with Nature and Her forces; but he did not have to work alone, for Instinctive Life has always been with him and will never depart from him. Instinctive Life desires that man shall express more, and yet more, of its own limitless possibilities.

Man is evolving from an Infinite basis; behind him is the great Unknown but not the great unknowable; for the unknown becomes known through man, and whatever more Instinctive Life is to do for him must be done through him. Nature must work through man in order to work for him. This is true all along the line of life and endeavor.

The first great discovery of man was that he could think, plan and execute. As the result of this discovery he has built up a great civilization and all that goes with it. He has harnessed electricity to his inventions, tied steam and compelled it to do his bidding. He has laid waste forests, built cities, made the desert to bloom, and has thrown the lines of his commerce around the globe; indeed, he has seemed to possess the earth.

THE INNER SENSE AWAKENS

But with all of man's powers he has still felt a vague sense of something more, something greater, something further along; a sort of mystical inner sense of things, an instinctive urge, a blind groping after a greater light. Disregarding all of his apparent power, man has still been unhappy, sick, lonely and afraid. The cities which he built have crumbled into dust, the nations which he fostered have, one by one, fallen into ruin, and history alone remains to tell the tale of most of his endeavors.

In spite of man's apparent power he has suffered greatly, and death has crowned his life and work with a pall of darkness and uncertainty.

THE GREAT QUESTION "WHY"

The great question "Why" has forever been upon his lips. Few indeed have been able to answer this question; and these few have been passed by, unheeded, in the struggle for existence.

Man has struggled along the weary road with a heavy heart and bleeding feet, only to be met by the grave. The lack of a sense of completion has beset his every pathway; and in his blind groping he has held up his hands in speechless anguish, and his broken cries have rent the air with supplications to an apparently unheeding Deity.

Why the suffering, the sorrow, the sin, the sickness and a lifetime of trouble, only to be met at last by the grim and sinister tomb?

Why, why, why? Man has sought the wise only to discover their foolishness; he has sought the learned only to find a lack of wisdom. Why, why, why? His cry has appeared to go forth into an empty nothingness. But hark! from somewhere a vague answer has come, some subtle inner sense of things; some unknown presence has given answer and a still small voice has said to him, "Man, know thyself." The Instinctive Man has again spoken and told him to search more deeply into his own nature; to look deep within himself for the answer to life. The hour has struck in the evolution of man when he can understand this voice and do its bidding.

THE GREATEST DISCOVERY OF ALL TIME—MIND

Man's response to this inner Instinctive Voice has caused him to start on the greatest adventure of his career, the discovery of Mind.

Man's first discovery of his ability to think was set aside as being too evident to take any notice of; he could think, but what of it. Of course, it was a proof that he was, but that was all; he had always been able to think; this simply gave him the ability to know his needs and try to supply them. This he had always done.

The ability to think seemed to be an automatic thing; it came with him and would doubtless die when he died; the brain seemed to be the organ of thought; and, of course, when death stilled the brain it would no longer operate—this was self-evident.

The Brain Does Not Think

But the day came when some wise man said that it is not the brain that thinks at all; for if the brain, of itself, could think, then one could cut it out and it would keep right on thinking. No, the brain of itself could not think; and yet, without a brain man could not think; which simply means that man needs a brain while here, but that the brain, of itself, does not think. The brain does not think and yet man thinks; so behind the brain there must be a thinker. But where is this thinker? We do not see him. Have we a right to say that there is a thinker when no one has ever seen him? Yes; for can we name a single force of nature that we can see? Have we ever seen electricity or any of the other forces of nature? No; and the only evidence we have of their existence is that we see what they do. We have light and motive power, so we have a right to suppose that there is a force which we call electricity. This is true all along the line, for we see effects and not causes.

We Do Not See the Thinker

But to return to the thinker; we do not see him, but the proof of his reality is in the evidence of his works. We know that the legs do not walk; for, if severed from the body, they could not carry any one very far. Cut off the hand and see if it could still hold anything in its grasp! Pluck out the eye and it cannot see; and so it is with all the organs of the body. There is a thinker and doer back of the organism who is using it for a conscious purpose.

The Body Unconscious Without the Thinker

This is a great discovery; for it means that the body without the thinker could neither be sick nor suffer; for without the thinker there could be no movement of the body. Why then are we sick? This inquiry will not be answered until every form of disease is swept from the face of the earth and numbered with the things that were once thought necessary. For man has discovered that the body, of itself, has no life nor power to act.

Let us follow the course of man's thought since he first made this discovery about the body and began to apply his knowledge. He first realized that Instinctive Man built up the body through evolution; and, after having created and evolved a perfect body, left it in man's keeping to do with as he willed. At first, man was ignorant of this, thinking that the body was self-operating; but as soon as he discovered that such was not the case he began to formulate certain new theories about himself. He discovered that while he could consciously think and decide, something happened to his thoughts after he had thought them. They went somewhere; for soon they would come back as remembrance. Man had now discovered that he could consciously think and that his thought would come back to him again. This led to the conclusion that memory is an active thing, an inner mental action. He said, "Memory is the storehouse of all my conscious thoughts and it is active. My body is not conscious of life, but my thought is conscious of my body; my body is operated upon by my thought; and it must also be operated upon by my memory, since memory is active. But, since memory is only the result of conscious thought, memory, of itself, is an unconscious operation of what was once a conscious thought."

The Conscious and the Unconscious Thought

Since man always has had the habit of naming things, he named his memory his "unconscious thought," and his conscious thought he called his "objective mind." He now came to the conclusion that he had two minds, one conscious and one unconscious, or sub-conscious. The conscious mind being the one that he used all of the time in his self-conscious state and the sub-conscious mind being the storehouse of all his conscious thoughts, as well as the seat of his memory. It follows, that as conscious thought acts, unconscious thought must also operate. This conclusion led to the discovery that the sub-conscious mind is the builder of the body; not that it really made the body in the first place, for Instinctive Man did that; but that the sub-conscious mind keeps the body going and is always acting on the thoughts of the conscious mind. After carefully watching this process, man discovered that he could consciously think and, by so doing, make such an impression on his unconscious thought that it would do what he directed. From these observations he deduced the law of suggestion to be one of action and reaction. Thus he found how habits are formed; that they are conscious ideas fallen into the inner thought and carried out to logical conclusions.

A New Basis of Thought

Therefore, he began to reason: "Instinctive Man within me is perfect and yet I appear to be imperfect. My apparent imperfection must be the result of an imperfect thinking; in reality I am, and always have been, perfect. I will now begin to think differently about myself and see what happens." And as he began to think from the new basis he found that the body responded and was healed. So he came to this conclusion: "God made me perfect but He also made me an individual, which means that I can do with myself as I will. I cannot really destroy my body but I can make it most uncomfortable. Since God made me and made me perfect, each one of the organs of my body represents a perfect idea."

Realizing this to be true, he began to think from this basis, and the organs of the body responded. He found that thoughts of peace produced a peaceful condition while thoughts of fear produced a disturbed condition; that confidence made him strong while fear made him weak. In fact, he was able to trace each mental attitude to its physical correspondent. He discovered that, asleep or awake, the inner mind works all the time. He also found that by analyzing his thought he could discover what ailed him. This he called psycho-analysis.

The Law of Mind

Then another idea came to him: the whole thing was in accordance with law. He had discovered a law of mind just as he, at another time, discovered a law of electricity. If it were law, then he could always use it and it would always respond. From this he gradually built up a definite technique for the practice of right thinking.

He found that if he always thought of himself as being perfect he would always feel better. But what should he do with his body when it appeared sick? How was he to think of himself when he was sick? Could he deny that he was sick when he was suffering? Yes; for his sickness was the result of thought, and by changing the thought he could change the effect. He learned to turn away from the body when it was sick and go back into mind and think of the body as being perfect; for his thought worked independently of the body. He turned from the image of sickness to the idea of health and said, "I am perfect, no matter what the appearance may be."

Unconscious Mind at Work

But some kinds of sickness had never entered his mind at all; that is, he had never consciously thought of them. How was he to reconcile this fact with his new theory? For a while this was a hard problem to solve; but by a still more careful study of his inner self, he discovered that what he called his subjective mind took all of his thoughts and did something with them. He found that there were certain combinations of thought which, brought to their logical conclusions, would produce certain kinds of diseases. He did not have to consciously think of a certain disease to have it; but if he thought certain kinds of thoughts they would produce their logical results. For instance, if he were excited all the time it would produce nervousness; if he became angry it would secrete poison in his system, and so on through the whole category of the human ailments; somewhere in mind they had their reason for being. Perhaps he could not always tell exactly where, but, by knowing that his body was perfect, he could still heal himself. He knew that as time went on and his knowledge grew he would find out more and more about himself and so be better able to heal himself. He was glad that he had started on the right track; he believed that he would know all in time and never be sick again.

ANOTHER GREAT DISCOVERY—THOUGHT REACHED OTHERS

Then a new discovery came, which was that he could think of others and heal them. It seemed to make no difference where they were; he could think of them and heal them. This was a most astounding fact, for it meant that there was a common mind somewhere through which his thought operated; for he could not reach another unless there were a medium between himself and the other person. This seemed strange; for what he had learned to think of as his individual subjective mind, was, after all, only the personal use that he was making of something which was around every one. He began to think for others, and found that mind responded to his thinking for them and caused some action to take place in their bodies. He called this medium "Universal Mind," or "the Law of God." It seemed to be as omnipresent as the law of electricity or any of the other forces of nature.

THE DISCOVERY OF RACE-THOUGHT

In this way he discovered how it was possible that the whole race might have held certain kinds of thoughts and how they might have operated through any one who was receptive to them. That is, if any one should feel discouraged, other thoughts of discouragement might gain entrance also and make him feel worse. This he called race-suggestion. But how was he to protect himself from it? By knowing that it could not operate through him; that he was a perfect idea and could not be affected by suggestion; for, after all, it was nothing but thought. He learned to build a mental wall around himself which could not be entered unless he chose. This he called "Divine Protection."

A Universal Medium Which All Must Come to Believe In

Man had now discovered that he could help and heal himself and others by thinking into some kind of a Universal Law of Mind. He found that, like all other forces of nature, it was a great Impersonal Law and could be consciously used whenever he wished to use It and that the use of It was through right thinking. He realized that the time must come when the race would be healed by knowing the Truth about itself. But because the Law was mental it could only work for those who believed in It, and since many did not believe, the thing to do was to heal himself and others who wished to be healed, waiting for the rest of the world to realize the fact.

Another Question Comes Up—Why Are People Poor?

But another thought came to him. If he could think into some kind of a Universal Medium of Mind and heal himself and others; if this Mind could produce such a physical effect on the body, why could it not also produce the same kind of an effect on conditions and in the affairs of life? Why was it that some were rich and some poor? Was this fate, or was it because there was not enough for all? If the One Mind made bodies, why did It not also create conditions? And if It did, why did it not give to all alike?

Why were some people happy and prosperous and others unhappy, weak and poor? Could the answer to this also be in Mind? Could it be that just as man had thought of himself as sick, and so made sickness, he had thought of poverty and made this condition possible in his experience?

Questions like these and many others came into the mind of man and caused him to search even more deeply into the nature of things. Looking about, he saw some succeed and some fail, though all was taking place in the same world and under common conditions. So he knew that it must be something *in* man, and not *outside* of him, that made all these things possible. He realized that conditions did not make themselves. Everything in man's life was run by man himself.

Man Begins to Realize That His Conditions Are Controlled by Thought

In this way man realized that even his affairs were controlled by thought working through the avenue of the One Mind. He discovered that by changing his thought he could remold his affairs, and that by right thinking he could bring into his life new conditions. But would there be enough to go around should every one become prosperous? Yes, for Instinctive Life is Limitless.

Realizes That He Must Think Correctly

So man discovered that he could control his affairs by right thinking; he could bring into his experience the things he wished to enjoy if he thought correctly; and since this was all in accordance with law he could do so consciously. He realized that the time would come when every one would think correctly; and poverty, unhappiness, and all that goes with them, would be swept from the face of the earth. They were never intended to be, but man had misused his power; now that he understood, he would change his whole manner of thinking and consequently he would become happy and have plenty. But every one did not believe this. Many said that it was a foolish idea, while others said that it was too good to be true. However, it was soon proven that whoever would believe and comply with the Law could prove it to be true. If some did not wish to believe, that was all right; there were plenty who would, and the direct proofs of their lives would in time convince others. In this way, eventually, all would be saved from unbearable conditions. The thing to do was to teach the Law to those who did believe.

And so the lessons which follow are for this purpose, to teach those who believe in the Law how to use It.

The race is made up of individuals, and the place to begin is with the person who believes in the greater possibility. Each one, for himself, must work out the law of his own being. It is within the power of every man to completely change his environment and completely heal his body. Whether or not he will do this depends entirely upon his own conviction and his own determination. Nature attends him on the way and is always ready to serve; but he is an individual and nothing will ever be forced upon him. Let any one follow the Law, comply with Its nature, and consistently apply himself to right thinking and living, and he will prove to himself that life holds all and more than he has ever imagined.

PART TWO
THE LESSONS

LESSON ONE: INTRODUCTION

In presenting these lessons in Mental Science to the public, it is my desire to make it possible for any one, who cares to take the time to study them, to demonstrate the truths that will be discussed. It is, perhaps, hard to set down in writing a complete teaching in Mental Science that will not appear difficult to understand; but this could be said as well of any science, and the Science of Mind is no exception to the general rule.

SCIENCE

Science is a knowledge of facts built around some proven principle. All that we know about any science is that certain things happen under certain conditions. Take electricity as an example; we know that there is such a thing as electricity; we have never seen it, but we know that it exists because we can use it; we know that it operates in a certain way and we have discovered the way that it works. From this knowledge we go ahead and deduce certain facts about electricity; and, applying them to the general principle, we receive definite results. No one has ever seen the power or the energy that we call electricity; and the only proof we have that it really exists is that from it we receive light, heat and motive power.

No one has ever seen any of the great causes that lie back of the manifestations of life, and perhaps no one ever will; but we know that such principles exist because we can use them.

How Laws Are Discovered

The discovery of a law is generally made more or less by accident, or by some one who, after careful thought and observation, has come to the conclusion that such a principle must exist. As soon as a law is discovered experiments are made with it, certain facts are proved to be true, and in this way a science is gradually formulated; for any science consists of the number of known facts about any given principle. As more and more facts are gathered and proven, the science expands and gradually becomes accepted by all and used by those who understand it. In this way all of our sciences have been evolved until to-day we have the use of powers and unseen forces of which our ancestors never even dreamed.

Proof of Mind

This is true of the Science of Mind. No one has ever seen Mind or Spirit, but who could possibly doubt their existence? Nothing is more self-evident than that we live; and since we live, we must have life; yet who has ever seen this life? The only proof of life we have is that we live; and the only proof we have of Mind is that we can think; so we are perfectly justified in believing that we have a mind and that we live.

Where Our Thoughts Go

As we watch the processes of thought we find that we think consciously, and we also find that something happens to our thoughts after we have thought them; for instance, they become memory. This proves that we have a deeper aspect of mind, which is called subjective, lying just below the threshold of the conscious. This subjective mind is the place where our thoughts go and from whence they eventually return to us again as memory. Observation proves this to be true; for it always happens this way.

Observation has proven that the subjective mind is the seat of memory and that it contains mental pictures, or impressions, of all that has ever happened to the individual. As these mental impressions come to the surface of the conscious mind they are called memories.

Moreover observation has shown that the subjective mind is the builder of the body. It has proven that it is not only the seat of memory; it is also the avenue through which Instinctive Man works. We mean by Instinctive Man that part of the individual which came with him when he was born—that inner something which makes him what he is. For instance, we do not have to consciously think to make the body function; so we say that the inner, or the Instinctive, Man, does this for us. This is true of most of the functions of the body; they appear to be automatic; they came with us and are nature's way of working through us. So we say that in the unconscious or the sub-conscious or the subjective, there is a silent process forever working away and always doing its duty, carrying on all of the unconscious activities of the body without effort on our part.

SUGGESTION BECOMES MEMORY

It has been observed that suggestions, planted in the sub-conscious, become memories, and eventually tend to externalize in the body. From this it has been deduced that the sub-conscious mind is the builder of the body and is the creative factor in man. It has also been proven that certain types of thought produce certain kinds of results. This shows that the subjective mind takes our suggestions and tends to act upon them, no matter what the suggestion may be.

While the Instinctive Man, or the Natural Man, must be perfect, it is known that the thoughts of the conscious man may hinder instinctive action, through adverse suggestion. That is, conscious thought, acting as memory, may build a false condition in the body, which condition we call disease. Conscious thought may also erase this memory and thereby heal the disease.

Through observations such as these, a science of the subjective mind has gradually been formulated, many facts have been put together; and, to-day, these facts constitute what we call the science of the subjective life in its relationship to mental healing,

MENTAL MEDIUM THROUGH ALL

It has also been proven that thought operates in such a manner as to make it possible to convey mental impressions from one person to another, showing that there is a mental medium between all people. When we think of it, how could we talk with each other unless there were some kind of a medium through which we talked? We could not; and so we know that there really is such a medium. While there is a place where our bodies begin and leave off, as form, there does not appear to be a place where our thought leaves off. Indeed, the observations made and the facts gathered show that the medium between men's minds is omnipresent; that is, it seems to be everywhere present. Radio also shows this, for messages are sent out through some kind of a universal medium, and all that we can say of it is that we know the medium is there. So it is with Mind; all that we can say is that everything happens just as though it were there. We have a perfect right, then, to say that such a medium exists.

This opens up a far-reaching theory, for it leads to the conclusion that we are surrounded by a Universal Mind which is the Medium of the communication of our thoughts. Perhaps this is the Mind of God! Who knows? That It is there, we cannot doubt.

READING THOUGHT

Other observations have shown even more wonderful possibilities. It is known that certain people can read our thoughts, even when we are not aware of the fact, showing that thought operates through a medium which is universal, or always present. This also shows that the medium is subjective; for it retains our thoughts and transmits them to others. This leads to the conclusion that what we call our subjective mind is really the use that we, as individuals, make of something which is universal. Perhaps, just as radio messages are operative through a universal medium, our thoughts are operative through the medium of a Universal Mind. Indeed, this has been believed for thousands of years by some of the deepest thinkers.

MENTAL LAW

As we think of the medium of radio transmission in terms of law, so we should think of the Mental Medium in terms of law; for it must be the law of mental action. While we might think of it as the Mind of God, we surely could not think of it as the Spirit of God; for the Mental Medium is automatic, while the Spirit must be Self-Knowing. We could not call the Universal Medium of Mind God, any more than we could call electricity God. It is but one of the many attributes of God or the Universe of Life. It is the avenue through which God operates as Law.

THE WORD OF GOD AS LAW

Since man has a self-conscious mind, a subconscious mind and a body, we know that he is threefold in his nature. First, he is conscious mind or spirit; next, he is subconscious mind or mental law; and then, he is body. The conscious mind controls the subconscious; and in its turn, the subconscious controls the body.

It is evident that man comes from God, Life or Nature, whichever we choose to call It. It is also evident that we can get from Life only that which is in It. Man must partake of the Divine Nature if he comes from It or is made out of It; for what is true of the Whole must also be true of any of Its parts. Something cannot come from nothing; something must come from something; for nothing comes from nothing and nothing is the result; but man is something, else he could not declare himself; and since he is something, he must be made from, or come out of, something; and that something must be what we call God.

THREEFOLD NATURE OF GOD

If we study the true nature of man, then, we shall have delved into the real nature of God, or First Cause, from which man springs; and as we have found that man is threefold in his nature, so we must also deduce that God is threefold in His Nature; that is, God is Spirit, or Self-Knowingness; God is Law and action; and God is Result or Body. This is the inner meaning of the teaching of "the Trinity." But let us elaborate: God, as Self-Knowing Spirit, means the Divine Being Whom we have always thought of and believed in; the Being to Whom we have prayed and Whom we have adored. God, as Law, means the way in which the Spirit works; and Law in this sense, would be the servant of the Spirit. God, as Body, means the manifestation of the Spirit. We might put it in another form and say, there is the Thing, the way that It works and the result of Its work. Still another form would be to say, Cause, Medium and Effect.

TRINITY OF BEING

A trinity of being appears to run through all Nature and all Life; for instance, there is electricity, the way it works and its result, which is light or motive power. There is the seed, the creative medium of the soil and the plant. Turn it as we may, we are confronted with the necessity of a trinity of being. There must always be the thing, what it does and the way that it operates. Always a trinity runs through life and through everything in it. But through the Trinity of God and man there runs a Self-Conscious Spirit, and this is what distinguishes man from the brute, or from a purely mechanical creation; and is the only thing that could make God a Self-Knowing Power.

CONSCIOUS MIND IN GOD AND MAN

In God and in man there is a power that, while it may not transcend law, yet consciously uses it for definite purposes. In God this knowledge must be complete, but in man it is, of course, but dimly perceived. Jesus, the wisest Man who ever lived, said that God and man are One in real nature, and no doubt this understanding was what gave Him His marvelous power.

UNITY

It is well to remember that the enlightened in every age have taught that back of all things there is One Unseen Cause. In studying the teachings of the great thinkers we find that a common thread runs through all—the thread of Unity. There is no record of any deep thinker, of any age, who taught duality. One of the great teachings of Moses was, "Hear, O Israel, the Lord our God is One Lord";[1] and the saying, "I AM that I AM,"[2] was old when Moses was yet unborn; for it had been inscribed over the temple entrances for generations. We may go back much farther than Moses and find the same teaching, for it crops out from the literatures and sayings of the wise of all ages. Jesus taught this when He said, "I and the Father are One,"[3] and in the saying, "The Father that dwelleth in me."[4]

This teaching of Unity is the chief cornerstone of the Sacred Scriptures of the East as well as of our own Sacred Writings. It is to-day the mainspring of the teachings of the modern philosophies, such as Christian Science, Divine Science, The Unity Teachings, The New Thought Movement, The Occult Teachings, The Esoteric or Inner Teachings, and even of much that is taught under the name of Psychology. Without this basic teaching of Unity these movements would have but little to offer. Science has found nothing to contradict this teaching, and it never will, for the teaching is self-evident.

WORSHIP OF GOD

That there is a God or First Cause no one can doubt. That the Being Whom we call God really exists from eternity to eternity is self-evident. In every age people have worshiped some kind of Deity. It is true that as the evolution of man has progressed the idea of God has expanded, and the more that people have realized of life, and of nature and her laws, the clearer has been the concept of Deity, for this is the logical result of an unfolding mentality.

MANY GODS

The first stages of human thought brought out the idea that there were many gods, the natural outcome of a life which experienced many kinds of misfortune and difficulties. As there were

---

1 Deut. 6 : 4.

2 Exodus 3 : 14.

3 John 10 : 30.

4 John 14 : 10.

many gods so there were many devils or evil powers; but as the understanding of man grew he began to realize that there could not be so many powers, since the Cause back of everything must be a Unity, else It could not exist. More than one power would indicate a universe divided against itself, and this kind of a universe could not hold together. However, it has taken a long time to come to this conclusion, and in the stages between many weird ideas have been formulated and believed in. At first there were many gods and many devils; but as thought progressed, this was narrowed down to One God and one devil or evil power. Duality has been believed in since time immemorial, and, indeed, is still believed in by many. By duality we mean a belief in more than One Power back of all things.

BELIEF IN DUALITY—ITS RESULTS

The belief in duality has robbed theology of power and has polluted philosophy with untruths; it has divided science against itself and has made countless thousands go through life with saddened hearts.

DUALITY IN THEOLOGY

The belief in duality has given rise in theology to the idea of a God and a devil, each with equal power to impose upon man a blessing or a curse, and men have worshiped a devil just as truly as they ever worshiped God. Even to-day this monstrous thought is robbing men of their birthright to happiness and a sense of security. Even to-day, and openly, men still teach that there is an evil power in the universe, that there is damnation to the souls of those who do not fall down and worship—they know not what. But the time is rapidly coming when such teachings will be thrown on the scrap heap and numbered among the delusions of a frantic mentality. It has been the habit of many religious teachers of all times to hold the crowd in awe before a mighty throne of condemnation and utter destruction, till the poor, ignorant population have rent the air with their lamentations of complete despair. This, indeed, was a good method to compel the attention with, the hope of salvation through some sacred rites to be performed by those whom God had appointed. In justice to such an awful performance, we would better give to these religious teachers the benefit of the doubt and say that they themselves have believed in the atrocious teachings which they have so unhesitatingly given out.

Be this as it may, the time has now come for a clearer understanding of the true nature of the Deity, in Whom we all believe, and Whom we all seek to know and to understand. That there is a God no sane person would deny; that there could be a God of vengeance and hate, having all the characteristics of a huge man in a terrible rage, no person can well believe and keep his sanity. We will say, then, and without mincing matters in the least, that the most we had better believe about such a God is that there is no such being.

DUALITY IN PHILOSOPHY

As the belief in duality has robbed theology of its greater message, so it has robbed much of the philosophy of the ages of a greater truth; for in philosophy the belief in duality has created a confusion that is almost as great as that in theology. It has made a philosophy of good and evil in which men have come to believe. True philosophy in every age, however, has perceived that the Power back of all things must be One Power; and the clearer the thought of Unity, the greater has been the philosophy. It has shone forth as a beacon light toward which weary souls have traveled, hoping to find reality. To the great philosophers of all times we owe the advancement of the world; for they have been the great way-showers and helpers of mankind. In reverence, we humbly bow before them as Messengers of the Most High; for God has spoken through their lips and has told us that we are not creatures of the dust but that we are Divine Beings, made in the image of Perfection and with an endless destiny.

DUALITY AND SCIENCE

The belief in duality has robbed science, in that it has created Spirit and matter; i.e., a dual universe. However, modern science is rapidly giving out a different idea of the universe; for with the passing of matter into a hypothetical and theoretical ether there is but little left on which to hang any belief in materialism. We now are told that all matter is in a constant state of flow; that it all comes from one source; and that it will eventually return to that source.

AN AWAKENING

The world is waking up to the fact that things are not at all what they appear to be; that matter and form are but the one substance appearing and disappearing; and that form is simply used to express something which is formless, but self-conscious life. What this life is, science does not attempt to explain. This has been left to theology, and whether or not it has been delegated to those competent to handle the problem time alone will tell.

PHILOSOPHY LEADS MAN'S THOUGHT

Philosophy has always transcended science and always will; for philosophy deals with causes while science deals with effects. A scientist observes the result of nature's work while a philosopher speculates as to its cause. Many things which philosophy has taught for thousands of years are to-day being demonstrated by science. The two should really go hand in hand; for one deals with causes and the other with effects. True philosophy and true science will some day meet on a common basis; and, working together, will give to the world a theology of reality. Then, indeed, will "God go forth anew into Creation."

A DEEP INQUIRY

The deep thinkers of antiquity as well as the philosophers of all ages have meditated long and earnestly on the nature of the Divine Being. Knowing that there could be but One Ultimate Reality back of all things, they have pondered deeply upon the nature of that Reality; and it is a significant fact that all of the greatest thinkers have come to about the same conclusion.

THE GREAT DIFFICULTY

The difficulty that has beset the path of true philosophy has been the necessity of explaining a multiplied Creation with a Unitary Cause. Nothing is more evident than that we live in a world of constant change. Things and forms come and go continuously; forms appear only to disappear; things happen only to stop happening; and it is no wonder that the average person, unused to trying to discover causes, is led to feel and to believe that there is a multiple cause back of the world of things.

The philosophers of all times have had to meet the difficulty of explaining how One Cause could manifest Itself in a multiplicity of forms without dividing or breaking up the One. This has not been easy, yet, when understood, the explanation becomes very apparent.

THE VOICE OF GOD IN CREATION

The argument has been something after this manner: The Ultimate Cause back of all things must be One, since Life cannot be divided against Itself; the Infinite must be One, for there could not be two Infinites. Whatever change takes place must take place within the One; but the One must be Changeless; for, being One and Only, It cannot change into anything but Itself. All seeming change, then, is really only the play of Life upon Itself; and all that happens must happen by and through It. How do these things happen through It? By some inner action upon Itself. What would be the nature of this inner action? It could not be physical, as we understand physics, but would have to be by the power of the inner Word of Life; that is, the Voice of God, God standing for the First great and Only Cause of all that Is.

THE WORD OF GOD

It is impossible to conceive of anything other than the Word of God being that which sets power in motion. This is why the Scriptures announce that, "In the beginning was the Word, and the Word was with God and the Word was God. All things were made by Him, and without Him was not anything made that was made."[5] God speaks and it is done.

It is evident that First Cause must be Self-Existent; that is, It must be Causeless. Nothing came before That Which was First; and, while it may be a little hard to understand this, yet we can all grasp the fact that whatever the Being is Whom we call God, It must be Self-Existent.

SPIRIT KNOWS ITSELF

God speaks and it is done; but if God speaks, His Word must be Law. The Word of God is also the Law of God. God is Word, God is Law and God is Spirit; this is self-evident. We arrive at the conclusion that God, as Spirit, is Self-Conscious Life. That Spirit is conscious is proven by the fact that we have evidence of this consciousness strewn through all time and space. God must know that God Is. This is the inner meaning of the teaching of the "I AM," handed down from antiquity. "The Spirit is the Power that knows Itself," is one of the oldest sayings of time.

LAW, SERVANT OF THE WORD

Spirit knows Itself, but the Law is the servant of the Spirit and is set in motion through Its Word. It is known that all law is some form of universal force or energy. Law does not know itself; law only knows to do; it is, therefore, the servant of the Spirit. It is the way that the Spirit works; and is the medium through which It operates to fulfill Its purpose.

Did God make law? As it is not possible to conceive a time when law did not operate, it is impossible to conceive that it was ever created; therefore, law must be coexistent and coeternal with Spirit. We might say that law is one of the attributes of Spirit.

The Spirit operated through law which is some part of Its own Nature; therefore, all action

---

5 John 1 : 1, 3.

must be some action of Spirit as Law. The Word of Spirit sets Its purposes in motion through the law; and since the law must be as Infinite as the Spirit, we could not think of a time when it was not, or a time when it would cease to be; neither can we imagine the law ever failing to operate when set in motion.

We have, then, an Infinite Spirit and an Infinite Law; Intelligence and the way that It works; God, working through Law, which is unfailing and certain.

FORMS OF SPIRIT OR CREATION

Next, we come to the forms of Spirit, which forms we call matter. But what is matter? Science tells us that matter is eternal and indestructible; that, at first, it is an invisible cosmic stuff; and that it gradually takes form through some law working within it. The worlds were formed by the power of His Word. We know that right now worlds are being formed in the vast reaches of space, and worlds are also ceasing to be; that is, they are gradually losing their form. In this way Creation is eternally going on. This proves a definite purposefulness, a definite law set in motion to work out this purposefulness, and a definite form as the result of the operation of this purposefulness. In other words, it shows that there is an Intelligence inherent in the universe which knows what It is doing, and how to do it, and which knows why It does it; and that there is a law obeying Its will. It also shows that there is something upon which It operates. This "something" we will call matter in its unformed state. Perhaps this is "the ether" of science; it is impossible to say; but surely there is something upon which the Spirit works.

The teaching of the great thinkers of all times is that we live in a threefold universe of Spirit, Soul and Body—of Intelligence, Substance and Form.

MEANING OF CREATION

With this in mind, we shall be better able to realize that Creation does not mean making something out of nothing, but means the passing of Substance into form through a law which is set in motion by the Word of Spirit. Creation is eternally going on; for we could not imagine a time when the activity of Spirit would cease. It is "the same yesterday, to-day and forever."[6]

The whole action of Spirit must be within Itself, upon the Law, which is also within Itself, and upon the Universal Stuff, or matter, which is also within Itself. The three must in reality be One; hence, "The Trinity."

------

6 Heb. 13 : 8.

THE WORD ALONE IS CONSCIOUS

One of the main facts to bear in mind is, that, of the three attributes of Spirit, the Word alone is conscious of Itself. The Law is force, and matter is simply stuff ready to take form. Since law or energy is proven to be timeless, that is, not added to or taken from; and since matter is known to be of the same nature, we have a right to suppose that both matter and law are co-existent and coeternal with Spirit. But Spirit alone is Conscious. Law, of itself, is only a force, and matter has no mind of its own. Law is not a thinker but is a doer, while matter cannot think but is thought upon.

THE THOUGHT OF GOD

Just what is meant by the Word of God? This must mean the Inner Consciousness, or Self-Knowingness, of Spirit; the Thought of God. The word "thought" seems to mean more to us than any other word; it seems to cover the meaning better, for we know that thought is an inner process of consciousness.

The Thought of God must be back of all that really exists, and, as there are many things that really exist, there must be many thoughts in the Mind of the Infinite. This is logical to suppose; for an Infinite Mind can think of an infinite number of ideas. Hence the world of multiplicity or many things. But the world of multiplicity does not contradict the world of Unity; for the many live in the One.

ETERNAL CREATION

There may be confusion in the minds of men but not in the Thought of God; and so we have a universe expressing the limitless Ideas of a Limitless Mind, and without confusion. We have, then, a Cosmic World, and an infinite and endless Creation. This is the inner meaning of those mystic words, "World without end." Creation always was and always will be. Things may come and things may go, but Creation goes on forever; for It is the Thought of God coming into expression. This is, indeed, a wonderful concept, for it means that there will always be a manifestation of the Divine Ideas. We need not worry about whether it will ever cease; it cannot cease so long as God exists; and since God will be forever, there will forever be some kind of manifestation.

The Universe Is Alive

The universe is alive with action and power, with energy and life. We touch it only in parts, but from these parts we do catch a glimpse of the nature of the Whole, "He hath not left Himself without a witness."[7] Modern science is revealing many things that the great thinkers of the ages have announced. One of them is that matter is in a constant state of flow; it is like a river flowing in, out and on; it is operated upon by an unseen force or law and takes its form through some agency which science supposes to be the Will and Purpose of Spirit. This we call the Word. All things were made by the Word.

Conclusion

To sum up: There is a power in the universe which acts as though It were Intelligent and we may assume that It is. There is an activity in the universe which acts as law. We know this to be true. And there is a formless stuff in the universe, forever taking form, and forever changing its form; this also is self-evident. We have every right, then, to assume that there is a threefold nature of Being which we will call Spirit, Soul and Body. We will think of the Spirit as the great Actor, the Soul as the medium of Its action, and the Body as the result of this action. We will think of Spirit as the only Conscious Actor, the only Power that knows Itself. We will think of Soul as a blind force, obeying the Will of Spirit; and we will think of Body as the effect of the Spirit, working through law, thus producing form. We will say that neither the Law nor the stuff from which form comes has any conscious intelligence, but must, because of its nature, take the form of the Word. This simplifies the whole matter and enables us to see that in the entire universe One Power Alone really acts, the Power of the Word of God.

The chart in lesson one of this series is an attempt to portray the Threefold Nature of the Universe; to show how the Spirit, acting through Law, becomes Form; for this is the inner meaning of Creation.

---

7 Acts 14 : 17.

SPIRIT
ABSOLUTE
FIRST CAUSE——GOD
THE GREAT I AM
CONSCIOUS MIND
PURPOSEFULNESS

ONLY——ALL	SELF-PROPELLING	PERSONALNESS
KNOWING NO OTHER	SELF-EXISTENCE	CONSCIOUS IDEA
FATHER——MOTHER GOD	VOLITION——LIFE——TRUTH	CHANGELESS
UNCONDITIONED ONE	POWER——CHOICE——WILL	OMNISCIENCE
UNITY——MACROCOSM	FREE SPIRIT	OMNIPOTENCE
THE GREAT HOUSE	PEACE——POISE	OMNIPRESENCE
MASCULINE	THE WORD	REASON DEDUCTIVE ONLY
ACTIVE	PERFECT LOGOS	

SOUL
CREATIVE MEDIUM
SUBJECTIVE——UNCHOOSING

BLIND FORCE——LAW	SUBCONSCIOUS MIND	KARMIC LAW
NOT KNOWING——ONLY DOING	IMMATERIAL	KNOWN AS
MEDIUM OF THOUGHT,	ILLUSION OF MIND	THE SERVANT OF THE
POWER AND ACTION	IMPERSONAL	ETERNAL SPIRIT
CINEMA PICTURES	FEMININE	THROUGHOUT
REASON——DEDUCTIVE ONLY	NEUTRAL	THE AGES
PASSIVE AND RECEPTIVE	PLASTIC	
	MAYA	

REFLECTION	BODY	RELATIVE MIRROR
ILLUSION OF MATTER	EFFECT	EMANATION
MULTIPLICITY——MANY	FORM	
	OBJECTIVE	
	CONDITIONS	
	RESULTS	
	TIME	
	SPACE	
	THINGS	

LESSON ONE: METAPHYSICAL CHART NO. 1.

This chart, which is called the Universal Chart, shows the Universe as a Trinity of Being. The upper section designates those attributes of Spirit which are Self-Conscious. The middle section shows the subconscious aspect of Law; and the lowest section shows the effect of Spirit working through the medium of Universal Mind. Read and carefully study the full explanation and meaning of the words used in this chart.

LESSON ONE:
METAPHYSICAL MEANING OF WORDS USED IN UNIVERSAL CHART

UPPER SECTION

SPIRIT.—The Intelligent Power back of and through everything; the First Person of The Trinity.

ABSOLUTE.—The Unconditioned, that which nothing can limit.

FIRST CAUSE.—That from Which everything comes. The Cause of all that is made manifest on any plane. That Which comes first. The first in any creative series. The Life back of Things.

GOD.—The same as Spirit. The Self-Knowing Mind back of everything. The Heavenly Father and the Eternal Mother of all. The Being Whom we worship and adore. The One and Only Conscious Mind in the Universe, personal to all who believe in Him. It is impossible to conceive of such a vast idea as God, and the only way that we can conceive of the Divine Being is through our own nature, for His Spirit is Our Spirit.

THE GREAT "I AM."—Revealed to Moses as the One and Only Real Mind or Power in the Universe. That beside Which there is no other. I Am is another way of saying God. The "I AM" in man is the Life of man; without this "I AM," man could not be.

CONSCIOUS MIND.—That Power of Consciousness which knows Itself. That which is conscious of Its Own Being. "The Spirit is the Power Which knows Itself." The Self-Knowing God. The Intelligence in the Universe which reveals Itself in all of Its Creation. If God were not Self-Conscious, then man could not be self-conscious, It is impossible for us to conceive of such a Universal Consciousness. We touch It only in spots, but the evidence of this Conscious Mind is strewn throughout all time and space; and the eternal activity of the Cosmos is proof enough that such a Conscious Mind really exists.

PURPOSEFULNESS.—When we speak of the purposefulness of Spirit we mean that Conscious Mind has the ability to know what It wishes to express and the power to express it. Dean Inge says that there can be no such thing as an infinite purpose because this would be a contradiction of the meaning of Infinite. This is probably true; but it does not follow that there could be no such thing as an element of purposefulness running through the Eternal Mind. Indeed, the evidence of this quality of being is so complete in the Universe that we cannot deny it. The evolution of creation on this planet alone would presuppose some kind of a purposefulness.

SELF-PROPELLING.—The Spirit must be Its own propelling power, Its own motive power. To suppose that Spirit had to go somewhere to get energy with which to energize Itself would be to suppose Spirit is not First Cause. Whatever the nature of that which comes first is, It must have within Itself all that It needs with which to express Itself. We must realize that, in dealing with Causation, we are dealing with That which is the First of everything and is absolutely Unconditioned. It does not need to be energized, but is the energy back of all form and all manifestation of Life.

SELF-EXISTENT.—It is difficult to grasp the idea of self-existence; but we can do so to a degree at least. For instance, we might ask the question, "Why is water wet?" There is no reason why; it is wet simply because it is its nature to be wet. If we were to ask the question, "Who made Life?", it could not be answered; because if we were to assume that some power made Life we would not be supposing that Life is First Cause. We must grasp the fact that, in dealing with Real Being, we are dealing with that which was never created. When did two times two begin to make four? Never, of course. It is a self-existent truth. God did not make God; God Is, This is the meaning of the saying, "I AM THAT I AM." All inquiry into Truth must begin with the self-evident fact that Life Is. The Truth is that which Is and so is Self-Existent.

> "Never The Spirit was born;
> The Spirit shall cease to be never;
> Never was time It was not;
> End and beginning are dreams."

VOLITION.—Volition means the power of conscious choice.

CHOICE.—Choice means the ability to choose consciously.

WILL.—Will means decision coming into execution.

Volition, choice and will must be attributes of Spirit. They mean practically the same thing. We must be careful, however, not to think of these qualities of Spirit in terms of human or limited thought. When we choose, we choose between different things; but when Spirit chooses, It simply announces that It is a certain thing. The Spirit does not have to will to make things happen; things happen because it is the will of Spirit that they should be. This will, then, is simply the execution of a purpose; and since Spirit is Absolute, there can be nothing to deny Its Will. Choice, volition and will are necessary and real attributes of Self-Existent Power; for without them there would be no channel through which the Ideas of God could be expressed. In man these qualities of mentality are limited but in God they are limitless.

POWER.—The energy by which everything lives.

LIFE.—Life means that Inner Something that makes everything live. Life and Power are necessary attributes of a Limitless Being, and go hand in hand to complete a Perfect Being. Life is That Which Lives, and Power is the Energy with which It operates. Considering Life and Power as a combined quality of Causation, we see that they combine to make the underlying basis of all manifestation visible and invisible. In the objective world, Life is the Power that binds everything together; It is the Intelligent Basis of all that exists. For instance, in the material world, It is the Power that holds the atoms together that they may produce form. In the mental world, It is the Power that enables us to think; and in the Spiritual World, It is the Power that enables us to live at all.

It appears that Life manifests on different levels. In the mineral world, and in the world of all material form, It seems to be unconscious; that is, It is not manifesting in a self-conscious state. We know, however, that a certain degree of intelligence runs through all Creation. Chemical Affinity is a manifestation of Life as the attraction of Itself to Itself. In plant life It seems to have a more developed degree of consciousness. That is, It manifests in the vegetable world as a power to express in one spot, but without volition to move about. This, however, does not limit The Spirit but is simply one of the ways that It works. In the animal world, we see different degrees of Life's manifestation, from the first cell life up to Man. For instance, a dog is more intelligent than a fish, yet each has the power to move about. The fish seems to move by instinct alone; the dog appears to have some degree of conscious being, although there is a difference of opinion on this score. At least, in most animal life, we find the ability to move about and, either from instinct or self-choice, the ability to express a certain degree of freedom. In man, Life expresses in terms of Volition and Self-Will; It is manifesting at the level of Self-Consciousness. While The Spirit, of Itself, must always know Itself, yet we are perfectly justified in saying that It manifests on different levels. This does not limit The Spirit, but on the other hand proves that It is really Limitless. For if It had to manifest on one level only, It would then be limited, but because It can manifest on as many levels as It wishes It is Limitless.

When Spirit manifests in the purely mechanical and material world we say that It is Unconscious Life; when It manifests in the animal world we say that It is manifesting in a state of simple consciousness; and when It manifests in and through man we say that It is in a Self-Conscious State. As this Self-Conscious state of man's mentality reaches a larger world of realization and comprehends something of Its Unity with the Whole, we say that It is in a Cosmic State. We now know of four different levels upon which Spirit manifests:—Unconscious State, Simple-Consciousness, Self-Consciousness and Cosmic-Consciousness. All of these are but different ways through which the One Power operates. Life, then, is that quality of Being, running through all, which enables anything to be what It is.

TRUTH.—The Truth is That which Is. It is the Reason, Cause and Power in and through everything. It is Birthless, Deathless, Changeless, Complete, Perfect, Whole, Self-Existent, Causeless, Almighty, God, Spirit, Law, Mind, Intelligence, and anything and everything that implies Reality.

FREE SPIRIT.—Means that which cannot be bound; It is free to do as It chooses, but cannot, of course, do anything that denies Its own Nature.

PEACE.—An inner calm so complete that nothing can disturb it. The Peace which comes only from the knowledge that It is All. Fathomless Peace is meant by the Peace of the Spirit. This is the peace to which Jesus referred when He said, "Peace I leave with you, My peace I give unto you."[8] The Infinite is always at peace because there is nothing to disturb It.

POISE.—That perfect balance which maintains everything in its proper place without effort. It is the law of equilibrium without which nothing could be maintained. It is the law of balance that must exist in the Infinite Mind, since there is nothing to disturb It. Poise or balance is the law back of what we call "the Law of Compensation." It is Life perfectly balancing Itself. Self-Existent Life alone could produce complete poise. We cannot fathom the full meaning of poise as it exists in Spirit; but we can understand that it means an Eternal Power, unruffled by conflicting emotions, always sure of Itself, unhurried and certain.

THE WORD.—The Word means, of course, the ability of Spirit to declare Itself into manifestation, into form. The Word of God means the Self-Contemplation of

---

8 John 14 : 27.

Spirit. The Manifest Universe, as we see It, as well as the Invisible Universe that must also exist, is the result of the Self-Contemplation of the Lord. "He spake and it was done." "The Word was with God and the Word was God. All things were made by Him and without Him was not anything made that was made."[9] The starting point of all Creation is in the Word of Spirit. The Word is the Concept, Idea, Image or Thought of God. It is the Self-Knowing Mind Speaking Itself into manifestation. Everything has a Word back of it as its Initial Cause.

THE PERFECT LOGOS.—"The Divine Creative Word." The Perfect Word of God.

ONLY—ALL.—Beside Which there is none other. That Which has within Itself all that really is. The Life of everything and the Love through everything. The One Presence and the One Infinite Person Whom we call God or Spirit. Within This One all Live.

KNOWING NO OTHER.—The Spirit could know nothing outside Itself. It is The Center and Circumference of everything that exists. It has no enemies, no differences, no otherness, no apartness, no separation from Itself; is Undivided, Complete and Perfect within Itself. It has no opposites and no oppositions. It knows only of Its own ability to do; and, since It is All, It cannot be hindered in any way, shape or manner. It is not possible to conceive of such a complete Life and Power; but we do catch glimpses-in moments of real inspiration when we realize, to a degree, at least, that God is All.

FATHER-MOTHER GOD.—The Spirit contains within Itself the Life Principle of both the masculine and feminine. It is both combined in One.

UNITY.—The Axioms of Reason declare that that Which is Infinite cannot be divided against Itself. The Infinite is, therefore, Indivisible and consequently a Perfect Unit. "Hear, O Israel, the Lord our God is One Lord."[10] It is also, "That Whose Center is everywhere and Whose Circumference is nowhere." All of It is present at any and every point within It. It is not approaching a point nor receding from it, but is always at it. The Whole of God is present at any and every point within God. It was to this Indwelling Spirit that Jesus prayed; for God is within man as well as throughout all Creation. It is, "That thread of the All-Sustaining Beauty Which runs through all and doth all unite." "His lines have gone out into all places."[11] "There is no place where God is not." This concept enabled Job to say,

---

9 John 1 : 1, 3.

10 Deut. 6 : 4.

11 Ps. 19 : 4.

"In my flesh shall I see God."[12] All Life is bound together by One common law of Love, and Love is the Self-Givingness of Spirit, manifested in and through all that is visible and invisible. It was the realization of this One Presence that illumined the saints and sages of the past. "I and the Father are One."[13] "The Father that dwelleth in Me, He doeth the works."[14] We must come to sense this Marvelous Presence; for It is the secret of metaphysical work; God in all and through all.

MACROCOSM.—Means the Universal World. It is another word for the Whole.

THE GREAT HOUSE.—Another way of saying The Universal.

MASCULINE.—The Assertive Principle of Being. The Self-Conscious, Self-Propelling Power of Spirit. The Projective Principle of Life, impregnating the Universal Soul with Its ideas and concepts.

ACTIVE.—The Self-Realizations of Spirit constitute Its Active Being. It acts upon Itself. Since we could not conceive of an unconscious consciousness, we could not imagine an inactive consciousness. The Spirit, by reason of Its Infinite Capacity to know Itself, must always be acting upon Itself. This action is what we call Creation. Creation is eternally going on. It may stop in one place and begin in another, but It is always going on; and, as we know that God will always be God, we know that Creation will never cease. This is the meaning of those mystical words, "World without end." This point must not be overlooked, for there are people who believe that some day Creation will cease. No more un-philosophical position could be taken than to suppose that the activity of Spirit would ever cease. There is another philosophical delusion that many believe in, namely, that there are periods when Spirit does not create. This is impossible, since we cannot conceive of a time when Spirit will cease to be conscious of Itself. ITS SELF-CONSCIOUSNESS IS ITS ACTION. We might imagine that It would not create more worlds like the one in which we live; but to suppose that It could stop creating would be to suppose that It could stop Being.

PERSONALNESS.—We do not think of God as a tremendous Person, but we do think of the Spirit as the Infinite Personalness in and through all Life. We must remember that Infinite as Spirit is, It is still Self-Conscious; and Infinite Self-Knowingness is the Infinite Essence of Personalness, or the Abstract Essence of all personality. To think of God simply as an Infinite Principle would be to resolve the Divine

---

12 Job 19 : 26.

13 John 10 : 30.

14 John 14 : 10.

Being into an Infinite It, a cold Impersonal Law containing no warmth or color, and certainly no responsiveness. Such a concept of God would rob man of his Divine Birthright and throw him, empty-handed, into an abyss of Law and Action without motive or direction. No worse state of mentality could be imagined than one in which man thought of God simply as a Principle. The very fact that man comes from the Universe in a self-conscious state proves that behind all manifestation there is a Power that knows Itself; and a Power that knows Itself must be Personal. It is not, of course, limited but must be Infinite. As wonderful as the concept may be, God is Personal to all who believe in Him. God is responsive to all who approach Him, and God is the Element of Personalness back of all personality.

CONSCIOUS IDEA.—No two ideas are alike. The Creative Mind of the Universe, being Infinite, thinks of a limitless number of things, and each thing is, therefore, separate and distinct in the great Whole. Just as the atoms of science are cemented together by the ether, so each idea of Divine Mind is united in One Spirit. No two things are alike; no two roses are alike; no two people are alike. All come from One Life; all are in One Life and all live by It; but each forever maintains its identity in the Perfect Whole.

CHANGELESS.—The One cannot change by reason of the fact that, being All, there is nothing for It to change into but Itself. It, therefore, remains Changeless. The One Cause back of all never changes, but It does constantly remain active; and so we perceive a changing form within that which is Changeless. Nothing changes, however, but the form. We know that matter and energy are indestructible and eternal, but we also know that within them a change is forever taking place. If we realize that nothing changes but form we will not become confused over the idea of the Changeless. Water may turn into ice and ice may be melted and again become water. Where was the water when it was ice? Where was the ice when it was water? Nothing really happened, except that a form took shape and again became formless. The Principle back of it did not change.

OMNISCIENCE.—The All-Knowing, All-Perceiving Mind of God.

OMNIPOTENCE.—The All-Powerful One.

OMNIPRESENCE.—The Constant Presence of the Undivided Whole. Read again the explanation of Unity.

REASON DEDUCTIVE ONLY.—The Spirit does not reason as man reasons; that is, It makes no inquiry into Truth, but Itself is the Truth. It knows intuitively; therefore,

It simply announces Itself to be That which It is. If we were to ascribe to It any reasoning power, we should be compelled to say that It reasons deductively only, or from the Whole to a part.

MIDDLE SECTION

SOUL.—Used in the sense of the World-Soul, or Medium through which Spirit operates. It is the Holy Ghost or Third Person of the Trinity.

CREATIVE MEDIUM.—Like the creative soil in which seeds are planted and from which plant life grows, the Soul of the Universe is the Creative Medium into which the Word of Spirit falls and from which Creation arises. We must be careful not to think of Soul and Spirit as separate; for they are really two parts, or aspects of the same thing, each being Self-Existent and Coeternal with the other. The simplest way to think of the World-Soul is to think of It as we would the soil in which we plant seeds.

SUBJECTIVE.—The dictionary defines "subjective" as "the impression which an object makes on the mind." The external object is a percept while the impression is a concept. The concept, or idea, would be subjective; for it would be the impression which the mind receives.

In the above chart we are interpreting the word "subjective" as meaning the receptacle of the thought forms of Spirit. The Soul is Subjective to the Spirit; that is, It receives impressions from It. Subjective always means something that receives.

SUBCONSCIOUS MIND.—The same as Subjective. The Spirit is Conscious Mind; the Soul is Subconscious Mind; It is like the soil or ground; It receives and acts. It is not a Knower as Spirit is, but is a Doer, or Executor, of the Will of the Spirit.

UNCHOOSING.—Unlike Spirit, the Soul has no choice of Its own. Being subjective, It is bound to receive but cannot choose. We must always bear in mind that Soul simply reflects the images that the Spirit casts into It.

IMMATERIAL.—The Soul is immaterial, as we think of matter; but It is the substance of Spirit and might be considered to be the Matter of Spirit. As all matter in the physical world is supposed to finally resolve into the ether from which it came, so we may think of the Substance of Soul as we think about the ether and realize that everything in form finally becomes Soul-Stuff again. Perhaps the simplest way to think of It, however, would be to think of It as the last and final analysis of matter.

We know that matter comes from somewhere, and the teaching is that Soul-Stuff is the thing from which it comes. We must, however, distinguish Soul-Stuff from Soul. Soul is Subjective Intelligence; for, while It may not have the ability to choose, It certainly has the ability to intelligently work out the commands of Spirit. We must never think of the subconscious as though it were unconscious. The Soul of the Universe is next in Principle to Spirit and but little lower than Spirit. Sub-conscious means subjective consciousness but not unconsciousness. While the Soul may not choose, having ho self-knowing consciousness of Its own, yet It has an intelligence of Its own, which is Infinite compared to the power of intelligence which we exhibit. For instance, the whole intelligence of the race could not create a buttercup or a pansy; yet the Intelligence in the creative soil in the earth will produce as many for us as we ask it to; that is, of course, if we plant the seeds. This same idea holds good in that greater Creative Medium of the Spirit which we call the Soul of the Universe. It has the intelligence and the power to produce things but no choice as to what It is to produce.

Soul and Soul-Stuff are two different things; but they belong together and must be placed in the category of the Creative Medium. Soul is Sub-conscious Mind working on Immaterial Stuff and creating from It the many forms which we see. Think of It as a seed working in the soil and the soil working on the seed.

ILLUSION OF MIND.—This does not mean that Subjective Mind is an illusion, but it does mean that forms could be projected into It which were not really true. For a more complete explanation of this, see chart in the lesson on Psychic Phenomena.

IMPERSONAL.—The Creative Medium is Impersonal, having no personality of Its own as the Spirit has. It neither knows nor cares who uses It, but is always ready to work for any or all alike. Remember this.

FEMININE.—The Universal Medium or Soul has been called the "Womb of Nature" and "The Holy Mother," because It is receptive to the Spirit and is impregnated with the Divine Ideas. It gives birth to the Ideas of the Spirit and is, therefore, the Feminine Principle of Nature.

NEUTRAL.—Soul is neutral. Like the soil it will produce any or all kinds of plants. Having no conscious mind of Its own, It receives all ideas and works them out into form. We must always remember that the Creative Medium is neutral. If It could choose, It could reject, and this is just what It cannot do. It is bound to accept and act, just as the soil does when we plant cabbages in the ground. It does not argue, but at once goes to work to produce cabbages. When we plant potatoes it does the same thing. We may plant cabbages and potatoes with roses and pansies; and we shall receive all four plants from the one neutral creative medium which knows neither good nor bad, but is conscious only of its ability to do.

PLASTIC.—This refers to Soul-Stuff, either formed or unformed. It is entirely an indeterminate stuff; that is, it has no mind of its own. Matter has no intelligence at all, but is the material which is formed by the power of the Word.

MAYA.—Refers to the illusion of mind.

BLIND FORCE.—Some of the early philosophers referred to the Soul or Creative Medium as a "Blind force not knowing, only doing." This we know to be true of all law. Law knows only to do but has no conscious volition of its own.

LAW.—It will be apparent by now that the Creative Medium of Spirit is the great Mental Law of the Universe. It is the Law obeying the Will of the Spirit. It is the Universal Law of Mind. All law is Mind in action.

MEDIUM OF ALL THOUGHT, POWER AND ACTION.—It is the one Medium through which all Law and all Power operate. It is the One Law within which all the lesser laws work.

CINEMA PICTURES.—Means that It is the Medium of all thought forms. See explanation of chart covering the lesson on Psychic Phenomena.

PASSIVE AND RECEPTIVE.—Means neutral and feminine.

REASON DEDUCTIVE ONLY.—Being subjective, the Creative Medium cannot analyze, dissect nor deny. Because of Its nature, It must always accept. Consequently, It is always deductive in Its reasoning powers.

KARMIC LAW.—Karmic Law means the law of cause and effect. The Karmic Law works through the Medium of the World-Soul.

THE SERVANT OF THE SPIRIT THROUGHOUT THE AGES.—The Universal Soul, being the Creative Principle of Nature and the Law of Spirit, has been called "The Holy Ghost or The Servant of the Eternal Spirit throughout the Ages."

Let us realize that neither the Soul of the Universe nor the Spirit were ever created. Each is Eternal.

LOWEST SECTION

BODY.—The entire manifestation of Spirit, both visible and invisible, is the Body of God. Within this One Body of God is included all lesser bodies, This One Body, coupled with the Intelligence running through It, is called the Son, or the Second Person of the Trinity. This, of course, includes man, both visible and invisible. It also includes every gradation of consciousness from the simple to the complex, from a cell to an archangel.

> "All are but parts of One stupendous Whole,
> Whose body Nature is, and God the Soul."

In short, it is the entire manifestation of Spirit on any and all planes. "In my Father's House are many Mansions."[15] We do not, of course, see all these mansions, but science has revealed to us that many exist which we do not see, and revelation has shown that the Universe is Infinite. "For we know in part."[16]

EFFECT.—That which follows cause. Effect is that which did not make itself, but which must have a power back of it causing it to be. All manifestation is effect and all effect is subject to its cause. The Creator is greater than His Creation. Everything that we see, touch, taste, feel, hear or sense with the physical senses is an effect. "Things which are seen are not made of things which do appear."[17] This means that what we see comes from what we do not see.

FORM.—Form is definite, the result of a definite idea. Form is real as form, but is not self-conscious; it is subjective to the power that created it. Forms come and go, but the power back of them remains forever and is changeless. Form is temporary, but Mind is Eternal. It is necessary that Spirit should manifest in SOME KIND OF FORM in order that It may come into Self-Expression through Self-Realization. This is the meaning of that Creation which is eternally going on.

OBJECTIVE.—Means the object, the external, the effect.

CONDITIONS.—The result of causes, another word for effect.

RESULTS.—What happens as a necessary result of the law of cause and effect. Results follow causes mathematically.

TIME.—Dean Inge says that "Time is a sequence of events in a Unitary Whole." This is an excellent definition; for, of course, time is not a thing of itself; it is simply a measure of experience in eternity. Time does not contradict Eternity, but allows

---

15 John 14 : 2.
16 I Cor. 13 : 9.
17 Heb. 11 : 3.

It to become expressed in terms of definite experience. Time is necessary since it allows experience to take place within the One, but time is never a thing of itself. It is really impossible to measure time; for yesterday is gone and to-morrow has not come, and to-day is rapidly slipping into the past. If we were to attempt to put a finger on any period of time it would be gone before we could point to it. But, illusive as time is, it is still necessary to experience.

SPACE.—Space, like time, is not a thing of itself, but is only the outline of form. It is a relative distance within the Absolute. Space, also, is necessary to the expression of Spirit; for without it no definite form could be produced. We must not be confused over the ideas of time and space, as they are not things of themselves. They are entirely relative, but none the less necessary.

THINGS.—Mean forms in time and space. Things are always results and never make themselves; they are the objectifications of Spirit. Things are necessary to the manifestation of Spirit. They are the result of the Self-Knowingness of the Word of God. Things vary in size and shape, in time and duration, from the planet to the peanut, from a moment to an eternity. Reflection.—The world of matter reflects the Thoughts of God.

ILLUSION OF MATTER.—Refers to false forms.

MULTIPLICITY, MANY.—From One come many. From Unity comes multiplicity, but multiplicity does not contradict Unity. It is like the soil from which come many plants. We grow many plants from one soil, but the Unity of the soil is never disturbed in the least. So the One Mind, working through the Creative Medium of the Universe, produces many things.

RELATIVE MIRROR.—Both the Absolute and the relative are reflected in the mirror of matter.

EMANATION.—Projection of Spirit into form.

LESSON ONE: THE NATURE OF BEING

The circle in Chart No. I signifies Universal Life, because it is without beginning and without end. We have divided it into three parts, calling one Spirit, one Soul and the other Body; not because the nature of Being is three distinct things, but because It is a Unity with three distinct attributes, i.e., Spirit, Soul and Body.

Spirit

We treat of Spirit as the Active and the only Self-Conscious Principle. We define Spirit as the First Cause or God; the Absolute Essence of all that is. It is also called the great, or the Universal, I AM. When Moses asked God who he should tell the Children of Israel had sent him, the answer was, "Thus shalt thou say, I AM hath sent me unto you."[18] The reason why "I AM" was given is because this is an absolute statement. Spirit is Conscious Mind, and is the Power Which knows Itself; It is conscious of Its own Being. The Spirit is Self-Propelling; it is Absolute and All. It is Self-Existent, and has all life within Itself. It is the Word, and the Word is volition. It has choice because It is Volition; It is will because It chooses; It is Free Spirit because It knows nothing outside Itself, and nothing different from Itself.

Spirit is the Father-Mother God because It is the Principle of Unity back of all things. The masculine and feminine principles both come from the One. Spirit is all Life, Truth, Love, Being, Cause and Effect; and is the only Power in the Universe that knows Itself.

Soul

The Soul of the Universe, not as opposed to the Spirit, but as the Principle just beneath It, has always been taught as the receptive medium into which the Spirit lets fall the forms of Its thought. It is subjective to the Spirit; that which is subjective is always impersonal, neutral, plastic, passive and receptive. Wherever you find subjective law you will find something that is compelled to receive and to act upon; consequently the Soul of the Universe has been called a "blind force, not knowing, only doing," and "The servant of the Eternal Spirit throughout the ages." It is the medium of the thought, power and action of the Spirit.

Two Ways of Reasoning

There are but two processes of reasoning known to the human mind; one is inductive and the other is deductive. Inductive reasoning is an inquiry into the truth; it is a process of analysis. Deductive reasoning is that process of reasoning which follows an already established premise. It is from the whole to a part. Here is an example of inductive reasoning: I look about and say, "John Smith is good; Mary Jones is good; my neighbors are good; consequently, God must be good." This is a process of analysis which leads to the conclusion that the Cause back of all things must be Good. Deductive reasoning would operate this way: "God is Good; conse-

---

18 Exodus 3:14.

quently, Mary Jones, John Smith and my neighbors must be good"; because God is Good they cannot be otherwise.

Since inductive reasoning is an analysis, which is always an inquiry into truth, it follows that God can reason only deductively. That which is Infinite does not have to inquire into the Truth; consequently, there can be no inductive process of reasoning, either in the Spirit or the soul of the Universe. There cannot be any inductive reasoning in the Spirit, because It already knows all things. There cannot be any inductive reasoning in the Soul of the Universe, because It is the Creative Medium, and, if It could reason inductively, It could reject certain thoughts, because It could analyze; and soul or subjectivity can never reject; but is bound by its own nature to accept. It is impersonal, and neither knows nor cares who uses it. It is plastic, because It is immaterial. It is formless, having no mind of Its own. It has been called the Universal Feminine or Holy Womb of Nature, because It is receptive and creative. It is Karmic Law, because It is subjective to the self-knowing mind. It is the medium of all Karmic Law and of all race suggestion.

Body

The Universe has been called the Great Trinity, or Triune Unity of Spirit, Soul and Body. The body is the result, the effect, the objectification of Spirit. Soul is the immaterial, plastic and receptive medium; It is primordial or Cosmic Stuff; It is unmanifest form. Body is the result of Spirit working through Soul or Law. There is but one Body of the Universe; It is both visible and invisible; and within this one body are all of the lesser bodies, all of the manifest Universe, including the body of man. "But now are they many members yet but One Body."[19]

Spirit is the Absolute Being; and is the only power in the universe which has self-knowingness, volition, choice or will. The soul has no will; It has no purpose to execute other than the purpose that is given It. Soul is the servant of the Spirit, while body is the result of the union of Spirit with Soul. There is the Power, the way that It works and the result of Its operation; the Word, the law, and the effect; Intelligence, substance, and form; the Active Principle, the passive receptivity, and the relative condition. The Spirit of the Universe cannot change; the Soul of the Universe cannot change; the Body of the Universe cannot help changing.

The Changeless

The Spirit cannot change because there is nothing for It to change into, Spirit being All; this is axiomatic. The Soul of the Universe cannot change; for it is simply Universal Substance and

---

19 I Cor. 12 : 20.

Law; and we know that energy and substance are indestructible and eternal. The Soul of the Universe cannot change; but, as stated above, the body of the universe is forever changing; and this is what constitutes the eternal activity of Spirit within Itself.

Creation does not mean making something out of nothing. If by Creation we mean making something out of nothing, there is no such thing; but if we mean the passing of Spirit into form, then Creation is eternally going on.

It is necessary to understand that the only Active Principle is Spirit—Self-Conscious, Self-Knowing Life, and that all else is subject to Its will. The Spirit is conscious of Its own Thought, Its own Desire and manifestation; and It is conscious that Its desire is satisfied; consequently, It is conscious of that which It manifests; but It is not conscious of any effort or process in Its manifestation.

It is necessary that Soul and Body should exist, because Spirit, without manifestation, would construct only a dream world, never coming into Self-Realization. Since Spirit must be manifested, in order to be Spirit, there must be a way in which It manifests, and there must be a manifestation; hence, Soul and Body.

CAUSE AND EFFECT

If all Cause is existent in Spirit, and if the Law which executes the volition of Spirit is entirely subconscious, or subjective to the Will of the Spirit, and if the body is only an effect, it follows that both cause and effect are spiritual. Involved within the seed, which the Spirit drops into the Creative Medium, is everything necessary to unfold the seed into form. This is why the Spirit never thinks of methods or processes; for that which the Spirit involves must evolve.

UNITY AND MULTIPLICITY

From Unity—which is the One back of all things, through the One Law, which is the medium of the One—multiplicity is manifested, but it never contradicts Unity. When we realize that we are dealing with an Infinite Intelligence, and with an Infinite Law within this Intelligence, we see that there can be no limit placed upon Creation. We think of the world as we see it, but we see it from the viewpoint of only one plane. We see it as matter, which we have divided into eighty or ninety odd elements; but we discover that all of these elements come from one substance. Suppose we should view it from ten different planes, what would happen? We should see ten times as much as we now see. The present hypothesis of science is that the ether is more solid than matter; and this means that there could be a form within the very form that one's body now occupies in space; there might even be a million bodies, each within the other;

and each would be just as real as the one that we now think we occupy. The Universe, as we see it, is not even a fractional part of the Universe that actually is. "Eye hath not seen,"[20] because it sees only on one plane, i.e., in part.

IMMORTALITY

From the standpoint of immortality, we may have a body within a body to infinity; and when this body is rendered useless, and is no longer a fit instrument through which to function, another one may be already there.

The physical disappearance of Jesus after His resurrection was the result of the spiritualization of His consciousness. This so quickened His mentality that His body disintegrated; and His followers could not see Him because He was on another plane. Planes are not places; they are states of consciousness.

Is it apparent that the Spirit can know nothing outside Itself; that whatever the Spirit knows must be a definite mental image, concept, or idea, in the Consciousness of the Spirit? Is it clear that as the Self-Consciousness of Spirit knows within Itself, It knows upon Itself as Law? Is it clear that the Law can never say, "I will not," but can only act? And is it clear that as the Spirit lets fall the forms of Its thought into the Soul, or Subjectivity of the Universe, these thoughts must manifest as things?

FORMS

Let us take a look at these forms. As we look at the many millions of forms, and see that they are all of different shape and color, and yet we know that they all came from One Stuff, are we not compelled to accept the fact that there is a specific cause, or concrete mental image, back of every idea or thing, a Divine Mental Picture? In the subjective world there must be a correspondent of everything in the objective world; and since the subjective world is a receptive or plastic substance, this correspondence can find its initial starting point only in real Intelligence. Therefore, Intelligence is ultimately all there is in the universe.

ALLNESS OF TRUTH

By a process of axiomatic reasoning, we arrive at the conclusion that Spirit knows nothing outside Itself. The Truth is that which Is; and being that which Is, It must be Infinite and All.

---

20 I Cor. 2 : 9.

Being Infinite or All, the Truth can have nothing outside Itself, other than Itself, or unlike Itself, by which to divide Itself; consequently, the Spirit is Indivisible, Changeless and Complete within Itself. Itself is all that is—both Cause and Effect, the Alpha and the Omega.

VOLITION

There is but one volitional factor in the Universe, and this is Spirit or the Self-Knowing Mind. God did not make God; this is self-evident; hence God is Self-Existent. God did not make Law; Law is coeternal with God. God did not make Substance; this, also, is coexistent and coeternal with God. But God did make, and does make, and is making, and will continue to make, from eternity to eternity—forms. We live in a universe of Infinite Substance and numberless forms wherein nothing is moved unless Intelligence moves it.

Mind is dual in its aspect; it is conscious, as the active principle of conscious intelligence, and subconscious, as the passive principle of impersonal receptivity. Body is the result of the knowing of Spirit through Soul. Matter, of itself, has no intelligence, no volition, no power. Since the Law is but a Universal Potential Possibility through which anything might happen, and since it is set in motion by the Word, it follows that every word specializes its own law and carries its own mathematics along with it.

It follows that everything that the Spirit thinks must take form. The Spirit, being Self-Conscious Life, knows and cannot stop knowing. To suppose that It could stop knowing would be to suppose that It could stop being. Since It cannot stop knowing, It must be forever setting in motion the Law of Its own Being, which Law must be forever projecting the forms of Its thoughts, thereby producing things. Creation is always beginning, but never ending. The slightest thought of Intelligence sets in motion a power in the Law to produce a corresponding thing.

When we speak of every thought dropped into the Creative Medium, do we think of God's thought and man's as the same? We think of each as thought; but, whereas man thinks both inductively and deductively, God thinks only deductively. "As he thinketh in his heart, so is he,"[21] i.e., as he lets fall the forms of his thought.

God is not conscious of matter, as we are. God is conscious of Himself as form, but not as size. God is conscious of Himself as definite purposefulness, but not as space. God is conscious of Himself as definite outline, but not as limitation. God is conscious of Himself as many, but not as division.

Would there be any difference between a conscious thought, for the purpose of a direct manifestation, and one that might be thought with no idea of the form that would be mani-

---

21 Prov. 23 : 7.

fested? There would be a great difference. Trained thought is far more powerful than untrained. If this were not true, the thoughts of the metaphysical practitioner could not neutralize those that caused his patient to be sick. We know a little right thought puts to rout that which is wrong. The day that you say to yourself, "My thought is powerful," you would better be careful. *Every thought must manifest according to its intensity*.

Ponder over the meaning of the words in Chart No. I. Think what Self-Existent Life is—Life within Itself; get an understanding of the Law which is the Servant of It, and what matter is, until you begin to feel your own self as part of this great scheme of Existence.

ONLY ONE MIND

There is no such thing as your mind, my mind, his mind, her mind and God's Mind; there is just Mind in which we all live, move and have our being. There is Mind and nothing but Mind. We think of Conscious Mind and Spirit as One and the Same.

Things are ideas. What else could they be? There is nothing out of which to make things, except ideas. In the beginning we behold nothing visible; there is only an infinite possibility, a Limitless Imagination, a Consciousness; the only action of this Consciousness being idea.

That which we call our subjective mind is, in reality, our identity in Infinite Mind; in other words, it is the result of our mental attitudes. It is our mental atmosphere or center in Universal Subjective Mind, in which are retained all the images, impressions, inherited tendencies and race suggestions as far as we accept them.

We see, then, that this is the Medium through which everything comes to us.

There is One First Cause, having three aspects: Spirit, Soul and Body, i.e., Cause, Medium and Effect; the Father, Son and Holy Ghost; Masculine Activity, Feminine Activity and Result.

We should not think of three Gods, but of the Triune Nature of the One God, the One Cause. We think of Spirit as Absolute, Self-Conscious Intelligence. We think of Soul as Receptive to Intelligence; and of the Intelligence as always acting upon It. Spirit and Soul intersphere each other; i.e., both have Omnipresence. The Spirit of the Universe permeates the Soul of the Universe, eternally impregnating It with ideas. The Soul of the Universe is the "Holy Womb of Nature," producing the forms which appear in the physical Universe.

The Body of the Universe is the result of the thought of Spirit, operating through the medium of Soul. This Trinity is called the Father, the Son and the Holy Ghost. The Father is Absolute, Positive Intelligence; the Son is the Offspring of the Father; the Holy Ghost is "the Servant of The Eternal Spirit throughout the Ages." Spirit is Absolute Intelligence, operating through the Soul of Receptive Intelligence, impregnating It with "The Divine Ideas."

Neither the Spirit nor the Soul of the Universe can change. That which changes is the Body of the Universe. Planets may appear and disappear as do people and things; but the Substance from which things are formed is Changeless.

INDIVIDUALITY

Individuality emerges from the Universal. Psychology teaches the personification of this individuality, which is true as far as it goes; but Metaphysics universalizes individuality by unifying it with the Whole.

There is a Universal Nature of Man, inherent within him, which causes the manifestation of his personality, i.e., The Spirit of God.

The next chart will be about man, and when that is explained you will begin to see the way out of your difficulties if you have any.

Note: Study carefully "The Edinburgh Lectures on Mental Science," by T. Troward; "Creative Mind," by Ernest S. Holmes; "The Axioms of Truth," by Burnell; "Philosophy of Plotinus," by Dean Inge.

LESSON ONE: RECAPITULATION

The evolution of man brings him automatically to a time when real individuality is produced. From that day any further evolution must be through his conscious coöperation with Life. All nature waits on man's self-recognition and is always ready to obey his will; but he must use nature's forces in accordance with her laws.

Science is the knowledge of certain facts built around some known principle of being. Man never creates; he discovers and uses. In this way all sciences are evolved. We live in a Universe of Law through which runs an element of Self-Knowing Intelligence. "All's Love, yet all's Law."

The Law has done all that it can do for man automatically. It has brought him to the point of individuality, and must now let him alone to make this discovery for himself. Man is potentially perfect, but free will and self-choice cause him to appear imperfect. In reality, all that he can destroy is the embodiment of himself, for the Divine Spark is always intact in Instinctive Man.

Man awakes to self-consciousness, finding himself already equipped with a mentality, a body and an environment. Gradually he discovers one law of nature after another until he conquers his environment through his acquisition of natural forces. Everywhere he finds that nature does his bidding, in so far as he understands her laws and uses them along the lines of their inherent being; for he must first obey nature, then she will obey him.

Man discovers his ability to think, and begins to realize that from within comes a reaction to his thought. He comes to realize that he is threefold in his nature; that he can consciously think; that he has within a mentality which acts upon his thoughts; and that he has a body which is affected by his thinking.

He next discovers that he can think for others, causing a corresponding action in and through their bodies. In this way he discovers that there is a mental medium through which thought operates. He now realizes himself to be a thinking center in a Universal Mind.

Man next discovers that his affairs are also controlled by thought, and that he can likewise think for others and aid in the control of their affairs.

He now realizes that everything in the visible world is an effect; that back of all effects there are ideas which are the real causes of these effects. The Divine Ideas are Perfect, but man has the ability to cause them to appear imperfect. Through right thinking he is able to uncover the appearance of imperfection and reveal the Perfect Idea.

Man's idea of the Deity evolves with his other ideas. After a belief in many gods, he comes to realize that there is One Mind and One Spirit back of all manifestation.

There is One Spirit or Self-Conscious Life acting through the Medium of One Mind or Subjective Law, producing many manifestations. Multiplicity comes from Unity without breaking up the Unity of the Whole.

Spirit is Self-Knowing, but Law is automatic and obeys the will of Spirit, having no alternative other than to obey.

Like all law, the Law of Mind is an Impersonal Force, and because of Its nature is compelled to act.

Soul and Universal Subjective Mind have the same meaning and are the Creative Medium of all thought and action. Soul is also the Substance of Spirit; i.e., It is the unformed Stuff from which all forms are evolved.

Spirit, acting upon Soul, produces Creation; Spirit, Soul and Substance intersphere each other; each has omnipresence. Creation takes place *within* Spirit and is the result of the *Contemplation of Spirit*.

Creation is eternally going on; change is always taking place within that which is changeless; forms appear and disappear in that which is formless.

God thinks or knows within Himself; and as the result of this inner action Creation manifests. Creation is the play of Life upon Itself through Divine Self-Imagination. Spirit must create in order to be expressed.

Spirit, Life, Soul, Substance, Law and Unity are all co-existent and coeternal with each other. The only thing that changes is form.

Life makes things out of Itself by becoming the thing that It makes; there is no effort in the process.

Conscious Mind and Spirit mean the same; they denote that part of the Trinity which is Self-Knowing or God.

Subconscious and Subjective Mind, Soul and Mental Medium, Universal Subjectivity or Law, all have the same meaning; they denote that part of the Trinity which acts as Law.

Body, Creation or the manifest Universe, is simply the result of the Trinity which acts as Law.

BODY—Creation or the manifest Universe—is simply the result of the Knowingness of Spirit through Law.

One element alone is really self-conscious and that is Spirit. Both Law and Manifestation are automatic and must react to Spirit.

Soul or Subjective? Mind, Substance or unformed matter, and Conscious Spirit permeate all things and all people. There is an Intelligence acting through everything, and everything responds to intelligence.

It cannot be too plainly stated that Spirit, or Conscious Intelligence, is the only Self-Assertive Principle in the Universe. "Spirit is the Power that knows Itself," and is the only power that is Self-Knowing. Everything else is subject to Spirit. The sole and only operation of Spirit is through Its Word. The Word, acting as Law through Substance, produces Creation.

LESSON TWO: INTRODUCTION

Mental Science, which is the Science of Mind and Spirit, makes a tremendous claim when it states that it can free the individual from the bondage of sickness, poverty and unhappiness; but it makes this statement without hesitation and without qualification; it does not retract from that claim and it never will. It does, however, carefully set forth the conditions under which it operates and the laws governing Life, warning man that, unless he understands these conditions and obeys these laws, he will not receive full benefit from the Science of Mind.

THE WORLD HAS LEARNED ALL IT CAN THROUGH SUFFERING

The world is beginning to realize that it has learned all it can through suffering and pain. Perhaps they were good in their place, but surely there can be no power in the Universe which wishes man to be sick, to suffer pain, to be unhappy and end in the grave. Surely God could not ordain that man should ultimately be other than a perfect expression of Life.

We should have no intellectual difficulty in realizing that even God Himself could not make an automatic individuality, and this explains why man must suffer on the road to self-discovery. He must suffer, not because pain is a necessity, but because he must have experience in order to become individualized.

WHAT INDIVIDUALITY REALLY MEANS

Perhaps it would be a good idea to elaborate on this and explain just what individuality really means. Individuality means self-choice, volition, conscious mind, personified Spirit complete freedom and a POWER TO BACK UP THAT FREEDOM.

We cannot imagine a mechanical or unspontaneous individuality. To be real and free, individuality must be created IN THE IMAGE OF PERFECTION AND LET ALONE TO MAKE THE GREAT DISCOVERY FOR ITSELF.

The answer to the question, "Why did not God make us free and compel that freedom?" is apparent when we realize that even God could not do this. A freedom under compulsion would produce a freedom that would ultimately amount to the very worst kind of bondage. There is no such thing as compulsory freedom; even God Himself could not ordain this; for He could do nothing that would violate His own nature. No; man must be created with the possibility of limitless freedom and then be let alone to discover the fact for himself. On the road to that discovery he must be subject to the Law of all Life, and if in ignorance he violates that Law, he must thereby suffer. This is not, however, because God imposes the suffering or desires it, but simply because it is the necessity of the case.

THE MEANING OF FREEDOM

Freedom of will means the ability to do, say and think as one wishes; to express life as one personally desires. To be able only to think and dream of freedom would not be liberty. To imagine, without the power to manifest that imagination, would be to remain in a sort of dream world which would never come to complete self-realization. This is not the world in which man lives at all, for man's world is one of self-expression, even though that expression appears at times to destroy him.

SIN AND PUNISHMENT. RIGHTEOUSNESS AND REWARD

We do not wish to enter into theological discussions in this course of instruction, but we do wish to make the thought clear to those who care to study it. There is no sin but a mistake and no punishment but an inevitable consequence. Wrong doing must be punished, for the Law of cause and effect must be eternally operative. Right doing must be rewarded for the same reason.

We do not say that man cannot sin; what we say is, that he does sin or make mistakes and that he is thereby automatically punished, AS LONG AS HE CONTINUES TO MAKE MISTAKES. This does not mean that there is an evil power in the Universe; but it does mean that there is an immutable Law of cause and effect running through everything. Sin is its own punishment and righteousness ITS OWN REWARD.

The age-long discussion of the problem of evil will never be answered until we realize that it is not a thing of itself but is simply A MISUSE OF THE LAW OF FREEDOM. The problem of evil will be met only to the degree that we *cease doing evil and do good*, for evil will disappear when we no longer indulge in it. When the whole world sees the right and does it; then, and not until then, will the problem of evil be solved for the entire race.

THE INCARNATION OF SPIRIT

To return to individuality; it is that which distinguishes man from the mere brute creation; it is the greater Incarnation of God in the human; the Indwelling Spirit of the Most High.

Man is created and left to discover himself, and on the road to this self-discovery he experiences the creations of his own imaginations which ultimately show him the Truth and lead to real freedom.

There is an interesting myth in regard to the creating of man which may serve to point out this fact. It is said that when the gods decided to make man, and make him a Divine Being, they held a long discussion as to where would be the best place to hide his Divinity. Some of the gods suggested that it be hidden in the earth, but others argued that some day man would penetrate the earth and so discover himself; it was then suggested that it be hidden in the depths of the sea, but this idea was rejected, for man would go under the sea and there discover his true nature; it was next suggested that his real nature should be deposited somewhere in the air, but this also was rejected, for he would surely fly through the air and find himself. After a long discussion it was finally agreed that the best place to hide man's Divinity would be IN THE INNERMOST NATURE OF MAN HIMSELF—this being the last place he would look to find it!

This discovery would not be made until he had had all the experience necessary to complete a well-rounded life. "The Word is very nigh unto thee, in thy mouth, and in thy heart, that thou mayest do it."[22]

Of course, this is a fable, but how clearly it sets forth the reality of the case! The word is really in our own mouths, and every time we say "I AM" we are repeating it; for "I AM" is the secret of nature and the emblem of Eternity.

The story of "The Prodigal Son" is the story of man's return to "His Father's House." How truly the poet puts it when he says that "Trailing clouds of Glory do we come from Heaven which is our home." This is the mystical meaning of that marvelous poem of Robert Browning's called "Saul." Saul had lost his sense of real life and lay in a stupor in his tent when David came to sing to him, to awaken him to the realization of his true nature. At first David sings of the wonders of Creation and of the delights of life; he tells Saul of his power and glory as a human being; and, as the song expands, he touches the secret spring of Saul's being—"He is Saul ye remember in glory, ere error had bent the broad brow from the daily communion." Then, he plainly tells Saul of the Christ. This revelation finally awakens Saul to "His old motions and attitudes kingly." The healing has taken place and the realization of the Truth has freed Saul from the thraldom of false belief.

DIFFERENT VIEWPOINTS

Some take the viewpoint that man was cast forth to discover himself; and others contend that man decided to do this for himself. It makes no difference what the case may be; man is certainly on the pathway to self-discovery, and everything in his experience points to the truth of this fact. We know that the forces of nature wait on man's discovery of them and obey his will as soon as he understands how to make use of her laws. We certainly have freedom enough when we understand how to use that freedom. The Pilgrim Fathers might have had steam cars if they had understood the nature of steam. It was not pushed into man's experience by any autocratic power, but served him only after he had discovered how to use it. We might say the same of any and all of the laws that we now understand and utilize.

---

22 Deut. 30 : 14.

The Lesson of Nature's Laws

If we find this to be true of the laws of the mechanical world, why should we not also find it true of those Mental and Spiritual Laws which transcend the mechanical world? No doubt, we shall find latent powers and capacities of which we have never dreamed; powers and abilities waiting to be understood and used. "Behold I stand at the door and knock." It certainly will pay man to spend much time and thought in the study of his own nature; for he will discover things about himself that will cause him to "Arise and shine." [23] Man is to-day, more than ever before, awakening to the real facts of the case, and from now on his evolution will become very rapid. Nothing is impossible; all things are possible to the Great Whole, and man is a part of that Whole.

The Relation of Man to the Universe of Spirit

As the evidence of design in the Universe proves a Designer, so the evidence of self-choice shows a Power that Knows Itself. The Spirit is Self-Knowing; God knows that God Is. But a Universal Self-Knowingness really means a Universal Personalness; and so we see how God can be Personal to every living soul who believes in Spirit. We could truthfully say—so it seems to me at least—that there is One Infinite Person, in whom we all "live, and move and have our Being"; [24] for we all live in the One.

Man's Experience

Let us assume that man is on the road to self-discovery. What is he to discover?—That he is really free, but that, in order to be free, he must first go through experiences which will teach him how to use his freedom properly; and, after the lesson is learned, he will be free indeed. Everything seems as if this were true. We have traced man's progress carefully through his journey on this planet from the time when the first face "Was turned from the clod," to now, and what have we discovered? That all nature waits upon man's self-discovery and is ever ready to serve him and do his bidding. Laws and forces undreamed of by our ancestors are now being employed; powers and forces which to prehistoric man would have seemed as gods, are to-day called nature's forces, and we consciously make use of them. Man has gradually merged with nature and her laws, and to-day stands forth as a new being so far as the mechanical world is concerned. It seems as if he had conquered nature and compelled her to serve him.

---

23 Isa. 60 : 1.
24 Acts 17 : 28.

Nature Waits on Man

Nowhere on this path has he found nature opposed to him. She has silently waited for his recognition and as silently done his bidding. She will never contradict herself nor operate contrary to her inherent laws; but she will serve whoever comes to understand and use them along the lines of her way of working. Man never created any of these laws but simply uses them, and he can do this only as he first obeys them. "Nature obeys us as we first obey it" is an old saying and a true one. We learn the fundamental principle of a law, obey its mode of operation and then have conscious use of it. It would be absurd to say that nature punished us because we did not make proper use of her laws. She simply will not work harmoniously for us until we harmonize with her; she will obey us only after we have obeyed her. This is, of course, true of any and all law. If we obey, it serves; if we disobey, it seems to punish us.

Mental and Spiritual Laws

It is the same with those great Mental and Spiritual Laws of our Being. We must come to discover and utilize the inner forces of Mind and Spirit, for they are the highest powers.

Man will be delivered from sin, sickness and trouble in exact proportion to his discovery of himself and his relationship to the Whole.

Law is law wherever we find it, and we shall discover that the Laws of Mind and Spirit must be understood if they are to be consciously used for definite purposes. THE SPIRIT KNOWS AND THE LAW OBEYS.

Hidden away in the inner nature of the real man is the Law of his life, and some day he will discover it and consciously make use of it. He will heal himself, make himself happy and prosperous, and will live in an entirely different world; for he will have discovered that LIFE IS FROM WITHIN AND NOT FROM WITHOUT.

God and Man

Man is made out of and from Life; and, as effect must partake of the nature of its cause, so man must partake of the Divine Nature from which he springs.

Man Reënacts the Nature of God

If we realize that God is "Triune" and that man is made in the Image and Likeness of God, we shall see that the whole scheme of Life and the whole nature of the Divine Being is reënacted through man. This, of course, does not mean that man is God; it means that, in his small world of individual expression, his nature is identical with God's. This is what Jesus meant when he said, "As the Father hath Life within Himself so hath He given to the Son to have Life within himself."[25]

A single drop of water is not the whole ocean, but it does resemble the ocean and does contain within itself the same qualities and attributes. We might say that man is in God and that God works through man. "I and The Father are One,"[26] "The Kingdom of God is within you";[27] and we might add, "God's in His Heaven, all's right with the world."

THE TWO WAYS TO REASON

There are but two processes of reasoning known to the human mind: inductive and deductive; and from these two ways of reasoning all our knowledge of life has come. Inductive reasoning is the systematic process of reasoning from a part to the whole. Deductive reasoning is the process of accepting certain conclusions as truths and drawing other conclusions from them; it is reasoning from the whole to a part. For instance, in inductive reasoning we would say that everything happens just as if there were what we call electricity and that it is everywhere present. Deductive reasoning says that since electricity is everywhere present, it is always where we are and can always be generated from any center.

Using these two methods of reasoning to deduce the nature of God, we may start with the assumption that God IS, drawing all our conclusions from this premise; or we may carefully study the nature of man and the Universe and so draw the conclusion that a God must exist. Whichever method we use will lead to the same conclusion; namely, that there is a Divine Being and that man is made in His Image and must reënact and portray the same attributes as the Life from which he came.

NOTHING HAPPENS BY CHANCE

Nothing in the Universe happens by chance. All is in accordance with Law, and the Law of God is as Omnipresent as is the Spirit of God. This Law is a Law of Mind, but back of the Law is the Word." All things were made by Him and without Him was not anything made that was made."[28]

---

25 John 5 : 26.

26 John 10 : 30.

27 Luke 17 : 21.

28 John 1 : 3.

Back of our lives is the Law of our Being; and through that Law runs the word which we speak; for "What things soever He (the Son) seeth the Father do, these also doeth the Son likewise."[29]

MANY ARE WAKING UP TO THE FACTS

Thousands of people to-day are beginning to realize this and put it into operation, and the results attained would fill more books than one man could read in a lifetime. Thousands to-day are using the silent power of Mind to heal their bodies and bring prosperity into their affairs; and the Law is always working in accordance with the belief of those seeking to use It. As the Universe is run by an Infinite Mind, so man's life is controlled by his thinking; ignorance of this keeps him in bondage; knowledge will free him.

One by one, people will investigate the Truth and put It into operation, and the time will come when disease and poverty will be swept from the face of the earth, for they were never intended to be. They are simply the by-products of ignorance, and enlightenment alone will erase them.

THE TIME HAS COME TO KNOW THE TRUTH

The hour of freedom has struck, the bell of Liberty is ringing, and "Let him that is athirst come."[30] Let us, then, plunge more deeply into our own natures and into the nature of the Universe and see if we shall not find treasures undreamed of, possibilities never imagined and opportunities which the fond thought—yearning for freedom—has often, in our vision of the greater Life, given us.

"Prove me now, herewith, saith the Lord of hosts, if I will not open you the windows of heaven, and pour you out a blessing that there shall not be room enough to receive it."[31]

A WONDERFUL EXPERIMENT

It would be a wonderful experiment for any one to make to begin to live as if this promise were true; to talk, think and act as though there were a Limitless Power attending him on his journey through life; as though his every act were directed and guided into expressions of

---

29 John 5 : 19.
30 Rev. 22 : 17.
31 Mal. 3: 10.

peace, health, happiness and harmony. It is surely worth while, and understanding will make the way so clear before us that we shall some day come to see the logic of it; and then, indeed, shall we really begin to live. Our lives, fortunes and happiness are in our own hands to mold as we will—provided we first obey the Law and learn how to make conscious use of It. "With all thy getting get understanding"[32]—an old adage—but to-day as true as ever.

It has been the teaching of all times that man reproduces the Divine Nature; and if he does, we shall expect to find in his nature the same qualities that we suppose must be in the Nature of Life Itself.

What Psychology Teaches About Man's Nature

A study of the psychological nature of man verifies the belief in "The Trinity" running through all Life. Man is self-conscious; of this we are sure, for he can say "I AM." This fact alone proves his claim to immortality and greatness. In psychology we learn that man is threefold in his nature; that is, he has a self-conscious mind, a subconscious mind and a body. In metaphysics we learn that the three are but different attributes of the same life. Man's self-conscious mind is the power with which he knows; it is, therefore, one with the Spirit of God; it is, indeed, His only guarantee of conscious being.

The Self-knowing Mind

It is from this self-knowing mind that man is able to realize his relationship with the Whole; for without it he would be unhuman and most certainly not Divine; but since he has it, he must be Divine.

It is the self-knowing mind alone that constitutes reality, personality and individuality. It is the "Image of God," the essence of Sonship, and the "Personification of the Infinite."

Man's Unity with the Whole

We recognize, then, in man's self-knowing mind his Unity with the Whole. For while a drop of water is not the ocean, yet it does contain within itself all the attributes of the limitless deep.

Man's self-knowing mind is the instrument which perceives reality, and cognizes or realizes Truth. All illumination, inspiration and realization must come through the self-knowing mind

---

32 Prov. 4 : 7.

in order to manifest in man. Vision, intuition and revelation proclaim themselves through man's self-knowing mind; and the Saints and Sages, the Saviours and Christs, the Prophets and Seers, the Wise and Learned, have all consciously perceived and proclaimed this fact. Every evidence of human experience, all acts of kindness and mercy, have interpreted themselves through man's self-knowing mind. All that we know, say or think, feel or believe, hope or long for, fear or doubt, is some action of the self-knowing mind. Subjective memories we have, and inner, unexpressed emotions we feel; but to the self-knowing mind alone does realization come. Without this capacity to consciously know, man would not exist as an expressed being; and, so far as we are concerned, would not exist at all. The self-knowing mind of man proclaims itself in every thought, deed or act, and is truly the only guarantee of his individuality.

Man a Center of God-Consciousness

With this vast array of facts at our disposal it would be foolish to suppose that man's self-knowing mind is any other than his perception of Reality. *It is his Unity with the Whole, or God, on the conscious side of life, and is an absolute guarantee that he is a Center of God-Consciousness in the Vast Whole.*

Unity with Law

We will say, then, that in Spirit man is One with God. But what of the great Law of the Universe? If we are really One with the Whole we must be One with the Law of the Whole, as well as One with the Spirit. Again psychology has determined the fact to be more than a fancy. The characteristics of the subconscious mind of man determine his Subjective Unity with the Universe of Life, Law and Action.

The Subjective Obeys the Objective

In the Subjective Mind of man we find a law obeying his word, the servant of his Spirit. Suggestion has proved that the subconscious mind acts upon our thought without question or doubt. It is the mental law of our Being and the creative factor within us. It is unnecessary, at this point, to go into all the details of the Subjective Mind and its mode of action; it is enough to say that within us is a mental law, working out the will and purposes of our conscious thoughts. This can be no other than OUR INDIVIDUAL USE OF THAT GREATER SUBJECTIVE MIND WHICH IS THE SEAT OF ALL LAW AND ACTION, AND IS "THE SERVANT OF THE ETERNAL SPIRIT THROUGH ALL THE AGES."

Marvelous as the concept may be, it is none the less true that man has at his disposal, in what he calls his subjective mind, a power which seems to be Limitless. This is because he a One with the Whole, on the subjective side of life.

Man's thought, falling into his subjective mind merges with the Universal Subjective Mind and becomes the law of his life, through THE ONE GREAT LAW OF ALL LIFE.

There are not two subjective minds. *There is but one Subjective mind; and what we call our subjective mind is really Only THE USE THAT WE ARE MAKING OF THE ONE LAW.*

Each individual maintains his identity in Law through his personal use of It; and each is drawing *from* Life what HE THINKS *INTO* IT.

TO LEARN HOW TO THINK IS TO LEARN HOW TO LIVE, for our thoughts go into a Medium that is Infinite in Its ability to do and to be.

MAN, BY THINKING, CAN BRING INTO HIS EXPERIENCE WHATSOEVER HE DESIRES, IF HE THINKS CORRECTLY AND BECOMES A LIVING EMBODIMENT OF HIS THOUGHTS. *This is not done by holding thoughts but by KNOWING THE TRUTH.*

THE BODY

But what about man's body? Is that, too, one with the Body of the Universe? Let us briefly analyze matter and see what it really is. We are told that matter is not a solid, stationary thing; but is a constantly flowing, formless substance which is forever coming and going. Matter is as indestructible as God, as eternal as Timeless Being; nothing can be either added to or taken from it. The very bodies we now have were not with us a short time ago. As Sir Oliver Lodge says, we discard many of them on the path through this life, for the material from which our bodies are composed is in a constant state of flow. Vistas of thought open up along the line of mental healing when we realize this fact; later we will thoroughly discuss and work out a definite technique for the purpose of healing.

Matter is not what we thought it to be; it is simply a flowing stuff taking the form that Mind gives it. How about the matter from which other things than the body are made? It is all the same—ONE SUBSTANCE IN THE UNIVERSE TAKES DIFFERENT FORMS AND SHAPES AND BECOMES DIFFERENT THINGS.

LAST STAGES OF MATTER

The last analysis of matter resolves it into a universal ether and leaves nothing more than a stuff which may be operated upon.

Matter, in the last analysis, is composed of particles so fine that they are simply supposed to be. In other words, it disappears entirely, and the place where it once was is again "without form and void."[33] Matter, as we know it, is only an aggregation of these particles arranged in such order as to produce definite forms, which are determined by something *WHICH IS NOT MATERIAL*.

There is no difference between the particles which any one form takes and the particles which all forms take; the difference is not in the minute particles but in their arrangement.

THE UNITY OF ALL BODY

Our bodies are One with the Whole Body of the Universe. Seeds, plants, cabbages and kings are made of the same substance; minerals, solids and liquids are made from *THE PRIMORDIAL SUBSTANCE WHICH IS FOREVER FLOWING INTO FORM AND FOREVER FLOWING OUT AGAIN INTO THE VOID*.

THE FORMLESS AND THE FORMED

Nothing could form a formless stuff, which has no mind of its own, except Intelligence operating upon it. Again we come back to the Word as the starting point of all Creation—God's Word in the Great World, man's word in the small world.

ONE SPIRIT, *ONE* MIND, AND *ONE* SUBSTANCE; *ONE* LAW BUT MANY THOUGHTS; *ONE* POWER, BUT MANY WAYS OF USING IT; *ONE* GOD IN WHOM WE ALL LIVE, AND *ONE* LAW WHICH ALL OPERATE; *ONE, ONE, ONE.* NO GREATER UNITY COULD BE GIVEN THAN THAT WHICH IS ALREADY VOUCHSAFED TO MANKIND.

But why is man so limited? Why is he still poor, sick, afraid and unhappy? Because he does not know the Truth—that is the only "Why." But why was he not so made that he would *have* to know the Truth? The answer is that even God could not make a real man, that is, a real Personified Expression of Himself, without *creating him in freedom and leaving him TO DISCOVER HIMSELF*. This is the meaning of the story of the Prodigal Son and the whole meaning of it.

INDIVIDUALITY MEANS SELF-CHOICE

Individuality means real individualized being and real personified self-choice. We could not imagine an individuality without self-choice; but what would be the use of self-choice unless the ability to choose were backed with the power to externalize that choice? It would remain

---

33 Gen. I : 2.

simply an idle dream, never coming into real self-expression. A little thought will make it clear that, if man is created to express freedom, he must be left to discover himself. Of course, during the process he will have much experience, but in the end he will come out a real being.

The day of man's discovery of himself marked the first day of the record of human history on this planet; and from the day when he first made this discovery he has constantly risen and continuously progressed. All the forces of nature attend him on his way, but he must first discover them in order to make use of them.

THE GREATEST DISCOVERY EVER MADE

The greatest discovery that man ever made was, that his thought has creative power; that is, that it uses creative power. His thought, of itself, would have no power unless it were operative through a creative medium. We do not have to compel Law to operate; all that we have to do is to use It. The Law of Mind is just like any and all other laws of Being. It simply Is.

A COMPLETE UNITY

We have now discovered a Unity with the Whole on all three sides of life or from all three modes of expression. We are One with all matter in the physical world, One with the Creative Law of the Universe in the Mental World, and One with the Spirit of God in the Conscious World.

What more could we ask or hope for? How would it be possible for more to be given? We could ask for no more, and no greater freedom could be given. From now on we will expand, grow and express, only to the degree that we consciously coöperate with the Whole.

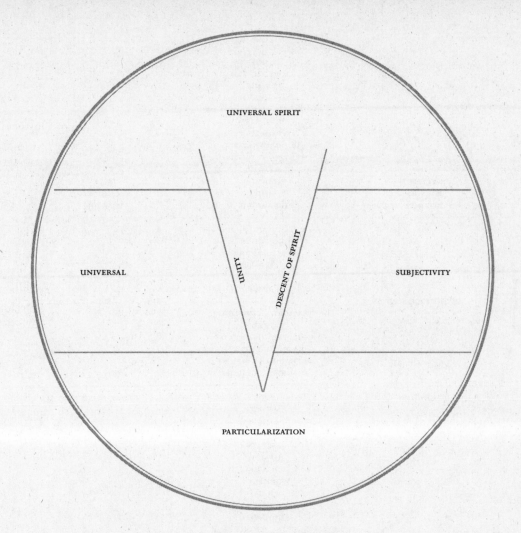

UNIVERSAL SPIRIT

UNITY

DESCENT OF SPIRIT

UNIVERSAL

SUBJECTIVITY

PARTICULARIZATION

LESSON TWO:
METAPHYSICAL CHART NO. II-A.

This chart shows, first, the Universal Spirit; then the Universal Soul or Subjectivity which is the medium of all thought, power and action; then the particularization or manifestation of Spirit.

The point drawn down through the center symbolizes the descent of Spirit into matter, or form. It is necessary that Spirit be manifested in order to express Itself. The word Unity on the descending line shows that all come from the One. Man reënacts the world Universal Life, and his nature is identical with Spirit. What is true of the Whole is true of any one of Its undivided parts. Man comes to a point of individualization in the Whole and is subject to the Law of the Whole.

	SPIRIT	
	CHRIST LOGOS	
	SONSHIP	
	MICROCOSM	
	EMMANUEL—GOD-WITH-US	
	PERSONALITY	
	INDIVIDUALITY	
	CONSCIOUS STATE	
	MENTAL—SPIRITUAL	
	REASON	
INTELLECT	INDUCTIVE	WILL
PURPOSE	AND	CHOICE
DECISION	DEDUCTIVE	VOLITION

	SOUL	
	SUBJECTIVE	
	SUB-CONSCIOUS	
	UN-CONSCIOUS	
	CONSCIOUSNESS	
	KARMA	
AUTO-SUGGESTION	AURA	REASON—DEDUCTIVE ONLY
	MEMORY—CONFLICT	
	PSYCHE	
	INHERITED TENDENCIES	
	RACE-SUGGESTIONS	
	PRENATAL CONDITIONS	
	IMAGES OF THOUGHT	

OCCUPATION	BODY	REASON—NONE
	EFFECT	
	AFFAIR	
	CONDITIONS	
	RESULTS	
	HEALTH	
	DISEASE	
	DESTINY	
	RICHES	
	POVERTY	
	BUSINESS	
	VOCATION	
	PROFESSION	

LESSON TWO:
METAPHYSICAL CHART NO. II-B.

This chart shows how man reënacts the Whole and is subject to the law of his own being. If the meaning of this chart is carefully studied it will be made plain that man thinks consciously and that his conscious thought becomes the law of his life. The upper section stands for the Self-Conscious man; the middle section stands for the subconscious man; and the lowest section stands for the man as he appears in the flesh and in the conditions of his life.

LESSON TWO: METAPHYSICAL MEANING OF WORDS USED IN INDIVIDUAL CHART NO. II-B

UPPER SECTION

SPIRIT.—That part of man which enables him to be self-conscious. That which he really is. We do not see the spirit of man any more than we see the Spirit of God We see what man does; but we do not see the doer.

CHRIST, LOGOS.—The Word of God manifest in and through man. In a liberal sense the Christ means the Entire Manifestation of God and is, therefore, the Second Person of the Trinity. Christ is a Universal Idea, and each one "Puts on The Christ"[34] to the degree that he surrenders a limited sense of Life to the Divine Realization.

SONSHIP.—We are all Sons of God and all partake of the Divine Nature.

MICROCOSM.—The individual world as distinguished from the Universal.

EMMANUEL—GOD-WITH-US.—Means that Christ is in every one.

PERSONALITY.—The external evidence of individualized being.

INDIVIDUALITY.—Each one is a separate identity in Mind and no two are alike. Each is an Individualized Center of God-Consciousness. Our personality is the use that we make of our Divine Individuality.

CONSCIOUS-STATE.—The conscious-state is the self-knowing mind of man. It is the only thing that distinguishes him from brute creation. Without a conscious-state of mind man would not be at all; or, at least, he would not know that he is. The conscious mind should be carefully guarded, as it is the real man.

MENTAL.—Means that man is mentally conscious.

SPIRITUAL.—Means that man is a Spiritual Being.

REASON: INDUCTIVE AND DEDUCTIVE.—The conscious mind of man can reason both inductively and deductively. It can reason from the Whole to a part or from a part to the Whole.

WILL.—Means conscious ability to determine.

CHOICE.—Ability to differentiate and choose.

VOLITION.—Power to act independently.

---

34 Gal. 3 : 27.

INTELLECT.—Mental quality of analysis.

PURPOSE.—Determination with incentive.

DECISION.—Ability to choose.

MIDDLE SECTION

SOUL.—*The Subjective Side of Life*. Man's place in the One Subjective Mind of the Universe; his identity in Mind. Man's soul life reënacts the Soul Life of the Universe with which it is at One.

SUBJECTIVE.—The Soul is subjective. Read again the meaning of subjectivity as given in the Universal Chart.

SUBCONSCIOUS.—The Soul is subjective to the conscious thought.

UNCONSCIOUS.—Word used in Psycho-analysis to denote soul. It is a poor way of expressing soul-life, for it really is not unconscious. It is subconscious but certainly not unconscious.

CONSCIOUSNESS.—Another way of saying soul. The Bible says, soul; the psycho-analyst says, unconscious; the psychologist says, subjective or subconscious; and the metaphysician says, consciousness. All have the same meaning.

KARMA.—The subjective law of tendency set in motion by the individual. The mental law acting through him. Karmic Law means the use that man makes of his mentality. Karma is not Kismet; for Kismet means "fate," and Karma simply means "the mental tendency." Karma is both individual and Universal.

AURA.—Mental atmosphere or vibration. It extends from a few inches to a few feet around the individual and can be seen by many people.

MEMORY.—The soul, or subjective mind, is the seat of memory, and retains within itself everything that the individual has ever said, thought, seen, heard, felt, read or been told; and, indeed, everything that has ever happened to him. It also contains race memory, and may, or may not, contain much of what we call Cosmic Purposes. Cosmic Purposes mean the Ideas of God. The soul of man, being in constant contact with the Soul of the Universe, might contact tremendous powers if it would turn to the One.

CONFLICT.—In the study of Psycho-analysis, which means the analysis of the soul, we learn that the subjective side of thought, being the seat of memory, often retains thoughts and suppressed emotions which more or less tear or bind. This is what is meant by inner conflict.

PSYCHE.—Means soul.

INHERITED TENDENCIES.—The subjective, being the seat of memory, contains the race characteristics and tendencies. We do not inherit diseases, but we do inherit tendencies. This is the way that family and race traits are handed down.

RACE-SUGGESTION.—The tendency to reproduce what the race has thought and experienced.

PRENATAL CONDITIONS.—The tendency to inherit family traits.

IMAGES OF THOUGHT.—The soul, or subjective mind, contains all of our thoughts as mental images or pictures.

AUTO-SUGGESTION.—The soul receives the suggestions of the individual.

REASON—Deductive Only.—That which is subjective can reason deductively only.

LOWEST SECTION

BODY.—The definite outline of flesh, containing all of the ideas which go to make the complete physical instrument.

EFFECT.—That which follows cause. The body is always an effect.

AFFAIRS.—That which happens to the external man.

CONDITIONS.—External things, the result of thought.

RESULTS.—Conditions.

HEALTH.—Result of correct thinking.

DISEASE.—Result of wrong thinking.

DESTINY.—Result of what man thinks.

RICHES.—Result of a consciousness of supply.

POVERTY.—Result of limited thought.

BUSINESS.—Also result of thought.

VOCATION.—The thing that our thought causes us to do.

PROFESSION.—Same as vocation.

OCCUPATION.—Same as vocation.

REASON—None.—Everything in the body of man, as well as in his affairs, is the result of what he thinks. Nothing in the external is a cause, and nothing that happens causes itself to happen. Things have no power to reason, but are always the result of some inner cause.

LESSON TWO: THE NATURE OF MAN

In the first lesson we studied the Universal Chart; we are now taking up the individual chart. Whatever is true of the Universe as a Whole must also be true of the individual as some part of this Whole. Man is evolved from the Universe, and is a self-conscious, thinking center of Living Spirit, and, as such, he must, in his nature and being, reproduce the Universe. This is what Jesus meant when He said, "As the Father hath (Inherent) Life in Himself, so hath he given to the Son to have (Inherent) Life in Himself."[35] Inherent Life means real Life. The whole Cosmic Scheme must be reproduced on the plane of the individual, if there is an individual.

We must expect to find in man, therefore, the same inherent attributes that we find in the universe from which he springs.

Chart No. II-A symbolizes, first, the Universal Spirit; next, the Universal Subjectivity, which is called the Soul of the Universe; and third, the particularization or manifestation of Universal Spirit. We have marked Unity on the descending line, because the Spirit emanates, or particularizes Itself, at the point of our personality becoming what we call man. It is essential that we realize the Unity of life, i.e., the Unity of God and man on all three planes.

Let us start with the objective plane: matter or body, devoid of mind or intelligence, has no volition; it may be permeated with intelligence, but it is not intelligent. It is one with the Body of the Universe.

Now, what do we know about the soul? Remember the things that were discussed in connection with the qualities of the Soul of the Universe; and you will find all of them depicted in what is called the psychological, subjective nature of man; for our subjective or subconscious mind reproduces all the attributes belonging to the Universal Mind. When we turn to the spirit of man, we find that it is one with the Spirit of God—that is, man is a self-conscious, thinking, choosing center of individualized intelligence, or God-Consciousness in the great Whole.

So we find man is one with all matter in the material world, one with the Soul of the Universe in the subjective world, and one with the Spirit of God in the conscious world. What we call our objective or conscious mind is as much as we know of God and Life. The objective mind is the spiritual mind for which we have been looking, but it is not fully developed; if this were not so there would be no mind with which to look. The objective mind must be the spiritual mind of man, since it is the only thing about him which knows that it has life and is conscious of itself.

---

35 John 5 : 26.

The whole of Spirit is potentially focused in our individual, objective consciousness; but we have not yet evolved to a realization of this, except in a small degree. Back of the objective mind is the subjective mind or soul, which is the medium through which intelligence operates.

There is but One Universal Subjective Mind or Soul; and what we call our subjective mind is simply our use of Universal Subjectivity; for our subjective mind is not a thing apart, but is our place in Universal Subjective Mind; and our place in It is the use that we make of It.

SPIRIT

Turning to the chart of man, Chart No. II-B, we find that the spirit of man is his conscious state of mental and spiritual being; that this mental state is equipped with decision, will, choice, volition, intellect and purpose. We find that it is individuality, personality, and is called Emmanuel or God with us. It is the microcosm within the Macrocosm, which means the little world within the big world; it is also called the Image of God; it is Sonship, the Sonship of the Father; it is the Christ or Logos, which means the Word. It can reason both inductively and deductively, and is the only thing known to us that can reason both ways.

SOUL

We find that on the subjective or soul side man is subconscious; but subconscious does not mean unconscious. Subconscious means subjective to the conscious thought, compelled by reason of its subjectivity to receive what is put into it. The term "unconscious" is used by psycho-analysts. Consciousness is the word that some use in speaking of the soul side of life. It is Karmic Law, because it is the use that we are making of Universal Subjectivity; Karma means the law of cause and effect. Soul contains the memory, because it is the receptacle for the seeds of our thought. It is psyche, soul, psychic; this is where we get the word "psycho-analysis," analysis of the soul. It contains the inherited tendencies, because it is the seat of memory. It also contains race-suggestion; for we are not dealing with a separated and isolated subjective mind, but with the one Subjective Mind. There is a vast difference between thinking of having three or four minds and thinking of having but One which all use. Its reasoning capacity is deductive only, yet it contains an intelligence which is infinite compared with the human concept of intelligence.

BODY

Next we come to the body of man, which is simply the effect of what his thought has been in Mind. Body, effect, affairs, conditions, health, disease, destiny, riches, poverty, business, vocation, profession, results, occupation, any word that stands for the externalization of man's thought and endeavor, we class as a part of the body.

"What a man has, as well as what he is, is the result of the subjective state of his thought." The thinker is conscious mind, but when he thinks, he lets fall the forms of his thought into Subjective Mind, which is the Universal Medium of all thought and action, and as the result of this, the Creative Medium at once sets to work to produce the thing thought of. This is the way that Nature works and it is the way that man works, although he is just waking to this realization.

Plotinus, who was one of the Neo-Platonic philosophers, personifying Nature, said, "I do not argue; I contemplate; and as I contemplate, I let fall the forms of my thought." This is the way Nature creates; It contemplates through Its Conscious Mind. As the result of Its contemplation, It lets fall the seeds of Its thought into the Universal Subjective, which, being Law, produces the thing thought of. Now we must expect to find, and we do find, the same thing reënacted in man. This means that whatever man thinks (whether it is what he calls good or bad) falls into this Universal Creative Medium, is accepted by It, is at once acted upon, begins to take form, and, unless neutralized, tends to become a thing in the objective world.

Limitless Medium

When we realize that as we deal with our own individuality we are dealing with Self-Conscious Mind, and when we realize that as we deal with subjective mind we are dealing with the Universal Subjectivity, we see at once that we have at our disposal a Power compared to which the united intelligence of the human race is as nothing; because the Universal Subjective Mind, being entirely receptive to our thought, is compelled by reason of Its very being to accept that thought and act upon it, no matter what the thought is. Since we are dealing with an Infinite Power, which knows only Its own ability to do, and since It can objectify any idea impressed upon It, there can be no limit to what It could or would do for us, other than the limit of our mental concept. Limitation could not be in Principle or in Law but only in the individual use that we make of It. Our individual use of It can only equal our individual capacity to understand It, to embody It. *We cannot demonstrate beyond our ability to mentally conceive, or to mentally provide, an equivalent.* We must have a mental equivalent of the thing we want, in order to demonstrate.

Subjectivity is entirely receptive and neutral, as we have learned, and It can take our thoughts only the way we think them. There is no alternative. If I say, "I am poor," and keep on saying, "I am poor," subconscious mind at once says, "Yes, you are poor," and keeps me poor, as long as I say it. This is all there is to poverty. It comes from impoverished thinking. We deal only with thoughts, for thoughts are things, and if the thought is right the condition will be right. An active thought will produce an active condition. Suppose I have thought poverty year after year, I have created a law, which keeps on perpetuating this condition. If the thought be unerased, the condition will remain. A law has been set in motion which says, "I am poor," and sees to it that it is so. This is, at first, auto-suggestion; then it becomes an unconscious memory, working day and night. This is what decides the law of attraction, because the laws of attraction and repulsion are entirely subjective. They may be *conscious to start with, but they are subconscious as soon as they are set in motion.* Now suppose I did not say I was poor, but came into the world with an unconscious thought of poverty; so long as that thought operated, I would be poor. I might not have understood the Law, but it would have been working all the time.

There is also a race-suggestion which says that some people are rich and some are poor; so we are all born or come into this world with a subjective tendency toward negative conditions. But we are also dealing with a subjective tendency toward ultimate good; because, in spite of all conditions, the race believes more in the good than in the evil; otherwise, it would not exist. It believes that everything will come out all right, rather than all wrong. This is the eternal hope and sense of all life.

No matter what may be in the soul, or subjective state of our thought, the conscious state can change it. This is what treatment does. How can this be done? Through the most direct method imaginable—by consciously knowing that there is no subjective state of poverty, no inherited tendency toward limitation, no race-suggestion operating through subjectivity; nothing in, around or through it that believes in or accepts limitation in any way, shape, form or manner. The conscious state must now provide a higher form of thought. What does it do? It supplies a spiritual realization, a self-conscious realization, and says, "I partake of the nature and bounty of the All Good and I am now surrounded by everything which makes life worth while." What happens then ? This Soul side of life, this Universal Medium, at once changes Its thought (because Its thought is deductive only) and says, "Yes, you are all of these things." *Whatever is held in consciousness until it becomes a part of the subjective side of thought must take place in the world of affairs. Nothing can stop it.* The reason we do not demonstrate more easily is that the objective state of our thought is too often neutralized by the subjective state. There is more fear of poverty than there is belief in riches. As long as that fear remains it is sure to produce a limited condition. *Whatever is subjective must objectify.* Matter is immaterial, unknowing, unthinking, and plastic in the hands of Law or Mind; and Law or Subjective Mind, which is entirely unvolitional, but not unintelligent, is compelled by its own subjectivity to receive the thought of the conscious mind, which alone can choose and decide. It follows then that whatever the conscious mind holds long enough is bound to be produced in external affairs; nothing can stop it, because we are dealing with Universal Law. This is called Divine Principle. It is the Medium in which we all live, move and have our being on the subjective side of life; our atmosphere in Universal Subjectivity; the medium through which all intercommunication takes place on every plane.

It follows from what we have said that any suggestion held in Creative Mind would produce its logical result, no matter what that suggestion might be. If it were a suggestion of destruction, it would destroy; for this is a neutral field. If it were a suggestion of good, it would construct.

CHRIST AND ANTICHRIST

The Spirit of Christ means that mentality which recognizes the Law and uses It for constructive purposes only. The spirit of Antichrist is the spirit of the individual, or class of individuals who, understanding the Law, use It destructively. The meaning of the Flood or Deluge (which is recorded in every sacred scripture we have read or heard of) is that a race of people were upon the earth who came to understand psychic, or subjective, law as being the servant of the Spirit. They understood themselves to be Spirit, but they did not understand the harmonious Unity of Spirit. They had arrived at an intellectual concept of the Law,—a very clearly defined mental concept; but that knowledge and wisdom were not used for constructive purposes. They used it destructively, and what happened? The confusion which took place in the psychic world (or the psychic atmosphere of this planet) caused its physical correspondence in the form of the Deluge or Flood.

Psyche also means "sea," and it was into this psychic sea that Jonah fell. This is the meaning of the story of Jonah and the whale and is also why, in Revelation, it says: "There was no more sea."[36] It does not mean that Law shall be eliminated, but that the time will come when It will be used for constructive purposes only. The misuse of this Law to-day is called "Malpractice." We have no fear of malpractice, because it can be practiced only upon the person who believes in it. If we say to Mind: "There is no such thing as malpractice," there being only One Ultimate Reality, as far as we are concerned, we are free from it. "Against such there is no law."[37] We recognize Subconscious Mind as the Great Servant of our thought. It is the Medium through which all treatment operates. How do we contact this Universal Subjective Mind, which is the Medium through which healing and demonstration take place? *We contact It within ourselves and nowhere else.* It is in us, being Omnipresent. Our use of It, we call our subjective mind; but It is Universal Subjectivity.

---

36 Rev. 21 : 1.

37 Gal. 5 : 23.

MAN IS IDENTIFIED IN MIND

Mental treatment recognizes that each individual has his identity in Mind and is known in Mind by the name he bears. This Subjective Law knows there is a John Smith and a Mary Jones. Why? Because John Smith and Mary Jones know that there is a John Smith and a Mary Jones. *But It only knows about them what they know about themselves.* Being subjective to their thought, It could not know anything else; consequently, whatever John Smith and Mary Jones say, It says, accepts and does. This is a marvelous concept. Unless we have thought it out, it may seem rather startling. But it means this:——that *the Law absolutely accepts us at our own valuation.* Now this does not mean that it accepts us at an *assumption* of *valuation*, but at the *actual valuation*. It can reflect to us only the actual embodiment of ourselves. *It is the deep inner conviction that we carry which decides what is going to happen.* So we are each known by the name we bear, and each is daily making some statement about that name. When we say "I am this or that," we are involving in Mind statements which Mind in turn produces as conditions.

TREATMENT

In treatment we turn entirely from the condition, because so long as we look at a condition we cannot overcome it. That is why the mystic said: "Behold my face forevermore." "Look unto me and be ye saved, all the ends of the earth."[38] That is, look up and not down. It is useless to treat one's business, because business is an immaterial thing. It is an unthinking, unknowing thing— a lot of stuff in form, a lot of forms in stuff. That which decides what the business shall be is in Consciousness or Mind. Consequently, we must involve in Mind a correct concept of the business, seeing it as we want it to be; and when we have seen it that way long enough, it will be so. How long will it take? *Until the subjective side of thought accepts the new concept as true, or until we have neutralized the old concept.*

Jesus had a great understanding and He gave a clew to that understanding when He said: "The Prince of this world cometh and findeth nothing in me."[39] He meant that race-suggestion found no mental correspondence or equivalent in Him. His consciousness was so clear that it operated directly from the Spirit.

---

38 Isa. 45 : 22.
39 John 14 : 30.

THE AIM OF EVOLUTION

The aim of evolution is to produce a man who, at the point of his objective thought, may completely manifest the whole idea of life—i.e., bring the concept of Unity to the point of particularization, finding nothing in the Law to oppose it. The reason Jesus was able to become the Christ was, that at the objective point of His thought there was a complete realization of the Unity of the Spirit and the Absoluteness of His word. His spiritual and psychical faculties, His objective and subjective mind, were completely poised and perfectly balanced.

It is evident that if this took place in any individual his word would be manifested likewise. It would have to be, because behind the word is Universal Soul, Omnipotent Law. Divine Principle is Limitless, but *It can only be to us what we believe It is*. Why must we believe It is? Because until we believe It is, we are believing It is not. The reason some people cannot demonstrate the Truth is, they do not realize It. The whole thing is a matter of belief; *but belief is scientifically induced into a subjective state through conscious endeavor and effort*. Treatment is the science of inducing within Mind concepts, acceptances, and realizations of peace, poise, power, plenty, health, happiness, and success, or whatever the particular need may be.

What does a practitioner do? He sets the Law in motion in Universal Mind. Let us suppose that Mary is sick, and that John is a practitioner. She comes to him, saying, "I am sick." He, being a metaphysician, understands that Mind is all; she does not understand this. She feels that she is sick. But he knows that all sickness is mental. He does not try to hold a thought over her, nor does he try to suggest anything to her; for that is not mental treatment. He simply declares the Truth about her; he speaks her name and says: "This word is for her; she is perfect; she is well." In other words, he contradicts what appears to be and declares the Truth about her. What happens? A law is being enacted on the subjective side of life. His word, operative through the Universal Sea of Mind (in which both live) sets in motion a law which objectifies through her body as healing.

Mary thinks a miracle has been performed. She exclaims: "I am healed. I did not have a bit of faith, but John healed me." No miracle has been performed. He used a law which all may use if they will. Suppose Mary were perfectly well, but wanted a position,—what would the treatment be? It would be the same. John would state in Mind what should be done for Mary. There is only One Law, and Mary could demonstrate just as well for herself if she understood It, but she must first see It demonstrated to realize It. This is the state of mind of most people who come for healing. They do not know what ails them; they think their condition is due to some external cause. Nevertheless, they are healed and exclaim: "This is a marvelous thing, though I do not understand what it is all about." Often they become superstitious about it, as people do about the things they do not understand; once they understand the Law, however, healing is no longer a mystery.

The only reason a man has difficulty in throwing off some weakness of character, while believing in Spirit implicitly and having faith that he is going to overcome his limitation, is because he has not induced the necessary mental images in Mind. If he had, he would have overcome his trouble; thinking of his weakness keeps the image of it before him.

In treating, turn entirely away from the condition. Disease and limitation are neither person, place nor thing; they are simply images of thought. Turn entirely from the condition, or the limited situation, to its opposite; that is, to the realization of health, happiness or harmony.

METHODS OF TREATMENT

Although several methods of treatment are used, there are but two distinct methods; one is called argumentative, and the other realization. The argumentative method is a process of mental argument in which the practitioner argues to himself about his patient. He is, consequently, presenting a logical argument to Universal Mind, or Divine Principle; and if that argument carries with it a complete evidence in favor of his patient, it is supposed that the patient will be healed.

The method of realization is one whereby the practitioner realizes within himself the perfect state of his patient; it is purely a spiritual and meditative process of contemplating the Perfect Man; and if the embodiment of the idea is really made, it will at once produce a healing.

Treatment is for the purpose of inducing an inner realization of perfection in the mentality of the practitioner, which inner realization, acting through Mind, operates in the patient.

Between John and Mary there is One Universal Medium which is also in John and Mary; It is not only between them, but in them. As John knows right where John is (since there is only *One*), he is at the same time knowing right where Mary is, because his work is operative through a field which is not divided but which is a complete Unit or Whole, i.e., Universal Subjectivity. As he knows within or upon himself, he is setting in motion the Law, which operates through the person whom he mentions in his treatment, no matter where the patient may be. There is no such thing as an absent treatment, as opposed to a present treatment.

Mary must have a consciousness of health before the healing can be permanent. It will have to become a part of her subjective thought. If the consciousness did not change she would perpetuate the old thought images and would get sick again; and that is why, in treating, people get well for a while and then become sick again. They are not permanently healed unless the consciousness is healed.

A treatment begins and ends within the thought of the one giving it. The practitioner must do the whole work within himself. He must know the Truth, and as he does that, he sets in motion the Law. A thing which is known by any part of the Universal Mind is known by every part of It, for It is an Undivided Whole. When you know in one place you know everywhere. When you give a treatment you do not send out a thought, or hold a thought, or give suggestion. A treatment is a positive thing.

If you are treating a certain John Smith, you say (if he is not present), "I am treating John Smith of such and such a place." Then you forget all about him as a personality and give your treatment. It is not necessary to specify the trouble. Once in a great while, you might find yourself mentioning a thing in order to make some statement against it, but probably that is not the best way. Of course there are certain thoughts back of certain things, and a knowledge of the disease might enable you to know better what thought to destroy.

It is like this: Mary Jones comes to John Smith and says, "I have tuberculosis." In answer to this he declares, "This word is for Mary Jones. She is a perfect and complete manifestation of Pure Spirit, and Pure Spirit cannot be diseased; consequently she is not diseased." This is an argument, trying to bring out the evidence in favor of perfection. It is an argument which produces a certain conclusion in the mentality of John Smith, and, consequently, it sets in motion a certain law for Mary Jones. As John does this, day after day, he gradually becomes convinced of her perfection and she is healed. If he could do it in one minute, she would be healed in one minute. *There is no process in healing. It is a revelation, an awakening, a realization of Life.* Man exists in Divine Mind as a Perfect Image; but he covers himself with the distorted images of his own thought along the pathway of his mental experience.

If using the method of realization, say, "This word or this thought is for Mary Jones." Then begin to realize the Perfect Presence, the *Only* Perfect Presence. "God is all there is; there is no other Life"; very little argument, but more and more a complete realization. This is very powerful, although it makes no difference which method you use, as they produce the same result. It is a good idea to combine both.

In the case of a child, the treatment should be the same. *It would have an effect commensurate with the absolute conviction that the practitioner has.* But in the case of an infant, who is subjective to the conscious thought of the people around it, you must teach those people how to think about the child, and see that they do think that way; else you might heal the child and their thought might make it sick again.

In case of failure, it is probable that the trouble is more with John than with Mary, as far as the immediate healing is concerned. However, diseases are the direct results of certain habitual mental attitudes which people entertain, and unless those mental attitudes are changed, there will be no permanent healing. It is the business of the practitioner to discover what those attitudes are and to change them. It is also the business of the practitioner to show people why they are as they are, and to teach them how to overcome undesirable attitudes.

In giving a treatment, you talk to yourself about somebody else.

We must grasp the idea of Universal Subjectivity, the Potentiality of all things, the Divine Creative Medium. This is the Principle through which we are to demonstrate the healing of the body or of the conditions; and It acts accurately and mathematically, because It is the Law of cause and effect.

SUBJECTIVE LAW

When we think, we think from conscious intelligence, or Spirit. We will say that the thought becomes subjectified; i.e., it goes into the subconscious mind. But what is man's subconscious mind? It is his atmosphere or mental vibration in Universal Subjectivity. There is no such thing as your subjective mind and my subjective mind, meaning two, for this would be duality. But there is such a thing as the subjective state of your thought and of my thought in Mind. This should be made very clear, for here is where psychology and metaphysics separate; i.e., their understandings are different. When we think, we think into a Universal Creative Medium, a receptive and plastic substance which surrounds us on all sides, which permeates us and flows through us. We do not have to think that we are thinking in It or upon It; for when we think we do think into and upon It; there is no other place that we could think, since It is Omnipresent.

As each subjectifies himself in consciousness he is building around himself a mental atmosphere; and nothing can enter this unless he allows it to, through the avenues of his own thought; but this thought might be conscious or unconscious; in most cases it is unconscious, but the student of Truth is learning to consciously control the stream of thought that he allows to enter his inner and creative mentality.

THOUGHT AND THE CREATIVE MEDIUM

Thought is an inner movement which is the result of one's perception of life and his reaction to it. Every time this movement takes place it takes place within Mind, upon Cause, according to law. We are, without question, dealing with the same Power that molds the planets and all that is upon them; and the limit of our ability to prove this is not in Principle, but is in our understanding of It; in our ability to incorporate within ourselves an embodiment of our ideals.

EACH IS THE LOGICAL RESULT OF HIS OWN THINKING

We are dealing with a neutral, creative power, just as we would be in the case of electricity or any other natural force. It is on a higher plane; for it is the power of intelligence. As we think into this Universal Mind, our thought, in its externalization, will reach its own level, just as water will reach its own level by its own weight and without effort. This is in line with necessity; for the Universe, in order to be at all, must be Self-Existent.

What is meant by the Self-Existence of the Universe? This means a Universe which is Its own reason for being; a Universe which exists by virtue of Itself, being All.

Each one of us is to-day the result of what has gone before, either consciously or unconsciously, no matter what kind of a condition he may be in. As soon as we realize this we shall be better off, because we shall see that since what we now are, or what we now have and experience, is the result of what we have thought; the answer to what we shall be is contained in what we now are; for we *can change* our thinking.

Man thinks and supposes that he lets go of the thoughts he thinks. But such is not the case; for thought becomes subjectified in Mind, like a seed planted in the soil; it stays there, unless neutralized, and decides the attraction and repulsion in the experience of the one thinking. There is a constant action on the subjective side of life; and it is this unconscious process which decides what is going to happen in the outer expression.

Whatever we think, act, believe in, feel, visualize, vision, image, read, talk about, in fact, all processes which affect or impress us at all, are going into the subjective state of our thought, which is our individualized use of Universal Mind. Whatever goes into the subjective state of thought tends to return again as some condition.

A Law of Belief

Jesus said, "As thou hast believed so be it done unto thee."[40] Knowing the nature of the law, He did not say, "It is done unto you as you wish." He announced the universality of law when He said, "As thou hast believed so be it done unto thee."[40]

We Are Dealing with Law

Some one may say, "I can't imagine God not caring." I cannot either; but we are dealing with law. Does the law of electricity care whether it cooks the dinner or burns the house down? Whether it electrocutes a criminal or warms the feet of a saint? Of course it does not care at all! Does the urge, which impels people to express, care whether a man kneels in ecstasy or lies drunk in the gutter? We are dealing with law. And it follows that, since we are dealing with law, it will ultimately bring back to us the results of the forces which we set in motion through it. Consequently, no person who is enlightened would seek to use this law destructively; for he

---

40 Matt. 8 : 13.

would know that, sooner or later, the very power set in motion by himself would ultimately destroy him. "All they that take the sword shall perish with the sword."[41] The Spirit of Christ is the spirit which constructively uses the law. The spirit of Antichrist is the destructive use of law. The Spirit of Christ, being in line with the Cosmic Life, will always transcend, neutralize, destroy, and utterly obliterate the spirit of Antichrist; and ultimately only the Spirit of Christ can succeed. "He that hath an ear, let him hear."[42]

THE CYCLE OF NECESSITY AND KARMIC LAW

The cycle of necessity means that those things which the individual sets in motion through the law must ultimately swing back to him again. This is the Karmic Law; "The law that binds the ignorant but frees the wise." This law has been announced by every great teacher who has ever lived. Jesus referred to this law when He said, "As thou hast believed so be it done unto thee";[43] and when He said, "Heaven and earth shall pass away: but my words shall not pass away."[44] It is the law to which Isaiah referred when he said, "So shall my word be that goeth forth out of my mouth; it shall not return unto me void, but it shall accomplish that which I please."[45] This is the law which to-day is called "Divine Principle," or the law of cause and effect; it means that once a tendency is set in motion through law, it is bound to objectify at the level of the subjective concept which entertains it. There is nothing fatalistic about this, for we may consciously change the currents of subjectivity with the conscious thought. Indeed, this is what treatment does.

THE LAW OF ACTION AND REACTION

This is simply the law of cause and effect, and instead of getting too occult or mystical a concept of it we would better think of it simply as something into which we think, and which returns to the thinker what he thinks into it. This law can be applied for concrete purposes, and once it is set in motion the rest works automatically. This is why we may absolutely trust Principle when we understand how it operates. It knows everything and can do anything; but in order to work for us, we must let it work through us. This is the power that Jesus used when He withered the fig tree and when He raised Lazarus from the dead.

---

41 Matt. 26 : 52.
42 Rev. 3 : 6.
43 Matt. 8 : 13.
44 Luke 21 : 33.
45 Isa. 55 :11.

WE ARGUE IN MIND

So we argue in Mind; and if we argue toward a belief in health, we will be healed. It isn't a question of suggestion or of the power of thought making us well, for this is but a limited sense of will power. It isn't something over which we must clinch our teeth and will to be; it is something which we have to know. Water doesn't have to will to be wet, it is wet; and if we go into it we will get wet. Life doesn't have to claim to be Life; It simply announces Itself to be what It knows that It Is. So we argue in Mind, not to convince Mind that It is or can accomplish, but to convince ourselves that we are *now* perfect.

WRONG USE OF MIND

There have been many controversies about the use and the misuse of this power. Some claim that we cannot misuse this power, since there is but One Mind, and It cannot act against Itself. Mind cannot act against Itself; and any person who knows this, and who knows that there is no human mind to destroy, or to be destroyed, is immune from malpractice. But let any one believe in malpractice, and he will open mental avenues of receptivity to it; for we can receive only that to which we vibrate.

Malpractice is the ignorant use of something which of itself is good. It is the wrong use of mental power and will never be indulged in by any one who understands the Truth; neither can one who understands the Truth be affected by it. There could be innocent, ignorant and malicious malpractice. Innocent malpractice, in the form of sympathy with disease and trouble, thereby accentuating these conditions, is often prolific of dire results. Ignorant malpractice would be about the same thing; for instance, when one sees a criminal, thinking of him as such helps to perpetuate the state in which he is manifesting. Malicious malpractice would be an act of centering thought for destructive purposes. When Jesus said, "The prince of this world cometh and hath nothing in me,"[46] He meant that he had neutralized all race thought about destruction and so was immune to all false suggestion. This we should all try to do.

SUBJECTIVE BUT NOT UNCONSCIOUS

The subjective mind can deduce only; it cannot, of itself, initiate anything; but this does not mean that it is unintelligent. We must be very careful not to labor under the delusion that

---

46 John 14 : 30.

because the subjective mind cannot reason it is unintelligent, for it is infinitely more intelligent than our present state of conscious mind, but is, nevertheless, controlled by it.

If our subjective consciousness were always clear, that is, if it never received any false impressions, the Spirit would always flow to the point of objectivity and we would never make mistakes; we would never be sick, poor, or unhappy.

How Habits Are Formed

Back in the subjective are the images of thought surrounding us, all acting as living intelligences. It is here that habits are formed; for when one has a habit that he cannot seem to break he is hypnotized by the thought and desire back of that habit; the thought force has grown too strong to be controlled. Habits are healed by neutralizing the thought forces behind them.

Law Is Mind in Action

There is One Infinite Life acting through Law, and this Law is mental; Law is Mind in action. We are surrounded by an Infinite, Subconscious, Impersonal, Neutral, Plastic, Creative, Ever-Present, Thinking Stuff from which all things come, which, in Its Original State, permeates and penetrates all things. By impressing our thought upon this Substance we can cause It to produce for us that which we think, to the limit of our ability to mentally embody the idea. Impressing our thought upon It is not an external act, for when we impress our thought upon ourselves, we are thinking into It; this is because of the Unity of all Mind. This is one of the great lessons to learn; we do not know anything outside ourselves. This is what Jesus meant when He said, "Ye shall know the Truth and the Truth shall make you free."[47] When we know within ourselves we are knowing at the point of that Individualized Spirit which we are; upon the very Heart of the Infinite, the Ever-Present Substance, which is ever responsive to Itself.

We Are Bound by Our Own Freedom

We are all bound, tied hand and foot, by our very freedom; our free will binds us; but, as free will creates the conditions which externally limit us, so it can uncreate or dissolve them. The Universe, being deductive only, cannot refuse man anything.

The very force that makes us sick an heal us; the force that makes us poor can make us rich;

---

47 John 8 : 32.

and the power that makes us miserable can make us happy. If this were not true there would be duality in the Universe, and this is impossible.

Oneness with All Law

When we know of our Oneness with God and Law, what a great burden will be removed which otherwise would cause us to struggle in making a demonstration! The sense of opposition must forever be removed from the consciousness which perceives Unity.

Instead of saying, "Here is a sick man to heal and I shall have to work hard on this case," we should realize that there is nothing but concept in the Universe and, therefore, say, "I am going to conceive of this man as being absolutely perfect," then the same power which made him sick will heal him. This is the reversal of thought.

That which we call our subjective mind is but a point in Universal Mind where our personality maintains its individualized expression of Spirit. If we think of ourselves as being separated from the Universe we will be limited by this thought; for it is a belief in separation from Good which binds and limits; we are bound by nothing except belief. "They could not enter in because of unbelief,"[48] and because they "limited the Holy One of Israel."[49]

There is but One Mind. Here is the point: everything we experience, touch, taste, handle and smell; environment, bodies, conditions, money, happiness, friends; all are effects. Is it clear that the infinite and limitless possibilities of that One of which man is a part, depend, in man's expression, upon his own concepts? If he is a point of personality in limitless Mind, which he is, and if all of his life must be drawn from this One Mind, which it must, there cannot be anything else, can there? And if there is nothing else, if there is nothing to move but Mind, and if man is a thinking center in Mind, nothing is going to happen to him that does not happen through him, whether this is the result of his own erroneous conclusions, those of his grandfathers, or the race to which he belongs. It is impossible to conceive of anything ever happening to any one unless the force back of it was set in motion by himself, sometime or somewhere. But this is not fatalistic, for we may change the chain of causation which we have set in motion.

Everything comes from Intelligence; there is nothing but Unity; there is nothing but freedom; there is nothing but completeness; there is nothing but Totality. Begin at the beginning and reason this out time after time till doubt disappears; for you will be neutralizing that subjectivity which rises to slay you. It is necessary that each do this for himself.

---

48 Heb. 3 : 19.
49 Ps. 78 : 41

DEMONSTRATION

As far as making a demonstration is concerned, when we get the correct consciousness this is the easiest thing in the world; but we cannot demonstrate beyond our ability to mentally embody an idea. The argument is between our experience, what the world believes, and what we are convinced is the Truth.

It should be understood that we can demonstrate in spite of our own selves, in spite of all weakness, in spite of every fear, in spite of all that is in us, because such is the power of the Truth. If we waited to be good before demonstrating, the wheel might turn a million times; but law is neither good nor bad; law is and responds.

The Possibility of demonstrating does not depend upon environment, conditions, location, personality or opportunity. It depends upon ourselves and upon nothing else. The Universe will never deny man anything, unless we conceive that it is possible for man to think of something that it is impossible for the universe to produce. Every one who asks receives, according to his belief.

KARMIC LAW

Annie Besant said of Karma, "It is the law that binds the ignorant but frees the wise." That which is called Karma in the Orient, we call cause and effect. The subjective state of consciousness is our Karma; this is the result of the thinking that has gone before, and of the race-suggestion operating through us. Karma is not fate; it is mental law; and it can be changed by right thinking and right action. Karma is not Kismet.

THOUGHT FORCE

Thought force is the movement of consciousness which sets law in operation. The movement of consciousness upon itself creates a motion or vibration in Intelligence and upon Substance, the force of which is equal to the reality of the thought set in motion. For everything that happens in the objective world, there must be something in the subjective world to perfectly balance it. Just suppose for a moment that the Universe is nothing but water, permeated by an Infinite Intelligence. Imagine that every time this Intelligence moves or thinks an icicle is formed in the water, exactly corresponding to the thought. We might have countless numbers of icicles of different forms, colors and sizes; but these icicles would still be water. If we could heat the whole mass, it would melt, and all the forms would again become fluent; nothing would have changed but form. This is all there is to matter; it is Spirit in Form; and as such is perfectly good; to deny matter is poor logic.

First is Intelligence; then the Word, the vision, the image, the concept; then the movement to the thing. Remember, thought is an actual working power; otherwise there would be nothing with which the Universe could be run.

CHOOSING THOUGHT

We have a right to choose what we shall induce in Mind. The way that our thoughts are to become manifested we cannot always see; but we should not be disturbed if we do not see the way, because effect is potential in cause; "I am Alpha and Omega,"[50] and all that comes between cause and effect. Cause and effect are really One, and if we have a given cause set in motion the effect will have to equal this cause. One is the inside and the other the outside of a concept or idea.

A practitioner's work begins and ends within himself. If, in doing mental work, the thought should come that the thing cannot be done, you must treat this thought as having no power, but only as an impersonal suggestion trying to gain entrance to your mentality. Realize that there is nothing in you that can hinder you from demonstrating the Truth.

If one says to himself, "I am filled with life, health, strength and vigor," and then goes down the street saying, "I see a poor blind beggar, a criminal and a sick person," he is still treating himself just as much as when he affirmed that he was perfect. We are only as perfect as we perceive others to be. This does not mean that we shut our eyes to those who are in trouble; for we may have sympathy with the one having trouble without having sympathy with his trouble. We must have sympathy with all, for, as one of the great prophets of the new age said, "The Divinity of Christ was made manifest through the Humanity of Jesus."

A certain, specific, intelligent form, or idea in Mind, will produce a certain, specific, concrete manifestation in matter, equal to itself. There is one Infinite Principle, One Infinite Thought-Stuff, One Infinite Creative Power and countless numbers of forms, which appear and disappear as the definite, specific, concrete thought behind them changes.

A practitioner is one who changes the false thought and builds on the Principle of Truth, which executes and manifests the truth that the practitioner embodies. He can demonstrate to the limit of his mental ability and his spiritual capacity to conceive of the Truth.

If one wishes to demonstrate prosperity he must first have a consciousness of prosperity; if he wishes health he must embody the idea of health. A consciousness of health, happiness and prosperity can be induced within through right mental and spiritual practice. By consciousness is meant the inner embodiment of an idea; the subjective image of the idea; the mental and spiritual equivalent of the idea.

---

50 Rev. 1 : 8.

Inducing Thought

While a certain consciousness may be mechanically induced, of course, the more spontaneity put into the mechanical word, the more power the word must have. Since we all must begin right where we are, most of us will be compelled to begin with a mechanical process. This is more than faith, for it is a sure knowledge that we are dealing with Law.

Principle is Changeless Reality. That which we call personality is the instrument through which Principle operates, but It can operate for the individual only by operating through him. It is never bound by the form that It takes, but is forever free. Principle fills all form, and not only fills all forms but surges around them, and is in and through them. Ice is water and water is ice; so God and man exist in an Eternal state of Unity.

When one realizes that he is depending upon Principle, he should educate himself to the point of realization of his ability to use It.

We should always be impersonal in mental work. We do not have to be impersonal in life, for we are brought to the point of personality in order that we might enjoy each other. But in mental work we are dealing with an impersonal Principle. It will operate for one just as quickly as for another, because It is Law. Dare to speak and to know that what you speak is the law unto the thing spoken. One, alone in consciousness with the Infinite, constitutes a complete majority.

Knowing this in your own thought, work in perfect peace and calm; always expect; have enthusiasm; and have a consciousness of love; that is, a radiant feeling flowing through the personality at all times. If one hasn't this he should treat himself until he does have it; for without it, he is diseased in mind. Treat until you feel an inner sense of Unity with the all Good. There is One Mind, and the moving impulse of this Mind is Love.

In choosing words in treatment, say anything that will induce the right mental attitude. Giving formulas is a mistake, for how can any one put a spontaneous thought into the mind of another? Any one can stand in front of a dead man and say, "Arise," but who is going to have the consciousness to make this happen?

Place No Limit on Principle

Know your own mind; train yourself to think what you wish to think; be what you wish to be; feel what you wish to feel; and place no limit on Principle. The word which you speak would be just as powerful as the words which Jesus spoke, if you knew it; but know this within and not only without.

After all, all there is, is mental action and reaction. If you have reached the point where the inner consciousness produces all things, then your word is simply an announcement of reality. There will come a time when demonstration will no longer be necessary.

Know that when you give a treatment, the act takes place in Infinite Mind. Infinite Mind is the Actor and you are the announcer. If you have a vague, subtle, unconscious fear, get still and think, "Who am I? What am I? Who is speaking? What is my life?" Think right back to Principle until your thought becomes perfectly clear again.

Such is the Power of right thinking that It cancels and erases everything unlike Itself. It answers every question, solves all problems, is the solution to every difficulty. It is like the sunlight of Eternal Truth, bursting through the clouds of obscurity and bathing all life in glory. It is the Absolute with which you are dealing and nothing less.

Note: Read carefully "Being and Becoming," F. L. Holmes; "Doré Lectures," T. Troward; "From Existence to Life," James Porter Mills; "Mind's Silent Partner," James Porter Mills; "History and Power of Mind," Richard Ingalese.

LESSON TWO: RECAPITULATION

Man reënacts the Divine Nature on all three planes; he is self-knowing in his conscious mind, creative through his subconscious mind, and has a body. He reënacts the Trinity of Being.

Man is in perfect unity with the Whole. His conscious mind is his understanding of God; his subjective mind is the use that he makes of the Universal Creative Medium; and his body is one with the Body of God.

There is but One Mind in the Universe, and man uses It. Man is an identity in the Universe; he is a center of God-Consciousness. At first he is ignorant of this and misuses his power, consequently bringing upon himself misfortune and sickness.

Man's thought operates through the medium of Universal Creative Mind. As he thinks within himself, he thinks upon Creative Mind and sets Law in motion. Since there is but One Mind a person may think for himself, or for some one else, and cause the Law to operate as he directs.

The use of Creative Mind is like the use of the creative soil. Man never creates; he simply uses a Creative Law.

Objective, conscious and self-knowing mind, all have the same meaning; they mean that part of man which knows that it exists.

Subjective, subconscious, unconscious, soul and consciousness have the same meaning; they mean the inner creative medium.

Body, effect and outward conditions all respond to the inner thought.

The Spirit of man, which is his self-knowingness, is the only part of him which has volition or self-choice; all else is automatic law.

Man's conscious thought, acting through Law, may change any condition in his experience, provided he can clearly conceive of that condition as being changed. There is no limit to the Law. The limit is not in the Law but in man's ability to embody the Truth and constructively use the Law.

Remember, there is but One Mind and One Law which all people use, consciously or unconsciously, constructively or destructively; One Spirit, One Mind, One Law, One Substance, but many forms. There is only One Ultimate Reality, but within this One there are many experiences. Man is within the One and draws from It any and all experiences in which he believes.

As man thinks he subjectifies thought and sets Law in motion through the Medium of the Universal Mind. *This Law works automatically until It is consciously changed.*

Man uses a Power which is Infinite as compared with the power of his conscious thought.

Divine Principle means Universal Subjective Law; It is the Medium of all thought and action.

Freedom and bondage, sickness and health, poverty and riches, heaven and hell, good and bad, big and little, happiness and misery, peace and confusion, faith and fear and all conditions that appear as opposites, are not really opposing powers, but are the way that the One Power is used.

Man has within himself the key to every situation, but he must come to realize his relation to the Whole. That relationship is one of Perfect Unity.

LESSON THREE: INTRODUCTION

HEALING

Mental healing means mind healing. The possibility of healing physical diseases through the power of right thinking rests entirely on the theory that we are surrounded by an Infinite Mind which reacts to our thought.

That people have been healed through prayer and by faith in all ages, there is no question. But we live in a Universe of Law and Order, and at no time can that Law or Order be broken; therefore, if people have been healed through prayer and faith, it is because they have somewhere contacted a Law which really exists. To suppose that God would heal one man any more readily than another, would be to suppose that God is human and subject to the changing emotions that we ascribe to the human mind. To believe that the Divine Power would operate for one man simply because he asked It to, but would not operate for all, would be to believe in a God more human than man himself. It is very evident, however, that many times people have been healed through prayer; and either God has especially answered them, while He left others to suffer, or else by the act of prayer they have complied with some law. Again, many people have prayed and their prayers have not been answered; yet they have prayed to the best of their ability. Why have some been heard and others not heard? The only possible answer is that some reached a place in their mentality where they believed, while others fell short of this mental attitude. After all, prayer is a certain mental attitude, a certain way of thinking, a certain way of believing. All prayer is mental; some prayers reach a state of belief, while others fall short of that state. This leads us to suppose that *the answer to prayer is in the prayer when it is prayed*. True prayer stimulates a belief in Good which nothing else can, and often causes the one who prays to rise to a point in mentality where the healing work may be done according to the Law of the Universe, which is a Law of Mind.

We have no objection to any form of healing. Anything that will help to overcome suffering must be good, whether it takes the form of a pill or of a prayer. We do not oppose doctors nor medical practitioners, but gratefully acknowledge the wonderful work that they have done and are doing. We hold no controversy with any one on the subject of healing. We are glad when any one is healed, or helped, by any method. We believe in any and all methods, and know that each has its place in the whole. We know that man's life is a drama which takes place on three planes—the physical, the mental and the spiritual. We know that each needs to be taken into account. We believe in proper food, proper exercise, proper clothing, proper sanitation and in everything that is real and sensible. We include all and exclude none.

But, while we do not hold arguments with any one, neither will we allow any one to hold controversies with us. We know that man's life, in reality, is spiritual and mental; and that until the thought is healed, no form of cure will be permanent. We will gladly coöperate with any and all; but we will not accept the judgment of any and all. We know that there is a Law higher than the physical, and we seek to use It. We, perhaps, shall not always succeed, but we shall not become discouraged or confused over the issue, but will continue until we arrive.

We hold no arguments over any form of theology. We believe in any and every church and in all forms of worship. Above all, we certainly believe in God. But we will not allow any one to tell us how to worship God, nor compel us to worship in any way other than the way we choose.

We reject the theory that the Truth has been once and for all time given and that It cannot be added to nor taken from. We know this to be true about the Truth; but we also know that no one, so far, has arrived at a complete understanding of Truth. We expect more light all along the line, and we repudiate any belief that says that all truth has been given.

We know that the authority of man is, in most cases, an assumption and not a reality, and we refuse to be hypnotized into believing in any man-made mandate.

WHAT WE UNDERSTAND ABOUT HEALING

We understand that health is a mental and not a physical state. We seek to heal men's mentalities, knowing that to the degree in which we are successful we shall also be healing their bodies. We know that to the degree in which we are able to see a perfect man he will appear. We feel that man is really perfect, no matter how he appears; and we seek to uncover that perfection which is within every man's life, for this is healing.

We realize that mental healing must also be spiritual healing, for the two cannot be divorced. We know that *a belief in duality has made man sick and that the understanding of Unity alone will heal him*. We seek to realize that Unity with God in all our healing work. Every treatment must carry with it a realization of God if it is to be a good treatment.

We are not superstitious about this, but understand that it is necessary since all Life is One. God stands to us for the One Life in which we all live.

THOUGHTS ARE THINGS

We know that thoughts are things. We know that thought is intelligent and has power within itself to objectify itself. We know that belief makes thought very powerful. We know that our thought lays hold of Causation and manipulates real Substance. We know that the word of man is the law of his life, under the One Great Law of all Life. We know that thoughts of sickness make man sick, and that thoughts of health and perfection will heal him. We know that a realization of the Presence of God is the most powerful healing agency known to the mind of man. We do not argue over the issue, nor seek to convince any one of its merits. We have passed the stage of doubt and uncertainty; for we KNOW. We also know that we can heal only to the degree that we can think from the higher motive; and we know that we should be constantly on the alert, seeking to embody higher thoughts. Meanwhile, we will use the best thought that we have and will expect to heal and help all who ask our aid.

Thought is the conscious activity of the one thinking, and works as he directs; it works through Law, but that Law is *consciously* set in motion. We know that Law will operate for us to the fullest extent of our belief in, and understanding of, it.

We realize that since our understanding is not yet complete, it is legitimate to use any and all methods that will help humanity; but we do look forward to the day when Truth alone will answer every need. That day will come to the degree that we know it is already here. The mental healer will do all of his work in Mind and will give his whole time and attention to correct knowing; but he will leave his patient free to use any method that will help him. In this way he will get the best results, for everything is good so far as it goes; but a consciousness of Truth alone can really and permanently heal.

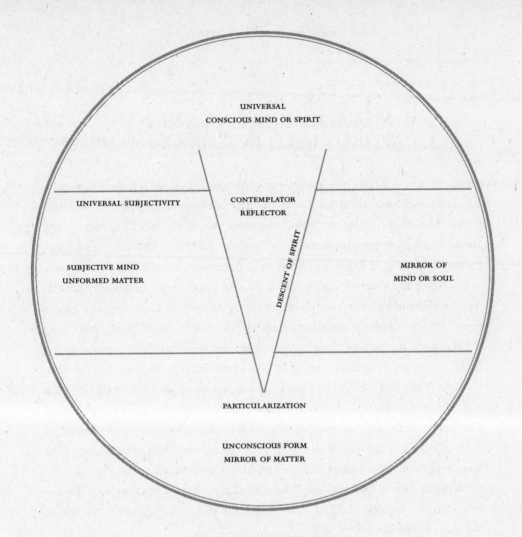

UNIVERSAL
CONSCIOUS MIND OR SPIRIT

UNIVERSAL SUBJECTIVITY

CONTEMPLATOR
REFLECTOR

DESCENT OF SPIRIT

SUBJECTIVE MIND
UNFORMED MATTER

MIRROR OF
MIND OR SOUL

PARTICULARIZATION

UNCONSCIOUS FORM
MIRROR OF MATTER

LESSON THREE:
METAPHYSICAL CHART NO. III.

The upper section of this chart shows how the conscious mind, or spirit of man, reflects or contemplates itself, through the medium of soul or subjectivity, into form or matter. The middle section represents the World-Soul or Subjectivity; the Mirror of Mind and unformed matter; the Servant of the Spirit; the lowest section shows the result of self-contemplation as it takes form in the world of matter. Read and carefully study the metaphysical meanings of the words used in the Individual Chart.

LESSON THREE:
METAPHYSICAL MEANING
OF WORDS USED IN CHART NO. III

UNIVERSAL SPIRIT.——Means the universe of conscious mind and self-determination. The Universal Subjectivity means the Creative Medium of the Spirit, or the Subjective Law of the Universe. Particularization means the world of matter and forms. Read again the explanation to Chart Number One. The descent of Spirit means the passing of Spirit into form——the particularization of Spirit into many things. The point, drawn from the top of the chart to the bottom section, symbolizes the Unity of all Life. Spirit passes through Law into Form. Multiplicity comes from Unity, but never contradicts Oneness. The many are within the One.

Man's life partakes of the Divine Nature, and this chart may be used in the Individual or the Universal sense. Our conscious mind is some part of the One Conscious Mind of the Whole. The Complete Nature of God is reflected in man, and he uses the same law that God uses; for there is but One Law, as there is but One Spirit, Both God and man use the same Creative Medium or the Universal Subjectivity. It is the law of all thought and all action. Things come from One Source through One Common Law and One Common Creative Medium. We think of our lives as One with the Whole on all three planes of expression. We are one with the Conscious Mind, one with the Creative Law, and in our bodies we are one with all matter.

No matter what we are treating or for what purpose, the Medium of all thought is the Universal Law. It particularizes Itself through the power of the word that is spoken into It. The word alone is conscious. The Law is Automatic and the form is without self-determination.

CONSCIOUS MIND OR SPIRIT.——Means the Self-Knowing Mind of the Universe. Contemplator, or Reflector, means the conscious thought of the Conscious Mind.

SUBJECTIVE MIND AND UNFORMED MATTER.——Mean the Substance and the Soul of the Universe.

MIRROR OF MIND, OR SOUL.——Means that the Subjective side of life acts like a mirror; that is, It reflects the forms of thought that are given It.

UNCONSCIOUS FORM OR MIRROR OF MATTER.——Means that the material world reflects the forms of thought which the Soul holds before it.

This depicts the Creative Process and sequence—first in the chain of Causation is the Word, and this Word is conscious of Itself; next comes the action of Law, reflecting the Word. (This Law is subjective and obeys the Word, reflecting It into form or matter; matter, being at first unformed, or a Universal unformed stuff.) It then takes form, through the power of the word acting upon It, on the subjective side of life.

Soul and Substance are both subjective to the Spirit; and form, or matter in form, has no volition.

In the Trinity of Unity, one attribute alone is really self-conscious, namely, the Spirit, or the Word.

This chart may be used in either the individual or the universal sense, for the individual reënacts the Universal on all three planes.

The manifest Universe is the result of the self-contemplation of Spirit or God. This self-contemplation, through law, reflects its images into the world of form or manifestation.

Man's world of affairs and his body are the result of his inner self-knowingness. He is the result of his self-contemplation.

LESSON THREE: MENTAL HEALING

Whatever exists at all must be the result of a definite image of thought held in the Mind of God or the Absolute, Who is the cause of all. Whether we think of man as a projection of God, an emanation of God, a manifestation or a reflection of God, we must realize that God, or the First Cause, holds man in His Consciousness as a Perfect Being, since the Perfect Mind could not conceive of an imperfect idea. If, on the other hand, we think of man as a part of God, which some schools of thought teach, we should then have to realize that man, as a part of the Divine Being, must inherently be perfect. This is a conclusion which is unavoidable. But man does not appear to be perfect; he certainly appears to have many experiences which are far from ideal. There can be no question but the human man suffers, is sick and has pain and eventually dies. To doubt this would be to doubt the evidence of the only quality we possess whereby we may consider ourselves conscious beings at all. We must, then, reconcile our conclusion of perfection with an experience which is apparently not perfect.

INDIVIDUALITY

While man must be, and is, a Divine Image or a Perfect Idea, yet he suffers and is sick. The answer to this is the same answer which can be given, philosophically, to the whole problem of evil—that man is an individual and does with himself what he wills. The Scriptures say, "God hath made man upright; but they have sought out many inventions."[51] Individuality cannot be automatically produced but must be spontaneous. It could not be real individuality unless it had the ability to think as it chose; and it could not be individuality unless its ability to think as it chose were backed by a power to produce this choice; because, if nothing ever happened as the result of man's choice, he would live in a dream world, and his dreams would never come to objectification. This would be a world of illusion. But man has the ability to choose and is unified with a Law which automatically produces his choice; whereas he does not have the ability to destroy the idea of himself, he does have the ability to deface it, to make it appear discordant; but he cannot destroy the Divine Image.

We live in a Universe of Love as well as in a Universe of Law. One is the complement of the other—the Universe of Love pulsating with feeling, with emotion; and the Universe of Law, the Executor of all feeling and all emotion.

In taking up this lesson on healing, then, let us remember that back of the man which we see is the Divine Image. There is a Perfect Concept, held in the Mind of the Universe as an already accomplished fact, but man is subject to the law of his own individuality.

Let us turn to the Law, and find what It says, in Chart No. III, viz., that man is conscious mind or spirit; this stands for his objective faculty. The objective mind of man is his recognition of life in a conscious state; it is the only attribute of man that is volitional, or self-choosing; consequently, it is the spiritual man. The conscious mind of man is the contemplator, the reflector. The Universe is the result of the Contemplation of the Divine Mind, or the Holy Spirit, which is God. God creates by contemplating His own I-AM-NESS; and this contemplation, through Law, becomes the objectification of the Self-Realization of the Infinite Mind.

MAN REËNACTS GOD

The Divine Nature is reënacted in man; he is conscious mind and spirit; and, as he contemplates, he reflects his thought into the Universal Subjectivity; it is received and acted upon.

As Mind, or Soul, accepts these images of thought, It operates upon unformed substance and causes it to take definite form as body, which is unconscious form. It becomes definite

---

51 Eccl. 7: 29.

form, but the form itself is unconscious, because it is made of immaterial substance. Body of itself, without Mind, has no consciousness nor volition. Devoid of mentality, the body neither thinks, sees, hears, feels, touches nor tastes. Take the mentality away from the body and it becomes a corpse. Having no conscious intelligence, it at once begins to disintegrate and to resolve again into the Universal Substance, or unformed matter, from which it came.

Conscious thought or contemplation is a reflector, reflecting through mentality into matter, the forms which consciousness entertains. Although man is inherently a perfect idea, his individuality covers this idea with the forms of thought which he images. Of course, these forms of thought may, or may not, be conscious. Man comes into this life subjective to the race consciousness and with a belief in his own environment; and as he unfolds his own personality he begins to create new subjective thought. He thinks and observes, draws certain conclusions and deductions, and incorporates them within his mentality, until, at last, they also become a part of the relative cause of his objective existence.

Healing is accomplished by uncovering, neutralizing and erasing false images of thought, and letting the perfect idea, or ideal, reflect itself through subjective mind into the body.

When one realizes that *everything is Mind and that nothing moves but Mind*, and that the only instrument of Mind is thought (which is contemplation in some form or other), he will see that nothing can permanently heal but right thinking. It is the only permanent form of healing that is known, i.e., mental and spiritual healing.

Not Limited by Principle

Realizing that conscious thought operates through a Power which is Infinite, we see that there can be no limit to the power to heal, other than the limit of our ability to conceive that Power as healing. We are limited, not by Principle, but by our ability to conceive perfection. Our thought can bring out a condition as perfect as we can conceive; therefore, the man whose thought is the most God-like will be the best healer. That is why we cannot divorce true mental healing from true spiritual work. The man whose thought is the most God-like, i.e., the truest, the highest, the most noble, the most complete, the most peaceful, will be the best healer because his thought reflects a greater perfection. When thought reaches a higher degree of perfection, it will bring out a still greater development, i.e., as the race consciousness unfolds and evolves.

Mental Treatment Is Real

Never forget that the Conscious Mind is the only Actor in the Universe and in man; that the unconscious or subjective mind is compelled, by reason of its nature, to accept; and that it can never reject; that the body is an effect, with no intelligence of its own. We can now see that a mental treatment is a real, tangible, specific operation, working in perfect accord with scientific Law.

When a practitioner treats any one, he does not just hope that his patient will get well; he does not ask that he may be healed; he does not simply desire that he may be healed; he is busy doing a definite piece of mental work, bringing out in his own consciousness (in his own self-contemplative, conscious mind) an understanding that the patient is healed and is perfect.

Treatment is the act, the art and the science of inducing thought within the mentality of the one treat-ing, which thought shall perceive that the body of the patient is a Divine, Spiritual and Perfect Idea. Treatment does not necessarily treat every organ of the body specifically, but it does declare the body to be harmonious and that every specific idea within it is harmonious. It then pays especial attention to what appears to be the physical disorder.

As the result of this treatment which the practitioner gives, Subjective Mind (which is Universal and Omnipresent) accepts the images of his thinking and reflects them in the direc-tion that he specifies.

He is not trying to send out a thought, hold a thought, or suggest a thought. Be sure that you differentiate between suggestion (which is all right, so far as it goes, but is limited) and real metaphysical healing. In metaphysical healing we are conscious that we are dealing with a Universal Principle, or Law, which takes the impress of our thought and acts upon it. Nothing can stop It. Some day we shall know that not even the thought of the patient can stop It, and then that argument will be ended! We are dealing with Something that cannot and does not answer back nor argue. We are directing It for definite purposes, telling It to do certain things which It does. This is what happens when we give a treatment.

Since the Law is Infinite, there is no incurable disease, as opposed to a curable one. The Law knows nothing about disease. It only acts. The practitioner says: "My word is the presence, power and activity of the Truth which is within me, which is Almighty, which is God. There is none other." This word then is the law of the thing whereunto it is spoken and has within itself the ability, the power, and the intelligence to execute itself through the great Law of all Life. This word, being the spontaneous recognition of Living Spirit—Infinite, Ever-Present, and Active—is now completely manifested in and through this person, or thing, about which the practitioner is thinking.

MAN COMES THROUGH SUBJECTIVITY

When man is born, he is born from pure subjectivity into objectivity. He is born from a subjec-tive state of consciousness into an objective state, and he gradually grows into intelligent, self-conscious, objective understanding.

When a baby is born into this world, it is purely subjective; it does not know enough to feed itself; it has no objective faculties, no judgment, no thought processes. But the minute it is born it begins to develop an objectivity through observation; however, it takes a baby longer than it does any other animal, as it is more helpless. A child does not always gain its objective faculties quickly—sometimes it never does during this lifetime. Irresponsible people never become completely objectified on this plane; they are still instinctively subjective.

Born Perfect

Since babies are born from subjectivity, they are born, generally speaking, from a perfect condition. You will find that practically everything, when it comes into the world, is perfect; it then takes on objectivity; but it brings with it, subjectively, certain tendencies. Very seldom does it bring disease. Very few diseases are inherited, in spite of all the claims that people make that they inherit heart trouble, tuberculosis, etc. They do not! What they do, however, is to inherit a subjective receptivity toward, and a belief in, those things.

At first, children are happy, free, spontaneous. That is why we like them; they live instinctively. As they grow older and their emotions become more complex and they hear people talk about death, trouble, divorce, love and marriage, and everything else that is good, bad or indifferent, they begin to react to these emotions subjectively.

Everything that opposes harmony and Spontaneous Unity will prove disastrous to the child's health, sooner or later. The inherited part is simply an inherited subjective tendency.

Race-Suggestion

Another prolific source of disease is race-suggestion. RACE-SUGGESTION MEANS THE ACCUMULATED SUBJECTIVE TENDENCIES OF THE HUMAN RACE; these tendencies are operative through any person who is receptive to them.

These, then, are the sources from which most diseases come—conscious observations, suppressed emotions, subjective inherited tendencies, and, perhaps three-fourths of them, from race-suggestion.

Disease Is Impersonal

Disease is an impersonal thought force operating through people, which does not belong to them at all. Recognize that it is neither person, place, nor thing; that there is no law to support it; that it is a coward, fleeing before the Truth; that there is nothing but the Truth. There is no

limitation imposed upon man anywhere. You must know that the Power you are using is definite, scientific, dynamic, Spiritual, Absolute and complete, and that It will work. Let no fear
come into your thought.

Remember that nothing can come through consciousness into objectivity but such thoughts
as you claim. The person who has clearly and subjectively realized the Unity of Mind, the Unity
of Good, the Presence of God, the Absoluteness of his own Being, the totality of things existing
at the point of his own personality, is immune from mental suggestion. He can surround himself with an armor of protection so that false suggestion cannot enter.

As a matter of fact, practically all the world is hypnotized through race concept, and what
we need to do is to dehypnotize it.

How to Heal

Disease is mentally contagious through suggestion; so we must surround our patients with
an aura, or atmosphere, of protection. This is nothing less than the realization of the Presence
and the Power of God, or Spirit, as their Life, as the only Life there Is, as Complete and Perfect
in them.

First recognize your own perfection; then build up the same recognition for your patient;
then directly attack the thought that binds him, recognizing that your word destroys it, stating
that it does, taking into account and specifically mentioning everything that needs to be
changed, every so-called broken law or false thought. Then finish your treatment with a great
realization of peace, sitting there a few moments in silent recognition that it is done, complete
and perfect.

The work must not be thought of as hard; and when we know that there is but One Mind,
we shall realize that it could not be hard. *Mental treatment is a direct statement in Mind of what we
wish to have done and a complete realization that it is done.*

Mind Is the Actor

We recognize that everything is in Mind and that nothing moves but Mind; that Intelligence is
back of everything, acting through a thought force which is concrete, definite and real. The
reason people do not realize that mental healing is possible is that they do not understand the
meaning of Causation; they do not realize that Intelligence is back of all things; that there is
but One Fundamental Intelligence in the Universe, One Common Mind or One Mind, Common to all people. *That which we appear to be is simply the point where this Mind manifests through*

us. (Man is an Individualized Center of God-Consciousness. Remember, all Law is Mind in Action.)

Every disease that we have must come through Mind in order to operate through us. There is but One Subjective Mind in the Universe. Upon this understanding alone is mental treatment possible (whether it be present or absent); if there were more than One, it would be impossible, for then there would be no Common Medium through which to work, think or act.

There is but One, and we are always thinking into It; so whether a patient is present or absent makes no difference. The only advantage in having him present is that you may talk to him and teach him, and, by analyzing his thought, remove any mental complex or conflict.

The question is often asked: "Is this Subjective Mind, or Law, all that there is to the Divine Nature?" No, of course not. There is the Spirit and the Soul of the Universe, a dual aspect of that which is One; but when you are practicing mental healing, you are dealing with Law, just as definitely as a physicist deals with law.

DISEASE IS NOT ALWAYS DUE TO CONSCIOUS THOUGHT

Any disease, in order to operate through the body, must first be a mental picture in the inner mentality; it must first be subjective, if it is to become objectified. "Disease is an image of thought held in Mind until it appears in the body." This is all there is to it. While every disease is an effect and must first have a subjective cause, the subjective cause, nine times out of ten, is not conscious in the thought of the person who has it; but is, perhaps, largely the result of certain combinations of thinking, which, gathering together around and through the individual who thought and received them, becomes operative through him. Certain combinations of thought, coalescing, produce a definite manifestation.

So, while it is true that every disease has a direct prototype in subjective mind, it is also true that the individual who suffers from the disease, nine times out of ten, never thought he was going to have that particular kind of trouble.

WE DEAL WITH IDEAS

You are dealing with ideas only. Let the physicians deal with bodies, if necessary. There is nothing wrong with medicine or manipulation, provided it relieves suffering, but lest the suffering come again, the mental cause must be removed. Never say to patients: "Don't take medicine, because if you do, the treatments will do you no good"; for this is untrue. Say, instead, "If you feel like taking medicine or going to the doctor, do so." If you follow this method, the time will generally come when your patient will realize that he no longer needs the medicine; *he will have unfolded out of the disease, rather than have broken away from it.*

Actually speaking, no one needs to be healed; that is, health is an omnipresent reality, and when the obstructions that hinder healing are removed, it will be found that health was there all the time. So, in your work, do not feel that you must heal any one. In fact, assume no responsibility for any one's recovery.

Have No Doubts

Suppose, when you treat a patient, you begin to feel a terrible sense of responsibility—what should you do? You should begin at once to treat yourself against that thought, for as long as you have it there is a barrier to healing. Why? Because when you sift that sense of responsibility down to its last analysis, it is a belief that you cannot heal. Do not give in to that belief, because it is nothing but a thought which says that you cannot heal. Nothing but a thought is saying, or could be saying, it. A chair could not say it, and since it is only a thought that says it, it is only a thought that can unsay it. Declare: "My word has the power to heal," and you will find that doubt has gone.

Thinking in Treatment

When you are giving a treatment, you are thinking; you are meeting, opposing, neutralizing, erasing and obliterating all suppression, fear, doubt, failure, morbid emotion and sense of loss—whatever the trouble may be. Every time your thought hits fairly and squarely, it erases just as definitely as one would erase a chalk line. Such is the mystery of appearance and disappearance.

Why doesn't God heal us? Because we are independent. We have made ourselves sick and we must heal ourselves. In the great world war ten or fifteen million people suffered agony, pain, sorrow and grief—it staggers the imagination to conceive of it. But water was just as wet and the birds sang just as sweetly through it all. Nothing happened, except in man's thought and act; he fought until he tired of fighting; then he stopped. We will be sick until we tire of it; then we will inquire into the cause, eliminate it and be healed.

Do Not Try to Go Beyond Your Understanding

Our understanding is not sufficient to enable us to set bones, and, since we cannot walk on the water, we take a boat. We can go only as far as we know. Principle is Infinite, but we can demonstrate only at the level of our own concept.

If a man struggles against a habit, he is building up a mental resistance, but if he does not resist it while you treat him, he will soon find himself liberated.

People say: "I can't take off my glasses." Then wear them; but begin to make the declaration that there is One Perfect Vision seeing through you. This is the Truth. *When this statement shall have become a subjective realization, you will be healed and will no longer need glasses.*

If a plaster will relieve, use it. If a pill does any good, take it; but gradually lead thought from where it is into the higher realms of consciousness where neither plasters nor pills are needed.

What a Practitioner Must Know

A practitioner knows that disease is mental. He not only knows this; he knows that disease is simply an impersonal thought force, operating through whatever channel it may find. He knows that it is a direct thought force; that there is nothing but Mind in the Universe; nothing to move but Intelligence. He is not dealing with a physical body, nor trying to heal a physical condition.

Right here, let me mention that many people think they must put their hands on their patients to heal them—that there is a certain magnetism, potent in healing. This has nothing to do with the power of which we are talking. Magnetic healing is the transmission of vital energy from one body to another and soon exhausts itself.

We treat man, not as a patient, not as a physical body, not as a diseased condition; neither do we treat the disease as belonging to him, the reason being that if we do, we will fasten the disease to him. We must not think of the disease as being connected with him or as a part of him. The practitioner realizes that man is born of Spirit and not of matter. Spirit is Changeless, Perfect, Complete, and in every respect Pure, Undefiled and Uncontaminated. He realizes this until he sees his patient as a living embodiment of Perfection.

A practitioner, then, is one who, recognizing that there is nothing but Mind to move, definitely, specifically, concretely and consciously speaks from his objective mind into Subjectivity and gives direction to Law, which is the Actor.

Healing Is Clear Thinking

Healing is the result of clear thinking and logical reasoning, which presents itself to consciousness and is acted upon by it. It is a systematic process of reasoning which unearths the mental cause or idea underlying disease, and presents the Truth about man's Being, thereby healing him.

For instance, say to yourself: "God is All there is. There is only One Life." When you are treating, if there is any little point that is not clear, stop at once and go back to the last analysis of Ultimate Reality and Absoluteness and build your whole argument upon It, in order to get a clear consciousness.

Repeat: "God is All. There is only One Power, Intelligence and Consciousness in the Universe, only One Presence. Now, that One Presence cannot change. There is nothing for It to change into but Itself. It is Changeless and It is My Life now. It is in me now." Claim that no form of race-suggestion, belief in limitation, subjective idea of limitation, thought of Karma, fatalism, theology or hell, horoscope, or any such beliefs have power. Accept none of them. If you have ever believed in them; if you have ever believed that the stars govern you, or that your environment governs you, or that your opportunities govern you, if you have ever been led to believe by any one that any of these things govern you, recognize that it is a hypnotic condition into which you have fallen, and deny every one of them, until there is no longer anything in you that believes in them.

This is the way to get your consciousness clear. You see what it does; it induces a clear concept of Reality which must reproduce Itself. This process of clear thinking, if carried out every day, would heal any disease, because it would bring a complete recognition of Life.

ONLY ONE LAW

The thing that makes you sick can heal you. You do not need to look for a law of health as opposed to a law of disease; for there is only One Law. This will give a great sense of relief, since it means that there is no power to oppose a correct mental treatment.

People often say to a practitioner: "I want you to hold a strong thought for me." This is a misconception; for there are no strong and weak thoughts in this sense. The most powerful thought is the one that carries the greatest conviction with it. We do not hold thoughts; we simply think them and let Mind operate upon them.

People often say: "It must be a drain to treat so many people; I should think that your will power would become exhausted." This also is a misconception; for will power has nothing whatever to do with real mental healing; its use would imply that the practitioner exercises a personal thought force over his patient. This is false suggestion, which is always some form of hypnotism.

NO SENSATION IN TREATMENTS

It is sometimes thought that in giving or receiving a treatment one must experience some physical sensation. A patient sometimes says, after having received a treatment: "I felt nothing during the treatment." It is not necessary that the patient should feel anything during the treatment, neither is it necessary that the practitioner should feel anything, other than the truth about the words that he speaks.

When we plant a seed in the ground, we do not have a great sensation, and it is not probable that the soil has any sensation. But the seed, planted in the creative soil, will, nevertheless, produce a plant. "What is true on one plane is true on all." Know that you are doing things just as definitely as the gardener. It is the person who knows what he is doing who gets results.

How to Remove Doubt

All thoughts of doubt concerning one's ability to heal come from the belief that it is the personality which does the healing, and not the Law. Never say: "I am not good enough to heal," or "I do not know enough to heal," or "I haven't understanding enough to heal." Know that you are dealing with Law and that It is the Actor. Recognize all such arguments as some form of suggestion and refuse to let them operate through you. You can heal; *but you must know that you can.*

The day will come when the entire world will believe the Truth, because of the great neutralizing power which It is exercising upon the race consciousness.

The Truth Demonstrates Itself

The reason people do not get better results is that they do not understand that Principle works independently; the Truth demonstrates Itself. At the root of every one's personality there is One Common Mind. There is but One Subjectivity in the Universe, and all use It. Think of yourself as being in Mind as a sponge is in the water; you are in It and It is in you.

Disease Is Mental

Every disease that comes up through subjectivity, or appears in the body, must come up through Mind. Bodies, of themselves, do not get sick. For instance, when the Life Principle deserts the body, it is what we call a corpse—a lifeless and inanimate thing; it no longer becomes sick; we understand that it could not get sick unless there were intelligence there to cognize the trouble.

Since the body, of itself, cannot become ill, or hurt, or contract disease, unless there is intelligence there to recognize and feel it, disease is primarily a mental thing. Without mentality it is not; and yet with mentality it appears to be.

For instance, a contagious disease is physically contagious between two living people; but it is not contagious between two dead people. There must be intelligence, even in a contagious disease, for the body to contract it. The dead body cannot catch it from the living because the intelligence has departed.

THE MEDIUM OF HEALING

The thing to *remember always* is, that *there is just One Subjective Mind in the Universe*. This is a point that people often do not realize, and because they do not, they cannot see how a person may be treated without touching him; or that a person can be healed at a distance through absent treatment.

If there is but One Subjective Mind in the Universe (and we all remember the meaning of Subjective Mind; It is Deductive, Receptive, Plastic, Neutral, Impersonal and Creative; It is the Stuff from which all things are formed)—you can impress upon It a certain image of thought, or a certain process of realization, and you will get a result; for It is the Actor.

DEPEND ON PRINCIPLE

Through the proper use of this great Subjective Law you can impress upon It a definite idea; and if you, yourself, do not withdraw that idea, or neutralize it by an opposite one, the law will bring it into manifestation.

What we need, then, is to learn the law governing this Principle. When you give a treatment, you are definitely setting in motion a Universal Law which must not only accept what you say, but the way in which you say it. If your treatment is given with a sense of struggle, it will manifest that way; if it is given with a sense of peace, then it will manifest in that manner.

Remember that you need assume no personal responsibility for the recovery of your patient. All that you have to do is to make certain statements which Mind is going to carry into effect through him.

One who understands the use of Divine Principle never tries to suggest, hypnotize nor personally influence any one; he is always impersonal in his work; he is stating in Mind directly what he wishes to have done.

When you have occasion to treat yourself, call your own name and then proceed with the treatment, as though you were treating some one else.

Disease will be healed, provided you get at its cause and remove it, and provided the one for whom you are working is willing to surrender that cause. *You cannot heal any one of his trouble if it is the result of some mental attitude which he will not surrender.* In this case, find out what the mental attitude is and remove it. It is a practitioner's duty to uncover false ideas of Life and replace them with the Truth. If this can be done before the disease destroys the body, a healing will always follow.

DEFINITE WORK IN HEALING

Principle is the Power that made everything; It is Absolute; It will not and cannot be denied. The only thing that can deny God is yourself.

Do not think of disease as an entity, but as an impersonal thought-force. In healing, you are separating the false from the true; the work is definite and dynamic, and is consciously done with a clear purpose always in mind.

If your own thought is clear, and you are able to completely realize the Presence of Spirit in your patient, all the power on earth cannot hinder you from healing.

REPEATING TREATMENTS

Always come to a complete conclusion while giving a treatment; always feel that it is done, complete and perfect. In the intervals between treatments, do not carry the thought of the patient around with you; to do so is to doubt, and this mental attitude must be completely overcome. Each treatment is a complete statement of the Reality of Being. The treatment should be repeated daily until a healing takes place. If it takes five minutes, five hours, five days or five years, the treatment must be kept up until a healing is accomplished. This is the only method that we know. It is not enough to say that everything is all right; this is true in Principle, but in fact, it is only as true as we make it. Treat until you get results. A healing takes place when the patient is no longer sick, and until that time mental work must be done.

REMOVE THE COMPLEX

Suppose one is constantly saying: "Everything is all wrong in the world; people are wrong; things are wrong; conditions are wrong; every one is sick; every one is unhappy; nothing is worth while." You, as a practitioner, must remove this complex; for these inner emotions create outer conditions in and through the body and are what cause a great deal of the sickness in the world.

Treatment straightens out consciousness by clear thinking. When the inner consciousness agrees with the Truth, when there is no longer anything within which denies the outer word of Truth, then, and not until then, a demonstration takes place. Specifically go over the thoughts that are wrong and use the power of your word to heal them.

HEALING PAIN

Use the thought of peace and the realization of a Perfect Presence; know that in this Presence there is no tension, there is no struggle, there is no fear, there is no sense of conflict. Know this until there comes to your own consciousness a deep, calm sense of peace and ease, and until every thought of pain is eliminated.

Do the same in the case of fever; treat until it is gone; usually it will go like heat off a stove.

HEADACHE

Suppose that every little while you have a headache. A physician may say that it is caused by some nerve strain; a chiropractor may say that it is something out of joint; the osteopath may say that it is something else; and some other practitioner may say that it is something else; for each has found some twist in the body to fit his theory. All of these twists may be there; but the body could not twist unless you were there to twist it. The metaphysician goes to the twister and untwists his thought, thus freeing the twists in the body. We recognize all the good that doctors are doing, but we insist that the mentality must also be taken into account.

Back of nearly every disorder there is some complex, or mental knot, that needs to be untied; generally, some suppressed emotion which, perhaps, is centered around the affections—the likes and dislikes, the loves and passions, and everything that goes with them. All these knots must be untied and it is the business of the practitioner to untie them.

WHAT RIGHT THOUGHT DOES

Right thought, constantly poured into consciousness, will eventually purify it. Disease is like a bottle of impure water; healing might be likened to the process of dropping pure water into the bottle, a drop at a time, until the whole is clean and pure. Some one might ask why the bottle could not be turned upside down and at once drain out all the impurities. Sometimes this happens, but not often; meanwhile, a drop at a time will finally eliminate the impurities and produce a healing.

In treating, go beyond the disease and supply a spiritual consciousness; never leave a person without the Great Realization of Life and Love, of God and Perfection, of Truth and Wisdom, of Power and Reality. Sense the Divine Presence in and through the patient at all times.

How Habits Are Healed

What is a habit? A habit is the form that desire takes; it is a desire for something that will give satisfaction. At the root of all habit is one basic thing, the desire to express life. There is an urge to express in all people, and this urge, operating through the channels of Creative Mind, looses energy into action and compels the individual to do something.

Back of all desire is the impulse of Spirit to express. In man, this impulse must express at the level of his consciousness:

> *"For each, for the joy of the working and each in his separate star,*
> *Shall paint the thing as he sees It for the God of things as they are."*

Some express constructively and some destructively.

Suppose a man who has the liquor habit comes to you to be healed. You would not pray that he be healed, for you would know that you are dealing with a man who has the desire to express life and who thinks that he must express it in terms of intoxication. He once thought this expressed reality to him; he now knows that it does not, but he has not the will power to stop; for the habit has appeared to take complete possession of him. (It is well to remember that unless we control thought, it will control us.)

In giving the treatment, first recognize who and what he is, saying something like this: "He is the full and complete expression of the Truth, and, as such, he is free from any sense of limitation. He is free from any delusion or fear of delusion. He knows that the Spirit of Truth within him is complete and always satisfied. That thing which calls itself the liquor habit has no power over him and cannot operate through him. By the power of this word, it is now completely destroyed and forever obliterated." Then see him free and satisfied. Wait until you, yourself, are sure of the statements made, realizing that the work is done. This is the treatment.

The Seed of Thought

Whether we say our thought goes out, or whether we say it is operated upon by Principle, makes no difference; it is very evident that until a thought is created there is no operation. For instance, a person is sick and he remains sick until some one knows that he is well. It is very evident, then, that as the result of some one's thinking he is healed. We know that the thinking sets in motion some law. Whether the word used heals, or whether it simply sets the Law in motion, really makes no difference. The practitioner is in the same Mind in which his patient lives; consequently, since each is in One Mind, the patient is sick in the same Medium and, in a certain sense, in the same Mind in which the practitioner lives; and because this Mind is In-divisible, the practitioner can, in his own mentality, reach the thought which causes the patient to be sick. Whether we say he sends out a thought, or whether he simply thinks a thought, makes no difference. *The simplest way is to say that the practitioner realizes within himself upon the One Mind, through the One Medium, in the One Law.*

The practitioner realizes a certain truth for his patient—within himself. Therefore he sets the Law in motion for his patient. (The operation of this Law may be thought of as the same as that of the law whereby water reaches its own level by its own weight.) The practitioner knows within himself; and that self-knowingness rises into the consciousness of his patient. So we do not have to worry about sending out thoughts. It is just like planting a seed in the ground; the practitioner sows the seed and the Creative Mind produces the plant. Does the ground operate on the seed, or does the seed operate upon the soil? We do not know, but we do know that when a seed is put into the ground, something operates upon it and a plant is produced; and that unless a seed is put into the ground, no plant will be produced.

WHAT CAN BE HEALED

What should we try to heal mentally? If we were dealing only with the power of our own thought, our limited concept, we could not heal anything mentally; but if we realize that we are dealing with Universal Principles, how can we set any limit to Its Power?

People are sick because they cover a perfect idea with imperfect thoughts; for sickness is the result of subjectified thinking. Everything which the objective mind has consciously thought has fallen into the subjective. All suggestions received have also fallen into the subjective thought; these suggestions may or may not have been consciously received. This will explain why people may be taken sick with diseases of which they never heard; somewhere, on the subjective side of thought, certain forces have been set in motion which, when objectified, produced certain conditions.

WHY PEOPLE GET TIRED

Let a person say to himself: "I have overworked," and at once there will come up through his consciousness a belief in weariness. People who are constantly complaining of being tired are simply hypnotized into this belief through the law of race-suggestion.

Suppose one had dropped complexes into his subjective thought; suppose desires had torn him, and conflicts had entered into his life; what would have happened? He would have been continually dropping opposing thoughts and concepts into his mentality; and as the mental action took place, they might produce a twisted body; and if over-chaotic, they might produce what is called nervous prostration. It would not, however, be the body that was sick but would be a condition brought about through wrong thought.

Now, if subjective thought were a thing apart from us, if we did not have conscious access to it, we could not change it; but being the result of the way thought has worked, we *can* consciously change it. If this were not true mental healing would be impossible.

THE IDEA MUST TAKE FORM

Healing, then, takes place to the degree that we send down the right kind of thoughts into subjectivity. This does not mean that we must sit around holding thoughts. We do not hold a seed in our hand when we wish to plant it, and it is the same in healing; we do not hold the thought but seek to realize it and let it work. By thinking consciously and with deep feeling, we implant the right idea in Mind, and Mind reproduces this idea as effect in the body. We must realize that we are using a Power compared to which the united intelligence of the human race is as nothing. This should not seem strange; for we know that the united intelligence of the entire race cannot produce a single rosebud, yet any gardener may produce as many roses as he wishes, if he goes about it in the right way. We must remember that what is true on one plane is true on all. Involution and evolution are the law, cause and effect. The practitioner involves an idea in Mind; it is Law and must operate.

If one wishes to treat a patient, he must first treat himself; as he treats himself, that is, as he treats his own mentality, which is simply a point in Mind, he reaches the mentality of his patient. The practitioner cannot erase the thought in the patient's mentality until he has first neutralized the idea in his own thought.

RESOLVE THINGS INTO THOUGHTS

A treatment is a specific thing. If you are treating some one against the belief in scarlet fever, you are making your word operate in such a way as to neutralize a belief in this disease. Each treatment must have, in itself, everything necessary to cover the case. When you treat, resolve things into thoughts; bodies, people, objects and all things. Having resolved everything into thoughts, know that disease is neither person, place nor thing; it has no location, does not belong to any one, cannot operate through any one, is not believed in by any one. Know that it is a false belief, a false image, with no power. Know that the whole thing is mental; then mentally dissolve it.

HEALING INSANITY

In treating some one whose mind appears to be deranged, realize that there is but One Mind, which Mind is God, and is Perfect. This is the only Mind that is; It is the Mind of your patient; It is your own Mind. This Mind, being a Complete, Perfect and Indivisible Whole, cannot labor under a delusion, cannot, for one moment, lose Its Self-Consciousness. After you have realized this Truth about Life, realize that it is also true about the one you are treating; his thought is perfect. If you have this realization in your own mentality, knowing there is just the One Mind, there will be no doubts or confusions; and the mentality of the patient will cease to be deranged.

WHAT A PRACTITIONER DOES

What a practitioner really does is to take his patient, the disease and everything that appears to be wrong right into his own mentality, and here he dissolves all false appearances and all erroneous conclusions. He takes the condition, not as a reality, but as a belief; and right at the center of his own being he neutralizes the whole false thought, thus healing the condition.

The more completely the practitioner is convinced of the power of his own word, the more power his word will have. There must be a complete realization that the power of the word, operating as the Truth and the Reality of Being, can do all things. Therefore, the person whose consciousness is the clearest, who has the most complete idea of Life, will be the best healer.

BACK OF THE APPEARANCE IS THE REALITY

HEALING IS NOT CREATING A PERFECT BODY OR A PERFECT IDEA; IT IS REVEALING AN IDEA WHICH IS ALREADY PERFECT. HEALING IS NOT A PROCESS. IT IS A REVELATION, through the thought of the practitioner to the thought of the patient. There may be a process *in* healing but not a process *of* healing. The process in healing is the mental work and the time it takes the practitioner to convince himself of the perfectness of his patient; and the length of time it takes the patient to realize this perfectness.

It is necessary that the practitioner realize a perfect body; he cannot realize this unless he has already become convinced that the perfect body is there. If he has come to this conclusion, he must not deny it. There is a perfect heart and a perfect idea of heart; there is a perfect head and a perfect idea of head; perfect lungs and a perfect idea of lungs. The practitioner must realize that back of the appearance is the Reality, and it is his business to uncover this Reality. He does this through a process of obliterating false thought; he must deny false conclusions, bring out the evidence of perfection, and produce the healing. Disease is a fact but not a truth; it is an experience but not a reality.

SEEING PERFECTION

When Jesus said to the man, "Stretch forth thine hand,"[52] He undoubtedly saw a perfect hand. Did he see the without or the within as being perfect? If everything is mental, and if He saw an imperfect hand instead of a perfect one, no good result could have come through His seeing, according to the law of cause and effect. This is true of all demonstration in healing. A practitioner does not treat a sick man; if he does, he not only will not heal him, but he might become sick himself. The reason for this is simple; he will have entered into the vibration of the patient's thought, and will, himself, experience the results of that vibration. This is an experience that many have when they first begin to practice; they take on the conditions of their patients. So, from what we know, Jesus must have seen only the perfect hand. Even though He might have recognized the false condition, as far as His word of healing was concerned it must have been a recognition of perfection, else it could not have healed.

We must think of the subjective state of our thought as our atmosphere in the Universal Mind; for we cannot separate ourselves from the Universe. There is but One Mind and we are in It; we are in It as intelligence; It accepts our thought and acts upon it. Destructive emotions, desires or ideas, unless they are neutralized, will grow into some bodily condition, and may produce disease. Disease is thought manifested, no matter what the disease may be. We are surrounded by a Receptive Intelligence which receives the impress of our thought and acts upon it.

HEALING LUNG TROUBLE

Suppose a person comes to a practitioner and says: "I am dying of tuberculosis." What is tuberculosis? It is a belief in lung trouble; but lung itself is a universal idea, a perfect idea; and nothing has ever happened to it. It was, is, and will be; but man, through the creative medium of his thought, has caused an appearance of disorder and disease in the lung. Back of all such trouble is a consuming passion, an unexpressed emotion, a strong desire. Healing will take place to the degree that the practitioner neutralizes this belief and perceives the presence of a perfect lung. He realizes that there is a perfect body, perfect lung, perfect being, perfect God, perfect man, perfect expression; he must bring his own thought up to this perception. The

---

52 Matt. 12 : 13.

word he speaks is law; it is power; it knows itself to be what it is. It is the law unto the case. He is now conscious that the word he speaks will neutralize and entirely destroy the false thought and condition. He says: "There is one body; this body is the Body of God; and it is Perfect; it is never depleted; its vitality is never lowered. There is no wasting away of substance or burning up of substance; for substance is eternal, changeless and perfect." He goes on until he covers what in his own thought appears to be the cause of the false condition. If he does this day after day, the patient begins to get better; though the practitioner never thinks of his patient, other than that his word is being spoken for him; and he never wonders whether his word is taking effect, because he speaks into Intelligence and lets It act. Perhaps, if it is a case that requires a great deal of attention, he treats morning, afternoon, and evening, each time for a few moments; otherwise ten or fifteen minutes each day should be sufficient.

Never think that a sick person is one who simply has a sick *body*. If you do you will find yourself treating the *body*. Why shouldn't we treat the body? Because the cause of the disease is not in the body. The body is an effect and not a cause. KNOW THAT BODIES AND CONDITIONS NEVER MOVE; THEY ARE ALWAYS MOVED UPON. A sick person is one who has a sick thought.

What about accidents? It is part of our belief that as soon as, and to the degree that, our minds become adjusted harmoniously to the Universe, we will be less and less likely to have accidents.

WE DO NOT SEND OUT THOUGHTS

In practice we do not try to send thoughts to our patients; for there is but One Mind in the universe. We will say "A" represents a man who is sick; "B" represents a practitioner. "B" thinks into Mind; and whether we say he is thinking within himself or somewhere else does not matter; he is always thinking into Mind, because he is in Mind. "But," one might say, "the patient thinks into his own subjective mind"; yes, but his subjective mind is only his atmosphere in the One Mind. We must get this very clearly, else some day there will be a wall between our thought and its ability to heal some condition, or some person who is at a physical distance.

Both the patient and the practitioner think into One Common Mind; therefore when a patient comes to a practitioner for healing the practitioner does not try to hypnotize him or suggest anything to him; he declares the Truth about him. And to the degree that he brings his own consciousness to a true recognition of perfection—provided there is a receptivity in the thought of the patient—that man will be healed; nothing can hinder it. The practitioner does not try to hold a thought or send out a thought; he simply tries to convince himself of the perfection of his patient. He does not try to make his word operate through his patient but only attempts to know the Truth of what he states. The patient must be receptive to the Truth, and then the Truth will heal him. The practitioner is dealing with Universal Law, backed by Omnipotent Power, which is Divine Principle. This is what Jesus meant when He said: "Ye shall know the Truth and the Truth shall make you free."[53]

Every time we think, we are thinking into a receptive, plastic Substance, which receives the impress of our thought. When we stop to realize how subtle thoughts are, how unconsciously we think negation, how easy it is to get down and out, we will see that each is perpetuating his own condition. This is why people go from bad to worse, or from success to a greater success.

VISION

Eye trouble is a belief in limited vision; it is a belief in a separated vision. God sees, and His is the Only Mind there is. It is our Mind; consequently, man sees, whether he knows it or not. Do not fear to claim this; because it is the truth. There is no obstruction to vision; there is no near vision nor far vision; there is no false vision; there is no weak vision nor blurred vision. There is One Perfect Seeing, which is Now seeing through and in me.

HEALING CONSTIPATION

Constipation is due to a belief in limitation or burden and is healed by knowing that there is no restriction, no inaction, no limited action, no bondage, no fear, no congestion. Make the thought realize that there is nothing but freedom; that all action is normal, harmonious and perfect.

Very often the word of healing is spoken and does not appear to operate because some obstruction hinders it. Some people are obstinate, resistant, stubborn; and they must be healed of these beliefs. There is no resistance to Truth, no thought anywhere which can hinder consciousness from perceiving the Truth. Whatever the false condition is, ARRAY MENTAL ARGUMENT AGAINST IT IN AN OPPOSITE MANNER. Turn the thought over and over, until, either by reason or by chance, you hit upon the thing that is wrong. Any one can heal if he will do this, just as any one, if he goes into the garden and drops seed into the ground, will cause plants to grow. Any one can heal who can get away from the effect long enough to perceive a different cause.

In every treatment the thought of fear must always be handled. One should realize that there is no fear, nothing to be afraid of; and that fear cannot operate through man.

---

53 John 8 : 32.

DISEASE NOT AN ENTITY

Man is fundamentally perfect; this is our whole premise; Perfect God, Perfect Man, Perfect Being; this is the whole basis of the argument. Always separate disease from the person suffering with it. Declare very frequently that disease is neither person, place nor thing; that it has no location, no avenue through which to express itself, no expression, no one through whom to express. Never locate disease, because thoughts are things, and if located they will operate. Always separate the belief from the believer, for nothing ails the real man; nothing ever did or ever will.

THROAT TROUBLE

In treating throat trouble the thought to handle is sensitiveness. No one would ever have throat trouble if his feelings were never hurt. You heal a person of sensitiveness by teaching him that no one desires to hurt him, and that no one could if he did so desire. When one becomes really individualized his feelings cannot be hurt; for he will feel complete within himself.

CONGESTION

In colds, congestion and like conditions, the thought to heal is confusion. There should be a consciousness of poise, a recognition of peace; and when this comes into the individual's experience he will no longer have colds.

PARALYSIS

People could be healed of all forms of paralysis through the elimination of the belief in bondage. Use the thought that Life cannot become paralyzed or inactive. As in constipation, there is a thought of restriction back of the thought of paralysis; and often there is a very emotional nature to deal with; and often, though not always, a lot of stubbornness and resistance to heal.

GROWTHS

If the thought of false growths can be erased the manifestation can be healed. Declare, "Every plant which my Heavenly Father hath not planted shall be rooted up." The Heavenly Father is the Reality of Man and is Eternal Presence and Perfection. Dissolve the idea of false growths by knowing that there is nothing for them to feed upon. Erase the belief in your own mentality and you will remove it from the mentality of your patient, and thereby heal his body.

TREATING CHILDREN

In the case of children, remember that the thoughts of the parents influence the child. We will suppose the child's mother is constantly saying: "The poor thing; the poor, little, sick thing!" From the human standpoint this is natural, but it makes the child sick just the same, no matter how loving it may be. This is called unconscious, or innocent, malpractice. It is malpractice, because it is the wrong use of thought; innocent, because it is not intended to harm; unconscious, because she doesn't know what she is doing; ignorant, because she doesn't know the results of such mental action. In such a case the practitioner must realize that there is no mental influence operating through the child, except a belief in perfection.

POWER OF THE WORD

Be specific in treating, be definite and direct in your mental work. You are dealing with Intelligence, so deal with It intelligently. The treatment must realize the patient as perfect; must recognize the word as power; must know that it breaks down every man-made law and casts it out; that it is the law of harmony and the recognition of the Presence of Good; that within itself it is unbounded, and equipped with the power to execute itself; and it must know that it does this. It must know that there is nothing that can change it; that there is no belief which can hinder it; that it cannot be reversed, mislaid, misplaced, neutralized or destroyed by any opposing force; but that it does the thing that it is supposed to do. And it must know that it is continuous and will operate until it does all that it is supposed to do.

Jesus said: "Heaven and earth shall pass away: but my words shall not pass away."[54] Isaiah understood something of this when he said: "So shall my word be that goeth forth out of my mouth: it shall not return unto me void."[55]

NO AGE

There are certain thoughts that should always be handled, such as thoughts of race-suggestion, inherited tendencies, prenatal conditions, environment, and mental influences and suggestion.

---

54 Luke 21: 33.
55 Isa. 55 : 11.

A treatment must be so formulated as to recognize that there is but One Mind; consequently, no thought can flow through It of depression, fear, or suggestion of imperfection, Man is Birthless, Deathless, Ageless Spirit; and this should be the consciousness of our work. This leaves nothing to be born, mature, decay and die. When this thought shall be made clear in the consciousness of the race, people will no longer grow old. Life cannot grow old; It is always the same.

MEMORY

Locke, in "Human Understanding," defines memory as: "The power to revive again in our minds those ideas which, after imprinting, have disappeared, or have been, as it were, laid aside out of sight." Memory is the ability to remember things that have happened; therefore, if something happened two years ago, of which we are not at present thinking, we can remember it, because it is in our subjective thought. We say that we are getting absent-minded, which means that we cannot recall thoughts. A person may be healed of this belief by knowing that the One Mind never forgets Itself. This Mind is our Mind now.

GUIDANCE IN TREATING

If, in treating, it seems impossible to know just what thought to handle, it is well to be still and know that Intelligence within will tell you what to say and how to say it. By doing this some idea will come and you will find that, by using it, you will reach the case.

HOW TO HEAL

Never say: "Here is a patient whom I must heal"; for, if you see him from this angle, how are you going to heal him? If you see a sick man he will remain sick, so far as you are concerned; you cannot heal while you see sickness. Disease is neither person, place nor thing; nobody believes in it; it has no action or reaction; it is neither cause nor effect; it has no law to support it and no one to operate through; there is no one to talk about it or believe in it.

You have nothing to do with the patient's thought as a personality, for as your own thought clears it will heal him. When you give a treatment, first eliminate all doubt and fear from your own thought. Realize that you are a Divine Idea and that your word is the law unto the thing unto which it is spoken. This is what gave Jesus His power; "For he taught them as one having authority, and not as the scribes."[56]

---

56 Matt. 7 : 29.

REMOVE DOUBT

Suppose a practitioner is not able to convince himself of the Truth of the statements which he makes; how is he going to bring himself to the point of belief? By repeating the affirmation, dwelling on its meaning, meditating upon the spiritual significance of it until the subjective state of his thinking becomes clarified. This is the only reason for repeating treatments; for one treatment would heal anything if there were no doubts. Repeated treatments induce within consciousness a definite concept of an already established fact, even though the fact may not already have become objectified; this is why mental healing is a science. There is no room for doubt in a treatment.

Realize that you treat with your understanding through the Law. Never say: "I am not good enough to treat." There are no good, better and best; this is a delusion; for one is as good as another in the Truth.

Do not allow yourself to become superstitious; for you are dealing with a normal, natural law in the mental and spiritual world. This law is just as real as any other known law. Don't say: "I am not sure that I have enough power to treat"; you cannot heal with this mental attitude. Say, "As I let fall the forms of my thought they are operated upon by Principles I believe. This is the Law of God, the law of man and the Law of the Universe." Never say: "This disease is hard to heal while another is easy." If you find yourself saying this, at once heal yourself. This comes from a belief that we are dealing with a limited power.

NO FEAR

Suppose when you begin to treat, a great surge of fear comes over you and attempts to tell you that you cannot give a good treatment. The thing to do is to treat this fear as a suggestion which has no power and which cannot convince you that you lack the power to heal. Say: "There is nothing in me which can doubt my ability to heal." This will neutralize the fear and free the effort to accomplish.

How do we know when we have treated a patient long enough? When he is well he will need no more treatments; until this time comes treat every day for a realization of perfection.

Does it make any difference whether or not the patient is taking medicine? Not a bit. If this form of healing gives him any relief, let him have it. We all need all the relief we can get. The patient is healed when he no longer needs medicine. Forget the medicine and heal him mentally and he will no longer take pills.

Some think that they dishonor God when they take a pill. God knows nothing about pills; this is superstition, pure and simple; mostly simple. Discard all such thoughts and give your entire attention to realizing perfection for your patient.

Healing is not accomplished through will power but by knowing the Truth; this Truth is that man is already Perfect, no matter what the appearance may be. Holding thoughts has nothing to do with treatment. If you find, when you begin to give treatments, that the process gives you a headache, know that you are doing your work on the mental plane and not through spiritual realization. A treatment should leave the practitioner in a better condition than before he gave it; otherwise it is not a good one.

One might ask: "Is all disease a thought held in the conscious mind of the patient?" No, not necessarily; it may be a subconscious thought; or it may be the result of many thoughts which, gathered together, produce a definite result.

Psycho-analysis

It may be necessary for the practitioner to diagnose the thought of his patient; in fact this is one of the main points in healing. This is psycho-analysis (from psyche or soul). Psycho-analysis is the analysis of the soul or subjective mind. Its teaching is, that within the soul, or subjective mind, all the seeds of our thought fall; and that most of man's physical troubles are caused by some conflict of the emotions and the will. The conscious mind, desiring certain things which it cannot have, sends into the subjective thought opposing desires, which conflict with each other and mentally tear or bind; and as they manifest in the body, they produce disease. It is claimed that seventy per cent of all diseases are the results of suppressed emotions; these emotions are not necessarily sex emotions, but may be any suppressed desires. These suppressed emotions cause what are called complexes.

It is probable that when Jesus forgave the man his sins, He realized that the man had a complex of condemnation within himself. The sense of condemnation which the race holds about itself weights it down, and it must be removed. This explains why Jesus said: "Thy sins be forgiven thee."[57] It is feeling that hurts. The thinking man thinks things out, resolves everything into its normal parts and so avoids complexes. It has been said: "Life is a comedy to him who thinks, a tragedy to him who feels."

The practitioner talks to his patient, shows him the Law of Mind, teaches him the way, diagnoses his thought, points out to him that certain mental attitudes produce certain physical results, teaches him how to be harmonious in his thinking, how to be at peace, how to trust and believe in the Good, lifts him up mentally and spiritually and supports his thought until he can stand alone.

A practitioner must be filled with a spirit of Divine Compassion; he must have a deep,

---

57 Matt. 9 : 2.

underlying sense of unity and sympathy, else he will do but little good; but he must not have sympathy with the disease. The only guarantee of our Divinity is in its expression through our Humanity. Consequently an enlightened soul understands the meaning of sympathy and exercises it, but not morbidly.

DEAL ONLY WITH THOUGHTS

In mental treatment, the practitioner deals with thoughts and does not treat bodies or conditions. He never manipulates, nor need he lay his hands on his patients. He does not hypnotize them; he does not care where they are when he is treating them, or what they are doing; for this would be a limited concept. The practitioner's work begins and ends within his own consciousness.

NERVOUSNESS

The thoughts to cover in nervousness are ones of peace, poise and power. There is no twitching of the nerves; there is no strain or struggle in the universe. Things move harmoniously, quietly and normally; and this action, which is the action of Life, is the truth about the one you are treating. A treatment lasts until the one treating is convinced of the truth which he states; it might last one minute or one hour, or longer.

STAMMERING

The treatment for stammering is one that covers the idea of correct speech. Speech is the Word of God and cannot become impaired, but must be a flow from that One Life which knows Itself to be what it is. Speech is perfect.

ARGUMENT IN TREATMENT

Just a word about argument in treatment; we do not argue to make Principle work but to convince our own thought that it already is operating.

To sum up the idea of treating, then—you are conscious mind: your patient is conscious mind; he has thought, or is thinking, or there has been thought through him, consciously or unconsciously, an idea of imperfection. You, as conscious mind, remove this something which says that he is imperfect. The treatment begins and ends within your own mentality; it must cover the case and leave nothing to be sick, sin or die; then it will be effective. Meditation in treatment; an uplifted receptivity to Spirit will always produce good results. A deep inner sense of the unity of all life enables one to feel that the Great Conscious Mind and Spirit of the Universe, flowing through his mentality, is the Presence and the Power of an Infinite Life, Truth and Love. We should sense that back of the word which we speak is the Power of the Universe surging to express Itself. Then speak the word consciously, knowing that it is Law.

Note: Read and carefully study "Teaching and Addresses," Edward S. Kimball; "The Law of Mind in Action," F. L. Holmes; "The Faith That Heals," F. L. Holmes; "Christian Healing," Fillmore; "Lessons in Truth," Cady; "Primary Lessons," Militz; "Outwitting Our Nerves," Jackson.

LESSON THREE: RECAPITULATION

Sickness is an experience but not an Ultimate Reality; it is an effect and not a cause. The body, devoid of mentality, could neither know nor have sensation; it is entirely an effect. The body is made of the same unthinking stuff from which all Creation is formed.

Instinctive Man is Perfect, but his individual use of Life and Law enables him to cover a perfect idea with an apparently imperfect cloak.

Man comes into objectivity with the tendency of the race already subjectified within him, through race-suggestion. The race believes in sickness and limitation, and this suggestion is more or less operative through all people. This suggestion works through the field of the subjective state of the race thought, and will operate through any individual who is receptive to it.

As man becomes individualized, he consciously thinks and continuously pours suggestions into his subjective thought which is the silent builder of the physical body. Through the field of subjectivity thought always works out to a logical conclusion.

Man does not, necessarily, consciously think that he is to have a certain type of physical trouble, but the physical correspondent is a logical outcome of what he thinks.

Disease, of itself, is neither person, place nor thing; it is an image of thought, consciously or unconsciously held somewhere in Mind and will externalize wherever it finds an avenue of operation.

Disease is entirely mental in its origin, since no person could be sick unless he had intelligence; it is the result of thinking about, and believing in duality, or a power apart from God.

Disease can be healed through reversing the thought and turning to the Spiritual Realization of Life. It is impossible to divorce real mental healing from true Spiritual Realization, since God is ALL.

The use of mental argument in healing rests upon the theory that we are surrounded by a Universal Mind which reacts to our thought.

Right mental practice is the constructive use of Mind, i.e., a mental argument given for the purpose of presenting the Spiritual Truth about man. Wrong mental practice is the destructive use of Mind, i.e., a mental argument given for the purpose of presenting a false claim about man.

Right mental practice is called the Spirit of Christ. Wrong mental practice is called the spirit of Antichrist; it is malpractice and may or may not be consciously used. To think of any one in a negative way is some form of malpractice and is harmful. Malpractice may be ignorant, innocent or malicious. It is always some form of suggestion.

Man is known in Mind by the name he bears, and any statement made in Mind about his name will cause some action to take place through Law towards him. This is the basis of all mental healing.

A practitioner is one who recognizes Man as a spiritual reality. *Since there is but One Mind, the practitioner does this within himself*. Through the medium of the One Mind these statements rise to objective conditions in his patient, according to the practitioner's belief and according to the ability of his patient to receive the Truth. Healing is accomplished through the act of setting Subjective Law in motion. The more Spiritual or Godlike the mentality of the practitioner, the more powerful the treatment.

A mental treatment begins and ends within the thought of the practitioner because he is in the same Mind in which his patient lives. Treatment is inducing right concepts within the subjective side of life.

Absent and present treatments are the same; *for there is no absence in the One Presence*.

One disease would be as easily healed as another if the thought were as sure of itself in one case as another.

There is no personal responsibility in healing; the practitioner directs the Power and lets It work. One does not hold thoughts in mental healing; he looses thought. A practitioner does not try to suggest, hypnotize or mentally influence; he simply knows that man is now a spiritual being and holds to that belief,—no matter what the appearance may be. Right mental treatment does not tire the one giving it.

Personal magnetism has nothing to do with mental healing. The whole basis of the possibility of mental healing rests upon the premise that we all live in One Creative Mind which reacts to our belief. It is as though there were a Universal Ear listening to, and hearing, everything that we say, feel or think, and reacting to it.

Healing is not a process, but a revelation; for the revealing of the perfect man always heals. The process is the time and thought that it takes to arrive at the correct understanding of man's perfect state in Spirit.

Any one can heal who believes that he can, and who will take the time to put that belief in motion through the Law.

To daily see the perfect man and to daily declare for his objective appearance is correct mental practice and will heal.

A treatment recognizes that all is Mind and that everything is mental; it resolves all disease into thought; neutralizes the false thought and recognizes the true. Nothing can stop it from operating except a lack of faith in the reality of the Truth and man's ability to use It.

In giving mental treatment the practitioner first realizes his own being as spiritual; he then recognizes the perfect state of his patient's being; then he attacks the false claim and brings the evidence of Truth to bear against it, thinking in such a manner as to completely destroy the false claim and to realize the Truth.

LESSON FOUR: INTRODUCTION

Mental Science is not a "get-rich-quick scheme," neither does it promise something for nothing. It does, however, promise the one who will comply with its teaching that he shall be able to bring into his life and experience greater possibilities and happier conditions.

The Science of Mind is based entirely upon the supposition that we are surrounded by a Universal Mind into which we think; this Mind, in Its original state, fills all space with Its Presence. Since It fills all space, It fills the space that man uses in the Universe. It is *in* man as well as outside of him. As he thinks into this Universal Mind he sets in motion a Law which is creative, and which contains within Itself a limitless possibility.

THE LAW IS INFINITE

The Law through which man operates is Infinite, but man appears to be finite; that is, he has not yet evolved to a complete understanding of It. He is unfolding from a limitless potential but can bring into his experience only that which he can conceive. There is no limit to the Law, but there appears to be a limit to man's understanding of It. As his understanding unfolds, his possibilities of attainment will increase.

It is a great mistake to say: "Take what you wish; for you can have anything you like." We do not take what we wish, but we do attract to ourselves that which is like our thought. MAN MUST BECOME MORE IF HE WISHES TO DRAW A GREATER GOOD INTO HIS LIFE. We need not labor under the delusion that all we have to do is to say everything is ours. This is true in reality; but in fact, it is only as true as we make it. We provide the mold for the Creative Law, and unless the mold which we provide is increased, the substance cannot increase in our experience; for Mental Science cannot hold forth a promise that will do away with the necessity of complying with law.

The Law is a law of liberty, but not a law of license. It is exact and exacting, and unless we are willing to comply with Its nature and work with It, along the lines of Its inherent being, we will receive no great benefit. Every man must pay the price for that which he receives, and that price is paid in mental and spiritual coin. An avenue must be provided through which the Law may work as a law of liberty, if It is to free us. This does not mean that we must please the Law; for It is impersonal and neither knows nor cares who uses It, nor for what purpose; but, because It is impersonal, It is compelled, by Its very nature, to return to the thinker exactly what he thinks into It. The law of mental equivalents must never be overlooked; for "Whatsoever a man soweth, that shall he also reap."[58]

The Possibilities of the Law

The possibilities of the Law are infinite; and our possibilities of using It are limitless. We may, and should, receive full benefit, and we will to the degree that we understand and properly use It.

There is a law of unfoldment in man which says that he can advance only by going from where he is to the place where he would like to be. This is not because the Law is limited but because It is law. As man unfolds in his mentality, the Law automatically reacts to him. The way to work is to begin right where we are, and, through constantly applying ourselves to the Truth, to gradually increase in wisdom and understanding; for in this way alone will good results be obtained. If, day by day, we have a greater understanding and a clearer concept; if daily, we are realizing more of Truth and applying it in our actions, then we are on the right path, and eventually we will be made free.

Spirit and Mental Law

It is impossible to divorce spiritual understanding from the proper use of mental law. The Spirit within man is God, and only to the degree that we listen to, and seek to obey that Spirit, shall

---

58 Gal. 6 : 7.

we really succeed. The Law is a blind force, and lest we misuse It, we should be very careful to FOLLOW ONLY A CONSTRUCTIVE COURSE. But the Law is Absolute, and we should trust Its impersonal action implicitly. It can do anything for us that we can conceive of Its doing. It is the law of freedom to all who believe in and obey It.

The highest realization that we can have is a recognition of the Omnipresence of Spirit. This will set in motion greater possibilities and will, automatically, provide a larger concept of life. We should daily train our thought to recognize the Spirit in everything we do, say, or think. There is no other way, and to try any other way would be to make a complete failure. "Render to Caesar the things that are Caesar's; and to God the things that are God's."[59]

A constant realization of the Presence of Spirit will provide a sense of Divine Companionship that no other attitude could produce. Why should we not take the highest and best? God Is,—and we should Realize this fact and make use of it; as soon as we recognize that God Is, we can turn to the Law and tell It what to do.

We have no record of Jesus ever asking God to do things for Him; He gave thanks, and then commanded the Law to work. This is the correct manner of approach to the Spirit and the Law. This is not superstition but the fact in the case, and we would better realize it.

The Law is subject to the Spirit and is Its servant. Man is Spirit, but until he knows this he will be only half using the Law; for he will not have a clear understanding to fall back upon.

DEMONSTRATION, OR BRINGING THINGS TO PASS

We hold no argument with any one over the possibility of demonstrating the Law. There is such a thing as Universal Law and Mind, and we can use It if we comply with Its nature and work as It works. We do not argue, ask, deny, nor affirm; WE KNOW. Thousands are to-day proving this Law, and in time, all will come to realize the Truth.

We can demonstrate to the level of our ability to know; beyond this we cannot go. But we will constantly expand and increase in knowledge and understanding, thereby continuously growing in our ability to make use of the Law; in time we will be made free through It.

It is a wonderful experiment and a great adventure to make conscious use of the Law, to feel that we can plant an idea in Mind and see it gradually take form.

The student should take time every day to see his life as he wishes it to be, to make a mental picture of his ideal. He should pass this picture over to the Law and go about his business with the inner assurance that on the invisible side of life something is taking place. There should

---

59 Mark 12 : 17.

never be any sense of hurry nor worry about this; just a calm, peaceful sense of reality. Let the Law work through, and express Itself in, the experience. There should be no idea of compulsion; we do not have to make the Law work; it is Its nature to work, and all that we need to do is to make use of It. In gladness, then, we should make known our desires, and in confidence we should wait upon the Perfect Law to manifest through us.

Our Part

Our part is to be ready and willing to be guided into truth and liberty. If, in the making of a demonstration, it becomes necessary to change our mode of living, then the Law will point the way and we will follow. Our correct choice will be part of the working out of the Law. All doubt and fear must go, and in their place must come faith and confidence; for we shall be led by the Spirit into all good.

Treatment

Treatment is not for the purpose of making things happen; it is to provide, within ourselves, an avenue through which they may happen. Treatment opens up the avenues of thought, expands the consciousness, and lets Reality through; it clarifies the mentality, removes the obstructions of thought and lets in the Light. We already live in a Perfect Universe, but It needs to be mentally seen before It can become a part of our experience. Treatment removes doubt and fear; lets in the realization of the Presence of Spirit; and is necessary while we are confronted by obstruction or obstacles. Every problem is primarily mental, and the answer to all problems will be found in Spiritual Realizations.

Medium Between Man and His Manifestation

The subjective state of man's thought decides what is going to happen to him. The subjective state of his thought is the sum-total of his thinking and knowing; It is the medium between the relative and the Absolute, between the Limitless and the conditioned. Whatever is involved in it will evolve; therefore, treatment is the act, the art and the science of systematically and consciously inducing such thoughts as we wish to see expressed. When there is no longer anything within our mentality that denies our word, a demonstration will be made; nothing can stop it, for the Law is Absolute. The question might be asked: "If this is true, why not affirm that we have what we desire and let it go at that?" This is true in Principle, but in practice and in fact, it is only as true as we make it; that is, we cannot demonstrate beyond our ability to know the Truth. We should begin, then, with the things that we do know, and from that basis evolve a greater knowledge.

We should approach the Law normally and naturally and with a sense of ease. There is nothing peculiar or weird about this; it is a natural Law, working in a normal way, and must be thought of in this light.

We should come to consider the Law and the Spirit as friends and think of them as such; in this way we will gradually go from good to more good and from peace to a greater peace. This is the natural unfoldment of Reality through man. We should expect the best and so live that the best may become a part of our experience.

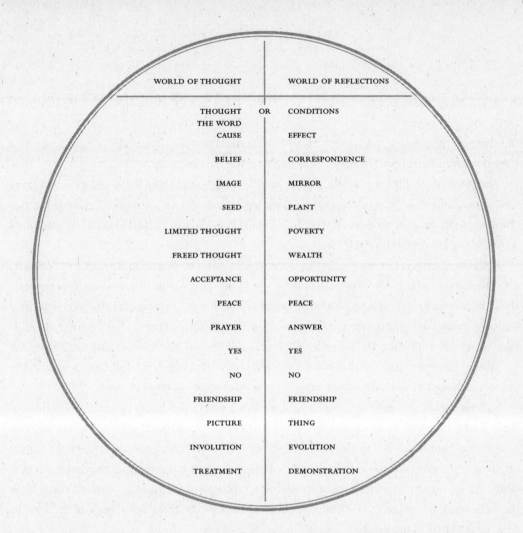

WORLD OF THOUGHT		WORLD OF REFLECTIONS
THOUGHT	OR	CONDITIONS
THE WORD		
CAUSE		EFFECT
BELIEF		CORRESPONDENCE
IMAGE		MIRROR
SEED		PLANT
LIMITED THOUGHT		POVERTY
FREED THOUGHT		WEALTH
ACCEPTANCE		OPPORTUNITY
PEACE		PEACE
PRAYER		ANSWER
YES		YES
NO		NO
FRIENDSHIP		FRIENDSHIP
PICTURE		THING
INVOLUTION		EVOLUTION
TREATMENT		DEMONSTRATION

LESSON FOUR: METAPHYSICAL CHART NO. IV.

How Ideas Manifest as Things

This chart is divided into two sides, representing the world of thought and the world of reflections. It represents the law of cause and effect. The world of thought is the world of ideas, while the world of reflections means the results of thought. The world of reflections is entirely a world of effects and is, of itself, unconscious and unknowing. Consider everything on the left side of this chart to be thoughts or ideas; and consider everything on the right side to be the automatic results of the law as it works out into effects. By using this chart in conjunction with the explanations already given, it will be plain just how the law of cause and effect works from the idea to the thing.

LESSON FOUR: THE CONTROL OF CONDITIONS

In taking up this subject, let us very clearly understand that we do not differentiate between Conscious Mind and Spirit; there is no difference, for they are One.

The Spirit of Intelligence, which is God, in order to do something for us must do that thing through us, and what It is to do must first become a part of our mentality before it can become an individual experience. OUR MENTALITIES ARE BUT THE SPIRIT WORKING THROUGH US AS INDIVIDUALS.

In the new schools of thought there are those who claim to demonstrate only by the Spirit; also those who claim to demonstrate only by the Mind. This is a distinction which is suppositional rather than real and is impossible, because, if there were two powers, we would at once have duality and our philosophy of Unity would be contradicted. There is but One Active Intelligence, whether it be the Universal Intelligence or Universal Spirit individualized in us.

We do, however, distinguish between the phase of mind which we call conscious and the phase which we call unconscious or subjective, as has already been explained.

In demonstrating conditions, the only inquiries we need to make are: Do the things that we want lend themselves to a constructive program? Do they express a more abundant life, rob none, create no delusion, but instead, do they express a greater degree of livingness? If they do, then all the power in the universe must be behind them. If it is money, automobiles, houses, lands, stocks, bonds, dresses, shirts or shoestrings, cabbages or kings,—all of which come from the same source,—there can be nothing, either in the Law or in the Spirit back of the Law, to deny us the right to the greatest possible expression of life.

So we need not hesitate to use the Law for personal motives, for we have a perfect right to do so. It is good for every one to express himself, provided that in so doing, he does not destroy the independence of others.

LAW OF REFLECTION

In turning to the Law, then, realize that It is a Law of reflection. "Life is the mirror of king and slave." Chart No. IV is divided into two parts with a suppositional line in the center; on one side is depicted the world of thought and on the other, the world of the reflections of thought. The world of thought is the world of our individuality; it is the part of us that knows. The other is the world of soul or receptivity and of reflections. In the thought is the cause that reflects the effect; the belief that reflects the correspondence. Here is the image; and here is a form. Here is the limited thought, the result of which reflects poverty. Here is the freed thought, the result of which reflects wealth. Here is a thought of peace which reflects peace. Here is a prayer and here is its answer; the answer to prayer is in the prayer when it is prayed, and the answer is identical with the prayer. Here is Yes and here is Yes; and here is No and here is No. Why is this? Because the Law takes us at our own valuation; if we say "Yes," It says "Yes"; and if we say "No," It says "No"; for It can only reflect; It cannot initiate anything. So here is friendship and over here is friendship. Emerson said: "If you want a friend, be a friend"; and so, as the idea of friendship dawns upon the consciousness, the law of attraction produces friends; for one is the picture and the other is the thing. This is the great teaching of Involution and Evolution, the thought involved and the result evolved; one is the treatment and the other is the demonstration.

We mean by demonstration, bringing into our experience something which we had not experienced before; bringing it in as the result of conscious thought; and unless it is possible to do this the whole science is a mistake and a delusion.

Unless there is a Divine Principle, Universal Soul or Subjectivity, or Medium, which, of Itself, without any help or assistance, can produce things, and will, then there is nothing in this teaching. But there is Divine Principle; and what It does for us, It must do through us. Our part in the demonstration is to set the word in motion, thus compelling, through the law of subjectivity, the result or manifestation.

Attracting Friends

When we are dealing with Causation, we are dealing with that which has involved within Itself all effect, as it unfolds. We may leave it to the Law to compel right action. With this in mind, let us go on to treatment.

Suppose we wish to attract friends. We must begin to image ideal relationships, be they social or otherwise; to sense and feel the presence of friends; to enjoy them in our own mentalities, not as an illusion, but as a reality; not as a dream, but as an experience; to declare that their presence is now here; that they know it and that we know it. But we must never look to see if they are here, because this would imply doubt and would neutralize our word. We can attract the kind of friends we wish if we specifically designate the kind; but we must never think of certain people, or that a particular individual must be one of them, for this would be hypnotic; just thinking the idea will bring the right kind of friends.

In order to have this friendship enduring, true, really worth while and a thing of beauty, we should cultivate an attitude of friendship toward everybody and everything.

THE PRINCIPLE OF PROSPERITY

We are surrounded by a Universal Subjectivity, a Subjective, Creative Consciousness, which is receptive, neutral, impersonal, always receiving the impress of our thought, and which has no alternative other than to operate directly upon it, thus creating the things which we think.

Each one should realize that there is nothing in him that denies that which he desires. Our unity with our good is not established while there is anything in us that denies it.

People often say: "How shall I know when I know?" If you knew you would not ask this question; the very fact that you can ask it proves you do not know; for when you know that you know you can prove it by doing.

Thought sets definite force in motion in Mind, relative to the individual who thinks. For instance, I am known in Consciousness as Ernest Holmes, for that is my name; and every claim made for me, which I accept, operates through avenues of mind-activity and returns to me as some condition.

In practice, always forget the limitations of individuality. Each treatment should embody a recognition of the Whole, because It is Omnipresent.

WE DEAL WITH ABSOLUTENESS

We deal with Absoluteness; this is the attitude that we should have. What we need is to know the Truth. This does not mean that we need not be active; of course we shall be active; but we need not compel things to happen. A good demonstration is made when the Truth, gathering Its own power, lifts one out of his environment; and until that time comes he should stay where he is, in order that he may know when he has made a demonstration.

It is not a good demonstration if, when we give our treatments, we have to struggle just as before. Principle is Absolute, and in so far as any individual can actually induce, within consciousness, upon Principle, a definite, concrete acceptance of his desire, it will manifest, even if every thought on earth had to change to compel it. If it were a bit of information that only one person on earth knew, and he was in the center of Africa, it would be produced.

PRAYER IS ITS OWN ANSWER

Cause and effect are but two sides of thought; and Spirit is both Cause and Effect. Prayer is its own answer. Now, if the one who prays only partly believes, then there is a tendency to set an idea in motion; if the next day he wholly doubts, this idea must be wiped out. In dealing with Mind, we are dealing with a Force which we cannot fool. We can fool ourselves; we can fool others; but we cannot cheat Principle out of the slightest shadow of our most subtle concept; for this is impossible. The hand writes and passes on, but the writing is left there, nevertheless; and the only thing that can erase it is a writing of a different character. We must either transcend all that has gone before, by walking above it, neutralize it by an opposite state of consciousness, or endure it.

Get a sense of self-mastery, of being equal to every occasion. There is nothing too great; there is no obstacle that you cannot surmount; no obstruction that you cannot dissipate by the power of Truth, if your concept of Truth is dynamic enough and clear enough, and if the embodiment is complete.

If You Know

If you know that the Power with which you are dealing is Principle and not personality; if you know and believe that Mind is the only Actor, Cause, Effect, Substance, Intelligence, Truth and Power that there is; and if you have a real embodiment of your desires, then you can demonstrate.

If you lack, if you are poor, if you are without friends, if you are without opportunity, don't fight anything; but be sure to erase from your consciousness any sense of that lack.

You erase thought from consciousness by pouring in an opposite thought; this opposite thought meets the other and neutralizes it; that is, it rubs it out, just as we rub a chalk mark off a board. Take a consistent, positive, aggressive mental attitude in the Truth.

We walk by falling forward; water falls by its own weight; the planets are eternally falling through space; for everything sustains itself in nature. The only reason that man is limited is that he has not allowed the Instinctive Life to come out through him, and the reason why this is possible, is that his own Divine Individuality, as soon as it was evolved, compelled Infinity to appear in his experience as duality, because he believed in duality.

Take no personal responsibility for making anything happen. Throw your word into Mind, and know that Mind receives it; Mind believes it; Mind accepts it; Mind acts upon it; and Mind produces it.

No Personal Responsibility

No matter how great a responsibility may rest in that which must be done, never let one minute's responsibility rest in your own thought about it, because that to which the mind gives birth is, and EVERY IDEA IS BOUND TO PRODUCE AN EFFECT EXACTLY LIKE ITS CAUSE.

When we make a demonstration we must take what goes with it. Therefore, all demonstrations should be made in peace, confidence and joy and in the realization of Divine Love and Perfection as permeating everything. The reason for this is evident, for we are dealing with the law of cause and effect. We are not depending upon chance, but upon Law.

We must know that we are dealing with the substance from which all things are made—people, brains, monkeys—everything that is. Nothing moves but Mind, and we are dealing with the Mind that is the Mover, the Creator, the Cause of all that is or is to be.

HELPING AN INVENTOR

Suppose an inventor came to you and said: "I am trying to perfect a piece of machinery and have not been able to work out the right plan." You sit with him for treatment; that is, you concentrate in Mind, in order to produce the desired idea through him. You know that all ideas come from Mind and that Mind is always unfolding Its Ideas through man. You say: "John Smith is an inventor; a certain idea is trying to operate through him and there is nothing in him that can obstruct this idea." Then state that this idea is known in Mind, and is now flowing through him. If you do this, thinking clearly, new ideas will begin to operate through him and he will discover the thing he needs.

LOOK ONLY AT WHAT YOU WANT

Never look at that which you do not wish to experience. No matter what the false condition may be, it must be refuted. The proper kind of a denial is based upon the recognition that, in reality, there is no limitation; for mind can as easily make a planet as anything else. The Infinite knows no difference between a million dollars and a penny. It only knows that IT IS. It would be just as easy to demonstrate a million dollars as it would be to demonstrate ten cents, if the mental concept embodied the idea of a million dollars.

It is the consciousness back of the word that forms the word. Consciousness means the inner embodiment of an idea through the recognition of Truth and a direct relationship to the Divine. The greatest Teacher Who ever lived was the most spiritual man; for the more universal and comprehensive the thought, the more Godlike it must become.

A good treatment is always filled with the recognition of the Presence of God or Good. Even in Spiritual Things we are still dealing with the law of cause and effect, for God is Law. The more exalted the thought, the more heavenly, the more boundless, the more Godlike or Christlike the thought, the more power it will have. This is why the greatest Teacher should become the Saviour; He couldn't help it. A great teacher would have to be a Saviour.

DEFINITE PLAN

We will say that there are four men, "A," "B," "C," and "D." "A" receives $15 a week, "B" receives $50, "C," $75, and "D," $100. Now these four are all without positions and they come to a practitioner for mental treatment. The practitioner takes the thought that there is nothing but activity; he neutralizes, in his own thought, any belief in inactivity and declares that each of these four men is divinely active and occupied. Without question he has set in motion a law which will respond and will reproduce something for each of these four. We will suppose that his treatment is a good and an effective one; they receive it, and consequently each one of them receives a position. You will find that each does not receive the same compensation, for in all probability "A" will receive $15 per week; "B," $50; "C," $75, and "D," $100. "But." one might say, "he spoke the same word for each; why did they not all receive $100 per week?" Because, while his word was used for each in a like manner, each could receive only his fill, his mental capacity to comprehend. Each was full, and no doubt running over; but the molds which their perceptions of life provided were limited to the subjective remembrance already set in motion by themselves. Each attracted to himself, out of the Universal Good, that which he could comprehend. It is the old statement that water will reach its own level by its own weight, and without effort. So a treatment will only level itself in the objective world at the level of the subjective thought and realization.

This does not mean that each of the above-stated men will always have to receive the same compensation; for with an enlarged consciousness he would receive more.

ATTRACTION

Every one automatically attracts to himself just what he is, and you may set it down that wherever you are, however intolerable the situation may be, it is just where you belong. There is no power in the Universe but yourself that can get you out of it. Some one may help you on the road to realization, but substantiality and permanence can come only through the consciousness of your own life and thought. Man must bring himself to a point where there is no misfortune, no calamity, no accident, no trouble, no confusion; where there is nothing but plenty, peace, power, Life and Truth. He should definitely, daily, using his own name, declare the Truth about himself, realizing that he is rejecting his statements into Consciousness, and that they will be operated upon by It.

This is called, in mysticism, High Invocation; invoking the Divine Mind; implanting within It seeds of thought relative to one's self. And this is why some of the teachers of older times used to teach their pupils to cross their hands over their chests and say: "Wonderful, wonderful,

wonderful me!" definitely teaching them that, as they held themselves, so they would be held. "Act as though I Am and I will Be."

One of the ancient sayings is that, "To the man who can perfectly practice inaction, all things are possible." This sounds like a contradiction until one gets down to the inner teachings; for it is only when one completely practices inaction that he arrives at the point of the true actor. For he then realizes that the act and the actor are one and the same, that cause and effect are the same; which is simply a different way of saying: "Know the Truth and the Truth shall make you free." To reduce the whole thing to its simplest form, whatever one reflects into Mind will be done.

How to Demonstrate a Home

Suppose you wish to demonstrate a home; daily, looking into Mind, visualize it just as you wish it to be, making the picture as clear as possible; for it is a lack of clearness of thought that hinders demonstration. Then sit there about ten minutes, saying, "It is, it is, it is." Perhaps thoughts will come in which say "that it is not." Pay no attention to such thoughts but return to your meditation, and seeing the picture anew, say again, "It is, it is, it is." Use no effort, but simply see the picture very clearly and declare for its presence.

Never look for results from treatment; for if you do you will not find them. This is in accordance with law, for what you look for you know that you do not have and are only trying to fool yourself into thinking that you do have. Treatment is not a process of hypnotism; it is a process of self-knowing; and if you really know you will be sure to demonstrate.

Treatment is the art, the science and process of systematically inducing within consciousness concepts of definite desires as already accomplished facts and experiences in life.

Resist Not

When Jesus said "Resist not evil,"[60] He meant that non-recognition of evil is the only way to avoid it. This is true according to the law of cause and effect; for what we persist in recognizing, we persist in holding in place. That which we non-recognize, we neutralize, and it is no longer there, so far as we are concerned. In making a demonstration, don't try to demonstrate; for demonstrations are not made through effort, because this would contradict one of the fundamental principles of the universe, which is the Self-Existence of Causation. In other words,

---

60 Matt. 5 : 39.

nothing can come before that which is, consequently everything must come out of that which is; and within that which is, is the inherent possibility of that which is to be. All things exist as a potentiality, as a possibility, now. "I Am Alpha and Omega."[61] Try to get a recognition of your desire and pass the whole thing over to Mind, and let It operate. Just know that the desire is already a fact, and quietly say to yourself, as often as the thought comes into mind: "It is done." The lighter the thought is, the less care or worry over it, the better. The best work is done when the element of struggle is entirely left out.

HEALING A MISUNDERSTANDING

Suppose one says: "I have had a terrible misunderstanding with a friend of mine and it has come to a point where we do not even speak to each other." What is the fundamental error which has brought about this condition? A lack of the realization of the Unity of all life, a belief in duality. Destroy this belief in duality; recognize that there is but One Mind; see God in each, and the trouble will be healed. We all live in the One Mind of God.

FATE

If one believes in fate he must be healed of this thought, for there is no such thing as fate. If one believes that planetary forces have anything to do with life he must be healed of this thought. Break down everything except the recognition of the One Perfect Power, which is not contingent upon any place, person, condition, time of year, or anything but Itself. A demonstration is made when it comes through straight from the Truth.

The one who wishes to make a demonstration must first clear up his own subjective atmosphere; the reason being that he may be objectively making statements which his subjective thought may be denying. In this way we often neutralize our word as fast as it is spoken.

A treatment is scientific in that it is the act of inducing into Subjectivity ideas which neutralize false images of thought and which let the Truth come through into expression. The reason that we need such a science is that we do not have a perfect faith; for if we had a perfect faith we would have washed clean the subjective thought and no doubts would be there. Until the time comes when one can say to the sick, "Get up and walk," and have them do so; or say, "There is money," and have it appear, he must take the process of inducing thought for the purpose of accumulating a subjective belief in the things which he desires; this belief, as soon

---

61 Rev. 1 : 8.

as it is complete, IS THE DEMONSTRATION. The demonstration takes place within and not without.

ATTRACTION OF PERSONALITY

One might say, "I have no personality with which to attract people." There is but One Person; this Person is manifested through every living soul. It is radiant, vibrant, dynamic; It is *The* Personality; It is Complete; It is, It is.

The ones to whom we are the most strongly attracted are not necessarily the ones who are the most beautiful physically; but are the ones from which we receive that subtle emanation, "that something." What is "that something"? It is not that which shows, but that which floats through from within. It is the inner recognition of Reality.

SEE LIFE EXPRESSED

One should analyze himself, saying, "Do I look at myself from a standpoint of restriction? Do I see life as limited to the eternal round of getting up in the morning, eating, going to work, coming home, going to bed, sleeping, getting up again?" and so on. Break the bonds of necessity and see life as one continuous expression of the Infinite Self; and as this conception gradually dawns upon the inner thought, something will happen in the outer conditions to let up on the greater demands of the law of necessity. If one were doing the work he should be doing, he would never become tired, because the energy which holds the Universe in place is tireless. The reason why we become tired is that we have cross currents of thought over our work. This arises from a belief in duality.

A treatment is the scientific act of inducing concepts in Mind, which operates upon them and manifests them in external affairs, just as the picture is held subjectively. During the process we meet, contact, neutralize and erase any and all opposing mental forces or conditions which deny our greater good.

Never limit your view of life by what you or any one else has ever accomplished. The possibility of life is inherent within the capacity to imagine what life is, backed by the power to produce this imagery or Divine Imagination. It is not a question of failing or of succeeding; it is simply a question of sticking to an idea until it becomes a tangible reality.

The illusion is in the way that we look at things. We have looked at some things and they have looked evil to us; we must look at them until they look good. We have looked at some one and he has looked sick to us; we must look at him until he looks well. We have seen discord; we must see harmony.

Look at harmony and people will become harmonious. We have looked at poverty, degradation and misery until they have assumed a gigantic form. Now we must look at harmony, happiness, plenty, prosperity, peace and right action until it appears.

Look to the Ultimate

In treating, we conceive of the ultimate of the idea, but never of the process. Never treat a process; never look for one. We plant a seed, and there is in that seed, operating through the creative soil, everything that is going to happen until it comes up, unfolds, and produces a plant. The ultimate of effect is already potential in cause. This is the mystical meaning of those words, "I am Alpha and Omega."[62] Our word should be the alpha and the omega, the beginning and the end of the thing thought of. All cause and effect are in Spirit. Cause and effect are bound together into one complete whole. One is the inside and the other is the outside of the same thing.

Once you have driven the peg into the ground, stick to it. Never let anything cause you to doubt your ability to demonstrate the Truth. Conceive of your word as being the thing. See the desire as an already accomplished fact and rest in perfect confidence, peace and certainty, never looking for results, never wondering, never becoming anxious, never being hurried nor worried. Those who do not understand this attitude will think that you are inactive, but remember, "To him who can perfectly practice inaction, all things are possible."

No Mistakes

In mental work, we must realize that there is One Infinite Mind, which is consciously directing our destiny. Declare every day that "no mistakes have been made, none are being made, and none can be made"; declare, "There is One Supreme Intelligence which governs, guides and guards, tells me what to do, when to act, and how to act"; then act with perfect assurance. Declare, "everything necessary to the full and complete expression of the most boundless experience, joy and life, everything is now"; know this, see it, feel it and be it. Do this every day for a few minutes; we should all do this until the time comes when it will no longer be necessary. When that time comes, we will know it, because our demonstrations will have been made.

Suppose one says: "I have made a lot of mistakes in my life. I had opportunities which I did not grasp." This is a direct belief that there is but one opportunity which comes to man, and if

---

62 Rev. 1 : 8.

he does not take it he will have no more. This is a belief in limited opportunities, and it must be denied completely and specifically. We exist in Limitless Opportunities, which are forever seeking expression through us, and are expressed in and through us.

Know that there is no condemnation; for nothing can condemn unless we believe in condemnation. Destroy the thought that would lay limitation or bondage upon any situation or condition. "Loose him, and let him go."[63]

Talk to yourself, not to the world. There is no one to talk to but yourself, for all experiences take place within. Conditions are the reflections of our own meditations, and nothing else. There is but One Mind to think, but one thing that It can think; that Mind is our Mind now. It never thinks confusion; It knows what it wishes, and how to accomplish what it desires. It is what It desires.

CAUSES AND CONDITIONS

Pay no attention to what happens in the objective world when you are making a demonstration. We interpret causes by conditions only as we realize that a condition must partake of the nature of its cause. If there appears to be confusion in the condition, then there must have been confusion in the thought back of it. Pay no attention to the objective expression so long as you know you are getting the right subjective recognition. The way to work out a problem scientifically is to take it up in thought daily and conceive of it as already being an accomplished fact in experience. Get the idea of the desire as already embodied in the Absolute. Unless one believes that there is an Absolute, how can he do this? We must believe that we are dealing with Reality and with nothing less than the Absolute.

If we are radiating thought into Divine Mind, what is there that can hinder It from operating on this thought? Nothing, for It knows no hindrances. Be sure that there is nothing destructive in the reaction; for there must be no element of destructiveness in our work. Daily hold your desire as an already accomplished fact and go about your business with joy and gladness, with peace and quiet confidence; the Law is then sure to act. During the process many things may happen that will appear to be destructive. You may pass through good fortune and bad; but if you can come to the point where you are not disturbed by what happens on the outside, you have found the secret. If, as Jesus said, we "Judge not according to the appearance, but judge righteous judgment,"[64] remembering that "things which are seen were not made of things which

---

63 John 11 : 44.
64 John 7 : 24.

do appear";[65] out of any chaos we can produce harmony, provided we keep our thought steady. The answer to prayer is already in the prayer when it is prayed.

PERFECT ACTION

Assume a case of treatment for prosperity. Suppose one comes to you and says: "Business is bad; there is no activity." How are you going to treat him? Are you going to treat activity or business, customers, conditions or what? There is but one thing to treat, as far as the practitioner is concerned, and that is HIMSELF. The practitioner treats himself, the reason being that his patient's and his own mind are in the One Mind.

There is but one activity, which is perfect. Nothing has happened to it; nothing can cut it off; it is always operating. There is no belief in inactivity. What is this statement for? To neutralize the belief in inactivity. A word spoken in Mind will reach its own level, in the objective world, by its own weight; just as in physical science we know that water reaches its own level by its own weight. You must destroy the thoughts of inactivity. Man cannot become either discouraged or afraid if he realizes that, there is but One Mind which he may consciously use. The real man knows no discouragement, cannot be afraid and has no unbelief.

> *"Who plants a seed beneath the sod*
> *And waits to see it turn away the clod,*
> *Has faith in God."*

And he who knows of the power with which he is dealing, and who plants a seed of thought in Subjectivity, knows that it will come up and bear fruit.

Bring out the idea of Substance. Make consciousness perceive that Substance is Spirit, Spirit is God, and God is all that there is. Once you acquaint the consciousness with this idea, it is implanted in the Creative Power which is externalizing in your life.

MENTAL EQUIVALENTS

The Law is Infinite and Perfect; but in order to make a demonstration we must first have a mental equivalent of the thing we DESIRE. Consequently, the range of our possibilities at the present time does not extend far beyond the range of our present concepts. As we bring ourselves to a greater vision, we can then induce a still greater concept and thereby demonstrate

---

65 Heb. 11 : 3.

more in our experience. In this way there is a continuous growth and unfoldment taking place. We do not expect to give a treatment to-day and have a million dollars to-morrow. But, little by little, we can unfold our consciousness through the acquisition of greater and still greater mental equivalents, until at last we shall be made free. The way to proceed is to begin right where we are. It is not scientific to attempt to begin somewhere else. This would be chaotic. One who understands the systematic use of the Law will realize that he is where he is because of what he is; but he will not say, "I must be where I am because of what I am." Instead, he will begin to disclaim what he appears to be. As his statements loosen wrong subjective tendencies and false mentality, providing in their place a correct concept of life and Reality, he will automatically be lifted out of his conditions; and impelling forces, which will sweep everything before them, will set him free, if he trusts in Spirit and in nothing else.

Stay with the One and never deviate from It; never leave It for a moment. Nothing else can equal this attitude. To desert the Truth in the hour of need is to prove that we do not know the Truth. When things look the worst is the supreme moment to demonstrate to yourself that there are no obstructions. When things look worst is the best time to work, the most satisfying time. The person who can throw himself, with a complete abandon, into that Limitless Sea of Receptivity, having cut loose from all apparent moorings, is the one who will always receive the greatest reward.

TREATING FOR ACTIVITY

Suppose you have a store and wish to attract customers, which means activity in this kind of business. Every day see the place filled with people. Make a mental picture of this. You are dealing with Intelligence, so work intelligently. Ask for what you wish and take it. If you were treating for activity in a store in Boston you would not be treating some one in Kalamazoo for the mumps. Remember that you are dealing with Intelligence; IT IS GOING TO EVOLVE YOUR CONCEPT EXACTLY AS YOU INVOLVE IT. If one could take a picture of his objective circumstances and his subjective mentality, he would find that they would be identical; for one is the cause of the other; one is the image and the other is the reflection of that image.

RECEIVING INFORMATION

Suppose that we wish a special piece of information; we should say, "I wish to know this thing and I do know it. Whatever instrument is necessary to present it to me is now in full operation." This is a direct declaration that we have the desired knowledge, that that which we wish to know we do know. Say, "The Spirit of Intelligence within me tells me what I should know," or, "Everything that I should know I do know." It does not matter how we get this knowledge; we would not care if we read it on a sign, or in the dictionary, or if it were told us, or if it were sent to us; but we should consider the demonstration complete provided we received it. Say, "Everything necessary for the complete fulfillment of this idea is now in full operation, and I accept it."

No Failures

If one appears to have failed he should realize that there are no failures in the universe. We should completely erase the idea of failure by stating that there are no failures. If one believes that he failed last year he will be likely to fail again this year, unless the false thought should be erased.

Now here is a place where it looks as though one were lying to himself, but he is not; for he is declaring the truth about the Spirit that indwells him; this Spirit never fails. Affirm, "This word blots from the book of my remembrance any sense of lack, limitation, want or fear of failure. There is no failure, no person to fail; failure is neither person, place nor thing; it is a false thought and has no truth in it; it is a belief in lack and there is no lack; it is a belief in a limitation which does not exist."

Thought is very subtle, and sometimes you may find, when you are making such a statement, that arguments will rise against it. Stop right here and meet those arguments; refuse to accept them.

Opportunity

Suppose you are treating your business and something from within says, "There are too many people in this business"; handle the thought of competition at once; say, "There is no competition or monopoly." You must do something to free the endeavor to express itself. Treatment is a thing of itself; it is an entity of Infinite Intelligence, Life and Action, and nothing can hinder its operation except unbelief or a lack of adequate mental equivalents. "They could not enter in because of unbelief,"[66] and they "tempted God and limited the Holy One of Israel."[67]

Never depend upon people, or say that things must come from this or that source. It makes

---

66 Heb. 3 : 19.
67 Ps. 78 : 41.

no difference where things come from. Say that they are and let them come from where they will; and then, if something appears to happen which points to a place for them to come from, it is correct to say, "If this is the place, then there is nothing which can hinder." This is not hypnotic, for you are simply guarding against the possibility of some false thought coming in and hindering your demonstration.

Nothing moves but Mind. God makes things through the direct act of becoming the things which He creates. This is what we do, for our thought becomes the thing thought of. The thought and the thing are one, in reality. "WHAT A MAN HAS AS WELL AS WHAT HE IS, IS THE RESULT OF THE SUBJECTIVE STATE OF HIS THOUGHT." Keep on subjectifying thought until the balance of your consciousness is on the affirmative side, and nothing can hinder it from demonstrating. This is inevitable, for this is the way that the Law operates.

No Mistakes

Regarding mistakes,—declare that there are none, that there never were and never will be any. Say, "I represent the Truth, the whole Truth and nothing but the Truth; It is unerring, It never mistakes; there are no mistakes in the Divine Plan for me; there is no fear; there is no limitation, poverty, want nor lack; I stand in the midst of eternal opportunity, which is forever presenting me with the evidence of its full expression. I am joy, peace and happiness; I am the spirit of joy within me; I am the spirit of peace within me, of poise and power; I am the spirit of happiness within me; I radiate Life; I am Life. There is One Life; that Life is my Life now." It is not enough to say, "There is One Life and that Life is God." We must complete this statement by saying, "That Life is my Life now," because we must couple this Life with ours in order to express It. We are not becoming This Life, but are now, in, and of, This Life. There is no other Life.

God is not becoming; God Is. God is not growing; God is Complete. God is not trying to find out something; God already knows. Evolution is not the expression of a becoming God, but is simply one of the ways that a God Who already Is, expresses Himself; and as such, it is the logical result of involution and is eternally going on.

Demonstration by Proof

If one is in a position which is distasteful, subject to circumstances over which he apparently has no control at the time, how should he act? He should not leave the place where he is until his thought has drawn him to a better one. In making a demonstration, we should not shove anything before us, carry anything with us nor drag anything after us. We should stay where we are until our word takes us somewhere else; for this is the only proof that we have demonstrated.

Handling a Schoolroom

A teacher, in dealing with the thought of pupils, should treat their thought as a unit. The individuality of the room, of which each pupil is a part, is a perfect idea. There is One Mind operating in, around and through all these pupils, controlling them, directing them and inspiring them; there are peace, calm, satisfaction and enlightenment here. Realize the Active Presence of the One Mind, working in, around and through all, and you will find that this will harmonize the most discordant state, provided the teacher, the one who is thinking, really knows the Truth.

The Law of Correspondence

The limit of our ability to demonstrate depends on our ability to provide a mental equivalent of our desire; for the law of correspondences works from the belief to the thing. But we can provide a greater mental equivalent through the unfolding of consciousness; and this growth from within will finally lead to freedom.

What we demonstrate to-day, to-morrow and the next day is not as important as THE TENDENCY WHICH OUR THOUGHT IS TAKING. If, every day, things are a little better, a little happier, a little more harmonious, a little more health-giving and joyous; if, each day, we are expressing more life, we are going in the right direction.

And so we meditate daily upon the Universe of the All Good, that Infinite Indwelling Spirit which we call God, the Father, Incarnate in man; trying to sense and to feel this Indwelling Good as the Active Principle of our lives. This is what the mystics call "The Man of the Heart," or "The Angel of God's Presence." This is why they taught that there are always Two; for there is what we seem to be and what we really are; and as we contact this Higher Principle of our own lives—Which is Perfect and Complete, needing nothing, wanting nothing, knowing everything, being happy and satisfied,—and as we daily meditate upon this Indwelling God, we shall acquire a greater mental equivalent.

For those who have thought small thoughts all of their lives a very good practice is to dwell upon the bigness of the universe. Think how many stars there are; think of how many fish there are in the seas, and how many grains of sand on the beach. Think of how big the ocean is; of the immensity of space, the bigness of everything, the grandeur of everything. Mechanically, if necessary, compel the mentality to cognize Reality. Compel the consciousness to recognize the Truth through pure reason, if no other conviction comes.

Think, see and feel activity. Radiate Life. Feel that there is that within which is the center and circumference of the universe. The universe is the result of the Self-Contemplation of the Lord. Our lives are the results of our self-contemplations, and are peopled with the personifications of our thoughts and ideas. Accept this without question, for it is true.

Nothing is real to us unless we make it real. Nothing can touch us unless we let it touch us. Refuse to have the feelings hurt. Refuse to receive any one's condemnation. In the independence of your own mentality, believe and feel that you are wonderful. This is not conceit; it is the truth. What can be more wonderful than the manifestation of the Infinite Mind?

"Awake thou that sleepest, and arise from the dead, and Christ shall give thee light."[68] "Prove Me, now herewith, saith the Lord of Hosts, if I will not open you the windows of heaven, and pour you out a blessing, that there shall not be room enough to receive it."[69] "Be firm and ye shall be made firm." "Act as though I am and I will be." "Onlook thou the Deity and the Deity will onlook thee." "As thou hast believed so be it done."[70] "Ask and it shall be given unto you."[71] "So shall my word be that goeth forth out of my mouth—it shall prosper."[72]

Note: Read and study "That Something"; "The Edinburgh Lectures," T. Troward; "The Law and the Word," T. Troward; "Creative Mind and Success," E. S. Holmes; "How to Visualize," Behrend; "Financial Success Through Creative Thought," Wattles.

LESSON FOUR: RECAPITULATION

Limitation and poverty are not things but are the results of restricted ways of thinking. We are surrounded by a Subjective Intelligence which receives the impress of our thought and acts upon it. This Intelligence is a natural Law in the Mental World, and consequently It is neither good nor bad. It can only be said of It, that It Is, and that we may consciously use It.

The Law is a Law of Reflection; for life is a mirror, reflecting to us, as conditions, the im-

---

68 Eph. 5 : 14.
69 Mal. 3 : 10.
70 Matt. 8 : 13.
71 Matt. 7 : 7.
72 Isa. 55 : 11.

ages of our thinking. Whatever one thinks tends to take form and to become a part of his experience.

The Medium of all thought is the Universal Mind, acting as Law. Law is always impersonal, neutral, receptive and reactive.

A sense of separation from good causes us to feel restricted; and a sense of our Unity with Good changes the currents of Causation and brings a happier condition into the experience.

Everything in the so-called material universe is an effect and exists only by virtue of some mental image behind it.

Man's individuality enables him to make such use of the Law as he desires; he is bound, not by limitation, but by a limited thought. The same power which binds him will free him when he understands the Law to be one of Liberty and not one of bondage. The power within man can free him from all distasteful conditions, if the Law governing this power is properly understood and utilized.

The Law of Mind, which is the Medium of all action, is a Law of perfect balance; the Objective World perfectly balances the images within the Subjective World. Water will reach its own level by its own weight; and, according to the same law, consciousness will externalize at its own level by its own weight. Cause and effect are but two sides of the same thing, one being the image in Mind and the other the objective condition.

The manifest universe is the result of the Self-Contemplation of the Lord. Man's world of affairs is the result of his self-contemplation. He is, at first, ignorant of this, and so binds himself through wrong ideation and action; reversing this thought will reverse the condition.

There is neither effort nor strain in knowing the Truth. Right action will be compelled through right knowing; therefore, when we know the Truth, It will compel us to act in the correct manner.

Attraction and repulsion are mental qualities, and may be consciously utilized for definite purposes. Man, automatically and according to Law, attracts from without the correspondences of his inner mental attitudes. Inner mental attitudes may be induced through right thinking and correct knowing. The subjective state of thought is the power always at work; it is the result of the sum total of all beliefs, consciously or unconsciously held. The subjective state of thought may be consciously changed through right mental action. The conscious thought controls the subconscious, and in its turn, the subconscious controls conditions.

Visualizing, or mentally seeing right action, tends to produce the picture in external affairs.

Since the Law is mental, one must believe in It, in order to have It work affirmatively for him; but It is always working according to our belief, whether we are conscious of this fact or not.

Demonstration takes place through the field of the One Universal Mind; we set the Power in motion; the Law produces the effect. We plant the seed and the Law produces the plant.

One should never allow himself to think of, or talk about, limitation or poverty. Life is a mirror and will reflect back to the thinker what he thinks into it.

God's plan for man is a perfect one, and when we harmonize with it we will become free from all bondage. The more spiritual the thought, the higher the manifestation. Spiritual thought means an absolute belief in, and reliance upon, Truth; this is both natural and normal.

All is Love yet all is Law; Love is the impelling force and Law executes the will of Love. Man is a center of God-Consciousness in the great Whole; he cannot deface his real being, but may hinder the Whole from coming into a complete expression through his life. Turning to the One with a complete abandonment and in absolute trust, he will find that he already is saved, helped and prospered.

There is One Infinite Mind from which all things come; this Mind is through, in and around man; It is the Only Mind that there is, and every time man thinks he uses It. There is One Infinite Spirit, and every time man says, "I am," he proclaims It. There is One Infinite Substance; and every time man moves, he moves in It. There is One Infinite Law, and every time man thinks he sets It in motion. There is One Infinite God, and every time man speaks to This God he receives a direct answer. One! One! One! "I Am God and there is none else."[73] There is One Limitless Life which returns to the thinker what he thinks into It. One! One! One! "In all, over all and through all."

Talk, live, act, believe and know that you are a center in the One. All the Power there is; all the Presence there is; all the Love there is; all the Peace there is; all the Good there is and the Only God that is, is Omnipresent; consequently, the Infinite is in and through man and is in and through everything. "Act as though I am and I will Be."

LESSON FIVE: INTRODUCTION

A mystic is not a mysterious person; but is one who has a deep, inner sense of Life and Unity with the Whole; mysticism and mystery are entirely different things; one is real while the other may, or may not, be an illusion. There is nothing mysterious in the Truth, so far as It is understood; but all things, of course, are mysteries until we understand them.

---

73 Isa. 45 : 22.

A mystic is one who intuitively perceives Truth and who, without mental process, arrives at Spiritual Realizations. It is from the teachings of the great mystics that the best in the philosophy of the world has come.

The civilization of to-day is built around the teachings of a few people who have intuitively perceived Spiritual Truth. Our great code of law was given by Moses, a map who through the mystic sense perceived that we live in a Universe of Law. Our greatest code of ethics was given through the perception of the prophets, culminating in such teachings as those of Jesus and Buddha. Who was there who could have taught such men as these? By what process of mentality did they arrive at their profound conclusions? We are compelled to recognize that Spirit Alone was their Teacher; they were, indeed, taught of God.

The mystic intuitively senses Reality and instinctively knows The Truth; and in this way all of the best in literature, music and art have come.

Our great religions have been given by a few who climbed the heights of spiritual vision and caught a fleeting glimpse of Ultimate Reality. No living soul could have taught them what they knew, and it is doubtful if even they themselves knew why they knew.

The great poets have been true mystics and have revealed, through their poems, the Presence of God. Men like Robert Browning, Tennyson, Wordsworth, Homer, Walt Whitman, Edward Rowland Sill, and others of like nature, have given us poetry which is immortal, because they had a mystic sense of life: the perception of a Living Presence.

All true philosophers are mystics; the old prophets were mystics; David, Solomon, Jesus, Plato, Buddha, Plotinus, Emerson, and a score of others, all had the same experience: the sense of a Living Presence.

The greatest music ever composed was written by the hand of a mystic; and the highest and best in art has come from the same source.

Man has compelled nature to do his bidding; he has harnessed electric energy, caught the wind, trapped steam and made them all obey his will. He has invented machines to do the work of thousands; he has belted the globe with his traffic and built up a wonderful civilization; but in few cases has he conquered his own soul.

The highest and best that we have in civilization is the result of the mystic sense which has been perceived by a few in each age. All that modern appliances and inventions give us in the way of comfort and luxury, good and necessary as they are, may be counted as nothing compared to the teachings of Jesus. By this, we do not mean to decry modern civilization, education or anything that goes with it; for we are firm believers in anything and everything that makes life interesting and worth living. We believe in science, art, religion, education, commerce, government, industry, agriculture, and all that goes to make up a well-rounded experience in life; but we repeat, what would they amount to, if thought of in any other light than as passing things?

The mystic has revealed things that do not pass as ships in the night; he has revealed Eternal Verities and has plainly taught us that there is a Living Presence indwelling All.

TRUE MYSTICISM AND THE PSYCHIC SENSE

There is a vast difference between mysticism and psychism, between a mystic and an ordinary psychic. The psychic capacity will be thoroughly discussed in Lesson Six, and the reader will remember that it is the power to read subjectively; it may be dealing with a reality or with an illusion. The average psychic must become more or less subjective in order to do good work. At best, and even though in a normal state of mind, he can only read subjective pictures and tendencies; at best, he is generally dealing with human thought. Should he penetrate that thought, he would then become a mystic.

A mystic does not read human thought but senses the Thought of God. The question might be asked, "How do you know that he senses the Thought of God?" Because the mystics of every age have seen, sensed and taught THE SAME TRUTH. Psychic experiences more or less contradict each other, because each psychic sees a different kind of mental picture; but the mystic experiences of the ages have revealed ONE AND THE SAME TRUTH.

WHAT THE MYSTICS HAVE TAUGHT

Without exception, all of the mystics have taught that there is but One Ultimate Reality; and that this Ultimate Reality is HERE NOW, IF WE COULD BUT SEE IT.

Strange as it may seem, the great mystics have all believed in a Personal God; that is, a God who is Personal to all who believe in Him. They have not, of course, believed in an ANTHRO-POMORPHIC GOD; but they have believed in a God who consciously works in and through man; and they have adored and worshiped this God.

The great mystics have been illumined, that is, they have, at times, seen through the veil of matter and perceived the Spiritual Universe. They have taught that the Kingdom of God is NOW PRESENT AND NEEDS BUT TO BE REALIZED; and they have, apparently, sensed that this Kingdom is within.

A psychic sees only through his own subjective mentality; consequently, everything that he looks at is more or less colored by the vibration of his own thought; he is subject to hallucinations and false impressions of every description. This is why, generally speaking, no two psychics ever see the same thing.

Mystics have all seen the same thing, and their testimony is in no way confusing; this is because the Spirit within them has borne witness to the Truth.

No Ultimate Evil

One of the most illuminating things that mysticism has revealed, is that evil is not an ultimate reality. Evil is simply an experience of the soul on its journey toward Reality; it is not an entity but an experience necessary to self-unfoldment; it is not a thing of itself but simply a misuse of power. It will disappear when we stop looking at, or believing in, it. We cannot stop believing in it as long as we indulge in it; so the mystic has always taught the race to turn from evil and do good.

Ultimate Salvation of All

The mystics have taught the ultimate salvation of all people and the immortality of every soul. Indeed, they have taught that immortality IS HERE AND NOW, IF WE WOULD BUT WAKE TO THE FACT. "Beloved, now are we the Sons of God."[74] Since each soul is some part of the Whole, it is impossible that any soul can be lost. "God is not the God of the dead, but of the living."[75] Damnation has been as foreign to the thought of the mystic as any belief in evil must be to the Mind of God.

Freedom from Burden

The great mystics have taught that man should have no burdens, and would have none, if he turned to "The One." "Come unto Me all ye that labor and are heavy laden and I will give you rest."[76] As Jesus must have known that it would be impossible for all men to come unto Him as a Personality, He must have meant that we should come into His understanding of Life and Reality; that is, to come unto the Great God. Some day we will learn to lay our burdens on the Altar of Love, that they may be consumed by the fire of faith in the Living Spirit. Man would have no burdens if he kept his "High watch" toward "The One"; that is, if he always turned to God.

Unity of All

Jesus prayed that all might come to see the Unity of Life. "That they may be One, even as we are One,"[77] was His prayer as He neared the completion of His great work on this planet. All

---

74 I John 3 : 2.
75 Matt. 22 : 32.
76 Matt. 11 : 28.
77 John 17:22.

mystics have sensed that we live in One Life. "For in Him we live, and move, and have our being."[78] The Unity of Good is a revelation of the greatest importance; for it teaches us that we are One with the Whole, and One with each other. This realization alone will settle the question of human inequality. The real Fatherhood of God and the Actual Brotherhood of Man will be made apparent on earth to the degree that men realize True Unity.

REALIZATION OF INDIVIDUALITY

No great mystic ever lived who denied the reality of individuality. The higher the sense of Truth, the greater will be the realization of the uniqueness of individual character and personality. The Real Self is God-given and cannot be denied; it is the place where God comes to a point of Individualized and Personified Expression, and should be thought of in this light. "I am the Light of the world."[79]

NORMALCY

All mystics have been normal people, that is, they have lived just as other people have lived. The only difference has been that they have sensed a greater Reality; namely, the Presence of the Living Spirit. The true mystic in every age has come into the world of affairs and lived among men, sometimes as a teacher, and sometimes in the ordinary walks of life, but always in a perfectly natural way. There is nothing peculiar or strange about a mystic. People who shroud themselves in a cloak of mystery are not true mystics but are laboring under mental delusions and subjective hallucinations. They may be sincere in their beliefs; but they are none the less wrong in their methods. It is a question if a real mystic would even realize that he is a mystic. He would be more liable to think of himself simply as one who understands that he is One with the Whole.

THE GREAT LIGHT

It is impossible, perhaps, to put into words or into print what a mystic sometimes sees, and it is as hard to believe it as it is to put it into words. But there is a certain inner sense which, at times, sees Reality in a flash which illuminates the whole being with a great flood of light. This, too, might seem an illusion unless the testimony were complete; for every mystic has had this

---

78 Acts 17: 28.
79 John 8: 12.

experience; but some have had it to a greater degree than others. Jesus was the greatest of all the mystics; and once, at least, after a period of illumination, His face was so bright that His followers could not look upon it.

In moments of deepest realization the great mystics have sensed that One Life flows through ALL; and that all are some part of that Life. They have also seen Substance, a fine, white, brilliant stuff, forever falling into everything; a Substance, indestructible and eternal. At times, the realization has been so complete that they have been actually blinded by the light. There are instances where for several days after such an experience, the one having it could not see on the physical plane; for he had seen the Inner Light. Remember, all this takes place when in a perfectly normal state of mind and has nothing whatever to do with the psychic state. It is not an illusion but a reality; and it is during these periods that real revelation comes. Perhaps a good illustration would be to suppose a large group of people in a room together, but unaware of each other's presence; each is busy with his own personal affairs. We will suppose the place to be dark and that some one comes in and takes a flash-light picture of the room and its occupants. Should this picture be shown to any one who was in the room before it was taken, it might be hard for him to believe that all of the objects in the picture were actually in the room. This is, of course, a poor analogy, but it does serve to elucidate a point. In flashes of illumination, the inspired have seen INTO THE VERY CENTER OF REALITY, and have brought back with them a picture of what they have seen and felt. Again, we know that this has not been an illusion or simply a subjective hallucination, for each age has had its mystics, and every age has produced the same results. ALL HAVE SEEN THE SAME THING. The testimony is complete and the evidence is certain.

What the Mystics Have Taught About the Individual

All of the great mystics have taught practically the same thing. They have all agreed that the soul is on the pathway of experience, that is, of self-discovery; that it is on its way back to its Father's House; and that every soul will ultimately reach its Heavenly Home. They have taught the Divinity to Man. "I have said, Ye are gods; and all of you are children of the most High."[80] They have told us that man's destiny is Divine and sure; and that Creation is Complete and Perfect NOW. The great mystics have all agreed that man's life is his to do with as he chooses; but that when he turns to "The One," he will always receive inspiration from On High.

They have told us of the marvelous relationship which exists between God and man, of a close Union that cannot be broken; and the greatest of the mystics have consciously walked

---

80 Ps. 82 : 6.

with God and talked with Him, just as we talk to each other. It is difficult to realize how this could be; it is hard to understand how a Being, so Universal as God must be, can talk with man; here, alone, the mystic sense reveals the greater truth and knows that, Infinite as is the Divine Being, It is still Personal to all who believe in Its Presence. It is entirely possible for a man to talk with the Spirit; for the Spirit is within men, and "He who made the ears" can hear.

INSTINCT AND INTUITION

That quality in an animal which directs its action and tells it where to go to find food and shelter, we call instinct. It is, really, Omniscience in the animal. The same quality, more highly developed, makes its appearance in man; and is what we call intuition. Intuition is God in man, revealing to him the Realities of Being; and just as instinct guides the animal, so would intuition guide man, if he would allow it to operate through him. Here again, we must be careful not to mistake a psychic impression for an intuitive one. *Psychic impressions seek to control man; intuition always remains in the background and waits* for his recognition. "Behold, I stand at the door."[81]

All arbitrary control of man stopped as soon as he was brought to a point of self-knowingness. From this point he must discover himself; but intuition, which is nothing less than God in man, silently awaits his recognition and coöperation. The Spirit is always there if we could but sense Its Presence. Mystics have felt this wonderful power working from within, and have responded to it; and, as a sure evidence that they were not laboring under delusions, they have all sensed the same thing; had the impressions been psychic only, each would have seen and sensed a different thing; for each would have seen through the darkness of his own subjective mentality.

ILLUMINATION AND COSMIC CONSCIOUSNESS

There is such an experience as Illumination and Cosmic Consciousness; It is not a mystery, however, but is the Self-Knowingness of God through man. The more complete the operation of that Power, the more complete has been man's conscious mentality; for the illumined do not become less, but more themselves. The greater the consciousness of God, the more complete must be the realization of the True Self,—The Divine Reality.

Illumination will come as man more and more realizes his Unity with the Whole; and as he constantly endeavors to let the Truth operate through him. But since the Whole is at the point

---

81 Rev. 3: 20.

of the Inner Mentality, it will be here alone that he will contact It. "Speak to Him, thou, for He hears."

The only God man knows is the God of his own Inner Life; indeed, he can know no other. To assume that man can know a God outside himself is to assume that he can know something of which he is not conscious. This does not mean that man is God; it means that the only God man knows is within. The only place that man contacts God is within; and the only life man has is from within. God is not external, but is Indwelling, at the very center of man's life. This is why Jesus said that the Kingdom of Heaven is within, and why He prayed, "Our Father Which art in Heaven."[82]

THE HIGHEST PRACTICE

The highest mental practice is to listen to this Inner Voice and to declare for Its Presence. The greater a man's consciousness of this Indwelling I AM is, the more power he will have. This will never lead to illusion but will always lead to Reality. All great souls have known this and have constantly striven to let the Mind of God come out through their mentalities. "The Father that dwelleth in Me, He doeth the works."[83] This was the declaration of the great Master, and it should be ours also; not a limited sense of life but a limitless one.

THE POWER OF JESUS

The occult significance of the power of Jesus is easily understood when we study His method of procedure. Consider His raising of Lazarus from the dead. He stood at the tomb and gave thanks; this was recognition. He next said, "I Knew that Thou hearest me always";[84] this was unification; then He said, "Lazarus, come forth";[85] this was command. The method is perfect and we will do well to study and follow it. This method can be used in all treatment. First, realize that Divine Power Is; then unify with It, and then speak the word as "one having authority," for the Law is "the servant of the Eternal Spirit throughout all the ages."

---

82 Luke 11: 2.
83 John 14: 10.
84 John 11: 42.
85 John 11: 43.

TURNING WITHIN

We should turn within, then, as have all of those great souls who have blessed the world with their presence; we should turn with and FIND GOD. It should seem natural to turn to the Great Power back of everything; it should seem normal to believe in the Power; and we should have a sense of a Real Presence when we do turn toward the One and Only Power in the entire Universe. This method is by far the most effective. It gives a sense of power that nothing else can, and, in this way, proves that it is a Reality. It would be a wonderful experiment if the world would try to solve all of its problems through the power of Spirit. Indeed the time will come when every one will, "From the highest . . . to the lowest."

A sense of real completion can come only to that soul which realizes its Unity with the Great Whole. Man will never be satisfied until his whole being responds to this thought, and then, indeed, "Will God go forth anew into Creation."

"To as many as believed gave He the Power."

THE TRIUNE UNITY

THE INDIVISIBLE WHOLE

WITHIN WHICH IS ALL OF ITS PARTS

THE ABSOLUTE WITHIN WHICH IS THE RELATIVE

THE UNCREATED WITHIN WHICH IS THE CREATED

THE CHANGELESS WITHIN WHICH IS ALL CHANGE

THE FORMLESS WITHIN WHICH IS ALL FORM

THE LIMITLESS WITHIN WHICH IS ALL SPACE

THE TIMELESS WITHIN WHICH IS ALL TIME

THE UNIVERSAL WITHIN WHICH IS THE INDIVIDUAL

THE ONE PERSON WITHIN WHOM ARE ALL PEOPLE

SOURCE AND CENTER OF ALL LIFE POWER AND ACTION

TRUTH, LOVE, MIND, SPIRIT, THE EVER, AND THE ALL

GOD

Our father
which art
in
Heaven

THE
SON

PERSONALITY....INDIVIDUALITY

M A N

LESSON FIVE: METAPHYSICAL CHART NO. V.

This is the mystic's chart and shows how the Universal becomes the Particularization of Itself through man. Man comes to a point in the Universal, or God, and is the Idea of God as man. The Father is represented as the Whole just back of, or above, or within, man. This is the Indwelling God to Whom we pray and with Whom we talk. The mystic has the ability to consciously talk to God and to consciously receive a direct answer from the Spirit. In this chart it is shown that the Absolute contains the relative, within Itself, but is not limited by the relative. We must remember that the relative does not limit, but expresses, the Absolute. All change takes place within the Changeless. All form subsists within the Formless. All conditions obtain within that which is Limitless; and Creation is eternally going on within that which is Uncreated. All are activities of the One Mind and Spirit of God. All people come to a point of individuality within that which is Universal.

LESSON FIVE: THE PERFECT WHOLE

Chart No. V represents the Triune Unity. The other charts were divided into Spirit, Soul and Body, symbolizing the Conscious part of Existence; the Law through which It operates; and the result of the operation. But those lines were entirely arbitrary. No such lines could exist, for the threefold Universe, with all of Its attributes, interspheres Itself. We find the Spirit, or Conscious Mind, the Soul or Subconscious Mind, and the Body, which is the manifestation of the union of Spirit and Soul, simultaneously present at every point. This chart represents the Indivisible Whole, within which are all of Its parts; the Absolute, within which is the relative; the Uncreated, within which is all Creation.

Creation is the giving of form to the Substance of Spirit. Spirit, being All and Only, there is nothing for It to change into but Itself; therefore, It is the Changeless, within which must take place all change or manifestation of Itself. Change is simply motion within Life.

The Infinite, of Itself, is Formless, but within It are contained all of the forms which are the expressions or the outlines of Its experiences.

Spirit is the Limitless, within which is all space; Spirit is Timeless, within which is all time. "Time is the sequence of events in a Unitary Whole." Creation and experience are eternally going on, but a particular experience is measured by time and has a beginning and an end.

The big circle represents the Universal, within which is the individual; the One Person within Whom are all people. There is really but One Person in the Universe; but within this One Person all people live, "for in Him we live, and move, and have our being."[86] It is the Source and center of all Life, Power, Action, Truth, Love, Mind, Spirit, the Ever and the All. It is, of course, God.

INDIVIDUALITY

The point within the big circle represents the personality and individuality of man, indicating that he is a center in the Divine Mind or God.

Man is the Personification of the Infinite Life; and so we place, just above this point and on the inside of it, "The Son"; and just above this (with no line to divide them) are written the words, "Our Father which art in Heaven,"[87] taken from the Lord's Prayer. There is no dif-

---

86 Acts 17: 28.
87 Luke 11: 2.

ference between God, the Absolute, which is Our Father in Heaven, and the Son, so far as actual Being is concerned. The Son is simply a point where God recognizes Himself as Personality or Individualized Being. It is within that we find the Unity of God and man; there is no separation.

Man, having his existence in the Unitary Whole, which is Indivisible, is compelled to accept the fact that his life is God or Spirit; but to say that man is God, which is equivalent to saying that any part equals the whole, is to contradict logic and reason, and limit the Limitless Idea. It is enough to say that we are at one with the Whole. It is both within and without. In perhaps a more liberal sense we could say man is in God; immersed in God; saturated with God. God permeates all life, and in man we find that this Infinite Mind or Intelligence comes to a point of Individualized Self-Consciousness.

Theoretically, we believe that the personality which we possess is on the pathway of self-discovery; for everything bears witness to this belief; as fast as we discover any truth, it is there to use. We never create Truth—we discover and use It. We believe, then, that as man continuously unfolds his personality, he will find latent capacities of which he has never dreamed.

FURTHER EVOLUTION

Since his whole life is the unfoldment of intelligence, according to law, man can only evolve as he recognizes greater possibilities—there could be no other way. The arbitrary process of evolution ceased when man became an individual; and any further evolution will be through self-recognition; but back of him is the whole of Life surging to express Itself. This is what is known as the Divine Urge. It is that Instinctive, Omniscient "I am" in man, always pushing him on and up; but It can only express for him as It flows through him. That person has the greatest power who the most completely recognizes himself to be one with this Infinite Mind. That is why Jesus said: "I speak not of myself" (it is not this individualized point); "but the Father, that dwelleth in Me" (that is, God, our Father, Which is in Heaven); "He doeth the works."[88]

The evolution of man, which is the unfoldment of Spirit through his personality, will be more complete when his objective and subjective faculties are more perfectly balanced; that is, when he has conscious control of the spiritual forces which surge for expression. The psychological nature has to change somewhat, and the subjective tendencies that hinder the Whole from coming to a point of conscious contact must be neutralized. This would produce illumination or the consciousness of his Unity with the Whole.

---

88 John 14 : 10.

In treatment, we work until we penetrate the false thought within and break through to Reality. There is no limitation, either in Infinite Intelligence or in Infinite Law. The whole limitation which we experience is not, of itself, a reality or an entity, but is simply one of the forms within the formless which we are outlining.

THE TRUTH IS KNOWN

Our conscious intelligence is as much of Life as we understand. We have stopped looking for the Spirit, because we have found It; It is what you are and It is what I am; we could not be anything else if we tried. The thing that we look with is the thing that we have been looking for. That is why it is written: "I have said, Ye are gods; and all of you are children of the most High."[89] We have stopped looking for the Law. We have found It. In the Universe we call It Universal Subjectivity or Soul; in our own experience we call It the subjective state of our thought, which is our individual use of Universal Law. We have found the Law and demonstrated It. We find that both the Law and the Spirit are Limitless. What is it that we need for a greater freedom? Nothing but a greater realization of what we already know.

We should never hesitate to say that we know the Truth, because we do; for the realization of the Unity of God and man *is* the Truth. We simply need a greater realization of this. How are we to get it? Only by penetrating deeper and yet deeper into our own Divine Nature; pushing farther and farther back into the Infinite. Where are we to do that? There is no place except within that we can do it. Who is to do it for us? No one. No one can. People can heal us; they can set the Law in motion for us and help us to become prosperous;—that is good and helpful; but the evolution of the individual, the unfoldment of personality, the enlightenment of the Soul, the illumination of Spirit, can come only to the degree that the individual himself purposes to let Life operate through him. "Let this Mind be in you which was also in Christ Jesus."[90] This is the Mind of God,—the only Mind,—the Supreme Intelligence of the Universe.

THE ANSWER IS IN MAN

The answer to every question is within man, because man is within Spirit and Spirit is an Indivisible Whole. The solution to every problem is within man; the healing of all disease is within man; the forgiveness of all sin is within man; the raising of the dead is within man; Heaven is

89 Ps. 82 : 6.
90 Phil. 2 : 5

within man. That is why Jesus prayed to this indwelling "I am" and said: "Our Father Which art in Heaven."[91] He also said: "The Kingdom of God is within you."[92]

Each of us, then, represents the Whole. How should we feel toward the Whole? In the old order, we thought of the Whole as a sort of mandatory power, an autocratic government, an arbitrary God, sending some to Heaven and some to hell; and "all for His glory." Now we are more enlightened and we realize that there can be no such a Divine Being. We have meditated upon the vastness of the Universe of Law, and we have said: "God is Law; there is a Divine Principle Which is God." In the new order, we are liable to fall into as great an error as the old thought fell into, unless we go much deeper than thinking of God simply as Principle. God is more than Law or Principle. God is the Infinite Spirit, the Limitless, Conscious Life of the Universe; the One Infinite Person within Whom all people live. The Law is simply a Force.

GOD—INFINITE PERSONALITY

God or Spirit is Supreme, Infinite, Limitless Personality. And we should think of the Divine Being as such—as completely responsive to everything we do. There should come to us a sense of communion, a spontaneous sense of Irresistible Union. If we had that, we would demonstrate instantaneously.

An evolved soul is always a worshiper of God. He worships God in everything; for God *is* in everything. God not only is *in everything, but He is more than everything He is in*. "Ye are the light of the world";[93]—that is, God in us. All that we are is God; yet God is more than all we are.

The nearer consciousness gets to the Truth, the more Cosmic sweep it has, the more power it has. Angels wait upon individuals who perceive Cosmic Purposes and Powers, because the Whole is crowding forth into expression. Let a man recognize a Cosmic Purpose, which is the expression of Life, Truth and Love; let his thought vibrate to the higher and grander realization of life, and see how—automatically—he becomes more powerful.

The process of healing and demonstration is, at first, mechanical and scientific; then the fire of Spirit is added to make it real. One is technique—the other is the pulsating life and glow. We need the recognition of love, coupled with a scientific understanding of what we are doing. Thoughts are things, and diseases are the direct result of specific thoughts somewhere in consciousness. Poverty is the direct result of a subjective state of thought which binds.

---

91 Luke 11 : 2.
92 Luke 17 : 21.
93 Matt. 5 : 14.

UNITY

All Manifestation of Life is from an invisible to a visible plane; and it is a silent, effortless process of spiritual realization. We must unify, in our own mentalities, with Pure Spirit. To each of us, individually, God, or Spirit, is the Supreme Personality of the Universe; the Supreme Personality of that which we, ourselves, are. It is only as the relationship of the individual to this Deity becomes enlarged that he has a consciousness of power.

There should always be a recognition in treatment of the Absolute Unity of God and man; the Oneness, Inseparability, Indivisibility, Changelessness; God as the Big Circle, and man as the little circle. Man is in God and God is in man; just as a drop of water is in the ocean, while the ocean is in the drop of water. This is the recognition Jesus had when He said: "I and my Father are One."[94] There is a Perfect Union; and to the degree that we are conscious of this Union we incorporate this consciousness in our word, and our word has just as much power as we put in it, no more and no less.

Within this Infinite Mind each individual exists, not as a separated, but as a separate, entity. We are a point in Universal Consciousness, which is God, and God is our Life, Spirit, Mind and Intelligence. We are not separated from Life, neither is It separated from us; but we are separate entities in It, Individualized Centers of God's Consciousness.

We came from Life and are in Life, so we are One with Life; and we know that Instinctive Life within, which has brought us to the point of self-recognition, still knows in us the reason for all things, the purpose underlying all things; and we know that there is nothing in us of fear, doubt or confusion which can hinder the flow of Reality to the point of our recognition. We are guided, daily, by Divine Intelligence into paths of peace wherein the soul recognizes its Source and meets It in joyful Union, in complete At-one-ment.

HOLD TO THE GOOD

Such is the power of clear thought that it penetrates things; it removes obstructions, the reason being that there is nothing but consciousness, nothing but Mind. The only instrument of Mind is idea. See with perfect clearness and never become discouraged nor overcome by a sense of limitation. Know this—that the Truth with which you are dealing is absolute. All of God, all of Truth, all there is, is at the point of man's recognition; and every time you give a treatment, and all the way through it, keep bringing this back to your remembrance.

---

94 John 10 : 30.

Never struggle; say, "There is nothing to struggle over; everything is mine by Divine Right; Infinite Intelligence is my Intelligence; Divine Love is my Love; Limitless Freedom is my Freedom; Perfect Joy is my Gladness; Limitless Life is my Energy."

Let us BLIND OURSELVES TO NEGATION, as far as we are mentally able to. LET US NOT TALK, THINK, OR READ ABOUT ANYTHING DESTRUCTIVE, whether it be war, pestilence, famine, poverty, sickness, or limitation of any kind. Looking at this from a practical standpoint, there is all to win and nothing to lose. The rapid progress we would make if we should do this would be wonderful.

We are always dealing with First Cause. Nothing else can equal the satisfaction that comes to one when he perceives himself, from the silence of his own soul and the activity of his own thought, actually bringing about a condition without the aid of visible instrumentalities. There is nothing else as satisfying as to heal some disease purely by the power of thought; this shows that we are dealing with First Cause.

We must definitely neutralize confusion and doubt. We should take time, daily, to conceive of ourselves as being tranquil, poised, powerful,—always in control of every situation; as being always the highest concept of the Divine which we can imagine. We should never hesitate to think of ourselves in this way. The Ancients used to teach their pupils to say to themselves— "Wonderful, wonderful, wonderful me!"—until they lost sight of themselves as Mary Smith or John Jones, and perceived themselves as Divine Realities. Then, when they came back to the objectivity of Mary Smith and John Jones, they brought with them that subtle power which distinguishes Spiritual Growth,—the Atmosphere of Reality.

THE INFINITE IS PERSONAL TO ALL

Undoubtedly the power of Jesus lay in His recognition of the Infinite Person as a Responsive, Conscious, Living Reality; while, on the other hand, He recognized the Law as an arbitrary force, which was compelled to obey His will. He combined the personal and the impersonal attributes of Life into a perfect whole. The Infinite is Personal to every soul who believes in the Infinite. It is a mistake to so abstract the Principle that we forget the Living Presence; it is the combination of the two that makes work effective.

THE CHRIST

Who is man? He is the Christ. Who is the Christ? The Son, begotten of the only Father—not the only begotten Son of God. Christ means the Universal Idea of Sonship, of which each is a Member.

That is why we are spoken of as Members of that One Body; and why we are told to have that Mind in us "which was also in Christ Jesus."[95] Each partakes of the Christ Nature to the degree that the Christ is revealed through him, and to that degree he becomes the Christ. We should turn to that Living Presence within, Which is the Father in Heaven, recognize It as the One and Only Power in the Universe, unify with It, declare our word to be the presence, power and activity of that One, and speak the word as if we believed it; because the Law is the servant of the Spirit.

If we could stand aside and let the One Perfect Life flow through us, we could not help healing people. This is the highest form of healing.

We have gone through all of our abstract processes of reasoning and have found out what the Law is and how It works; now we can forget all about It, and know that there is nothing but the Word; the Law will be working automatically. We must forget everything else, and let our word be spoken with a deep inner realization of love, beauty, peace, poise, power, and of the great Presence of Life at the point of our own consciousness.

REALIZATION

We do not dare to throw ourselves with abandonment into a seeming void; but if we did, we would find our feet planted firmly on a rock, for there is a place in the mentality, in the heights of its greatest realizations, where it throws itself with complete abandonment into the very center of the Universe. There is a point in the supreme moment of realization where the individual merges with the Universe, but not to the loss of his individuality; where a sense of the Oneness of all Life so enters his being that there is no sense of otherness; it is here that the mentality performs seeming miracles, because there is nothing to hinder the Whole from coming through. We can do this only by providing the great mental equivalents of Life, by dwelling and meditating upon the immensity of Life; and yet as vast, as immense, as limitless as It is, the whole of It is brought to the point of our own consciousness.

We comprehend the Infinite only to the degree that It expresses Itself through us, becoming to us that which we believe It to be. And so we daily practice in our meditations the realizations of Life—"Infinite, indwelling Spirit within me, Almighty God within me, Perfect Peace within me, Complete Satisfaction within me, Real Substance within me; that which is the Truth within me." "I am the Truth," Jesus said. He said: "I am the way; I am the Life; no man cometh unto the Father but by Me."[96] How true it is! We cannot come unto the Father Which art in Heaven except through our own nature.

---

95 Phil. 2 : 5.
96 John 14 : 6.

Right here, through our own nature, is the gateway and the path that gradually leads to illumination, to realization, to inspiration, to the intuitive perception of everything.

The highest faculty in man is intuition, and it comes to a point sometimes where, with no process of reasoning at all, he realizes the Truth intuitively. So we should daily meditate, particularly if we are practicing right along.

MEDITATION

Any practitioner should take a certain time every day to meditate within himself, to realize that the words which he speaks are the words of Truth. Being the words of Truth, they cannot fail to be fulfilled; they are a law unto themselves within the Great Law. They know themselves to be what they are. They are immutable, irresistible, unassailable; they are eternal and complete, having intelligence, knowledge and understanding within themselves.

Every treatment must be a complete thing within itself. It is an unqualified statement of Being and pays no attention to appearances. If it did, it would not be efficacious. It rises above all appearance and may contradict every experience the human race has ever had; but it is real just the same. *The treatment begins and ends within the mentality of the one giving it; and the demonstration takes place within the mentality of the one giving it; and, to the degree that it does take place there, it is a good treatment and will be a good demonstration.*

If you have a patient who says: "I am sick," and you are able to neutralize your belief of that man as being sick, or any man as being sick, and can see him perfect, he will come to you and say: "I am healed." *The practitioner must know within himself.* He never thinks of projecting his thought, sending it out or holding it. He simply takes the whole condition and brings it into the great realization of Life.

Declare:——"Perfect Life within me, God within me, Spirit within me, Good within me, Almightiness within me, Loving Intelligence within me, Peace, Poise, Power, Happiness and Joy within me, Life, Truth and Love within me, Omniscient Instinctive I am within me, Almighty God within me." It is not enough to say that God is. The concept must be brought home to the mentality of the individual and unified with it, in order to have it expressed through him.

If we need financial healing, we should say: "Infinite Substance within me, Infinite Activity within me, flowing through me into everything I do, say or think, quickening into action all those things that my mentality touches; Infinite Activity within me, unerring, never mistaking, always doing the right thing at the right time, always knowing what to do, knowing how to do it and doing it; Infinite Executive Power within me, the Great Executive, the great I am, the All-Knowing and All-Seeing, the All-Wise within me; Infinite Substance within me, forever expressing Itself through me; Infinite Supply flowing through me and flowing to me;——irresistible supply, unassailable supply, limitless." As you say this, stop and think of the things you want—seeing them as realities—much as one would look at pictures on the wall.

Repeat:—"Infinite Substance within me, Infinite Supply flowing through me and to me, Infinite Activity around me and within me, Infinite Intelligence within me, directing me, guarding me, governing me, controlling me; the One and Only within me and through me, that is, Almighty God within me. There is no other, or beside which there is none other. Infinite love within me, seeing all, knowing all, loving all, One in and through all." Carry this concept out until you see that you live in everybody and everybody lives in you. Then continue: "Infinite One, comprehending, seeing, knowing, understanding, living in and including the All, within me." Realize what this means. "I am One with all people. There are no enemies. There is only the One, in all and through all."

If we would spend half the time making such affirmations that we spend complaining, finding fault, fussing, being sad and sorry for ourselves, we would soon be healed. "Infinite Wisdom within me"; stop and think what this means,—the Intelligence that operates through everything, visible and invisible. "Infinite Wisdom within me; Infinite Intelligence within me; Infinite Power within me";—feel what this means: The Power that holds the planets in place; a power to which the united force of the human race is as nothing. "Infinite Intelligence and Infinite Power within me, the great Executor; Infinite Energy and Wisdom within me,—the All-Knowing, the Unerring Mind of the Universe;—Infinite Peace within me, Infinite Peace, undisturbed and unalterable; Infinite Life, Infinite Peace within me"; that means there is no disturbance, no commotion, no trouble. There is only Infinite Peace; the power that stilled the waves and told the winds to be calm is the Power with which we deal. "Infinite Peace within me, Infinite Joy within me, the Joy that causes the leaves of the trees to clap their hands." It is the Joy that sings in the brook, the music of the spheres, the Joy of the sense of completion. "Infinite Joy within me, not somewhere else, but within me"; It is the Good which is urging Itself forth through every act which we call human or humane. We see it in the hand that gives and in every human act. That is the "Infinite Good that is within me,"—Infinite everything, whatever the need may be. Meditate upon the abstract essence of the thing; then bring it to a concrete point within your own mentality and see what it means as it manifests, declaring that it is.

This great teaching plainly shows the way to liberty and freedom. It is a pathway continuously unfolding from a Limitless Source to a Limitless Source. "Arise, shine, for thy light is come."[97] "I am that I am."[98]

---

97 Isa. 60: 1.
98 Exodus 3: 14.

Note: Read and study "Cosmic Consciousness," Bucke; "Twelve Lessons in Mysticism," Hopkins; "The Impersonal Life" and "Creative Process in the Individual," T. Troward; "Bible Mystery and Meaning," T. Troward; "Sayings of Jesus," Red Letter Testament.

LESSON SIX: THE LAW OF PSYCHIC PHENOMENA—INTRODUCTION

It is taken for granted that the average person of to-day is more or less acquainted with the facts concerning psychic phenomena. It would be useless, in a course such as this, to attempt any exhaustive research work; this has already been done by those eminently able to furnish the data.

There is within man a power that can communicate without the tongue, hear without the ear, see without the eye, talk without the mouth, move ponderable objects and grasp things without the hand; and perform many other feats that are usually connected only with the physical instrument. All these facts have been completely proved, and it is no longer necessary to produce evidence to substantiate these facts.

While the above-stated facts have all been proved, the reason for their being has not been so thoroughly or logically discussed, and it is the purpose of this article to explain the fundamental reasons behind the law of mental action which is called psychic; for if a thing happens, there must be a reason for its happening and a law through which it operates.

The only excuse for taking up this topic in a course of lessons in Mental Science is that, being the phenomena of Mind, it should come under the category of known mental actions.

PSYCHIC PHENOMENA AND IMMORTALITY

Psychic phenomena are closely associated with immortality in people's minds for the reason that they deal with those unseen powers which we think of as being attributes of the soul; and also because many people have attributed the phenomena largely to the agency of discarnate spirits.

NO APOLOGIES

While no apologies are made for the ensuing pages, yet, in justice to the Truth, it must be said that many of the world's eminent scientists have investigated the subjects to be discussed, and so far, to the author's knowledge, none of them have ever refuted the ensuing facts.

The powers which are exhibited through the psychic life do really exist in man, and some day he will make conscious use of them and will, thereby, be greatly benefited. Meanwhile, every one is urged to be most careful in his approach to the subject. A little knowledge is a very dangerous thing, and it is to be regretted that very few people exhibiting psychic powers appear to know what the law is that underlies the phenomena. Many are led astray through ignorance, and one should be most careful in handling the topic. But, as stated above, this subject, coming under the known laws of mental action, must be dealt with.

God has given us a mind with which to know, and a power with which to discern the Truth, and it is a terrible mistake to misuse that power. The whole end and aim of evolution is to produce a man who, in his self-conscious state, may depict the Divine Nature. We can do this only to the degree that we remain ourselves at all times.

We will take up the study of this subject just as we would approach the study of any other law, with an open mind, without any superstition and free from any sense of the unnatural. Nature is always natural, and only those things are mysteries which we do not understand.

SPIRIT OR CONSCIOUS MIND

ONE AND ONLY KNOWING

POWER IN GOD OR MAN

THE PSYCHIC SEA—SUBJECTIVE

FALSE OR TRUE—MIRROR OF MIND

MEDIUM OF ALL PSYCHIC PHENOMENA

THOUGHT FORMS OR MENTAL PICTURES

OBJECTIVE

ILLUSION OF MATTER

FALSE OR TRUE

MIRROR OF MATTER

LESSON SIX: METAPHYSICAL CHART NO. VI.

This is the psychic's chart and should be carefully considered, as it shows that the Spirit, or Conscious Mind, operates through a mental field, or law, which is a world of reflections. Thought is first reflected into Mind and then into matter. Read again the meaning of the conscious and the subconscious aspects of being. The world of Subjectivity is the Psychic Sea and the Medium of all subjective action. From the standpoint of man's thoughts it may be false or true, according to the way in which he thinks. It is the picture gallery of the soul, both from the universal and the individual sense. The illusion of matter means that the false mental pictures will produce a false form in the world of objectivity. Mind is not an illusion, but might contain false pictures which would be illusions; matter is not an illusion but may take on false conditions. We must learn to separate the false from the true.

LESSON SIX:
METAPHYSICAL MEANING OF WORDS USED IN CHART NO. VI

The upper section represents the Conscious Mind, the Self-Knowing Mind, which we call Spirit. The middle section represents the Psychic Sea, that is, the Subjective World; this is the world of thought forms and mental pictures. This has been called "The illusion of Mind," because it contains many pictures, which are pictures only, and have no real form behind them. As a picture that is hung on the wall is not really a person—but is simply a picture—so the Psychic Sea may contain pictures which, while they are real as pictures, are not real from any other sense. It does not follow that everything in the psychic world is an illusion, for it contains much that is true. We should be very careful to distinguish the false from the true.

The lower section of the chart represents the objective world. This world also reflects many false forms, such as disease and limitation. They are not things of themselves, but are the results of wrong mental pictures in the Subjective World.

Neither the psychic pictures nor the world of forms are self-creative; both are effects.

LESSON SIX: PSYCHIC PHENOMENA

Psyche means soul; psychic phenomena are the phenomena of the soul. We have already seen that what we call the soul is, really, the subjective part of us. We do not have two minds, but we do have a dual aspect of mentality in what we call the objective and subjective phases of mind. The objective mind is that part of the mentality which functions consciously; it is the part of us which really knows itself; and without it we would not be real or conscious entities.

THE SUBJECTIVE MIND

Our subjective mind is our mental emanation in Universal Subjectivity; it is our individual use of mental law. It is also the avenue through which Instinctive Man works, carrying on the functions of the body; for it is the silent builder of the body. The subjective mind of the individual is the working of Instinctive Man within him, plus all of his conscious and subconscious experiences.

SEAT OF MEMORY

The subjective mind is the seat of memory and of instinctive emotion. Being the seat of memory, it contains a remembrance of everything that has ever happened to the outer man. This memory is perfect and retains every experience of the individual life. The subjective mind also contains many of the family and race characteristics which have been experienced by individualized man. It retains these memories, partly, at least, as mental pictures or impressions. This is proven by the fact that pictures have been taken of the subjective thought and definite outlines developed. This does not necessarily mean that every impression is retained as a mental picture, but that, in all probability, anything that the outer eye has definitely seen is retained as a more or less distinct picture.

The subjective mind is a picture gallery, upon whose walls are hung the pictures of all the people whom the individual has ever known and all the incidents which he has ever experienced.

SUGGESTION AND SUBJECTIVITY

The subjective mind being deductive only in its reasoning powers is compelled by its nature to retain all the mental impressions that it has ever received. It, therefore, contains much that the objective mind has never consciously known. When we realize that the individual's subjectivity is his use of the One Subjective Mind, we shall see that a subjective unity is maintained between all people, and that individual mentalities which are in sympathetic vibration with each other must, more or less, mingle, and receive suggestions from each other. This is the meaning of mental influence, which is, indeed, a very real thing. This also means that the subjective mind receives suggestions from the race and is, more or less, influenced by its environment; all this takes place on the silent side of life and is mostly unknown to the receiver.

Race-suggestion is a very real thing, and each individual carries around with him, and has written into his mentality, many impressions that he never consciously thought of or experienced; for there is a silent influence going on at all times between people under this law.

SUBJECTIVE COMMUNICATION

It is almost certain that between friends there is, at all times, a silent communication, a sort of unconscious mental conversation going on subjectively. When this rises to the surface of conscious intelligence, it is called mental telepathy. This communication with others is going on at all times, whether the conscious mind is aware of the fact or not. We are always receiving impressions that are more or less vague, and it is seldom that they come to the surface; but they are there nevertheless and are gradually building into our mentalities impressions and forms of thought that are unconsciously and silently perceived.

Subjective Mind and Inspiration

Since the subjective mind is the storehouse of memory, it retains all that the eye has seen, the ear heard or the mentality conceived. Since it contains much that the outer man never consciously knew, and is the receptacle of much of the race-knowledge, through unconscious communication, it must, and does, have knowledge that far surpasses the objective faculties.

Realizing that the subjective draws to itself everything that it is in sympathy with, or vibrates to, we see that any one who is sympathetically inclined toward the race, or vibrates to the race-thought, might pick up the entire race-emotion and experience, and, if he were able to bring it to the surface, he could consciously depict it. Many of the world's orators, actors, and writers have been able to do this; which explains the reason why many of them have been so erratic; for they have been more or less controlled by the emotions which they have contacted.

Our greatest speakers are able to contact the subjective mentality of their audiences and in this way, not only to tell the audience what it wishes to be told, but also to send out a strong vibration that will make an equally strong subjective impression on those who are listening. It is a well-known fact that many speakers are able to connect with the mentality of an audience in such a manner as to be able to completely control it. Napoleon seemed to be able to do this, which was one of the reasons why he had such tremendous influence over his followers.

Singers and poets generally enter into more or less of a subjective state while singing or writing. In the case of a singer or actor, this enables him to respond to the emotion of his listeners and to be able to reflect back to them an equally strong emotion. It might work the other way; that is, he might, himself, awaken the emotion in his hearers. This we call temperament, and no singer, speaker or actor can be a great success without it.

In the case of a writer, this enables him to enter into the race-thought and perfectly depict race-emotion and race-endeavor. Poets are an especially good example of this ability; for poetry, like song, is the language of the soul, and none can write good poems unless he allows the soul to come to the surface. We could not imagine a great poem written mechanically. Artists lose themselves in their work and musicians often do the same; this we call inspiration.

In preaching, it is probable that the orator of the pulpit often so enters into the longings of men's hearts that he reveals them to themselves. He is able to depict their thoughts and emotions, and coupling his own with theirs, give birth to a great discourse; we say that he is inspired.

Any one contacting the subjective side of the race-mentality with the ability to permit it to come to the surface, will have at his disposal a knowledge that many lifetimes of hard study could not possibly accumulate. But, if one had to surrender his individuality in the process, he would be better off to remain ignorant.

Enough has been said on this subject to show the source of human inspiration. There is, of course, a much deeper seat of knowledge than the subjective mind; that is, the Spirit. But direct contact with Spirit is Illumination, and is a quality which has been developed in but few people; the few who have developed this quality have given the world its greatest literature, religion and law.

MENTAL ATMOSPHERES

Each person has a mental atmosphere which is the result of all that he has thought, said, done, and consciously or unconsciously perceived. This mental atmosphere is very real and is that subtle influence which constitutes the power of personal attraction; for personal attraction has but little to do with looks; it goes much deeper and is almost entirely subjective. This will explain the likes and dislikes for those with whom we come in daily contact. We meet some, only to turn away without a word, while others we are at once drawn toward, and without any apparent reason; this is the result of their mental atmosphere or thought vibration. No matter what the lips may be saying, the inner thought out-speaks them and the unspoken word often carries more weight than the spoken. As Emerson said: "What you are speaks so loudly that I cannot hear what you say."

In contacting people, we are instantly attracted or repelled, according to the vibrations which we feel. A person whose atmosphere is one of love and sunshine, whose nature is to be happy, who lives a clean, wholesome life in a free atmosphere, will always attract friends.

Children feel mental atmosphere very keenly and are drawn to those who are inwardly right, shunning those who are inwardly wrong. It has been truly said that people whom children and dogs do not like are dangerous. Animals are almost entirely subjective and feel mental atmospheres more keenly than do most people. A dog instinctively knows one's attitude toward him and, acting accordingly, is immediately a friend or foe. Personal atmospheres vary in their intensity, there being as many varieties as there are people; for each creates his own atmosphere in Mind.

HOW TO CREATE PERSONAL CHARM

Personal charm may be easily created by learning to love all and hate none. Truly did the great Emerson say: "If you want a friend, be one." If one wishes to have friends, he should become friendly; if he wishes love, he should learn to love. There is no excuse for any one being without a power of attraction, since it is a mental quality and may be consciously induced through right practice.

THE ATMOSPHERE OF PLACES

As all people have a mental atmosphere, so do all places; and as the atmosphere of people is the result of their thoughts, so the atmosphere of places is the result of the thoughts that have been created in them. Places are permeated with the thoughts of the people who inhabit them; in this way, mental atmospheres are created and may be easily felt by those contacting them.

How often we have had the experience of going into a place, only to feel that we were not wanted, and became so disturbed that we wished immediately to leave. How often, on the other hand, we have gone into places where we felt such a warmth and inner glow that we wished to remain. This is the result of the mental atmosphere surrounding the place or room. This is why we love our homes; they are filled with love and affection and we feel at peace within their walls. This is why one likes to return home after his day's work; for he knows that here is a place where he will be away from the world with all of its cares and worries. It is a wise wife who understands this law and who keeps the atmosphere of the home pleasant. Such a one will seldom lose her mate, but will hold him through the strong ties of love and affection with which she floods his abode. Many an unhappy home could be harmonized if this law were better understood and practiced.

The atmosphere of the home should never be clouded with the uncertainties of the outside world. Here, in the palace of human love, all else should be forgotten and an atmosphere maintained which will be a shelter from the world. Here love should be the ruling passion and harmony should reign supreme. Here, above all other places, should the Kingdom of God be established and families should dwell together in peace and joy.

Too often, jealousy and deceit rob the home of its joy, while mistrust and doubtings make it so unpleasant that it becomes an impossible place in which to live. But all this can be changed by reversing the wrong thoughts and in their place creating thoughts of love and tenderness toward one another.

There is nothing more unfortunate for a child's mind than to be compelled to live in an unhappy home. The home should stand for heaven on earth, and unless it does, it will not stand long, but will be buried in the ashes of dead hopes.

The atmosphere of the desert is wonderful, for it is free from the thoughts of men's confusion and fear, and so is a place of great peace. Here, indeed, away from the haunts of men's terrible struggles, quiet may be found and peace regained. It is the same with the mountains, the lakes and the trackless deep. This is what we love about Nature; her marvelous calm and deep peace; for she speaks to us and tells of a life undisturbed by the strife of man. She does, indeed, bear a message from On High, and happy is the one who can talk to her and learn from her, for she is wonderful and filled with light.

Even the slightest things seem to be possessed of a soul, or subjective atmosphere. How often we see a familiar coat or hat hanging on a peg, while in it we seem to see the person who wears it; it seems to look like him, and so it does, for it retains the emanation of his atmosphere, and really is permeated with his personality. Everything has an atmosphere which we sense and to which we react accordingly; if it is pleasant we like it, and if unpleasant we dislike it.

THE RACE-MIND

Just as each person, place or thing has a subjective atmosphere or remembrance, so each town, city, or nation has its individual atmosphere. Some towns are bustling with life and action, while others seem dead; some are filled with a spirit of culture, while others seem filled with a spirit of commercial strife. This is the result of the mentalities of those who live in these places. A city given over to the pursuit of the higher endeavors will react with an atmosphere of culture and refinement, while one whose dominant thought is to acquire wealth will react to an atmosphere of grasp and grab. This is very definite and is felt by all who enter such places.

Just as a city has its atmosphere, so does a whole nation; for a nation is made up of the individuals who inhabit it; and the combined atmospheres of all the people who inhabit a nation creates a national mentality which we speak of as the psychology of that people.

THE MIND OF HISTORY

When we remember that Subjective Mind is Universal, we will come to the conclusion that the history of the race is written in the mental atmosphere of the globe on which we live. That is, everything that has ever happened on this planet has left its imprint on the walls of time; and could we walk down their corridors and read the writings, we should be reading the race history. This should seem simple when we realize that the vibrations of the human voice can be preserved in the receptive phonographic disc, and reproduced at will. If we were to impress one of these discs with the vibration of some one's voice and lay it away for a million years, it would still reproduce those vibrations.

It is not hard, then, to understand how the walls of time may be hung with the pictures of human events and how one who sees these pictures may read the race history.

TELEPATHY

Telepathy, or thought-transference, is such a commonly known fact that it is useless to do other than to discuss it briefly. However, there are some facts which might be overlooked unless we give them careful attention. The main fact to emphasize is that mental telepathy would not be possible unless there were a medium through which it could operate. This medium is Universal Mind; and it is through this medium that all thought-transference or mental telepathy takes place. Forms in matter and solid bodies may begin and end in space, but thought is more fluent.

Telepathy is the act of reading subjective thought, or of receiving conscious thought without audible words being spoken. But there must be a mental tuning in, so to speak, just as there must be in radio. We are surrounded by all sorts of vibrations, and if we wish to catch any of them distinctly, we must tune in; but there is a great deal of interference, and we do not always get the messages clearly. We often get the wrong ones, and sometimes many of the vibrations come together and seem to be nothing but a lot of noises, without any particular reason for being. It is only when the instrument is properly adjusted to some individual vibration that a clear message may be received.

This is true of mental telepathy, which is the transmission of thought. The receiver must tune in with the sender. It does not follow, however, that the sender knows that he is being tuned in on; in other words, one might pick up thoughts just as he picks up radio messages; and just as the one broadcasting may not know who is listening in, so the one sending out thought may not know who is listening in. Happily, but few people can listen in mentally, and these few only with more or less certainty of success. It would be terrible to be compelled to listen in on all the thoughts that are floating around. But, fortunately, we can only receive those messages to which we vibrate; and so the whole thing is a matter of our own choice. We are individuals in the mental world just as in the physical; and a wise person will protect himself mentally just as he would physically.

TUNING IN ON THOUGHT

Some seem to have the ability to tune in on thought and to read it, much as one would read a book. These people we call psychics; but all people really are psychic, since all have a soul or subjective mind. What we really mean is, that a psychic or medium is one who has the ability to objectify that which is subjective; to bring to the surface of conscious thought that which lies below the threshold of the outer mind. The medium reads from the book of remembrance; and it is marvelous how far-reaching this book of remembrance is.

Mental Pictures

As everything must exist in the subjective world before it can in the objective, and as it must exist there as a mental picture, it follows that whatever may have happened at any time on this planet is to-day within its subjective atmosphere; i.e., the experiences of those who have lived here. These pictures are hung upon the walls of time, and may be clearly discerned by those who can read them.

Accordingly, since the Universal Subjectivity is a Unit and is Indivisible, all these pictures really exist at any, and every, point within It simultaneously; and we may contact anything that is within It at any point, because the whole of It is at every point. Consequently we may contact at the point of our own subjective mind (which is a point in Universal Subjective Mind) every incident that ever transpired on this planet. We may even see a picture that was enacted two thousand years ago in some Roman arena; for the atmosphere is filled with such pictures. This has been called "The Illusion of Mind" (the psychic sea). This does not mean that Mind is an illusion, but that it might present us with an illusion unless we are very careful and are quite sure that what we are looking at is a real form and not simply a picture.

It is very important that we understand this; for each person in his objective state is a distinct and individualized center in Universal Mind; but in his subjective state every one, in his stream of consciousness, or at his rate of vibration, is universal, because of the Indivisibility of Mind. Wherever and whenever any individual contacts another upon the subjective side of life, if he is psychic, i.e., if he objectifies subjectivity, he may see a thought form of that person, but it does not necessarily follow that he would be really seeing the person.

Conditions Necessary for the Best Results

The conditions necessary for the best results in psychic work are faith and expectancy; for the subjective responds to faith and seems clouded by doubts. Doubt appears to throw dust in its eyes, while sympathetic faith and willing belief render the veil much thinner and the consequent messages much clearer. This explains why many unbelieving investigators fail to receive the desired results, and go away saying that the whole thing is a fraud. Whatever the nature of the subjective may be, we did not make and we cannot change it; we shall be compelled to use this force, like all other forces in nature, according to its own laws, and not according to the way we think it should act.

It has been completely proved that the subjective mentality responds more completely when fully believed in; and any one wishing to investigate the psychic life would much better accept this fact and act upon it, rather than dispute it and receive no results. If the law is complied with the results will be certain.

Some psychics go into a trance while giving subjective readings, while some can do this in a normal state. The trance state varies from a slight subjectivity to a completely submerged mentality, i.e., from simply getting in tune with thought while in a conscious state of mind, to becoming completely submerged in an unconscious state in order to get in tune with thought. It is never good to lose one's self-control, but many people do this and, in so doing, have brought to light remarkable evidence of the ability of the inner mind to perform wonderful tasks.

Deep Telepathic Messages

It is possible, at times, for a psychic to tell one most of the incidents that have happened in his life, and also to tell of his friends and many of the incidents that have happened to them. This is done by entering the subjective realm of the individual and reading the thoughts and mental pictures that are hung on the wall of his memory. When a psychic tells one something about his friends, he is entering their thought through the sympathetic vibration of the one whose thought he is reading. We are always in mental contact with our friends on the subjective side of life; and a psychic, tuning in on these vibrations, reads the thoughts that come over the mental wireless.

Reading the History of the Individual

Often a psychic will enter a person's mentality and give him a fairly complete history of his past and of the family from which he came, going back, perhaps, for several generations, naming ancestors and the things that engaged their attention while on earth. He is reading the records of what has already happened and is a subjective remembrance of his family.

For instance, people have often said to me: "I saw Emerson standing behind you this morning." Of course they did not see Emerson; what they saw was a mental picture of him; the reason being that I am a student of Emerson, and each is surrounded by the forms of the people he knows and the forms of those whose thought he studies.

Personal Readings

One is surprised when he goes to a medium and is told his own, and perhaps his mother's, name, and is told by the medium that his mother stands beside him. The psychic often tells just how she looked while in the flesh. Now it might or might not be, that what the medium says is true; for, while this personality might be consciously near, the chances are more than even that she is not, but that the medium is simply looking at a picture of her as she once was while in the flesh.

A medium might, by reading one's subjectivity, be able to tell something about people who were not present at the time; because each, through a sympathetic vibration of thought, is connected with the subjective emanations of those whom he likes, of those with whom he is associated and of those to whom he vibrates. These people might be in the flesh or out of it.

The personal reading appears to be limited either to the immediate individual or to some one with whom he is in contact. The value of subjective mind reading is more or less uncertain. Generally all that a psychic can tell is about something that has already happened or something that might happen as the result of a subjective tendency already set in motion. There are, however, deeper messages than these.

STREAMS OF CONSCIOUSNESS

Each, being an individual identity in Mind, is known by the name he bears, and by the vibration which he emanates. For, while we are all One in Mind and Spirit, we each have a separate and an individualized personality. This is the only way that Spirit can individualize, making it possible for many to live in the One.

Each, then, is represented by his stream of consciousness; and each, continuously functioning in Mind, builds around himself an aura or mental atmosphere, which, in its turn, is constantly flowing out as a stream of consciousness.

Because of the Unity of Mind, each is one with the All; and at the point where he contacts the All, he universalizes himself. This will be easily understood when we realize that man always uses the One Mind. He is in It and thinks into It; and because It is Universal, his thought may be picked up by any one who is able to tune in on that thought, just as we pick up radio messages. A radio message, broadcast from New York City, is immediately present all around the world. Hard as this concept may be to grasp, we know it to be the truth.

Let us shift the basis to mentality and we shall see that the same thing happens when we think. We think into the One Mind, and this thought is immediately present everywhere. It is in this sense that each one is universal. According to the Unity of Mind, thought is everywhere present, and so long as it persists it will be. What is known in one place may be known in all places.

No Obstructions to Thought

Time, space and obstructions are unknown to Mind and thought. It follows, then, that any one tuning in on our thought will enter into our stream of consciousness, no matter where we are or where he may be. And if we still persist after the body shall have suffered the shock of physical death, this law must still hold good; for past and present are one and the same in Mind. Time is only the measure of an experience, and space, of itself, is not apart from, but is in, Mind.

Entering the Stream of Thought

A psychic can enter the stream of thought of any one whose vibration he can mentally contact, be that person in the flesh or out of it; and since we are all psychic, all having a soul element, we are all, doubtless, communicating with each other to the degree that we sympathetically vibrate toward each other. (This explains the medium through which absent treatment takes place.)

We do not all have the ability to objectify psychic impressions, and ordinarily they never come to the surface; however, they are there just the same. This is the reason why we often feel so uneasy when in the presence of certain people, or when we mentally contact some condition, having an uneasy inner feeling but without any apparent reason.

The Vibration of a Book

As we read and study people's thought, we gradually enter into the current of their consciousness and begin to read between the lines; we are unconsciously reading their inner mentalities. This is why we enjoy reading the thoughts of the great mentalities of all ages. More that is unwritten comes to us than mere words could possibly convey.

Why Saints Have Seen Jesus

Many of the saints have seen Jesus in this way. That is, through studying His words and works, they have so completely entered His thought that they have seen a picture of Him; for the pictures of everything and everybody are hung on the walls of time and any one who can enter may read. It does not follow that these saints have seen Jesus, but that they have, without doubt, seen His likeness, or what the world believes to be His likeness, hung on the walls of time. When we look at a picture of a person we are not looking at the person, but at a likeness of him.

Many Mental Pictures

We are all surrounded by mental pictures, and a good psychic sees these pictures clairvoyantly and reads our thoughts telepathically. A good medium has the ability, more or less clearly, to bring these pictures and thoughts to the surface and objectify them; but it does not follow that he is really communicating with the people whose pictures he sees.

The Human Aura

Every one constantly radiates some kind of a vibration, and consequently is always surrounded by some kind of a mental atmosphere. This is called the aura: it extends from a few inches to a few feet from the body and sometimes even farther. It varies in color and density with the varying degrees of consciousness. In moments of spiritual realization the aura is bright yellow, merging into almost a pure white; and in moments of rage it is dark and murky in appearance. There are as many colors in the aura as there are varying degrees of thought-activity in the mentality.

Halo

The halo which artists have portrayed around the heads of the saints is real, and not an idea of the artists. There is a more pronounced emanation from the head than from any other part of the body, because thought operates through the brain more than through any other part of the human instrument.

It is said that the face of Jesus shone so brightly, at times, that His disciples could not look upon it without becoming blinded by its brilliancy.

Unpleasant Atmospheres

In a combat of wills the atmosphere sometimes appears to strike sparks as though a battle were being waged on the subjective side of life. Unpleasant people always have a disagreeable atmosphere and morbid people always depress. A radiant aura emanates from the one who lives a normal, happy life, and who is always at peace within himself.

HABIT

Habits are formed by first consciously thinking, and then unconsciously acting. But few realize that when one consciously thinks, something must happen to his thoughts. What one thinks to-day will to-morrow be a part of his memory; and since memory is active, what he thinks to-day as a conscious thought will to-morrow be submerged but active thought.

This is how a habit is formed: first it is a desire, then comes the expression of this desire, then the desire becomes subjective and the subconscious action of thought causes it to be performed automatically. First we control thought, then thought controls us.

> "First the man takes a drink,
> Then the drink takes a drink,
> Then the drink takes the man."

Constant repetition gradually forms such a thought force on the subjective side of life that the very force created, in its turn, controls the one who created it. How careful we should be about what we let down into the deeper currents of mentality! All habits are formed in much the same way; they are at first conscious; then they become unconscious or subconscious. A person may create such a strong desire that it will compel him to put it into execution; this is called mania.

MANIA

Literally speaking, mania is a desire too strong to be controlled. We speak of one having a mania for certain things; that is, he has subjectified so much desire along some particular line that he becomes controlled by the very power which he has set in motion. Morbid people are more liable to do this than normally minded ones. For instance, let a sensitive person become despondent and he may think of committing suicide. This thought, at first, may be put aside as unworthy, but as it returns it receives a little more attention, until at last it may become so strong that it is irresistible.

Most murders are committed from this mental attitude; and most murderers are people who are mentally sick. Some day this will be better understood; such people will be considered sick and will be healed mentally. This shows how very careful we should be to control our thinking, never allowing the mentality to conceive ideas which we do not wish to see manifest. After all, these things are mental attitudes, and the best way to heal them is through mental treatment.

Obsession

Obsession is another form of mental control and may or may not be conscious at its inception. People may become obsessed with desires, thoughts, ambitions, habits, suggestions or other mental influences; and if the spirits of undeveloped entities surround us, it seems entirely possible that people may become obsessed by them.

The obsession of desire produces a mania to express that desire; for thought demands an outlet. Some are so obsessed by their ambitions that they are constantly driven to the accomplishment of them. Some are obsessed by the suggestion of their environment, for the mental atmosphere of places often obsesses people, compelling them to do certain things and without any apparent reason. In studying a case of obsession we should take all the facts into consideration and reason from effect back to cause.

Personal Influence and Obsession

People often become mildly obsessed by the mentalities of those surrounding them; this is called personal contagion. Many take on the color of their environment, and this should be guarded against, for it is a mild form of hypnotism. It is, of course, brought about through the suggestive power of unconscious mental action, and may or may not be malicious. We should never allow ourselves to become controlled by anything that we do not consciously allow to enter the thought. If one feels an influence silently demanding attention, he should at once declare that there is no power, in the flesh or but of it, that can control him, except, of course, the One Perfect Mind.

Obsession of Discarnate Spirits

If we are surrounded by discarnate spirits, they, also, might control us through suggestion; that is, if we allowed them to do so. By thinking toward us with a strong desire, they might so implant this desire on the subjective side of our thought that it would come up from within, causing us to do certain things which we never consciously thought of doing. This, of course, is hypnotic influence; but all mental influence is hypnotic, varying only in degree. If it is true that discarnate spirits are around us (and it appears to be true), we should carefully guard against the possibility of any mental influence from them. The statement that ONLY THE ONE MIND CONTROLS will protect us from any and all wrong mental influences of whatever nature, whether emanating from those in the flesh or out of it.

General Theory of Obsession and Mental Influence

All obsession, of whatever character, is some form of mental influence, and can easily be destroyed by making the above stated affirmation. We should never for one instant allow the suggestions of other mentalities to control us. The day will come when people will choose the thoughts that they allow to enter the mind as carefully as they now choose the food they eat. Staying close to the thought of the One Mind is a safe and sure protection from any and all wrong mental influence.

Insanity

Insanity is the complete control of the conscious mind by the unconscious or subjective mind. Dwelling too long on one idea, or some sudden shock, seems to produce this state. It is easily healed by knowing that there is but ONE MIND, AND THAT IT CANNOT FORGET ITSELF. THERE IS ONE MIND IN GOD, AND THIS MIND IS OUR MIND NOW.

The Psychic Power Must Be Controlled

The psychic power should always be under full control of the conscious mind; otherwise, all sorts of influences may be picked up, which, operating under the guise of seemingly real individualities, control the one who admits them. When the psychic power is under full control of the conscious mind, it furnishes a wonderful storehouse of knowledge; for, being the seat of memory of both the individual and the race, it contains much that we do not consciously know.

Normal State

A normal condition would be a complete balance between the objective and subjective mentalities. This would give an immediate access to all the wisdom of the human race, and might even extend much farther, for it could give access to a higher state, which is now more or less clogged by contrary suggestions.

The subjective side of thought is the sole and only medium between the relative and the Absolute. If one were in full control of his inner mentality he could, at once, enter the Absolute, and his every word would bear fruit. Jesus was such an One.

In attempting to accomplish this we do not have to come under control of any power other than that of our inner selves and our higher selves; anything less than this is dangerous. Many seem to think that simply because they are under control they must be dealing with spiritual power. NO GREATER MISTAKE WAS EVER MADE. Jesus, Who was fully illumined, always kept His full state of conscious thought and personal volition.

THE AIM OF EVOLUTION

The aim of evolution is to produce a man who, at the objective point of his own self-determination, may completely manifest the inner life of the Spirit. Even the Spirit does not seek to control us, for It lets us alone to discover ourselves.

The most precious thing that man possesses is his own individuality; indeed, this is the only thing that he really has, or is; and for one instant to allow any outside influence to enter or control this individuality is a crime against man's real self.

THE STATE OF TRANCE

The trance state is any state of mentality that allows itself to become submerged. It varies in degree from simply allowing the mind to become receptive, which is harmless, to a complete self-denial of the objective consciousness, i.e., allowing any and all influences to be picked up. This is very dangerous.

There are many normal psychics who can, while in a perfectly objective state, read people's thoughts and perform many other wonderful feats of the mind. This is normal and no harm can come from it. It is, indeed, one of nature's ways of working and is most interesting.

NORMAL PSYCHIC CAPACITIES

Any psychic power that can be used while in a normal state of mind is harmless and helpful; that is, any psychic power which can be used while one is in a perfectly conscious state of mentality. Many have this power and find that it is helpful as well as interesting. This power can be developed by knowing that the WITHIN AND THE WITHOUT ARE REALLY ONE.

ABNORMAL PSYCHIC POWERS

Abnormal psychic powers are developed in the full trance state; that is, when the medium becomes controlled by surrounding influences. In this state some wonderful and hidden powers of mind are revealed.

In certain psychic states people can see, hear and read others' thoughts; travel abroad and perform many other marvelous feats, which in the conscious state seem impossible. No doubt the time will come when all these powers will be under the control of the conscious mind; man will then be much less limited.

CLAIRVOYANCE

Clairvoyance is a state of mentality wherein the medium is able to see things that the objective eye cannot see under normal conditions. It is the physical eye reproduced on the mental side of life, only with a greatly extended vision. Time, space and obstructions are swept away, and the operator can as easily look through a closed door as, in a normal state, he looks through a window.

PSYCHOMETRY

Psychometry is a clairvoyant state wherein the operator is able to psychometrize, or read from the soul or subjective side of things. Mention has already been made of the fact that everything has its mental atmosphere which is the result of the thoughts surrounding it. To psychometrize anything means to read from this mental atmosphere and to tell what it radiates. Sometimes the operator seems able to take a piece of ore or metal and give a perfect description of the location from which it was taken. This will explain why some mediums wish to hold an object which has been used by the sitter; for through this avenue the medium is able to enter the inner thought of the person sitting.

CLAIRAUDIENCE

Clairaudience may be called the ear of the soul; it is the ability to hear the inner voice speak, and is a most remarkable mental attribute. Some hear these voices silently, while to some they come as independent voices.

It appears as though the instinctive man tries to tell the outer man of certain things or to give him warnings. Sometimes these warnings come as visions and sometimes in dreams. This power is uncertain and should be carefully watched, as we are not always able to tell whether the impression is real or simply some suggestion of a surrounding mental influence. A good way to test this is to know that all impressions must come from the Perfect Mind.

INDEPENDENT VOICES

Sometimes independent voices speak forth, apparently from the air, and may be conversed with by the hour. I have talked with these voices, but, so far, have not been able to determine whether or not they ever told anything beyond the subjective knowledge of those present. I have been unable to satisfy myself as to whether they were caused by those present in the flesh or whether they were caused by some form of spirit life. The fact remains that such voices do speak and that they are real. I have held animated and interesting conversations with such voices hours at a sitting, and it has been a most wonderful experience; but, so far, it seems impossible to determine their exact nature. Time and a more complete investigation alone can give the real proof.

APPARITIONS

Apparitions, or thought forms, often appear during mental stress. For instance, people often see some friend just before he passes from this life. Sometimes the apparition appears before the incident takes place; an explanation of this will be made later in this chapter. This type of phenomenon is not at all uncommon; nearly every one has some record of such experiences. When one is asleep he is entirely subjective, and this will explain why so many of the above referred to incidents take place during sleep. But impressions received while in the sleeping state do not always come to the surface.

GHOSTS AND PHANTASMS OF THE DEAD

People often see the forms of those who have passed from this life. Many have been alarmed over seeing such forms, as though there might be danger from them; but whether or not we believe them to be the forms of the dead or the living, they certainly can do no harm.

It is claimed by some that ghosts are always the result of some form of violent death, and that those who pass out in a state of peace never leave a ghost behind. Of the truth of this statement I am NOT absolutely sure, since all must leave behind the forms used while in the flesh, and each must leave behind him a thought form of himself.

GHOSTS SOMETIMES CAN SPEAK

It is a well-known fact that ghosts sometimes have the ability to speak or convey some kind of a message to the living. And it is also generally conceded by those who have investigated such matters, that once a ghost has had the opportunity to speak, it is seldom ever seen again.

If we suppose a ghost to be a real entity, we can easily see how it could speak or telepathically convey a message. If, on the other hand, we assume that a ghost is only a form of thought, we can imagine that it might be equipped with the power to convey a message, after which it would gradually fade away. For thought has some power to express itself. I hold no brief for either case, since I have been unable to make up my own mind as to just what a ghost really is.

In such a case as this it is a mistake to assume anything, other than the fact that such appearances do make themselves known to people under certain conditions. The matter will have to rest at this point until further investigation proves what a ghost is.

PROJECTING THE MENTALITY

Under certain states of mentality it is possible to project the mentality and travel far from the body. Just what it is that projects is difficult to say; and we are not so much concerned about what it is that projects as we are interested in the fact that there is something about the mentality which can project itself. Since there is but One Mind, perhaps nothing has to project; perhaps we simply see through the One Mind, which must have and hold, within Itself, all that is.

CRYSTAL GAZING

Crystal gazing is a form of concentrating the mentality in such a manner as to make it possible for the subjective to come to the surface. The operator, looking steadily at a bright object, gradually becomes subjective and consequently able to read thought.

BLACK MAGIC

Black Magic has been taught and practiced from time immemorial. It is the act of thinking toward some one for the purpose of doing him an injury.

THE MODERN CURSE

To-day, black magic is called by another name, but "a rose by any other name would smell as sweet." To-day it is called malpractice. Malpractice takes several different forms; namely, malicious, ignorant and unconscious. Malicious malpractice is the act of arguing in Mind that some certain person is something that he ought not to be. In some cases it is supposed to even take the form of saying that he is not present in the flesh. If this were persisted in, and the one being damned should receive the condemnation, he might begin to feel sick; and if this were carried to a final conclusion, he would, perhaps, "pass from this vale of tears."

Mention is made of this, not as being something to fear, but as one of those things which to-day is being more or less discussed and believed in by many. So far as we are concerned, we believe only in the One Mind, AND WE KNOW THAT IT CANNOT BE DIVIDED AGAINST ITSELF. This will settle the question of malicious malpractice for all time.

We hear of people who live in constant terror of malpractice, and it seems certain that some do try to use this force to do injury to others; but no one with real understanding of the Truth will be affected by it, nor seek to use it; for this would be playing with fire; and we are the servants to the things which we obey.

If our thought is still operating on a level where such things are possible, we had better find it out, straighten up our thought and be healed; for, after all, malpractice is only wrong thought suggestion, and we do not believe in wrong thought suggestion.

Innocent and ignorant malpractice causes much disease and discomfort, through sympathy with sickness and fear for people's safety. We should sympathize with the one suffering, but never with that from which he suffers; for this would make him worse instead of better.

Automatic Writing

Automatic writing is an interesting phenomenon of the mind. It is a mental control which uses the arm and hand for the purpose of writing messages.

There are several forms of automatic writing; one, the ouija board, which is a small smooth board, upon which is written the alphabet. Upon this board is placed a small, pear-shaped, three-legged instrument, which points to the letters and spells out words. Another form is to put a pencil through the board; and still another form, and one even more interesting, is when the pen is held in the hand, which is controlled by some force not known, but supposed to be the subjective thought of either the operator or of some one present.

Some believe that the arm is under control of a discarnate spirit. Many and long have been the discussions on this point, and I do not care to enter into them; but one thing is certain, the phenomenon transpires, and many wonderful messages come through in this manner.

Independent Writing

The most interesting writing of all is what is called independent writing; that is, where the pencil simply tips up and writes without any one touching it. I have seen this done and can vouch for its reality. Here, indeed, is ample cause for speculation, and we are compelled to admit that either some unconscious force of those present grasps the pencil, or that some spirit force does.

HUDSON'S THEORY

I am well aware of the theory which Hudson worked out along these lines, but I have not been able to explain everything on his basis; and I fear that he overworked his theory.

His idea was that we have no right to assume the presence of an unknown agency when there is a known one present. In other words, he said that the phenomenon is caused by some form of mental action which he called subjective; and that we have no right to assume a spirit to be the cause when we know that there are people present in the flesh; and that, since people in the flesh, as well as those out of it, have a mind, we must assume that the phenomena are caused by those present in the flesh. By the same token, and with the same logic, it could be proved either way. That psychic phenomena are caused by some form of mental power, there can be no question; and the student of the workings of mind will rest content here, knowing that mental power can operate in independence of the physical instrument; for this is the great lesson to learn.

SMELLING WHERE THERE IS NOTHING TO SMELL

A most peculiar and interesting phenomenon takes place in the act of smelling where there is, apparently, nothing to smell. The mentality, in connecting with the vibrations of a rose, can produce its odor independently of the presence of the flower.

I have seen a case where the vibrations of a certain man were brought into the room when he was in an intoxicated condition. The smell of whiskey was so strong that the influence was asked to remove its presence. Perhaps this is what is meant by occult perfume.

GRASPING OBJECTS WITHOUT THE HAND

It is a commonly known fact, to those who have spent time investigating these things, that objects are grasped and held independently of the physical touch. This is shown in independent writing and in telekinetic energy.

TELEKINETIC ENERGY

Telekinetic energy is defined as "the ability to move ponderable objects without physical contact." This form of energy is displayed in that class of mental phenomena which cause objects to move without any physical agency, and is, therefore, caused by some form of mental energy, or by some agency other than physical.

TABLE TIPPING

Table tipping is so common as to cause but little comment, but it does help to prove a principle of mind, namely, that an object can be moved about from place to place without the aid of any physical contact.

RAPPINGS

Rappings on the walls and floor are also too common to mention, but should be classed in the category of telekinetic energy.

THEORY OF ECTOPLASM

One of the investigators has advanced the theory of ectoplasm, which is a formless stuff emanating from the body of the medium. I have no doubt but this theory is correct as far as it goes; but am not willing to advance it as being sufficient to explain all the phenomena. For instance, according to this theory, if any one stands in front of the medium the emanation is blocked and no results will follow. I have sat in a room and had a glass of water brought from another room and held to my lips while I drank it. It was a real glass and real water and I was really there, and in a perfectly normal state of mind. I could not possibly account for the above-stated incident on the theory of ectoplasm; but I could account for it through the theory of mental power.

LEVITATION

The theory of ectoplasm certainly will not account for levitation, where the body of the medium is lifted from a chair and carried to some other place in the room. This can be accounted for only on the theory that there is a power that transcends the better-known physical laws. Experience has taught that there are many things in life that cannot be accounted for on any other basis than that of a mind power which operates independent of any, and of all, physical agencies.

INTERESTING THOUGHTS

It is interesting to realize that we have such marvelous powers; and no doubt the time will come when we shall make common use of them. They are for some purpose and, as we live in a Timeless Universe, this purpose will be made known just as soon as we are ready for it.

WHAT IS THE CAUSE?

Whether psychic phenomena are caused by the agency of spirits or by some inner power of our own mentality makes no difference. That they are caused by mind power is apparent; for they are not caused by what we call physical force at all, but by some finer power than we, at present, well understand.

CAUSE FOR THOUGHT

It gives reason for thought when we realize that such inner powers exist. Some power, independent of the body, can see, hear, feel, smell, touch and taste without the aid of the physical instrument. Some power of intelligence within us can travel, communicate, project itself, recognize and be recognized, without the aid of the physical instrument. That there is a reason for this is certain; that this reason is natural and normal, no one can doubt, for nature is always natural, and only that is a mystery which is not understood.

TIME WILL PROVE ALL THINGS

Time and experience, alone, will unravel the mysteries of the human mind, with its many and varied activities. So far we have but touched the outskirts of its garments. To deny these inner attributes is not only intolerant, but is downright ignorance. It is all right to say that we do not understand them; but to openly deny them is to place us, not among the unbelievers, but among those who do not know the facts.

THE SPIRIT OF PROPHECY

Subjective mind can deduce only; it has no power of initiative or self-choice, and is compelled, because of its very nature, to retain any and all suggestions that it receives. The best illustration of this is in the creative soil, in which the gardener puts his seed. The soil does not argue nor deny, but goes to work on the seed and begins to create a plant which will represent the type of manifestation inherent, as an idea, in the seed. That is, from a cucumber seed we get cucumbers; and from a cabbage seed we get cabbages. Always the law maintains the individuality of the seed as it creates the plant; never does it contradict the right of the seed to be what it really is. Involved within the seed is the idea of the plant, as are also those lesser ideas which are to act as a medium between the seed and the plant. Involved within the seed are both cause and effect; but the seed must first be placed within the creative soil if we wish to receive a plant. In the creative soil, or in the seed, the full and perfect idea of the plant must exist as a completed thing, else it could never be brought forth into manifestation.

The idea of the full-grown plant must exist somewhere in the seed and soil if it is ever going to materialize.

A Lesson in Subjectivity

This teaches us a lesson in subjectivity. Thoughts going into the subjective are like seeds; they are concepts of ideas, and acting through the creative medium of Mind, have within themselves the full power to develop and to express themselves. But how could they express unless they were already known to Mind? They could not, and so Mind must view the thought as already completed in the thing; and Mind must also contain the avenue through which the idea is to be expressed. Every thought sets in motion in Mind the fulfillment of its purpose, and Mind sees the thing as already done.

Mental tendencies set in motion cast their shadows before them; and a psychic often sees the complete manifestation of an idea before it has had the time to materialize in the objective world.

This is what constitutes the average spirit of prophecy; for prophecy is the reading of subjective tendencies, and seeing them as already accomplished facts. The subjective mind can deduce only, but its power of logic and sequence appears to be perfect.

Explanation

For illustration, suppose that there is a window one mile away; I am throwing a ball at this window, and the ball is halfway to it, going at the rate of one mile a minute. Now you come in, measure, the distance, compute the speed with which the ball is passing through the air and say, "The ball is halfway to the window; it is traveling at the rate of one mile a minute; in just one half a minute the window is going to be broken by the ball passing through it." Let us suppose that you are the only one who sees the ball, for the rest are looking at the window; and in half a minute it is broken. How did you prophesy that the window was to be broken? By drawing a logical conclusion of an already established premise.

This is much like what happens when a psychic exercises a spirit of prophecy. They are generally unconscious as to why they do what they do, because they are getting their own subjective contact with the condition and simply interpreting what comes to them. But this is the logical, deductive, conclusive power of their subjective thought, seeing a thing completed, by first seeing a tendency set in motion, and computing the time that it will take to complete it. There are but few, however, who have any reliable spirit of prophecy.

Let us carry this thought further; the race has its subjectivity, from an individual to a nation. This is its karma, its subjective law set in motion. Each nation has its subjective causation, and the prophet of a nation could, and would, read its subjective tendency; and this is what the old prophets did, for they were psychics, every one of them, from Moses down. They were able to interpret the subjective causation of their race and so predict that certain things must follow.

There is, however, a still higher spirit of prophecy which but few have perceived, and those who have perceived it have been illumined. Within the subjective mirror of Mind there must also exist the Divine and Cosmic Purposes,—the very Thoughts of God. An illumined person, who is also psychic, might read these great Cosmic Purposes; and in this manner some of the great prophets have read the destiny of the race. They have told us that the destiny of man is divine, that he is immortal now, that he need not die to become immortal, but that HE IS IMMORTAL. It was in contact with this great Law, and from It, that Moses received the Ten Commandments, the Mosaic Law. It is through the avenue of subjectivity, which is the medium between Spirit and man, between the Absolute and the intellect, that all of the prophets have prophesied and all of the sages have taught; for it contains Infinite Wisdom, Knowledge and Law.

The subjective mind is the source of much inspiration; for it contains all the thoughts which the race has ever created, and at times one contacts these thoughts and becomes inspired by them. The subjective mind is the source of much revelation because it contains the Purposes of God, and if the soul were to turn to the One, it surely would reflect into the outer mind the Light of the Eternal.

Summary

We have shown that mind, independent of the body, can, and at times does, perform each and every function which we usually associate with the physical being. While most people may have to go into a trance state to perform these acts, there are a few who can produce the same results while in a perfectly normal state, that is, while in a self-conscious state. I wish to make this very plain, for there is a belief that an abnormal state must be entered into before these phenomena can be produced. I not only challenge such a statement, but entirely refute it as being altogether wrong. I have myself, while in a perfectly normal state, seen or experienced nearly everything that has been discussed under this heading.

I am willing to admit that ordinarily a trance state is developed before the best results can be obtained; but to say that it MUST be developed is to contradict my own experience and refute my own observations. I have never, at any time, gone into a trance state, and would no more consider doing so than I would consider jumping from the roof of a ten-story building. If, then, I were to refute my sanity during these experiences, by what manner of judgment could I consider myself to be sane at all? It is useless for those who know nothing at all about psychic phenomena to deny its reality. I can understand any one saying that he does not understand it, but I cannot grasp the position of an individual who denies something of which he is entirely ignorant.

We will say then THAT EVERY ACT OF THE HUMAN INSTRUMENT WHICH WE CALL THE BODY CAN BE REPRODUCED THROUGH SOME AGENCY WHICH IS NOT PHYSICAL, OR THROUGH SOME AGENCY THAT PHYSICS CANNOT EXPLAIN. We will call this agency some power of mind with which we are not yet well familiar. It is all simple enough, anyway, for our bodies could not move unless we were here to move them, and so every act is mental, even though we use the body as an instrument.

I can find no explanation for the above-stated facts, unless we suppose that we have a mental body which reproduces the physical one; and which can function without its counterpart, and is entirely independent of it.

It makes no difference whether we attribute the phenomena to spirits or whether we say that we are unconsciously producing it ourselves, THE FACT WILL STILL REMAIN THAT THE PHENOMENA ARE PRODUCED and can be accounted for only on the basis that we either have a mental body, which acts independent of the physical one, or that the power of thought alone, and without any physical instrument, can operate upon matter. Personally, I prefer to accept the theory that we have a mental body, since this appeals to me as being more reasonable and certainly much more human.

If we assume that spirits have the ability to move ponderable objects without physical contact, we are assuming that they have a mental body, or that they operate their thought to produce the phenomena. For, once granted that the phenomena are really produced, it is self-evident that some kind of an explanation must be forthcoming.

There are but two possible answers from what is to-day known: either the minds of departed souls or the minds of those present in the flesh produce the phenomena. This eliminates any other possible agency, for the theory of ectoplasm cannot answer all of the facts.

LESSON SIX: PSYCHIC PHENOMENA AND IMMORTALITY

The Meaning of Immortality

Immortality means to the average person that man shall persist after the experience of physical death, retaining a full recollection of himself and the ability to recognize others. If his full capacities go with him beyond the grave, he must be able to think consciously, to reason, will, affirm, declare, accept, reject, know and be known, communicate and be communicated with; he must be able to travel about, see and be seen, understand and be understood; he must be able to touch, taste, smell, hear, cognize and realize. In fact, if he is really to continue as a self-conscious personality, he can do so only to the degree that he maintains a continuous stream of consciousness and self-knowingness.

This means that he must carry with him a complete remembrance; for it is to the remembrance alone that we must look for the link that binds one event to another, making life a constant stream of self-conscious expression. To suppose that man can forget and still remain himself is to suppose that he could cut off the entire past and at this moment be the same personality that he was a moment ago. Remembrance alone guarantees personality. Individuality might remain without remembrance, but not so with personality; for what we are is the result of what we have been, the result of what has gone before.

Man, then, if he is to have an immortality worthy of the name, must continue, as he now is, beyond the grave. DEATH CANNOT ROB HIM OF ANYTHING IF HE BE IMMORTAL.

Where Did Man Come from and Why?

It is useless to ask why man is. It can only be said of man that he is; for if we were to push his history back to some beginning, we should still be compelled to say that he is. If man's life is of God, then it comes from a source which had no beginning; and so the question as to why he is must forever remain unanswered.

God could not tell why God is; to suppose that Life could give an excuse or reason for being would be to suppose an absurdity. Life Is, and right at this point all inquiry into Truth starts, and from this point alone must this inquiry continue.

We are not so much interested in why we are, as we are interested in what we are. That we are some part of Life, no one can deny and keep faith with reason. Let us not bother about questions that can never be answered, but pay attention to those which have an answer.

MAN AWAKES WITH A BODY

When man first woke to self-consciousness, he had a body and a definite form, showing that Instinctive Life, which is God, had already clothed Itself with the form of flesh. Body, or form, is the necessary outcome of self-knowingness. In order to know, there must be something that may be known; in order to be conscious there must be something of which to be conscious. Some kind of a body or expression there always was and always will be, if consciousness is to remain true to its own nature.

WHAT IS THE BODY?

Body is a concrete idea, existing in time and space, for the purpose of furnishing a vehicle through which Life may express Itself. The physical universe is the Body of God; it is a manifestation of the Mind of God, in form. It is that Creation which, while It may have beginnings and ends, of Itself neither begins nor ends. The Manifestation of Spirit is necessary if Spirit is to come into Self-Realization; hence, Body.

MATTER

We say that body is composed of matter, but what is matter? Science tells us that matter is an aggregation of small particles arranged in some kind of form; we are also told that matter is in a continuous state of flow. Strange as it may seem, we do not have the same physical bodies that we had a few months ago; they have completely changed; new particles have taken the place of the old; and the only reason why they have taken the same form is, that Instinctive Man has provided the same mold. Our bodies are like a river, forever flowing; the Indwelling Spirit alone maintains the identity.

If we assume that immortality simply means persisting in the physical body, then we already have immortalized ourselves many times right here on earth.

THE ETHER OF SCIENCE

We are now being taught that the ether is more solid than matter. We know that the ether penetrates everything; it is in our bodies, at the center of the earth, and throughout all space. This means that within our present bodies there is a substance more solid than the body which we see. This idea is very far-reaching; for it shows that we might have a body right within the physical one, which could be as real as the one of which we are accustomed to think. If Instinctive Man has molded the outer body in form, why should It not also mold the inner one into definite form? There is every reason to suppose that It does and no reason to suppose the opposite. In all probability, there is a body within a body to infinity. "In my Father's house are many mansions."[99]

We do not depart from reason when we assume this; for, while we used to say that two bodies could not occupy the same space at the same time, we must remember that we were talking about only one plane of expression. The new idea of matter and ether has PROVED THAT MORE THAN ONE BODY MAY OCCUPY THE SAME SPACE AT THE SAME TIME; for it has been proved that there is a substance which can occupy the same space that our body does. No doubt, as time goes on, it will also be proved that there is something still finer than the ether; this may go on to infinity. There is every reason to suppose that we have a body within a body to infinity, and it is our belief that we do have.

The Resurrection Body

The resurrection body, then, will not have to be snatched from some Cosmic shelf as the soul soars aloft, but will be found to exist already WITHIN; EVERYTHING IS FROM WITHIN, FOR LIFE IS WITHIN. The resurrection body of Jesus shone so that it could not be looked upon, because it was a more spiritual one than the physical eye is used to beholding.

Conclusive Facts

The facts are conclusive that we have a spiritual body now, and do not have to die to receive one. We now remember the past, and have already outlived the physical body many times during life. It looks as though we were already immortal and would not have to die to take on immortality.

If there are many planes of Life and consciousness, perhaps we only die from one plane to another. This thought makes a strong appeal and seems to answer the question completely.

In What Mental State Do We Go Out?

Some think that death robs us of the objective faculties, and that we pass out in a purely subjective state; but we are unable to follow the logic of such an assumption. To suppose that the

---

99 John 14: 2.

objective faculties die with the brain, is to suppose that the brain thinks and reasons. This is proved to be false through the experience of death itself; for, if the brain could think, it would think on and on forever. No; the brain does not think; the thinker thinks through the brain, perhaps; but of itself, the brain has no power to think or feel. Detach the brain and it will not formulate ideas, nor work out plans. THE THINKER ALONE CAN THINK.

It is logical to suppose that we pass from this life to the next in full and complete retention of all our faculties. Jesus revealed Himself to His followers after His resurrection, to show them that death is but a passing to a higher sphere of life and action. To know that we maintain an identity independent of the physical body, is proof enough of immortality. This, together with the fact that remembrance maintains a constant stream of recollection, and the realization that mentality can operate independently of the body, performing all of its normal functions without its aid; and that the new theory of matter and ether furnishes proof of the possibility of a body within a body to infinity; and that the Instinctive Man is constantly forming matter into the shape of a body, should prove to any one that we are not going TO ATTAIN IMMORTALITY; BUT THAT WE NOW ARE IMMORTAL.

What Causes Psychic Manifestations?

It would be interesting to know whether the spirits of the supposed dead cause the manifestations which we see in the séance chamber. One thing is certain: these manifestations are either caused by those who are supposed to be dead, or else they are caused by those now in the flesh; for, since they happen, something must make them happen. Whether the manifestations are caused by the dead or the living, the agency used is either a mental body or the direct power of thought operating upon objects. Of course, in the conveyance of mental messages, telepathy explains the agency; but in physical manifestations, some kind of contact either takes place or else thought directly works on objects.

Hudson, in his "Law of Psychic Phenomena," carefully goes through an elaborate process of reasoning, the result of years of painstaking investigation, and completely proves that all of the manifestations do take place. He then goes through an extensive argument to show that they are not caused by spirits, saying that we have no reason to suppose the presence of an unknown agency, when we know that there is one present who could be producing the phenomena. Now, if our reasoning power is correct, and it is proved that physical manifestations take place through some power that is mental, and if it is proved that those who have passed on might still be near us, then we cannot see where the argument against spirit agencies could be considered perfect. We are inclined to feel that the very facts in the case prove that these manifestations could be produced by either the living or the dead; and such, we believe, to be the case.

Telepathy Does Not Explain Everything

Telepathy does not explain everything. It may explain much, but certainly not all. Telepathy could not explain certain visions which people sometimes have when passing out. We once knew a woman who practically passed out and was, indeed, thought dead for nearly a day and night; but was finally restored to consciousness to continue here for another year. She plainly saw and talked to several members of her family who had gone on some years earlier. It is not strange that those who have gone before are interested in us and wish to see us when we go over. If we had friends in London and were to send word that we were coming over, they would certainly wish to meet us. Our friends on the other side must be just as interested in us as they ever were.

Telepathy cannot explain how Jesus could take some of His more advanced disciples aside and let them talk with the departed. It clearly states that this incident took place; and, if we cannot believe this, how can we believe any of the other events in the life and experience of this most remarkable Person?

Spirit Communication

There are thousands of cases on record where people have penetrated the veil of flesh and seen into the beyond. If we cannot believe the experience of so many, how can we believe in any experience at all? Of course, there is a large field for deception, and it is not probable that all communications are real; but, to state positively that they are all illusions, is to throw the lie into the face of human thought and say that it never sees clearly. There is certainly more argument and evidence in favor of the theory of spirit communication than against it, and, so far as we are concerned, we are entirely convinced of the reality of this evidence.

If spirits really exist, and if we all live in One Mind, and if mentality can communicate with mentality without the aid of the physical instrument, then spirit communication must be possible; and since we know that the above-stated facts are true, we have no alternative other than to accept the conclusive evidence and realize that while it may be difficult to communicate with the departed, yet it is possible.

Communication Must Be Mental

It is evident that any such communication must be mental; it would be thought transference or mental telepathy, at best. Now if the supposed entity knows that we wish to communicate with it, and if it is consciously present trying to communicate with us, then it must, by the power of its thought, cause its message to come up through our subjectivity to an objective state of recognition; consequently how very difficult to receive a coherent message! For instance, suppose that one tries to think a lecture to an audience, how much would they receive? Yet this is exactly what would happen under the very best condition if the departed were trying to impress our thought. I believe that they do seek to communicate with us and that they often succeed, perhaps more often than we realize; but I repeat, "How difficult it must be!"

Whether or not the spirits are present is uncertain. Just because a psychic sees the picture of a person around us, does not mean that he is really there; for the pictures of all our friends are always in our mental atmospheres. It is quite absurd to suppose that at any time we wish we can call any one we ever knew and make him talk to us. We are unable to do so here; and psychological and metaphysical laws are the same on every plane.

WE DO NOT CONTROL SPIRITS

To suppose that we can compel the attention of one out of the flesh, any more than of one in it, is an absurdity. And if we could, what would we hope to gain? People out of the flesh know no more than they did when in the body. I believe that we do communicate with the subjectivity of those who are departed, whether they know that we are doing so or not; but the messages that come, in our present state of evolution, are very incoherent. I believe that an unconscious communication goes on, more or less, all the time, and that those people whom we have greatly loved are still conscious of us; and are, without doubt, seeking to influence us; but it could only be a mental influence. We might feel a vague sense, much as the niece of Oom Peter did in "The Return of Peter Grimm." She felt a vague sense of her uncle; that he was trying to impress her with his thought and desire. She felt a blind groping, and that is probably the best that we would get.

THE PSYCHIC POWER SHOULD NOT BE FORCED

We all have psychic capacities, but they should never be forced; for it is only when the subjective comes to the surface while in a normal state that a normal psychic power is produced. The average psychic must go into a semitrance to let the subjective come through; this is never good nor right, but is always destructive. The psychic capacity is normal only to the extent that it can be used while in a self-conscious state. Don't misunderstand what I am saying. It is known as the "power of darkness," but is all right if understood. Many people are bothered by their psychic powers, constantly seeing things, continually getting impressions; they are very near the surface of subjectivity, and it bothers them. This can easily be healed and should be.

There is a normal psychic capacity, and some are able to discern mental causes with perfect ease. Jesus was such a One; He was able to tell the woman that she had been married five times, and that the man with whom she was living was not her husband. He read that out of her thought; but He did it while in an objective state; for He was able to consciously and objectively exercise His subjective faculties. This is perfectly normal; but to let go of the volitional and choosing faculties, which alone constitute individuality, and become immersed in subjectivity, is very dangerous. One might become obsessed by discarnate spirits, earth-bound entities, elementals, thought forms, desires or other forces floating around; for we cannot close our eyes to the fact that all of these things do exist.

It is a crime against individuality to allow the conscious faculties to become submerged. We should control the subjective and not let it control us. The teaching of the illusion of mind sprang up because men of wisdom perceived that people might mistake the shade for the reality, the form for real substance, the hollow voice for revelation, and thereby be misled. That is why they warned against these things and against having familiar spirits; and they were absolutely right. Never let any voices speak to you unless you are in perfect control of the situation. Never admit any mental impressions or images that you do not wish to receive or that you cannot receive consciously. Say: "There is no power in the flesh or out of it but the One, which can enter my consciousness. Anything that obeys the One, conforms to the One, believes only in the One and comes only through the consciousness of the One, is perfectly welcome, but anything other than that cannot come."

The only value that an understanding of psychic phenomena can have, is that without it we do not understand the complete workings of mind. We do not understand experiences people often have; and in a consistent philosophy which deals with mind, the lack of an understanding of psychic phenomena would be inexcusable. For any one in this day to say that powers of clairvoyance, telepathy, thought transference, clairaudience or telekinetic energy are not exercised, is to admit his own ignorance.

These things do happen and are continuously happening in more and more instances. The thing to do is not to deny what happens, but to find a logical and scientific explanation of it. It is our business to explain all mental action, in so far as it is explainable; and so we must find an answer which will cover the law of psychic phenomena. Mind, with the laws governing It, is the whole answer, for each plane reproduces the one next to it; and psychic phenomena are reproductions of man's physical capacities on the mental plane. "What is true on one plane is true on all."

Note: Read and carefully study "Law of Psychic Phenomena," Hudson; "Life After Death," Hyslop; "The Unknown Guest," Maeterlinck; "Science and Immortality," Lodge; "The Hidden Power," Troward; "From the Unconscious to the Conscious," Geley.

LESSON SIX: RECAPITULATION

Psychic phenomena are the phenomena of the soul, or subjective mind. The subjective mentality is man's atmosphere in Universal Mind; it is the seat of his memory and the avenue through which Instinctive Life works.

The subjective mentality, being deductive only in its reasoning power, is compelled to retain all of the impressions that it receives, but, of course, these impressions can be erased, consciously.

Man is Universal on the subjective side of life, and in this way is connected with the subjectivity of all with whom he is in harmonious vibration.

Mental suggestion operates through the subjective mind, and a silent influence is always going on through this avenue in the form of race-suggestion. A silent communication takes place at all times between friends on the subjective side of life; when it comes to the surface, it is called mental telepathy.

The subjective mind, being in contact with the race-thought, has a much greater knowledge than the conscious mind. It is through this avenue that human inspiration comes. Orators and actors contact the subjective side of their audiences and, in this way, wield a tremendous influence. Singers, poets and writers enter the subjective race-thought and interpret it; this enables them to depict the race-emotions.

Each person has a subjective mental emanation or atmosphere which is the result of all that has ever been consciously or unconsciously said, thought or done by that person. The mental atmosphere of a person is his power of attraction. It is the result of his inner thoughts. The mental atmosphere of a place is the result of all that has been thought, said or done in that place. The mental atmosphere of a place is its power of attraction. We love those places whose mental atmosphere is one of love and peace; this is why we like our homes. The home should always be kept sacred and its atmosphere should always be one of love.

Things are possessed of a soul element and continuously emanate this atmosphere.

Each city or town has a special atmosphere which is the result of the mental emanations of those who inhabit it. The same may be said of nations; each has its national mentality.

The history of the whole race is subjectively written on the unseen walls of time, and may be reproduced by one who can read the race-mentality.

Telepathy, which is the act of reading subjective thought, takes place through the medium of Universal Subjectivity. In order to mentally receive a message, and bring it to the surface, one must be in tune with the vibration of that message.

Since the whole field of subjectivity is Universal, it follows that everything that has ever been thought, said or done, is retained in the race-thought; and since this field is a unit, all of the vibrations are ever present, and may be contacted at the point of any one's mentality.

In his objective state, man is separate and distinct, but on the subjective side of life he is universal.

The conditions necessary for the best results in psychic work are faith and expectancy; this is because the subjective mentality is the seat of the instinctive emotions and responds to feeling.

A psychic, going into more or less of a subjective state, is able to enter the vibration of an individual's thought and read from the book of his remembrance. The personal reading seems to be limited to the subjective remembrance, although this is often very far-reaching.

Each maintains a stream of consciousness in the One Mind, and any one contacting this stream may objectify it. Because of the Universality of the Medium, the individual stream of consciousness is always omnipresent, whether the one from whom it emanated be in the flesh or out of it.

Time and space are unknown in Mind, the past and the present are one. In reading the thought of people set down in books, we enter their vibration, and in studying their thoughts we enter their stream of consciousness.

Every one who ever lived on earth has left behind a mental picture of himself; these pictures are often seen when one is in a subjective state. This does not mean that we really see the person; what we see generally is the picture.

The human aura is the mental vibration or emanation of the individual. The idea of the halo surrounding the heads of the saints is explained in this way. The personal atmosphere varies with the changing thought and emotion, and is sometimes pleasant and at other times unpleasant.

Habits are formed through conscious thought becoming subjective, and in its turn, controlling the one through whom it operates. Mania is a strong desire, subjectified, which becomes an obsession.

People may become obsessed with their own ideas or with those that operate through them from some foreign source, whether this source is from some one in the flesh or out of it. Obsession is always some form of mental suggestion. Insanity is the loss of the objective faculty.

The psychic power must always be controlled. A normal state is a perfect balance between the objective and the subjective faculties. This is the aim of evolution: to produce a man who, at the point of his objective faculty, may perfectly control the subjective. A trance state is abnormal, and only that psychic faculty is normal which is under full control of the self-discerning mind.

Clairvoyance is the ability to see without the physical eye. Psychometry is a clairvoyant state wherein the medium is able to enter the subjective side of things and read the atmospheres surrounding them; this is why mediums often wish to hold some familiar object in their hands while giving readings.

Clairaudience is the ear of the soul. Independent voices sometimes come from the air, proving that some inner power is able to express itself audibly. Apparitions are thought forms, and may come from the living or from the dead; at times they come as a warning.

Crystal gazing is for the purpose of concentrating the mind, in order that it may become subjective.

Black magic, the curse of malpractice, all mean the use of thought power for destructive purposes.

Automatic writing takes place when the arm is under control of the subjective mind of the operator or by the subconscious mind of some one else, either in the flesh or out of it; it is a form of suggestion, either conscious or unconscious. Independent writing is where the pencil writes without physical contact. This shows that some inner power has the ability to grasp solid objects without physical contact. Table tipping and rappings are from the same source. It is thought by some that these manifestations come from the agency of what is called "ectoplasm," or a subtle emanation of the body; this theory, however, does not explain all of the facts. Mind alone can do this. Levitation or the ability to move the body is another fact well known to investigators.

The power of prophecy is limited to some subjective tendency already set in motion; for mental tendencies cast their shadows before them. There is a higher power of prophecy which contacts the Cosmic Purposes and reads the thought of God.

Man reproduces, on the mental plane, all of the physical faculties.

IMMORTALITY

Immortality means that the individual shall persist after the experience of physical death, carrying with him a complete remembrance and an unbroken stream of consciousness; for if man be immortal, death cannot rob him of anything.

Man cannot conceive of himself, either as being born or as dying; he lives, and cannot think of himself from any other standpoint. Even though a person should conceive of himself as dying and imagine his own funeral, he would still have to conceive of himself as consciously being there, and so prove that he did not die at all. It is the same with birth; we can imagine being born into this world, but we cannot imagine the self as being non-existent; for, while thinking of the self as being born, we are still consciously thinking; thus proving that we were before we were physically born.

All inquiry into the Truth starts with the self-evident proposition that Life Is.

When man first woke to self-consciousness on this plane he already had a body. Consciousness always clothes itself in some kind of form.

Matter, from which the body is made, is a fluent substance, forever taking the form that intelligence gives it; it flows in and out like a river; we yearly immortalize ourselves, so far as the body is concerned.

The ether, being more solid than matter, proves that we could have a body within the one that we now occupy. Since matter in form is only a certain rate of vibration, it follows that, in dealing with Infinite Life, we are dealing with an infinite number of vibrations; consequently, we might have a body within a body to Infinity.

In reality, the body is a spiritual idea; the flesh simply covers it for the purpose of providing a physical instrument through which Spirit may function on this plane.

Man departs this body only to find himself already equipped with another one. He carries with him every attribute that he now possesses, and goes forth in complete retention of his individuality.

Since there is but One Mind, it follows that it is possible to communicate with the departed; but, as the communication must come through the subjective, it is difficult to receive clear messages; and it is impossible to know whether or not the ones with whom we think we are communicating are consciously present.

It is never safe to go into a trance state in order to communicate with the departed, as in so doing, one might subject himself to the mental influences of lesser mentalities. Individuality is sacred and must never be tampered with nor controlled, except by the conscious mind.

The value of an understanding of psychic phenomena lies in the fact that they are the phenomena of Mind and must be accounted for.

Every plane reproduces the one just below or just above it; psychic phenomena are the reproductions, on the mental plane, of the principle just below the mental, which is the physical.

PART THREE

SPECIAL ARTICLES

ABSOLUTENESS AND RELATIVITY

Absolute is defined as, "Free from restrictions, unlimited, unconditioned." "The Unlimited and Perfect Being, God."

Relativity is defined as, "Existence only as an object of, or in relation to, a thinking mind." "A condition of dependence."

The Absolute, being Unconditioned, is Infinite and All; It is that Which Is, or the Truth. It is axiomatic that the Truth, being All, cannot be separated, limited nor divided; It must be Changeless, Complete, Perfect and Uncreated.

Relativity is that which depends upon something else; and if there be such a thing as relativity, it is not a thing of itself, but only that which functions within the Absolute and depends on It.

We wish to affirm relativity without destroying Absoluteness. This can be done only by realizing that the relative is not a thing apart from, but is an experience in, the All-Comprehending Mind. The relative does not contradict the Absolute, but affirms It; and the relative alone guarantees that there is an Absolute.

The Absolute is Cause, the relative is effect; the Absolute depends upon Itself, being Self-Existent; the relative must depend upon the Absolute.

We should be careful not to deny the relative, simply because it is not absolute. To suppose that there could be an Absolute without a relative, would be to suppose that there could be an unexpressed God or First Cause; this is unthinkable and impossible. The Consciousness of God must be expressed, hence the relative. The relative is not apart from, but is in the Absolute; and, as such, it is perfectly good and necessary. Time, space, outline, form, change, movement, action and reaction, manifestation and creation, all are relative; but all are real.

Relativity subsists within existence and inherent Life is potential and latent with limitless possibilities.

The relative and the Absolute do not contradict each other.

THE PROBLEM OF EVIL

Evil will remain a problem as long as any one believes in it. This may sound rather startling until one has taken the time to think the matter through to a conclusion. Evil, of itself, is neither person, place nor thing, but is only a certain use that we make of life. We call that evil which we feel is the wrong thing to do; but our ideas of good and evil change with the unfoldment of our thought about, and belief in, life; for what was thought to be good yesterday, is to-day considered evil; and what, yesterday, was considered to be evil, is to-day called good.

Generally speaking, we may consider evil to be that which is destructive in its nature, and good to be that which is constructive.

Evil, then, will disappear in the exact proportion that we cease using destructive methods; and good will appear to the degree that we embody constructive methods. To turn from evil and do good is the desire of every soul who is consecrated to the Truth; this we can do only as we cease talking about, believing in, or doing evil.

The problem of evil will continue to be a problem just as long as we believe in it. Good will appear only as we embody it. Each soul has within a sure test, a something which directs and guides it. This Something is the Spirit of God and It knows no evil.

As there is no sin but a mistake, so there is no punishment but an inevitable consequence. As long as we make mistakes we shall be sinning; and just so long, we shall automatically be punished; for the law is certain and sure. As we turn to the Good, we will stop doing evil and, therefore, stop sinning.

The problem is solved as we turn from all that hurts, all that is destructive, all that denies the Good, and turn with our whole being into the Light and toward the Truth. Evil is swallowed up in the Good as we learn to live daily in the Presence of God. "I will forgive their iniquity and I will remember their sin no more."[100] That is, it will be completely blotted out; it will cease to be.

With our whole heart, with our whole being, in sincerity and honesty, with a complete trust in the Good, yearning toward It with a soul-desire that will be satisfied, we should turn to God, as the Supreme Presence, as the Complete Life, forsaking any belief in evil; we should turn so completely to the Spirit that our souls will become illumined by the Light Eternal.

Evil will cease to be when we stop looking at it; it never really was and is but a supposition. Let us, then, turn to the Path of Light and look to the God Within. Let us say, "Thou Infinite, Indwelling God, within me, knowing no evil, teach me of Thy ways, and in Thy wisdom make me wise. Almighty God within me, direct me into the way of the All Good." Let us turn completely from any and every belief in evil and do good. The problem will thus be solved and we shall realize that only the Good remains.

THE MEANING OF THE FALL

The story of the fall typifies race-experience as brought about through its belief in duality. Man is created perfect; that is, he starts on his journey as a perfect being, but he also starts as an individual; and this, of course, means that he starts with self-choice. Self-choice would have no real meaning unless it were backed by the power to externalize this choice and experience the effect of it. Man has the ability to choose and to externalize his choice; for he is a real individual.

THE GARDEN OF EDEN

The Garden of Eden typifies man's original state of perfection before he began to have experience. The Tree of Knowledge means the Life Principle which can be used both ways. It bore the fruit of the knowledge of both kinds of experience, good and evil, freedom and limitation. Man must choose which kind of fruit he will eat. "Choose ye this day whom ye will serve."[101] Man makes his choice consciously but generally in ignorance. The serpent typifies the Life

---

100 Jer. 31: 34.
101 Josh. 24: 15.

Principle viewed from the materialistic viewpoint; it casts man from his perfect state through his belief in duality and separation. Man chose to depart from Good, and man alone must choose to return to It. God lets him alone; for he is a free agent and may do as he wills with himself. When man decides to return to his Father's House, he will find that his Father is still there. "Act as though I am and I will be." "Onlook the Deity and the Deity will onlook thee," "Be firm and ye shall be made firm." "As thou hast believed so be it done unto thee."[102] "Ask and it shall be given unto you; seek and ye shall find; knock and it shall be opened unto you."[103] God's Creation is Perfect and we must wake to the fact and know that we are now in the Kingdom of Heaven.

SALVATION AND GRACE

As the fall of man was brought about through his own act, so the rise of man will be accomplished through his own act. God already Is. Salvation is not a thing but a Way; the way of salvation is through the realization of man's unity with the Whole. Grace is the givingness of the Spirit to Its Creation and is not a special law, but is a specialized one. In other words, Grace Is, but we need to recognize It. It is not something that God imposed upon us, but is the logical result of the correct acceptance of life and of a correct relationship to the Spirit.

We are saved by Grace to the extent that we believe in, accept and seek to embody, the Law of Good; for the Law of Good is ever a Law of Liberty and never one of limitation. Limitation is not a thing, but is a belief. Freedom is a Divine Reality, while limitation is an illusion, a false belief.

Salvation is an act of man and not an act of God. Man damned himself and man must save himself, if he ever is saved. He will save himself to the exact degree that he stops damning himself. He will live in Heaven when he stops living in hell. He will be healed when he stops being sick. He will become rich just as soon as he stops being poor. He will become as God when he stops masquerading as the devil. He will be happy when he stops being miserable. He will be at peace when he stops becoming confused. He will be filled with joy when he stops thinking sadness. He will live when he stops dying. He will be perfect when he stops looking upon imperfection; and he will be saved when he stops damning himself. HE WILL BE ONE

---

102 Matt. 8:13.
103 Matt. 7:7.

WHEN HE STOPS BEING TWO. MAN, MAN, MAN, MAN, MAN, MAN, MAN; "The great Thou—*I*—and the great I—Thou."

THE PERFECT UNIVERSE

We must realize the Perfect Universe if we wish to embody the greatest good. If the Universe were not Perfect It could not exist for a single moment. It is self-evident that we live in a Perfect Universe; and, if so, then everything in It must also be perfect.

The Truth is Indivisible and Whole. God is Complete and Perfect. A Perfect Cause must produce a Perfect Effect. Disregarding all evidence to the contrary, the student of Truth will maintain that he lives in a Perfect Universe and among perfect people; he will regulate his thinking to meet this necessity and will refuse to believe in its opposite. At first he may appear to be weak; but as time goes on, he will prove to himself that his position is a correct one; for that which appears imperfect will begin to slip from his experience.

To daily meditate on the Perfect Life and to daily embody the Great Ideal is the way to sure salvation; this is a royal road to freedom and is happiness to the soul of man. We cannot afford to believe in imperfection for a single instant. Let us learn to look as God must look, with a Perfect Vision; let us seek the Good and the True and believe in them with our whole heart; let us say daily to our inner selves: "Perfect God within me; Perfect Life within me, Which is God; Perfect Being within me, Which is God, come forth into expression through me and become that which I am; lead me into the paths of perfection and cause me to see only the Good."

By this practice, the soul will become illumined and will acquaint itself with God and be at peace. "Be ye therefore perfect, even as your Father Which is in heaven is Perfect."[104]

IMAGINATION AND WILL

Coué announced a great truth when he said that imagination is superior to the will; but he did not explain the philosophy behind this truth. It is a fact that what he said is true, but we wish

---

104 Matt. 5 : 48.

to analyze the fact and discover the reason back of it; for if anything is true there is always a reason for its being true.

Will is an assumption, pure and simple. We do not will to live; we live because we have life and cannot help living. The use of the will could not make us anything that we are not; for it is not possible to get out of a bag anything that the bag does not contain. We live because life is within us. Perhaps this is what Jesus meant when He said, "Which of you, by taking thought, can add one cubit to his stature?"[105]

We did not make Life and we cannot change It, but we can use It; and the use of Life is through the imagination; because this faculty has, at its roots, the very well-spring of life and action. Imagination carries with it feeling and conviction, which mean life and action; it awakens within us all the finer forces of nature and stirs into action latent powers which otherwise would never come to the surface.

At the very root of the whole matter we find that the Creative Power of the universe does not create through will, but through imagination; imaging, feeling, and knowing. To suppose that God must will things to happen would be to suppose that God had some opposing force to contend with.

Will power may be necessary in its place, but as a creative agency it is non-existent; it is not creative but directive; and used from this standpoint it is a wonderful force; whereas, used from any other angle, it becomes destructive and will mentally weary the one using it. To feel that we have to will things to happen casts doubt into the face of Creation and presupposes that Life is not Self-Existent and Self-Propelling.

Imagination taps the very roots of Being and utilizes the same Power that brought the worlds forth from Chaos. "The worlds were framed by the word of God."[106] Imagination is the power of the word, while will is the directive agency, denoting the purpose for which the word is spoken.

Man reproduces the power to create and, in his own life, controls his destiny through the activity of his word. This word cannot be willed; but it can be imagined, or imaged forth, into expression.

---

105 Matt. 6: 27.
106 Heb. 11: 3.

HOW TO VISUALIZE

Visualizing means mentally seeing the things that you wish to have or to do. When you mentally see the things you desire, and see them very clearly, you are presenting Universal Mind with images of thought; and, like the creative soil of the ground, It at once tends to project them into form. If the thought image is clear it provides a good mold; if it is imperfect the mold is a poor one. This does not mean that one must set his mind or hold thoughts; it simply means that he must think clearly. There is no power in holding thoughts; indeed, the real secret of successful mental work is to loose thought and let Mind operate upon it.

The first thing to do is to decide what you wish to image into Mind. After having become composed in thought, begin to see the complete outcome of your desires, in mental pictures. Suppose that you wish to demonstrate a home; you should know just what kind of a home you wish. Of course, if you simply thought of house you would get something, but the more definite the picture the better the results will be. In order to make the picture complete, decide just what kind of a home you wish to live in; then, in the silence of your thought, mentally look at this house; go from room to room, stopping here and there to look at some piece of furniture or at some picture on the wall. Make the whole thing real, as far as possible; enter the house, sit down and feel that you are actually living there, saying, "I am now living in this house." You have set a word in motion through the Law which will bring a realization of your desire, unless you, yourself, neutralize the picture by doubting it. Do this every day until the house appears. Use the same process in visualizing anything.

In order that you may fully understand just what I mean, I will illustrate by drawing a mental picture which I will ask you to follow as you read these lines. Imagine that you are with me; we will suppose that I am a man about six feet tall, with light hair and complexion. We are sitting on the front porch of a house that is painted green; it is a two-story house and sits quite far back from the road; there are tall trees standing in front of the house through which the sun is shining. We can see the little shadows as they play upon the porch through the open spaces between the trees. The breeze is gently blowing and the leaves are waving back and forth. I am talking to you, saying, "Let us take a walk together." We immediately rise from our seats, which are made of wicker, and walk down three stone steps to a gravel walk, leading to the street. As we go out through a stone gate we are suddenly met by a dog which is running along the street; he is a large, yellow dog, and is running rapidly. We watch him as he runs, barking, down the street, till he turns a corner,—and our picture is at an end. Now, if you have carefully imaged each step in the above picture, you will understand what visualizing means.

THE SEQUENCE OF THE CREATIVE ORDER

In the creation of any form it is necessary for its image to exist in Mind before it can come into realization in the external. The Law, being only a neutral force, cannot initiate anything, and cannot, of Itself, choose to create anything. It is a Doer only, not a Knower. The Word alone knows; so we may assume that each word is a law unto itself, through the One great Law of all Life.

MAN'S CREATIVE POWER MARVELOUS

Man's creative power in his world is marvelous; for every time he thinks he sets the Law in motion. As his thought sets the Law in motion it is specializing It for some definite purpose; and in this way his word becomes the law unto the thing which he speaks. Of course man never really creates, but his use of Creative Power makes his word creative through the Medium of Mind. This should give to all a sense of freedom and a realization that there is neither competition nor monopoly. It leaves each to work out his own salvation, not with fear or even trembling, but with a calm sense of peace and assurance.

CONCENTRATION

To concentrate means to bring to a point. To concentrate the mentality means to bring the thinking to bear on one point of interest and to hold it there. Concentration has little to do with will power. Indeed, the misuse of will often renders concentration impossible.

The simplest practice for concentration is always the best. Nature always works along the lines of least resistance; and mental power is only a force of nature and should always be thought of in a natural way.

If you wish to concentrate on some particular idea or thought, bring the attention to it; then hold it there, but without effort. At first you may find that the thought wavers; do not oppose this, but mentally brush the wrong thought aside, much as you would brush a fly from the face with the hand. Be sure that you make no great mental effort, feel at ease and at peace, gently bringing the thought back to the point of attention.

Let us illustrate this by supposing that one is going to concentrate on the thought of happiness. Taking the word "happy" into the mentality, say, "I am happy"; without effort or mentally trying, just think the words, "I am happy." In a few minutes you may find that your thought has begun to wander. Right here be sure and not bring the attention back with a bang; just say again, "I am happy," making no effort to destroy the other thought, but returning to the starting point, "I am happy." Make the whole thing easy and natural, and soon you will find that you can hold the attention as long as you desire.

It is always a mistake to oppose thoughts that interfere; when one begins to do this he will at once find that he is resisting something, thereby disrupting his whole meditation.

It is unnecessary to concentrate on an external object; for CONCENTRATION IS ALWAYS FROM WITHIN AND NEVER FROM WITHOUT. The only place that the mind can know is within itself.

In concentrating, lay aside all will power and resistance, letting the thought realize the words upon which you wish to concentrate. This will be found a simple but most effective method, and by far the most prolific of results.

In teaching a child to concentrate, it is well to have him take something in which he is particularly interested. As a child's mind wanders more or less aimlessly about, it is well to have him write some thought on paper; and, looking at it, see how long he can center his interest on the mental picture that the words suggest.

THE MIRROR OF THE SUBJECTIVE

It has truly been said that Mind is a mirror. If we could realize how completely this law works, no doubt we would greatly alter our manner of thinking. It is impossible to create even the slightest thought without causing some reflex action in Mind; and the deeper the emotion the deeper will be the penetration of thought and the more complete will be the reaction.

Thought is the most subtle of all the forces which we know anything about, and but few understand what a tremendous power it has, either for good or for ill. To learn how to control one's thought means knowing how to control one's body and destiny.

Subjective mind can reason only deductively; consequently, it is compelled, by reason of its nature, to accept whatever thought gains entrance to it. So the mirror of Mind is, in reality, the working of the law of cause and effect through the mentality. The subjective mind, being the seat of memory, must contain all the thoughts which have ever gone into it, whether these thoughts have been conscious or not. But when a person is told that he has thoughts which he never consciously created it is a little hard to understand. He must realize, however, that constant contact with life opens the door to many impressions which were never consciously created. This fact, together with the realization that whatever falls into the subjective mind must be acted upon, answers the question.

Of course, we do not imagine that certain things are going to happen to us; but we do think certain kinds of thoughts which, brought to their logical conclusions, would produce definite effects. Remember that the subjective mind reasons deductively only; and all this becomes quite evident.

The subjective side of thought, being the creative agency within, must at once set to work to produce anything which is given it, no matter what the emotion may be. How wonderful! But this shows how very careful one should be in choosing the kind and type of emotion to be made into form; for something must happen to all the thoughts which submerge.

The subjective mind never argues nor contradicts what is put into it; the thought is at once accepted and acted upon. If one says that he is sick, it at once begins to create a sick condition; for, like a mirror, it reflects; and being creative, what it reflects it tends to create and to cast forth as a condition.

Like any other natural force, subjective mind was not created by man and he cannot change its mode of operation; but, while he may not change a natural force, he may change his manner of approach to it. Man cannot change his own inherent nature; but he can, and should, learn to make the best use of all his forces. Subjective mind will never change its own nature, but will always reflect to the thinker what he thinks into it. Man did not make this law nor can he change it; but, like any other law, once understood, it becomes an obedient servant.

The use of this law is entirely mental and is within the grasp of every one; it is so simple that all can understand; it is the law of mind in action, and this law is set in motion by correct thinking and knowing.

But how few know why they think or what they think! How few control even the slightest emotion or allow the emotions to express in a constructive manner! No doubt the time will come when a complete control of the subjective will be gained and man will then be much less limited.

But the race is made up of individuals, and the place to begin is right at home. We, who have affirmed these great laws of mind to be realities in the human experience, must so prove them in our expressions of life that the rest, looking on, may read the sign and follow the signal. It is possible to do this, and the reward is great.

At first the road may be hard and beset with many difficulties; there may be failures and discouragements; but the end is certain. We fall, only to rise again into a greater realization of life and action; and, like the pilgrim of old, to renew the journey. We shall need a backbone instead of a wishbone here as in all other places. It is not in wishing but in knowing and in doing that we shall find the reward of true merit. It behooves each one to make the effort to consciously control the processes of his thought.

This does not mean sitting around in some dark corner with the hand at the brow, impersonating Socrates or Plato; it means out in the world, in the midst of affairs, at home and abroad, wherever our work takes us. We need not leave the world; for we may engage in all of its activities without being controlled by them; we may be in the world of affairs as masters and not as slaves.

Surely this hope, held before the waiting thought, will so stimulate our endeavors that we shall go forth into life and the great game of living with a new song upon our lips and a new joy within, springing forth into the dawn of a new day.

PERSONALITY

Personality is the result of man's experience; it is the sum total of all that he has said, done, felt, thought, hoped for and believed in; it is the result of his reactions to the events of life as they come and go. Factors to be considered in the development of personality are heredity, race-suggestion, environment, child training, education, auto-suggestion and, indeed, anything and everything that impinges upon consciousness. Therefore, we are what we are and where we are because of the nature of our accumulated consciousness.

Factors Necessary for a Dynamic Personality

It goes without saying that all people desire a dynamic, radiant personality; and it is self-evident that certain qualities are essential to produce this result. The external personality really reflects the soul, and its building may be likened to a mental garden where the harvest depends upon the kind of seed that is sown. Each one chooses for himself just what kind of materials he will use and each builds according to the pattern of his own desires. "Whatsoever a man soweth, that shall he also reap."[107] Just as a fine architect uses only the best materials and plans most carefully how to construct his building, so should we, in the building of personality, choose most carefully the kind of materials we wish to use.

---

107 Gal. 6: 7.

HIGH CHARACTER.—First of all, it should be founded upon the rock of high character, high ideals, and built for Eternity as well as for to-day.

SINCERITY.—Sincerity in every human relationship is essential.

ABILITY.—To be a master of one thing and to daily improve.

ENTHUSIASM.—A keen interest in people and things at home and abroad; it has been called "The Fortune-Teller of Life." Enthusiasm is compelling and sweeps everything before it.

SERVICE.—Service is the keynote to success and implies constructive work; also, loyalty to your work and to all concerned in it.

WHOLESOMENESS.—A clean-minded man with high ideals is always sought after. The reading of fine books, listening to good music and becoming acquainted with the best in art and literature will soon implant in the mentality a quality of wholesomeness that is most desirable.

SUCCESS.—A consciousness of success must be developed; this can be done by creating clear pictures of success and working toward them daily. Decision and assertion are aids to this end and must not be overlooked.

SELF-CONFIDENCE.—Implies peace and poise and knowing what to do in every situation.

POWER AND STRENGTH.—Are also born of peace and poise.

SENSE OF HUMOR.—This is most necessary to have, as it lightens the burdens of life and makes one's self and others happy. Without it things seem dull and drear. This has no barb or sting and implies the ability to laugh at one's own expense.

GOOD MANNERS.—Not servile but courteous.

TACT.—Saying or doing the right thing at the right time.

THOROUGHNESS.—Implies system and the ability to carry things out to a definite conclusion. This quality is essential to success.

CHARM.—Personal charm is that indefinable something which makes every one a friend. It is the result of genuine friendliness, sympathy, kindliness and unselfish interest in others.

MAGNETISM.—The result of an abundant vitality on the physical plane; of intellect and temperament on the mental plane; and of atmosphere or consciousness on the Spiritual plane.

TENDERNESS.—Sympathetic union with people; real compassion.

LOVE.—The Universal Urge to express, the Self-givingness of Spirit.

ORIGINALITY.—Try to create; do not imitate; think for yourself. Read Emerson's Essay on "Self-Reliance."

INCENTIVE.—Have wholesome ambitions and definite objectives which are constructive in their nature. Any ambition is wholesome which brings only good results to one's self and all concerned.

SUITABLE HUMILITY, SIMPLICITY AND GENUINENESS.—These attributes keep one from being over-ambitious and from being too aggressive.

EMOTIONAL CONTROL.—Presupposes poise and self-mastery.

SPIRITUALITY.—Looking for the good in all and having faith, belief, and trust.

HEALTH.—Is a great factor in creating a dynamic, vibrant personality.

VOICE.—A clear, resonant, well-modulated tone at all times.

DRESS.—Clothes reflect one's idea of "The Eternal fitness of things." Colors particularly have a peculiarly subtle effect on the wearer and upon those with whom he comes in contact.

Strictly speaking, personality is the use that we make of our individuality. Individuality means that which we really are; it means the point in Life where we exist and can say, I AM. Perhaps it could be defined as a point in Mind where Life recognizes Itself as some Person. Each person is an Individualized Center of God-Consciousness, a self-knowing center of Life and Action.

It follows, then, that personality is much greater than it seems to be; for it is the use of Divine Individuality and has, back of it, a limitless possibility. It is the coming forth of God, or Life, into Self-Expression.

Man's personality is not a thing to be lightly spoken of or decried as human or ineffective. Within and behind it are boundless possibilities, and few, indeed, realize what a tremendous power it wields, either for good or for ill.

To-day we are hearing much about this power and the way to develop it; for as yet we express only in part, being unaware of the Whole. Latent forces surge to express through man; Divine impulses seek expression through him; a Cosmic Urge forever beats against the threshold of his consciousness, demanding expression; hence, all his subtle longings and unspoken thoughts.

To develop or express the self is the great need of the human race; but though feeling, sensing, inwardly knowing and realizing a greater good, man stumbles blindly along the pathway of life, expressing only in part.

Like all the other faculties of the Great Within, personality may be consciously unfolded and expressed, if we let it come through.

We all desire a powerful personality, and all may have one if they pay attention to a few fundamental facts of Being; for personality is the expression of something that already exists and simply needs to be allowed to come forth.

Any one wishing to develop a pleasing personality must first become pleasant. He must think pleasant thoughts. All animosity and vindictiveness must be swept aside if the soul is to express itself in terms of greatness.

There is no place for smallness in the full life and no place for meanness in the liberal mind. A broad-minded, tolerant attitude must be maintained toward all. This is not a goody-goody idea but a plain statement of fact.

A sense of calm and peace is essential to a well-rounded personality. The din and roar of the outer struggle for existence must not find entrance to the soul if Reality is to be expressed.

Poise and balance are the mainsprings of reality and cannot be overlooked. We are not attracted to people who are always fussed up and fretful, who are never satisfied and are always unhappy. Misery and unhappiness are unknown to the Spirit of man, and we should make them unknown to the outer man.

Sensitiveness and morbidity must be swept aside as unworthy of the great Ideal. Refuse to have the feelings hurt. Friends do not wish to hurt the feelings of those whom they love, and none but friends need be admitted.

Personality is but half expressed until we realize that within we are complete. Wholeness is the keynote to perfection and self-esteem is not egotism but is self-realization. Completion is from within and not from without; and no one can add to, or take from, that which is already complete. The Soul and Spirit are already perfect and whole.

Love is the great loadstone of Life; and without this quality of Spirit, shining through Life's action, everything becomes dull and drear. Goodness and human kindness are the handmaids of Love and Life, and cannot be separated from Reality.

Irritation, vexation and confusion go hand in hand to rob man of his birthright to peace, comfort and harmony. As children of the dust they must be brushed aside as unfit companions of the soul.

Anger and malice, revenge and animosity cannot breathe the same atmosphere as goodness and purity, and they will fall away as we climb to those heights where the Indwelling Spirit lives.

Self-confidence and courage go hand in hand with real worth and are but the declarations of man's Wholeness. There is nothing petty or little about greatness.

Mental alertness and animation but signify that man lives in a life of everlasting interests and activities.

Honesty and sincerity show forth the fundamental principles of Being, and without them man expresses only a makeshift of himself, a false and deluded sense of Reality. No real person can be dishonest or insincere. Truth alone shines to Eternal Day.

The complete, well-rounded, dynamic personality contains all of these qualities and attributes; and they will come forth into expression to the exact degree that we allow them to flow through us.

Personality is not false but real; it is the shining through of the Real Self,—the man God made.

Physical appearance has but little to do with those inner, subtle powers of attraction which decide what the Indwelling Ego is to attract to Itself. The Inner Man transcends all that is external and compels attention without effort. To be conscious of this Inner Self is to know the Real Man, to know the truth about personality and the power of attraction. As a rose unfolds, so the personality of man unfolds and blossoms forth into complete expression.

A few simple practices will soon develop such a powerful personality that it will become a magnet, drawing to its center with a force that cannot be denied. THESE PRACTICES BEGIN AND END WITHIN MAN; FOR HE IS THE CENTER OF HIS OWN UNIVERSE, AND NOTHING HAPPENS TO HIM UNLESS HE LETS IT.

Know that Life flows through you and cannot be hindered in Its expression. Know that the All Good is yours now. Act, think, believe, speak as though you were now all that you have ever dreamed. AND BE SURE THAT YOU BELIEVE THE SAME THING ABOUT ALL PEOPLE FOR NONE OF US LIVES UNTO HIMSELF ALONE, BUT EACH LIVES UNTO ALL, WITHIN THE ONE LIFE.

Live constantly from this inner conviction, never stooping to anything less than the All Good; and you will soon discover that something is taking place that never took place before in your experience. DO NOT TRY TO MAKE THINGS HAPPEN; SIMPLY KNOW THAT THEY ARE HAPPENING.

Daily realize your Unity with the Whole and the Unity of the Whole with you. YOU WILL SOON DEVELOP SUCH A POWERFUL PERSONALITY THAT ALL WHO COME IN CONTACT WITH YOU WILL WISH TO REMAIN IN YOUR PRESENCE.

REPRESSION AND SUBLIMATION

The Spirit of Sex

We have discovered, from the preceding chapters, that the Universe is threefold in Its nature. It is Spirit, Soul and Body; Spirit as the active, projective, masculine factor; Soul as the receptive, creative, feminine factor; and Body, which is the result of the union of Spirit with Soul. The Spirit impregnates the Soul with Its Ideas, and the Soul gives form to these Ideas and clothes them with flesh. But this is the Trinity of Unity, a Triune Oneness; for the Three are really one.

Life is Androgynous, i.e., It contains within Itself both the masculine and the feminine factors. The male and the female of Creation come from One Principle; all come from the One and all will return to the One: all are now in the One and will forever remain in the One.

DESIRE

Back of all manifestation must be the desire to create, the urge to express; this is called the "Divine Urge." But this Urge, operating as Law, produces energy. Desire gathers energy for creative purposes and utilizes power to express itself. So dynamic is this Urge that it will cause a little seed to break open the most solid earth, in order that it may express itself in the form of a plant. It is the coming forth of Spirit into expression, the loosing of energy into action, and is apparent in all Creation.

THE SPIRIT IS EXPRESSED

The Spirit, being Absolute, is always expressed; It has no unfulfilled desires. IT IS ALWAYS SATISFIED AND HAPPY BECAUSE IT IS ALWAYS EXPRESSED. Creation is the result of the desire of Spirit to express Itself; It is the unfoldment of the Divine Ideas, Evolution is the time and process of this unfoldment. Involution is the idea in Mind, and evolution is the coming forth of the idea into expression. Involution precedes evolution, and evolution follows involution with a mathematical precision, propelled by an Immutable Law.

That which is involved must evolve, else the Spirit would remain unexpressed. As this is unthinkable, we may set it down that evolution, or the manifestation of desire and energy, is bound to take place whenever desire sets power and energy in motion. From this law we cannot hope to escape, and it would be useless to make the attempt.

MAN REËNACTS THE DIVINE NATURE

Man, as we have discussed, reënacts the Divine Nature and makes use of the same Laws that God uses. We find in man the same androgynous nature that we find in God. This nature we call his objective and subjective faculties. His objective mentality impregnates his subjective with ideas; and in its turn, the subjective, gathering force and energy, projects these ideas into forms.

Back of every act of man is some form of desire to express. This desire, of course, is purely mental in its nature. All that man is, is his mentality, both conscious and subconscious, plus what he expresses.

The Divine Urge is strong in man and constantly causes him to seek some form of self-expression. It is Divine because It is the desire of Spirit to express Itself through him; and like all the other forces of Nature, this energy can work through man only at his bidding; consciously or unconsciously, for he is an individual and has self-choice.

This Urge or Energy is called "Libido," which means "The emotional craving, or wish, behind all human activities, the repression of which leads to psycho-neuroses."

Congested Emotions

The energy set in motion through this urge is the dynamic power of Mind, and unless it becomes expressed, it will congest and cause a conflict within the mentality.

Inhibited action produces conflicts and complexes which mentally tear and bind; and as they manifest their physical correspondents, they produce nervous disorders. It is claimed that a large percentage of diseases is caused by the suppression of some form of emotion. This does not necessarily mean the suppression of the sex emotion, but might mean any desire that remains unexpressed. Some form of desire is back of every impulse that the mind can conceive, some impulse to express life. Any unexpressed desire will eventually cause a complex. Things will stand just so much pressure and no more; when the limit is reached an explosion will follow, unless some avenue for expression is provided.

Irritation, Agitation and Fear

People who are constantly being irritated have suppressed some desire to speak their minds. It may not appear as though this were the cause, but thought is very subtle, and only a careful study of its workings reveals the real facts. All irritation and agitation are mental in their cause, and a sense of calm and peace alone can heal them.

Fear is an intense emotion, and if bottled up, secretes poison in the system. Fear must be removed from the mentality if one is to be healed and is to function normally.

Anger, malice, vindictiveness and kindred emotions are but subtle forms of fear arising from a sense of inferiority. All of these emotions must be swept off the board if one is to gain peace, calm and poise. The union of peace, with calm and poise, alone can give birth to power; for without these attributes of reality, power is dissipated and lost in the shuffle.

IF WE WERE EXPRESSED

If we were completely expressed we would never become sick or unhappy. The average person goes through life expressed only in part and always with a sense of incompletion and dissatisfaction. Something must be done to make the individual complete if he is to remain normal and happy and really live.

EMOTION AND INTELLECT

Emotion is strong in man, and in the well-balanced person it is controlled by the intellect; but in many people there is a conflict between the emotions and the intellect; and in too many cases the emotion gains the ascendency.

Our strongest emotions center around the ideas of fear, hate, love, sex, and worship, with all of their many ramifications and meanings.

Emotion, uncontrolled, produces chaos; unexpressed it produces confusion, conflict and complex; for energy will have an outlet. Bottled up, it creates a pressure that is the cause of much damage to the physical man, and produces most of our nervous disorders. Expression is normal when the intellect decides how the emotion is going to manifest. "He that is slow to anger is better than the mighty; and he that ruleth his spirit than he that taketh a city."[108]

THE CONFLICT OF DESIRE

When an emotion conflicts with the will and becomes suppressed it returns to its subjective state, but remains active; it will come up in some other form; it will not be put down. It may remain in a subjective state for years; but eventually, unless neutralized, it will manifest. Let one go for years with some unexpressed longing and he will have created such a desire that it will have become irresistible in its inclinaton toward expression.

People often become seething caldrons within because of inhibited action. Energy must find an outlet.

THE EMOTION OF SEX

Human love and the affections often go hand in hand with sex desire, even when not recognized as such. An affectionate nature is generally a passionate one. Love is the most wonderful thing

---

108 Prov. 16 : 32.

in the world and creates the highest form of energy known to the mind of man. It will be expressed at the level of the passions or else become transmuted into Spiritual Coin of real and lasting value. But the ideas on sex are likely to become over-emphasized in modern literature along these lines. Sex is normal in its proper sphere; if it were not, it would not be; for nature does nothing without some good and ample reason.

The True Meaning of Love

The true meaning of love is a wonderful thing; for it is the desire of the soul to express itself in terms of creation. Creation is brought about only through the self-givingness of the lover to the object of his love. This is why, when we love people, we will go to the limit to help or serve them; nothing is too great, no sacrifice is enough. The true lover gives all and is unhappy in not having still more of himself to give to the object of his adoration.

Because of our emotional nature, love is generally expressed through the sex desire. But too great an expression of this desire is destructive, for it depletes the vitality and demagnetizes the one who overindulges. This is the meaning, and the whole meaning, of the story of Samson and Delilah. "He that hath an ear, let him hear."[109] All people look, and occasionally some one sees.

Sex Not Necessary to the Expression of Love

The sex relationship is not necessary to the expression of real love. Love is the givingness of the self, and if this givingness is complete sex will take care of itself. But energy must have some outlet. It is only when the unexpressed desire remains in the subjective that destruction follows in its wake and strews the shores of time with human derelicts. Liberty and license, freedom and bondage, heaven and hell, happiness and misery, good and bad, all, all, are tied up in human desires. Energy is energy and will be expressed or blow the top off, just as a pipe will stand only so much pressure before bursting. Millions are daily being blown up, mentally, and physically, through the suppression of desires. Desire is a dynamic force and must be taken into account.

When Sex Becomes Destructive

Sex desire becomes destructive only when it remains an unexpressed longing. This theory is not put forth to encourage free love nor to advocate indiscriminate relationships; for neither

---

109 Rev. 2 : 7.

the one nor the other is believed in by the writer. It is stated as a fact patent to any thinking person. "Libido," may be expressed through more than one avenue; through transmutation, freeing life's energies and lifting them into an avenue of constructive expression; or through sublimation, transfusing the essence of energy into high action and producing a magnetism that is irresistible and wonderful in its scope. The atmosphere of one thus charged is complete; for the energy then takes the form of real Love and is the highest and most powerful vibration on the physical plane.

MALE AND FEMALE

Man, coming from Unity, is both male and female, and has, within himself, both attributes of reality. In some the male predominates; in others the female. We have two distinct types in man and woman; but they are types of one fundamental principle. There is also an intermediate sex; that is, one in which the two attributes seem to be almost equally balanced. The greatest men and women of the ages have belonged to this type, for it is a more complete balance between the two which are really one. But this is too great a topic to discuss in this course of lessons.

THE SOLUTION

The solution to the problem of desire is to transmute any destructive tendency into some form of action that is constructive. However, an intellectual form of expression alone will not do this, for only those things to which we may give the complete self will solve the problem. Love is the givingness of the self to the object of its adoration. We should all have something that we love to do, something that will completely express the self, something that will loose the energies of Life into action and transmute the power into creative work. We should learn to love all people and not just some people.

It is very disastrous to feel that we cannot live unless we possess some one individual, body and soul. This is not love but is an idea of possession, which often becomes an obsession. No soul is really complete until he feels complete within himself.

This does not exclude the great human relationships which mean so much to all of us; but it does take the sting out of life and does free the individual to love all, adore some, and find happiness everywhere.

To feel that love is unrequited creates a longing so intense that it tears the very heart out of life, and throws the one so feeling into a fit of despondency from which it is, indeed, hard to recover. This feeling is met in the Truth by knowing that Love is Eternal and Real and cannot be added to nor taken from.

This may seem like a hard teaching; but the problems of humanity deal largely with the human relationships, and until they are harmonized, there can be no lasting happiness.

Happiness is from within, like all the other qualities of the Spirit. Within, Man is already complete and perfect; but he needs to realize this truth.

I can imagine some one saying: "This is too impersonal a teaching." It is not impersonal at all; this does not mean that we care less for people; indeed, we shall find that for the first time in life we shall really care; but the sting will have gone.

Refuse to have the feelings hurt. Refuse yourself the pleasure and morbidity of sensitiveness. Come out of the emotional intoxication and be YOURSELF. Never allow the thought to become depressed nor morbid. Engage in some form of activity that will express the better self. Do not attempt to draw life from others; live the life that God gave you; it is ample and complete. "But," people will say, "I believe in affinities." If by this one means that each is only one-half of a real person and must find the other half in order to be expressed, he is mistaken. Such persons usually find a second affinity as soon as the first disappears. We all have a natural affinity for each other, since we all live in One Common Mind and in One Unified Spirit. It is all right if we wish to specialize on some particular love; but the hurt will remain unless love has a broader scope than when narrowed down to one single person.

Live, love and laugh! Let the heart be glad and free; rejoice in the thought of life and be happy. Realize God, in and through all, and unify with the Whole. Why take fragments when the Whole is here for the asking?

Psycho-analysis

Psycho-analysis is a system of analyzing the soul, or the subjective mentality. It is a mental process of diagnosis which seems to be technically perfect when used by those who understand it. It goes into the past and unearths the objectively forgotten emotions, brings them to light and causes them to be self-seen and so dissipated. It is based upon the theory that Nature is Perfect and when let alone will flow through man in a perfect state of health. The purpose of the analysis is to uncover the complex and heal the conflict, through removing it. It takes into account every experience that the individual has ever had, paying much attention to his early training, and more especially to his mental reactions to life.

It is a wonderful system, and in the hands of the right people, is prolific of much good. But, in the thought of the writer, it is a thing without a soul, a skeleton without flesh. It lacks the warmth, the fire and the reality of spiritual realization. It is useless to remove a mental complex, unless at the same time we place in its stead a real realization of what life means. It is useless to tear down unless, at the same time, we build up. The proper analysis of the soul, coupled with real spiritual recognition, will do wonders, however, and is well worth while.

SELF-ANALYSIS

Go through a process of self-analysis; look into your own past and carefully remove every complex. This is easily done by the one who is not afraid to look himself in the face. Find out what you are afraid of and convince the mentality that there is nothing to fear. Look the world squarely in the face; sift the mentality to its depths, removing every obstruction that inhibits the free flow of those great spiritual realizations, such as will be found in the meditations that follow these lessons.

METAPHYSICS

The right kind of mental work will go beneath the surface and destroy the subjective cause of the complex, thereby easing the conflict. It will then supply a Spiritual Realization that will open the avenues of thought to the great Whole. This alone is real and lasting.

THE ATONEMENT

Atonement is defined as reconciliation: "To make an expiation for sin or a sinner," and "To be at one." The definition for sin is, "To commit sin, transgress, neglect or disregard the Divine Law; to do wrong or offend." Literally speaking, sin means missing the mark or making a mistake. "There is no sin but a mistake and no punishment but a consequence." To assume that man could sin against God would be to suppose that a Divine Law could be broken. To suppose that Divine Law could be broken would be to assume that man has the power to destroy Divine Harmony and wreck the universe with his actions.

Man may have power to go contrary to Law, but certainly he has no power to break it. Man cannot break a law, but the law can break him if he goes contrary to it.

There is no doubt but that all of man's troubles come from his disregard of law, through ignorance. There can be no doubt that much of his trouble will be over when he comes to understand the law, and to consciously coöperate with it.

We live in a Universe of Law and a Universe of Love. The Law of God is Perfect, and the Love of God is also Perfect. The Law of God is the way in which the Spirit works; the Love of

God is the Self-Givingness of the Spirit to Its Creation. The unity of Love and Law produce a harmonious Universe and a Perfect Creation.

Man, because of his individuality and the use that he makes of it, may go contrary to both Love and Law; but so long as he does this he will suffer. This is the real meaning of sin and punishment.

Man has gone contrary to the Law of Harmony and Love, and no doubt this is the reason for all his troubles. He will be saved to the degree that he returns to a state of harmony and unity with God and with Life. He can do this only as he first comes to realize that God is Love and that he lives in a Universe of Law.

The greatest lesson that can be taught to the race is the lesson of Love and of Law. The lesson of Love teaches us that Life gives and that God is Good; while the lesson of Law teaches that there is a way to freedom through real Love.

If Love is the Self-Givingness of Spirit, then that man who most completely loves, will most completely give of himself to Life. The man who loves his work gives himself to it; the one who loves his art gives himself to it. We give ourselves to our friends and to our families and to the causes which we really love. Love is always the giving of the self to something; but the idea of self-givingness is not a morbid one and should never be thought of in this light.

We have always thought of the Atonement of Jesus as the act of His giving Himself, through suffering on the cross, as a sacrifice for the sins of the world. But God surely does not need that any man shall suffer for Him, nor sacrifice himself to please Him. This would, indeed, be a limited idea of the Divine Being. God does not need an At-one-ment, since He is already at one with Himself and with all Creation. It is man; not God, who needs an At-one-ment. The act of atonement must be on the part of man and not of God. Man may need salvation, but God is already conscious of Complete Life and Being.

MAN'S WHOLE TROUBLE

Man's whole trouble lies in the fact that he believes himself to be separated from the Source of Life. He believes in duality. The At-one-ment is made to the degree that he realizes the Unity of Good. Man needs, and always has needed, to know the Truth about himself and God; and anything that helps to fill this need would be an act of atonement.

Now a man who had reached the understanding at which Jesus must have arrived would find the ordinary channels of expression inadequate to portray His concept of Life. Jesus could have had no desire to become rich; neither did He wish to be made a king, nor to receive the plaudits of the world. He wished to show to the world what the Love of God could really mean in the lives of men; He wished to show that the Self-Givingness of Spirit is complete; to prove that Life completely gives of Itself to Its Creation. This He could do only to the degree that He let God become Man through His own Individuality.

CAREFUL PREPARATION

The whole thought and attention of Jesus was given to the accomplishment of one supreme purpose: to show that God is a Living Reality in the lives of all men. He must show the Nature of the Divine Being; he must take the place of God and reveal the Love and tender care of the Creator for Its Creation. No more complete plan was ever organized in the mentality of an individual than the plan of Jesus to prove the reality of Spirit.

His thought, being psychic, that is, being able to read mental causes, told Him just what would happen if He did this. (See chapter on Prophecy in lesson on Psychic Phenomena.) He knew that he would have to suffer physical agony, and for a time, at least, be misunderstood and abused. He also knew that the lesson would prove for all time that God is Love. He knew that in the end the lesson which He was to teach would be accepted by all; and in this way He would become a Living Witness to the reality of Divine Love and Goodness.

Carefully He worked out His plan and patiently He waited for the right time to come to complete His life work; and when this time came, He unflinchingly gave of Himself to the necessity of the case. Man must come to understand God if he is ever to realize his own nature; he must come to know Spirit as a Living Reality and not as a myth.

THE VICARIOUS ATONEMENT

The Vicarious Atonement was the conscious giving of the Self to the needs of the human race— an example for all time that God is Love. Jesus perfectly understood the Law of Life and consciously chose to make an example of Himself that would cause all people to see what a real At-one-ment could mean. In order to do this, He had to take on the sins of the world; that is, He had to enter into men's mistakes in order to rectify them; not because God demanded this, but because man needed the example.

The suffering of Jesus, as He contacted the disorders of men's minds, was His vicarious atonement for the race. It was a wonderful example of what one man could do in proving the Unity of Good.

Any person who contacts the race-mind with the desire to lift it above its own level, will, thereby, go through a vicarious atonement. But the thought of morbidity that theology has given to the message of atonement is entirely erroneous. It is not a morbid thing but a glorious one. Atonement could not be morbid, but must always produce a realization of Unity and of

Good. The life of Jesus is not a sad story, but is the account of a Man Who so completely realized His own At-one-ment that He had realization to spare and to give to all who believe in His teaching. His life was a triumphant march from the cradle into Eternity, and not from the cradle to the grave. He swallowed the grave in victory, because of His At-one-ment. Jesus left no grave and no dead man behind Him.

The At-one-ment, then, is a glorious recognition of fulfillment and completion. The vicarious part is lost in the greater realization of Unity and of Good. Jesus is the most Triumphant Figure of all history and the only Man, of Whom we have record, Who completely knew His own Nature. All thought of sin, shame, iniquity, poverty, sickness, obscurity and death are swept away with the empty tomb. No wonder that this lesson still remains and His teachings still hold good, for Reality never changes.

The Givingness of Spirit

As the human side of Jesus gave way, more and more, to the Divine Realization, He more and more completely became Divine; that is, He more completely became God, Incarnated in and through Man. In this mystic way He took the place of God, and we may, perhaps, bay that through Him God proved the Love of God. Of course this is a crude way of putting it, but it does serve to point a moral and is, perhaps, the best way that we can conceive of the greatest lesson of all history.

The World Has Learned All That
It Should Through Suffering

The world has learned all that it should through suffering. God does not demand that man suffer; and man suffers simply because he is ignorant of his own nature and because he misuses his power. Jesus proved the Truth and departed this life in joy, having fulfilled His Divine Mission. The lesson has been taught and the evidence is complete. The grave has been swallowed up in the Victory of Life and Love; and the tomb is empty for all time. "Why seek ye the living among the dead?"[110] The time has come for rejoicing and not for sorrowing; for the fulfillment of that peace which was promised. "Peace I leave with you."[111] There need be no more sorrowing nor crying; for Reality is now known. Life is Triumphant and Love reigns Supreme.

---

110 Luke 24:5.

111 John 14:27.

OUR PART IN THE ATONEMENT

The Vicarious Atonement is over, but the real At-one-ment has only begun. We are just beginning to realize what Love and Life mean. Every time we give of ourselves to others, helping them to overcome their troubles, we are performing an At-one-ment; we are proving the Unity of Good.

THE PERSONALITY OF GOD

In our metaphysical abstractions we have come to the conclusion that God, or First Cause, must be Infinite; and it is difficult to perceive how a power which is Infinite can, at the same time, be personal. Yet the soul longs for a responsive universe; and the heart yearns for a God Who responds to the human desire.

To take from the individual his idea of God as a personally responsive Intelligence, and leave him only a cold, unresponsive Law, is to rob the individual of his greatest birthright and to throw him, naked and bare, into the midst of an Eternity which holds no attraction.

To think of the Universe in terms of Law only, is to make of God only an Infinite It, a cold and bitter Principle, lacking that warmth and color which the soul craves.

This difficulty is removed when we realize that the Law of Mind is like any other law; it is a natural force, and, like all law, should be thought of from this angle. But back of, and working in and through the Law, there is a responsive Intelligence and a knowing Spirit, Which is God, the Father of all; and Who responds to all.

We will think of Mind, then, as Law, and of God as Love; we will use the Law and love the Spirit back of, and through, the Law. In this way, we will be robbed of nothing, but will see that the way to freedom is through Love and by Law.

JESUS AS A SAVIOUR

Jesus stands forth from the pages of human history as the greatest Figure of all time. His teachings contain the greatest lesson ever given to the human race; and His life and works, while on earth, provide the grandest example that was ever given to man.

In the Higher Thought no attempt is made to rob Jesus of His greatness or to refute His teachings; indeed, the Higher Thought Movement is based upon the words and the works of this, the most remarkable Personality that ever graced bur planet with His presence; and, until a greater figure appears, Jesus will still remain the great Wayshower to mankind, the great Saviour of the race.

Let us not waste time, then, in theological discussions which lead nowhere; but, following the example set before us, let us also do the works which He did. "The works that I do, shall he do also; and greater works than these shall he do, because I go unto my Father."[112]

SELF-EXISTENT LIFE

The most important thing that any student of the Truth can understand is the real meaning of self-existence. Whatever the nature of First Cause is, It must be Self-Existent, or else It could not be at all. It is, perhaps, hard to comprehend that there must be, and is, a Power which exists simply because It is what It Is; and yet this is the mainspring of all right metaphysical work and endeavor.

We must come to believe in, and trust, that Power of Life and Intelligence which is God, or First Cause. We must understand that we deal with First Cause whenever we think, at any, and at all, times. If we had to gather energy with which to energize the Creative Principle of Life, where should we go to get the energy with which to energize It?

We are constantly thrown back upon the fundamental proposition that Life already Is; and that we use a Power which already Is. Let us then, without doubt or fear, throw our word into that Great Receptivity and trust It to do the work.

THE SUPREME AFFIRMATION

Strange as it may seem, the human thought can affirm only; it can never deny; for, even at the moment of denial, it really affirms the presence of that which it denies.

We speak of denials and affirmations as though they were opposed to each other, but such is not the case. Fear and faith are but different ways of expressing positive beliefs about something. Fear is a positive belief that we will experience something that we do not wish to have happen, while faith is a positive belief that we will experience something that we do wish to have happen.

---

112 John 14 :12.

The nature of Being is such that real denial is impossible; for there is but One Mind in the Universe, and It is always "yea and amen."

We are constantly affirming our way through life; and since affirmation is the only mental action possible, it behooves us to find the greatest affirmation and use it.

The Supreme Affirmation is "I AM"; and, as such, It was given to Moses. This affirmation is constantly with us, and every time we speak we use it in some form. We must be careful to use it only as an upbuilding force.

CHRIST AND ANTICHRIST

The Spirit of Christ is the spirit of one who understands the Law and who uses It for constructive purposes only.

The spirit of Antichrist is the spirit of one who, understanding the Law, uses It for destructive purposes.

The Law, of Itself, is neither good nor bad, but is a Neutral Force, obeying all, and may be used for any purpose. But those truly instructed in the Law will never attempt to use It destructively; for they will understand that, by so doing, they would subject themselves to the very power which they have set in motion.

There is a power surrounding us which can be used either way, that is, constructively or destructively; but one instructed in the Truth will use this power only for the good of all. A most solemn warning is given to any one who would be so rash as to misuse his power.

If the thought is kept close to Good, to Love and to the Spirit, and if there is never any desire to do other than that which is constructive, there is no danger.

The Law is there to use and It is a Law of Liberty to all who constructively contact It. Anything which makes for a greater expression of life, either for the individual or for the race, and which has no element of destruction in it, is good.

We should not hesitate to use the Law for the benefit of our personal affairs or those of our friends or for any who ask our help; but we should be very careful to use It constructively.

EVOLUTION

All emerge from that One Whose Being is ever present and Whose Life, robed in numberless forms, is manifest throughout all Creation.

Creation is the logical result of the outpush of Life into self-expression. It is the coming forth of Spirit into manifestation the externalization of an internal idea, through the objectification of a subjective image.

The One encompasses and flows through the All, spilling Itself into numberless forms and shapes. These forms and shapes, propelled by a Divine Urge which brings them into being, seek still further expression because of the dynamic power with which they are equipped.

This is the real meaning of evolution; for evolution is the result of intelligence and not its cause.

Each evolving thing has, within itself, an impulse implanted by the Divine; and since the Divine is Limitless and Perfect, It must and will, ultimately, bring all Creation to a state of perfect manifestation.

That which, to the human eye, appears as imperfect, is imperfect only because the human eye sees imperfectly or in part; i.e., the human does not see the real idea back of the external image.

There is a philosophy which states that there is a "Becoming God," and which attempts to prove this assertion through evolution; but this philosophy is inconsistent with the ultimate nature of Reality; for, if ultimate Reality were in a state of "becoming," from what source would It gather Its impulse to become, and from whence would It draw Its power to express Itself?

A "becoming" or evolving God, or First Cause, is not consistent with true philosophy; while, on the other hand, an unfolding God, or First Cause, is consistent with Reality.

It is one thing to say that God is unfolding through His Idea of Himself but quite another thing to say that He is gradually becoming conscious of Himself. One is true while the other is false.

A "becoming" God implies a state of imperfection, or a state of being which does not recognize its perfection, at the very root of all being. An unfolding God implies a forever-outpouring Spirit and a forever-manifesting Deity, or First Cause.

The unfoldment of this First Cause is what we call evolution. Since this unfoldment is not yet complete, i.e., since the idea is still in an unfolding state, it appears as though we lived in an imperfect universe.

To a few, who have been able to see behind the veil of matter, the perfect idea has been apparent; and these few have given to the world its greatest code of law, morals and ethics. These few have been the great mystics of the race, and to them the world owes a debt which can be paid only to the degree that the world comes to understand their teachings.

Evolution is the time and the process through which an idea unfolds to a higher state of manifestation; and since ideas are Divine Realities, evolution will forever go on.

PART FOUR

DAILY MEDITATIONS FOR SELF-HELP AND HEALING

In these short meditations I have tried to set forth some ideas which my experiences in mental healing have given me. I have found that a few brief statements, mentally affirmed, followed by a silent meditation, have been most effective in the healing work.

Most of these meditations have been written in the first person in order that those using them may be able to do so just as they are written.

It is not claimed that there is any occult power in the words, but that words similar to these are effective in inducing a greater realization of life. They contain thoughts which I have found to be most helpful.

Try them, my good reader, and see if they will not bring to life a deeper meaning and a greater joy. Whatever brings to the mentality a greater realization of life has, within itself, a healing power. I believe that these meditations will help all who take the time to use them.

First, decide which meditation you wish to use; then become quiet and composed. The body should be relaxed but the mentality should be active. Then carefully read the meditation several times, phrase by phrase, endeavoring to realize the meaning of the words and trying to enter into the atmosphere of the thought. After having done this, meditate upon the words, following that meditation until you feel a sense of realization.

BODILY PERFECTION

COME, AND LET ME HEAL YOU

Come to me and I will heal you.
The inner power of Life within me is God,
    and it can heal anything.
I will to heal and help all who come to me.
I know that the realization of Life and Love
    within me heals all who come into Its
    presence.
I love the thought that I silently bless all who
    enter my atmosphere.
It is not I, but The Father Who dwelleth in
    me; He doeth the works.

I heal all who come near me.

HE IS MIGHTY WITHIN ME TO HEAL

God within me is mighty to heal.
He healeth me of all my diseases and cures
    me of all.
God within is now healing me of all my in-
    firmities, sickness and pain and is bring-
    ing comfort to my soul.
God is my life; I cannot be sick.
I hear the voice of Truth telling me to arise
    and walk, for I am healed.

I am healed.

I DO NOT INHERIT DISEASE

There is no inherited tendency to disease,
    nor ill health.

I am born of Pure Spirit and am free from
    the belief in material existence.
False ideas cannot be transmitted from one
    to another, and I am free from all race-
    suggestion.
My Life is from Above, and I remember that
    I was always Perfect and Complete.
An Inner Light shines forth and frees me
    from the bonds of all false belief.

I came from the Spirit.

NO CONGESTION

There is no congestion nor stoppage of
    action.
Life, flowing through me, is Perfect and
    Clear;
It cannot be stopped, retarded nor hindered.
I feel the One Life flowing through me now.
It eliminates all impure secretions and
    washes me clean from all suggestion of
    false deposits in the flesh.
I am Clean, Pure and Perfect, and my Word
    eliminates all else.

There is no congestion.

NO FALSE GROWTH

"Every plant which my Heavenly Father hath
    not planted, shall be rooted up."
There is no false growth and nothing for one
    to feed on.
I am free from all thought of, or belief in,
    anything false or fearsome.

I cast out all fear and with it all manifestation
of Fear.

A false idea is neither person, place nor
thing, and has no one to believe in it nor
experience it.

I am now One with The Perfect Life of
Complete Wholeness.

My Word casts out all fear.

. .
.

NO WEARINESS

There is no weariness.

Mind and Spirit do not become tired nor
weary, and I am

Mind and Spirit.

The flesh cannot become weary, since it has
no mind of its own.

I am free from all illusions of weariness.

My whole being responds to the thought of
Life.

I am alive with the Great Vitality of the
Spirit.

I am alive with Spirit.

. .
.

PERFECT HEARING

My hearing is perfect.

It is God in me hearing His own voice.

I hear That Voice, and no belief in inaction
can hinder that hearing.

There are no impaired organs.

Every idea of the body is now complete and
perfect and functions according to the
Divine Law.

I open my ears to hear.

I am receptive to Truth and can understand it.

Open my ears that I may hear.

. .
.

PERFECT VISION

There is One Vision and One ability to see,
One perfect seeing.

My eyes are open and I see and behold one
Perfect Life.

No suggestion of imperfect vision can enter
my thought.

I perceive that all people can see, and that
the One, looking through all, sees and
cannot be limited in vision.

I am one with that complete ability to see, to
know and understand the Truth.

I do open my eyes and do see.

Nothing in me can hinder this Word from
operating through me and manifesting
through my eyes.

Open my eyes that I may see.

. .
.

THE ALL-SEEING EYE

The Eye of the Spirit cannot be dimmed,
neither can it be impaired in Its ability to
see.

My eyes are the Vision of my Indwelling
Lord; they are the Windows of my Inner
Spirit and are always open to the Vision
of Truth.

I see with the Vision of the Spirit, and that

ability cannot be weakened nor lost; it is
forever effective.

My word which I now speak is the Law of
Perfect Sight and my eyes are opened
and I see.

Spirit sees through me.

. . .

THE HEALING OF THE FLESH

My flesh is the Manifestation of the Spirit in
my body.

It is kept perfect through the Law of God.

"In my flesh shall I see God."

The mantle of flesh is perfect and complete
here and now.

It is one with the Body of God, and cannot
be sick, nor suffer.

My flesh is perfect.

. . .

THERE IS NO PAIN

There is no pain nor inflammation.

All fear is swept away in the realization of
Truth.

I am free from every belief in pain.

The Spirit cannot pain, and I am Pure Spirit
and cannot be hurt nor harmed.

I am free from all pain.

. . .

COMPLETENESS

HAPPINESS AND COMPLETION

I am happy and complete to-day and
forever.

Within me is that which is Perfect and
Complete.

It is The Spirit of all Life, Truth and Action.

I am happy in the sure knowledge of the
Inner Light.

I cannot be sad nor sorry, but must radiate
Joy and Life, For Life is within me now.

I am happy and complete.

. . .

HERE AND NOW

Perfection is already accomplished.

I do not have to wait for the Perfect Life.

I am that Perfect Life here and now.

To-day I express the Limitless Life of the All
Good.

To-day I manifest my Completion in every
part of me.

To-day I am saved.

Here and now I am healed.

. . .

MAJESTIC CALM

The Inner Mind is still.

The Soul reflects the Most High.

The Spirit of man is God.

In the great calm of the All Good,

I rest in peace and security.

My life is now reflecting the Perfect Whole.
I am Peace; I am Calm
I am security and complete satisfaction.
I am One with God.

I am filled with peace.

∴

NO LOSS

There is no loss.
Nothing can be lost, misplaced nor
forgotten.
There was never any loss nor confusion.
Creation is Perfect and Complete, and
within the One are all
things, and all are known to the One.
I am now in complete harmony with the
Whole and I cannot lose nor misplace
anything.
I am constantly finding more and more
Good.

I know that there is no loss.

∴

OH, FOR A TONGUE TO EXPRESS

Oh, for a tongue to express the Wonders
which the Thought reveals!
Oh, for some Word to comprehend the
boundless idea!
Would that some Voice were sweet enough
to sound the harmony of Life.
But Within, in that vast realm of thought
where the Soul meets God, the Spirit
knows.

I will listen for that Voice and It will tell me
of Life, of Love and Unity.

Speak to me, Spirit.

∴

O SOUL OF MINE,
LOOK OUT AND SEE

O Soul of mine, look out and see; look up
and know Thy freedom.
Be not cast down nor dismayed; be uplifted
within me and exult, for Thy Salvation
has come.
Behold the wonders of the Great Whole and
the marvels of the Universe.
Look out and see Thy good. It is not afar off,
but is at hand.
Prepare Thyself to accept and believe; to
know and live.
Let Life enter and live through Thee, Soul of
mine, and rejoice that Thou hast vision so
fair and so complete.
Rejoice that the Perfect Whole is so completely reflected through Thee.

My light has come.

∴

SEEING THE PERFECT

My eyes behold the complete and perfect in
all Creation,
"In all, over all and through all."
I see the perfect; there is nothing else to see,
and no suggestion of otherness can enter
my thought.

I know only the perfect and the complete.
I am perfect and whole, now.

I see the Good.

THE CIRCLE IS COMPLETE

The Circle of Love is complete.
It comprehends all, includes all, and binds all
    together with cords of Everlasting Unity.
I cannot depart from Its Presence nor wan-
    der from Its care.
My Love is complete within me.
The Love of God binds me to Itself, and will
    not let me go.
I shall make a home for you, O my wonder-
    ful Love, and we shall journey through
    life hand in hand.
I shall sit in your Presence and learn the
    wondrous things You will tell me;
For You are God.

Love sits within me.

THE THINGS THAT ARE

The things that are, were and evermore
    shall be.
Time, Chance and change begone from my
    thought!
The Changeless is here to stay, and the Time-
    less cannot cease from Being.
The things that are shall remain,
    though heaven and earth should
    pass away.

I rest secure and safe within the Life of End-
    less Perfection and Completion.
My whole Being responds to the Realization
    of the Complete Whole.

I am that which Is.

DIVINE COMPANIONSHIP

A SONG OF HOPE

My Life is in Thee, O Inner Presence.
I look upon Thee and hope springs forth into
    realization.
O Hope within me, undying evidence of
    Good,
Thou dost completely hold me in Thy loving
    embrace,
And from this fond caress assurance shall be
    born, and confidence and love.

My hope is in Thee.

BE STILL AND KNOW

"Be still and know that I am God."
I am still in Thy Presence.
I am quiet and peaceful, for I put my trust
    in Thee.
A great stillness steals over me and a great
    calm quiets my whole being, as I realize
    Thy Presence.
The heart knows of Thee, O Most High
    within.

It is still in Thy Presence, and it puts its
whole confidence in Thee alone.

In Thy Presence I am still.

. .

CAST ASIDE ALL DOUBT

Cast aside all doubt, O Soul of mine, and
be unafraid, for Thy power is from
On High.
He Who sitteth in the heavens shall be Thy
champion;
Thou need not fear; Come forth, O Spirit,
from within and express Thyself through
me and let not my doubts hinder Thy
approach.
My faith shall go forth to meet Thee, and my
confidence shall embrace Thee.
My waiting thought shall bid Thee welcome
to my house of Love,
And Joy shall accompany us through the ages
yet to come.

I lay aside all fear and doubt.

. .

DIVINE COMPANIONSHIP

I have an Inner Friend who walks and talks
with me daily.
He is not afar off, but is within me, a con-
stant companion.
I shall never become lonely, for my Friend is
always near.
I have but to speak and He answers.
Before ever my lips spoke He told me of
His love.

O my kind Friend, how dear to me is Thy
presence.

The Spirit within me is my Friend.

. .

HIS EYE IS ON THE SPARROW

"His eye is on the sparrow and I know He
watches me."
This is a blessed thought, for it means that
we cannot wander from His Presence,
nor depart from His care.
Always He will watch over us and comfort us.
Forever we shall sit in His house and ceaselessly He will care for us.
The All-Seeing Eye cannot overlook any one,
and all, all shall be kept in His care.

All are kept in His care.

. .

HOPE CANNOT DIE

Hope cannot die. Eternal Hope is forever
warm and fresh within me; the deathless Hope built upon the rock of sure
knowledge.
O Hope Sublime, O Life Supreme, behold I
come to Thee as a tired child, and Thou
dost rekindle within me the fires of Faith.
Strong, swift and sure, Faith springs forth
into action and my entire Being rises to
meet the Dawn.

Hope, Faith and Love are in me.

. .

I AM NOT ALONE

I am not alone, for a Presence goes with
   me and daily accompanies me on my
   travels.
Always I shall find this Divine Companion
   with me.
He will not desert nor allow me to go alone.
He will always be with me and near me, and
   will always provide for every want.

My life is hid with Christ in God.

I WENT INTO A MOUNTAIN

I have discovered a Secret Place within,
   where the thought goes into a mountain
   high above the din of the world.
I have found in this mountain a Place of
   Peace and rest,
A Place of joy and comfort to the heart.
I have found that the Secret Place of God is
   within my own Soul.

I will listen for Thy Voice.

THE JOY OF THE SOUL

My Soul within me rejoices at the realization
   of Life.
I am made glad as I behold my inner Light;
I cannot be sad nor depressed, for the All
   Good has claimed me as Its own.
O Soul within me, rejoice and become glad,
   for Thy Light has come and Thy Day of
   Salvation is at hand.

Be still within me and behold Him Who
   sitteth On High.
Reflect to me Thy revelation and flood me
   with Thy marvelous Light.

I rejoice in my Life within me.

FREEDOM

FREEDOM

Yes, I know that the Truth has freed me
   from the bonds of fear.
I am not afraid. I adore thee, Most
   High within me; I trust in Thee and
   abide in that hope that knows no fear;
   I am Free Spirit and cannot be bound.
The One Life flowing through me is Perfect
   and Complete.
I am not apart from It. I am One with It in
   Marvelous Unity and Freedom; One with
   the Complete Whole.
I was born free and must always remain free.
   The realization of freedom permeates my
   whole being and sinks into the innermost
   parts of me.
I love it, I adore it, I accept it.

I am free.

FREEDOM FROM SIN

I am free from belief in sin; there is neither
   sin nor sinner.
There is no judgment against any one.

God does not condemn, and man cannot.

All fear of sin is removed from me; all theological belief in punishment is gone from me.

I do not allow myself to receive such suggestions, for I perceive that they are lies.

I am free from all lies and from all liars.

I live by the One Power, and no thought can enter to disturb me.

There is neither sin nor sinner.

. .
.

FREE FROM SENSITIVENESS

My feelings cannot be hurt.

No one wishes to harm me, and there is nothing in me that can believe in any separation from the All Good.

I perceive that I am free from all people, and I cannot be harmed nor mistreated.

I have such a sense of unity with all that the circle is complete and perfect.

I love my friends and they love me, and that love is in, and of, God, and cannot be marred nor hindered.

I am filled with joy and love, forever.

. .
.

I KEEP THE PROMISE

I shall keep the promise that I have made to myself.

I shall never again tell myself that I am poor, sick, weak nor unhappy.

I shall not lie to myself any more, but shall daily speak the truth to my inner

Soul, telling It that It is wonderful and marvelous; that It is One with the Great Cause of all Life, Truth, Power and Action.

I shall whisper these things into my Soul until it breaks forth into songs of joy with the realization of Its Limitless possibilities.

I shall assure my Soul.

. .
.

LOVE GLEAMS THROUGH THE MIST

Through the mist of human fear love gleams and points the way to freedom.

I now decree and declare that I am free from all sense of bondage.

I am made perfect and whole through knowledge of the Real Life within me.

No illusions can enter my thought.

I know that there is One Power, and I know that this Power now protects me from all harm.

As Perfect Love casts out all fear, so my fear flees before the knowledge of Truth.

I am not afraid.

. .
.

NO BONDAGE

There is no bondage nor limitation.

Every part of me moves in perfect harmony and freedom.

I cannot be tied, bound nor made inactive, for I am Free Spirit, and the Power of my Life is from on High.

There is no inaction nor false action, And I am now completely Free.

I am free.

. .
.

NO CONDEMNATION

There is no condemnation in me nor operating through me.

I am free from the belief or thought of men.

I walk my own way, immune to all suggestion of condemnation.

Only those thoughts can enter my mentality which I allow to enter.

I do not, and cannot, receive adverse thoughts.

Only those thoughts which are helpful and life-giving can find entrance to my house.

There is no condemnation.

. .
.

NO FALSE HABIT

There are no vicious nor false habits.

Every desire of my thought and heart is satisfied in the Truth.

I do not long for anything nor feel the lack of anything.

I am complete within myself; I am perfect within myself; I am happy and satisfied within myself.

I am One with All Life within me.

I am free.

. .
.

NO HYPNOTISM NOR FALSE SUGGESTION

There is no hypnotism nor false suggestion.

I represent the One Mind which cannot act against Itself nor can It act against me.

I am immune to all suggestion and cannot receive false thoughts, nor harbor them.

I am surrounded with a circle of Love and Protection.

Asleep or awake, I am free from false thoughts.

I see the nothingness of all belief in, or fear of, otherness; and I know that The One and Only Mind, alone, can act.

Only the Good can enter.

. .
.

NO MISTAKES

There are no mistakes; none have ever been made and none ever will be made.

Nothing ever happened in the past to hinder or hurt.

There is no past, and I know, and can see, that there is no belief in any past to rise against me.

I live in the Now, free from any yesterdays or to-morrows

Now, I am Happy, Free and Complete.

My Word erases any and all beliefs in mistakes and sets me free.

I Am Free!

I am free from any beliefs in the past.

. .
.

THERE ARE NO RESPONSIBILITIES

The Spirit has no responsibilities.

Its work is already accomplished and Its purposes are already fulfilled.

The Spirit knows no want nor fear.

It is complete within Itself and lives by virtue of Its own Being.

I am Spirit and cannot take on the fears of the world.

My work is accomplished and my ways are made straight before me.

The pathway of Life is an endless road of Eternal Satisfaction and Perfect Joy.

My Life within me is Complete and Perfect, and has no cares nor burdens.

It is Free Spirit and cannot be bound.

I rejoice in that Freedom.

I rejoice in freedom.

THE TIME HAS COME

The time has come, the hour has struck.

The power from within has come forth and is expressing through my word.

I do not have to wait; to-day is the time.

To-day I enter into all Truth; to-day I am completely saved and healed and made happy.

To-day I enter into my inheritance.

To-day the Truth has made me free.

WITHIN THY LAW IS FREEDOM

Within Thy Law is freedom to all who will believe.

I believe in Thy Law and I love Thy precepts.

I know that Thy Law is perfect and It is a delight to my Soul, for It is illumined with Thy Words of Power.

Thy Law is complete freedom to me, and to all for whom it shall be spoken.

I speak the Word of freedom to all, and all shall receive it.

I am free in Thy Law.

HARMONY OF LIFE

BEAUTY

I behold the Beautiful and the Pleasant.

My eyes see only that which is beautiful to look upon.

I will not see anything else nor believe in anything else.

I know that beauty has entered into my life, and will always remain there.

I see only the beautiful.

FRIENDSHIP OF THE SPIRIT AND OF MAN

The Friendship of the Spirit and of man is mine now and forever.

Even now I see the countless numbers of friends coming and going around me.

I enter into this friendship and this companionship with gladness and rejoicing.

I receive my friends.

.·.

HE WILLS ME TO BE

It was God Himself who willed that I
    should be.
I have no cares nor burdens to bear,
I am reminded of the great command:
"Come unto Me all ye who labor and are
    heavy laden and I will give you rest."
I do come into the Light and I do know that
    all cares
And responsibilities fall from me as I let the
Light of Wisdom direct my ways.

He wills me to be; therefore, I am.

.·.

I SERVE

I serve the world.
I wait upon the Lord within all men;
I call forth glory from On High through the
    minds of all people.
I obey the will of Him Who inhabits
    Eternity.
I do the works of Him Who dwelleth among
    the heavens.
My Lord within commands and I obey.

I do good to all people.

.·.

I SHALL NOT DOUBT NOR FEAR

I shall not doubt nor fear, for my salvation is
    from On High, and the day of its appearing is now at hand.
I shall not doubt nor fear, for my whole
    being responds to the realization of Life
    within and around me.
I shall not fear, for the Hosts of Heaven are
    waiting upon me and the Law of the Universe is my Salvation.

I shall not fear.

.·.

I WAS TOLD TO LIVE

I was told to live and to love, to laugh and to
    be glad.
I was told to be still and know of the One
    Almighty Power, in and through all.
I was told to let that Power work through
    and in me.
I believed that voice and I received my Good.

I am healed——The joy of Life.

.·.

LAW

I meditate upon the Law of God.
It is a Perfect Law and is now working for
    me and in and through me.
"The Law of the Lord is perfect."
I speak into that Law and it is done unto me.

Thy Law is in my heart.

.·.

LOVE

The Love of the All Good is within me and
  through me.
That Love goes out to meet all who come
  into my atmosphere.
It radiates to all and is flowing through all.
My Love within me is Perfect.

Thy Love within me is Perfect.

∴

LOVE DISSOLVES ALL FEAR

Greater than fear is Love.
Love dissolves all fear, casts out all doubt and
  sets the captive free.
Love, like the River of Life, flows through
  me and refreshes me with its eternal
  blessings.
Love cannot be afraid; it is fearless and
  strong, and is mighty in its works.
It can accomplish all things through the Inner
  Light of that faith in the All Good,
Which fills my very Being with a Powerful
  Presence.

Love casts out all fear.

∴

MY AFFAIRS

My affairs are in the hands of Him Who
  guides the planets in their course, And
  Who causes the Sun to shine.
Divine Understanding attends me on the
  Way, And I shall not be hindered in
  my work.

My affairs are controlled by Perfect Intelligence, And cannot be hindered from
  expression.
I know that all that I do is done from
  the One Motive: To express Life;
  and Life will be expressed In and
  through me. I cannot hinder it.

I am controlled by Intelligence.

∴

MY BUSINESS

My business is directed by Divine
  Intelligence.
The All-Knowing Mind knows what to do
  and how to do it.
I do not hinder, but let It operate in my
  affairs.
It prospers and directs me and controls
  my life.
My affairs are managed by Love, and di-
  rected by
Wisdom, and they cannot fail to prosper and
  expand.

My affairs are in His hands.

∴

MY PROFESSION

My profession is the Activity of the Great
  Mind working through me.
As such It is a Divine Activity and is con-
  stantly in touch with Reality.
I am inspired in my work from On High
  with lofty ideals,

And my thought is illumined by the All-
Knowing One.

I am inspired.

. .
.

NO DELAYS

There are no delays in the Divine Plan
    for me.
Nothing can hinder the operation of this Law
    unto my Life and Action.
Obstructions are removed from my
    path, and
I now enter into the realization and manifes-
    tation of complete fulfillment of right
    desires.
I do not have to wait, for the Law waits upon
    me at every turn in Life's road.

Now it is done unto me.

. .
.

NO MISREPRESENTATIONS

No one can lie to me; none can mislead me.
I am free from the belief in all lies and un-
    truths;
I know and speak only the Truth, and the
    Truth alone can be spoken to me.
I know the false and can understand
    the Real.
I cannot be fooled nor misled; I am guided
    by Truth alone.

There is no lie nor liar.

. .
.

NO OBSTRUCTIONS

There are no obstructions to Life's Path; no
    hindrance to man's endeavors.
Let my Word be the Law of elimination to all
    thought of hindrance or delay,
And let the thing that I speak come forth
    into manifestation at once.
I behold it and see that it is even now done,
    complete and perfect.

I receive now.

. .
.

NO OVER-ACTION NOR INACTION

There is no over-action nor inaction in
    Divine Law, for everything moves accord-
    ing to perfect harmony.
Every idea of my body functions in accor-
    dance with this
Law of Perfect Life.
I now perceive that the action within me is
    perfect, complete and harmonious.
Peace be unto every part of me, and perfect
    Life to every member of my body.
I act in accordance with Divine Law.

I am Perfect Life throughout my whole Being.

. .
.

ONE WITH PERFECT ACTION

I am One with Perfect Action. Everything
    that I do, say or think is quickened into
    action through this right understanding
    and this correct knowing.
The harmonious action of the Great Whole

operates through me now and at all times.

I am carried along by this Right Action and am compelled to do the right thing at the right time.

There is nothing in me that can hinder this action from flowing through me.

The action of God is the only action.

PEACE, POISE AND POWER

Peace, Poise and Power are within me, for they are the witnesses of the Inner Spirit of all Truth, Love and Wisdom.

I am at peace within me, and all about responds to that Great

Calm of the Inner Soul which knows its rightful place in the All Good.

Power is born from within me and passes into my experience without effort or labor.

I rest in Security and Peace, for the Inner Light shines forth and illumines the way.

I rest in Thee.

STILLNESS AND RECEPTIVITY

I am still and receptive to Life.

I let Life flow through me into all that I do, say or think.

I shall let my Life be what it is, and shall not worry nor complain.

I am now entered into the Secret Place of the Soul where complete quiet reigns supreme and where God talks to me.

I receive.

THANKSGIVING AND PRAISE

I will give thanks to my Inner Life for all Its Marvelous

Wonders, and for all Its Wonderful Works.

I will sing and be glad, for I know that I am hid with Truth in a Perfect Life.

The fullness of Joy is mine.

THE DIVINE PROMISES ARE KEPT

The Divine Promises are all kept; not one is changed.

God has told me that my Life is Perfect;

He will never desert nor leave me to travel alone.

I know that from this day on and forevermore

I shall live under Divine Protection and Love.

I live under Divine Protection and Love.

THE INNER LIGHT

The Light of Heaven shines through me and illumines my Path.

The Light Eternal is my guide and my protection.

In that Light there is no darkness at all.

It is a Perfect Light shining from the altar of a perfect Love.
O Light and Love within me, Thou art welcome.

Light shines through me and illumines the Way.

. .
.

THE NIGHT IS FILLED WITH PEACE

I wrap myself in the mantle of Love and fall asleep, filled with Peace.
Through the long night Peace remains with me, and at the breaking of the new day I shall still be filled with Life and Love.
I shall go forth into the new day confident and happy.

I rest in Thee.

. .
.

THE SEAL OF APPROVAL

The Seal of Approval is upon me, and I am not condemned by the thought or the act of man.
I will fear no evil, for I know that the Great Judge of all controls my every act.
Let every fear of man be removed from me and let the Silence of my soul bear witness to the Truth.

God approves of me.

. .
.

THE SECRET WAY

There is a Secret Way of the Soul which all may know.

It is the Way of Peace and Love.
This Secret Way leads into places of joy
And into the house of good.
It is the Way of the Spirit, and all may enter who will.
I tread the Secret Way of good, the Path of Peace,
And I enter into "The Secret Place of The Most High."

The Secret Place of The Most High is within me.

. .
.

THE SHINING PATH

The Pathway of Life shines before me unto the Perfect Day.
I walk the pathway of the Soul to the Gate of Good.
I enter into the fulfillment of my desires.
Nothing need be added and nothing can be taken from the All
Good which is forever expressing Itself in me.
Daily shall I receive Its great blessings and my Soul shall rejoice forevermore.

I am now entered into my good.

. .
.

THE THINGS I NEED COME TO ME

Whatever I need comes to me from the All Good.
Divine Intelligence working through me always knows just what I need and always supplies it when I need it.

This Law is unfailing and sure, and cannot be broken.

I receive my Good daily as I go along the pathway of Life, and I cannot be robbed of my birthright to freedom and happiness.

I receive my Good.

THE WAY IS MADE CLEAR BEFORE ME

The Way is made clear before me; I do not falter nor fall.

The Way of the Spirit is my Way, and I am compelled to walk in it.

My feet are kept on the Path of Perfect Life.

The Way is prepared before me, and that Way is a Path of

Peace, of Fulfillment and Joy.

The Way is bright with the light of Love and Kindness.

The Way I tread is a pleasant and a happy one.

I see the Way and I walk in It.

IMMANENT POWER

AS LOVE ENTERS, FEAR DEPARTS

As Love enters, fear vanishes.

I am so filled with Love that no fear can enter my thought.

I am not afraid, for I know that a Perfect Intelligence guards and governs my every act.

Perfect Love casteth out all fear.

I am unafraid and strong in my faith in Him Who keeps me from all harm.

Perfect Love casteth out all fear.

HE WILL KEEP THEE

The Inner Spirit of man is God, and my Inner Spirit is the Realization of my life.

I know that my Inner Spirit will keep me from all harm, and will not let destruction come near me.

I am unafraid in the midst of confusion, and unmoved in the face of calamity.

I am confident in the presence of seeming danger, and fearless before any sense of trouble.

He will keep me.

INFINITE LIFE WITHIN

Infinite Life within me, which is God, guard Thou my feet and keep Thou my way.

Let me not stray from Thee, but compel me to do Thy will.

I am guarded and governed by an Infinite Intelligence and an Omnipotent Power.

No mistakes can be made and none ever have been made.

An unerring judgment operates through me and I am led by the Spirit of Truth into all Good and into all Peace and Happiness.

Infinite Life within me.

MY FEET SHALL NOT FALTER

My feet shall not falter, for they are kept
    upon the path of
Life through the Power of the Eternal Spirit.
Guide Thou my feet; compel my way; direct
    my paths and keep me in Thy Presence.
My feet are guarded, and I am guided into
    The All Good.

He guides my feet.

NO HARM SMALL BEFALL THREE

No harm shall befall you, my friend, for a
    Divine Presence attends your way and
    guards you into The All Good.
Loving kindness awaits you at every turn of
    Life's road.
Guidance is yours along the pathway of ex-
    perience,
And an Infallible Power protects you.
God, Himself, and no other is your
    Keeper.

I proclaim this for you.

POWER TO LIVE

I have the power to live the life of good.
My power is from On High; it cannot be
    taken from me;
It will not leave me desolate.
Power flows through me and is in
    me, and
I can now feel and sense it.

The Power to live is in me and it cannot
    desert me.
It is my power and is continually
    present.

I am the power to live.

THE CIRCLE OF LOVE

A circle of love is drawn around me and
    mine, and all.
No harm can enter that Sacred Circle, for it
    is the Love of God.
It is a complete protection from all evil.
"I will fear no evil, for Thou art with me."
There is no evil and no harm.
I am free from all sense of fear.

Love surrounds and protects me.

THE CIRCLE OF PROTECTION

I draw around me a circle of love and pro-
    tection.
No harm can enter nor find place within that
    charmed circle of life and love, for it rep-
    resents God's Loving Care and Eternal
    Watchfulness.
I will rest within me now, and I will speak
    comfort to my
Soul and tell It of all the wonders of its life,
    safe from the din of strife and fear.

I am protected from On High.

THE POWER WITHIN BLESSES ALL

The Power within me is blessing all mankind, and is forever healing all with whom I come in contact.

The Power within me is God, and It must bless and help and heal all who come near It.

Silently the work goes on, and silently all are being helped by this Inner Power which is operating through me.

I will give thanks that my Power within is silently blessing and helping every one to whom my thought reaches.

The Life within me blesses all mankind.

. .

THE QUICK ANSWER

My answer comes quickly and surely back to me from On High.

My answer will not fail me, for the Law of the Universe is the Power through which it comes.

I shall not doubt nor fear, for the answer is swift and certain.

My answer comes.

. .

INSPIRATION

A SONG OF JOY

There is a Song upon my lips to-day; it sings of the glad heart and the happy ways of Life.

I will listen to my song, for it carols to me the glad tidings of Great Joy, of Love and Life.

It tells me of the Wondrous Journey of the Soul and the Boundless Life in which my life is hid.

I am filled with joy.

. .

BORN OF ETERNAL DAY

Child of All Good, you are born of Eternal Day.

There is no evening of the Soul, for it shall live forever.

It is Deathless and Perfect, Complete and One with the Everlasting.

No thought of to-morrow can disturb the calm of him who knows that Life is one Eternal Day.

No fear can enter where Love reigns, and Reason keeps faith with Hope.

The thoughts of the to-morrows and the yesterdays are swallowed up in the great realization of the Perfect Here and the Complete Now.

To-day I completely accept my wholeness.

. .

I ARISE AND GO FORTH

I arise and go forth into the Dawn of the New Day, filled with faith and assurance in the All Good.

I arise, I arise, I sing with joy!

I proclaim the One Life: "In all and through all."

I arise, I arise, I shout with gladness that is
within me.
I declare this day to be Complete, Perfect
and Eternal.

I respond to Life.

. .
.

INSPIRATION

Come, Thou Great and Infinite Mind and in-
spire me to do great deeds.
Acquaint me with Thy knowledge and in Thy
wisdom make me wise.
I would be taught of Thee, Inner Light, and
inspired by Thy presence.
I will listen for Thy Voice and it will tell me
of great things to be done.
I will walk in Thy Paths and they will lead
me into All Good.
I will be inspired from On High.
O Wonderful Presence, flooding me, filling
me with Thy Light,
Thou dost inspire me!

I feel the inspiration of Spirit.

. .
.

THE DAWN HAS COME

Out of the darkness of the long night the
Dawn has come.
I rise to meet the new day, filled with confi-
dence and strength.
I arise and go forth into the dawn, inspired and
refreshed by the Living Spirit within me.
O Day, you shall never die; the sun shall
never set upon your perfect glory.

For the Lamp of the Soul has been re-kindled
with the oil of Faith,
And Love has cleansed the windows
of Life with the spirit of
gladness.
They shall nevermore grow dim with
fear, for Perfect Love casteth out all
fear.
I am renewed in strength through knowing
Good.

My light has come.

. .
.

I AM COMPLETE IN THEE

Almighty God, Everlasting Good, Eternal
Spirit, Maker of all things and Keeper of
my Life, Thou art All.
Infinite Presence within, in Whom all live;
Joy Supreme, flooding all with gladness, I
adore Thee.
Eternal Peace, undisturbed and quiet, I feel
Thy calm.
O Thou Who dost inhabit Eternity and dost
dwell within all Creation, Who Dost live
through all things and in all people, hear
Thou my prayer.
I would enter Thy gates with joy and live at
peace in Thy House.
I would find a resting place in Thee, and in
Thy presence live.
Make me to do Thy will and from Thy wis-
dom teach me the ways of Truth.
Compel me to follow Thee and let me
not pursue the paths of my own
counsel.

O Eternal and Blessed Presence, illumine my mind and command my will that my Soul may be refreshed and that my life may be renewed.

As deep cries unto deep, so my thought cries unto Thee and Thou dost answer.

I am renewed and refreshed; my whole being responds to Thy love, and I am complete in Thee.

All my ways are guarded and guided, and I shall live with Thee eternally.

O Lover of my Soul and Keeper of my Spirit, none can separate us, for we are One.

So shall Thy Wisdom guide me, Thy Presence dwell within me, Thy Love keep me and Thy life envelop me now and forever-more.

I rest in Thee.

• •
•

PRESENCE OF THE ALL GOOD

A MARVELOUS SENSE

A marvelous sense steals over him who waits on Good, and in patience bides his time.

A feeling of some Unseen Presence silently creeps over the waiting thought, and the Voice of God speaks through the mist and says: "Be not afraid."

It is all for a purpose; and when you cannot trace, you must trust. This is not an illusion, but a reality; for time proves all things, and he who will wait for his time to come shall be rewarded; and Good

shall come to him, for God Himself shall be his Companion and Champion.

I wait on Thee.

• •
•

COMPLETE CONFIDENCE

My confidence in The All Good is complete.

My faith in the Power of Spirit is supreme.

I have no doubts nor uncertainties.

I know that my Good is at hand, and

I realize that no fear can hinder

That Good from making Its appearance in my life and affairs.

I know that my Life and Good are complete.

Evil cannot touch nor hinder my work.

I rest in security, for

THE ONE MIND IS MY COMPLETE REF-UGE AND STRENGTH.

I am serene and confident.

• •
•

DRAWING THE GOOD

I draw my Good to me as I travel along the Way of Life, and nothing can keep It from me.

My Good will always follow me.

I accept the Good and rejoice that it is with me.

I accept the Good.

• •
•

I FEAR NO EVIL

"I will fear no evil, for Thou art with me."
I will not be afraid, for the All Good is constantly with me and is always near at hand
to guide and comfort.
There is no evil in the Truth, and no power
of darkness to hinder the Light from
shining.
I will not be afraid, for there is One within
Who protects and keeps me from all
harm.

I fear no evil.

I HAVE KNOWN, ALWAYS

I have always known the Truth, and no fear
can keep my inner knowledge from me.
My wisdom from within comes forth into
daily expression.
Knowledge from On High is given to me,
and I shall always be led of the Spirit.

I know the Truth.

I MEET MY GOOD

To-day I meet my Good; it knows me and
will not let me depart from it.
My Good is at hand, and I cannot be robbed
of it.
Good is forever expressing itself to me and
mine.
I can even now see and hear and feel the All
Good in and around me.

It presses itself against me, and fills me with
a great surge of Life.

My Good is at hand.

MY ATMOSPHERE

My atmosphere is attracting the Good; it is
constantly on the alert to see and know the
Good, and to bring it into my experience.
There is that within me that calls forth abun-
dance and happiness from Life. I am sur-
rounded with an atmosphere of Peace,
Poise and Power.
All who come in contact with that great
Calm of my Life are made strong and
confident, are healed and blessed.
"Bless the Lord, O my Soul, and all that is
within me, bless His Holy Name."

I am hid with Christ in God.

MY GOOD IS COMPLETE

My Good is complete; it is finished; it is now
here and is conscious of me and of mine.
I do not have to wait for my Good; it is at
hand and ever ready to spring forth and
express itself to me.
I accept my Good and gladly acknowledge it
to be my daily companion.
My Good is mine now, and I can see it and
feel it and know it.

To-day I claim my Good.

MY OWN SHALL COME TO ME

From far and near my own shall come to me. Even now it is coming to me, and I receive it.

My own is now manifesting itself to me, and I see and know its presence. My own shall know and respond to me.

The drawing power of that inner Spirit within me is now attracting and drawing into my experience all that is good and perfect. There is nothing within me to hinder nor to delay it.

My own cannot be kept from me, neither can I keep my good away from me. I receive it now.

I now receive my good.

. .
.

MY OWN SHALL FIND ME

My Own shall find me; no matter where I go, It will follow and claim me.

I cannot hide myself from my Own.

My Own shall come to me, even though I deny it; for there is nothing in me that can hinder it from entering and taking possession of my Soul.

My own is now expressed.

. .
.

MY SOUL REFLECTS THY LIFE

My Soul reflects Thy Life and rejoices in the happy thought that it looks on Thee alone.

O Soul of mine, look out and up and on; and reflect to me the wondrous Life of the All Good.

Look thou upon The One, and be saved.

Behold thou His Face forevermore.

My Soul reflects Thy Life.

. .
.

OUT OF THE DEPTHS OF LIFE

Out of the deep places of life my Soul has cried unto Thee and Thou hast made answer.

Out of the turmoil and struggle and strife I have come unto Thee, and Thou hast heard me and understood.

I shall nevermore be sad, for I have found what the Soul craves—the Inner Life and Love of the All Good.

Thou hast heard.

. .
.

SORROW FLEES FROM ME

As the Great joy of Life comes into my Soul, flooding me with its wondrous light, all sorrow and sadness flee from me.

I shall not grieve, for nothing is lost nor gone from me.

My own cannot be kept from me.

My own knows me and will follow me wherever I go.

I am filled with the Joy of living and the Great Peace that comes to all who believe.

I am made glad forevermore.

. .
.

SUBSTANCE AND SUPPLY

The Substance of the Spirit is my Daily
　　Supply.
I cannot be without my Good.
I can see that the constant stream of Life
　　flowing to me brings into my experience
　　all that makes Life happy and worthwhile.
I rest in security, knowing that Infinite Good
　　is within and is expressing through me.

I receive my good.

• •
•

THE EVER AND THE ALL

Life always was and evermore shall be,
　　"World without end."
All the Power there is, is mine now.
All the Life, Truth and Love of the Universe
　　is now and forever
Flowing through my Soul.
The All Good cannot change.
I shall always have access to my Eternal God
　　within me.

I am Changeless Life within me.

• •
•

THE HOUSE OF LOVE

I dwell in the house of Love;
"A house not made with hands, eternal in
　　the heavens."
My dwelling place is filled with peace and
　　eternal calm.
Love attends me in my home of the Soul,
　　and

Joy awaits upon me in the "Secret Place of
　　the Most High."
My house is built for me by the hand of
　　Love, and
I shall never leave this Home of the Spirit,
　　for it is always present.
I shall abide in this home
　　forevermore.

My house is a house of love.

• •
•

SPIRIT OF GOD WITHIN

ARISE, MY SPIRIT

Arise, my Spirit, arise and shine.
Let Thy light illumine my path, and let Thy
　　wisdom direct my way.
Compel my will to do Thy bidding, and
　　command my Soul to look to Thee.
I will follow Thee, my Spirit, and will learn
　　of Thee all that I need to know.
I will sit in the Silence and listen and
　　watch, and
I will see Thy light and hear Thy voice.
I will follow Thee and will not depart from
　　Thee,
For in Thee alone is Peace.

Arise and shine.

• •
•

BIRTHLESS AND DEATHLESS

The Spirit within me is Birthless and Death-
　　less; It was not born and It cannot die.

I have no fear of death, for I perceive
that
Death is an illusion and not the Truth.
I was born of the Spirit, and I live in the
Spirit, And shall continue to live in and
by the Spirit.

The Spirit within me lives forever.

• •
•

COMMAND MY SOUL

Spirit within me, command my Soul to do
Thy bidding;
Compel me to follow the course of Truth
and Wisdom.
Control my inward thoughts and my out-
ward ways,
And make me to understand Thy Laws.
Command my Soul to turn to Thee for guid-
ance and light;
To turn to Thee for wisdom and knowledge.
Let the paths of my Life be made straight
and sure;
Let the Journey of my Soul find its comple-
tion in Thee.

Command my Soul to do Thy bidding.

• •
•

DESPAIR GIVES WAY TO JOY

Despair gives way to joy at the thought of
Thee, Indwelling Good.
I cannot be sad when I think of Thee.
My sorrow is turned to gladness and my
shame to rejoicing.
My tears are wiped away and the sunlight of

the Spirit shines through the clouds of
depression and lights the way to Heaven.

Thy Joy has made me glad.

• •
•

FREE SPIRIT WITHIN ME

Free Spirit within me, Unbound and Perfect,
teach me Thy ways and make known to
me Thy Limitless Completion.
O Spirit of Life, control my every action and
thought.
Compel me to follow Thy light that I too
may be free and complete.
I will follow Thy footsteps and learn of Thee
all the wondrous secrets of Life.
I will follow Thy Light into the Perfect Day.

Free Spirit within me.

• •
•

FULNESS OF LIGHT

The Light of Life is full within me and
around me.
It shines forth into the Perfect Day.
O Light within, lighting my path to peace,
I adore and love You and I let You shine.
Go forth and bless all who come to You,
Light within.
My Light radiates to all and through all.

My Light has come.

• •
•

HE WHO INHABITS ETERNITY

He Who inhabits Eternity keeps watch over
    me and mine.
"He Who neither slumbers nor sleeps" for-
    ever keeps watch over all.
I will rest in the assurance of Love and
    Protection.
O Thou Great Overshadowing Presence,
I am conscious of Thy care; I am aware of
    Thy loving kindness. I rest in Thee.

Be still and know.

. .

I LISTEN

I will listen for Thy voice, Inner Presence.
It will guide me and acquaint me with all
    knowledge.
Thy voice is sweet and tender; it is always
    kind and gentle.
O Lover of my Soul, how I adore Thee! How
    I love Thee!
How I love Thy voice; it thrills me with glad-
    ness and joy.
It fills me with peace and calm, and it
    soothes me.
It quiets me and gives me wonderful rest.
I listen, O Divine Speaker, I listen to Thee
    alone.

I listen for Thy voice.

. .

JOY HAS COME TO LIVE WITH ME

Joy has come to live with me. How can I be
    sad?
I do so love Thy presence, which is joy
    within me.
It makes me glad, and I sing, for I am so
    filled with Thy
Spirit that I cannot be depressed nor unhappy.
I am filled with the joy of the Spirit, and I
    overflow with the gladness of life.
Thou art a Happy Companion to travel with
    me through
Life, wonderful Joy, Thou art so radiant and
    beaming.
It is impossible to be sad in Thy presence.
I shall give myself to Thee and remain
    with Thee, for Thou art complete and
    satisfying.
I find fulfillment in Thee and joy forever-
    more.

I am filled with the Spirit of Joy.

. .

KNOWLEDGE AND WISDOM

All Wisdom and Knowledge is from within,
And my God, Who is All-Knowing, is also
    within.
I am guided and guarded along Life's road
    into the All Good.
My Mind is instructed from On High,
And my Wisdom cometh from afar.

The Spirit within me is All Wisdom.

. .

MY THOUGHT IS IN THEE

My thought is in Thee, Inner Light.
My words are from Thee, Inner Wisdom.
My understanding is of Thee, Inner God.
I cannot be hid from Thee, my Inspiration
and my Life.

My thought is in Thee.

. .

O LOVE DIVINE

O Love Divine within me, I am overpowered
by Thy Presence.
I am speechless, for words cannot utter the
things that Thou hast revealed to me.
Why dost Thou love me so, and why clasp
me so close to Thy Eternal Heart?
O Blessed Presence, I know, for Thou hast
claimed me as Thine own.
I shall nevermore walk apart from Thee.

The love of God is within me.

. .

PEACE STEALS THROUGH THE SOUL

Peace steals through the waiting Soul, and
the comfort of the Spirit comes into the
stillness of the heart.
Peace, like an ocean of Infinite Life, reflects
itself through me and calms every turbu-
lent feeling.
I am at peace and rest in the knowledge of
the All Good which is at hand.

I rest in peace.

. .

STAND FORTH AND SPEAK

Stand forth and speak, Spirit within me.
Proclaim Thy presence, announce Thy
course.
Declare through me Thy wondrous works and
Let the children of men hear Thy voice.
Behold, He maketh all things new.
The Spirit within speaks words of Truth and
Life to all.
The Spirit within me is God.

I speak the Truth.

. .

SUBTLE ESSENCE OF SPIRIT WITHIN ME

Subtle Essence of Spirit within me, flowing
through me;
Elixir of Life in my veins purifying me with
Thy marvelous Life,
I let Thy Spirit cleanse me from all false
thought and idea;
I let Thy Life flow through me in a complete
and Perfect Whole.

I feel the presence of Spirit within me.

. .

THE CHRIST WITHIN

My Life is "hid with Christ in God";
The Inner Man is the image and likeness of
the Spirit of God.
I let that Inner Man come forth into expres-
sion in my life;
He will guide my feet into all Truth and
Wisdom.

The Christ within me is free from all worry,
and cannot be hindered by any opposing
force.
My Christ within me is now perfect.

My Christ is within me.

. . .

THE EVERLASTING ARMS

His Arms enfold me, His Strength upholds
me,
His Presence fills me with Life and Joy.
I shall nevermore be sad nor depressed, for I
know that I do not walk Life's path alone.
There is One Who goes with me and tells
me all the things that I should know.
There is a Presence with me guiding me into
the Perfect Way.

I rejoice in knowing that I am not alone.

. . .

THE MANTLE OF LOVE

Like a cloak His Love is wrapped around me.
Like a warm garment It shelters me from
the storms of life.
I feel and know that an Almighty Love envel-
ops me in Its close embrace.
O Love Divine, My Love, how wonderful
Thou art. I am open to receive Thy great
blessing.

Love envelops me.

. . .

THE VOICE OF TRUTH

The Voice of Truth speaks to me and
through me.
The Voice of Truth guides me and keeps me
on the Path of the Perfect Day.
I will listen to the Inner Voice and It will tell
me what to do in the hour of need.
I shall be told everything that I ought to
know when the time of need arrives, and
I shall not be misled.
The Voice of Truth cannot lie, but always
speaks to me from On High.
Nothing enters but This Voice, for it is the
Voice of God.

God speaks to me.

. . .

THE WITNESS OF TRUTH

There is a Witness within me who knows the
Truth and who will not let me enter into
falsehood.
My Inner Guide keeps me on the Pathway of
Life and directs me at all times to that
which is right and best.
I shall never be without this witness of the
Spirit, for I believe in It and accept It as
the Great Companion of the Soul.

The Spirit within me is perfect now.

. . .

THROUGH THE LONG NIGHT WATCHES

Through the long night watches Thou hast
been with me.

In the dark places of human ignorance Thy
hand hath guided me,

Thy light hath lighted the pathway of desolation to a land of plenty.

I have perceived Thee from afar, and my soul
hath yearned to Thee, O Thou Mighty One!

The Spirit within me hath urged me on to
the goal, and I have not been misled.

I have been guided and guarded through the
long journey, and

Thy Presence hath been made known to me.

I awake from the dream and reënter the
house of my Lord clothed with Peace and
robed in colors of Light.

The Spirit of Truth watches over me.

THY STRENGTH IS SUFFICIENT

O Spirit of man and God within me, Thy
Power is great, and Thy Knowledge goes
beyond the range of human experience.

Thy Wisdom excels that of all else, and beside Thee there is none other. In Thy
Strength do I daily walk and live; In
Thy Presence do I always rest in
peace and joy.

Spirit within me and without, Powerful Thou
art, and Great; Wonderful is Thy Might,
and Complete is Thy Understanding.

I let Thy Mighty Strength flow through me,
And out into all the paths of my human
endeavors.

Life from within expresses through me.

WAITING ON THEE

In waiting on Thee there is fulness of Life.

I wait on Thee, my Inner Lord; I listen for
Thy voice.

I hear Thy word; I do Thy will; again I wait
on Thee.

And listening, I hear Thee say: "Be perfect,
be complete; live love, be glad."

Sit thou in the stillness and let thy Lord speak.

WHOSE RIGHT IT IS TO COME

He has come Whose right it is.

He has made His home within me, and will
nevermore depart from me.

I shall walk no more alone, for One walks
with me

Who knows the path of Life, and Whose feet
will never falter nor fail.

My Inner Light shines through the mist of
human beliefs

And frees me from the bondage of fear and
limitation.

I shall walk with You, my Friend, and
shall learn of You the ways of Life
and Freedom.

We shall travel together from this day, and
none can part us,

For we are united in the perfect bonds of an
everlasting unity.

I walk with Thee.

THE POWER OF THE WORD

I CONTROL MY MENTAL HOUSEHOLD AND CONQUER ALL FEAR AND DOUBT

I conquer my mental household and cast out
all fear and doubt.
Let my Word cast out all sense of fear
and doubt and let my thoughts be
lifted unto Him Who lives
Within.
My Word has dissolved all fear within me,
and has cast out all doubt.
My Word shall guard my thought and
make me receive only that which is
Good and Perfect.

I control my life.

• •
•

MY WORD COMES BACK TO ME

My word comes back to me laden with the
fruits of its own speech.
My word is the Law unto my Life, and the
Law unto everything that I speak.
O Word, go forth and heal and bless all
humanity.
Tell them of their Divine Birthright.
Tell the stranger that he is not alone, but that
One goes with him Who knows and
cares.
Tell the sick that they are healed and the
poor that they cannot want.
Tell the unhappy of the joy of the Soul, and
break the bonds of those who are in
prison.

*My Word shall come back to me blessed of God
and man.*

• •
•

MY WORD SHALL BEAR FRUIT

The Word of my mouth shall bear fruit.
It shall accomplish and prosper, and shall not
return unto me void.
My Word is the law unto the thing whereunto it is sent, and it cannot come back
empty-handed.
I send out my Word, and it is the law unto
my life.

My Word is Power.

• •
•

NOTHING CAN HINDER

Nothing can hinder my Word from working;
It will work, and nothing can stop it.
My word is the Law unto that thing whereunto it is spoken, and will become fulfilled in the right way and at the right
time.
My Word is complete and perfect, and is the
presence and the
Power of the One Mind that is in and
through all.
I speak that Word and know that it will
accomplish.
I wait in perfect confidence for the Word to
fulfill itself in my life.

My Word is law.

• •
•

O MAN, SPEAK FORTH THY WORD

O man, speak forth thy word and be not
    afraid.
Did you not know; have you not heard?
His Divinity is planted within thee, and thy
    word is one with all power.
The Spirit of the Most High is thy Spirit, and
    the word of God is thy word.
Thy freedom is hid within thee, and thy
    inner light shall illumine thy way.
Speak, man, and be free! Announce and pro-
    claim thy works!
Let thy word go forth with power, and thy
    Spirit shall conquer all.

Spirit within me, speak.

. .
.

THE POWER OF THE WORD

The Word is a mighty Power, and that Word
    is in me and through me now.
My Word is one with the All Good and can-
    not fail to accomplish the desired ends.
My Word goes forth with Power unto every-
    thing that I do, say or think.
The Word is my Power by day and by night.
I will speak that Word and trust in the great
    Law of Life to fulfill it.

I speak the word in full confidence.

. .
.

THE WORD OF POWER

My Word is a Word of Power, for I know that
    it is the

Word of the Great God within me.
My Word shall accomplish and prosper, and
    shall do good unto all who call upon my
    name.
My Word is a tower of strength and cannot
    be denied.
It is complete and perfect here and now.
My Word is the Word of God.

My word is the word of God.

. .
.

THE UNASSAILABLE TRUTH AND THE
IRRESISTIBLE WORD

The Truth within me is unassailable, and the
    Power of the Word is irresistible.
I can even now feel that my Word has gone
    forth with Power and Reality, and that it
    will accomplish that purpose for which it
    was created.
Limitless is its Power and wonderful are its
    works.
It can be nothing less than the Almighty
    working in and through me.
I will let this Word of the Spirit go forth
    from my mouth, and heal and bless the
    world.
It shall be as a strong tower unto all who call
    upon it.
The Truth is Complete and Perfect, and is
    within me now.

My Word is complete and perfect, now.

. .
.

I BEHOLD IN THEE HIS IMAGE

I behold in thee His Image.

In thee, my friend, I see God, and through
you I feel His presence.

I see in the hand that gives, His hand;

And in the voice that speaks of Love, I hear
Him speak.

For His lines have gone out into all places,

And from the highest to the lowest, all, all
partake of His nature.

"For He is all in all, over all and through all."

I perceive that God is in all people.

. ·.

UNITY

I SEE NO EVIL

I see no evil; I behold only the good.

I have seen the drunkard lying in the gutter,
and the saint kneeling in ecstasy before
the high altar of his faith; but I have found
no difference.

I have perceived that each, in his own tongue,
is seeking to express the One Life.

I will not separate and divide; I cannot condemn nor censure, for I know that there
is but One in All.

I know that all came from the One, and all
will return to the One.

I know that all are now in the One, and that
each is seeking to express the One.

I know and love all.

. ·.

I SHALL NEVER DIE

I shall never die, for the Spirit within me is
God and cannot change.

My life is hid within the Universe of Love
and Light, and that Light shall live forever.

Go, fear of death and change; begone
from my thought, fear of death and
uncertainty.

That which is cannot become that which is
not; and that which I am can never change.

The Spirit of Eternity is enthroned within
me, and the Life of Endless Ages flows
through my being.

From Eternity to Eternity my Life flows
along its way of peace and harmony.

Time brings but more glory to crown me
with its pleasures.

My life is forever.

. ·.

LOVE TO THE WORLD

My Love goes out to every one in the world;

I do not exclude anything, for I love all Nature and everything that is.

My Love warms and lightens everything that
it touches, and it goes out into all places.

The Love flowing through me is a Power to
all who come into contact with it, and all
feel and know that I love.

Love within me is Complete and Perfect.

Love within me is Complete.

. ·.

MY LIFE IS ONE WITH GOD

My life is in God; it cannot be hurt nor hindered in its expression.

God lives and expresses through me; His work is complete and perfect in me now.

I know His life to be my life, and I know that my life is complete and perfect.

My Life is in God.

. .

NO MISUNDERSTANDINGS

There are no misunderstandings.

All is made clear between the ideas of Good.

No false sense of separation can come between people, nor disturb the realization of the Unity of All Life.

I perceive that I am one with all people, and all are One with me.

There is no separation.

There is no separation.

. .

THE DIVINE PLAN FOR ME

The Divine Plan for me is Perfect. I am held in the Mind of God as a Complete and Perfect Expression of Life and Truth.

No power can hinder nor mar this Inner Image of Reality, for It is God-given and God-kept.

God gave and God will keep.

. .

THE PERSONALITY OF GOD

The Great Personality of God is my Personality; the Limitless Knowingness of The Spirit is my Knowingness, and the One Mind is my mind.

All, All live in One Infinite Person, and each manifests the One Who is formed through and in all.

Man is the Personality of God in manifestation and cannot be left without the Inner Witness of the Spirit.

I now realize that the Infinite Personalness of the Spirit is my Personality, and I rejoice to know the Truth about myself.

God is my Personality.

. .

THE RADIATION OF LIFE

The life of God within me radiates and shines forth from me in a constant stream of Light to all.

The One Life flowing through me is Life to all who come near.

The One Power operating through me is flowing into everything that I contact.

Life radiates from me.

. .

UNITY

To-day I realize that I am One with the All Good; my God and I are One.

I cannot be hid from His face.

I behold Thee, O Most High, enthroned in
my temple of flesh.

Thy secret place is within me. I feel Thy
presence,

I hear Thy voice, I rejoice in Thy Light.

To-day my body responds to the Divine Be-
hest: "Be perfect."

I know of my perfection and wholeness; I am
complete and perfect now.

Let every thought of disease flee from me,
and let Thy Light shine.

O Light Eternal, O Light of my Life, I come
into Thy presence with joy and thanksgiving.

So be it.

. .
.

WITHIN THEE IS FULNESS OF LIFE

Within Thee is fulness of Life.

Within Thee is complete Joy and everlasting
Peace.

Within Thee is all.

Thou art in me as I am in Thee, and we are
all in all.

My Life is full and complete within
me, and that Life I give to all
men freely;

And from all I receive again that which I
have given,

For it is One in All.

I am One with the fulness of All Life.

. .
.

Glossary

This glossary gives the Metaphysical meaning of the words as used in these lessons. It is not claimed that the definition of the words used in this glossary will, in every case, keep faith with the regular dictionary definition. The words are defined in such a way as to bring out the meaning with which they are used in this course of instruction.

It will be necessary for the student to carefully study the meaning of these words, together with the explanation of the words used in the different charts; in this way, the desired objective will be obtained, and there will be no confusion.

ABSOLUTE.—"Free from restriction." See Chart No. I.

ACCUMULATED CONSCIOUSNESS.—The sum total of all that one has ever said, thought, done or seen, consciously or unconsciously.

ACTIVE PRINCIPLE OF LIFE.—The Self-Conscious Spirit.

AFFIRMATION.—To state positively and maintain as being true.

ALL-GOOD.—God or Spirit.

ALPHA.—That which is first.

ANALYSIS.—Resolving things into their first elements.

ANDROGYNOUS.—Having the characteristics of both sexes.

APPARITION.—"A specter of phantom. The act of appearing."

ATTRIBUTE.—The being, essence, nature and substance of.

AURA.—The mental atmosphere surrounding a person.

AXIOM.—A self-evident truth.

AXIOMATIC REASONING.—The deductions drawn from self-evident truths.

BEING.—That which has existence.

BIBLE.—"The sacred books of any race or people."

BLESSING.—Constructive thought directed toward any one.

BODY.—The outward form.

BODY OF THE UNIVERSE.—The manifest Creation, the Body of God, both visible and invisible.

CAUSATION.—That which stands back of things as the Intelligent Cause.

CHANGE.—The appearance and disappearance of forms.

CHRIST.—The total manifestation of God, from the plant to an angel; from a peanut to the entire Universe of expression. Christ in Man means the idea of Sonship, the Perfect Man as He must be held in the Mind of God.

CLAIRAUDIENCE.—The ability to perceive sounds without the ear.

CLAIRVOYANCE.—The ability to see mentally. Seeing without the eye.

COETERNAL.—Always existing. Uncreated.

COEXISTENT.—That which exists with.

COMPENSATION.—The law of balance in the mental world. Cause and effect.

COMPLEX.—The result of mental struggle, conscious or unconscious.

CONCEIVE.—To give birth to an idea.

CONCENTRATION.—Bringing the attention to a focus.

CONCEPT.—An idea in mind.

CONCRETE CAUSE.—Definite idea.

CONDITIONS.—That which follows cause; the effect of law.

CONFLICT.—Inner mental struggle, conscious or unconscious.

CONSCIOUS MIND.—The self-knowing mind in God or man.

CONSCIOUSNESS.—The perception of existence.

CONTEMPLATE.—To know within the self.

CORRESPONDENT.—The mental picture or cause of anything.

COSMIC CONCEPTION.—The Divine Mind giving birth to Its Ideas.

COSMIC CONSCIOUSNESS.—Perception of The Whole.

COSMIC MIND.—The Mind of God.

COSMIC PURPOSE.—The ideas of Spirit propelling themselves into outer expression. The desire of Spirit executing itself.

COSMIC STUFF.—The stuff from which all forms are made.

COSMIC URGE.—The desire of Spirit to express Itself.

COSMOS.—The Universal World, visible and invisible.

CREATION.—Passing of Spirit into form.

CREATIVE MEDIUM.—From the Universal Sense, it is the World-Soul; and from the individual sense, it is the subjective state of man's thought.

CREATIVE MIND.—The Universal Soul or Subjectivity. The Feminine Principle of the Universal Life.

CREATIVE SERIES.—Any particular and concrete manifestation of Spirit.

CURSE.—Mentality used to destroy.

DEDUCTIVE REASONING.—Reasoning from the whole to a part.

DEITY.—God.

DENIAL.—The mental act of denying the false appearance.

DESIRE.—Life wishing to express Itself.

DEVIL.—The personification of evil.

DIAGNOSIS.—Unearthing mental causes.

DISCARNATE SPIRITS.—Entities out of the flesh.

DISEASE.—The result of inhibited mental and spiritual action.

DIVINE IDEAS.—The Ideas of God.

DIVINE NATURE.—The true nature of all things.

DIVINE PRINCIPLE.—Spiritual Causation operating through Universal Law.

DIVINE SCIENCE.—The facts known about mental and spiritual law.

DIVINE URGE.—The inner desire to express life.

DREAM WORLD.—World of thoughts that are unexpressed.

EARTH-BOUND.—An entity unable to leave this plane.

EFFECT.—That which follows a cause. The result of some inner action.

EGO.—The real self. The inner man.

ELEMENTALS.—Unevolved entities in the invisible world.

EMANATE.—To flow forth from.

EMMANUEL.—"God with us."

EMOTION.—Mental energy, set in motion through feeling.

ENTITIES.—Anything that exists, visible or invisible.

EQUIVALENT.—The mental likeness of a thing. The mental cause back of anything. The idea of the thing in the Subjective World.

ESOTERIC.—Inner.

ETERNAL.—Everlasting, without beginning or end.

ETHER.—A universal medium which is supposed to be the last known analysis of matter; it interspheres all things and all space. The fine particles of matter, or electrons, are supposed to be cemented together by the ether. Ether seems to be, to the material world, what mind is to the mental world; i.e., a universal medium.

EVIL.—That which seems destructive.

EVOLUTION.—The passing of Spirit into form.

EXISTENCE.—Having real being within itself. The cause of its own being, depending upon nothing but itself. Different from subsistence.

EXOTERIC.—Outer.

FACULTY.—"Any mode of bodily or mental behavior regarded as implying a natural endowment or acquired power—the faculties of seeing, hearing, feeling, etc."

FAMILIAR SPIRITS.—Refers to the control of consciousness through the instrument of some invisible agency.

FATHER-MOTHER GOD.—The Masculine and Feminine Principles of Being as included in the Androgynous One, or First Cause.

FEMININE PRINCIPLE.—The Universal Soul. In man, the subjective or subconscious intelligence.

FIRST CAUSE.—That which is the cause of all things. The Uncreated, from which all Creation springs. The First Cause is both Masculine and Feminine in Its Nature, and includes the Intermediate Principle of Creative Activity.

FORM.—Any definite outline in time and space. Forms may be visible or invisible. In all probability, all space is filled with many kinds of forms.

FORMLESS SUBSTANCE.—The ultimate stuff from which all forms are created, universally present, in an unformed state, and acted upon by conscious and subconscious intelligence. It is the nature of the Soul to give form to the ideas with which It is impregnated; hence, Soul contains Substance within Itself.

FUNCTION.—"The normal action of any organ."

GHOST.—The mental form of any person in the flesh or out of it.

GOD.—The First Cause, the Great I Am, The Unborn One, The Uncreated, The Absolute or Unconditioned, The One and Only. Man comprehends God only to the degree that he embodies the Divine Nature.

HABIT.—Any act that has become a part of the subconscious mentality.

HALO.—The emanation that appears around the head.

HEAVEN.—A harmonious state of being.

HELL.—A discordant state of being.

HOLY GHOST.—The third Person of the Trinity. The Servant of the Spirit. Used in the sense of the World,—Soul or Universal Subjectivity.

HUMANITY.—The multiplied expression of God as people. The many who live in the One.

HYPNOTISM.—The mental control of another.

I AM.—From the universal standpoint, means God; and from the individual, means the Real Man.

IDEA.—A concept. The Ideas of God are the Divine Realizations of His own Being. The real Ideas are eternal.

ILLUMINATION.—Inspiration reaching a Cosmic state. A direct contact with Reality or God. A complete intuitive perception.

ILLUSION OF MIND.—Means looking at a picture in Mind which may be real, only as a picture, but not as substance. As a picture of a person is not the person, so there are many pictures, drawn in Mind, which are real only as pictures. Mind is not an illusion, but might present us with illusions, unless we are very careful to distinguish the false from the true.

IMAGE.—The mental likeness of anything.

IMAGINATION.—The imaging faculty.

IMMACULATE CONCEPTION.—All things are immaculately conceived, as all things come from the One.

IMMORTALITY.—The Deathless Principle of Being in all people.

IMMUTABLE LAW.—Absolute in its ability to accomplish.

IMPERSONAL RECEPTIVITY.—The Creative Mind is impersonal receptivity, in that It receives all seeds of thought.

INCARNATION.—The Spirit of God in all Creation.

INDIVIDUALITY.—The Real Idea of man, as distinguished from the outer personality.

INDUCE.—The act of planting seeds of thought in Creative Mind.

INDUCTIVE REASONING.—Reasoning from effect to cause.

INDWELLING CHRIST.—Generic man, manifesting through the individual. The idea of Divine Son-ship. The Real Man. As much of this reality appears as we allow to express through us.

INDWELLING EGO.—The Spirit of man as differentiated from his soul or subjective mentality. The Real Man which is the conscious part of him.

INDWELLING GOD.—The Real Man is as much of God as he is able to embody. The Divine Spark, Birthless and Deathless.

INFINITE.—That which is beyond all comprehension.

INHERENT LIFE.—Real life as distinguished from latent life.

INNER SIGHT.—The spiritual capacity of knowing the Truth. It is a mental quality which brings the mentality to a comprehension of Reality.

INSANITY.—The loss of the objective faculties.

INSPIRATION.—From the human side, means contact with the subconscious of the individual or the race. From the Divine, means contact with the Universal Spirit.

INSTINCTIVE LIFE.—The One in everything.

INSTINCTIVE MAN.—The Spiritual Man.

INTELLECT.—The reasoning faculty.

INTUITION.—The ability to know without any process of reasoning. God knows only intuitively.

INVOLUTION.—Ideas involved in Mind. Involution precedes evolution.

JESUS.—The name of a man. Distinguished from the Christ. The man Jesus became the embodiment of the Christ as the human gave way to the Divine Idea of Sonship.

KARMA.—The subjective law of cause and effect.

LATENT LIFE.—Life that depends upon reality. Distinguished from inherent life.

LAW.—Mind in action.

LAW OF ATTRACTION.—Subjective tendencies set in motion which are bound to attract.

LAW OF CORRESPONDENCES.—The subjective image of a desire. In the subjective world there is an exact image of everything that is in the objective world.

LEVITATION.—Where the body is lifted without the aid of any physical medium.

LIBIDO.—The emotional urge within life which causes it to express itself.

LIFE.—The animating Principle of Being.

LOGIC.—Reasoning which keeps faith with itself.

LOGOS.—The word of God.

LOVE.—The givingness of the self.

MACROCOSM.—The Universal World.

MALPRACTICE.—The destructive use of Mind Power. It may be conscious or malicious, innocent or ignorant.

MAN.—The objectification of God in the human form. The idea of God manifested in the flesh. The Sonship of the Father. Generic man is the Type, and the personal man is the concrete expression of the Type.

MANIA.—An irresistible desire controlling personal action.

MANIFESTATION.—The objectification of ideas.

MASCULINE PRINCIPLE.—The Self-Assertive Spirit, either in God or man.

MATERIAL MAN.—The objective man. Not opposed to Spirit, but the logical outcome of the Self-Knowing Mind.

MATTER.—Any form which substance takes in the world of sense and objectivity.

MAYA.—World of mental illusion.

MEDIUM.—One who objectifies subjectivity.

MEMORY.—The subjective retention of ideas.

MENTAL ATMOSPHERE.—The mental emanation of anything, any person or any place. Everything has some kind of a mental atmosphere.

MENTAL CORRESPONDENTS.—The inner image in mind which balances the outer objectification of itself. Every objective thing has an inner mental correspondent.

MENTAL EQUIVALENT.—Having a subjective idea of the desired experience.

MENTAL IMAGE.—Subjective likeness.

MENTAL PLANE.—Just between the Spiritual and the physical. The three planes intersphere each other.

MENTAL SCIENCE.—The science of Mind and Spirit. A systematic knowledge of the laws of the Mental and Spiritual World.

MENTAL TREATMENT.—The act, art, and science of inducing thought in Mind, which thought, operated upon by Mind, becomes a manifested condition.

MENTALITY.—An individual use of Universal Mind. There is One Mind, but within this One Mind are many mentalities. The One Mind is God and the mentalities are people.

MESMERISM.—The influence of personality.

METAPHYSICAL PRINCIPLE.—The Universal Creative Mind; as Spirit, It is conscious; as Law, it is subjective.

METAPHYSICS.—That which is beyond the known laws of physics.

MICROCOSM.—The individual world or universe of man.

MIND.—Mind is both conscious and subconscious. Conscious Mind is Spirit, either in God or man. Unconscious Mind is the law of conscious Mind acting and is, therefore, subconscious or subjective.

MIRROR OF MATTER.—The external form of an inner concept.

MIRROR OF MIND.—The subjective world, reflecting the images of thought that are projected into it by the conscious mind.

MONEY.—The idea of Spiritual supply, objectified.

MULTIPLICITY.—The many things and people which come from the One. All come from the One, and all live in, and by, the One.

MYSTIC.—One who senses the Divine Presence.

MYSTICISM.—Not a mystery, but a mystic sense of the presence of Ultimate Reality.

NATURAL MAN.—Instinctive or Spiritual Man.

NEUTRAL.—Not caring which way it works.

NEUTRALIZING THOUGHT.—The act of mentally erasing thought images.

NORMAL.—Natural.

OBJECTIFICATION.—The act of objectifying.

OBJECTIVE MIND.—The conscious mind.

OBJECTIVE PLANE.—The outer world of expression.

OBJECTIVE SIDE OF THOUGHT.—The conscious side of thinking.

OBSESSION.—Being controlled by thoughts, ideas or entities.

OCCULT.—Hidden.

OMEGA.—The last.

OMNIPOTENT.—All-powerful.

OMNIPRESENT.—Everywhere present.

OMNISCIENT INSTINCTIVE I AM.—God in man and things.

OMNISCIENT.—All-knowing.

THE ONLY.—The One Power.

PARTICULARIZATION.—Concrete forms produced by the Spirit.

PASSIVE RECEPTIVITY.—Willing to receive any and all forms of thought.

PEACE.—A state of inner calm.

PERCEPT.—An external object perceived by the mind. Distinguished from a concept which is an inner idea.

PERFECTION.—The real state of being.

PERSONALITY.—The objective evidence of individuality. The man as we see him in the relative world.

PHILOSOPHY.—A man's idea of life.

PLANES.—Different rates of vibration.

PLASTIC.—Easily molded.

POISE.—Mental balance.

POTENTIAL.—Inherent possibility.

POVERTY.—A limited thought.

POWER.—The union of peace with poise.

PRACTITIONER.—One who practices mental healing or demonstration.

PRENATAL.—Conditions before human birth.

PRIMORDIAL SUBSTANCE.—The ultimate formless stuff from which all things come.

PRINCIPLE.—Any law of nature.

PROPHET.—One who prophesies.

PSYCHE.—Soul or subjective.

PSYCHIC.—Subjective capacity. All people are psychic, but all are not mediums. A medium is one who objectifies the psychic sense.

PSYCHIC PHENOMENA.—Phenomena of the soul or subjective mentality.

PSYCHIC WORLD.—The world of subjectivity.

PSYCHO-ANALYSIS.—A systematic analysis of the subjective thought.

PSYCHOLOGY.—Study of the workings of the human mind.

PSYCHOMETRY.—Reading from the soul side of things.

PURPOSE.—Definite intention.

RACE-SUGGESTION.—Human beliefs, operating through the mentality of the individual.

REALITY.—The truth about anything.

REALIZATION.—Subjective comprehension of Truth.

REASON.—The mental ability to analyze, dissect and figure out the cause of things. The human mind can reason both inductively and deductively. The Divine Mind can reason only deductively.

REINCARNATION.—Rebirth in the flesh.

RELATIVE.—That which depends upon something else.

RELIGION.—A Man's idea of God or gods.

RESURRECTION.—Rising from a belief in death.

REVELATION.—Becoming consciously aware of hidden things.

RICHES.—Idea of abundance.

SAGE.—One versed in spiritual truths.

SAINT.—A holy man.

SCIENCE.—Knowledge of laws and principles.

SEER.—One who sees into causes.

SELF-CONSCIOUSNESS.—Personally conscious. Distinguished from Cosmic Consciousness, which is a consciousness of the Unity of the Whole.

SELF-EXISTENT.—Living by virtue of its own being.

SELF-KNOWING MIND.—The conscious mind.

SELF-PROPELLING.—Having power within itself.

SELF-REALIZATION.—A consciousness of the self as a reality.

SILENCE.—The inner realization of the One Life.

SIMPLE CONSCIOUSNESS.—Consciousness, as in an animal.

SIN.—Missing the mark. There is no sin but a mistake and no punishment but an inevitable consequence.

SONSHIP.—Man as the Son of God.

SOUL.—The Creative Medium of Spirit.

SOUL OF THE UNIVERSE.—The Universal Creative Medium.

SPACE.—The Cosmic World. The distance between two specific forms. Space is a relative condition within the Absolute.

SPECIALIZE.—To bring into concrete form.

SPIRIT.—God, within Whom all spirits exist. The Self-Knowing One. The Conscious Universe. The Absolute.

SPIRIT OF MAN.—God in man.

SPIRIT OF THE UNIVERSE.—The Self-Knowing Mind of God.

SPIRITS.—Personalities.

SPIRITUAL.—The atmosphere of God.

SPIRITUAL CONSCIOUSNESS.—The realization of the Divine Presence.

SPIRITUAL MAN.—Man in a conscious state.

SPIRITUAL REALIZATION.—The realization of the Divine Presence.

STREAM OF CONSCIOUSNESS.—The automatic, mental emanation of the subjective state of thought.

SUBCONSCIOUS.—The same as subjective.

SUBJECTIVE.—Beneath the threshold of the conscious. The inner side.

SUBJECTIVE ACTIVITY.—The inner action of the automatic law.

SUBJECTIVE CAUSATION.—The mental law set in motion.

SUBJECTIVE SIDE OF LIFE.—The inner side of life, as law.

SUBJECTIVE STATE OF THOUGHT.—The sum total of all one's thinking, both conscious and unconscious.

SUBJECTIVE TENDENCY.—The subjective trend of thought.

SUBJECTIVE TO SPIRIT.—The Law is subjective to the Spirit.

SUBJECTIVITY OF THE UNIVERSE.—The Universal Soul or mental Law.

SUBLIMATE.—To transmute energy into another form of action.

SUBSIST.—To live by virtue of spirit.

SUBSTANCE.—The formless back of all forms.

SUGGESTION.—Receiving the thoughts of another. Suggestion accepts the ideas of others and believes in them. It may be conscious or unconscious.

SYMBOL.—Mental impressions denoting spiritual or mental truths.

TELEKINETIC ENERGY.—Moving ponderable objects without physical contact.

TELEPATHY.—Thought transference.

THEOLOGY.—That which treats of the nature of God.

THOUGHT FORMS.—All thought has definite form on the subjective side of life.

THOUGHT.—The movement of consciousness.

TIME.—"Sequence of events in a Unitary Whole."

TRANCE.—A subjective state.

TRANSMUTATION.—Same as sublimation.

TREATMENT.—The art, act and science of inducing thought on the subjective side of life. Setting the Law in motion.

TRINITY.—The Threefold Universe.

TRIUNE UNITY.—The Trinity.

TRUTH.—That which Is.

UNCONSCIOUS MEMORY.—Subjective memory.

UNCONSCIOUS THOUGHT.—Unconscious subjective thought.

UNITY.—The Oneness of God and man.

UNIVERSAL LAW.—Divine Principle.

UNIVERSAL MIND.—The Creative Medium of Spirit.

UNIVERSAL SOUL.—The Universal Subjectivity.

UNIVERSAL SPIRIT.—The Conscious Mind of God.

UNIVERSAL SUBJECTIVITY.—The Creative Medium or the Universal Mind.

UNIVERSE.—The Cosmic World.

VIBRATION.—Law in execution.

VISUALIZATION.—The art of mentally projecting a thought form into the Universal Creative Medium.

WORD.—The thought of God or man.

THE CALL

This I saw, or else some inner presence made it known to me;
The Universe is filled with life; the air, the sky, the sea
Teem with intelligence, with majesty and might;
And deep within me, some subtle inner sight
Beholds and sees, comprehends and knows the All,
Nor fears nor falters, but answers the Divine Call
To be as one beyond the bounds of time and space,
To overcome the bondage of the human race,
And leap, with trust undaunted, free,
Into the deeps of that Infinite Sea
Whose waters, calm, are ready to receive
Those who, in simple faith, believe.

THE
SCIENCE
OF MIND

1938 Edition

These lessons are dedicated to that Truth
which frees man from himself and sets him on the pathway
of a new experience, which enables him to see
through the mist to the Eternal and Changeless Reality.

PEACE BE UNTO THEE, STRANGER

Peace be unto thee, stranger, enter and be not afraid.

I have left the gate open and thou art welcome to my home.

There is room in my house for all.

I have swept the hearth and lighted the fire.

The room is warm and cheerful and you will find comfort and rest
within.

The table is laid and the fruits of Life are spread before thee.

The wine is here also, it sparkles in the light.

I have set a chair for you where the sunbeams dance through the
shade.

Sit and rest and refresh your soul.

Eat of the fruit and drink the wine.

All, all is yours, and you are welcome.

Contents

INTRODUCTION

I. THE THING ITSELF   309

The Universe Never Plays Favorites • *Nothing Supernatural about the Study of Life* • *There Are Not Two Minds, Only Two Names* • *Limitless Power at Man's Disposal* • *All Thought Is Creative* • *The Road to Freedom Is Not Mysterious* • *Learning to Trust Will Make Us Happy* • *Divine Nature Is in Every Man.*

II. THE WAY IT WORKS   316

Universal Mind, or Spirit, Is God • *The Seed of Perfection Is Hidden Within* • *Spirit Works for Us by Working Through Us* • *How Much Can We Believe?* • *Good Only . . . Not Good and Evil.*

III. WHAT IT DOES   320

The Universe Impersonal • *A Riddle of Simplicity* • *Love Rules Through Law* • *The Scientific Method* • *Contains All Knowledge* • *Mental Work Is Definite* • *The Principle Re-stated* • *The Secret Already Known* • *Treatment Active, Not Passive* • *No Mystery in Truth* • *Hope a Subtle Illusion* • *No Limit to Thought.*

IV. HOW TO USE IT   328

All Principles Are Intangible • The Law Is Infinite • God Does Not Punish the Mathematician, the Unsolved Problem Does • Bring Thought into Line with Reality • Fill the Mind with the Expectancy of Good • Let Your Conversation Be in Heaven • We Must Trust the Invisible • Treatment a Spiritual Entity in a Mental World • True Thought Deals Directly with First Cause.

Part One

THE NATURE OF BEING

What we believe about God and man.

1. "IN THE BEGINNING, GOD!"   337

The Beginning • The Story of Creation Simplified • Describing the Infinite • Absolute Intelligence • A Deep Inquiry • The Voice of God in Creation • The Thought of God ... The Word of God • Spirit Knows Itself • Volition.

2. MIND . . . THE GREATEST DISCOVERY   343

Nature Waits on Man's Self-Recognition • The First Great Discovery • The Greatest Discovery of All Time ... Mind • Memory • Science • How Laws Are Discovered • The Science of Mind • Where Do We Get Our Mental Impressions? • Reading Thought • Mental Laws • The Threefold Nature of God • Trinity of Being.

3. SPIRIT   350

The Definition of Spirit • Its Nature • Spirit, the Changeless • The Action of Spirit Within Itself • How We Understand Its Operation • Metaphysics and Physics • Only One Mind • The "Personalness" of God.

4. SOUL   356

Creative Medium • Subjective Intelligence • Law • How We Use the Creative Principle • Mind and Ether • How Can Spirit Create? • The Soul Reasons Deductively • Subjectivity Never an Entity.

5. BODY   362

Definition • That Which Changes • Form Within the Formless • Cause and Effect • Unity and
Multiplicity • Immortality • A Divine Mental Picture.

6. MAN'S RELATIONSHIP TO THE SPIRITUAL UNIVERSE   368

Man Re-enacts the Nature of God • The World Has Learned All It Should Through Suffering •
Freedom or Bondage • Punishment and Reward • Spirit, Soul, and Body • Limitless Medium • Christ
and Antichrist • Unity • Subjective Law • The Result of Our Own Thinking • Law Is Mind in
Action • The Destructive Use of the Law • Oneness with All Law.

7. SUMMARY OF PART ONE: THE NATURE OF BEING   384

What we believe about God and man.

Part Two

SPIRITUAL MIND HEALING

FIRST DIVISION: IDEATION

*A recognition of the Power, and the
thought and purpose back of mind healing.*

8. THE POWER OF THOUGHT   391

Spiritual Mind Healing • The Basis for Mental Healing • The Act of Incarnation • Activity of the One
Mind • It Is Done unto Us • Thought Force • The Atmosphere of Our Thinking • Inducing
Thought • Choosing Thought • Thoughts Are Things • One with God • The Power Within • We Set
Our Own Limitations • Understanding.

9. PRAYER   399

The Difference Between Prayer and Treatment • Laws Governing Prayer • Prayer Is Essential to
Happiness • Prayer Is Its Own Answer.

10. FAITH 403

The Mental Approach • Always a Power • Misplaced Faith • Understanding Faith • No Confusion • Available to All • Vitalizing Faith • The Technique of Acquiring Faith • Conviction.

11. MENTAL AND SPIRITUAL TREATMENT 409

Treatment: What It Is • The Purpose of Treatment • The Way of Treatment • Treatment Not Explained in the Bible • What Is a Practitioner? • The First Requisite • A Practitioner's Business • Different Methods of Treatment • When and What Is a Demonstration? • Let Us Not Fool Ourselves.

12. SUMMARY OF PART TWO: SPIRITUAL MIND HEALING, FIRST DIVISION: IDEATION 419

A recognition of the Power, and the thought and purpose back of mind healing.

Part Three

SPIRITUAL MIND HEALING

SECOND DIVISION: PRACTICE

Determining destiny. The technique by which
we lay hold of mind power, and prove its practicability.

13. CAUSES AND CONDITIONS 425

Mental Practice Deals Only with Thought • Changeless Reality • The Perfect Universe • Turn Entirely from the Condition • Look Only at What You Want • Never Limit Your View of Life • Place No Limit on Principle • God Never Compromises.

14. PHYSICAL PERFECTION 430

What We Understand about Healing • We Are Allowed to Choose • Man Re-enacts God • Only Our Own Concepts Limit Us • Spiritual Mind Healing • Disease Is Impersonal • Disease Is Not Always Due to Conscious Thought • How to Heal • Healing Is Clear Thinking • No Sensation in Treatments • The Medium of Healing • Treating Children • The Power of the Word • Seeing Perfection.

15. PHYSICAL PERFECTION, CONCLUDED   *452*

What Can Be Healed? • *Suggestions for Treatments* • *Do Not Try to Go Beyond Your Understanding* • *Depend upon Principle* • *How Habits Are Acquired and Treated* • *Treating Pain* • *Repeating Treatments* • *Headache* • *Why People Become Fatigued* • *Treating Insanity* • *Treating Lung Trouble* • *Vision* • *Constipation* • *Skin* • *Arms and Hands* • *Feet and Legs* • *False Growths (Tumors, Cancer, Gallstones)* • *Removing the Complex* • *Heart Trouble* • *Poison of Any Kind* • *Paralysis* • *Asthma and Hay Fever* • *Nerve Troubles* • *Blood Troubles and Skin Diseases (High Blood Pressure, Hardening of the Arteries, Eczema, Boils)* • *Fevers* • *Obstetrics* • *Colds, Influenza and Grippe* • *Obesity* • *Treating Kidney, Bladder and Liver Disturbances* • *Treating Stomach and Bowel Troubles* • *Treating Insomnia* • *Deafness* • *Weather Conditions* • *Thoughts about Food* • *Rheumatism* • *Healing Intemperance* • *Supply* • *A Treatment for Peace of Mind.*

16. THE PRINCIPLES OF SUCCESSFUL LIVING   *481*

Not Something for Nothing • *The Law Is Infinite* • *Demonstrating the Law* • *Spirit and Mental Law* • *Success and Happiness.*

17. MENTAL EQUIVALENTS   *490*

If We Know • *What Do We Mean by Mental Equivalents?* • *The Prayer of Faith* • *Definite Plan* • *How to Demonstrate a Home* • *See Life Expressed* • *Perfect Action . . . No Mistakes.*

18. THE LAW OF ATTRACTION   *500*

Thought Atmosphere • *Attraction of Personality* • *Attracting Friends* • *Attracting Success* • *No Failures* • *No Personal Responsibility* • *The Law of Correspondence.*

19. SUMMARY OF PART THREE:

THE PRACTICE OF SPIRITUAL MIND HEALING   *510*

The healing of conditions, the technique by which we lay hold of mind power and prove its practicability in determining destiny.

Brief Reminders on How to Give Spiritual Treatment   *517*

Part Four

THE PERFECT WHOLE

The Indivisible Whole, within which are all of Its parts.

20. WHAT THE MYSTICS HAVE TAUGHT   523

What Is a Mystic? • *Unity* • *Individuality* • *Ultimate Salvation for All* • *Evolution* • *Cosmic Consciousness . . . Illumination.*

21. SOME PHASES OF THE SUBJECTIVE LIFE   536

The Subjective Mind • *Race-Suggestion* • *Subjective Mind and Inspiration* • *Mental Atmospheres* • *Tuning in on Thought* • *Streams of Consciousness* • *The Spirit of Prophecy.*

22. FINDING THE CHRIST   543

Who Is Christ? • *God . . . Infinite Personality* • *The Indivisible Whole* • *The Triumphant Christ.*

23. IMMORTALITY   554

The Meaning of Immortality • *Where Did Man Come from and Why?* • *What Is the Body?* • *Shall We Have a Body Hereafter?* • *The Ether of Science* • *Is There Spirit Communication?* • *What of Reward and Punishment?* • *Shall We Rest in the Hereafter?* • *Personal Convictions of Life Eternal.*

24. GENERAL SUMMARY OF ALL FOUR SECTIONS OF THE SCIENCE OF MIND AND A FINAL CONCLUSION   567

Part Five

TEACHINGS FROM THE NEW TESTAMENT

FROM THE TEACHING OF JESUS   593

Why Jesus Had Such Power • Man Shall Not Live by Bread Alone • The Meek Shall Inherit the Earth • They That Hunger Shall Be Fed • The Merciful Shall Obtain Mercy • The Pure in Heart Shall See God • The Altar of Faith • The Father Who Seeth in Secret • The Secret of Prayer • How God Forgives • The Single Eye • The Divine Bounty • Judge Not, That Ye Be Not Judged • Religious Morbidities • Thought Retards or Quickens • Self-Healing Must Come First of All • Scientific Prayer • God and Creation • Entering the Kingdom of Reality • The Healing of the Centurion's Servant.

Jesus Forgives a Man and Heals Him • God Knows No Evil • New Cloth and Old Garments • Thy Faith Hath Made Thee Whole • The Law of Circulation • Whom Shall We Try to Help? • Nothing Can Be Hidden • A Man's Foes • The Reward of True Visioning • Wisdom Is Justified of Her Children • The Child-Like Faith • The Real Father and Son • The Power at the Heart of God • The Great Search • The Need of Spiritual Experience • The Cause of Human Troubles • How to Approach the Spirit • The Purpose of the Science of Mind.

And Jesus Knew Their Thoughts • Good Thoughts and a Good Harvest • The Father-Mother God • To Him Who Hath Shall Be Given • The Concept of a Successful Man • The Seeing Eye • The Kingdom and the Mustard Seed • The Kingdom Is Like Leaven • The Pearl of Great Price • That Which Defiles • When the Blind Lead the Blind • Who Would Save His Life Shall Lose It • Fasting and Prayer • Healing the Lunatic • As Little Children • Whatsoever Ye Shall Bind on Earth • Divine Forgiveness • A Formula for Effective Prayer • The Two Great Commandments • History Proves the Reality of Truth.

God Turns to Us as We Turn to Him • The Two Sons • God Does Not Argue • The Far Country • Why We Are in Want • The Fallen Man • No One Gives to Us but Ourselves • The Great Awakening • Self-Condemnation • And the Father Saw Him Afar Off • God Does Not Condemn • God Knows No Sin • The Best Robe • The Father's House Always Open • The Stay-at-Home Son • The Application of the Story • God Can Only Give Us What We Take • The Universe Holds Nothing Against Us • The Eternal Completion • The New Birth • Heaven • The Son of Man.

When We Are Strong • The Word of Power • The Meat Which Perisheth • The Three Planes of Life • The Light of the World • Love • Let Not Your Heart Be Troubled • In My Father's House Are Many

Mansions • Who Sees the Son Sees the Father • The Holy Comforter • Abiding in the One • That Ye Bear Much Fruit.

OTHER TEACHINGS FROM THE NEW TESTAMENT 638

The Law of Correspondents • There Is No Condemnation • The Spirit That Raised Jesus • The Spirit of Adoption • Joint Heirs with Christ • The Inner Light • Predestination • God's Will for His Creation • The Renewing of Your Mind • Bless and Curse Not • The Great Awakening • The Law of God Is One of Liberty • How to Demonstrate Liberty • Mental Expansion • The Ascending Scale of Life • The Divine Ideas • Immortal Clothing • The Inner Man • The Endless Creation • The Unity of Life • The Renewing of the Mind • Be Strong in the Lord • Wickedness in High Places • The Armor of God • The Mind That Jesus Used • A Pattern for Thought • Rejoice Evermore • Constant Prayer • Quench Not the Spirit • Ask in Faith, Believing • Evil Is Created by Man • Doers of the Word • The Law Is No Respecter of Persons • The Prayer of Faith • The Confession of Mistakes • Now Are We the Sons of God.

Part Six

MEDITATIONS

MEDITATIONS FOR SELF-HELP AND HEALING 657

Come, and Let Me Heal You • He Is Mighty Within Me to Heal • I Do Not Inherit Disease • No Congestion • No False Growth • No Weariness • Perfect Hearing • Perfect Vision • The All-Seeing Eye • The Healing of the Flesh • There Is No Pain • Happiness and Completion • Here and Now • Majestic Calm • No Loss • Oh, for a Tongue to Express • O Soul of Mine, Look Out and See • Seeing the Perfect • The Circle Is Complete • The Things That Are • A Song of Hope • Be Still and Know • Cast Aside All Doubt • Divine Companionship • His Eye Is on the Sparrow • Hope Cannot Die • I Am Not Alone • I Went into a Mountain • The Joy of the Soul.

Freedom from Sin • Free from Sensitiveness • I Keep the Promise • Love Gleams Through the Mist • No Bondage • No Condemnation • No False Habit • No Hypnotism nor False Suggestion • No Mistakes • There Are No Responsibilities • The Time Has Come • Within Thy Law Is Freedom • Beauty • Friendship of the Spirit and of Man • I Serve • I Shall Not Doubt nor Fear • I Was Told to Live • Law • Love • Love Dissolves All Fear • My Affairs • My Business • My Profession • No Delays • No Misrepresentations • No Obstructions • No Over-Action nor Inaction • One with Perfect

Action • Peace, Poise and Power • Stillness and Receptivity • Thanksgiving and Praise • The Inner Light • The Night Is Filled with Peace • The Seal of Approval • The Secret Way • The Shining Path • The Things I Need Come to Me • The Way Is Made Clear Before Me.

As Love Enters, Fear Departs • Infinite Life Within • My Feet Shall Not Falter • No Harm Shall Befall You • Power to Live • The Circle of Love • The Circle of Protection • The Power Within Blesses All • The Quick Answer • A Song of Joy • Born of Eternal Day • I Arise and Go Forth • Inspiration • The Dawn Has Come • Complete Confidence • Drawing the Good • I Fear No Evil • I Have Known, Always • I Meet My Good • My Atmosphere • My Good Is Complete • My Own Shall Come to Me • My Soul Reflects Thy Life • Sorrow Flees from Me • Substance and Supply • The Ever and the All • The House of Love.

Arise, My Spirit • Command My Soul • Despair Gives Way to Joy • Free Spirit Within Me • Fullness of Light • He Who Inhabits Eternity • I Listen • Joy Has Come to Live with Me • My Thought Is in Thee • O Love Divine • Peace Steals Through the Soul • Stand Forth and Speak • Subtle Essence of Spirit Within Me • The Everlasting Arms • The Mantle of Love • The Voice of Truth • The Witness of Truth • Through the Long Night Watches • They Strength Is Sufficient • Waiting on Thee • Whose Right It Is to Come.

I Control My Mental Household • My Word Comes Back to Me • My Word Shall Bear Fruit • O Man, Speak Forth Thy Word • The Power of the Word • The Word of Power • The Unassailable Truth and the Irresistible Word • I Behold in Thee His Image • I See No Evil • I Shall Never Die • Love to the World • My Life Is One with God • No Misunderstandings • The Divine Plan for Me • The Personality of God • The Radiation of Life • Unity • Within Thee Is Fullness of Life • I Am Complete in Thee.

MEDITATIONS, CONCLUDED

*A Treatment for Alcoholism or Other Drug Addiction • A Treatment to Heal Confusion or Discord •
I Accept the Fullness of My Own Divine Well-Being • The Gifts of God Are Mine Today • Abundance Is
My Inheritance • My Vibration Attracts Friends to Me • Peace Is the Power at the Heart of God • God
Restores Me to Perfect Health • I Allow Myself to Dip Deeply into My Divine Nature • Perfect
Intelligence Directs My Thought • I Am Not Bound by Any Mistake • My Ideal Merges into the Real • I
Represent the Principle of Perfection • I Take the Christ Way to Fulfillment • The Eternal Cycles of Life
in Motion Fulfill My Faith.*

Charts   703

Glossary   711

Index   759

INTRODUCTION

I. THE THING ITSELF

II. THE WAY IT WORKS

III. WHAT IT DOES

IV. HOW TO USE IT

I

THE THING ITSELF

We all look forward to the day when science and religion shall walk hand in hand through the visible to the invisible. Science knows nothing of opinion, but recognizes a government of law whose principles are universal. Yet any scientist who refuses to accept intangible values has no adequate basis for the values which he has already discovered. Revelation must keep faith with reason, and religion with law—while intuition is ever spreading its wings for greater flights— and science must justify faith in the invisible.

To suppose that the Creative Intelligence of the Universe would create man in bondage and leave him bound would be to dishonor the Creative Power which we call God. To suppose that God could make man as an individual, without leaving him to discover himself, would be to suppose an impossibility. Individuality must be spontaneous; it can never be automatic. The seed of freedom must be planted in the innermost being of man, but, like the Prodigal Son, man must make the great discovery for himself.

We see abundance in the Universe. We cannot count the grains of sand on a single beach. The earth contains untold riches, and the very air is vibrant with power. Why, then, is man weak, poor and afraid? The Science of Mind deals with these questions. The Divine Plan is one of Freedom; bondage is not God-ordained. Freedom is the birthright of every living soul. All instinctively feel this. The Truth points to freedom, under Law. Thus the inherent nature of man is forever seeking to express itself in terms of freedom. We do well to listen to this Inner

Voice, for it tells us of a life wonderful in its scope; of a love beyond our fondest dreams; of a freedom which the soul craves.

But the great Love of the Universe must be One with the great law of Its Own Being, and we approach Love through the Law. This, then, is the teaching: Love and Law. As the love of God is perfect, so the law of God also is perfect. We must understand both.

Whatever the nature of any principle may be—in so far as it is understood by anyone—it may be understood by all who take the time to investigate. This does not require an unusual degree of intelligence, but, rather, a practical application of what we now know in order that we may increase our knowledge. The study of the Science of Mind is a study of First Cause, Spirit, Mind, or that invisible Essence, that ultimate Stuff and Intelligence from which everything comes, the Power back of creation—the Thing Itself.

We accept this "Thing" and believe in It. What we desire is to know more about It, and how to use It. From proof alone, we know we are dealing with a definite principle. If one (through the conscious use of his knowledge) can produce a certain result, he must know with what he is dealing.

It may seem as though, in dealing with metaphysics, we are dealing with something that is too abstract. But what is tangible other than results? Principles are forever hidden from our eyes. We accept the deductions of science in so far as they are proved, and we recognize that they are built upon immutable, but invisible principles.

The Universe Never Plays Favorites

We are so used to the thought that if we mix certain colors we get certain other colors, that we do not realize we are dealing with a principle. We know that *whoever* blends these particular colors will get the same result, but we do not know why; THE WISEST MAN LIVING DOES NOT KNOW WHY! We do not have to stretch our credulity any more in metaphysics.

We think of metaphysics, perhaps, as something that only the most profound thinkers have known about, but we should remember that we also are thinkers. The profound thought of all ages has stood in awe of Life itself, realizing that here is a power and potentiality, the highest possibilities of which the human intellect cannot fathom.

Universal principles are never respecters of persons; the Universe has no favorites. Therefore, it is written: "And let him that is athirst come. And whosoever will, let him take the water of life freely" (Rev. 22:17).

Nothing Supernatural about the Study of Life

Let us then approach the Science of Mind—the Science of Spiritual Psychology—with awe, but not with fear; with truly a humble thought, but not with a sense that we are unworthy. Let us approach it normally, happily, willing to accept, glad to experiment, hoping and believing that as the result of our efforts we shall each derive a great good—a sound understanding of the natural laws of Life, as they apply to the individual and his relationship to the whole universal scheme of things.

This is the simple meaning of true metaphysical teaching, the study of Life and the nature of the Law, governed and directed by thought; always conscious that we live in a spiritual Universe; that God is in, through, around and for us. There is nothing supernatural about the study of Life from the metaphysical viewpoint. That which today seems to us supernatural, after it is thoroughly understood, will be found spontaneously natural.

We all know that many have been healed of physical disease through prayer. Let us analyze this. Why are some healed through prayer while others are not? Can we believe that there is a God who picks out some man and says, "I will honor your prayer, but I do not think so much of Mr. So and So"? It is superstitious to believe that God will answer the prayer of one above another. Jesus said that God "maketh His sun to rise on the evil and on the good, and sendeth rain on the just and on the unjust" (Matt. 5:45).

Since some people have been healed through prayer, while others have not, the answer is NOT that God has responded to some and not to others, but that some have responded to God more than others. Their prayer (their thought) has responded by corresponding. The answer to prayer is in the prayer. But what is a prayer? A prayer is a movement of thought, within the mind of the one praying, along a definite line of meditation; that is, for a specific purpose.

What is the mind? No man living knows. We know a great deal about the mind, *but not what it is*. By mind, we mean consciousness. We are now using it. We cannot locate mind in the body, for, while the body is a necessary vehicle for consciousness while we are here, it is not consciousness. We cannot isolate mind. All we know about it is not what it is, but *what it does*, and the greatest philosopher who ever lived knows no more than this . . . except that he may tell us more of how it works.

There Are Not Two Minds, Only Two Names

Mind—the Thing, Spirit, Causation—is beyond, and yet not beyond, our grasp. *Beyond*, in that It is so big; *within*, in that wherever we grasp at It, *we are It to the extent that we grasp It;* but, since It is Infinite, we can never encompass It. *We shall never encompass God, and yet we shall always be in God and of God!*

Mind comes under two classifications. There are not *two minds*, but rather two names employed in describing states of consciousness: the *objective*, or conscious and the *subjective*, or unconscious. We think of the conscious state as our conscious use of mind. The subconscious (or subjective) state of mind—sometimes called the unconscious state—is that part of mind which is set in motion as a creative thing by the conscious state.

In the body of this textbook, under the heading of "Subjective Mind," we say: "In the Subjective Mind of man, we find a law obeying his word, the servant of his spirit. Suggestion has proved that the subconscious mind acts upon our thoughts. It is the mental law of our being, and the *creative factor* within us. It is unnecessary, at this point, to go into all the details of the Subjective Mind and its mode of action; it is enough to say that within us is a *mental law*, working out the will and purposes of our conscious thoughts. This can be no other than *our individual use of that Greater SUBJECTIVE MIND, which is the seat of all mental law and action*, and is 'The Servant of the Eternal Spirit throughout the ages.'"

Limitless Power at Man's Disposal

Marvelous as the concept may be, it is none the less true that man has at his disposal—in what he calls *his* Subjective Mind—a power that seems to be Limitless. THIS IS BECAUSE HE IS ONE WITH THE WHOLE ON THE SUBJECTIVE SIDE OF LIFE! Man's thought, falling into his subjective mind, merges with the Universal Subjective Mind, and becomes the law of his life, through the one great law of all life.

There are not two subjective minds. There is but one Subjective Mind, and what we call *our subjective mind* is really the use we are making of the One Law. Each individual maintains his identity in Law, through his personal use of It. And each is drawing from Life what he thinks into It!

To learn how to think is to learn how to live, for our thoughts go into a medium that is Infinite in Its ability to do and to be. Man, by thinking, can bring into his experience whatsoever he desires—if he thinks correctly, and becomes a living embodiment of his thoughts. This is not done by *holding thoughts* but by knowing the Truth.

Within us, then, there is a creative field, which we call the subjective mind; around us there is a creative field which we call Subjective. One is universal and the other is individual, but in reality they are one. THERE IS ONE MENTAL LAW IN THE UNIVERSE, AND WHERE WE USE IT, IT BECOMES OUR LAW BECAUSE WE HAVE INDIVIDUALIZED IT. It is impossible to plumb the depths of the individual mind, *because the individual mind is really not individual but is individualized*. Behind the individual is the Universal, which has no limits. In this concept alone lies the possibility of eternal and endless expansion. Everyone is Universal on the subjective side of life, and individual only at the point of conscious perception. The riddle is solved, and we all use the creative power of the Universal Mind *every time we use our own mind*.

All Thought Is Creative

Since this is true, it follows that we cannot say that one thought is creative while another is not. We must say that all thought is creative, according to the nature, impulse, emotion or conviction behind the thought. Thought creates a mold in the Subjective, in which the idea is accepted and poured, and sets power in motion in accordance with the thought. Ignorance of this excuses no one from its effects, for we are dealing with Law and not with whimsical fancy.

The conscious mind is superior to the subjective and may *consciously* use it. Great as the subconscious is, its tendency is set in motion by the conscious thought, and in this possibility lies the path to freedom. The Karmic Law is not Kismet. It is not fate but cause and effect. It is a taskmaster to the unwise; a servant to the wise.

The Road to Freedom Is Not Mysterious

Experience has taught us that the subjective tendency of this intelligent Law of creative force may consciously be directed and definitely used. *This is the greatest discovery of all time.* There is no mystery here, but a profound fact and a demonstrable one. The road to freedom lies, not through mysteries or occult performances, but through the intelligent use of Nature's forces and laws. The Law of Mind is a natural law in the spiritual world.

But what do we mean by the *spiritual world?* We mean the world of conscious intelligence. The Subjective is a world of Law and of mechanical order; in our lives, it is largely a reaction, an effect, a way. IT IS NEVER A PERSON THOUGH IT OFTEN APPEARS TO ACT AS THOUGH IT WERE ONE. Right here, many are completely misled, mistaking subjective impulses for actual personalities. This, however, is a field of investigation not fully to be considered here.

The simplest way to state the proposition is to say that we have a conscious mind that operates within a subjective field, which is creative. The conscious mind is Spirit, the subjective mind is Law. One is a complement of the other and no real individuality could be expressed without a combination of both.

No man has ever plumbed the depths of either the conscious or the subjective life. In both directions, we reach out to Infinity, and since we cannot encompass Infinity, we shall always be expanding and always enlarging our capacity to know and to experience.

We need not ask *why* these things are so. There can be no reason given as to why the Truth is true. We do not create laws and principles, but discover and make use of them. Let us accept this position relative to the laws of Mind and Spirit, and see what we can do with them—rather than how we may contradict the inevitable. Our mind and spirit is our echo of the "Eternal Thing" Itself, and the sooner we discover this fact, the sooner we shall be made free and happy. The Universe is filled with Spirit and filled with Law. One reacts to the other. We are Spirit and we are Law. The law of our life reacts to our spiritual or material concepts, and builds and re-builds according to our beliefs and faith.

LEARNING TO TRUST WILL MAKE US HAPPY

All men seek some relationship to the Universal Mind, the Over-Soul, or the Eternal Spirit, which we call God. And Life reveals itself to whoever is receptive to it. That we are living in a spiritual Universe, which includes the material or physical universe, has been a conclusion of the deepest thinkers of every age. That this spiritual Universe must be one of pure Intelligence and perfect Life, dominated by Love, by Reason and by the power to create, seems an inevitable conclusion.

There is a Power in the Universe that honors our faith in It; there is a Law in the Universe which exacts the "uttermost farthing." We all wish to feel that the power behind everything is good, as well as creative, an Eternal and Changeless Intelligence, in which man lives and moves and has his being. Intuitively, we sense that every man, in his native state, is some part or manifestation of this Eternal Principle; and that the entire problem of limitation, evil, suffering, and uncertainty is not God-ordained, but is the result of ignorance. It has been written that the Truth shall make us free, provided we know the Truth, and we note that the evolution of man's consciousness brings with it the acquisition of new powers and higher possibilities.

We find ourselves torn by confusion, by conflict, by affirmation and denial, by emotion congested by fear, congealed by pride. We are afraid of the Universe in which we live, suspicious of people around us, uncertain of the salvation of our own souls. All these things negatively react and cause physical disorders.

Nature seems to await our comprehension of her and, since she is governed by immutable laws—the ignorance of which excuses no man from their effects—the bondage of humanity must be a result of our ignorance of the true nature of Reality. The storehouse of Nature may be filled with good, but this good is locked to the ignorant. The key to this door is held in the mind of Intelligence, working in accordance with Universal Law. Through experience, man learns what is really good and satisfying, what is truly worthwhile. As his intelligence increases, and his capacity to understand the subtle laws of Nature grows, he will gradually be set free. As he learns the Truth, the Truth will automatically free him.

When we learn to trust the Universe, we shall be happy, prosperous and well. We must learn to come under that Divine Government, and accept the fact that Nature's table is ever filled. Never was there a Cosmic famine. "The finite alone has wrought and suffered, the Infinite lies stretched in smiling repose." God is always God. No matter what our emotional storm, or what our objective situation, may be, there is always a something hidden in the inner being that has never been violated. We may stumble, but always there is that Eternal Voice, forever whispering within our ear, that thing which causes the eternal quest, that thing which forever sings and sings.

DIVINE NATURE IS IN EVERY MAN

This is The Thing Itself. Briefly, let us recapitulate. There is that within every individual which partakes of the nature of the Universal Wholeness and—in so far as it operates—is God. That is the meaning of the word *Emmanuel*, the meaning of the word *Christ*. There is that within us which partakes of the nature of the Divine Being, and *since it partakes of the nature of the Divine Being, we are divine*. It reacts to us according to our belief in It; and it is an immutable Law, subject to the use of the least among us; no respecter of persons, It cannot be bound. Our Soul will never change or violate its own nature; all the denying of it will never change it; all the affirming of it will never make it any more than it is. But since it is what it is, and works in the way that it works, it appears to each through his belief. It is done unto each one of us as we believe.

We will say, then, that in spirit, man is One with God. But what of the great Law of the Universe? If we are really One with the Whole, we must be One with the Law of the Whole, as well as One with the Spirit of the Whole.

If we try to find something difficult to grasp, then we shall never grasp it, because we shall always think of It as being incomprehensible. The mind which we discover within us *is the Mind that governs everything*. This is The Thing Itself, and we should recognize its simplicity.

11
THE WAY IT WORKS

The Science of Mind is not a special revelation of any individual; it is, rather, the culmination of all revelations. We take the good wherever we find it, making it our own in so far as we understand it. The realization that Good is Universal, and that as much good as any individual is able to incorporate in his life is his to use, is what constitutes the Science of Mind and Spirit.

We have discussed the nature of The Thing as being Universal Energy, Mind, Intelligence, Spirit—finding conscious and individualized centers of expression through us—and that man's intelligence is this Universal Mind, functioning at the level of man's concept of It. This is the essence of the whole teaching.

UNIVERSAL MIND, OR SPIRIT, IS GOD

There is a Universal Mind, Spirit, Intelligence, that is the origin of everything: It is First Cause. It is God. This Universal Life and Energy finds an outlet in and through all that is energized, and through everything that lives. There is One Life back of everything that lives. There is One Energy back of all that is energized. This Energy is in everything. There is One Spirit back of all expression. That is the meaning of that mystical saying: "In Him we live, and move, and have our being" (Acts 17:28).

The life which we live is the Universal Life expressing through us, else how could we live.

Our thought and emotion is the use we make—consciously or unconsciously—of this original creative Thing that is the Cause of everything. Therefore, we shall say that the mind, spirit, and intelligence which we find in ourselves is as much of this original, creative God as we understand. That this is not robbing God is a self-evident fact. Since we are, then we are real and actual and have existence; and since we can reduce all that is to a fundamental unit, we find that we have this proposition:

There is Spirit—or this Invisible Cause—and nothing, out of which all things are to be made. Now, Spirit plus nothing leaves Spirit only. Hence there is One Original Cause and nothing, out of which we are made. In other words, we are made from this Thing. That is why we are called the "son of God."

We now know that this is what we are—because we could not be anything else—but we do not know how much of this we are! When we see It as It is, then, we shall see ourselves as we are. We can only see It by looking at It through our own eyes. Hence, we shall find a better God when we shall have arrived at a higher standard for man. If God is to interpret Himself to man, He must interpret Himself *through* man. And the Spirit can make no gift that we do not accept.

The Seed of Perfection Is Hidden Within

This Original Life is Infinite. It is good. It is filled with peace. It is of the essence of purity. It is the ultimate of intelligence. It is power. It is Law. It is Life. It is in us. In that inner sanctuary of our own nature, hidden perhaps from objective gaze, "nestles the seed, perfection."

In our ignorance of the truth, we have misused the highest power we possess. And so great is this power—so complete is our freedom in it, so absolute the domain of law through it—that the misuse of this power has brought upon us the very conditions from which we suffer. We are bound because we are first free; the power which appears to bind us is the only power in the universe which can free us. This is why Jesus summed up His whole philosophy in this simple statement: "It is done unto you as you believe." The great Teacher looked so deeply into Nature, that She revealed Her fundamental simplicity to him. That "believe" and that "as" symbolize heaven and hell. And so we suffer, not because suffering is imposed upon us, but because we are ignorant of our true nature.

Spirit Works for Us by Working Through Us

The Thing, then, works for us by working through us and is us, always. It cannot work for us in any other way. It spreads Itself over the whole universe and shouts at us from every angle, but It can become power to us ONLY WHEN WE RECOGNIZE IT AS POWER.

We cannot recognize that It is, while we are believing that It is not. Hence, it is written: "they . . . entered not in because of unbelief" (Heb. 4:6). We may enter in because of our belief, but we cannot enter while there is unbelief. Here we come to a house divided against itself. If we say we can only experience a little good, then we shall experience but a little good. But, if we say, with Emerson, "There is no great and no small to the soul that maketh all," then we may experience a greater good because we have conceived it.

Therefore, our belief sets the limit to our demonstration of a Principle which, of Itself, is without limit. It is ready to fill everything, because It is Infinite. So, it is not a question of Its willingness, nor of Its ability. It is entirely a question of our own receptivity.

How Much Can We Believe?

That we must go the way of the Law, is a fundamental tenet of this Science, because Nature obeys us as we first obey It, and our obedience to It is our acceptance of It. How much can we believe? AS MUCH AS WE CAN BELIEVE will be done unto us.

When the consciousness speaks, the law receives and executes. When a farmer plants a seed, he invokes the law. That which follows is done by the mechanical side of Nature, which has no volition of Its own. Involution is the cause and evolution is the effect. When a practitioner thinks, or gives a treatment, or makes a prayer, he is dealing with involution—the first step of the creative order. This is what the Bible calls the Word. That which follows is evolution, or the unfoldment of the word, or concept, into objective existence.

We are thinking, willing, knowing, conscious centers of Life. We are surrounded by, immersed in, and there is flowing through us, a creative Something . . . call It what you will. The sum total of all our thought, will, purpose, and belief, creates a tendency in this Law that causes It to react to us according to the sum total of that belief.

Ignorance of the law excuses no one from its effects. If, then, certain specific ways of thought and belief have produced limitations, other beliefs will change them. We must learn to believe. The approach should be direct, and it should be specific.

Suppose one is laboring under the idea of limitation. His whole thought is a picture of limitation. Where is he placing himself in Mind? Is he not, in substance, saying: "I cannot have and enjoy good things"? And he is demonstrating that he cannot have, or accomplish, good. It may take time to reshape the basis of his thought; he must commence by saying, "I perceive that because I am what I am—because of this Infinite Thing that over-shadows eternity and finds Its abiding place in me, I know that good is now mine—all good." There is no mental coercion in this. We do not will things to be done; things are brought into being, not by will, but by the power of the self-assertive Truth.

How much can one demonstrate? Just what one can believe. How much can we see, how much can we accept, how much can we find in our consciousness that is no longer repudiated by our own denials? Whatever that is, THAT MUCH WE CAN HAVE.

GOOD ONLY—NOT GOOD AND EVIL

The gardener goes forth in faith to sow his seeds. He has learned that as he sows, so shall he reap; that the law works for all alike. We must accustom ourselves to the concept of the impersonalness of the law, the availability of the law, and the mechanical accuracy of the law. If we can conceive only a little good, that is as much as we can experience.

We must instill into the mind the fundamental proposition that good is without bounds. Only good and loving-kindness shall "follow me all the days of my life" (Psalms 23). We must get this concept, rather than continuing to think there is a power of evil as opposed to the power of Good. We experience good and evil because we perceive a presence of duality rather than unity.

Then, knowing that The Thing can work for us only through us, let us begin to accept today more good than we experienced yesterday, and to know that we shall reap a harvest of fulfilled desires. The time must come when we shall have left the apparent evil behind; when it shall be rolled up like a scroll and numbered with the things which were once thought to be.

Let us realize and work with this sound knowledge and perfect faith: That as high as we shall make our mark in Mind and Spirit, so high shall be Its outward manifestation in our material world.

III

WHAT IT DOES

We should approach the study of this Science rationally, never expecting to derive any benefits from it that its Principle does not contain. For while it is true that we are immersed in an Infinite Intelligence, a Mind that knows all things, it is also true that this Intelligence can acquaint us with Its ideas only as we are able and willing to receive them. The Divine Mind is Infinite. It contains all knowledge and wisdom, but, before It can reveal Its secrets, It must have an outlet. This outlet we shall be compelled to supply through our own receptive mentalities.

All invention, art, literature, government, law and wisdom that has come to the race has been given to it through those who have deeply penetrated the secrets of nature and the mind of God.

Perhaps the simplest way to state the proposition is to say that we are surrounded by a Mind, or Intelligence, that knows everything; that the potential knowledge of all things exists in this Mind; that the abstract essence of beauty, truth and wisdom co-exist in the Mind of the Universe; that we also exist in It and may draw from It. BUT WHAT WE DRAW FROM IT WE MUST DRAW THROUGH THE CHANNEL OF OUR OWN MINDS. A unity must be established, and a conscious connection must be made, before we can derive the benefits which the greater Mind is willing to reveal or impart to us.

The Spirit can give us only what we can take; It imparts of Itself only as we partake of Its nature. It can tell us only what we can understand. The Infinite Knowingness becomes our wisdom only in such degree as we embody Its Intelligence. It has been said that we can know God only in so far as we can become God. This is a far-reaching thought and should be carefully scrutinized. It is to be taken figuratively and not too literally, for we cannot really become God, but we can and do partake of the Divine Nature, and the Universal does personify Itself through man in varying degrees, according to man's receptivity to It.

THE UNIVERSE IMPERSONAL

The Universe is impersonal. It gives alike to all. It is no respecter of persons. It values each alike. Its nature is to impart, ours to receive. When we stand in the light, we cast a shadow across the pathway of our own experience. Emerson advises that we get our *bloated nothingness* out of the way of the divine circuits.

A RIDDLE OF SIMPLICITY

It is a beautiful and true thought to realize that *every man stands in the shadow of a mighty Mind, a pure Intelligence, and a Divine givingness!* Not alone unto the great comes the soft tread of the Unseen Guest. The arrogant have not perceived the simplicity of faith, but the pure in heart see God. The farmer has seen the Heavenly Host in his fields. The child has frolicked with Him at play. The mother has clasped Him to her breast and the fond lover has seen Him in the eyes of his beloved. We look too far away for Reality.

The intelligence by and through which we perceive that there is a Spiritual Presence and an Infinite Mind in the Universe, constitutes our receptivity to It, and decides Its flow through us. We have made a riddle out of simplicity; therefore, we have not read the sermons written in stones, nor interpreted the light of love running through life.

To return to a sane simplicity is one of the first and most important things to do. All men receive *some* light, and this light is always the same light. There is one nature diffused throughout all nature; One God incarnated in all peoples.

The Divine Incarnation is inherent in our nature. We are immersed in an Infinite Knowingness. The question is, how much of this Reality are we going to express in our own lives? The direct approach is always the best and the most effective. In so far as any man has spoken the truth, he has proclaimed God—it matters not what his particular approach may have been. The scientist and the philosopher, the priest and the professor, the humanitarian and the empire builder, all have caught some gleam of the eternal glory and each has spoken, in his own tongue, that language which is of itself Universal.

Let us do away with a ponderosity of thought and approach the thing simply and quietly. It is the nature of the Universe to give us what we are able to take. It cannot give us more. It has given all, we have not yet accepted the greater gift.

Spiritual wisdom says that God manifests through everything and is incarnated in all men; that all is Divinity and that Nature herself is the body of God. The mechanical laws of nature are set and immutable, but the spontaneous recognition of these laws gives us the power to bring them into practical use in everyday life and experience.

Here we have a dual unity; law and order, spontaneous choice, volition, conscious action, and automatic reaction. The laws of the universe are to be trusted but we must come to understand them before we can use them. Once understood, any law is available and is impersonally responsive to each and all alike.

LOVE RULES THROUGH LAW

In an intelligent study of the teachings of the Science of Mind, we come to understand that all is Love and yet all is Law. Love rules through Law. Love is the Divine Givingness; Law is the Way. Love is spontaneous; Law is impersonal. We should study the nature of Reality with this in mind, and in this way we shall avoid two grave mistakes: either viewing life as made up only of mechanical laws, or viewing it as made up only of spontaneous actions, irrespective of law and order.

As we gain the broader viewpoint, we shall see that Life must contain two fundamental characteristics. We shall see that there is an Infinite Spirit, operating through an Infinite and Immutable Law. In this, Cosmos, and not chaos, finds an eternal existence in Reality. Love points the way and Law makes the way possible.

THE SCIENTIFIC METHOD

If we observe any scientific discovery, we shall see that this is the way it works. Some man's mind discovers the law, or principle, governing the science; this is the way of Love, of personal volition, of choice—this is the spontaneous element in the universe. Following this knowledge of the way the principle works—having discovered the operation of the Law—the spontaneous element now rests its case on immutable reactions inherent in the Law. All science is based upon proven principles.

But we should not overlook the significant fact that it is the MIND which discovers and makes use of the mechanical law! Is not this mind the Spirit in us? We can never completely fathom the Infinite Mind: we shall always be discovering new lands. Consequently, evolution is an eternal unfoldment of the more yet to be.

Since it is the mind which must first come to see, know and understand—and since all future possibility for the race must first find an avenue of outlet through someone's mind—we shall do well to look to the mind for the answer to all our problems.

Undoubtedly we are surrounded by, and immersed in, a perfect Life: a complete, normal, happy, sane, harmonious and peaceful existence. But *only as much of this Life as we embody will really become ours to use.* As much of this Life as we understand and embody will react as immutable law—the reaction of the mechanical to the volitional. The concept is wonderful and fraught with tremendous significance. In it is bound up our hopes and fears, our expectations, and our future and present realizations.

Since an understanding of any law must pass first through our conscious mind before we can make use of it, it follows that with all our getting, we should get understanding. Should we wish to know a certain truth, we should state that this truth is already known in Mind and this statement will be true, but the Over-Mind must be accepted into our mind before we can understand It. How, then, are we to accomplish the desired result? By stating and feeling that *our mind* knows the truth about the thing we desire to know. In this way we draw the Infinite Mind into our mentalities, for definite knowledge of some particular good.

CONTAINS ALL KNOWLEDGE

The Universal Mind contains all knowledge. It is the potential ultimate of all things. To It, all things are possible. To us, as much is possible as we can conceive, according to law. Should all the wisdom of the universe be poured over us, we should yet receive only that which we are ready to understand. This is why some draw one type of knowledge and some another, and all from the same source—the Source of all knowledge. The scientist discovers the principles of his science, the artist embodies the spirit of his art, the saint draws Christ into his being—all because they have courted the particular presence of some definite concept. Each state of consciousness taps the same source, but has a different receptivity. Each receives what he asks for, according to his ability to embody. The Universal is Infinite; the possibility of differentiating is limitless.

Life always becomes to us the particular thing we need *when we believe that It becomes to us that particular thing.* The understanding of this is the essence of simplicity. As all numbers proceed from the fundamental unit, as all material forms are but different manifestations of one formless stuff, so all things proceed from that which is neither person, place nor thing, but is of the essence of all things.

Our thought and conscious receptivity differentiate this Universal Possibility, by drawing It through our minds and causing It to flow into particular channels, through the conscious receptivity of our different faiths. One state of consciousness will differentiate one kind of a result, another mental state a different manifestation.

MENTAL WORK IS DEFINITE

Mental work is definite. Each state of thought taps the same Principle, each uses the same Law, is inspired by the same Spirit, but each draws forth a different result. Here is multiplicity proceeding from Unity. This is what Emerson meant when he said that Unity passes into variety.

But, someone will ask, can we bring out both good and evil from the One Source? Of course not. The First Principle is goodness, and only in so far as our thought and action tend toward a constructive program, will it eventually succeed.

We cannot fight the Universe. It refuses to be budged from Its course. We can only go with It.

But there is ample latitude for personal expression. How then, are we to know what is right and what is wrong? We are not GOING to know; we already do know. Every man knows right from wrong, in its broadest sense.

It should be considered right to live and to enjoy living. To be well, happy, and to express freedom, is to be in accord with Divine Law and Wisdom. Here is latitude enough for the most expectant, and the most enthusiastic.

THE PRINCIPLE RE-STATED

Let us restate our Principle. We are surrounded by an Infinite Possibility. It is Goodness, Life, Law and Reason. In expressing Itself through us, It becomes more fully conscious of Its own being. Therefore, It wishes to express through us. As It passes into our being, It automatically becomes the law of our lives. It can pass into expression through us only as we consciously allow It to do so. Therefore, we should have faith in It, and Its desires and Its ability to do for us *all that we shall ever need to have done*. Since It must pass through our consciousness to operate for us, we must be conscious that It is doing so.

The one who wishes to demonstrate some particular good must become conscious of this particular good, if he wishes to experience it. Therefore, he must make his mind receptive to it and he must do this consciously. There is no hocus-pocus in a mental treatment. It is always definite, conscious, concrete and explicit. We are dealing with Intelligence, and should deal with It intelligently.

There is no occult trick in giving scientific treatments. It is just the reverse. Simplicity should mark our every effort and positivity should accompany all statements that we make into the law of Good.

The Secret Already Known

A *treatment* is a statement in the Law, embodying the concrete idea of our desires and accompanied by an unqualified faith that the Law works *for* us, as we work with It. Let us waste no further time looking for the secret of success or the key to happiness. Already the door is open and whosoever will may enter.

Undoubtedly, each of us is now demonstrating his concept of life, but *trained* thought is far more powerful than *untrained*, and the one who gives conscious power to his thought should be more careful what he thinks than the one who does not. The more power one gives to his thought—the more completely he believes that his thought has power—the more power will it have.

Treatment Active, Not Passive

A treatment is an active thing. When one gives a treatment, he is not sitting around, hoping that something may happen. He is definitely, constructively, actively stating, sensing, knowing some specific good. This is in accord with the Principle which we seek to demonstrate. If we give treatments without a definite motive in mind, the most we can accomplish will be to promote a salutary atmosphere. A *passive* meditation will never produce an active demonstration, any more than an artist can paint a picture by sitting down with his paints but never using them.

The mind must conceive before the Creative Energy can produce; we must supply the avenue through which It can work. It is ready and willing. It is Its nature to spring into being through our thought and action.

In an iron foundry, the pig iron is thrown into a great furnace and melted. That which was solid becomes liquid, and is then poured into molds which are fashioned in different shapes. The iron itself neither knows nor cares what particular form it takes, it is formless, ready to take any form supplied. If we did not place it in the proper molds, the liquid would assume no particular form.

This is the way it is in dealing with the subtle energy of Spirit, but the molds are made in our own subjective minds, through conscious and specific thought, purpose and direction. We should be very careful not to think that because we make the mold, we must create the substance. It already exists; It is part of the Life in which we live, a part of the Universal Energy.

Definite molds or concepts decide the shape which is to be created from the general liquid. This should prove to us that there is a specific technique in mental treatment which we should not overlook. If we wish a *certain* good, we must instill into our own minds a realization of this specific good and then—as this idea is the mold we place in mind—it will be filled by the substance necessary for the complete manifestation of this good in our lives.

Therefore, if a man is seeking to demonstrate, he must tell himself that he has faith in his power, in his ability, in the Principle, and in the certainty of the demonstration for which he works. Faith, being a mental attitude, is according to law; and even though one doubts, he can overcome his doubts and create the desired faith, definitely. If this were not so, only those who by nature have faith in God could ever hope to understand the Principle of the Science of Mind and Spirit, which is subject to certain, definite, immutable and impersonal laws. However, even though faith is a necessary attitude, it is something that can always be established by explaining the theory and proving the Principle.

No Mystery in Truth

Faith in a certain specific statement has power consciously to oppose, neutralize, erase and obliterate the opposite mental attitude. It is because of this fact that this study is a science that can definitely be used, and we must accept it as such. The mystery with which most people surround the search for Truth, relative to this Principle, is not read out of It, but is read into It.

It stands to reason that if thought and faith, prayer, hope and appreciation are anything at all, they are definite; and if they are definite, they must be specific; if they are specific, then they unquestionably must accomplish their desire.

Hope a Subtle Illusion

Many people correctly begin their treatment in this manner: "I know that the Principle of Intelligence within me will direct me, etc.," then they complete it with the thought: "Well, I certainly hope it does." This is entirely forgetting any definite statement, and is simply wondering if possibly some good will come along. This is not a correct treatment, and is not the scientific use of this Principle.

Hope is good; it is better than despair, but it is a subtle illusion and is an unconscious compromise, and has no part in an effective mental treatment. We should say to doubt: "Where did you come from, who is your father, etc. . . . . You have no place in my mind. Get out! I know that the faith within me now neutralizes ALL doubt." This is the scientific use of a mental statement. There must be no compromise with the consciousness.

We have discovered what the Principle is and How It Works, and now this is What It Does. Specifically turn to that thought which tells us we do not know how to use It, and repudiate the falsehood. The Principle that we have to demonstrate is perfect, and—in so far as we can compel the mind to perceive this perfection—so far it will automatically demonstrate. Experience has proved this to be true.

We waste much time in arguing over things that cannot be answered. When we have arrived at the ultimate, THAT IS THE ULTIMATE. It is the way the Thing works. Therefore, we have a right to say that there is a law involved, and that this Law executes the word. We discover laws, find out how they work and then begin to use them. Therefore, this question is answered, when we say it is the nature of thought and of the Creative Energy, and the nature of Being TO BE THIS WAY. We would say that Law is an attribute of God. God did not make Law; It co-exists with the Eternal. The Infinite Law and the Infinite Intelligence are but two sides of the Infinite Unity. One balances the other and they are the great personal and impersonal principles in the universe. Evolution is the out-working of the mechanical, and involution is the in-working of the conscious and the volitional.

No Limit to Thought

When we think, something happens to thought. The field through which thought operates is Infinite. There is no reason to doubt it. No matter how it is approached, to thought there can be no limit, so we will say that it is the nature of Being to react in this way. Here and now, we are surrounded by, and immersed in, an Infinite Good. How much of this Infinite Good is ours? ALL OF IT! And how much of It may we have to use? AS MUCH OF IT AS WE CAN EMBODY.

IV

HOW TO USE IT

One of the great difficulties in the new order of thought is that we are likely to indulge in too much theory and too little practice. As a matter of fact, we only know as much as we can prove by actual demonstration. That which we cannot prove may, or may not, be true but that which we can prove certainly must be, and is, the truth.

Of course, the *theory* of any scientific principle goes beyond its application, at any given stage of the unfoldment of that principle, and the evolution of its accomplishments. If this were not true, there would be no progress in any science. The sciences are objectively real to us only in so far as we demonstrate them, and until demonstrated they are suppositional, so far as practical results are concerned. If there is *any* field of research where the practical application is necessary, it is in the metaphysical field, the reason being that the principle of metaphysics seems less tangible to the average person than does the principle of other sciences. As a matter of fact, *all principles are as intangible*, but the world at large has not yet come to consider the Principle of mental practice in the same light that it considers other given principles of life and action. *Its apparent intangibility is lessened whenever and wherever anyone actually demonstrates the supremacy of spiritual thought force over apparent material resistance.*

It is easy enough to rush about shouting that there are no sick people, but this will never heal those who appear to be sick. It is easy to proclaim that there are no needy. Anyone can *say* this, whether he be wise or otherwise. If we are to *prove* such statements to be facts in our experience, we shall be compelled to do more than *announce a principle*, no matter how true it may be.

There is no doubt about the immutability and the availability of the Law. The Law is Infinite. It is right where we happen to be at any given time. It occupies all space and fills every form with differentiations of Itself. The Law also flows through us, because It flows through everything, and since we exist, It must be in and through us. This is the crux of the whole matter. Infinite and immutable as the Law is—ever-present and available as It must be, the potential possibility of all human probability—It must flow *through* us in order to manifest *for* us.

It has been proved that by thinking correctly and by a conscious mental use of the law of Mind, we can cause It to do definite things for us, through us. By conscious thinking, we give conscious direction to It, and It, consciously or unconsciously, responds to our advance along the line of our conscious, or subjective, direction.

It must and will respond to everyone, because It is Law and law is no respecter of persons. We are surrounded by an intelligent force and substance, from which all things come—the ultimate Essence, in the invisible and subjective world, of all visible and objective forms and conditions. It is around us in its original state, ready and willing to take form through the impulse of our creative belief. *It works for us by flowing through us.* This law we did not create; this law we cannot change. We can use It correctly only as we understand and use It according to Its nature.

Hence, it follows that if we believe that It will not work, It really works by appearing to "not work." When we believe that It cannot and will not, then, according to the principle, It DOES NOT. But when It does not, It still does—only It does according to our belief that It will not. This is our own punishment through the law of cause and effect; we do not enter in because of our doubts and fears. It is not a punishment imposed upon us by the Spirit of God, but an automatic result of failing constructively to use the Law of God.

God does not punish the mathematician who fails to obtain the right answer to his problem. The thought of the unsolved problem *does* punish him until he applies the right principle and thus secures the desired result. Thus sin and punishment, righteousness and salvation, are logical reactions of the Universe to the life of the individual.

When we are dealing with real Life—with thoughts, impulses, emotions, etc.—we are dealing with Causation, with original Cause, and we should be most careful how we deal with such powers and forces. In dealing with this subtle power of Mind and Spirit, we are dealing with a fluent force. It is forever taking form and forever deserting the form which it has taken. Thus a practitioner of this Science should not be confused over any given form, but should know that any form which is not of the original harmony is subject to change. The Original Spirit is Harmony. It is Beauty and Truth and everything that goes with Ultimate Reality. The Universe is not divided against Itself.

We should learn to control our thought processes and bring them into line with Reality. Thought should tend more and more toward an affirmative attitude of mind that is positive, stable, and—above all else—toward a real unity with Spirit that is already complete and perfect.

We should be able to look a discordant fact in the face and deny its reality, since we know its seeming reality is borrowed from illusion, from "chaos and old night." Our standard is one of perfection. "Be ye therefore perfect, even as your Father which is in heaven is perfect" (Matt. 5:48). We should be able to look at a wrong condition with the knowledge that we can change it. *The realization that we have this ability must be gained by the application of our knowledge.*

The practice of the Science of Mind calls for a positive understanding of the Spirit of Truth; a willingness to let this inner Spirit guide us, with the conscious knowledge that "The law of the Lord is perfect" (Psalms 19:7). And we must believe this to be a fact. IN SO FAR AS OUR THOUGHT IS IN ACCORD WITH THIS PERFECT LAW, IT WILL ACCOMPLISH AND NOTHING CAN HINDER IT. "Heaven and earth shall pass away, but my words shall not pass away" (Matt. 24:35), said the beautiful Jesus, as he strove to teach his disciples the immutability of the Law of Righteousness.

A practitioner uses thought definitely and for specific purposes, and the more definitely he uses the Law, the more directly will It respond to him. A false fact is neither person, place nor thing to the one who uncovers it, and once uncovered it has no place in which to hide. The *illusion*, seen and understood, is made negative in the experience of the one who suffered by it. While it is true that wrong conditions exist, they could not remain unless there were someone to experience them. Consequently, the experience must be in consciousness. Change the consciousness and the false condition will disappear. Conditions are not entities, we are entities. Cannot that which is conscious cast out that which has no consciousness? If we properly understood, we would be able to remove false conditions as easily as Jesus did. He *knew*, but our faith is weak. We must strengthen it and we can.

Let us analyze this: One finds himself impoverished. He wishes to change this condition. He knows that it is not in accord with Ultimate Reality; that the Spirit imposes no limitations. Therefore, he knows that his apparent limited condition has no real law to support it; it is simply an experience of consciousness. He wishes a definite result in the opposite direction. First, he realizes that the Law of Life is a Law of Liberty, of Freedom. He now states that this Law of Liberty is flowing through him and into all his affairs. But the image of his limitation persists. Here is a definite contradiction of his statements of freedom.

Right here, he must stop and declare that these images of limitation are neither person, place nor thing; that they have no power, personality nor presence and no real law to support them. He does not believe in them and they cannot operate through him. He is free from their influence, forever. He then begins to fill his thought with the idea of faith, the expectancy of good and the realization of plenty. He senses, and mentally sees, right action in his life. He puts his whole trust in the Law of Good, and It becomes very real to him as he definitely speaks It into being—into his being and into the being of his affairs. He denies anything and everything that contradicts his realization of this truth.

At this point of realization, he meets a friend(?) who immediately begins a tale of woe about hard times, bad business conditions, etc., and, should he listen to this "tale of the serpent," he might reverse his previous affirmations and make negative his former mental and spiritual concept! This does not mean that he should refuse to hold conversation with people, for fear they will neutralize the position which he has taken in his mind, but that he should refuse mentally to accept the false position. Then he can talk with anyone and not be disturbed.

The time will come when we will let our "conversation be in Heaven," and refuse to talk about, read or think about, those things that ought not to be. But, someone will say, "Should we refuse to look at sickness, poverty and unhappiness?" This is not what we are discussing. We will not refuse to help the helpless or lift up the fallen, but we will refuse to wallow in the mud because of our sympathies. "And if the blind lead the blind, both shall fall into the ditch" (Matt. 15:14).

Of all the people in the world, the ones who have come the nearest to touching the seamless garment of Truth have been the most sympathetic and the greatest lovers of the race. Jesus said, "And I, if I be lifted up, . . . (not dragged down) will draw all men unto me" (John 12:32).

We are in the world and of it and it is good that it is so. The world is all right when we view it correctly. Who knows what would transpire if all men would speak the truth? It has never yet been tried, but let not the mouth of the profane hinder those who would enter, thereby keeping them from entering. The world has never yet followed the simple ethics of Jesus, yet it is loud in its proclamation that it is Christian. This statement is not written in a spirit of controversy, it is one of conviction, and will make its appeal only to those who are convinced. "A man convinced against his will is of the same opinion still."

Let us return to the man who really wishes to demonstrate the supremacy of spiritual thought force over apparent material resistance. Let us put his treatment in the first person—impersonating him for the purpose of clarity.

"I am a center in the Divine Mind, a point of God-conscious life, truth and action. My affairs are divinely guided and guarded into right action, into correct results. Everything I do, say or think, is stimulated by the Truth. There is power in this word that I speak, because it is of the Truth and it is the Truth. There is perfect and continuous right action in my life and my affairs. All belief in wrong action is dispelled and made negative. Right action alone has power and right action *is power*, and Power is God . . . the Living Spirit Almighty. This Spirit animates everything that I do, say or think. Ideas come to me daily and these ideas are divine ideas. They direct me and sustain me without effort. I am continuously directed. I am compelled to do the right thing at the right time, to say the right word at the right time, to follow the right course at all times.

"All suggestion of age, poverty, limitation or unhappiness is uprooted from my mind and cannot gain entrance to my thought. I am happy, well and filled with perfect Life. I live in the Spirit of Truth and am conscious that the Spirit of Truth lives in me. My word is the law unto its own manifestation, and will bring to me or cause me to be brought to its fulfillment. There is no unbelief, no doubt, no uncertainty. I know and I know that I know. Let every thought of doubt vanish from my mind that I may know the Truth and the Truth may make me free."

The Truth is instantaneous in its demonstration, taking only such time in Its unfoldment as is inherent in the law of a logical and sequential evolution. In this invisible law of unfoldment, we must come to trust, and although we do not see the way, we must believe that the way IS and IS OPERATIVE. We must trust the Invisible, for It is the sole cause of that which is visible . . . ". . . things which are seen were not made of things which do appear" (Heb. 11:3).

Healing and demonstration take place as our minds become attuned to the truth of Being. There is no *process of healing*, but there is generally a *process in healing*. This process is the time and effort which we undergo in our realizations of Truth.

The one who wishes scientifically to work out his problems, must daily take the time to meditate and mentally treat the condition, no matter what the apparent contradictions may be. He is working silently in the Law and the Law will find an outlet through his faith in It. This Law is the Law which puts the act into all action. It is the invisible actor, working through us to will and to do. As a result of right treatment, the mold formed in the subjective mind by the treatment makes possible a concrete manifestation. The treatment is an intelligent Energy in the invisible world. It is a spiritual entity, working through the Law of Mind, and it is an actual force now consciously directed. Therefore, it must produce specific results.

This will not seem strange to those who have given thought to the subject. As the primordial Word of the Creator is the only thing which explains creation, so *every man's word*—partaking of this original nature as it does—must reproduce the creative function in his life, at the level of his consciousness of One Life back of, in, and through all.

A treatment is a spiritual entity in the mental world and is equipped with power and volition—as much power and volition as there is faith in it, given to it by the mind of the one using it—and, operating through the Law, It knows exactly how to work and what methods to use and just how to use them. *We do not put the power* into this word, but we do let the power of the Law flow through it, and the one who most completely believes in this power will produce the best results. This is the Law of cause and effect, again.

When one gives a treatment for right action, and does not believe that right action will be the result, he makes his own treatment negative. Therefore, we should spend much time in convincing ourselves of the truth of our treatments. Now this is not a power of will, but a power of choice. We do not put the power into the treatment, and we will take out of the treatment ONLY AS MUCH AS WE BELIEVE IS IN IT!

If one doubts his ability to give an effective treatment, he should specifically treat himself to remove this doubt. He should say something like this, but not necessarily these words: "I am convinced that this word has power, and I firmly believe in it. I trust it to produce the right results in my life, (or in the life of the one for whom I am using my word)."

We should work, not with anxiety but with expectancy; not by coercion but with conviction; not through compulsion but in a state of conscious recognition and receptivity. We do not have to drive or push but we must accept and believe. We should, then, leave everything to the Law, expecting a full and complete proof of our faith. We shall not be disappointed nor chagrined, for the Law is our faithful servant.

One should treat any given proposition until he proves his Principle, no matter how long it takes. We should treat until we get results—until there comes into our objective experience the actual outpouring of our subjective words. When working for someone else, speak the name of this person—into Mind—then proceed with the treatment. Should someone come to you with the question, "Am I too old to find my rightful place?," what are you as a practitioner to reply? You explain that there is no recognition of age in the Truth; that everyone has his place in Truth; that God does not withdraw Himself from us at a certain age, for God is Omnipresence. In this Presence, every being is fully provided for at every age.

A practitioner consciously removes the apparent obstruction, and leaves the field open to a new influx of Spirit. He resolves things into thoughts, dissolves the negative appearance in the condition, by recognizing only perfection. THE PRACTITIONER MUST KNOW, AND MUST STATE, THAT THERE ARE NO OBSTACLES IN THE PATHWAY OF TRUTH. He must know that his word, being the activity of the Truth, removes all obstructions from the pathway of his patient, or the one for whom he is working.

If the obstruction is the result of a "hang-over" of belief from past years, the practitioner must know that no past mistake can hinder or obstruct the flow of Divine Intelligence through God's idea—which is perfect man, manifesting the attributes of God in freedom, happiness, activity and power, and that this Truth is now made manifest in his life.

The patient should try to be receptive, not to the will of the practitioner, but to the purpose of the Universe. That is, the patient should expect results and should be willing to give up anything and everything that would hinder the demonstration. Perfect belief is the beginning and the end of all good mental work.

The mental attitude of the practitioner is one of denial toward every false condition that opposes the principle of Life as one of absolute perfection. God's world is perfect, and this is the Principle we have to demonstrate. Spiritual things must be spiritually discerned and when we are ready and willing spiritually to discern, we shall find a ready response from the Invisible into the visible. Let us do our work conscientiously and thoroughly and leave the results to that Law which is perfect.

A new light is coming into the world. We are on the borderland of a new experience. The veil between Spirit and matter is very thin. The invisible passes into visibility through our faith in it. A new science, a new religion, and a new philosophy are rapidly being developed. This is in line with the evolution of the great Presence and nothing can hinder its progress. It is useless, as well as foolish, to make any attempts to cover this Principle, or to hold It as a vested right of any religion, sect or order. The Truth will out; the Spirit will make Itself known. Happy are we if we see these things which, from the foundation of the human race, have been longed for by all aspiring souls.

True thought deals directly with First Cause; and this Science is the study of First Cause, Spirit, or the Truth, that Invisible Essence, that Ultimate Stuff and Intelligence from which everything comes—the Power back of creation—The Thing Itself.

PART ONE

THE NATURE
OF BEING

What we believe about

God and man.

CHAPTER ONE
"IN THE BEGINNING, GOD!"

*The Beginning • The Story of Creation Simplified • Describing the Infinite •
Absolute Intelligence • A Deep Inquiry • The Voice of God in Creation • The
Thought of God . . . The Word of God • Spirit Knows Itself • Volition.*

THE BEGINNING

We wish to discover what to believe in, why we believe in it, and why such a belief is reasonable; and in so far as possible to enter into the nature of the invisible Cause of this manifest life of ours. We wish to discover how this Cause works; Its relationship to us and our relationship to It, and how we may use this knowledge. The world is tired of mysteries, does not understand symbols, and longs for Reality. What is Reality, where may It be found and how used? These are some of the questions one should like to have answered.

"In the beginning, God!" In the beginning, Spirit or Intelligence only. No manifest universe! No system of planets! No visible form, nothing but the Life Principle. God, the Spirit, had not yet moved upon the waters. Then this All-Being moved or began to create. *Where* did Spirit move? Upon *what* did It move? From *whence* came Its pattern? What means or power did It employ? Through what agencies did It work? In short, out of *what* is the world, ourselves included, made? How did we and all other physical manifestations come into being?

If we suppose Spirit to be the Life Principle running through all manifestation, the Cause of all, then we must suppose that It has Substance within Itself. It is Self-Existent Consciousness, and also Self-Existent Substance. SPIRIT MAKES THINGS OUT OF ITSELF THROUGH SOME INNER ACT UPON ITSELF. This inner act must, of course, be an act of consciousness, of self-perception, of self-knowingness. What God knows IS. This has been called the *Word* of God and the *Self-Contemplation* of God.

THE STORY OF CREATION SIMPLIFIED

Without repeating the well-known account (rather accounts, for there are two) of Creation, as given in the Bible, let us say that someone—generally thought to have been Moses—in expounding *his idea* of how Creation came into being, put his thoughts into the form of an allegory or symbolic story. Let us re-state this story, in our own words, and see what we shall have:

God (meaning the Supreme Spirit or Intelligence of the Universe) was conscious of Himself, prior to the creation of any special world system. Being thus conscious, and desiring to manifest in form, He did so manifest through the power of His Word, which is Law. God is not only pure Spirit or Intelligence, He is also perfect and immutable Law. As pure Spirit, He governs the Universe through the power of His word. Hence, when He speaks, His Word becomes Law. The Law must obey. The Law is mechanical, the Word is spontaneous. God cannot speak a word which contradicts His own nature.

Since God is pure Intelligence and endless Being, He is always creating. It is His nature to create but being All He must act within Himself.

The Word of God, spoken within Himself, sets the Law (which is also in Himself) in motion. The result is Creation. The Word is the mold, which acting through Law produces form. As there are many words so there are many forms, each distinct and each an individualized idea of God.

Since the Word of God is permanent, when He speaks that Word is equipped to perpetuate Itself, even as the seed contains within itself all that is necessary for the reproduction of its kind. It does not become *another* kind for this would produce confusion and the Divine Mind is never confused.

God made the mechanical universe, the plant and animal life, but this did not satisfy Him, for He wished to create a being who could respond to and understand Him. So He created a being who had real life within *himself*.

He could do this only by imparting His own nature to this being whom He called man. He must make him in His own image and likeness. Man must be created out of the stuff of Eternity, if he is to have *real* being. Humanity must partake of the nature of Divinity if it is to have real life. So God made man from the essence of Himself and clothed this subtle essence with definite form.

And God said within Himself something after this fashion: "If I wish to have a man who is a real being, I must give him self-choice. He must be spontaneous, not automatic. He must have dominion over everything that is of less intelligence than himself. I will let him name everything I have created and he shall have all things to enjoy, for his life must be full and complete if he is to express My nature."

So God gave man dominion over all earthly things. Man was not given the power to govern the universe, but he was given the power to *have dominion*.

And God viewing all that He had created saw that it was good, "very good." How could it be otherwise since He had created it? How could God, being Goodness, see other than good?

This, briefly, is the story of Creation. The reader need not be startled by this rather human narrative. Remember we are putting into human language a story which can only be imagined. Let us see how much of this may have meaning for us—how much of it we may prove.

DESCRIBING THE INFINITE

Any account of Creation however brief implies, first of all, a Universal Intelligence which is omniscient, all-knowing. We call this Intelligence *God*. In philosophy, the word *Reality* is used. In science, the word *Principle*. The Reality of philosophy, the Principle of science and the God of religion all have much the same meaning—the nature of the Universe in which we live. We describe It as God, Spirit, Reality, Truth—Absolute Intelligence.

ABSOLUTE INTELLIGENCE

We believe in an Absolute Intelligence because such an intelligence is manifest throughout the universe in which we live. Wherever we look we see It at work, whether it be the intelligence in the atom or the convolutions of thought operating through the brain of a Socrates or an Einstein. Consequently, we state our First Principle as an Absolute Intelligence. It is impossible for thought—whether it be philosophic, scientific or religious (and these are the founts from which we gather knowledge)—to deny such Intelligence.

We believe in an Absolute Intelligence and an Absolute Consciousness. We are in the universe and we are conscious, so we have reason to believe that consciousness exists.

Creation means the giving of form to the Substance of Mind or Spirit. Spirit being All and Only, there is nothing for It to change into but Itself. Therefore, It is the Changeless, within which must take place all change or manifestation of Itself. The Infinite of Itself is Formless but within It are contained all the forms which give expression to Its consciousness. Spirit is the

Limitless within which is all space. Spirit is Timeless, within which is all time. Creation and experience are eternally going on, but any *particular* experience is measured by time and has a beginning and an end.

In the beginning of any creative series there is Absolute Intelligence alone, pure Spirit, all-inclusive, everywhere, infinite. This All-Spirit could not have the impulse to move unless It were conscious. Therefore, "Spirit is the Power that knows Itself." The account of Creation, which says "In the beginning, God created the heavens and the earth," does not refer to a time when there was no creation, but rather to the process of an eternal creation, which is a continual manifestation of Spirit. An eternal creation is proved by the fact that we must suppose Spirit to be Conscious Intelligence, and *there can be no Conscious Intelligence unless It is conscious of something!* Spirit is conscious and must be conscious of something. Therefore, *It must always create.* What a glorious concept is such an idea of an Eternal Creative Principle. There is no stagnation in Spirit, nor should there be any in our idea of spirituality. *To be spiritual is to create!* The Spirit is alive, conscious, aware and active.

A DEEP INQUIRY

If we were to examine the basic principles of the religions of the world, we would find a great similarity. Each points to One central Life, from Whose Self-Existence all draw their livingness, and without which nothing could exist. The Christian Religion gives more value to the individual life than do most of the others. That is why it has made such an appeal to the more vital races of the world. In many respects, the Christian Bible is the greatest book ever written, and does truly point a way to eternal values. But it is only ONE explanation and cannot be considered the ONLY light on religion, for there are many others whose combined teachings weave the story of Truth into a complete and unified pattern.

The deep thinkers of antiquity, as well as the philosophers of all ages, have meditated long and earnestly upon the *nature* of the Divine Being. Knowing that there could be but One Ultimate Reality back of all things, they have pondered deeply as to the nature of that Reality, and it is significant that most of the great thinkers have arrived at similar conclusions.

THE VOICE OF GOD IN CREATION

The argument has been something after this manner: The Ultimate Cause back of all things must be ONE, since Life cannot be divided against Itself. The Infinite must be ONE, for there *could* not be *two* Infinite Beings. Whatever change takes place must take place within this ONE. But this ONE must be Changeless, for being One and Only, It could not change into anything but Itself.

All *seeming* change is merely the play of Life upon Itself; and all that happens must happen by and through some inner action upon Itself. What would be the nature of this inner action? It could not be physical—as we understand physics—but would have to be by the Power of some inner movement of Life, i.e., the Voice of God—God standing for the First Great and Only Cause of all that is.

The Thought of God . . . The Word of God

The *Word of God* means the power of Spirit to declare Itself into manifestation, into form. The *Word of God* means the Self-Contemplation of Spirit. The manifest universe, as we see it, as well as the Invisible Universe which must also exist, is the result of the Self-Contemplation of God. "He spake and it was done." "The Word was with God, and the Word was God. All things were made by Him and without Him was not anything made that was made." The starting point of all creation is the Word of Spirit. The Word is the Concept, Idea, Image, or Thought of God. It is the Self-Knowing Mind, speaking Itself into manifestation. The Word back of everything is its Initial Cause.

The term "thought" seems to mean more to us than any other term, in this connection. It seems to cover the meaning better, for we know that *thought* is an inner process of consciousness. The Thought of God must be the Cause of all that really exists; and as there are many existing things, there must be many thoughts in the Mind of the Infinite. This is logical to suppose, for an Infinite Mind would necessarily conceive an infinite variety of ideas. Hence the world of multiplicity or many things. But the world of *multiplicity* does not contradict the world of *Unity*, for the many live in the One. This concept of Unity is the mystical secret of the ages, the key to spiritual wisdom and to the teaching of Jesus.

Spirit Knows Itself

It is impossible to conceive of anything other than the Word of God being that which sets power in motion. God speaks and it is done! It is evident that First Cause must be Self-Existent, i.e., It must be Causeless. Nothing could come before That Which was First. Hence the Being Whom we call GOD must be Self-Existent. GOD SPEAKS AND IT IS DONE. If God speaks, His Word must be Law. The Word of God is also the Law of God. GOD IS WORD, GOD IS LAW, GOD IS SPIRIT. This is self-evident. We arrive at the conclusion that God as Spirit is Conscious Life. This is the inner meaning of the teaching of the "I AM."

VOLITION

There is but one volitional factor in the Universe, and this is Spirit, or the Self-Knowing Mind. God did not make God, this is self-evident. God did not make Law; Law is Co-Eternal with God. God did not make Substance, this is also Co-Existent and Co-Eternal with God. BUT GOD DID MAKE, AND DOES MAKE, and IS MAKING AND WILL CONTINUE TO MAKE, FROM ETERNITY TO ETERNITY, *FORMS*. We live in a universe of Infinite Substance and numberless forms, wherein nothing is moved unless Intelligence moves it, in accord with law.

It follows that everything that Spirit thinks must take form. The Spirit, being Self-Conscious Life, knows and cannot stop knowing. To suppose that It could stop knowing would be to suppose that It could stop being! Since It cannot stop knowing, It must forever be setting in motion the Law of Its being, which Law must forever be projecting the form of Its thoughts, thereby producing things. Creation is always *beginning* but never *ending*. The slightest thought of Intelligence sets power in motion through the Law, producing a corresponding thing. Things may come and things may go, but Creation goes on forever. This is, indeed, a wonderful concept, for it means that there will always be a manifestation of Divine Ideas. They cannot cease so long as God exists, and since God will forever be there will forever be some kind of manifestation. The Invisible will always be made manifest on some plane.

CHAPTER TWO

MIND . . . THE GREATEST DISCOVERY

Nature Waits on Man's Self-Recognition • *The First Great Discovery* • *The Greatest Discovery of All Time . . . Mind* • *Memory* • *Science* • *How Laws Are Discovered* • *The Science of Mind* • *Where Do We Get Our Mental Impressions?* • *Reading Thought* • *Mental Laws* • *The Threefold Nature of God* • *Trinity of Being.*

NATURE WAITS ON MAN'S SELF-RECOGNITION

Nothing is more apparent than that man, as he now appears, is the result of evolution. But in order to evolve, he had to have a Principle from which to unfold. Since man is intelligent, he must have evolved from an Intelligent Cause.

In studying the order of man's evolution, it seems certain that it was necessary—from the time that he was brought to a point of self-choice—that he be left alone to discover his true nature. If man is endowed with the attributes of self-choice and free will, he must be allowed to make this great discovery for himself. Even God could not make a mechanical individual. Consider any of Nature's forces, they must have existed always, but, so far as man is concerned, they exist to be used only after he has discovered them and learned how to make use of them. Electricity was a reality in the universe when Moses led the children of Israel out of the land of Egypt, but neither Moses nor any of his followers knew anything about it. This is true of all natural laws; they have always existed but only when understood may they be used. In this way, Life waits upon man's discovery of natural laws, his discovery of himself, and his discovery of his relationship to the great Whole.

The *principle* of any science is invisible, theoretical, as is our idea of Spirit. No one has seen God; no one has seen Life; what we have seen is the manifestation of Life. No one has *seen* Intelligence; we *experience* It. No one has ever *seen* Causation; we see what It does, we deal with Its effects. We do not see Beauty. The artist feels beauty and depicts it as best he can, and the result of his effort is what we call the beautiful. The mathematician solves a problem, but the problem is not the Principle of Mathematics; the solution of the problem is an effect or a result of the application of the principle. We do not see Life, we experience living. Causation is invisible.

THE FIRST GREAT DISCOVERY

The first great discovery man made was that he could think. This was the day when he first said "I am." This marked his first day of personal attainment. From that day, man became an individual and had to make all further progress himself. From that day, there was no compulsory evolution; he had to work in conscious union with Life.

The basis from which man is evolving is Infinite. Behind him is the Great Unknown but not the great unknowable. As the result of the discovery that he could think, plan and execute, man has built up a great civilization; he has perceived that Nature works *through* him in order to work *for* him. He has harnessed electricity, compelled steam to do his bidding, conquered the air, built cities, made the desert to bloom, and has thrown the lines of his commerce around the globe. Indeed, he has seemed to possess the earth during this process, even though little attention has been given to that still, small voice which said: "Man, know thyself."

THE GREATEST DISCOVERY OF ALL TIME . . . MIND

Man's first discovery of his ability to think was taken as a matter of fact. He had always been able to think. It was proof that he existed; it gave him the ability to know his needs and to supply them. It appeared to be an automatic thing; it came with him and would doubtless die when he died. The brain seemed to be the organ of thought, and, of course, when death stilled the brain it would no longer operate.

However, a day came when some wise man claimed that it is not the brain that does the thinking, for if the brain could think it would keep on thinking when removed from the body; yet without a brain a man could not think, *which proved that something behind the brain used it as an instrument.* Man does think, so behind the brain there must be a thinker. But where is the thinker? We do not see him. Have we a right to say there is a thinker, when we have never seen him? Yes, for the proof of this reality is the evidence of his thought. Back of the organism is the thinker and the doer—the Mind. *This was the greatest discovery of all time, for it meant that the body without the thinker could not function.* At first, man did not perceive this and thought only of his body as self-operating, but when he discovered this was not the case, he found that he could consciously think and decide, and *that something happened to his thoughts after he thought them;* they went somewhere and returned to him as memory.

MEMORY

Pondering on this, man came to the conclusion that memory was an active thing, and he reasoned after this fashion: "Memory must be the storehouse of all ideas that have passed through my mind. Memory is *active*, for my thoughts come back to me. My thought is conscious of my body; my body is operated upon by my thought, and it must be operated upon by my memory, since memory is active; but since memory is the result of conscious thought, *memory of itself is an unconscious operation of what was once a conscious thought.*" THIS IS ONE OF THE MOST IMPORTANT CONCLUSIONS WHICH THE MIND OF MAN HAS EVER MADE. By changing his thought, he could re-mold his affairs; and by right thinking he could bring new conditions into his life! Tremendous!

SCIENCE

Science is the knowledge of facts based upon some proven principle. The scientific investigation of anything is, of necessity, a cold-blooded proposition. We speak about *knowing*, about science being absolute knowledge; science *is* absolute knowledge, in so far as the facts of science are demonstrable!

HOW LAWS ARE DISCOVERED

In the scientific discovery of laws, certain theories are postulated; such theories may develop through research and investigation. When a theory proves to be correct, after many experiments, then, a principle is announced. In this way scientific truth is demonstrated; but no one has ever *seen* any of these principles which science announces, as no one has ever seen the great Cause which lies back of all the manifestations of life.

As soon as a law is discovered, experiments are made with it, certain facts are proven to be true, and in this way a science is gradually formulated. *Any* science consists of the number of known facts about its invisible principle. As more and more facts are gathered and proven, the science expands and gradually becomes accepted by all and *may be used by those who understand it.*

THE SCIENCE OF MIND

Let us, then, approach the Science of Mind with awe, but not with fear; with a truly humble spirit, but not with any sense that we are unworthy, and certainly with no superstition. Let us approach it normally, happily, willing to accept it, glad to experiment with it, believing that as a result of our efforts we shall derive this great good—a better understanding of the natural laws of Life as they apply to the individual and his relationship to the universal scheme of things.

The Science of Mind, then, is the study of Life and the nature of the laws of thought; the conception that we live in a spiritual Universe; that God is in, through, around and for us. There is nothing supernatural anywhere, on any plane; that which today seems to us supernatural, after it is understood will be found spontaneously natural.

We say there is a Universal Mind; but no one ever saw It. We say God is Spirit; but no one ever saw God. The Bible says, "No man hath seen God at any time; only the Son, he hath revealed Him." To express this idea in our language: No one has seen Cause; because we see an effect, we know there must be a Cause. Nothing is more evident than the fact that we live; and since we live, we must have life, and since *we* have life there must be Life. The only proof we have of Mind is that we think. The Eternal Principle is forever hidden.

WHERE DO WE GET OUR MENTAL IMPRESSIONS?

The paramount problem of philosophy now as in the past is, how and from whence do we get our mental impressions? Kant says: We are able to perceive an object because it awakens an intuitive perception within us. How could it awaken an *intuitive perception* within us, unless the medium which created the object already existed *within* us? The intuitive perception was not the *result* of perceiving the object, *but was itself the cause of the object perceived!* This is what Emerson would have us understand when he says "There is one mind common to all individual men."

That which is apparently outside can become known to the individual through intuition, because the perception and the perceiver must be in one and the same Mind. *No object can appear to exist in the objective world unless there is first a subjective world to perceive the object.* There is no object on the *outside* of Reality; but Reality must be an Infinite Perceiver or an Infinite Mind. . . . One Mind common to all men.

The Bible says: "In Him we live and move and have our being." . . . "Him" . . . "It" . . . or "God." Jesus said Reality is not in the mountain, nor afar off, but within us. So without trying to define, without making any attempt to explain, we make the simple statement: "Mind is."

Mind is, and Mind is both Universal and individual, i.e., It is not only Universal and abstract, It is also individual and concrete. The Mind which is personified is the same Mind which is Universal.

This is the perception that Buddha, Jesus and other great spiritual leaders had. They understood that the Universe *has* to be *One* in order to be at all. Jesus saw it, when he said in substance: If I cast out devils by Beelzebub, the prince of devils, that is a house divided against itself, which cannot stand; and he also said, "Who hath seen me hath seen the Father." Jesus had arrived at a perception of Oneness.

Images of thought, although they appear to arise from without, *actually arise from the objective side of that which is part of a subjective within.* In order that Nature may be coherent and come into self-expression, there must be an objective, a manifest world; but *that which is physically outside of us still exists in the same medium in which we have our being, and the intelligence by which we perceive it is the SAME INTELLIGENCE THAT CREATED IT.* Therefore, while it is objectively separate, it is subjectively unified. Our images of thought arise from within a medium in which both the one who sees, and that which is seen, exist in a state of inner unity. God exists in everything. God exists in me, and because God exists in me, I am able to recognize other beings in whom God exists. Spirit is the medium through which I am conscious of myself, of others, and of my environment.

READING THOUGHT

Recognizing that we are surrounded by a Universal Mind, it does not seem strange that certain people should sense our thoughts even when we are not aware of the fact, because thought operates through a medium which is Universal . . . always present.

It is almost certain that between friends there is at all times a silent communication, a sort of unconscious mental conversation, going on. When this arises to the surface of the conscious intelligence, it is called mental telepathy. This communication with others is going on all the time, whether the conscious mind is aware of it or not. These impressions are more or less vague and seldom come to the surface. They are there, nevertheless, and are gradually building into our mentalities impressions and forms of thought that are unconsciously and silently perceived.

This all leads to the conclusion that what we call our subjective mind is really the use that we, as individuals, make of a Universal Subjectivity. Just as radio messages are operative through a universal medium, so our thoughts are operative through a Universal Medium.

MENTAL LAWS

As we think of the medium of radio transmission in terms of law, so we should think of the Mental Medium in terms of law, for the Mental Medium must be the Law of mental action. While we might think of It as the Mind of God, we could not think of It as the Spirit of God; for the Mental Medium is automatic, while the Spirit must be Self-Knowing. We could not call the Universal Medium of Mind "God" anymore than we could call electricity "God." The Universal Medium of Mind is but one of the many attributes of God, the avenue through which God operates as Law.

We should differentiate between Universal *Mind* and Universal *Spirit*. As we examine the Subjective, we find It to be both intelligent and conscious, without knowing that It is intelligent, and without being self-conscious. All law must be subjective; the soil knows how to take a seed and make a plant from it; it does not know whether it is making a tomato or a potato. If this were not true of the laws of nature, we could not depend upon them, we should be confronted with caprice. One of the most difficult problems to realize is that when we are dealing with the Law of Mind, we are dealing with an absolutely impersonal thing. It knows how to create without knowing what It creates. Therefore, we must distinguish between the Law of Mind and the Spirit which uses the Law. The ancients taught that there is an Infinite Self-Knowing Spirit (one of the oldest sayings in the world is: "Spirit is the Power that knows Itself"). in addition to which there is an Infinite Law which knows *how* to do but does not care what It does. This Law is the Karmic Law of Buddha: "the Law that binds the ignorant and frees the wise," as Anna Besant stated it. It is the Cause and Effect of the West; but It is not to be confused with Kismet, which is fate, because *Its tendency can be changed.*

There is a Law in the Universe which operates in a certain way according to the tendency set in motion, and does so mathematically, inexorably. We cannot destroy the Law but we can re-direct Its movement. Just as we plant seeds and later decide we wish something else, we go out and uproot the first seeds and plant others in their place. We are not thereby destroying the soil; we have simply determined to use it in a different way. *When we are dealing with Subjectivity, we are always dealing with that which is subject to the conscious volition.*

The conscious volition in the Universe is what is meant by the Spirit or God. The Mental Medium, the Universal Subjectivity, the Law, is the *doer* of the Word! Plotinus speaks of it as a *doer* but not a *knower*. He called it a blind force, not knowing only doing.

This is the principle which we use in practice. We should distinguish between conscious volition as Spirit, and the Subjective Law, which works with intelligence but not self-conscious awareness. When this is realized, we shall no longer be superstitious about our use of the Law. It has been difficult to get away from such a superstitious reaction, because of a theological rather than a scientific approach to the subject. The Law we are discussing is simply a law of Nature, a force of Nature. It happens to be a mental force, and an intelligent and creative one, like electricity, which will either light our house and cook our food or will electrocute us if we use it incorrectly.

THE THREEFOLD NATURE OF GOD

We find, then, as we study our own being we begin to deduce what the nature of God, or the Universal Being, is. There is no way we can know God except by studying man. Someone may say, "God reveals Himself"; yes, we think God reveals Himself to us, *but only by revealing Himself through us.* We know about God only as we judge what God must be, by studying the nature of those things which we can somewhat analyze, plus that intuitive feeling we have of eternal verities.

If we study the true nature of man, then we shall have delved into the real nature of God, or First Cause, from which man springs. As we have found that man is threefold in his nature, we must deduce that God is threefold in His Nature, i.e., that God is Spirit, or Self-Knowingness; God is Law and action; God is result or Body. This is the inner teaching of "The Trinity." God, as Self-Knowing Spirit, means the Divine Being Whom we have always thought of and believed in, the Being to Whom we have prayed and Whom we have adored. God as Law means the *way* in which Spirit works, and Law in this sense would be the servant of the Spirit. God as Body means the manifestation of the Spirit.

TRINITY OF BEING

This trinity of being appears to run through all Nature and all life. For instance, there is electricity, the way it works and its results, which is light or motive power. There is the seed, the creative medium of the soil, and the plant.

Turn it as we may, we are confronted with the necessity of a Trinity of Being. Throughout the ages, this Trinity has been taught. Every great religion and every great spiritual philosophy has taught this Trinity. Father, Son, and Holy Ghost is the Christian Trinity. It is the Thing, the Way It Works, and What It Does. The Thing is Absolute Intelligence; the *way* It works, is Absolute Law; and What It does, is the result—manifestation. The action of the Thing Itself is what the Bible calls "The Word." . . . Absolute Intelligence.

CHAPTER THREE

SPIRIT

The Definition of Spirit • Its Nature • Spirit, the Changeless • The Action of Spirit Within Itself • How We Understand Its Operation • Metaphysics and Physics • Only One Mind • The "Personalness" of God.

THE DEFINITION OF SPIRIT

The definition of Spirit is: "Life or intelligence conceived of entirely apart from physical embodiment. It is vital essence, force, energy, as distinct from matter."

Probably the definition of God as "Spirit" is more easily understood, more readily accepted, than any other term used in describing Deity. Jesus in talking with the woman of Samaria, explained: "God is Spirit, and they that worship him must worship him in spirit and in truth."

The nature of Being is a Unity, with three distinct attributes: Spirit, Soul, and Body.

Spirit is the active and Self-Conscious Principle. Spirit is First Cause or God—the Absolute Essence of all that is. It is the Great or Universal I AM. Spirit is Conscious Mind and is the Power which knows Itself. It is conscious Being.

The Spirit is Self-Propelling. It is Absolute and All. It is Self-Existent and has all life within Itself. It is the Word and the Word is Volition. It has choice because It is Volition. It is Will because It chooses. It is Free Spirit, because It knows nothing outside Itself, and therefore nothing different from Itself.

Spirit is the Father-Mother God, because It is the Principle of Unity back of all things. The masculine and the feminine principles both come from the One. Spirit is all Life, Truth, Love, Being, Cause and Effect. It is the only Power in the Universe that knows Itself. The Spirit *could know nothing outside Itself*, that would be God *and* something else. SPIRIT IS ALL—the Center and Circumference of everything that exists—both manifest and unmanifest. It has no enemies, no differences, no otherness, no apartness, no separation from Itself. It is Undivided, Complete and Perfect within Itself, having no opposites and no opposition. It knows only Its own ability and since It is All, It cannot be hindered in any way, shape or manner.

It is impossible for a finite mind to comprehend such a complete Life and Power. In moments of real inspiration, we realize, to a degree at least, that God is All—That which has within Itself all that really is—the Life in everything and the Love through everything. The One Presence and the One Infinite Person, Whom we call God or Spirit; within this One all live.

Its Nature

The fundamental premise upon which the philosophy of the Bible is developed is that *Spirit is One*, and that CREATION IS THE RESULT OF SPIRIT'S ONE MODE OF ACTION.

Perhaps the one point on which we are all agreed is that whatever the Nature of First Cause or Spirit, It is *creative*. If this were not true, nothing could come into existence. It is impossible to think of Creative Life expressing Itself other than in livingness. Jesus undoubtedly meant just this, when he explained that he had come "that they might have life, and that they might have it more abundantly."

Another point on which we are all agreed as to the Nature of First Cause is, that It is harmonious. If there were an element of inharmony, discord or decay anywhere in Its Nature, It would destroy Itself.

It has always been taught that the Soul of the Universe is that *receptive medium* into which the Spirit breathes forth the forms of Its thought. It is subjective to the Spirit. That which is *subjective* is always impersonal, neutral, plastic, passive and receptive. Wherever we find subjective law, we shall find something that is compelled to receive that which is given it, and compelled also to act upon it. Consequently, the Soul of the Universe has been called "a blind force, not knowing, only doing." It has been called "The Servant of the Eternal Spirit throughout the ages." It is the medium of the thought, power and action of Spirit.

Spirit, the Changeless

Creation does not mean making something out of nothing. Creation is the passing of Spirit into form and is eternally going on. Spirit cannot change, for being All, there is nothing for It to change into. This is self-evident.

It is necessary for us to understand that the only active Principle is Spirit . . . Self-Conscious, Self-Knowing Life . . . and that all else is subject to Its Will. The Spirit is conscious of Its own

Thought, Its own Desire, Its own manifest Action; and It is conscious that Its Desire is satisfied. Consequently, It is conscious of that which It manifests; *but It is not conscious of any effort or process in Its manifestation.*

It is necessary that Soul and Body should exist because Spirit, without manifestation, would construct only a dream world, never coming to Self-Realization. In order to express, there must be a medium through which Spirit manifests and there must be a manifestation, hence, Soul and Body. The teaching of the great thinkers of all time is, that we live in a threefold Universe of Spirit, Soul and Body—of Intelligence, Substance and Form.

The Action of Spirit Within Itself

God, the Self-Existent First Cause, speaks and it is done. His Word is Law. God is Word, God is Law, God is Spirit. Spirit knows Itself; the Law is the servant of the Spirit, and is set in motion through Its Word. All law is some form of universal force or energy. Law does not know itself; Law knows only to do. It is the *medium* through which the Spirit operates to fulfill Its purpose.

Did God make Law? It is impossible to think of a time when Law did not operate; it is impossible to conceive that It was ever created. Therefore, Law must be Co-Existent and Co-Eternal with Spirit, a part of the Causeless Nature of the Divine Reality.

The Spirit operates through Law, which is some part of Its own Nature; therefore, *all action must be some action of Spirit as Law!* The Word of Spirit moves through the Law and, since the Law must be as timeless as the Spirit, we could not think of a time when Law was not, or a time when It would cease to be; neither can we imagine the Law ever failing to operate once It is set in motion.

We have then, an Infinite Spirit and an Infinite Law. . . . Intelligence and the Way It works. GOD WORKING THROUGH LAW, which is unfailing and certain. Creation—he activity of God, the activity of Spirit—the passing of Substance into form, through a Law, which is set in motion by the Word of Spirit. Spirit is "the same yesterday, today and forever," so our thought cannot picture a time when the activity of Spirit will cease.

The whole action of Spirit must be within Itself, *upon* the Law (which is also within Itself) and upon the Universal Stuff, which is also within Itself. The three in reality are One—the Trinity. There is something called God that makes things out of Himself (or Itself) by becoming the things It makes, according to law and order. As nearly as the intelligence of the human race is able to judge, Spirit creates by contemplation.

How We Understand Its Operation

The philosophy of applied metaphysics rests upon two or three very simple, theoretical propositions. ALL INVISIBLE PRINCIPLES ARE THEORETICAL, in that we cannot appraise them with our physical senses; we cannot weigh and measure them. Life, love, and beauty may be considered theoretical, in that no one has ever seen them. We see only their manifestations; but because of such manifestations, we reason that the reality exists.

Metaphysical work rests upon the theory that the Universe is a thing of Absolute Intelligence, that this Intelligence is Self-Existent—Spirit was not created. It was, is, and ever will be. We are compelled to assume the actuality of an Original Creative Energy and Intelligence, before which nothing comes. God, the Divine or Universal Life Principle, or whatever we choose to call It, is an Original, Uncreated, Changeless Being. Not a Being with parts, but BEING with potentialities. There is a vast difference.

A present interpretation of the Universe, according to one learned physicist, is that of "an Infinite Thinker, thinking mathematically." The Infinite Thinker is a spontaneous Thinker. The Infinite Thinker thinks, and what follows is in a sequence of law and order, of cause and effect; this is the mathematics. The Infinite Thinker, in *movement*, is Principle. *The Being* of the Infinite Thinker is pure Spirit, and may be thought of (in a sense which we but dimly comprehend) as the Infinite or abstract Essence of concrete personality, and the Cause of all objective and subjective manifestation.

To express this more simply, God thinks. As the result of God's thought, Law is set in motion—or the Thought moves as Law—in a field of Cause and Effect. Its movement is now mathematical. The only thing that is spontaneous is the Creative Thought Itself—the Contemplation of Spirit.

Metaphysics and Physics

The laws of Mind, or Spirit, are not different from the laws of chemistry and physics. Metaphysics begins where physics leaves off. Everything is movement; everything we can take hold of and analyze, all things in the physical world or the world of form are in a certain rate of vibration and *are an effect*. This is the *result* of "an Infinite Thinker thinking mathematically."

To reduce this proposition to the practical life of the individual, our belief is that anything the mind thinks, it can *unthink*. If, therefore, by the law of cause and effect we have produced unpleasant conditions, we should be able by this same law to produce an entirely different effect.

Another principle which is fundamental to our practice is, that not only what is set in motion can be changed; but that the Truth known is demonstrated. The knowledge of Truth and its demonstration is both simultaneous and instantaneous. Since we are dealing with that which is Limitless, knowing no big and no little, the possibility of our demonstration rests not in the Principle, but in our acknowledgment of, and embodiment in it, of the ideas we desire experienced! The saying of "peace" will not produce peace unless back of the word is a realization of the meaning of peace. So in the simplicity of our own language, we try to convince ourselves of the reality of that for which we are treating, knowing that in such degree as we have an embodiment of the idea, it is thrown into a mechanical field and *must* operate.

"Spirit is the Power that knows Itself." Whatever that power within us is that knows itself, constitutes the part of us which is spirit or spiritual. *To be self-conscious, is to be a spiritual entity.* Mind, in Its self-conscious form, cannot be differentiated from Spirit. Mind, in Its subjective or subconscious state, is the Law of Spirit. Man is *a* spirit while God is *The* Spirit. Man is an individual, while God is the Universal; but since the individual comes from and is in the Universal, it follows that man is a little world within himself. This is what Jesus meant when he said that man has inherent life within himself. The meaning of *inherent* life is *real* life . . . creative life.

No limit can be placed upon the spirit of man. It merges with the Universal Spirit for the two are really One. God is in us as we are in God—the same essence, the degree apparently different. The one finite and the other Infinite, and since the Infinite cannot come from the finite, it follows that the finite *must* come from the Infinite—a little circle within the big circle.

Metaphysically, we recognize the Universal Spirit as the Source of all life and inspiration; an Infinite Self-Knowingness, which we grasp only in part but which is ever available, since the Infinite is omnipresent. The mind of man is an extension of the Eternal Mind or Spirit, and his evolution is the unfolding of this everlasting Mind or Spirit through his thought.

ONLY ONE MIND

There is no such thing as your mind, my mind and God's Mind. There is only Mind, in which we all "live and move and have our being."

Things are ideas in form. What else could they be? There is nothing from which to make things except ideas. In the beginning, we behold nothing visible; there is only an Infinite Possibility, a Limitless Imagination, a Consciousness—the only action of this Consciousness being Idea.

That which we call *our* subjective mind is, in reality, our identity in Infinite Mind. It is the result of our mental attitudes. It is our mental atmosphere, or center, in Universal Subjective Mind, in which are retained all of the images, impressions, inherited tendencies and race suggestions. We see then that our subjective mind is the *medium* through which experiences come to us.

There is One First Cause—Spirit, Soul and Body—Cause, Medium, and Effect; the Father, Son and Holy Ghost. Not three gods, but the Triune Nature of the One God, the One Cause. We think of Spirit as Absolute, Self-Conscious Intelligence. We think of Soul as receptive to Intelligence and the Intelligence as always acting upon It. Spirit and Soul intersphere each other and both have omnipresence. The Spirit of the Universe permeates the Soul of the Universe, forever impregnating It with ideas. The Soul of the Universe is the "Holy Womb of Nature," producing the forms which appear in the manifest universe.

The Body of the Universe is the result of the thought of Spirit, operating through the medium of Soul. The Father is Absolute, Positive Intelligence; the Son is the Offspring of the Father; the Holy Ghost is "The Servant of the Eternal Spirit throughout the ages." Spirit is Absolute Intelligence, operating through the Soul of Receptive Intelligence, impregnating It with "the Divine Ideas."

The "Personalness" of God

We should think of God, not only as Principle, forever pushing forward into expression; but as Infinite Person. In other words, if we merely think of an abstract Principle, and a mathematical Law of Cause and Effect, we shall lose all warmth and color. *We should be very careful in abstracting the Principle not to forget the Essence.*

There is something in the human mind that desires to think of God or Spirit as Person. Anything which has been in the human mind since time began—anything we are unable to erase from the human mind as a deep urge—arises out of Reality.

Let us not forget that there is inherent necessity for warmth and color. The Universe is more than an inexorable Law of Cause and Effect. PERSONALITY CANNOT EMERGE FROM A PRINCIPLE WHICH DOES NOT CONTAIN THE INHERENT POSSIBILITY OF PERSONALITY. In each one of us, to each one of us, through each one of us, something is personalized and *that which is personalized is personal to its own personification!* Spiritual evolution should make the Infinite not more distant; but more intimate.

CHAPTER FOUR

SOUL

Creative Medium • Subjective Intelligence • Law • How We Use the Creative Principle • Mind and Ether • How Can Spirit Create? • The Soul Reasons Deductively • Subjectivity Never an Entity.

CREATIVE MEDIUM

We have spoken of the threefold Nature of Reality or God—the Trinity of Being—as Spirit, Soul and Body: Conscious Intelligence, Subjective Law, and Form. This threefold unity of Reality has been taught by most of the great spiritual philosophies and religions that have been given to the world.

We are using the word "Soul" in the sense of a Universal Soul, or Medium, through which Spirit operates. It is the Holy Ghost, or Third Person of the Christian Trinity. Like the creative soil, in which seeds are planted and from which plant life comes, the Soul of the Universe is the Creative Medium into which the Word of Spirit falls and from which Creation arises.

We should not, however, think of Soul and Spirit as separate from each other. They are really two parts or aspects of the same thing, each being Self-Existent and Co-Eternal with the other. The term *Subjective Mind* is used in speaking of the Universal Soul, rather than the term *Subconscious* Mind, to avoid the impression that *subjective* means *unconscious*. MIND NEVER COULD BE UNCONSCIOUS! The Soul is subjective to Spirit, receives impressions from Spirit. The Subjective Mind which we call Soul, is not a knower in the sense that Spirit is, i.e., It is not Self-Conscious. It knows only to do without knowing why It does. It is a doer or executor of the will of the Spirit and has no choice of Its own. It is the business of Soul to reflect the images that Spirit casts into It.

356

SUBJECTIVE INTELLIGENCE

The Soul is immaterial as we think of matter, but It is the Substance of Spirit and perhaps we could use the expression, "the matter of Spirit." As all matter in the physical world is supposed finally to resolve into the ether from which it came, we may think of the Substance of Soul as we think of the ether of science, and realize that all form finally becomes Soul-Stuff again.

Perhaps the simplest way would be to think of It as the last and final analysis of matter. (We continue to use this word in the face of the knowledge that scientists, in theory, have already done away with matter.) We know that matter comes from somewhere, and the teaching is that Soul-Stuff is the source from which it comes. We must, however, distinguish Soul-Stuff from Soul. Soul is Subjective Intelligence, the Principle just beneath Spirit; for, while Soul may not have the conscious Intelligence to choose, It certainly has the Intelligence to execute the desire of Spirit. IT IS NEVER IN ANY SENSE UNCONSCIOUS. The Soul of the Universe is next in Principle to Spirit and is the servant of Spirit. The term "Soul-Stuff" refers to the primordial or undifferentiated Substance from which all things are made.

While the Soul may not choose, having no self-consciousness of Its own, yet It has an Intelligence which is infinite, compared to the intelligence which we exhibit. For instance, the combined intelligence of the race could not create the life of a plant, yet the Intelligence in the creative soil of the earth will produce as many for us as we ask, when we plant the seed of that which we wish to have created.

The same principle holds good in that greater Creative Medium of the Spirit, which we call the Soul of the Universe. It has the Intelligence and Power to produce, but no choice as to *what* It is to produce. Having no conscious mind of Its own, It receives all ideas given It, and tends to create a form around them. If It could choose, It could *reject*, and this is as impossible as for the soil to say, "You must not plant spinach this year, you must plant cauliflower." We can imagine what consternation would prevail throughout the world if *just once* the soil failed to function according to the law of its nature. We need not be disturbed by such a fear. It is bound to accept and to act. It does not argue but at once begins to create a likeness of the pattern given it. If we say "petunias," right back to us it says "petunias," and begins immediately the business of producing them. Being a neutral, creative medium which knows neither good nor bad, it is conscious only of its own ability to *do*. This is why some of the earlier philosophers referred to the Universal Soul, or Creative Medium, as a " blind force, not knowing, only doing." This we know to be true of the nature of all law. We are not discussing the Nature of the Spirit. We are talking about Law.

Law

It must be apparent by now that the Creative Medium of Spirit is the great Mental Law of the Universe. It is the Law, obeying the Will of the Spirit; It is the Universal Law of Mind. All law is Mind in action. Soul is the Medium through which all Law and all Power operate. Being subjective, It cannot analyze, dissect or deny. Because of Its Nature, It must always accept. The Karmic Law, which means the Law of Cause and Effect, works through the medium of the Universal Soul, which is the Creative Principle of Nature and the Law of Spirit.

Let us bear in mind that neither Spirit nor the Soul of the Universe were ever created. Each is eternal. Because this impartial, impersonal Soul is the medium through which Spirit works, and because It is a "blind force not knowing, only doing," It was called by the ancients "Maya," from which arose the teachings of the illusions of the mind—the mirror of the mind.

What is termed Subjective Mind, as the average person comprehends it, has no existence. In reality, there is no such thing as *your* subjective mind and *my* subjective mind. If our subjective minds were isolated and things of themselves, we would be so completely separated that there would be no means by which we could communicate with each other. The next great bridge that psychology must cross is a recognition that what is called your subjective mind and my subjective mind is merely the place where Universal Subjectivity, the Creative Medium Itself, reacts to our personal use of It.

Within us, then, there is a creative field which we call subjective mind, and around us there is a field which we call Universal Subjectivity. One is Universal, the other individual, but in reality they are one. There is One mental Law in the Universe and where we use It, It becomes *our* law, because we have individualized It. It is impossible to plumb the depths of the individual mind, because it is not really *individual* but *individualized*.

Behind or within the individualized point is the Universal, which has no limits. In this concept alone lies the possibility of an endless and an eternal expansion. Everyone is Universal on the subjective side of life and individual only at the point of conscious perception. We use the power of the Universal Mind every time we think!

How We Use the Creative Principle

If, through the Law, thought is creative, we cannot say that one thought will create while another will not. We must admit that all thought is creative, according to the impulse, emotion or conviction behind the thought. Our theory is that the medium is a Universal, simultaneous Presence and in this Presence all live; and *that whatever is known at one point in It is known at all points, instantly!* So if we, practicing this Principle in Los Angeles, declare the truth about some

John Smith who lives in New York (or at any other place in the world) the speaking of his name draws the Law into the vibration of his personality, his individuality. Mentally, physically, spiritually, he is now in It. We have, so to speak, tuned into the keynote of his being. This being is also at the center of our being, therefore, the *mental work is done in our being*, for him; but it must, and does, operate through Law. This Law is subjective.

MIND AND ETHER

In an interesting article by Sir Oliver Lodge (in which he writes about ether and the laws of the physical universe) he says that no two physical particles really touch each other, no two electrons. They are all divided from each other by a space which is relative to the space between the planetary bodies, and *they never once touch each other, throughout their existence, other than through the medium of this ether*. Lodge calls the ether "the cement of matter." His theory is that just as the laws of attraction and repulsion, gravitation, adhesion and cohesion, operate *through* the ether, so there must be a Universal Mind that operates *upon* the ether, or upon Mind; or that Mind must operate upon mind, through the medium of the ether; or *perhaps the ether is Mind?* His conclusion is that Mind and ether interact.

We think of the ether of Mind as a Universal Subjectivity, the Soul of the Universe. Just as the ether of space is a medium for physical action, so this Universal Subjectivity is the medium for mental action. Anything that has ever been thought at any time in the history of man, exists today in a subjective state in Universal Mind. When we get into the field of Mind, there is no past, present or future. They merge into one medium.

HOW CAN SPIRIT CREATE?

No one has ever plumbed the depths of either the conscious or the subjective life. In both directions we reach out to Infinity, and, since we cannot encompass Infinity, we shall always be expanding and always enlarging our capacity to know and to experience. We do not need to ask *why* these things are so. There can be no reason given as to why the Truth is true. How can Spirit of Itself create a new form? I do not know. As Newton said, the fact that we are able to announce the mystery *is* the mystery. We do not say to the physicist who has studied and photographed the atom "WHY does it act as it does?" He knows no more about the *reason* for its action than we do. All that he knows is, that he has learned something of the way the laws of its nature operate. We do not create laws and principles, but discover and make use of them. Let us accept this position relative to the laws of Mind and Spirit and see what we can do with them, rather than how we may contradict their existence.

THE SOUL REASONS DEDUCTIVELY

Before we leave this subject of Soul, we should understand perfectly that *it is impossible to divide Mind*. We speak of the conscious and the subjective; the self-conscious and the unconscious, and the terms are confusing unless we remember that consciousness is always a unity. We arbitrarily divide the different activities of consciousness in order that we may discuss how thought works.

There are two ways of reasoning, the inductive and the deductive method. Inductive reasoning is an *inquiry* into the truth; it is a process of analysis. Deductive reasoning follows an already established premise. It is from the whole to the part.

Since inductive reasoning is an analysis, an *inquiry* into Truth, it follows that God can only reason deductively, since God *is* Truth. That which is Infinite does not have to *inquire* into the Truth. Consequently, there can be no inductive reasoning either in the Spirit or the Soul of the Universe. There can be no inductive reasoning in Spirit, *because It already knows all things*. There can be no inductive reasoning in the Soul of the Universe, because It is the Creative Medium, and if It could reason inductively, It could reject certain thoughts because It could analyze; and Soul or Subjectivity can never reject. It is bound by Its own Nature to accept. It is impersonal and neither knows nor cares who uses It. It is formless, having no mind of Its own. It has been called the Universal Feminine or the Holy Womb of Nature, because It is receptive and creative. It is Karmic Law because It is subjective to the Self-Knowing Mind. It is the medium of the law of cause and effect, of all race-suggestion.

If a convicted felon in a prison garden were to plant pink roses, the soil would produce just as lovely flowers for him as for the most beautiful picture star. All that would be necessary in either case would be a compliance with the Law regarding the planting of roses. So, the Soul is without *conscious* consciousness, but is conscious in relationship to the impressions It has received (whether they be Truth or only belief) and with mathematical certainty and precision, backed by the law of Its own being, it proceeds to execute the ideas given It. Thus it is plainly seen that the Soul can only reason deductively.

SUBJECTIVITY NEVER AN ENTITY

The Subconscious, or Subjective, is never an entity, although It acts as though It were. The Creative Medium is a medium only, never a person. It is necessary that we understand this, because one of the first things a practitioner has to do is to separate the belief from the believer. From the standpoint of the *spiritual* man, disease, poverty, unhappiness and misery, are neither person, place nor thing.

When we give a treatment, that treatment is a spiritual entity in a subjective world, and it has ways and means and methods to project itself, which the conscious mind knows nothing of, *and yet it is subject to the conscious thought!* Plotinus had a clear concept when he said: "Nature is the great No Thing, yet It is not exactly nothing, because it is Its business to receive the impressions of Spirit." He spoke of that which we call *undifferentiated substance* as an indeterminate thing having no mind of its own. Its mind is always made up for it.

Most of this chapter has dealt with the Universal Soul, but in another chapter we shall discuss more fully the manner in which *man* re-enacts the Nature of God.

CHAPTER FIVE

BODY

Definition • That Which Changes • Form Within the Formless • Cause and Effect • Unity and Multiplicity • Immortality • A Divine Mental Picture.

DEFINITION

The Universe has been called the Great Trinity, or Triune Unity of Spirit, Soul and Body—the Body being the result, the effect, the objectification of Spirit. Soul is the immaterial, plastic and receptive Medium. It is primordial or Cosmic Stuff, *unmanifest* form. Body is the result of Spirit working through Soul or Law. THE ENTIRE MANIFESTATION OF SPIRIT, BOTH VISIBLE AND INVISIBLE, IS THE BODY OF GOD. There is One Body of the Universe. Within this One Body is included all lesser bodies.

Body means the entire manifestation of Spirit on all planes. "In my father's house are many mansions," said Jesus. We do not, of course, see all these mansions. Science has revealed to us that many exist which we do not see, and revelation has shown that the Universe is Infinite. . . . "For we know in part, and we prophesy in part."

The word "body" as used in the Science of Mind means all objective manifestations of the invisible Principle of Life. The body is distinguished from the idea, in that the body is seen while the idea is invisible. The physical universe is the Body of God—the invisible Principle of all life. Our physical being is the body of the unseen man. Behind the objective form of the rose is the idea that projects the rose.

Body is always an *effect*, never a *cause*. Body expresses intelligence, its apparent intelligence being lent by the consciousness which permeates it. We would not say that consciousness is in the body, but rather that *body is in consciousness!* If one is unconscious he has neither pain nor fear. Pain and fear are in consciousness, but consciousness so completely envelops the body that it appears to be intelligent.

Perhaps the human body is an exact counterpart of an invisible body which is non-material as we now understand matter and physical form. The physical body is evolved for the purpose of allowing consciousness to function on this plane. The body is necessary to this plane, since only through a physical body can we properly function here. When the body is no longer a fit instrument the soul deserts it and continues to function on another plane.

To say that the body is unreal is a mistake. It is real but is an effect, not an entity. It may yet be proven that the mind *completely* controls the body, and that the body is but a reflection of the mind. In no way would this contradict the reality of the body nor the experience of pain and sickness, but it might help in an understanding of these experiences. While we may affirm that the body is not a thing of itself, we cannot say there is *no* body. The simplest way to think of body is to realize that it is the objective manifestation of a subjective mind and consciousness; and if we are to be well and happy, not only the body but the mind also must be peaceful and harmonious.

Psychology has shown that psychical (or subjective) disturbances produce physical reactions in the body. If the body is to be permanently well, the soul or subjective life must be in poise, the mind peaceful and happy. It may be considered as a general rule that when the soul is poised in true spiritual realization the body will be normal and healthy. This is the purpose of mental healing, whether it be approached from the psychological or metaphysical angle. Psychology and metaphysics are but two ends of the same thing. So we treat the body as a legitimate effect, controlled by the soul life.

That Which Changes

We have learned that Spirit is the Absolute Being, that It is the only thing in the universe which has self-knowingness, volition, choice or will. The Soul is the servant of the Spirit and has no choice and no purpose other than to execute the purpose given It. The Spirit of the Universe *cannot* change; being ALL, there is nothing for It to change into. The Soul of the Universe must obey the Will of the Spirit. THE *BODY* OF THE UNIVERSE CANNOT HELP CHANGING! This is what constitutes the eternal activity of Spirit within Itself; the Spirit passing into form— creation eternally going on. Since Spirit must be manifest in order to be conscious, there must be a *way* in which It manifests and there must be a manifestation. So we have Soul and Body. Body, the manifestation and Soul, the Way, or Law by which It manifests.

FORM WITHIN THE FORMLESS

Our physical body is like other physical manifestations. The *idea* of body is an image derived from the fountain of all ideas. The *form* is a materialization from the Substance of all forms. All bodies are made out of the same stuff. This one stuff is an inanimate and infinite stuff, and is equally distributed in the universe—much like the modern idea of the ether of space—and IT IS THE NATURE OF THIS STUFF TO TAKE FORM! Therefore, *form is entirely in the realm* of effect. Form comes and goes but it is not self-knowing. Form is within the formless. Form is not an illusion, even when it is the form of disease; it then represents a false conclusion, but is as real as it is supposed to be. If the formless did not take form Spirit would never arrive at self-realization.

The Formless takes form in what we call "time." "Time is a sequence of events in a unitary wholeness"; it is recollection, attention, and anticipation—past, present, and future—simply the measure of experience. Of course time is real, but never a thing of itself. If the Timeless did not manifest in what we call *time*, it would never come to self-fruition. Therefore, we have form and time, and what we call space, which is never a thing of itself but the possibility of outline. If there were not such outline we would walk through each other without recognition. Form is real as *form* but is not self-conscious, it is subjective to the power that created it. Forms come and go but the Power back of them is Changeless. Form is temporary but Mind is eternal.

CAUSE AND EFFECT

Effect is that which did not make itself but must have a power back of it, causing it to be. All manifestation, all body, is *effect, and is subject to its cause!*

The Creator is greater than His creation. Everything we see, touch, taste, feel, hear or grasp with the physical senses, is an effect. "Things which are seen are not made of things which do appear." What we see comes from that which we do not see.

If self-knowingness is in Spirit, and if the Law which executes the volition of Spirit is entirely subconscious, or subjective to the Will of Spirit, *it follows that both cause and effect are spiritual!* Involved within the idea which the Spirit drops into the Creative Medium, is everything necessary to bring this idea into form. Spirit never thinks of methods or processes, *for that which the Spirit involves must evolve!* The contemplation of Spirit, the Self-Knowingness of God, produces involution. Evolution is the passing of thought into manifestation.

To put it in another way: All is Infinite Being and all is eternally becoming. Infinite Being is Infinite Knowingness; as the result of this Infinite Knowingness, there is an Infinite Becomingness or Creation. The Infinite Knowingness produces what is called involution through the self-contemplation of Spirit. As the result of this contemplation—this *Word* of the Bible—Creation is made manifest. This is evolution.

Evolution is the process, the way, the time, and the experience that transpires as Thought—or Intelligence, or Idea, or Contemplation—passes from abstract Being into concrete expression. Consequently, *evolution is an effect of intelligence and not the cause of it!* EVOLUTION IS NOT CREATING INTELLIGENCE; INTELLIGENCE IS PROJECTING EVOLUTION. We do not deny the theory of evolution; we affirm its cause to be Intelligence, operating as Consciousness and Law.

UNITY AND MULTIPLICITY

The stuff out of which our human bodies are made is the same etheric substance from which all things are made. The One Mind conceives all things. From Unity—which is the One, back of all things, through the One Law, which is the Medium of all action—multiplicity is manifested, but the many never contradict the Unity of the whole. When we realize that we are dealing with an Infinite Intelligence, and with an Infinite Law *within* this Intelligence, we see that no limit should be placed upon the Creative Principle.

Could we understand Absolute Causation, we should perceive It to be pure Intelligence operating through perfect Law, and producing effects which live and have their being, not by virtue of an isolated life but by reason of a Universal Unity which permeates all things. We should then see that the world of multiplicity is deep-rooted in a Universe of Unity; that nothing happens by chance; that we live under a government of Law—from the vast planetary system to a garden of roses; from the Archangel (the Christ), to the saint and the sinner; through good and in what is called evil. Through cosmic activities and in human destinies, we behold the vast objective panorama of invisible, but adequate, subjective causes.

We should not separate Life from living, Spirit from matter, nor Divine Principle from a Universal Creation. God is "All in all." That is, God IS, and is *in* everything. The gardener finds a divine idea concealed in the seed; loosed into action this idea produces a plant. The geologist finds the imprint of invisible forces in the rock. The evolutionist reads the history of cosmic activities on this planet, as he deciphers the unfolding of an Intelligent Life Force carrying creation forward to its consummation point here, which is the production of self-conscious life. The scientist finds an energy concealed in the atom, and the spiritual genius discloses an intuitive knowledge, which can be accounted for only on the theory that we lie in "the lap of an Infinite Intelligence."

So close is the union of creation with the Creator, that it is impossible to say where one begins and the other leaves off. Emerson tells us that *nature* is Spirit reduced to Its greatest thinness; and Spinoza says that Mind and matter are the same thing; while Jesus proclaimed that the very words which he spoke were Spirit and were life. Robert Browning writes of the spark which we may desecrate, but never quite lose, and he further announces that all are gods, "though in the germ." Wordsworth sings that Heaven is the native home of all mankind, and Tennyson exclaims that more things are wrought by prayer than this world dreams, while Shakespeare perceived sermons in stones and good in everything.

We are on the verge of disclosing a spiritual Universe, and will ultimately conclude that what we call the physical universe is a spontaneous emergence, through evolution of inner forces which cannot be explained, but which must be accepted. How, then, can we doubt that the very mind which we now use is the Intelligent Principle from which all life draws its power to be and its intelligence to express?

The furtherance of evolution depends upon our ability to sense a unity with Nature and her forces. When the knowledge of this unity comes alike to all, the tread of armies will cease and the bugle call will echo the soft notes of brotherly love.

IMMORTALITY

Suppose we should be able to view the world, not as we do now from one plane but from ten different planes, what would happen? We should certainly see ten times as much as we do now. The present hypothesis of science is, that ether is more solid than matter; and this means that there *could* be a form *within the very form that one's body now occupies in space;* there *might* be innumerable bodies each within the other; and each would be just as real as the one we now think we occupy. The Universe as we see it is not even a fractional part of the Universe that actually is, "Eye hath not seen . . . etc. . . ." because it sees only on one plane and only in part.

From the standpoint of immortality we may have a body within a body to infinity. When this physical body is rendered useless and is no longer a fit instrument through which to function, another one may be already there!

The physical disappearance of Jesus after his Resurrection was the result of the spiritualization of his consciousness. This so quickened his mentality that his body disintegrated, and his followers could not see him because he was on another plane. Planes are not places; they are states of consciousness.

Is it apparent that Spirit can know nothing outside Itself; that whatever the Spirit knows must be a definite mental image, concept or idea, in the Consciousness of the Spirit? Is it clear that as the Self-Consciousness of Spirit knows *within* Itself, It knows *upon* Itself as Law?

Is it clear that the Law can never say "I will not," but can only act as instructed? And is it clear that as the Spirit lets fall the form of Its thoughts into the Soul or Subjectivity of the Universe, these thoughts must manifest as things? As Form? As Body?

A Divine Mental Picture

As we look at the many millions of forms all of different shape and color, and yet know that they all come from One Stuff, are we not compelled to accept the fact that there is a specific cause, or concrete mental image back of every idea or thing, a Divine Mental Picture? In the subjective world, there must be a correspondent of everything in the objective world; and since the subjective world is a receptive or plastic substance, this correspondence can find its initial starting point only in real Intelligence. Therefore, *Intelligence is the ultimate creative agency of the Universe!*

CHAPTER SIX

MAN'S RELATIONSHIP TO THE SPIRITUAL UNIVERSE

Man Re-enacts the Nature of God • The World Has Learned All It Should Through Suffering • Freedom or Bondage • Punishment and Reward • Spirit, Soul, and Body • Limitless Medium • Christ and Antichrist • Unity • Subjective Law • The Result of Our Own Thinking • Law Is Mind in Action • The Destructive Use of the Law • Oneness with All Law.

MAN RE-ENACTS THE NATURE OF GOD

Whatever is true of the Universe as a Whole must also be true of the individual as some part of this Whole. Man is evolved from the Universe as a self-conscious, thinking center of Living Spirit, and as such he must, in his nature and being, reproduce the Universe.

If we realize that God is "Triune" and that man is a spiritual likeness of God we shall see that the whole scheme of Life, and the whole nature of the Divine Being, is reenacted through man. This, of course, does not mean that man is God. It means that in his small world of individual expression, his nature is identical with God's.

This is what Jesus meant when he said, "As the Father hath life within Himself, so hath He given to the Son to have life within himself." This refers to inherent Life, *real* Life. That is the only life God *could* have. We must expect to find in man, therefore, the same inherent attributes that we find in the Universe from which he springs. A single drop of water is not the whole ocean, but it does contain within itself the same qualities and attributes.

Man is made out of and from Life. As effect must partake of the nature of its cause, so man must partake of the Divine Nature from which he springs. We did not create our nature; we cannot change its inherent reality; we are what we are and we use this nature for better or for worse. Being what we are there are certain responsibilities that go with our natures—certain obligations; if our thought is creative and if we have selectivity—that is, volition and choice—and if we are unfolding to a discovery of our true nature, which must already be perfect, then the obligation and responsibility of this nature could impose freedom or bondage upon us temporarily, *but our bondage cannot be real from the standpoint of the Absolute.*

The World Has Learned All It Should Through Suffering

The Science of Mind and Spirit, makes a tremendous claim when it states that the individual should be free from the bondage of sickness, poverty and unhappiness. It does, however, carefully set forth the conditions under which freedom operates and the laws governing Life, stating in no uncertain terms that unless man understands these conditions and obeys these laws, he will not receive full benefit from its teachings.

The world is beginning to realize that it has learned all it should through suffering and pain. Surely there can be no Intelligence in the Universe that wishes man to be sick, suffer pain, be unhappy and end in oblivion. Surely if God or Universal Intelligence is imbued with goodness, then It *could not* ordain that man should ultimately be other than a perfect expression of Life.

We have shown that man's nature is the same as God's Nature; we should have no intellectual difficulty in realizing that an Infinite Intelligence could not make an automatic individuality, and this explains why man suffers on his road to self-discovery. His suffering is not God-ordained, because he creates his own experience as he becomes individualized. By individuality is meant self-choice, volition, conscious mind, personified Spirit, complete freedom, and a POWER TO BACK UP THAT FREEDOM. We cannot imagine a mechanical or unspontaneous individuality; to be real and free, *individuality must be created in the image of Perfection and let alone to make the great discovery for itself.*

Freedom or Bondage

We, therefore, arrive at the conclusion that *while bondage is an experience, there is a Reality to which bondage is not real.* To that Reality bondage is not even an illusion or hallucination; there is a part of us that is never fooled. That is why, in the midst of the greatest trial, death, or any human suffering, something rises from within and says with Job: "Though I die, yet shall I live."

Freedom of will means the ability to do, say, and think as one wishes; to express life as one personally desires, to be able merely to think and dream of freedom would not be liberty. A prisoner under a life sentence can do that. To imagine, without the power to manifest such imagination, would be to remain in a dream world which would never come to self-realization; this is not the world in which man lives at all, for man's world is one of self-expression, even though this expression appears to limit him.

We are in an Infinite Mind and Infinite Mind is also in us. It is by this Mind that we think. This Mind is eternal, therefore, *we* are eternal. This Mind is complete, therefore, we are spiritually complete, though we do not *appear* to be so. This does not alter the fact that potential man is just as perfect as is the inherent God. As Jesus said: "Fear not, little flock, it is your Father's good pleasure to give you the Kingdom"; if it is the Father's good pleasure to give us the Kingdom we should learn how to receive and use It.

A freedom under compulsion would amount to the worst kind of bondage. The Bible says: "If there had been any law whereby this freedom could be compelled, then verily by the law would that freedom have been given." If there had been a way by which the Divine Creative Principle could have compelled man to suddenly appear on the scene of experience full-orbed with all his freedom—and still be an individual—then verily by the law would this have been done. But even God could not do this. The only way God can evolve a spontaneous individual is to let him alone and allow him to awaken to himself. "Behold I stand at the door and knock. . . ."

So man must be created with the possibility of limitless freedom and let alone to discover himself. On the road to self-discovery he must be subject to the Law of Reality, and if in ignorance he violates this Law, he must thereby suffer. This is not, however, because any Divine decree ordains suffering but simply because it is the necessity of the case. God never intended man to suffer. Suffering may be salutary in that it leads us to a place where we learn that it is unnecessary! We shall cease to suffer as we more and more comply with the Laws of the Universe, all suffering is the result of some infringement of these Laws. It is a solace to the mind when we come to understand that all human limitation, from the standpoint of the Divinity within us, is unnecessary. We recognize that we experience pain, but how could there be an eternal reality to pain? If this were true, we would have a suffering Universe, a suffering God, an agonizing Deity, all of which seem untrue, unreal and impossible.

We must know definitely and consistently that the Universe is for us and not against us. But someone will say, "The Universe is *not* for us, look at the evil, the limitation, lack and physical pain and anguish of the human race." We shall have to learn that evil is neither person, place nor thing of itself, but is an experience which we are allowed to have—because of our divine individuality— until through negative experiences we learn to use the Law affirmatively, to cooperate with It, and thus to enjoy Its full benefits, for the true Law is a Law of Liberty and not of bondage. The Universe is fool-proof. It does say we can have what we can take, *while at the same time we must expect to experience the logical result of our thought and act, be it good or what we call evil.*

The meaning of freedom implies the *possibility* of suffering, because if we are free we are free only by virtue of the possibility of choosing more than one course of action as an experience. There is no freedom or happiness, as a spontaneous individuality, unless there can be a temporary restriction of bondage and unhappiness through the wrong use of freedom. (All things are possible to the Infinite, but the Infinite forever remains true to Its own nature and never contradicts Itself.)

If man takes his images of thought only from his previous experiences, then he continues in the bondage which those previous experiences create. If we talk about discord, we shall become more discordant. The more the world arms for war, the more certain it is that there will be war. People who spend all their time talking about their unhappiness become more unhappy. Jesus understood these great laws of cause and effect in the Universe, which work sometimes with apparent slowness but always with sureness. Eventually we shall understand that all human bondage is an invention of ignorance.

PUNISHMENT AND REWARD

Before we leave this subject of bondage and freedom, we wish to make clear that there is no sin but a mistake, and no punishment but an inevitable consequence. Wrong doing must be punished, for the Law of Cause and Effect must be eternally operative. Right acts are rewarded in the same manner.

We do not say that man cannot sin; what we say is, that he does sin—or make mistakes—and he is thereby automatically punished AS LONG AS HE CONTINUES TO MAKE MISTAKES; but bondage is not real to the Universe and sin is not real to God. This does not mean that we can do whatever we wish, with disregard for the consequences; nor does the fact that we are punished for our mistakes mean that there is an evil power in the Universe; it *does* mean that there is an immutable Law of Cause and Effect running through everything. We are not punished *for* our sins but *by* them. Sin is its own punishment and righteousness is its own reward!

The age-long discussion of the problem of evil will never be answered until we realize that evil is not a thing of itself. It is simply a *misuse of the Law of Freedom*. The problem of evil will be met only to the degree that we cease doing evil and do good, for evil will disappear when we no longer indulge in it. When the whole world sees the right and does it; then, and not until then, will the problem of evil be solved for the entire race.

SPIRIT, SOUL, AND BODY

It is necessary that we understand the Unity of all life, the Unity of God and man on all three planes. We have studied Universal Spirit; Universal Subjectivity, which is called the Soul of the

Universe, and Universal Spirit in manifestation, which is called the physical Universe, or the Body of God.

Studying man, we find that his body—like the physical Universe—devoid of mind or intelligence, has no volition. It may be permeated with intelligence, but it is not intelligent. It is one with the Body of God, the physical universe.

What did we learn about the Soul of the Universe? Remember the qualities that were discussed under the head of Subjectivity, and you will find all of them depicted in what is called the subjective nature of man; for our subconscious or subjective mind *reproduces all of the attributes belonging to Universal Subjective Mind.* When we turn to the spirit of man, we find that it is one with the Spirit of God, i.e., man is a self-conscious, thinking, choosing center of individualized intelligence, or God-Consciousness, in the great Whole.

So we find that man is one with everything physical in the physical world; one with the Soul of the Universe in the subjective world; and one with the Spirit of God in the conscious world. Through that which we call our objective or conscious mind, comes what we know of God and Life. The objective, or conscious, mind is the *spiritual mind* for which we have been looking, but it is not fully developed. *If this were not so, there would be no mind with which to look.* The objective mind must be the spiritual mind of man, since it is the only thing about him which knows that he has life and is conscious of itself!

The whole of Spirit is potentially focused in our individual objective consciousness, but we have not yet evolved to a realization of this, except in a slight degree. We approach and contact the Larger Spirit through our own spirit or conscious mind. *The doorway to the Absolute stands open at the center of our intuitive perception.* We enter the Absolute through that which appears to be finite, because the finite must be drawn from the Infinite. This Spirit which animates us is the same Spirit which animates all life and everything that lives. Emerson said that we animate what we see and see what we animate, the reason for this being, that only as we truly see can the Divine Harmony be reflected through us and animate that which is seen.

The spirit of man is equipped with decision, will, choice, volition, intellect and purpose. It is the microcosm within the Macrocosm, which means the little world within the big world. It is also called the Image of God; it is Sonship, the Sonship of the Father; it is Emmanuel or God with us; it is the Christ or Logos, which means the Word, it can reason both inductively and deductively.

The spirit of man seems to have an external and an internal perception. Its external perception is by appearance; its internal, through intuition. Appearances would limit the future possibility of man to the uses he has already made of Life, and thus circumscribe the Infinite, hence we are told to judge righteously and not by appearances. Plotinus tells us that there are three ways by which we gather knowledge: through science, through opinion, and through intuition or illumination. *These channels represent spiritual capacities since each is an avenue leading to self-knowingness, and self-knowingness is the very nature and essence of Spirit.* Science is Spirit *inducing* Its own laws. Intuition is Spirit *knowing* Itself. Opinion is our *estimate of Reality*. All are spiritual faculties and should be so considered in the study of this Science. The race is growing into a broader divinity, from age to age, as more and more of Reality opens before its onward march in its eternal progress.

We should think of our spirit as being some part of the Universal Spirit, and of our minds as open to the Divine Influx. As any specific knowledge must come from the center of all knowledge, it follows that whenever and wherever the mind of man is open to the Divine Influx, it will receive instruction directly from the center and source of All. Science, invention, art, literature, philosophy and religion, have one common center from which, through experience, is drawn all knowledge.

We should neither separate Spirit from matter . . . physical form from that which gives form . . . nor Life from living. To suppose that one must retire from the world to be spiritual is one of the greatest possible mistakes. This is directly opposed to the self-evident truth that Spirit enjoys Itself only in Its own works, which is Its self-manifestation. We enter into the Spirit of Life only as we enter into the spirit of living.

There can be no real enjoyment of life until we see that everything is animated by the Spirit, and as we see that things *are* thus animated, we are beholding the real Universe. The Essence of Reality is invisible, but the substance of the invisible is seen and heard, and *is a part of the everyday life of all!*

We find that on the subjective or soul side, man is subconscious; but subconscious does not mean unconscious. Subconscious merely means subjective to the conscious thought, compelled by reason of its subjectivity to receive what is put into it. It is Karmic Law, because it is the use we are making of Universal Subjectivity. Karma means the Law of Cause and Effect. Soul contains the memory because It is the receptacle for the seeds of our thought, and because It is the seat of memory it contains our inherited tendencies. It also contains the race-suggestion, for we are not dealing with a separated or isolated subjective mind, but with the One Subjective Mind—there is a vast difference between thinking of having three or four minds, and thinking of One Mind which all use.

We treat of *soul* as being that part of our mental being which is subjective to the conscious mind. From this viewpoint, the individual soul is an effect and not a cause. This understanding of soul life is in accord with the deepest thought of the ages, and is a legitimate point of view in the light of recent investigations, in both the psychological and metaphysical fields.

The soul is the seat of memory, the mirror of mind in the individual. It is the creative power within us, creating from the patterns given it, and from the memories it contains. We gather soul, or subjective force, as we accumulate the right kind of experiences. The law of the soul is subject to the conscious spirit; tendencies set in motion in the soul, or subjective life, tend to produce their like in the objective world. From this is deduced the possibility of the healing power of the spoken word, operating through mental law, for the law of mind is always subjective.

The soul, being the seat of memory, already contains a record of everything that has ever happened to us. These memories as a whole, constitute the subjective tendency of the individual life; *this tendency can be changed* through constant effort and a determined persistency of purpose. The soul life of all people merges, more or less, and this creates the soul life of the race—the collective subjectivity of all humanity—called by some the "collective unconscious." This "collective unconscious" contains a record of all human events that have ever transpired. We are all, more or less, subject to this collective thought, since it acts as a powerful race suggestion. The sum total of all erroneous human belief, *binds until the individual mentally lifts himself above the law of averages into the higher law of Spiritual Individualism.*

In studying man's relationship to the Universal, we have discovered how the spirit and soul of man are like the Spirit and Soul of the Universe. Let us now consider the idea of *body*. Body— effect, affairs, conditions, health, disease, destiny, riches, poverty, business, vocation, profession, results—any word which stands for the externalization of man's thought and endeavor, we class as a part of this *body*.

Man's outward life is a result of the subjective state of his thought. The *thinker* is conscious mind, but when he thinks he lets fall the forms of his thought into Subjective Mind, which is the Universal Medium of all thought and action and, as a result of this, the Creative Medium at once sets to work to produce the thing outlined.

Plotinus, perhaps the greatest of the Neo-Platonic philosophers, in personifying Nature said: "I do not argue, I contemplate; and as I contemplate, I let fall the forms of my thought," this is the manner in which Nature creates—It contemplates. As a result of Its contemplation, It lets fall the seed of Its thought into the Universal Subjective which, being Law, produces the object thought about. We must expect to find—and it is exactly what we do find—the same principle reproduced in man. This means that whatever man thinks (whether it is what he calls *good* or *bad*) falls into this Universal Creative Medium, is accepted by It, is at once acted upon and *unless neutralized* tends to take objective form.

The objective man is *body*. By objective or physical man, we mean the man who is formed, who has flesh and blood. This physical man is in unity with all other physical or objective elements in the Universe, and in unity with the invisible Source from which they come. We analyze the body and find it is made of the same stuff from which a brick is made, not different in its essence, but different in its composition, its vibration. There is One Universal Substance whose business it is to take form in multiplicity.

We are told that matter is not a solid, stationary thing; but a constantly flowing formless substance, which is forever coming and going—"an etheric whirl of energy" it has been called. Whatever its nature is, it is as indestructible as God, as eternal as Timeless Being; nothing can be added to or taken from it. The bodies we now have were not with us a short time ago; we discard many of them on our path through this life; for the substance of which they are composed is in a constant state of flow—a flowing substance, taking the form that Mind gives it. How about the *matter* from which other things than the body are made? It is all the same—ONE SUBSTANCE in the Universe, taking different forms and shapes and becoming different things. Unity is expressed in multiplicity.

The last analysis of *matter* resolves it into a universal ether, and leaves nothing more than a stuff which may be operated upon; a force and energy, without volition, ready to become molded. In the theoretical beginning of creation, the world was "without form and void." There is no difference in the ultimate and minute particles which take innumerable forms—only a difference in the arrangement. Our bodies are One with the Whole Body of the Universe; seeds, plants, cabbages and kings are all made of the same substance. Minerals, solids, and liquids are made from this primordial Substance which is forever flowing into form and forever flowing out again into the void.

Nothing could give form to a formless stuff, which has no mind of its own, but some Intelligence operating through it. Here, then, we come back to the *Word* as the starting point of all Creation—God's Word in the Great Creation, the Great World, and man's word in the small world; One Spirit, One Mind, and One Substance. One Law, but many ideas, one Power but many ways of using It. One God, in Whom we all live, and One Law, which we all use. ONE, ONE, ONE!! No greater unity could be conceived than that which is already given.

So we find that man is one with the physical universe in which he lives. The physical universe has no self-determination; we find that man's *physical* body is a latent mass of matter. Our body is really one with the Body of God, with the physical universe, *but body does not know it is body*. If feet knew they were feet with the physical capacity to walk, they might be cut off and still be able to run down the street on an errand. IT IS ONE THING TO SAY THAT OUR FEET DO NOT KNOW THEY ARE FEET AND QUITE ANOTHER THING TO SAY THAT THEY ARE ILLUSIONS, yet all are agreed that they have no intelligence of their own. Of itself, the physical universe is an *effect*. So it is with the physical part of man which we call his body.

LIMITLESS MEDIUM

When we realize that in dealing with our own individuality, we are dealing with Self-Conscious Mind, and when we realize that in dealing with subjective mind, we are dealing with a Universal

Subjectivity, we shall come to understand that we have a Creative Intelligence at our disposal, compared with which the united intelligence of the human race is as nothing. The Universal Subjective Mind, being entirely receptive to our thought, is compelled by Its very nature, to accept that thought and act upon it no matter what the thought may be.

Since we are dealing with an Infinite Power, which knows only Its own ability to do, and since It can objectify any idea impressed upon It, there can be no limit to what It can or would do for us, other than the limit of our inward embodiment. *Limitation is not in Principle nor in Law, but only in the individual use we make of Principle.* Our individual use of It can only equal our individual capacity to understand It, to embody It. We cannot demonstrate beyond our ability to provide a mental equivalent of our desire.

Subjectivity is entirely receptive and neutral as we have learned, and It can take our thoughts only the way we think them—It has no alternative. If I say, "I am unhappy," and continue to say it, the subconscious mind says, "Yes, you are unhappy," and keeps me unhappy as long as I say it, for thoughts are things, and an active thought will provide an active condition for good or evil.

Suppose one has thought *poverty* year after year, he has thereby personified a law which continues to perpetuate this condition. If the thought is not erased the condition will remain. A law has been set in motion which says "I am poor," and sees to it that this is so. This is at first an auto-suggestion, then it becomes an unconscious memory, working day and night. This is what decides how the Law of Attraction works for us, because *the laws of attraction and repulsion are entirely subjective.* Our use of them may be conscious to start with, but it becomes subconscious as soon as used.

Suppose I do not *say* I am poor, but that I came into the world with an unconscious thought of poverty. So long as this thought remains, I am likely to remain poor. I may not understand the Law, but it will be working all the time. We come into this world with a subjective tendency toward conditions, but we must not forget that *we are also dealing with a subjective tendency toward ultimate good,* because in spite of all conditions, the race believes more in good than in evil; otherwise it would not continue to exist. This is the eternal hope and sense of our life.

The encouraging message in all of this is, *no matter what may be in the subjective state of our thought, the conscious state can change it;* this is what treatment does. How can this be done? Through the most direct method imaginable: by consciously *knowing* that there is no inherited tendency toward limitation, no race suggestion operating through subjectivity, nothing in, around or through us that believes in or accepts limitation in any way, shape, manner or form. We do not stop here, this is only half the treatment. The conscious state must now provide a higher contemplation, a spiritual realization, which says: "I partake of the nature and bounty of the All Good and I am now surrounded by everything which makes life worth while." The

Universal Medium at once changes Its thought (because Its thought is *deductive* only) and says: "Yes, I am all these things in you," and immediately begins the work of bringing such conditions to pass. *Whatever is held in consciousness until it becomes a part of the subjective side of thought, tends to take place in the world of affairs.* The reason that we do not demonstrate more easily is that the subjective state of our thought is too often neutralized by the objective state, though often this is an unconscious process of thought.

Whatever our subconscious mind holds long enough, is bound to be produced in our external affairs. Our subconscious Mind is the Medium in which we all live and move and have our being on the subjective side of life—our atmosphere in Universal Subjectivity—the Medium through which all intercommunication takes place on every plane.

It follows from what we have said, that any suggestion held in Creative Mind would produce its logical result, no matter what such suggestion might be. If it were a suggestion of destruction, it would destroy; if it were a suggestion of good, it would construct, for this is a neutral field.

CHRIST AND ANTICHRIST

The Spirit of Christ means that mentality which recognizes the Law and uses It for constructive purposes only. The spirit of Antichrist means the spirit of the individual who understanding the Law, uses It destructively. The meaning of the Flood or Deluge (which is recorded in every sacred scripture we have ever heard of or read) is that a race of people once lived upon the earth who came to understand the psychic or subjective Law as being the servant of the Spirit. They understood themselves to be Spirit, but they did not understand the harmonious Unity of Spirit. They had arrived at an intellectual concept of the Law—a very clearly defined mental concept—but that knowledge was not used for constructive purposes. They used the Law destructively, and what happened? The confusion which took place in the psychic world (or the psychic atmosphere of this planet) caused its physical correspondence in the form of a Deluge or the Flood.

There have been many controversies about the use and misuse of the Power of Mind. Some claim that we *cannot* misuse this Power, since there is but One Mind and It cannot act against Itself. MIND CANNOT ACT AGAINST ITSELF; AND ANY PERSON WHO KNOWS THIS, and KNOWS THERE IS NO HUMAN MIND TO DESTROY, IS IMMUNE FROM MALPRACTICE.

We need have no fear of the misuse of this Law, if we protect ourselves by the realization that there is but One Ultimate Reality, for "against such there is no law." We recognize Subconscious Mind as the Great Servant of our thought, the Medium through which all treatment operates; and this Universal Subjective Mind *we contact within ourselves and nowhere else!* Being omnipresent, It is in us; our use of It we call our subjective mind, but of Itself It is Universal.

UNITY

Our teaching is that man actually has a body; that he actually has a subjective life and that he actually is a spirit. Body, soul, and spirit represent a point where individuality is accentuated in Universality. It is only through this conception that we can arrive at a consciousness of the Unity of the Whole. In other words, if I have one mind and you have one mind and God has another Mind . . . three separate minds . . . I cannot talk with you and you cannot talk with God. If your mind and my mind were not the same mind, we would have no way by which to communicate with each other. Thus we are forced to the conclusion that there is but One Mind. Each individual, however, is a unique variation in the Universe; no two people are alike, and yet all people are rooted in that which is identical.

We recognize, then, in man's self-knowing mind his Unity with the Whole; for while a drop of water is not the ocean, yet it does contain within itself all the attributes of the limitless deep. Man's self-knowing mind is the instrument which perceives Reality and cognizes or realizes Truth. All illumination, inspiration, and realization must come through the self-knowing mind in order to manifest in man. Vision, intuition and revelation proclaim themselves through man's self-knowing mind; and the saints and sages, the Saviours and Christs, the prophets and seers, the wise and learned have all consciously perceived and proclaimed this fact.

Every evidence of human experience, all acts of kindness and mercy, have interpreted themselves through man's self-knowing mind. All that we consciously know, say or think, feel or believe, hope or long for, fear or doubt, is some reaction of the self-knowing mind. Subjective memories we have, and unexpressed emotions we feel, but to the self-knowing mind alone comes realization. Without this capacity to consciously know, man would not exist as an expressed being; and so far as we are concerned, would not exist at all. The self-knowing mind of man proclaims itself in every thought, deed or act, and is truly the only guarantee of his divinity. *It is his unity with the Whole, or God, on the conscious side of life, and is an absolute guarantee that he is a center of God-consciousness in this vast Whole.*

We will say, then, that in Spirit man is One with God. But what of the great Law of the Universe? *If we are really One with the Whole, we must be One with the Law of the Whole,* as well as One with the Spirit. Again psychology has determined the fact to be more than fancy. The characteristics of the subconscious mind of man determine his Subjective Unity with the Universe of Life, Law and Action.

In the subjective mind of man we find a law obeying his word, the servant of his spirit, the mental law of his being, the creative factor within him. This is our individual use of that greater Subjective Mind of the Universe, which is the seat of all law and action. Marvelous as this concept may be, it is none the less true that man has at his disposal in what he calls *his* subjective mind, a power which is Limitless. Man's thought becomes the law of his life, *through the one great Law of all Life*. There are not two subjective minds; there is but One Subjective Mind, and what we call *our* subjective mind *is really the use we are making of this One Law.*

Each individual maintains his identity in Law, through his personal use of Law, and each is drawing *from* Life *what he thinks into it*. To learn how to think is to learn how to live. Man, by thinking, can bring into his experience whatever he desires *if he thinks correctly*. This is not done by *holding thoughts*, but by knowing the Truth. There is a vast difference, a difference which too few realize.

Modern science tends toward a teaching of Unity; tends to resolve the material universe into a physical universe, and the physical universe into energy. The tendency of modern thought is to return, by the route of inductive science, to the great spiritual deductions of the ages—that All is One. But men are still puzzled, trying to reconcile the world of multiplicity—the objective world of many things—to their belief in the final necessity of Unity. Every great spiritual teacher has known that God is One—not two. They have also known that evil exists in the world—what we mean by evil is apparent limitation—poverty, sickness, death and what we call sin, which is nothing more than a mistake.

How are we going to reconcile suffering and lack with the Goodness of God? The difficulty is solved when we realize that all creation is an *effect*. It is real enough—as real as it is supposed to be. As you look about you, the mountain is a mountain, and the molehill is a molehill, the dust storm is a dust storm; *but they are all effects*. As you enter your garden and observe the bamboo tree, the grape fruit, and the many other variations of form, you see each is rooted in the one creative soil, and each is individualizing out of this creative soil that which is unique. The type maintains its integrity always.

We observe in creation an atomic intelligence, then a simple consciousness; after which comes a personal consciousness, then a Cosmic consciousness. These variations of consciousness are definitely defined and accepted by most investigators. As we watch the transition from the atomic to the simple intelligence, from the simple to the personal, from the personal to the Cosmic, we find that *we are merely going up a scale of Unity*. The Spirit is not something apart from matter so-called, but is something working through matter; the potential possibility of what we call the highest and the lowest is inherent in everything. They are not different things. *They are the same thing functioning at different levels.* "It is neither Lo here nor Lo there, for behold the Kingdom of God is within."

There are different mental depths and heights from which we may look out upon life; from whatever level we look, that which we see comes back to us by an invariable law of attraction. That which we look upon is real while we look at it. *We arrive at a consciousness of Unity only in such degree as we see that what we are looking FOR, we are looking WITH, and looking AT.* Heaven is lost merely for the lack of a perception of harmony. Hell is the phantom abode of our morbid imaginations. Heaven and Hell are states of consciousness.

SUBJECTIVE LAW

We should grasp the idea of Universal Subjectivity, the Potentiality of all things, the Divine Creative Medium. This is the Principle through which we are to demonstrate the healing of the body or of conditions; and It acts accurately and mathematically, because It is the Law of Cause and Effect.

When we think, we think from conscious intelligence, or Spirit. The thought then becomes subjectified; it goes into the subconscious mind. What is man's subconscious mind? It is his atmosphere or mental center in Universal Subjectivity. It is held in our philosophy that there is no such thing as *your* subjective mind and *my* subjective mind, meaning two, for this would be duality. *But there is such a thing as the subjective state of my thought and of your thought in Mind.* This should be seen clearly, for here is where psychology and metaphysics separate, where their interpretations differ.

When we think, we think into a Universal Creative Medium, a receptive and plastic medium which surrounds us on all sides, which permeates and flows through us. When we think, we must and do think into and upon It, since It is omnipresent.

As each subjectifies a consciousness about himself, he is surrounding himself with a mental atmosphere; and nothing can enter this except through the avenues of his own thought. But *this thought might be conscious or unconscious.* In most cases it is unconscious. However, the student of metaphysics is learning to consciously control the stream of thought that he allows to enter his inner and creative mentality.

THE RESULT OF OUR OWN THINKING

Thought is an inner movement, which is largely the result of one's perception of life and his reaction to it. Every time this movement takes place it takes place within Mind, upon Cause, according to Law. We are dealing with the same Power that molds the planets and all that is upon them, and the limit of our ability to use this Power is not in Principle, but in our understanding of It!

We are dealing with a neutral, creative Power, just as we would be in the case of electricity or any other natural force. It is on a higher plane for It is the Power of Intelligence. Our thought, in its externalization, will reach its own level, just as water reaches its own level by its own weight and without effort. This is in line with necessity for the Universe, in order to be at all, must be Self-Existent. By the Self-Existence of the Universe is meant a Universe which is Its own reason for being; a Universe which exists by virtue of Itself being All.

Each one of us today is the result of the use he has made of the Law, either consciously or unconsciously. As soon as we realize this we shall see that what we are now (or what we now have and experience) is the result of what we have thought; and the answer to *what we shall be* is contained in what we are now thinking, FOR WE CAN CHANGE OUR THINKING!

Man thinks, and supposes that he lets go of those thoughts, . . . that he is finished with them; but such is not the case, for thought becomes subjectified in Mind like a seed planted in the soil, and, unless neutralized, it stays there and determines the attraction and repulsion in the experience of the one thinking. There is a constant action on the subjective side of life; and it is the unconscious process which decides what is going to happen in the outer experience. Whatever we think, act, believe in, feel, visualize, vision, image, read and talk about—in fact all processes which affect or impress us at all—are going into the subjective state of our thought, which is our individualized use of Universal Mind. Whatever goes into the subjective state of our thought tends to return again as some condition. So we, and we alone, control our destiny.

Law Is Mind in Action

There is One Infinite Life acting through Law, and this Law is mental. Law is Mind in action. We are surrounded by an Infinite, subconscious, impersonal, neutral, plastic, and ever-present Thinking Stuff, from which all things come, and which, in Its Original State, permeates and penetrates all things.

By impressing our thought upon this Substance, we can cause It to produce for us that which we think. Impressing our thought upon It is not an external act, for when we impress our thought upon ourselves, we are thinking into It. This is because of the Unity of all Mind.

Jesus said: "As thou hast believed, so be it done unto thee." Knowing the nature of Law, He did not say: "It is done unto you as you *wish*." He announced the universality of the Law when he called it a Law of Belief.

THE DESTRUCTIVE USE OF THE LAW

Someone may say, "I cannot imagine *God not caring*." I cannot either, but we are dealing with Law. Does the law of electricity care whether it cooks the dinner or burns the house? Whether it electrocutes a criminal or warms a saint? Of course, it does not. Does the Urge which impels people to express, care whether a man kneels in ecstasy or lies drunk in the gutter? We are dealing with Law, and it follows that since we are dealing with Law, It will ultimately bring back to us the result of the forces which we set in motion through It.

Consequently, no person who is enlightened would seek to use this Law destructively, for he would know that, sooner or later, the very power set in motion by himself would ultimately destroy him. "All they that take the sword shall perish by the sword." The Spirit of Christ is the spirit which *constructively* uses the Law. The spirit of Antichrist is the *destructive* use of the Law. The Spirit of Christ, being in line with the Cosmic Life, will always transcend, neutralize, destroy, and utterly obliterate the spirit of the Antichrist. Finally, only the Spirit of Christ can succeed.

ONENESS WITH ALL LAW

When we know our Oneness with God and Law, what a great burden is removed. *Any sense of opposition is removed from the consciousness which perceives Unity.* That which we call OUR subjective mind is but a point in Universal Mind where our personality maintains its individualized expression of Spirit. If we think of ourselves as being separated from the Universe, we shall be limited by this thought, for it is a belief in separation from God which binds and limits. WE ARE BOUND BY NOTHING EXCEPT BELIEF. "They could not enter in because of their unbelief, and because they limited the Holy One of Israel."

There is but One Mind. Here is the point: everything we experience, touch, taste, handle and smell—environment, bodies, conditions, money, happiness, friends—all are *effects*. Is it clear that the infinite and limitless possibilities of that One of which man is a part, depend *in man's expression*, upon his own concept? If he is a point of personality in Limitless Mind, which he is; and if all his life must be drawn from this One Mind, which it must be, there cannot be anything else, can there? And if there is nothing else, if there is nothing to move save Mind—and if man is a thinking center in Mind—*nothing is going to happen TO him that does not happen* THROUGH him, whether it be the result of his own erroneous conclusions, those of his grandfather, or those of the race to which he belongs! This is not in any sense fatalistic, for WE MAY CHANGE THE TREND OF CAUSATION WHICH HAS BEEN SET IN MOTION AT ANY TIME WE DECIDE TO DO SO.

Everything comes from Intelligence. There is nothing but Unity; there is nothing but freedom; there is nothing but completeness; there is nothing but Totality. Begin at the beginning and reason this out, time after time, until all doubt disappears. It is necessary that each one do this for himself.

Such is the power of right thinking that it cancels and erases everything unlike itself. It answers every question, solves all problems, is the solution to every difficulty. It is like the Sunlight of Eternal Truth bursting through the clouds of obscurity and bathing all life in a celestial glory. It is the Absolute with which we are dealing and nothing less.

CHAPTER SEVEN

SUMMARY OF PART ONE:
THE NATURE OF BEING

WHAT WE BELIEVE ABOUT GOD AND MAN.

There is a Universal Presence that acts as though It were intelligent, and we may assume that It is. There is a Universal Intelligence acting as Law—we may also assume this to be true. There is a formless Stuff in the Universe, forever taking form, and forever changing its form—this we may accept as being self-evident.

We have every reason to postulate a three-fold nature of the Universal Being, which we shall call Spirit, Soul, and Body. We shall think of Spirit as the great Actor, Soul as the Medium of Its action, and Body the result of Its action. We shall think of Spirit as the only Conscious Actor—the Power that knows Itself. We shall think of Soul as a blind Force, obeying the Will of Spirit; and we shall think of Body as the effect of Spirit, working through Law to produce form. We shall assume that neither Law, nor the Stuff from which form comes, has *conscious* intelligence, but must because of their nature be formed by the Word. This simplifies the whole matter and enables us to see that in the entire Universe, One Power alone really acts—the Power of the Word of Spirit, God, or Universal Conscious Intelligence.

The evolution of man brings him arbitrarily to a place where true individuality functions. From that day, a further evolution must be through his *conscious* co-operation with Reality. All Nature waits on man's recognition of and cooperation with her laws, and is always ready to obey his will; but man must use Nature's forces in accordance with her laws, and in co-operation with her purpose—which is goodness, truth, and beauty—if he wishes to attain self-mastery.

Man never creates; he discovers and uses. Through this method all sciences are evolved. We live in a Universe of Law, through which runs a spirit of self-knowing Intelligence. "All's Love, yet all is Law," mused Robert Browning.

The Law has done all it can automatically do for man. It has evolved him to a point of individuality and must now let him alone to discover the secrets of life for himself. Man is potentially perfect but free-will and self-choice cause him to appear imperfect. In reality all he can destroy is some particular embodiment of himself. The Divine Spark is always intact in potential man.

Man awakes to self-consciousness, finding himself already equipped with a mentality, a body and an environment. Gradually he discovers one law of nature after another, until he conquers his environment through his knowledge of the nature of those laws. Everywhere he finds that nature does his bidding, in so far as he understands her laws and uses them along the lines of their inherent being. He must first obey nature and she will then obey him.

Man discovers his ability to think and realizes that from within there comes a reaction to his thought. He can think consciously and mental law acts upon his thought; and his physical body is affected by his thinking.

He next discovers that he can think for others, causing a corresponding action in and through *their* bodies. In this way, he discovers a mental medium through which thought operates. He now realizes himself to be a thinking center in a Universal Mind.

Man next discovers that his affairs are primarily a thing of thought, and that being able to think for others he can also aid in the control of their affairs. He now realizes that *everything* in the visible world is an EFFECT; that back of all effects are *ideas* which are the real Cause of these effects. The Divine Ideas are perfect, but man's freedom of individuality causes them to appear imperfect. Through right thinking, he is able to uncover the appearance of imperfection and reveal the Perfect Idea. "Behold, thou, my face forevermore."

Man's idea of Deity evolves with his other ideas. After a belief in many gods, he comes to realize there is One Mind and One Spirit back of all manifestation. One Spirit, or Self-Conscious Life, acting through the medium of One Mind or Subjective Law, producing many manifestations. Multiplicity comes from Unity without breaking up the Unity of the Whole.

Spirit is Self-Knowing, but Law is automatic and obeys the Will of Spirit, having no alternative other than to obey. Like all law, the Law of Mind is an impersonal force, and because of Its nature It is compelled to act.

Soul and Universal Subjective Mind have the same meaning, and are the Creative Medium of all thought and action. Soul is also the Substance of Spirit, the unformed Stuff, from which all forms are evolved.

Spirit, acting upon Soul, produces Creation. Spirit, Soul and Substance intersphere each other, each being omnipresent. Creation takes place *within* Spirit, and is the result of the contemplation or the self-knowingness of Spirit. Creation is eternally going on; change is always taking place within that which is Changeless. Forms appear and disappear in a Medium which of Itself is formless.

Spirit thinks or knows within Itself, and, as a result of this inner action, Creation manifests. Creation is the play of Life upon Itself, through Divine Self-Imagination. Spirit must create in order to be expressed. Spirit, Life, Soul, Substance, Law and Unity are all Co-Existent and Co-Eternal with each other. The only thing that changes is form. Spirit makes things out of Itself by becoming the thing It makes. There is no effort in the process.

Conscious Mind and Spirit have the same meaning: that part of Reality which is Self-Knowing.

Subconscious and Subjective Mind, Soul and Mental Medium, Universal Subjectivity and Law, all have the same meaning: that part of Reality which acts as Law.

Body, Creation, or the manifest universe is the result of Spirit acting through Law. Body, Creation, or the manifest Universe is a result of the *Knowingness* of Spirit.

Spirit alone is Self-Conscious. Law and manifestation are automatic reactions to Spirit.

Soul, or Subjective Mind, Substance or unformed Stuff, and Conscious Spirit permeate all things and all people. There is an Intelligence acting through everything, and everything responds to this Intelligence.

It cannot be too plainly stated that Spirit, or Conscious Intelligence, is the only Self-Assertive Principle in the Universe. "Spirit is the Power that knows Itself," and is the *only* Power that is self-knowing, everything else is *subject* to Spirit. The sole and only operation of Spirit is through Its Word, acting as Law through Substance, producing Creation.

Man re-enacts the Divine Nature on all three planes. He is self-knowing in his conscious mind, creative through his subconscious reactions, and he has a body. He personifies the Trinity of Being. He is the son within the Father. The Father is greater than the son, but the son has the same life Essence as has the Father or Parent Mind.

Real man is in an eternal state of complete unity with the Whole. His conscious mind is his understanding of God; his subjective mind is his use of the Universal Creative Medium; and his body is one with the Body of Reality.

There is but One Mind in the Universe and man uses It. Man is an identity in the Universe . . . a center of God-Consciousness. At first he is ignorant of this and misuses his power, consequently bringing on himself misfortune and negation.

The Spirit of man, which is his self-knowingness, is the only part of him which has volition or self-choice; all else acts as automatic law. Man's conscious thought, acting through Law, may change any condition in his experience, provided he can clearly conceive of such conditions being changed. There is no limit to the Law. Limitation is not inherent in the Law, but is a result of man's inability to embody the Truth and constructively use the Law. Man has at his disposal, in what he calls his subjective mind, a power that is Limitless; this is because he is One with the Whole on the subjective side of Life.

There is but One Mind and One Law, which all people use, consciously or unconsciously, constructively or destructively: One Spirit, One Mind, One Law, One Substance . . . but many forms. There is One Ultimate Reality, but within this One are many experiences. Man is within the One and draws from It all of his experiences.

As man thinks he subjectifies thought and sets Law in motion, through the Medium of the Universal Mind. *This Law works automatically until it is consciously changed.* To learn how to think is to learn how to live, for our thoughts go into a Medium that is Infinite in Its ability to be and to do. Man is using a Power which is Infinite, as compared with the power of his conscious thought.

Great as the subconscious is, its tendency is set in motion by the conscious thought, and *in this lies the possibility of and the pathway to freedom.* Freedom and bondage, sickness and health, poverty and riches, Heaven and Hell, good and bad, big and little, happiness and misery, peace and confusion, faith and fear, and all conditions which *appear* to be opposites, are not really a result of the operation of *opposing powers*, but ARE THE WAY THE ONE POWER IS USED.

We are bound because we are first free, and the power which binds us is the only thing in the universe which can free us. Man already has, within himself, the key to freedom but he must come to realize his relation to the Whole. This relationship is one of complete Unity.

PART TWO

SPIRITUAL MIND HEALING

FIRST DIVISION: IDEATION

A recognition of the Power, and the thought

and purpose back of mind healing.

CHAPTER EIGHT
THE POWER OF THOUGHT

*Spiritual Mind Healing • The Basis for Mental Healing • The Act of Incarnation •
Activity of the One Mind • It Is Done unto Us • Thought Force • The Atmosphere
of Our Thinking • Inducing Thought • Choosing Thought • Thoughts Are Things •
One with God • The Power Within • We Set Our Own Limitations • Understanding.*

SPIRITUAL MIND HEALING

It has taken humanity thousands of years to learn that it has the power to control its own destiny. From the Bible we have the assurance: "As a man thinketh in his heart, so is he." The old Greek philosophers understood something of the meaning of thought. *What we expect*, said Aristotle, *that we find. What we wish*, said Demosthenes, *that we believe*. And Shakespeare is accredited with the saying: "There is nothing either good or bad but thinking makes it so." It is one thing to *know* a principle, another to *apply* it.

The modern commercial world accepts the slogan: "He can who *thinks* he can." Throughout the ages many persons have realized that causation is from within. True, the thousands of unhappy beings would indicate that a comparatively small number have used this knowledge for their benefit; yet the day for incredulous skepticism or shallow criticism of the power of thought has passed. Unless we discredit all human testimony, we are forced to the conclusion that bodily healing of all manner of sickness by mental and spiritual means, is a fact. Physicians of highest repute are assiduously betaking themselves to a serious study of mental phenomena and mental processes. They are realizing the incredible possibilities of dominion resident in the dynamic forces of the mental realm. A belief in and an acceptance of mental healing has arrived in the most orthodox of medical circles, and is being increasingly approved as a legitimate and useful healing agent.

The Basis for Mental Healing

Much in this field is as yet obscure and imperfectly understood, for the scientific study of mind is still in its infancy; but the fact that a misuse of mental and spiritual laws is at the root of many unhappy conditions incident to the physical life, stands out clear and sharp.

The first principle fundamental to the understanding of the operation of thought is that we are surrounded by an Infinite Intelligence. The possibility of healing physical disease, changing environment, attracting friends and demonstrating supply through the power of right thinking, rests entirely on the theory that we are surrounded by an Infinite Mind, which reacts to our thought according to Law.

We comprehend the meaning of Infinite Intelligence only in a small degree, but because we are spiritual beings, we do sense the presence of an Intelligence which is beyond human comprehension—an Intelligence which is great enough to encompass the past, to understand the present, and to be Father of the future. It is the Cause of everything that has been, and is that out of which must unfold everything that is to be. Our own intelligence is one of Its activities and is of like nature to It.

The Act of Incarnation

At the level of our self-comprehension, we know and understand the nature of God. This self-knowing, which is God-knowing, has the possibility of an eternal expansion. As individual intelligence, we communicate with each other—are able to respond to each other—and in so doing we establish the fact that intelligence responds to intelligence. This same law must hold good, whether we think of finite intelligence responding to finite intelligence, or Infinite Intelligence responding to finite intelligence—*for intelligence is the same in ESSENCE wherever we find it.* We may conclude that Infinite Intelligence responds to us by the very necessity of being true to Its own Nature.

But how does It respond? It can respond only by corresponding, which means that the Infinite Intelligence responds to us by a direct impartation of Itself through us. "The highest God and the innermost God is One God." So with Jesus we may say: "The Father and I are One." Whatever intelligence we possess is some degree of the One Intelligence, which we call God.

The Infinite Mind, then, imparts Itself to the finite, through the act of incarnation. The progress of the human race is a result of that process whereby Intelligence passes, by successive degrees of incarnation, through evolution, into the human mind.

ACTIVITY OF THE ONE MIND

We are living in an Intelligent Universe, which responds to our mental states. To the extent that we learn to control these mental states, we shall automatically control our environment. This is why we are studying *the power of thought* as we approach the subject of spiritual mind healing. This is what is meant by the practical application of this Science to the problems of everyday living. The result of this mental work is what is meant by demonstration.

In the great Universal Mind, man is a center of intelligence, and every time he thinks he sets Mind in action. Because of the Oneness of Mind, It cannot know anything outside Itself, and therefore cannot contradict any thought given It, but must reflect whatever is cast into It. We are immersed in an Infinite Creative Medium which, because of Its Nature, must create after the pattern our thought gives It. Jesus understood this, and in a few simple words laid down the law of life: "It is done unto you AS you believe." No more simple and yet no more profound statement could be made.

IT IS DONE UNTO US

What a marvelous thought to bear in mind: that it is done unto us! We need not coerce, we do not *create* the power, but we must LET this Great Power operate through us.

In the Infinity of Mind, there is nothing but Mind and what Mind does—Its operations. *This Mind is acted upon by our thought, and in this way thought becomes the law of our lives.* It is just as much a law in our individual lives as God's thought is in the larger life of the Universe. WE DO NOT CREATE. WE USE THE POWER OF THE ONE MIND, WHICH CREATES FOR US! Our beliefs and our deep-seated convictions inevitably out-picture and reflect themselves in our experience and environment, both in the physical condition of the body, and in the larger world of our affairs. What we outwardly are, and what we are to become, *depends upon what we are thinking*, for this is the way we are using Creative Power. The sooner we release our minds from the thought that we have to create, the sooner we shall be able to work in line with Spirit. Always man *uses*; he never *creates* anything. The united intelligence of the human race could not make a single rosebud; but our thought, centered in Mind, is *using* the Creative Power of the Universe.

Law of Life is a law of thought—an activity of consciousness—the Power flows through us. The Spirit can do for us only what It can do through us. Unless we are able to provide the consciousness, It cannot make the gift. The Power behind all things is without limit, but in working for us It must work through us. Realizing, then, that while the Power is limitless, It must become operative through our own thought, we shall see that what we need is not some greater power, but a greater consciousness, a deeper realization of life, a more sublime concept of Being, a more intimate concept of an already indwelling God, *Who is personal to us by virtue of being personified through us.*

THOUGHT FORCE

Thought force is a movement of consciousness in a field of mechanical but intelligent Law. The movement of consciousness upon itself creates a motion or vibration upon Substance, *the force of which is equal to the embodiment of the thought set in motion.* For everything that happens in the objective world, there must be something in the subjective world which perfectly balances it.

Let us suppose, for illustration, that the Universe is nothing but water, permeated by an Infinite Intelligence. Imagine that every time this Intelligence moves, or thinks, ice is formed in the water, exactly corresponding to the thought. We might have countless pieces of ice of different form, color and size, but *these pieces of ice would still be water!* If we could heat the entire mass, it would melt, and all forms would again become fluid. Nothing would have changed except form. The physical universe is Spirit in form.

First is Intelligence; then the Word, the idea, the image, the concept; then the movement toward the thing. Thought is an actual working power. Otherwise, there would be nothing by which the Universe could be governed.

THE ATMOSPHERE OF OUR THINKING

We are all immersed in the atmosphere of our own thinking, which is the direct result of all we have ever said, thought or done. This decides what is to take place in our lives. Thought attracts what is like itself and repels what is unlike. We are drawn toward those things which we mentally image. Most of the inner processes of our thought have been unconscious, but *when we understand the Law, we learn to consciously embody what we wish, and think of this only, and then we are drawn silently toward it.*

The emphasis on true mental healing is insistently on God, the One Mind, the One Soul, the One Being, ever-present and ever-available; and on man's ability and right to make himself receptive to this healing Presence—a realization of the essential divinity of our own nature, and the truth that no evil can live in this Presence. We must unify ourselves with the great Whole. The man who dares to fling his thought out into Universal Intelligence, with the assurance of one who realizes his divine nature and its relation to the Universe—and dares to claim all there is—will find an ever-creative good at hand to aid him. God will honor his request. To the soul that knows its own divinity, all else must gravitate. Let us, then, enlarge our thought processes, and dare to think in Universal terms. Let us dare to believe that every constructive word is invincible!

INDUCING THOUGHT

That which thought has done, thought can un-do. Life-long habits of wrong thinking can be consciously and deliberately neutralized, and an entirely new order of mental and emotional re-action established in Mind. Merely to abstain from wrong thinking is not enough; there must be active right thinking. We must become *actively* constructive and happy in our thinking—not merely *passively* so. New and wholesome ideas of life, vitality and hope must be accepted and incorporated into the sub-stratum of our mental life, so that a more wholesome externalization may manifest in our bodily condition and environment.

Since we must all begin right where we are, most of us will be compelled to begin our healing work with a mechanical process. We should take the highest thought we have, and attempt to enlarge on this consciousness until it embraces a more vital concept of Reality. Consciousness in this sense means an inner embodiment of ideas. If one wishes to demonstrate prosperity, he must first have a consciousness of prosperity; if he wishes health, he must embody the idea of health. This is more than faith; it is the knowledge that we are dealing with Law. While a certain consciousness may be mechanically induced, of course, the more spontaneity put into the me-chanical word, the more power the word must have.

CHOOSING THOUGHT

We cannot live a choiceless life. Every day, every moment, every second, there is choice. If it were not so we would not be individuals.

We have the right to choose what we wish to experience. We have the right to choose the kind of companions with whom we wish to associate; to say in what city and in what type of house we would like to live. We are individuals and the only way we can be individuals is to be spontaneous. There is no such thing as a mechanistic individuality, it must have the essential elements of spontaneity. There is no spontaneity and no individuality without prerogative. There can be no choice unless there is something from which to choose, otherwise the ability to choose would be merely a fantasy. Therefore, there must be not only the possibility of choice; but the liability of experiencing that which is chosen.

We have a right to choose what we shall induce in Mind. The *way* in which our thoughts are to become manifest, we cannot always see—or should we be disturbed that we do not see the way—because effect is potential in cause. "I am Alpha and Omega," and all that comes between cause and effect. Cause and effect are really one, and if we have a given cause set in motion, the effect will have to equal the cause. One is the inside and the other the outside of the same thing. A certain, specific, intelligent idea in Mind, will produce a certain, specific, concrete manifestation equal to itself. There is One Infinite Principle, One Infinite Thought-Stuff, One Infinite Creative Power, but countless numbers of forms, which change as the specific idea behind them changes.

THOUGHTS ARE THINGS

Health and sickness are largely externalizations of our dominant mental and spiritual states. An emotional shock, or a mind filled with thoughts of fear, has been known to cause the momentary stoppage or acceleration of the heart. Physicians now testify that, under emotional stress, particularly anger, the blood leaves a chemical deposit around the joints in the body. Worry, fear, anger, jealousy, and other emotional conditions, are mental in their nature, and as such are being recognized as the hidden cause of a large part of all the physical suffering to which the flesh is heir. A normal healthy mind reflects itself in a healthy body, and conversely, an abnormal mental state expresses its corresponding condition in some physical condition. Thoughts are things!

Modern psychology affirms that all the thoughts and emotions we have experienced since we came into conscious existence are still present in Mind, where ceaselessly active, they manifest themselves as subjective tendencies that mold the body in health or sickness; and determine, as well, our reactions to all life and experience.

We do not maintain that this or that specific disease is always the result of thinking about such a condition; but we do assert that a prolonged discordant mental state is certain to eventuate in some form of physical ailment. People have died of great grief; of broken hearts; of outbursts of temper; of deep and continued resentment; of excessive worry, and many other mental states, in which there was no specific thought of sickness at all. The point to remember is, *that all mind activity inevitably tends to create its physical correspondent*, so that an unhealthful and morbid mental state projects itself into the physical body.

Thoughts are things, they have the power to objectify themselves; thought lays hold of Causation and forms real Substance. The word of man is the law of his life, under the One Great Law of all Life. Thoughts of sickness can make a man sick, and thoughts of health and perfection can heal him. Thought is the conscious activity of the one thinking, and works as he directs, through Law; and this Law may be consciously set in motion. This Law will work for him to the fullest extent of his belief in, and understanding of, It. A realization of the Presence of God is the most powerful healing agency known to the mind of man.

ONE WITH GOD

Until we awake to the fact that we are One in nature with God, we shall not find the way of life. Until we realize that our own word has the power of life, we will not see clearly. The Bible points out that man has the same power, in his own life and in his own world, that it claims for God. "The Word was with God and the Word was God," is an oft-repeated but little understood statement. The promise to man is equally positive: "The word is nigh thee, even in thine own mouth that thou shouldst know it and do it." If any word has power, it follows that all words have power. It means that every word which we hear, speak or think, has some power.

THE POWER WITHIN

Through spiritual discernment, we see that we have within us a power which is greater than anything we shall ever contact; a power that can overcome every obstacle in our experience and set us safe, satisfied, and at peace, healed and prosperous in a new light and a new life. "If God be for us who can be against us?"

God's Creative Power of Mind is right here. We have as much of this power to use as we believe in and embody. The storehouse of nature is filled with infinite good, awaiting the touch of our awakened thought to spring forth into manifestation in our lives; but *the awakening must be within our thought!* The word that we speak is the law of our lives, and nothing hinders its operation but ourselves. We may use this creative word for whatever purpose we desire, and this word becomes the law unto the thing for which it was spoken. We are given the power to sit in the midst of our lives and direct their activities. Strife and struggle are unnecessary. We only need to *know*, but we must know *constructively*.

Just so far as we depend upon any condition, past, present or future, we are creating chaos, because we are then dealing with conditions (effects) and not with causes. Could we but comprehend the fact that there is a Power that makes things directly out of Itself—by simply becoming the thing It makes—could we but grasp this greatest truth about life; and realize that we are dealing with a Principle, scientifically correct and eternally present, *we could accomplish whatever it is possible for us to conceive*. Life externalizes at the level of our thought.

WE SET OUR OWN LIMITATIONS

Do we desire to live in a world peopled with friends who love us, surrounded by things beautiful and pleasing? There is but one way, and this way is as certain as that the sun shines. DAILY WE MUST CONTROL ALL THOUGHT THAT DENIES THE REAL; AFFIRM THE DIVINE

PRESENCE WITHIN US; then, as the mist disappears before the sun, so shall adversity melt before the shining radiance of our exalted thought!

The Prodigal Son remained a prodigal as long as he chose to do so. When he chose to, he returned to his "Father's house" and was greeted with outstretched hands. So shall our experience be when we return to the world which is perfect; there will be something that will turn to us. We shall behold a new heaven and a new earth, not in some far off place but here and now. "Act as though I am and I will be." The Spirit of Truth will lead us into all good. This is the highroad to the fulfillment of our lives.

There is, then, no limitation outside our own ignorance, and since we can all conceive of a greater good than we have so far experienced, we all have the ability to transcend previous experiences and rise triumphant above them; but *we shall never triumph over them while we persist in going through the old mental reactions.*

UNDERSTANDING

Before we attempt to improve our conditions; before we proceed further on the subject of *healing* it is necessary that we be certain in our own minds that *thought is creative*, as upon this basis our entire superstructure rests. Since Spirit creates by contemplation—purely mental action—then everything in the manifest world is *some effect* of Its thought. Our own minds are an expression of the Divine Mind and must be of the same essence.

That we find ourselves in an undesirable condition in the face of all this, is merely proof that we have limited ourselves by our very freedom. Shall we not, then, reverse our thinking and take for our starting point the inherent nature of mental powers?

We have gone far in the right direction, when we have determined that *Creation could have originated only in Intelligence*; and have realized further that our own mental power must be the same in kind with the Creativeness of God. Thus we begin to sense, even though dimly, that as our minds become more like the Divine Mind, we shall expand into a greater livingness—*our world created by our consciousness, and our consciousness taking its color from the perception of our relation to the Infinite!*

We should strive toward a perfect vision, a perfect conception. We should expand our thought until it realizes all good, and then cut right through all that *appears* to be, and use this Almighty Power for definite purposes. We should daily feel a deeper union with Life, a greater sense of that Indwelling God—the God of the seen and of the unseen—within us. When we speak into this Mind, we have sown a seed of thought in the Absolute and we may rest in peace. We need not make haste, for it is done unto us as we believe. "In that day they that call upon me, I will answer."

CHAPTER NINE
PRAYER

The Difference Between Prayer *and* Treatment • *Laws Governing Prayer* • *Prayer Is Essential to Happiness* • *Prayer Is Its Own Answer.*

THE DIFFERENCE BETWEEN *PRAYER* AND *TREATMENT*

One of the questions most frequently asked about the Science of Mind is, "Are *prayers* and *treatments* identical?" The answer to this question is both *Yes* and *No*.

If when one prays his prayer is a recognition of Spirit's Omniscience, Omnipotence, and Omnipresence, and a realization of man's unity with Spirit, then his prayer is a spiritual treatment.

If, on the other hand, one is holding to the viewpoint that God is some far off Being, Whom he would approach with doubt in his thought; wondering if by some good luck he may be able to placate God or persuade Him of the wisdom of one's request—*then*, there is but little similarity between *prayer* and *treatment*. Nothing could bring greater discouragement than to labor under the delusion that God is a Being of moods, who might answer *some* prayers and not others.

It would be difficult to believe in a God who cares more for one person than another. There can be no God who is kindly disposed one day and cruel the next; there can be no God who creates us with tendencies and impulses we can scarcely comprehend, and then eternally punishes us when we make mistakes. God is a Universal Presence, an impersonal Observer, a Divine and impartial Giver, forever pouring Himself into His Creation.

LAWS GOVERNING PRAYER

Most men who believe in God believe in prayer; but our idea of prayer changes as our idea of God changes; and it is natural for each to feel that his way of praying is the correct way. But we should bear in mind that the prayers which are effective—no matter whose prayers they may be—*are effective because they embody certain universal principles which, when understood, can be consciously used.*

IF GOD EVER ANSWERED PRAYER, HE ALWAYS ANSWERS PRAYER, since He is "the same yesterday, today and forever." If there seems to be any failure, it is in man's ignorance or misunderstanding of the Will and Nature of God.

We are told that "God is Spirit, and they that worship Him must worship Him in spirit and in truth." The immediate availability of the Divine Spirit is "neither in the mountain nor at the temple; neither Lo, here, nor lo there, for behold the Kingdom of God is within."

This is a true perception of spiritual power. The power is no longer I, but "the Father who dwelleth in me." Could we conceive of Spirit as being incarnate in us—while at the same time being ever *more* than that which is incarnated—would we not expand spiritually and intellectually? Would not our prayers be answered before they were uttered? "The Kingdom of God is within you." When we become conscious of our Oneness with Universal Good, beliefs in evil, sin, sickness, limitation, and death tend to disappear. We shall no longer "ask amiss," supplicating as though God were not willing, begging as though He were withholding.

"If ye abide in me and my words abide in you, ye shall ask what ye will and it shall be done unto you." This gives great light on an important law governing the answering of prayer. *Abiding in Him*, means having no consciousness separate from His consciousness—nothing in our thought which denies the power and presence of Spirit. Yes, we can readily see why prayers are answered when we are *abiding in Him.*

Again we read, "Whatsoever ye shall ask in my name, that will I do." This sounds simple at first, but it is another profound statement like unto the first; its significance lies in the phrase: "in my name." *In His name*, means like His Nature. If our thought is as unsullied as the Mind of God, if we are recognizing our Oneness with God, we cannot pray for other than the good of all men. In such prayer we should not dwell upon evil or adversity. The secret of spiritual power lies in a consciousness of one's union with the Whole, and of the availability of Good. God is accessible to all people.

God manifests Himself through all individuals. No two people are alike; each has a unique place in the universe of Mind; each lives in Mind; each contacts It through his own mentality, in an individual way, drawing from It a unique expression of Its Divine Nature. If one makes himself receptive to the idea of love, he becomes lovable. To the degree that he embodies love, he is love; so people who love are loved. Whoever becomes receptive to the idea of peace, poise and calm—whoever embodies these divine realities—finds them flowing through him and he becomes peaceful, poised and calm.

There is a place in us which lies open to the Infinite; but when the Spirit brings Its gift, by pouring Itself through us, It can give to us only what we take. This taking is mental. If we persist in saying that Life will not give us that which is good ("God will not answer *my* prayer"), it cannot, *for Life must reveal Itself to us through our intelligence*. The pent-up energy of life, and the possibility of further human evolution, work through man's imagination and will. *The time is now; the place is where we are, and it is done unto us as we believe.*

Prayer Is Essential to Happiness

Prayer is not an act of overcoming God's reluctance, but should be an *active* acceptance of His highest willingness. Through prayer we recognize a spiritual law, that has always existed, and put ourselves in alignment with it. The law of electricity might have been used by Moses had he understood this law. Emerson said: "Is not prayer a study of truth, a sally of the Soul into the unfound Infinite?"

Prayer is constructive, because it enables us to establish closer contact with the Fountain of Wisdom, and we are less likely to be influenced by appearances around us—to judge "according to appearance." Righteous prayer sets the "law of the Spirit of Life" in motion for us.

Prayer is essential, not to the salvation of the soul, for the soul is never lost; but to the conscious well-being of the soul that does not understand itself. There is a vitality in our communion with the Infinite, which is productive of the highest good. As fire warms the body, as food strengthens us, as sunshine raises our spirits, so there is a subtle transfusion of some invisible force in such communion, weaving itself into the very warp and woof of our own mentalities. This conscious commingling of our thought with Spirit is essential to the well-being of every part of us.

Prayer has stimulated countless millions of people to higher thoughts and nobler deeds. That which tends to connect our minds with the Universal Mind lets in a flood of Its consciousness. If we think of God as a Heavenly Dictator—something apart from that which lives and moves and has Its being where we are—then we are certain to believe ourselves disconnected from this Infinite Presence; and the inevitable consequence of such thinking would be a terrible fear that we should *never* be able to make contact with Him! But if we know God as an Indwelling Presence, our prayer is naturally addressed to this Presence in us. We long for, and need, a conscious union with the Infinite. This is as necessary to the nature and intellect of man, as food is to the well-being of his physical body.

PRAYER IS ITS OWN ANSWER

Cause and effect are but two sides of thought, and Spirit, being ALL, is both Cause and Effect. Prayer, then, is its own answer. The Bible tells us: "Before they call will I answer." Before our prayer is framed in words, God has already answered, *but if our prayer is one of partial belief, then there is only a tendency toward its answer*; if the next day we wholly doubt, then there is no answer at all. In dealing with Mind, we are dealing with a Force we cannot fool. We cannot cheat Principle out of the slightest shadow of our most subtle concept. The hand writes and passes on, but the writing remains; and the only thing that can erase it is writing of a different character. There is no obstruction one cannot dissipate by the power of Truth.

So we learn to go deeply within ourselves, and speak as though there were a Presence there that knows; and we should take the time to unearth this hidden cause, to penetrate this inner chamber of consciousness. It is most worthwhile to commune with Spirit—to sense and feel It. The approach to Spirit is direct . . . through our own consciousness.

This Spirit flows through us. Whatever intelligence we have is this Spirit in us. Prayer is its own answer.

We can be certain that there is an Intelligence in the Universe to which we may come, that will guide and inspire us, a love which overshadows. God is real to the one who believes in the Supreme Spirit, real to the soul that senses its unity with the Whole.

Every day and every hour we are meeting the eternal realities of life, and in such degree as we co-operate with these eternal realities in love, in peace, in wisdom, and in joy—believing and receiving—we are automatically blessed. Our prayer is answered before it is uttered.

CHAPTER TEN

FAITH

The Mental Approach • Always a Power • Misplaced Faith • Understanding Faith • No Confusion • Available to All • Vitalizing Faith • The Technique of Acquiring Faith • Conviction.

THE MENTAL APPROACH

The Universe is a Spiritual System. Its laws are those of intelligence. We approach it through the mind, which enables us to know, will and act. Prayer, faith and belief are closely related mental attitudes.

Prayer is a mental approach to Reality. It is not the symbol but *the idea symbolized* that makes prayer effective. Some prayers are more effective than others. Some only help us to endure, while others transcend conditions, and demonstrate an invisible law which has power over the visible. In so far as our prayer is affirmative, it is creative of the desired results.

ALWAYS A POWER

Faith has been recognized as a power throughout the ages—whether it be faith in God, faith in one's fellowmen, in oneself, or in what one is doing. The idea that faith has only to do with our religious experience is a mistake. Faith is a faculty of the mind that finds its highest expression in the religious attitude, but always the man who has faith in his own ability accomplishes far more than the one who has no confidence in himself. Those who have great faith, have great power.

Why is it that one man's prayers are answered, while another's remain unanswered? It cannot be that God desires more good for one person than another. It must be that all persons, in their approach to Reality, receive results—not because of what they believe in, but because of their belief. Faith is an affirmative mental approach to Reality.

MISPLACED FAITH

Someone has said that the entire world is suffering from one big fear . . . the fear that God will not answer our prayers. Let us analyze the fears which possess us and see if this is true. The fear of lack is nothing more than the belief that God does not, and will not, supply us with whatever we need. The fear of death is the belief that the promises of eternal life may not be true. The fear of loss of health, loss of friends, loss of property—all arise from the belief that God is not all that we claim: Omniscience, Omnipotence, and Omnipresence.

But what is fear? *Nothing more nor less than the negative use of faith* . . . faith misplaced; a belief in two powers instead of One; a belief that there can be a Power—opposed to God—whose influence and ability *may* bring us evil. In other words, *to correct all the evils of the world, would be but to have the positive faith*, faith rightly placed, a faith that lays hold of the integrity of the Universe, the beneficence of God and the Unity of all life. Nevertheless, we cannot have faith in that which we do not in some measure understand.

UNDERSTANDING FAITH

We wish a faith based on the knowledge that there is nothing to fear! "Faith is the substance of things hoped for, the evidence of things not seen." The thought of faith molds the undifferentiated substance, and brings into manifestation the thing which was fashioned in the mind. This is how faith brings our desires to pass.

When we use our creative imagination in strong faith, it will create for us, out of the One Substance, whatever we have formed in thought. In this way man becomes a Co-Creator with God. There will never be an end to any of the eternal verities like Truth, Love, Beauty. There will never be an end to God, nor to any of the attributes which are co-eternal and co-existent with God. If we are wise, we shall cultivate a faith in these realities. This is not a difficult *task*, but a thrilling *experience*.

Spiritual Substance is all around us, waiting to be formed. Thus we see what Jesus meant when he said: "And I say unto you, Ask and it shall be given unto you." The Law must work in compliance with our demand. The Divine Urge within us is God's way of letting us know that we should push forward and take that which is awaiting our demand. *If the good were not already ours in the invisible supply, it would be impossible for us to procure it in any manner.* "He openeth his hand and satisfieth the desire of every living creature."

No Confusion

History has recorded many instances of healing through faith. This is an undisputed fact. Yet we cannot believe in a Divine Power that responds more quickly to one than to another. We are compelled to see that prayer is not an end of itself; it is a means to an end. Like the practice of the Science of Mind, it is *a way*. The principle governing faith is, that when the one praying becomes convinced his prayer will automatically be answered. Jesus announced the law of mind, saying: "It is done unto you as you believe." The Universe exists by Its own self-pronouncement, by Its own affirmation. It only knows "I AM." It knows nothing else. Therefore, wherever prayer, in faith, touches Reality, prays aright—prays according to whatever the Truth is—*then prayer must be answered.*

Available to All

Persons familiar with Biblical history hardly need a lesson about faith, for the eleventh chapter of Hebrews is full of instances proving its sustaining power. Paul enumerates at length the experiences of Enoch, Noah, Abraham, Moses, Gideon, Samuel and the prophets, and many more, "who through faith subdued kingdoms, wrought righteousness, obtained promises, stopped the mouths of lions, quenched the power of fire, escaped the edge of the sword; out of weakness were made strong, waxed mighty in power, turned to flight armies of aliens, women received their dead raised to life again."

Our ancestors believed these records and embodied this living faith in their consciousness, thereby leaving us a great legacy of faith. Whatever they did, they were able to do because they grasped an instinctive faith and marched boldly on with it.

Since faith is a quality unconfined to age or station, it may be ours today as much as it has been any man's at any time. We are not going through a harder time today, a longer or darker night, than has ever been experienced before. It only seems darker because we have lost faith—the beacon light.

If one will have faith in himself, faith in his fellowmen, in the Universe, and in God, that faith will light the place in which he finds himself, and by the light of this faith, he will be able to see that ALL IS GOOD. And the light shed by this faith will light the way for others. We become conscious of darkness only when we are without faith—for faith is ever the light of our day and the light on our way, making that way clearly visible to us, even when to all others it may be beset with obstacles and the ongoing rough.

VITALIZING FAITH

In order to *have* faith, we must have a conviction that all is well. In order to *keep* faith, we must allow nothing to enter our thought which will weaken this conviction. Faith is built up from belief, acceptance and trust. Whenever anything enters our thought which destroys, in any degree, one of these attitudes, to that extent faith is weakened.

Our mind must be steady in its conviction that our life is some part of God, and that the Spirit is incarnated in us. Affirmations and denials are for the purpose of vitalizing faith—for the purpose of converting thought to *a belief* in things spiritual. The foundation for correct mental treatment is perfect God, perfect man, and perfect being. Thought must be organized to fit this premise, and conclusions must be built on this premise. We must keep our faith vital, if we hope to successfully treat for ourselves or others.

All sciences are built upon *faith principles*. All principles are invisible, and all laws accepted on faith. No man has seen God at any time, nor has he seen goodness, truth or beauty, but who can doubt their existence?

Not only must we have complete faith in Spirit, and Its ability to know and to do, but we must have complete confidence in our approach to It. We must not be lukewarm in our conviction. *We must know that we know.* We are to demonstrate that spiritual thought force has power over all apparent material resistance, and this cannot be done unless we have abounding confidence in the Principle which we approach.

Pure faith is a spiritual conviction; it is the acquiescence of the mind, the embodiment of an idea, the acceptance of a concept. If we believe that the Spirit, incarnated in us, can demonstrate, shall we be disturbed at what *appears* to contradict this? We shall often need to *know* that the Truth which we announce is superior to the condition we are to change. In other words, *if we are speaking from the standpoint of the Spirit, then there can be no opposition to It!* It is only when we let go of all human will, and recognize the pure essence of the Spiritual Principle incarnated in us, that thought rises above a belief in duality. We should constantly vitalize our faith by the knowledge that the Eternal is incarnated in us; that God Himself goes forth anew into creation through each one of us; and that in such degree as we speak the Truth, the Almighty has spoken!

THE TECHNIQUE OF ACQUIRING FAITH

One cannot be a good student of the Science of Mind who is filled with fear and confusion. He must keep himself in a state of equilibrium, in a state of poise, peace and confidence . . . in a state of spiritual understanding. By *spiritual understanding*, is not meant anything strange or unnatural, but merely that the belief in goodness must be greater than any apparent manifestation of its opposite. It is this science of faith we are seeking to uncover—a definite technique that will conduct our minds through a process of thought, if necessary, to that place which the sublime minds of all ages have reached by direct intuition.

There is no one who believes more in faith, more in prayer, or more in the necessity of the Divine Will being done, than he who practices daily the Science of Mind. He has relieved his mind of the morbid sense that the Will of God *can* be the will of suffering; for if there were a suffering God, and if we are eternal beings, then we should suffer through all eternity. But a suffering God is an impossibility. We suffer because we are not in both conscious and subjective communication with the affirmative side of the Universe. All human misery is a result of ignorance; and nothing but knowledge can free us from this ignorance and its effect.

As students of the Science of Mind, we find in the remarkable character of Jesus, a great impetus toward faith and conviction. The Centurion came to Jesus and asked Him to heal his servant, and Jesus said: "Go thy way; and as thou hast believed, so be it done unto thee." The Centurion had what we call a mental equivalent of Divine authority. In the realm in which he lived, he was accustomed to speak his word with authority. He accepted the word of Jesus as having authority on the invisible plane. Jesus said, "I have not found so great faith, no, not in all Israel."

It is wonderful to contemplate the mental attitude of people who are not afraid to believe their prayers will be answered, and are not afraid to say, "I know." We shall all arrive at this same assurance, this perfect faith, in such degree as we cease contemplating the Universe as opposed to Itself; as we cease having the will to do or to be that which is contrary to the Universal Good.

There is nothing in the universal order that denies the individual's good, or self-expression, so long as such self-expression does not contradict the general good, does not contradict Goodness Itself. There is nothing in the Universe that denies us the right to be happy, if our happiness does not deny or interfere with the general good. The Universe remains unlimited, though the whole world has suffered a sense of limitation.

We should be careful not to divide our mental house against itself. Having announced the law of liberty, we must not deny it. When we shall all know the Truth, then ways and means and methods will be found for the freedom of all. The mold of acceptance is the measure of our experience. The Infinite fills all molds and forever flows into new and greater ones. Within us is the unborn possibility of limitless experience. Ours is the privilege of giving birth to it!

CONVICTION

Mental Science does not deny the divinity of Jesus; but it does affirm the divinity of all people. It does not deny that Jesus was the son of God; but it affirms that all men are the sons of God.

It does not deny that the kingdom of God was revealed through Jesus; but it says that the kingdom of God is also revealed through you and me.

Jesus said: "If ye have faith as a grain of mustard seed, ye shall say unto this mountain, remove hence to yonder place, and it shall remove; and nothing shall be impossible unto you." Faith is centered in, and co-operates with, Divine Mind.

Because we fail to realize that Principle is not bound by precedent, we limit our faith to that which has already been accomplished, and few "miracles" result. When, through intuition, faith finds its proper place under Divine Law, there are no limitations, and what are called *miraculous* results follow.

While Jesus remained with the disciples, their faith for the most part was of the same essence as his, but as the years passed and his followers became more and more immersed in objective organization, they ceased to preach the necessity of a living faith. In fact, a few hundred years later, the Christians were teaching that the early "miracles" merely proved the divinity of Jesus!

If we are to have an active faith—the faith *of* God instead of merely a faith *in* God—our thought must be centered in Universal Mind. We are convinced that under Divine Law all things are possible, if we only *believe*, and work in conformity with the principles of that Law. Such a faith does not spring full-orbed into being, but grows by knowledge and experience. No matter what the outside appearance, we must cling steadfastly to the knowledge that God is good, and God is all, underneath, above and round about. Thus we shall be able to say, with conviction: "I know in whom I have believed. . . ."

CHAPTER ELEVEN

MENTAL AND SPIRITUAL TREATMENT

Treatment: What It Is • *The* Purpose *of Treatment* • *The* Way *of Treatment* • *Treatment Not Explained in the Bible* • *What Is a Practitioner?* • *The First Requisite* • *A Practitioner's Business* • *Different Methods of Treatment* • *When and What Is a Demonstration?* • *Let Us Not Fool Ourselves.*

TREATMENT: WHAT IT IS

Effective mental treatment is propelled by a consciousness of love and a realization that the Creative Spirit is always at work. The practitioner does not feel that he must compel the Force to work. It is the nature of the Creative Power to take form, and it is the nature of man to use It.

A treatment should be given in a calm, expectant manner and with a deep inner conviction of its reality, without any fear or any sense that the human mind must make it effective. The work is effective because the Law is always in operation.

THE PURPOSE OF TREATMENT

Mental or spiritual treatment should bring into actual manifestation the health and happiness which are mankind's normal and divine heritage. Such healing includes the emancipation of the mind from every form of bondage through a new concept of God, which causes the heart to beat with joy and gladness. This healing power is a consciousness of the Unity of all Life and the spiritual nature of all being. Man's life is rooted in the Universal and the Eternal, which life is none other than the Life of God. The healing process, in so far as it may be termed a process, is in becoming conscious of this eternal truth.

Treatment should incorporate a *conscious recognition* that health has always been ours, abundance has always been ours, happiness and peace have always been ours; they are ours now, for they are the very essence and Truth of our being. All there is of evil, of whatever name or kind, is an inversion of eternal good.

THE *WAY* OF TREATMENT

In treatment, we turn entirely away from the condition, because as long as we look at it, we cannot overcome it. By thinking upon a condition, we tend to animate it with the life of our thought, and thereby it is perpetuated and magnified. Treatment is the science of inducing, within Mind, concepts, acceptances and realizations of peace, poise, power, plenty—health, happiness and success—or whatever the particular need may be.

Treatment is not *willing* things to happen; it is to provide within ourselves an avenue through which they may happen. Treatment opens up the avenues of thought, expands the consciousness, and lets Reality through; it clarifies the mentality, removes the obstruction of thought and lets in the Light; it removes doubt and fear, in the realization of the Presence of Spirit, and is necessary while we are confronted by obstructions or obstacles. We already live in a Perfect Universe, but It needs to be seen mentally before It can become a part of our experience. Every problem is primarily mental, and the answer to all problems will be found in Spiritual Realization.

It is hardly necessary to state here that without an understanding of the limitless medium of Subjectivity there can be no full comprehension of how Law operates, when a treatment is given. Unless we understand the three-fold nature of both man and the Universe: as active consciousness, which we call Spirit; receptive or creative Law, which we call the medium or Universal Subjectivity; and manifestation, which we call form or Creation . . . unless we realize further, that as we deal with our own individuality, we are dealing with the Universal, which has projected out of Itself that which is like Itself on a miniature scale . . . unless we have this understanding, we shall be working much of the time on a basis of blind faith.

As an illustration of the importance of this understanding, take the following: Suppose a man in New York wired a practitioner in Los Angeles, explaining to him that he had been unable to sleep for weeks and that he wished treatment for insomnia. How would the practitioner go about this? The practitioner in Los Angeles knows that the man in New York fails to sleep because there is lack of peace in his consciousness; there is a mental disturbance, and the mind keeps working all night. The practitioner begins to think *peace* about this man. He does *not* say: "Now, John (supposing the man's name is John), you are going to be peaceful"; rather, he says *to himself*, "John *is* peaceful." The practitioner does not send out thoughts nor suggestions; he realizes, in his own mind, the truth about this man. *The practitioner treats the practitioner, for the patient, always!* The practitioner begins to pour the uplifting truth into his own mind: "John sleeps in peace, wakes in joy, and lives in good. There is no fear, no worry, no doubt, no confusion. He has not acquired the habit of wakefulness, because his consciousness is filled with peace."

Universal Mind, being Omnipresent, is wherever the man is who asked for help. If he is receptive to the harmony of the belief which the practitioner has poured into Subjective Mind, it will externalize for him at the level of the embodiment of the thought of the practitioner. Thus the man "John" in New York is helped through the work of the practitioner in Los Angeles.

A practitioner works through the Law of Mind, definitely, for someone else. He declares the truth about the person whom he is treating, stating that this person is a Divine Being, complete, happy, satisfied, conscious of his own spiritual being; that this thing which is causing him to suffer now is not a law, has no right to be, is no longer effective through him, cannot suggest anything to him; that he is free from it; that this word—which the practitioner is speaking—removes any obstruction in mind, or obstruction in manifestation, and allows the flow of life through this individual. He makes such statements to himself, about this individual, as tend to clear up, in his own thought, his belief about the person whom he is treating, until finally he comes to a place in his treatment where he says that the person is *now* all right; he is free from that condition. It can never return. That this is the Truth about him; that this *now* is the Truth. This is a formed treatment, stated definitely—a scientific treatment.

To the average person, when a result is obtained by this method of work, it looks as though a miracle has happened, but such is not the case. It is only a miracle as everything else in life is a miracle. A definite, conscious idea has been set in motion in the Subjective World, which accepts ideas at their own valuation and tends to act upon them.

Treatment Not Explained in the Bible

From beginning to end, in one way or another, the Bible teaches the law of cause and effect, based upon the premise that the Universe is a spiritual system, that man is included in this spiritual system, that the Infinite creates by the power of Its word or the contemplation of Its consciousness, and, as a complement to this, that man reproduces the Universal on an individual scale.

The Bible does not tell us how to give a treatment. It is only within the last hundred years that the science which we are studying has been given to the world. It is not an old system of thought. The old systems of thought did contain the Truth, but one would never learn *how* to give an effective mental treatment by studying them. We would no more learn how to give a treatment by studying the Bible, than we would learn how to psycho-analyze a person. The principle of spiritual treatment is implied in the Bible as well as in other sacred writings of antiquity, but one could not learn how to give a treatment from reading any of these Sacred Books. From all of these sources we gain a tremendous spiritual inspiration, *but they do not teach how to give a treatment*.

What Is a Practitioner?

The one who attempts to heal himself or another through a recognition of the creative power of Mind and the ever availability of Good, is a mental or spiritual practitioner. Such a one refuses to allow negative thoughts to control his consciousness. He endeavors to greet the divinity in every man he meets.

The one seeking to demonstrate the power of spiritual realization in everyday affairs should believe in Divine guidance. He should affirm that his mind is continually impressed with the images of right action, and that everything in his life is controlled by love, harmony and peace; that everything he does prospers, and that the Eternal Energy back of all things animates everything which he undertakes. Every objective evidence contrary to good should be resolutely denied, and in its place should come a sense of right action. He should feel a unity of Spirit in all people, and running through all events. He should declare that the Spirit within him is God, quickening into right action everything he touches, bringing the best out of all his experiences, and forever guiding and sustaining. The greatest good which his mind is able to conceive should be affirmed as a part of his everyday experience. No matter what the occupation of such a man, he is a mental and spiritual practitioner, and from such daily meditation he should venture forth into a life of action, with the will to do, the determination to be, and a joy in becoming!

The *professional* mental and spiritual practitioner is one who has dedicated his life—his time, his energies, his intelligence—to helping others, through mental and spiritual means and methods.

The First Requisite

The first requisite for the mental and spiritual practitioner is a full sense of the sacredness of his trust; the sacredness of the confidence of his patient, which impels him to pour out his very soul. *This confidence, a practitioner should keep sacred, inviolate.* He should no more betray this trust than would a priest who officiates at the confessional, a lawyer who handles the business and finances of his client, or a physician who cares for the physical well being of his patients.

Practitioners do meet occasionally and discuss cases, as doctors might in a clinic, but they should never mention the names nor the personal affairs of those under treatment.

A Practitioner's Business

It is the practitioner's business to uncover God in every man. God is not sick. God is not poor. God is not unhappy. God is never afraid. God is never confused. God is never out of His place. The premise upon which all mental work is based is perfect God, perfect man, perfect being.

First, perfect God, then perfect man. There is a spiritual man who is never sick, who is never poor, unhappy; never confused nor afraid . . . who is never caught by negative thought. Browning called this "the spark which a man may desecrate but never quite lose."

These are the tools of thought with which a practitioner works. Where does he do his work? IN HIS OWN MIND. Never anywhere else. Always in his own thought. A practitioner never tries to get away from the mind within.

We are practicing scientifically when the mind refuses to see the apparent condition and turns to the Absolute. A scientific treatment cannot be conditioned upon anything that now exists, upon any experience less than perfection. In treatment, we turn entirely away from the relative—entirely away from that which appears to be. We might begin a treatment with the statement: "With God all things are possible, God can find a way." We might say: "They that dwell in the Secret Place of the Most High, etc." It does not matter so much what one says, it is what one believes when he says it that counts. He must *believe*, if he is going to be a successful practitioner, that his word is the law of that whereunto it is spoken.

We treat man, not as a patient, not as a physical body, not as a diseased condition; neither do we treat the disease as belonging to him. We must not think of the disease as being connected with him or as any part of him. The practitioner realizes that man is born of Spirit and not of matter. He realizes this until he sees his patient a living embodiment of Perfection.

A practitioner, then, is one who, recognizing the power of Mind, definitely, specifically, concretely and consciously speaks from his objective mind into Subjectivity and gives direction to a Law, which is the Actor.

What the practitioner really does is to take his patient, the disease and everything that appears to be wrong, into his own mentality, and here he attempts to dissolve all false appearances and all erroneous conclusions. At the center of the practitioner's own being, the healing work must be accomplished.

The more completely the practitioner is convinced of the power of his own word, the more power his word will have. THERE MUST BE A RECOGNITION THAT THE POWER OF THE WORD, OPERATING AS THE TRUTH AND REALITY OF BEING, CAN DO ALL THINGS. Therefore, the person whose consciousness is the clearest, who has the most complete faith, will be the best healer.

DIFFERENT METHODS OF TREATMENT

Although several methods of treatment are used, there are but two distinct methods; one is called the *argumentative* and the other *realization*.

The argumentative method is just what the word implies, though the argument is never with another person—it is a process of mental reasoning in which the practitioner argues to himself about his patient. He is presenting a logical argument to Universal Mind, or Principle, and if it carries with it complete evidence in favor of his patient, the patient should be healed.

The realization method is one whereby the practitioner realizes within himself—without the necessity of step by step building up a conclusion—the perfect state of his patient. It is purely a spiritual and meditative process of contemplating the perfect man, and if the practitioner arrives at a perfect embodiment of the idea, without confusion or doubt, it will at once produce a healing. *Treatment is for the purpose of inducing an inner realization of perfection in the mentality of the practitioner, which inner realization, acting through Mind, operates through the patient.*

Another illustration: Let us suppose that Mary is sick and John is the practitioner. She comes to him, saying: "I am sick." He understands the power of Mind; she does not understand it. He does not try to hold a thought over her or for her, nor suggest one to her. He speaks her name and makes his declarations about this name. He contradicts what appears to be wrong and declares the Truth about her. What happens? *His word, operative through Universal Mind, sets a law in motion, on the subjective side of life, which objectifies through her body as healing.*

Mary thinks a miracle has been performed. No miracle has been enacted. John used a law, which all men may use if they will. If Mary had been perfectly well, and her need had been for a position, the treatment would be of like nature; John would have declared into Mind what should be done for Mary. There is only One Law; Mary could set It in operation for herself if she understood Its nature; sooner or later she must come to understand and make conscious use of this Law.

Between "John" and "Mary" there is One Universal Medium, which is also *in* John and *in* Mary. It is not only between them but in them and around them. As John, right where he is, knows the Truth, since there is only One, he is at the same time knowing the Truth *right where Mary is,* because his work is operative through a field which is not divided, but a complete Unit or Whole. As he knows within himself, he is knowing within the same Mind which operates through the person whom he mentions in his treatment, no matter where that person may be. There is no *absent* treatment, as opposed to a *present* treatment. When you know in one place, you know everywhere. When you give a treatment, you never send out a thought, or hold a thought, or make a suggestion. *A treatment is a conscious movement of thought, and the work begins and ends in the thought of the one giving the treatment. The practitioner must do the work within himself.* He must know the Truth within himself, and as he does this the Law unfolds; a thing which is known by any part of Universal Mind is known by every part of It, for It is an undivided Whole.

If one were treating "Henry Black," who is in another city, he would say: "I am treating Henry Black of such and such a place." Then he would forget all about Henry Black as a personality and give the treatment. It is not necessary to specify the trouble. Occasionally, there might be reason to mention a thing, in denying its existence, but this is not the best method. Of course, there are certain thoughts back of certain things, and a knowledge of the disease might better enable some practitioners to know what thought to deny.

Another illustration of the difference between the *argumentative* method of treatment and the *realization* method, will be found in the following:

Mary Jones comes to *John Smith* and says, "I have tuberculosis." In answer to this, he states: "The word I now speak is for Mary Jones. She is a perfect and complete manifestation of Pure Spirit, and Pure Spirit cannot be diseased, consequently, she is not diseased." This is an argument in the mind of "John Smith" trying to bring out the evidence in favor of "Mary Jones'" perfection; it is an argument which produces certain conclusions in his mind, and as a result it sets a certain law in motion for Mary Jones. As John does this, day after day, he gradually becomes convinced of her spiritual perfection. This is the *argumentative* method of treating. *All argumentative statements merely conduct the mind of the practitioner to a place where he believes what he is saying!*

In using the method of *realization*, "John Smith" would say: "The word that I now speak is for Mary Jones." Then he would begin to realize the Perfect Presence, the ONLY Perfect Presence. "God is all there is; there is nothing else. God is in Mary Jones, she is now a perfect being, she is now a spiritual being."

It makes no difference, however, which method one uses as each produces the same results. One method is a logical argument in the mind of the practitioner, by which he convinces himself of the Truth of Being; the other is the instant cutting through of all appearances to the Reality back of all things. Undoubtedly, when we can pursue only the way of *pure realization*, we will have attained the ideal method.

But since we do not at all times realize man's perfection, we go through this process called "treating" to find it out. Do not be afraid of this scientific approach; do not be afraid to set down on one side all of the negative appearances, admitting them as a condition; and on the other side bringing all the arguments, one at a time, which offset these apparent conditions, and finally realization will come.

This *argumentative* method of treatment is a series of affirmations and denials, for the purpose of building up in the mind of the practitioner a state of realization and acceptance. The power is in the realization, but there is also power in the argument. The one giving the treatment believes that there is a Power and a Presence that responds to his thought. No matter what all the world believes, no matter what anyone says, *he must believe that this Power does respond to his word.* As Jesus said, "Heaven and earth shall pass away, but my words shall not pass away." This is conviction, and if a practitioner does not have such conviction he must acquire it. After much experience, he will learn how best to build up a faith in the Power of Spirit. We are to approach this Presence simply, directly and easily, for It is *within us.* We can never get outside ourselves; we shall always be interior in our comprehension, we are here and It also is here.

In giving spiritual treatments we find that the more completely the mind turns away from lack, the more completely the thought stops trying to figure out how the demonstration can be made, the more completely it refrains from will power, and, strange as it may seem, the less it tries to concentrate, THE MORE POWER IT HAS. Treatment has nothing to do with any effort which attempts to concentrate the Energy of God. The Energy of God is already concentrated *everywhere.* The gardener does not *will* potatoes and cabbages into being, but he has a willingness to comply with the law of nature, and provides the conditions which make it possible for this law to produce them.

When and What Is a Demonstration?

In the language of metaphysics, a "demonstration" is made when the thing is accomplished which the one treating desires to achieve . . . whether it be health, happiness, or abundance. A demonstration is a manifestation. It is prayer answered. When the word of a practitioner takes form, this is a demonstration. When desire is given a subjective mold and then becomes objectified in the life of the one for whom the practitioner is working, this is demonstration. The practitioner, of course, gives thanks as he makes his demand on the Infinite, knowing that supply and demand are one, and that his request is instantly manifest on the invisible plane. "Before they call, will I answer," is the divine promise.

We cannot demonstrate beyond our ability to mentally embody an idea. The argument is between our experience, what the world believes, and what we are convinced is the Truth.

It should be understood that we can demonstrate in spite of ourselves—in spite of all weakness, in spite of all fear, in spite of all that is in us—because such is the power of Truth. We wait only for our own awakened thought. The Law is neither good nor bad. Law is and responds.

The possibility of demonstrating does not depend upon environment, condition, location, personality or opportunity. It depends solely upon our belief and our acceptance, and our willingness to comply with the Law through which all good comes. The Universe will never deny us anything, unless we conceive that it is possible for us to think of something that is impossible for the Universe to produce! Everyone who asks receives, according to his belief.

LET US NOT FOOL OURSELVES

But we should not fool ourselves about any demonstration. We know there is a state of consciousness which can heal instantly, but if we do not arrive at this in a moment, we should never admit defeat. Let us not despise our sums in addition because we cannot at the outset extract the cube root.

The kind of demonstration we believe in is the kind that can be checked by a physician, if one so desires. If we are treating for the removal of a cancer, we have not made a demonstration until the cancer is gone and the wholeness of the body is evident to anyone. This is not a process of saying "Peace" when there is no peace.

A practitioner working for one whose blood pressure is high might say, "Go every week or so and have your blood pressure tested." If one's blood pressure is high, a demonstration will not have been made until it is reduced to normal. To claim that he is perfectly normal, while the blood pressure remains high, would be to affront the intelligence of any sane individual.

While it is possible that we might have to work on a case for some time, *there should be some sign of improvement from the first treatment*. If the practitioner admits to himself that it is going to take a long time, he is losing sight of the fact that he is dealing with the instantaneous *now* and the ever-present *here*.

Our theory rests entirely upon the supposition that it is impossible to have a true subjective concept, without there being a positive, absolute and equal objective fact. The two will exactly balance. For every action there is always an opposite and equal reaction. If this is true and the equal and opposite reaction is automatic—like a reflection which nothing can stop—then the practitioner does not try to create the reflection; he tries to embody the image. There cannot be an embodiment of the image without the appreciation of what the image means. A man who is always distraught cannot give a good treatment for peace. *So there must not only be the image in the man's mind who is giving the treatment, but there must be an appreciation of what the image means, before the image can reflect itself*; otherwise, it is a word and not an embodiment. There is a great difference between the two. The word which carries power is the one which has conviction back of it. Let us not blithely repeat words, and say the treatment has gone forth and the healing work accomplished, unless we have the evidence that our word has accomplished "that, whereunto it was sent." Let us not deceive ourselves about our treatments.

This matter of self-deception about the truth of a demonstration is the most prolific field for delusion in our system of thought. There is nothing in all our teaching which calls for lying to ourselves or others. The more natural we can be, the more spontaneous we can be, and the more we can discharge the obligation of giving the treatment without taking on the responsibility of healing the condition—of putting the power into the treatment—the more power we shall have.

There is nothing in the world more specific than a scientific treatment, but there is nothing that should be so released from outline as a scientific treatment. However, there is no secret in this business of demonstrating. The only secret is the persistent ability to use the Law, and the determination to continue to use It until we prove It.

CHAPTER TWELVE
SUMMARY OF PART TWO: SPIRITUAL MIND HEALING

FIRST DIVISION: IDEATION

A recognition of the Power, and the thought
and purpose back of mind healing.

The possibility of spiritual mind healing, changing environment, controlling conditions, etc., through the power of right thinking, rests entirely upon the theory that we are surrounded by a Universal Mind, which reacts to our thought—and always according to Law.

Spiritual Man is Perfect, but his individual use of Life and Law enables him to cover a perfect idea with an apparently imperfect cloak.

Sickness is not a spiritual Reality; it is an experience—an effect and not a cause. The body, devoid of mentality, could neither know nor experience sensation—it is entirely an effect. The body of man is made from the same undifferentiated Spiritual Substance from which all Creation is formed.

Man comes into objectivity with the tendency of the race already subjectified within him, through race-suggestion. The race experiences sickness and limitation, and this suggestion is more or less operative through all people. It works through the subjective race thought and operates through the individual.

Man need not consciously think negation in order to produce physical disturbance, but the physical correspondent is a logical outcome of what he thinks. Thus we see not only how important it is to entertain right thoughts, but also the necessity for having a constructive basis for our thinking.

We find that prayer is essential to happiness, for righteous prayer sets the law of the Spirit of life in motion for our good. Prayer is essential to the conscious well-being of the soul. Prayer has stimulated countless millions to higher thoughts and better lives. Prayer is its own answer. Before our prayer is framed in words the possibility of its answer already exists.

We find that faith in God is a spiritual quality of the mind; and an understanding faith is based on Immutable Principle. Its action is higher than that of the intellect, because it is born of intuition.

One should have faith in himself, faith in his fellowman, in the Universe, and in God. Our mind must be steady in its conviction that our life is some part of God, and that the Spirit is incarnated in us. "Faith is the substance of things hoped for; the evidence of things not seen."

A spiritual practitioner is one who recognizes man as a Spiritual Reality. *Since there is but One Mind, the practitioner makes this recognition within his own mind.* Through the medium of the One Mind, his statements rise to objective conditions in his patient, according to his belief and the patient's receptivity. Healing is accomplished through the act of setting Subjective Law in motion. The more spiritual or Godlike the mentality of the practitioner, the more powerful the treatment.

A mental treatment begins and ends within the thought of the practitioner, because he is in the same Mind in which his patient lives. Treatment is the act of inducing right concepts on the subjective side of life.

Absent and present treatments are the same, *for there is no absence in the One Presence.* So far as the practitioner is concerned, there is no difference between an absent and a present treatment. He needs only to know whom he wishes to help, realizing that in the field of Mind and Spirit there is no apartness, and then he speaks the word for the other person, in full confidence that the Law will operate upon it. He is not concerned where the person *is* whom he desires to help, or what he may be doing at that particular time. He is concerned only with his own thought relative to this person, endeavoring to bring out in his own mind the realization that this person is a spiritual entity, governed by a perfect Law, directed by positive Intelligence, and animated by Divine Life, Love and Law.

There is no personal responsibility in healing. We should not feel that *we put the power into the word.* The practitioner directs the Power and lets It work. One does not *hold thought* in mental healing; he looses thought. A practitioner does not try to suggest, hypnotize or mentally influence; he simply seeks to *know* that man *is now* a spiritual being, and he holds to that belief no matter what the appearance may be. Right mental treatment does not tire the one giving the treatment.

Personal magnetism has nothing to do with mental healing. The whole basis of the possibility of mental healing rests upon the premise that we all live in One Creative Mind which reacts to our belief. It is as though there were a Universal Ear, listening to and hearing everything that we say, feel or think, and reacting to it.

Healing is not a process but a revelation; for the revealing of the perfect man always heals. The process, if there is one, is the time and thought that it takes to arrive at the correct understanding of man's perfect state in Spirit.

Anyone can heal who believes that he can, and who will take the time to set that belief in motion through the Law. To daily see the perfect man, and to daily declare for his objective appearance, is correct mental practice and will heal.

A treatment recognizes that all is Mind, and that everything is mental. It dissolves all disease into thought; neutralizes the false thought and recognizes the true. Nothing can stop it from operating except a lack of faith in the reality of Truth and man's ability to use It.

In giving mental treatment, the practitioner first realizes his own being as spiritual; he then recognizes the spiritual state of his patient's being; then he attacks the false claim and brings the evidence of Truth to bear against it, thinking in such a manner as to completely destroy the false claim and realize the Truth. In such degree as this acknowledgment is complete, petition is transmuted into acceptance, and the mind actually feels that the object of its desire is already an accomplished fact.

The greatest good that can come to anyone is the forming within him of an absolute certainty of himself, and of his relationship to the Universe, forever removing the sense of heaven as being outside himself.

Such an understanding teaches us that there can never come a time when we shall stop progressing; that age is an illusion, that limitation is a mistake, that unhappiness is ignorance. This understanding will rob man of his loneliness and give him a sense of security which knows no fear, a peace without which no life can be happy, a poise which is founded on this peace, and a power which is the result of the union of peace with poise.

PART THREE

SPIRITUAL MIND HEALING

SECOND DIVISION: PRACTICE

Determining destiny. The technique

by which we lay hold of mind power,

and prove its practicability.

CHAPTER THIRTEEN

CAUSES AND CONDITIONS

Mental Practice Deals Only with Thought · Changeless Reality · The Perfect Universe · Turn Entirely from the Condition · Look Only at What You Want · Never Limit Your View of Life · Place No Limit on Principle · God Never Compromises.

MENTAL PRACTICE DEALS ONLY WITH THOUGHT

The philosophy of spiritual mind healing is based upon the conception that we are living in a universe of Intelligence—a spiritual Universe; that thoughts are things, that definite states of consciousness, as they become subjective, operate through a creative field and tend to reproduce themselves in form.

Therefore, it logically follows that this system of treatment is for the purpose of uncovering and neutralizing the wrong states of thought . . . of building in mind a concept of our spiritual birthright. Thought which is built upon a realization of the Divine Presence has the power to neutralize negative thought, to erase it, just as light has the power to overcome darkness; not by combating darkness, but by being exactly what it is: LIGHT. "And the light shineth in the darkness; and the darkness comprehended it not."

Therefore, spiritual treatment does not concern itself with unpleasant conditions nor with imperfect manifestations, either in one's body or the body of one's affairs. Treatment is for the purpose of inducing an interior awareness—an inner realization—in the mind of the practitioner, pertaining to the spiritual perfection of the person for whom he is working.

CHANGELESS REALITY

Spirit is Changeless Reality. That which we call personality is the instrument through which Spirit operates, but Spirit can operate *for* the individual only by operating *through* him. Spirit is never bound by the form It takes, and *is not affected by any apparent cause or condition*, but is forever free. Spirit not only fills all forms but surges around them and through them. Ice is formed from water, all ice is some form of water. Just so, God and man exist in an eternal state of Unity—the solid and the liquid are one substance.

We are dealing with an impersonal Principle. It will operate for one just as quickly as for another, because It is Law. Dare to speak, and to know that what you speak is the law unto the thing spoken regardless of what conditions exist. One, alone, in consciousness with the Infinite, constitutes a complete majority. Knowing this in your thought, work in perfect peace and calm. ALWAYS EXPECT THE GOOD. Have enthusiasm and, above all, have a consciousness of love—a radiant feeling flowing through your consciousness at all times. Treat yourself until you have an inner sense of unity with all Good.

THE PERFECT UNIVERSE

We must seek to realize the spiritual Universe, regardless of any condition which appears, if we would embody the greatest good. If the spiritual Universe were *not* perfect, It could not exist for a single moment.

The Truth is Indivisible and Whole. God is Complete and Perfect. *A Perfect Cause must produce a perfect effect.* Disregarding all evidence to the contrary, the student of Truth will maintain that he lives in a Perfect Universe and among people potentially perfect. He will regulate his thinking to meet this necessity and will refuse to believe in its opposite. At first he may be influenced by conditions, and he may appear to be weak, but as time goes on he will prove to himself that his position is a correct one, for that which appears imperfect will begin to slip from his experience.

To daily meditate on the Perfect Life, and to daily embody the Great Ideal, is a royal road to freedom, to that "peace which passeth understanding," and is happiness to the soul of man. Let us learn to see as God must, with a Perfect Vision. Let us seek the good and the true and believe in them with our whole heart, even though every man we meet is filled with suffering, and limitation appears at all sides. We cannot afford to believe in imperfection for a single second, to do so is to doubt God; it is to believe in a Power apart from God, to believe in another Creator. Let us daily say to ourselves: "Perfect God *within me*, Perfect Life *within me*, which is God, come forth into expression through me as that which I am; lead me ever into the paths of perfection and cause me to see only the Good." By this practice, the soul will become illumined and will acquaint itself with God and be at peace. "Be ye therefore perfect, even as your Father which is in heaven is perfect."

TURN ENTIRELY FROM THE CONDITION

"Behold thou my face forevermore." "Look unto me and be ye saved, all the ends of the earth." That is, look up and not down. The reason a man has difficulty in throwing off some weakness of character—while believing in Spirit implicitly and having faith that he is going to overcome his limitation—is because he has not induced the necessary images in mind. If he had, he would have overcome his trouble. Thinking of his weakness keeps the image of *it* before him. We cannot be too insistent on this all-important point: in treating, we must TURN ENTIRELY AWAY FROM THE CONDITION. Disease and limitation are neither person, place, nor thing. Turn entirely from the condition, or limited situation, to its opposite, to the realization of health, happiness and harmony. Spiritual treatment starts with Perfect God, Perfect Man, and Perfect Being, which statement consciously removes any belief which denies such manifestation.

LOOK ONLY AT WHAT YOU WANT

Never look at that which you do not wish to experience. No matter what the false condition may be, it must be refuted. The proper kind of a denial is based upon the recognition that, *in reality*, there is no limitation, for Mind can as easily make a planet as an acorn. The Infinite knows no difference between a million dollars and a penny. It only knows that IT IS.

It is the consciousness back of the word that forms the word. Consciousness means the inner embodiment of an idea through the recognition of Truth and a direct relationship to the Divine. The greatest teacher who ever lived was the most spiritual man, for the more universal and comprehensive the thought, the more Godlike it must become.

A good treatment is always filled with the recognition of the Presence of God, or Good. This automatically wipes out any picture of undesirable conditions, for *the Spirit of God is a law of elimination and obliteration to everything unlike Itself!* Even in what we term *spiritual things*, we are still dealing with the law of cause and effect, for God is Law. The more exalted, the more heavenly, the more boundless, the more Godlike or Christlike the thought is, the more power it will have. This is why the greatest teacher became the Savior. A spiritual genius would have to be a Savior.

NEVER LIMIT YOUR VIEW OF LIFE

Never limit your view of life by any past experience. *The possibility of life is inherent within the capacity to imagine what life is, backed by the power to produce this imagery, or Divine Imagination.* It is not a question of failing or succeeding. It is simply a question of sticking to an idea until it becomes a tangible reality. The illusion is in the way we look at things. We have looked at poverty, degradation and misery until they have assumed gigantic proportions. Now we must look at harmony, happiness, plenty, prosperity, peace and right action, until they appear.

When we are making a demonstration, we pay no attention to what happens in the objective world. We interpret causes by conditions, only as we realize that a condition must partake of the nature of its cause. If there appears to be confusion in the condition, then there must have been confusion in the thought back of it. We pay no attention to the objective expression, so long as we know we are getting the right subjective recognition. The way scientifically to work out a problem is daily in thought to *conceive of it as already being an accomplished fact in experience.* We realize the desire is already embodied in the Absolute. We are dealing with nothing less than the Absolute—with REALITY.

During the process, many things may happen that *appear* to be destructive. We may pass through good fortune and bad, but if we can come to the point where we are not disturbed by "things" we have found the secret. If, as Jesus said, we "judge not according to appearance, but judge righteous judgment," remembering that "things which are seen are not made of things which do appear"; if, I repeat, we can judge in this manner, OUT OF ANY CHAOS WE CAN PRODUCE HARMONY.

PLACE NO LIMIT ON PRINCIPLE

Know your own mind. Train yourself to think what you wish to think; be what you wish to be; feel what you wish to feel, and place no limit on Principle!

The words which you speak would be just as powerful as the words which Jesus spoke, if you knew your word was the Law whereunto it was sent, but you must KNOW this WITHIN and not merely accept it with your intellect. If you have reached a point where the inner consciousness believes, then your word is simply an announcement of Reality!

KNOW—without a shadow of doubt—that as a result of your treatment, some action takes place in Infinite Mind. Infinite Mind is the actor and you are the announcer. If you have a vague, subtle, unconscious fear, be quiet and ask yourself, "Who am I?" "What am I?" "Who is speaking?" "What is my life?" In this manner think right back to Principle, until your thought becomes perfectly clear again. Such is the power of right thinking, that it cancels and erases everything unlike itself. It answers every question, solves all problems, is the solution to every difficulty. It is like the sunlight of Eternal Truth, bursting through the clouds of obscurity and bathing all life in glory. It is the Absolute with which you are dealing. ALL THERE REALLY IS, IS GOD!

GOD NEVER COMPROMISES

In demonstrating over conditions, the only inquiries we need to make are: "Do the things we want lend themselves to a constructive program? Do they express a more abundant life, rob no one, create no delusion, and express a greater degree of livingness?" If we are able to answer these questions affirmatively, *then all the power in the Universe is back of our program!* If it is money, houses, automobiles, lands, stocks, bonds, dresses, shirts or shoe strings—all of which come from the same source—there can be nothing, either in the Law or in the Spirit back of the Law, to deny us the right to the greatest possible expression of life.

Good never compromises with Its opposite. The one practicing must be able to look a fact in the face, and know that all manifestations are effects and can be changed by changing the mental cause. He must be able to look at the sick man who has come to him for help, and know that only *perfection* stands before him; he must see beyond the appearance to that which is basically perfect. This will not be irrational to the one who has made a careful study of the Science of Mind and Spirit.

Truth knows no opposites. When we take away the belief in evil—the belief that the outward appearance is the same as the inner reality—*evil* flees. We must continually remind ourselves of the power of the Word, and of our ability to use it. We must know that Truth produces freedom because Truth *is* freedom. Our work will best be done in quiet expectancy and in calm confidence. The *results* rest in the Eternal Law of Good.

CHAPTER FOURTEEN

PHYSICAL PERFECTION

What We Understand about Healing • We Are Allowed to Choose • Man Re-enacts God • Only Our Own Concepts Limit Us • Spiritual Mind Healing • Disease Is Impersonal • Disease Is Not Always Due to Conscious Thought • How to Heal • Healing Is Clear Thinking • No Sensation in Treatments • The Medium of Healing • Treating Children • The Power of the Word • Seeing Perfection.

WHAT WE UNDERSTAND ABOUT HEALING

There is no question that people throughout the ages have been healed through prayer and faith, that they have mentally contacted a healing Law in this spiritual Universe of Law and Order. How did they contact this Law? All prayer is mental, being a certain mental attitude, a certain way of thinking, a certain way of believing, an uplifting process, a belief in God. Some prayers fall short of this state, while others reach a state of spiritual awareness.

We come to understand, then, that *the answer to prayer is in the prayer when it is prayed*—the belief of the one praying sets in motion the Law of Love, which is the fundamental Law of the Universe.

Man's life, in reality, is spiritual and mental, and until his thought is healed, no form of cure will be permanent. We understand that *health is a mental as well as a physical state*. We seek to heal men's mentalities, knowing that to the degree in which we are successful, we shall also be healing their bodies. We know, too, that to the degree in which we are able to see a perfect man, he will appear. We feel that the spiritual or real man is perfect and we seek to uncover this perfection which *is* within every man's life. This is spiritual mind healing.

Man will deliver himself from sickness and trouble in exact proportion to his discovery of himself and his true relationship to the Whole. Law is Law wherever we find it, and we shall discover that the Laws of Mind and Spirit must be understood, if they are to be consciously used for definite purposes. The SPIRIT KNOWS and the LAW OBEYS. Hidden away in the inner nature of real man, is the law of his life.

As the Laws of God are broad, so should we be in dealing with them. In this Science, we believe that man's life is a drama which takes place on three planes: the physical, the mental, and the spiritual. We should have no objection to any form of healing, for anything that helps to overcome suffering is good, whether it be a pill or a prayer. We believe in any method which produces results, for each has its place in the Whole.

We believe in every church and in all forms of worship. Above all, *we certainly believe in God!* Because Truth is Infinite, It must be continuously unfolding in the consciousness of man and no one will ever have a *complete understanding of Truth*. A complete understanding of Truth would be a complete understanding of God, and a complete comprehension of God would be to become God. We know that more light will be given as we use that which we have, and we repudiate any belief which says that *all* of Truth has been given.

We realize that mental healing must also be spiritual healing, for the two *cannot* be divorced. We know that a belief in duality—a belief in the power of Good *and* the power of evil—has helped to destroy man, and the understanding of Unity alone will heal him. We seek to realize this Unity with God in all our healing work. *Every treatment must carry with it a realization of God*, if it is to be a good treatment. We are not in any way superstitious about this, but understand that it is necessary since all life is One, and God is the ONE Life in which we all live.

We realize that since our understanding is not yet complete, it is legitimate to use all methods which will help troubled humanity, but we do look forward to the day when Truth *alone* will answer every need! The mental healer will do all of his work in mind, and will give his whole time and attention to correct *knowing*, but he will leave his patient free to use any method that will benefit him. In this way, the practitioner will get the best results, for everything is good as far as it goes, but *the consciousness of Truth alone is the tool of a spiritual practitioner*.

Too much cannot be said against the belief that will power is creative. The will is directive but not creative. Will is the conscious, directive power of the intellect and as such has a very important place in the creative order but in no case is it to be used as though it could force things to happen. Any idea of using the will to influence people is a mistake.

If we agree that we can influence others by will power, then we are also admitting that someone else with a greater power of will can influence us. There is no law of nature that works only one way since all natural laws are impersonal. The temporary effects of will power continue only so long as the will forces them to. They have no real life within themselves and must disintegrate as soon as the unnatural force is withdrawn.

Moreover this use of will power contradicts the main foundation upon which all true mental science is built, that we use a Creative Power which does not need to be urged or forced into action. It is Its nature to act and because we are as we are, it is Its nature to act creatively upon the images of thought that we impress It with. We do not create energy, we distribute it, and in the natural sciences we know that we can transform energy from one type to another. So the will may decide what form the energy is to take but it cannot nor does it need to create the energy.

The Energy of Mind like other natural energies already exists. We merely use It and it is within our province to use It in any way we may desire, we have it within our power to cause it to take varying forms for us, no particular one is permanent. The imagination is creative, the will is directive.

Through will we decide just what we wish to have done. We may wish to use the creative power of mind for helping someone else, for self-help, or for some other purpose. The will holds attention to the mental viewpoint until the creative power has time to work through the law of unfoldment. We may wish on the other hand to draw some information to ourselves; the will then holds to the idea that we are receiving the desired information. It can become active or receptive or it may pass into a state of neutral contemplation where its purpose is merely to sense the wonders of the spiritual life. But in no case does the will become creative.

The will is given us to protect ourselves with. Nothing should be allowed to pass into the creative currents of our thought until the will has first admitted it. The will must first analyze, dissect and then decide what it wishes the inner imagination to work on. True spiritual work will strengthen the will without exhausting the mind; if our mental work tires us then we are using the will in the wrong way. The right way would be to determine to think peace whether there appeared to be any reason to expect that peace would be forthcoming in the experience.

As we should understand the proper use of the will, so we should understand the true meaning of concentration. So many different ideas have been promulgated that a great deal of confusion results. To concentrate means to bring to a center, and in Mental Science it means focusing the mental attention on some definite and desired thought, image, idea or thing. Of course we are dealing with the idea as though thoughts were things. The spirit of the thing is in the thought. This is its essence, law and cause.

Concentration of thought is not an effort to compel, but the desire to permit, the stream of Creative Energy to take definite form. To try to force, through concentration, would be to give ourselves an adverse suggestion and bring upon ourselves the very opposite to our wishes through recognizing an opposite to the power of Good. And all in accord with well known and defined mental law in the Spiritual World.

We concentrate our attention. The Law creates the form. This will solve one of those Divine Riddles which arise out of the teachings of Jesus. He was always telling his followers to believe, to have faith and then he as plainly said, "Who by taking thought can add one cubit to his stature?" Here he tells us not to take thought. The riddle is solved the moment we place thought, imagination, will and concentration where they rightly belong in the creative order.

A good psychological balance is struck when the will and the emotions are rightly poised. That is, when the intellect first decides what the emotions are to respond to. After the intellect has made this decision, then the imagination is called into play and the game of living commences. It is the office of the will to determine that to which the imagination is to respond.

One of the most important things for us to remember is that we are always causing something to be created for us. And that whatever cause we have set in motion must produce some kind of an effect. Are we producing the effects we should like to experience? The creative process will go on willy nilly. We cannot beat Nature at its own game for we are some part of the game She is playing. Shall the result, in our lives, be a comedy or a tragedy? We are given the WILL to decide the issue.

We should carefully consider whether we are willing to experience the results of our thoughts. There should never be any hurt in them, for ourselves or for anyone else. We may be sure that if there is hurt for others there must also be hurt for ourselves. As we sow, so we must reap, but here is no real limitation, for the Creative Life wishes us to have all that we can use. If we keep our thought fixed upon the idea that this Energy, which is also Intelligence, is now taking the form of some desire in our lives, then it will begin to take this form. If we change the desire then It will change the form. Therefore, there must be a definite purpose in our imagination.

We are so One with the Whole that what is true of It is also true of us. We are one with unmanifest Substance whose business it is to forever take form and we are one with the Law which gives form. The entire order is one of spontaneous being and spontaneous manifestation. The Law follows the word just as the word follows the desire. The desire arises from the necessity of the Universe to become self-expressed. The Law follows the word. The word follows the desire. The word gives form to Substance and the Principle of subjective Law produces the manifestation. There is no effort in the process whatsoever.

What we concentrate, then, is attention. This is done through intention and the willingness to hold thought centered until the form appears. It is unnecessary to learn any methods of concentration whatsoever if these simple rules are followed.

WE ARE ALLOWED TO CHOOSE

Man has the ability to choose what he will do with his life, and is unified with a Law which automatically produces his choice. While he does not have the ability to *destroy* the idea of himself, he does have the ability to deface it, to make it appear discordant, but he *cannot destroy the Divine Image*. Man is an individual and does with himself what he wills. The Scriptures say: "God hath made man upright; but they have sought out many inventions." Individuality cannot be automatically produced; it must be spontaneous. It would not be individuality without the ability to think as it chose.

We live in a Universe of Love as well as a Universe of Law. One is the complement of the other—the Universe of Love pulsating with feeling, with emotion, and the Universe of Law, the Executor of all feeling and all emotion. In this lesson on healing, then, let us remember that back of the man which we see is the Divine Image. *There is a Perfect Concept of Man, held in the Mind of the Universe as an already accomplished fact, hut man is subject to the law of his own choice.*

MAN RE-ENACTS GOD

Man is conscious mind or spirit; this stands for his objective faculty. The objective mind of man is his recognition of life in a conscious state—it is the only attribute of man that is volitional, or self-choosing. Consequently, it is the spiritual man. The conscious mind of man is the contemplator.

Let us bear in mind what we have already learned: that the Universe is the result of the contemplation of the Divine Mind, or the Holy Spirit, which is God. God creates by contemplating His own I-AM-NESS, and this contemplation, through Law, becomes the objectification of the Self-Realization of the Infinite Mind.

The Divine Nature is re-enacted in man; he is conscious mind and spirit, and, as he contemplates, he reflects his thought into the Universal Subjectivity where it is received and acted upon.

As Mind, or Soul, accepts these images of thought, It operates upon unformed substance and causes it to take definite form as body, which is unconscious form. It becomes *definite form*, but the form itself is unconscious, because it is made of immaterial substance. Body, of itself, without Mind, has neither consciousness nor volition. Devoid of mentality, the body neither thinks, sees, hears, feels, touches nor tastes. Take the mentality away from a body and it becomes a corpse. Having no conscious intelligence, it at once begins to disintegrate and to resolve into the Universal Substance, or unformed matter, from which it came.

Although man is inherently a perfect idea, his individuality covers this idea with the forms of thought which he images. Man comes into this life subjective to the race consciousness and to his own environment, he unfolds his own personality and begins to create new subjective thought. He thinks and observes, draws certain conclusions and deductions, and incorporates them within his mentality, until at last they also become a part of the *relative cause* of his objective existence.

Healing, then, is accomplished by uncovering, neutralizing and erasing false images of thought, and letting the perfect idea reflect itself through subjective mind into the body.

When one realizes that *everything is Mind and that nothing moves but Mind*, and that the only instrument of Mind is thought (which is contemplation in some form or other) he will see that nothing can permanently heal unless it be accompanied by right thinking.

Only Our Own Concepts Limit Us

Realizing that conscious thought operates through a Power which is Infinite, we see there can be no limit to the power to heal, other than the limit of our ability to conceive that Power as healing. We are limited, not by Principle, but *by our own inability to see perfection*. Our thought can bring out a condition as perfect as we can conceive. Therefore, the man whose thought is the most God-like—that is, the truest, the highest, the most noble, the most complete, the most peaceful—will be the best healer. His thought reflects a greater perfection. That is why we cannot divorce true mental healing from true spiritual work. When thought reaches a higher degree of perfection, as the race consciousness unfolds and evolves, it will bring out a still greater development of life than we know now.

Spiritual Mind Healing

Never forget that Conscious Mind is the only Actor in the Universe and in man; that the unconscious or subjective mind is compelled—by reason of its nature—to accept. It can never reject. The body is an effect, with no intelligence of its own. We can now see that a mental treatment is a real, tangible, specific operation, working in perfect accord with known law.

When a practitioner treats anyone, he does not just *hope* that his patient will get well, he does not *ask* that the patient may be healed, he does not simply *desire* that he may be healed; he convinces his own mind that the patient is perfect—a definite piece of mental work, bringing out in his own consciousness (in his own self-contemplative, conscious mind) an understanding that the patient *is healed* and *is perfect*.

Treatment is the act, the art, and the science of inducing thought within the mentality of the one treating, which thought shall perceive that the body of the patient is a Divine, Spiritual, and Perfect Idea. Treatment does not necessarily treat every organ of the body specifically, but it does declare the body to be harmonious, and that every specific idea in it is harmonious. It then pays especial attention to what appears as the physical disorder.

As a result of this treatment, Subjective Mind—which is Universal and Omnipresent—accepts the images of the practitioner's thinking, and reflects them in the direction he specifies . . . to his patient.

The practitioner is not trying to send out a thought, hold a thought, or suggest a thought. The practitioner is trying to realize the state of perfection of the patient. We must be certain that we differentiate between *suggestion* (which is all right as far as it goes, but limited) and real metaphysical healing. In metaphysical healing, we are conscious that we are dealing with a Universal Principle or Law, which takes the impress of our thought and acts upon it. We are dealing with Something that cannot, and does not argue. We are directing It for definite purposes, telling It to do certain things, which It does. This is what occurs when we give a treatment.

We leave the field of materia medica to do its own work. Our work is done entirely in the field of mind. Without controversy, we work side by side with any doctor the patient may desire—we, in the field of mind, the physician in his own field. If this is persisted in over a period of years, the two fields will be brought closer together. This will be one of the greatest steps ever undertaken in the curative art.

When one begins treatment for another, there is sometimes a great sense of personal responsibility. The practitioner, through sympathy, may feel a sense of doubt and burden, but always this is built *upon the idea that he, himself, has to accomplish the results!* Should this occur, the practitioner should begin at once to treat himself against this thought, for as long as he has it there is a barrier to healing. Why? Because, *when you sift that sense of responsibility down to its last analysis, it is a belief that you cannot heal!* Do not give in to that belief—not even for a second—because it is nothing but a *thought* which says you cannot heal. Nothing but a thought is saying, or could be saying it, and since it is only a thought which says it, it is only a *thought* which can unsay it. Declare: "My word has the power to heal," and you will find the doubt slipping away.

The practitioner must treat himself to know that the word he speaks is entirely independent, *even of himself*. If we walk out on the roof of a high building and drop a chair over the side, it will fall to the ground. There is a law which draws it there, we are not responsible for the law, we do not have to make the chair hit the ground. In like manner, if this treatment is through the medium of a Law on the subjective side of life, it is our business to give the treatment: *it is the business of the Law to execute it*.

However, as practitioners, we do have an obligation—to treat a case if we take it. If someone says to you casually, "Hold a good thought for me today," you should reply: "Do you mean you wish me to give you a treatment, to take a definite time—thirty minutes, more or less—and do specific mental work for you? Is that what you wish?" People unfamiliar with this work may still be under the impression that the work done consists of "holding a good thought."

People must come to realize that treatment is a specific thing. Each case is specific, and no two can be treated entirely alike. One is dishonest if he contracts to take a larger number of cases than he has time to intelligently treat.

DISEASE IS IMPERSONAL

The word disease means lack of ease—dis-ease. Ab-normal, absence of a normal condition. In order to do his work, it is necessary for the practitioner to know that disease is not an entity, any more than darkness (which is the absence of light) is an entity. From the standpoint of the mental practitioner, disease is an impersonal thing, attempting to operate and personify itself, a thought force, a misconception, a conviction in the mind of the one who has it, and of course, an actual experience to the one who is suffering from it.

Regardless of its particular source, disease is an experience operating through people, which does not belong to them at all. Recognize that it is neither person, place nor thing, that there is no spiritual law to support it, that it is discord fleeing before harmony, that there is nothing but the Truth. You must know that the Power you are using is definite, scientific, dynamic, spiritual, absolute, complete, and *that It will work*. Let no fear come into your thought.

The first thing a practitioner does is to separate the belief from the believer. It is a personal, not a Cosmic problem. Evil is not a problem to God, it is only a problem to the individual. Therefore, we separate the belief from the believer, and begin to perceive the individual as a spiritual being, no longer subject to this belief, and even now the embodiment of perfection. If the practitioner is able to see only *perfection*, wholeness, he will see health manifested in his patient. The practitioner, then, recognizing that Mind, or Intelligence, or Spirit—whatever he chooses to call It—is the groundwork of all movement, definitely, specifically and consciously, speaks his word into this creative medium.

Begin to use this principle, no matter how slight you feel your knowledge, and the result will inspire you to perceive new ways and methods of approach, until you gradually grow into deeper assurance.

Man is fundamentally perfect, this is our whole premise—Perfect God, Perfect Man, Perfect Being—this is the whole basis of our argument. Always mentally separate disease from the one suffering from it. In mental practice, NEVER LOCATE DISEASE, because thoughts are things. Separate the belief from the believer, for the spiritual man has no disease, and you are talking only about the spiritual man.

DISEASE IS NOT ALWAYS DUE TO CONSCIOUS THOUGHT

Diseases which are mental in their origin must arise from some inner state of consciousness. While most disease must first have a subjective cause, this subjective cause (nine times out of ten) is not conscious in the thought of the person who suffers from it, but is perhaps largely the result of certain combinations of thinking.

So while it is true that disease has a prototype in subjective mind, it is also true that the individual who suffers from the disease, frequently has never *thought* he was going to have that particular kind of trouble.

But this does not alter the fact that every disease which comes up through subjectivity, and appears in the body, *must come through mind*.

HOW TO HEAL

In our work, we treat man, not as a physical body, neither do we treat the disease as belonging to him, *the reason being that if we do, we cannot subsequently free him from it*. We do not think of the disease as being connected with him or a part of him. The practitioner seeks to realize man as *perfect*, not needing to be healed of anything. This is nothing less than the realization of the Presence and the Power of God, or Spirit, as Man's Life, as the only life there is, as complete and perfect in him right now.

First recognize your own perfection, then build up the same recognition for your patient. You are then ready to directly attack the *thought* that binds him, *recognizing that your word destroys it, and stating that it does*. You may then take into account and specifically mention everything that needs to be changed, every so-called broken law or false thought. Then finish your treatment with a realization of peace, remaining for a few moments in silent recognition *that your work is done, complete and perfect*.

The work must not be thought of as hard. When we know that there is but One Mind, we shall realize that this work could not be difficult or laborious. *Mental treatment is a direct statement of belief into Mind, coupled with a realization that the work is already an accomplished fact.* The spiritual man needs no healing, health is an omnipresent reality, and when the obstructions that hinder healing are removed, *it will be found that health was there all the time*. So in your work, do not feel that you must heal anyone. Your only responsibility is to uncover the Truth.

Never say: "Here is a patient whom I must heal," for if you think of him from this viewpoint, how are you going to heal him? If you mentally see a sick man, he will remain mentally sick. *We cannot heal successfully while we recognize sickness as a reality to the Spirit*. In spiritual healing by this method, no one believes in disease, it has no action nor reaction, it has neither cause nor effect, it has no law to support it and no one through whom it can operate. There is no one to talk with about it, and no one to believe in it. While we maintain that disease is primarily a thing of thought, we do not deny the actuality of its experience nor the suffering it causes, instead we seek to heal it, and we co-operate with all, no matter what method they are using to relieve distress.

You have nothing to do with the patient's thought as a personality, for as your own thought clears, he will be helped. First eliminate doubt and fear from your own thought; realize that your patient is a Divine Being, and that your word is the law unto the thing unto which it is spoken. This is what gave Jesus His power: "For He taught them as one having authority, and not as the scribes."

Healing Is Clear Thinking

Scientific mental healing is the result of clear thinking and logical reasoning, which presents itself to consciousness and is acted upon by Mind. It is a systematic process of reasoning, which unearths the mental cause or idea underlying disease, and presents the Truth about man's being.

For instance, say to yourself: "God is all there is. There is only One Life." When you are treating, if there is any slight point which is not clear, do not continue with the treatment. Stop at once, go back to your analysis of Ultimate Reality, and build your whole argument upon It, in order to get a clear consciousness.

Repeat: "God is All. There is but One Power, Intelligence and Consciousness in the Universe, but One Presence. This One Presence cannot change. There is nothing for It to change into but Itself. It is Changeless, *and It is my life now, It is in me now*." Claim that no form of race-suggestion, belief in limitation, subjective idea of limitation, thought of karma, fatalism, theology or hell, horoscope, or any other false belief, has power. Accept none of them. If you have ever believed in them, if you have ever believed that the stars govern you, or that your environment governs you, or that your opportunities govern you, recognize this as an hypnotic condition into which you have fallen, and deny every one of them until there is no longer anything in you that believes in them.

This is a good way to clear your consciousness. We can readily see what it does: it induces a clear concept of Reality, which must reproduce Itself. This process of clear thinking, if carried out every day, will heal.

When you are giving a treatment, you are *thinking*. You are meeting, opposing, neutralizing, erasing and obliterating suppression, fear, doubt, failure, morbid emotion and sense of loss—

whatever the trouble may be. Every time your thought hits fairly and squarely, it erases just as definitely as one would erase a chalk line. Such is the mystery of the appearance and the disappearance of thought.

Right thought, constantly poured into consciousness, will eventually purify it. Discord might be likened to a bottle of impure water; healing might be likened to the process of dropping pure water into the bottle, a drop at a time, until the whole is clean and pure. Someone might ask why the bottle could not be turned upside down and at once drain out all the impurities. Sometimes this happens but not often. Meanwhile, a drop at a time will finally eliminate the impurities and produce a healing.

In treating, go beyond the disease and supply a spiritual consciousness. A treatment is not complete without a great realization of Life and Love, of God and Perfection, of Truth and Wisdom, of Power and Reality. Sense the Divine Presence in and through the patient at all times.

Whether we say that thought *goes out*, or that it is operated upon by Principle, makes little difference. It is very evident that until a thought is created, there is no operation. It is evident that THINKING SETS CAUSATION IN MOTION. Whether the word used heals, or simply sets the law in motion, really is of small import.

The practitioner is in the same Mind in which his patient lives; consequently, since each is in the One Mind, the patient is sick in the same medium and in a certain sense in the same Mind in which the practitioner lives; and because this Mind is Indivisible, the practitioner can, in his own mentality, reach the thought which causes the patient to be sick. Whether we say he *sends out a thought*, or that he simply *realizes a thought*, makes no difference. The simplest way is to say that *the practitioner realizes, within himself, upon the One Mind, through the One Medium, in the One Law*.

The practitioner realizes a certain truth for his patient within himself. Therefore, he sets the Law in motion for his patient. (The operation of this Law may be thought of in the same way we think of the law whereby water reaches its own level by its own weight.) The practitioner knows WITHIN HIMSELF, and this self-knowingness rises into the consciousness of his patient. It is like planting a seed in the ground, the practitioner sows the seed and the Creative Mind produces the plant. Does the soil operate on the seed, or does the seed operate on the soil? We do not know, but we do know that when a seed is put into the ground, the law pertaining to growth operates and a plant is produced, and that unless a seed is planted, no plant will be produced.

In practice, we make no attempt to send thoughts to our patients! We know there is but One Mind. We will say that "A" represents one who is sick and desires help. "B" represents a practitioner. "B" thinks into Mind; and whether we say that he is thinking within himself or somewhere else does not matter, *he is always thinking into Mind, because he is in Mind!* But one might say, "The patient thinks into his own subjective mind." Yes, if you wish to designate it as his subjective mind, but his subjective mind is only his atmosphere in the One Mind. We must understand this very clearly, else someday there will be a wall between our thought and its ability to heal some person who happens to be at a physical distance.

Both the patient and the practitioner think into one common Mind. Therefore, when a patient comes to a practitioner for healing, the practitioner does not try to hypnotize him, nor suggest anything to him. He declares the Truth about the patient. *To the degree that the practitioner brings his own consciousness to a true recognition of perfection*—provided there is a subjective receptivity in the thought of the patient—that man will be helped.

The practitioner does not try to *hold a thought* nor to *send out a thought*. He simply tries to convince himself of the perfection of his patient. The practitioner does not try to *make* his word operate through his patient, but only attempts to know the Truth of what he states. The patient must be receptive to the Truth, then the Truth will heal him. The practitioner is dealing with Universal Law, backed by omnipotent Power, which is Divine Principle. This is what Jesus meant when he said: "Ye shall know the truth and the truth shall make you free."

Every time we think, we are thinking into a receptive, plastic Substance, which receives the impress of our thought. When we stop to realize how subtle thoughts are, how unconsciously we think negation, how easy it is to get "down and out" mentally, we shall see that each is perpetuating his own condition. This is why people go from bad to worse or from success to a greater success.

Only as we gradually, definitely, and intelligently take true ideas and build them into the structure of our own thought, can there come the desired reaction. In mental treatment, the practitioner deals solely with ideas, and treats neither bodies nor conditions. He never manipulates, nor should he lay hands on his patient. . . . He does not care where the patient is when he is treating him, or what he may be doing. *The practitioner's work begins and ends within his own consciousness.* This should be constantly borne in mind.

No Sensation in Treatments

It is sometimes thought that in giving or receiving a treatment, one must experience some physical sensation. A patient sometimes says, after receiving a treatment: "I felt nothing unusual during the treatment." It is not necessary that the patient should feel anything unusual. There is no peculiar sensation which accompanies a treatment, neither is it necessary that the practitioner should feel anything, other than the truth of the words that he speaks.

When we plant a seed in the ground we do not have a great sensation, and it is not probable that the soil has any; but the seed planted in the creative soil will, nevertheless, produce a plant. "What is true on one plane is true on all." Know what you are doing just as definitely as the gardener does. It is the person who knows what he is doing who gets results.

Sometimes people who are being treated, as well as the practitioner, feel a great sense of peace, or elation, a vibration of light. Such a treatment—if it could be seen—might appear as light. People often do have a sense of light during a treatment; but it is not at all necessary that either the practitioner or the patient should experience any sensation out of the ordinary during a treatment. The practitioner does not work himself up into an emotional state. While it is true that the treatment is creative, it is also true that *whatever feeling there is, must be an effect and not a cause*. It must be the result of a conviction.

The Medium of Healing

The thing to remember is, that THERE IS JUST ONE SUBJECTIVE MIND IN THE UNIVERSE. This is a point that people often do not realize, and because they do not, they cannot see how a person may be treated without touching him, or that a person at a distance can be helped through absent treatment.

If there is but One Subjective Mind in the Universe (and we have already learned the meaning and nature of Subjective Mind: It is deductive, receptive, plastic, neutral, impersonal and creative, It is the Stuff from which all things are made) you can impress upon It a certain image of thought, or a certain process of realization, and you will get a result, for It is the Actor.

When we speak of *every thought dropped into the Creative Medium*, do we think of God's thought and man's thought as the same? We think of each as thought; but, *whereas man thinks both inductively and deductively, God thinks only deductively.*

God is not conscious of matter as we know it. God is conscious of form, but not of size. God is conscious of manifestation but not of space. God is conscious of outline but not of limitation. God is conscious in many forms, *but not as division.*

There is a great difference between conscious and unconscious thought for trained thought is far more powerful than untrained. If this were not true, the thoughts of the metaphysical practitioner could not neutralize those which caused his patient to be sick. Even a small amount of right thought puts to rout that which is wrong.

We have learned that Subjective Mind can deduce only, that It cannot of Itself initiate anything; but this does not mean that It is unintelligent. We must be very careful not to labor under the delusion that because Subjective Mind cannot reason, It is unintelligent, *for It is infinitely more intelligent than our present state of conscious mind*, but is, nevertheless, controlled by it.

If our subjective consciousness were always clear, if it never received false impressions, the Spirit would always flow to the point of objectivity, and we would never make mistakes, would never be sick, poor or unhappy.

The Universe being deductive only, cannot refuse man anything. The very force which makes us sick can heal us, the force which makes us poor can enrich us, and the power which makes us miserable can make us happy. If this were not true, there would be a duality in the Universe and this is impossible.

You do not need to look for a *law of health* as opposed to a *law of disease*, for there is only One Law. This gives a great sense of relief since it means that THERE IS NO POWER TO OPPOSE A TREATMENT. We are bound by our very freedom, our free will binds us, but as free will creates the conditions which externally limit us, so it can uncreate or dissolve them. Instead of saying, "Here is a sick man to heal, and I shall have to work hard on this case," we should realize that there is nothing but Spirit in the Universe and, therefore, say, "I am going to conceive of this man as being Spirit, and the same power which made him sick will heal him."

People often say: "It must be a drain on one to treat so many people. I should think the practitioner's *will power* would become exhausted." This is a misconception. Our reference to "free will" means merely the matter of self-choosing, the matter of deciding *what* we shall think. WILL POWER HAS NOTHING WHATEVER TO DO WITH MENTAL HEALING! Its use would imply that the practitioner exercises a personal thought force over his patient. This is a false suggestion, which is always some form of hypnotism. Knowing our Oneness with God and the Creative Medium, Law, our treatments are free from any thought of control.

All thoughts of doubt concerning one's ability to heal, come from the belief that it is the personality and not the Law which does the healing. Never say: "I am not *good* enough to heal," or "I do not *know enough* to heal." Know that you are dealing with Law, *It* is the Actor. Recognize all such arguments as some form of suggestion, and refuse to let them operate through you. YOU CAN HEAL, but *you must know that you can!* The day will come, and is rapidly approaching, when the entire world will believe the Truth, because of the great neutralizing power which right thought is exercising upon the race consciousness.

The reason people do not get better results is that they do not understand that Principle works independently . . . the Truth demonstrates Itself!

TREATING CHILDREN

In the case of an infant—who is subjective to the conscious thought of the people around it—it may be necessary to teach the parents how to think about the child, else one might heal the infant and have the parents' thought make it sick again. Explain to them the result of entertaining fears for the health of their children. Remember that the thought of the parents influences the child.

We will suppose the mother is constantly saying: "The poor thing; the poor, little sick thing." From the human standpoint, this is natural, but it does not help the child, no matter how loving the thought may be. This is called unconscious, or innocent, malpractice. It is malpractice because it is the wrong use of thought; innocent because it is not intended to harm; unconscious because the mother does not know the result of such mental action. In such a case, it is the business of the practitioner to realize that there is no mental influence operating through the child except a belief in perfection.

At first, children are happy, free, spontaneous. That is why we like them, they live instinctively. As they grow older and their emotions become more complex, and they hear people talk about death, trouble, divorce, love and marriage and everything else, good, bad and indifferent, they begin to react to these emotions subjectively. Everything that opposes harmony and spontaneous unity, will prove disastrous to the child's health, sooner or later. After a certain age, children have to be re-educated, just as do adults, that their subjective mind may not reproduce false impressions.

THE POWER OF THE WORD

Be specific in treating, be direct and definite in your mental work. You are dealing with Intelligence, so deal with It intelligently. The treatment *must realize the patient as perfect*, must *recognize the word as power, must know that it breaks down every* man-made law and casts it out, that it is the law of harmony and the recognition of the Presence of Good, that within itself it is unbounded, and equipped with the power to execute itself—and *it must know that it does this*. It must know that there is nothing that can change it, that there is no belief which can hinder it; that it cannot be reversed, misplaced, mislaid, neutralized or destroyed by any opposing force; that *it does the thing it is supposed to do*. And it must know that it is continuous and unremitting *and will operate until it does* all it is supposed to do.

Jesus said: "Heaven and earth shall pass away, but my words shall not pass away." And Isaiah understood something of this when he said: "So shall my word be that goeth forth out of my mouth; it shall not return unto me void."

SEEING PERFECTION

When Jesus said to the man, "Stretch forth thine hand," *he undoubtedly saw a perfect hand!* If everything is mental, and if Jesus saw an imperfect hand instead of a perfect one, no good would have resulted, according to the law of cause and effect. A practitioner does not treat a sick man, he deals only with the idea, a spiritual man; otherwise, he would enter into the vibration of suffering and *might* himself experience the result of such vibration. From what we know, Jesus must have seen only the perfect hand. Even though he might have recognized the false condition, as far as his word of healing was concerned, it must have been a recognition of perfection . . . else it could not have healed.

Healing is not *creating* a perfect idea or a perfect body; it is revealing an idea which is already perfect. Healing is not a process, it is a revelation, through the thought of the practitioner to the thought of the patient. There may be a process *in* healing, but not a process *of* healing. The process *in* healing is the mental work and the time it takes the practitioner to convince himself of the perfectness of his patient; and the length of time it takes the patient to realize this perfectness.

Back of what we call the human body, there must be a Divine Body. It is not necessary to visualize this spiritual body, but we should sense body as a spiritual idea, that the flow and circulation of life through it is complete. It is not inhibited . . . not congested.

It is necessary that the practitioner believe in a perfect body. He cannot realize this unless he has already become convinced that the perfect body is there. If he has come to this conclusion, he must not deny it. There is a perfect heart and a perfect idea of heart, a perfect head and a perfect idea of head, perfect lungs and a perfect idea of lungs. The practitioner must realize that back of the appearance is the Reality, and it is his business to uncover this Reality. He does this through a process of obliterating false thought. He must deny false conclusions, bring out the evidence of perfection, and produce the healing. *Disease is a fact but not a truth; it is an experience but not a spiritual reality.*

We must transcend the appearance, even though we admit it as a fact. We are not so cold-blooded as to say to a person with pain that there is no such thing as pain. That is not our idea or purpose. We admit the fact. IT IS QUITE A DIFFERENT THING TO ADMIT ITS NECESSITY. We admit that there is unhappiness, but it would be unthinkable to admit that *one has to be unhappy*. Can it be true that there *could be* a Universal necessity for unhappiness? IT CANNOT. And the time will come when no one will be unhappy! I do not know *when* it will come. I am not going to wait for it to come, but it is certain that such a time will arrive; and it will come to you and to me NOW in such degree as we will let it come. We shall be able to let it come in such degree as we are able to convince our consciousness that it is there, and when it finally does come, we shall find that *it was always there!*

Disease, accordingly, is a fact but not a truth. It is not an eternal verity. It was a *fact* in human experience for ages that people did not broadcast over a radio, but it was not a *truth* that they could not. It was not a divine Reality, because had they known how to manufacture a radio and talk over it, they *could* have broadcast in any age. So we must try to see and sense that always, back of the appearance, PERFECTION IS.

CHAPTER FIFTEEN

PHYSICAL PERFECTION, CONCLUDED

What Can Be Healed? • *Suggestions for Treatments* • *Do Not Try to Go Beyond Your Understanding* • *Depend upon Principle* • *How Habits Are Acquired and Treated* • *Treating Pain* • *Repeating Treatments* • *Headache* • *Why People Become Fatigued* • *Treating Insanity* • *Treating Lung Trouble* • *Vision* • *Constipation* • *Skin* • *Arms and Hands* • *Feet and Legs* • *False Growths (Tumors, Cancer, Gallstones)* • *Removing the Complex* • *Heart Trouble* • *Poison of Any Kind* • *Paralysis* • *Asthma and Hay Fever* • *Nerve Troubles* • *Blood Troubles and Skin Diseases (High Blood Pressure, Hardening of the Arteries, Eczema, Boils)* • *Fevers* • *Obstetrics* • *Colds, Influenza and Grippe* • *Obesity* • *Treating Kidney, Bladder and Liver Disturbances* • *Treating Stomach and Bowel Troubles* • *Treating Insomnia* • *Deafness* • *Weather Conditions* • *Thoughts about Food* • *Rheumatism* • *Healing Intemperance* • *Supply* • *A Treatment for Peace of Mind.*

WHAT CAN BE HEALED?

What should we try to heal through spiritual treatment? If we were dealing *only* with the power of a thought, we should not expect to heal anything; but if we are dealing with a Universal Principle, why should we set any limit to Its power?

Since the Law of God is Infinite, from the spiritual viewpoint, there is no *incurable* disease, as opposed to a *curable* one. The Law knows nothing about disease; It only acts. The practitioner realizes that his word is the presence, power, and activity of Truth, which is in him, which is Almighty, which is God, "beside which there is none other."

446

This word is the law unto the thing whereunto it is spoken, and has within itself the ability, the power, and the intelligence to execute itself, through the great Law of all life. This word being the spontaneous recognition of Living Spirit—Infinite, Ever-Present, and Active—is now made manifest in and through this person, or thing, about which the practitioner is thinking.

To Spirit there can be no *incurable* disease. The word "incurable" means not susceptible of being cured. The root definition of *cured* is "cared for." If we say that a disease is *incurable*, we are saying that it is not sensitive to care. As long as any cell is alive it is sensitive to care, which means that as long as a person is alive, the cells of the body respond to care. Naturally, they are not being cured if they are not being properly cared for. We have already learned that disease is largely a state of mind, and we could hardly say that a state of mind is *incurable*, could we? We know that thought is constantly changing, forever taking on new ways of expression. It cannot possibly remain permanent. It has to change. Can we not, accordingly, change it to a better state instead of to a worse?

Materia medica is using the term "incurable" less and less frequently, for most disease in the field of medicine is being cured. Let us then free ourselves from the assumption that any disturbed state of thought need be permanent ("incurable").

Suggestions for Treatments

In giving mental and spiritual treatments, it is better not to dwell too much on the negative, since we are liable to give it undue importance. To affirm the presence of God is better than to deny the presence of evil. However, if the presence of evil persists in making its appearance, it is sometimes well to deny it, to know it is neither person, place nor thing, that it does not belong to us, and that it cannot operate through or around us. It is neither cause, medium, nor effect. It is neither imagination, idea, nor reflection. It is neither visible nor invisible. It cannot emanate from God, and does not emanate from man. The devil is a myth, and heaven is lost merely for the lack of an idea of harmony. "Stand still and watch the sure salvation of the Lord." This Lord is always an indwelling Presence. The individual "I" which is an incarnation of the Universal "I Am."

A practitioner should think of his patient as a perfect entity, living in a perfect Universe, surrounded by perfect situations and governed by perfect Law. The entire Universe is devoted to his good. "All the Father hath is thine." "Arise, O Son, and take." This taking is better accomplished through an affirmative attitude of mind than by dwelling too much on the negative. "Behold! The kingdom of heaven is at hand," but this kingdom must be recognized. The recognition is a mental act. We must know that the All-Powerful Spirit is ever available and ever equal to the healing of any discordant condition of body, mind or affairs, but we must never look outside of ourselves to find this Spirit, since It is indwelling. What we really do is to look within our own consciousness, and "pray to the Father who is in secret and the Father who seeth in secret, shall reward us openly." The sincere practitioner will be sure his own thought is clear, that his own faith is equal to the demands made upon it. Above all else he must be careful not to be caught in the negative stream of consciousness. Jesus could not have raised Lazarus from among those who were believed to be dead if he had been afraid to "roll away the stone," nor if he had listened to the wailing of those about him. To be spiritually minded is to enter that tranquil atmosphere of pure thought, that "Heavenly Consciousness" which is "the secret place of the Most High" in man.

In beginning a series of treatments for any person, we start with the idea of Perfect God, Perfect Man, and Perfect Being. In every case it is well to begin by the removal of doubt and fear, to assure ourselves that the one whom we are seeking to help is complete and perfect, harmonious and whole. Next we must conform our arguments, statements and realizations so that they may measure up to this high ideal.

It is easy to believe that God is perfect. We must also believe that the spiritual man is perfect, and since it is difficult to believe that the objective man is perfect, we must confine our statements to a realization of the spiritual perfection of man. In such degree as our realization becomes a subjective embodiment, the objective healing will automatically take place. We know the background of human thought is, to a great extent, one of negation, a denial of an harmonious and spiritual Universe; consequently, our outlook on life must be transformed by the renewing of the mind, and even when the results are not immediately forthcoming, we must still maintain a calm serenity of thought. We must relight the torch of our imagination by "fire caught from heaven." We must remain faithful to this vision for a realization of the Presence of God is the secret power of our work.

The following examples are not to be considered dogmatic; they are merely suggested ways by which one may do effective work. The practitioner must realize that all power is given unto him. He must believe that man is spiritual and he must be certain that his statements about the spiritual man will find a corresponding outlet in the physical man. However, he is very careful never to treat the physical man, but to think of man's entire being as spiritual, and if man's entire being is spiritual, then his physical being must reflect spiritual ideas. The practitioner supplies these spiritual ideas and lets the Law of Mind do the rest. To begin the treatment by a silent assurance that man, being spiritual, is exempt from negation, is a correct starting point. Infinite Love harmonizes man's entire being. The healing currents of Life flow through him, taking away every negative thought and manifestation, and adjusting his whole physical being to the idea of Divine Harmony.

Do Not Try to Go Beyond Your Understanding

Since our spiritual understanding is not sufficient to enable us to mentally set bones, we call in a surgeon; since we cannot walk on the water, we take a boat. We can go only as far as our spiritual knowledge takes us. Principle is Infinite, but we shall demonstrate Its power only at the level of our concept of It. Every day we have the announcement from scientists that they have made new discoveries—laws which have always existed but which have not as yet been utilized.

Do not let any one discourage or belittle your efforts by asking, "Why don't you walk on the water? Jesus did." Do not be sidetracked by any of these futile suggestions, these mental obstructions which an unbeliever would seek to throw in your path. If we had the understanding which Jesus had, we *would* be able to walk on the water. I am not at all confused by the fact that we do not do this today. Someday one will come along who knows how to walk on or over water.

We are probably on the verge of a great spiritual awakening. People are so tired of looking for things where they do not exist, that they are going to more and more completely open their thought to the realization that Spirit is an active Presence. But *if we spend our entire time trying to find out why It does not work, we shall never find out how and why It does work.* Arguing is often a waste of time. Somehow there must come to each individual an interior conviction that we are One with the Universe, and that the Spirit flows through us at the level of our recognition and embodiment of It. For this is "the way, the truth and the life."

People say: "I can't take off my glasses." Then wear them, but begin to make the declaration that there is One Perfect Vision seeing through you. This is the Truth. *If this statement becomes a subjective realization, you will be healed, will no longer need glasses.*

If a plaster will relieve, use it. If a pill does any good, take it, but gradually try to lead the thought from where it is into the higher realms of consciousness where the soul recognizes its own I-Am-ness.

Suppose one is unable to convince himself of the Truth of the statement which he makes, how is he going to bring himself to a place of belief? By repeating his affirmation, dwelling on its meaning, meditating upon the spiritual significance of it, until the subjective state of his thinking becomes clarified. This is the only reason for repeating treatments, for *one* treatment would heal if there were no subjective doubts. Repeated treatments induce, within consciousness, a definite concept of an already established truth, even though the fact may not as yet have become objectified. This is why mental healing is scientific. There is no room for doubt in a treatment.

Realize that you treat with your understanding; by your own choice you decide to give a treatment, *but the treatment becomes operative through the Law*. Never say: "I am not good enough to treat." In God there are no good, better or best.

Do not allow yourself to become superstitious, for you are dealing with a normal, natural law in the mental and spiritual world. This law is just as real as any other known law. Never say: "I am not sure that I have enough power to treat." You can never heal with this mental attitude, *for that implies that you think you are doing the healing*. Rather, say: "As I let fall the forms of my thought, they are operated upon by Principles in which I believe. This is the law of God, the law of man, and the law of the Universe." Never say, or think: "*This* disease is hard to heal, while that presented yesterday was easy." If you find yourself saying this, *at once heal yourself*. Such a belief comes from the thought that we are dealing with a limited power, and that such power knows degrees of discomfort. The truth is that there is but One Power and that Power knows only Perfection.

Depend upon Principle

Principle is the Power that made everything. It is Absolute, It will not and cannot be denied. The only thing that can deny God is yourself.

Do not think of disease as an entity, but as an impersonal thought-force. In healing, you are separating the false from the true. The work is definite and dynamic, and is consciously done, always with a clear purpose in mind.

If your own thought is clear, and you are able to realize the Presence of Spirit in your patient, your work will be effective. Through the proper use of this great Subjective Law, you can impress a definite idea upon it, and if you, yourself, do not withdraw that idea, or neutralize it by an opposite one, the Law will bring it into manifestation.

What we need, then, is to learn the Law governing this Principle. When you give a treatment, you are definitely setting a Universal Law in motion, *which must not only accept what you say but the way in which you say it*. If your treatment is given with a sense of struggle, it will manifest in that way. If it is given with a sense of peace, then it will manifest in a peaceful manner.

Remember that you need assume no personal responsibility for the recovery of your patient, *but you do have a definite obligation, which is to give the treatment* . . . properly, clearly, fully, and conscientiously . . . when you have agreed to. Back of all appearance to the contrary, it is your business to mentally see the spiritual perfection of your patient.

When you have occasion to treat yourself, call your own name, and proceed with the treatment as though you were treating someone else. Or you may say, "I am thus and so. . . ."

Disease will be healed, provided you get at its cause and remove it—and by *getting at its cause*, we mean getting at the mental cause—and provided the one for whom you are working is willing to surrender that cause. *You cannot heal anyone of his trouble, if it is the result of some mental attitude which he will not surrender.* In this case, find out what the mental attitude is and remove it, by showing the patient the right mental attitude. It is the practitioner's duty to uncover false ideas of life, and replace them with the truth. If this can be done before disease destroys the physical body, a healing will always follow.

How Habits Are Acquired and Treated

What is a habit? A habit is desire objectified—"the continuous character of one's thoughts and feelings"—desire for something that will give satisfaction. At the root of all habit is one basic thing: *the desire to express life.* There is an urge to express in all people, and this urge, operating through the channels of Creative Mind, looses energy into action, and compels the individual to do something. Back of all this desire is the impulse of Spirit to express. In man, this impulse must express at the level of his consciousness.

> *"For each, for the joy of working and each in*
> *his separate star,*
> *Shall paint the thing as he sees It, for the*
> *God of things as they are."*

Some express themselves constructively and some destructively. Suppose a man who has the liquor habit comes to you to be healed. You would not treat that *habit.* You would not pray for the man to be healed. You would know that you are dealing with a man who has the desire to express life and who, for the moment, thinks he must express it in terms of intoxication. He once thought this expressed reality to him. He now knows that it does not, but he cannot with mere will power stop it, for the habit appears to have taken complete possession of him. (We might well remember always that unless we control thought, it will control us.)

In giving treatment, first recognize who and what this man is, saying something like this: "This man is the full and complete expression of Truth, and as such he is free from any sense of limitation. He is not bound by any sense of inferiority, which he needs to cover up, for he is a unique individuality, expressing all the attributes of God. He is free from any delusion or fear of delusion. He knows that the Spirit of Truth within him is complete and always satisfied. He has no longing outside of the longing to express his own divinity, and he has the assurance that he shall be able to gratify this: 'Blessed are they who do hunger and thirst after righteousness (right living) for they shall be filled.' This thing which calls itself the liquor habit has no power over him and cannot operate through him. By the power of this word which I am now speaking, this habit is completely destroyed and forever obliterated." Then mentally see him free and harmoniously expressing life and happiness.

TREATING PAIN

Use the thought of peace with the realization of a Perfect Presence. Many times, just the statement: "Right where pain seems to operate, the Presence of God is," will instantly obliterate the pain. The *perfect realization* of this Presence would always do so. Know that in this Presence there is no tension, no struggle, no fear, there is no sense of conflict. Know this until there comes to your consciousness a deep, calm sense of peace and ease, and until every thought of pain is eliminated.

Healing takes place to the degree that we send down the right kind of thoughts into subjectivity. We mean, by thinking consciously and with deep feeling (knowing) we implant the right idea in Mind, and Mind reproduces this idea, as effect, in the body. We must realize that we are using a Power, compared to which the united intelligence of the human race is as nothing. The practitioner involves an idea in Mind; it is the Law which creates. As the practitioner treats his own mentality, which is simply a point in Mind, he reaches the mentality of his patient. The practitioner can erase the thought of pain from the patient's mentality when he has first neutralized the idea in his own thought.

REPEATING TREATMENTS

A treatment is a specific thing. When you are treating to neutralize *any* particular *form* of disease, your word should be spoken in such a way as to neutralize a *belief* in the necessity of the condition. Each treatment must have in itself everything necessary to cover the case. When you treat, resolve things into thought—bodies, people, objects and all things—everything is a thing of thought. Having resolved everything into thought, know that disease is neither person, place, nor thing. It has no location, does not belong to anyone, cannot operate through anyone. Know that it is a false image, with no power, and then you are ready to mentally dissolve it.

Always come to a complete conclusion when giving a treatment. Always feel that it is done, complete and perfect, and give thanks for the answer, as if it were already objectified. In the interval between treatments, do not carry the thought of the patient around with you. To do so is to doubt, and this mental attitude must be completely overcome. Each treatment should be a complete statement of the Reality of Being. The treatment *should be repeated daily until a healing takes place*. If it takes five minutes, five hours, five days, or five years, the treatment must be kept up until a healing is accomplished. This is the only method we know. It is not enough to *say* that everything is all right. This is true in Principle, but in fact and in human experience, it is only as true as we make it. Treat until you get results. A healing takes place when the patient is no longer sick, and until such time, mental work should be done.

HEADACHE

Confused, worried, anxious, tense thoughts can produce a congestion in the head. Those who worry over trifles, and think they are subject to the conditions which surround them, often suffer from headaches, but a realization of the vitalizing power of Spirit through the entire body quickly removes tension and brings a sense of relaxation to the body.

Back of nearly every discord or disorder, there is some subjective complex, or mental knot, that needs to be untied; generally, some suppressed emotion, which perhaps is centered around the affections——the likes and dislikes, the loves and passions, and everything which goes with them. These knots must be untied, and it is the business of the practitioner to untie them.

A treatment for peace, alone, often brings quick results when one is suffering from head-ache. If one can stop long enough to realize: "Infinite Intelligence within me lifts me out of worry, confusion and doubt," many times nothing else is necessary. And a safe rule for the *prevention* of headache is thinking correctly. Think only "whatsoever things are true, whatsoever things are honorable, whatsoever things are just, whatsoever things are pure, whatsoever things are lovely, whatsoever things are of good report." Following is a suggested treatment:

"There is neither congestion nor confusion in Spirit, and this man is spiritual. There is neither ache nor pain in the Consciousness of God as It flows through man. All ideas are assimilated, find perfect expression in joy through the life-giving Source which cannot be congested, retarded, nor strained. Ideas are comprehended fully and com-pletely, their spiritual significance is assimilated, and there is no strain as they pass into self-expression. The flow of Life-Force to the brain centers is always unretarded, suffi-cient and sustained."

WHY PEOPLE BECOME FATIGUED

Let a person say to himself, "I am overworked," and at once there will come up through his consciousness a belief in weariness. People who are constantly complaining of being tired are hypnotized into this belief through the law of race-suggestion. An instance of this is the belief that one more than forty years of age is easily fatigued, cannot engage in strenuous exercise of any kind, and must work fewer hours each day. This race-suggestion has hypnotized the entire world. Only a few people past forty dare to undertake new endeavors and engage in activities with the same enthusiasm they did at twenty-five. At what we term middle-age, all too many complain of habitual fatigue. Usually this is attributed to over-exertion, or general dissipation of the reserves, but frequently, when analyzed, the mental cause will be discovered as a deep-seated resistance to conditions which the patient has found himself unable to change.

Suppose someone had been bound by mental confusion, that desires had torn him and conflicts had entered into his life, what would have occurred? He would have been continually dropping *opposing thoughts* into his mentality; and as the mental action—the friction—took place, it might produce a very tired body; and if over-chaotic, it might produce what is known as nervous prostration. It would not, however, be the body that was sick, but a condition brought about through wrong thought.

Now, if subjective thought were a thing apart from us, if we did not have conscious access to it, we could not change it; but being the result of the way thought has worked, we *can* consciously change it. If this were not true, mental healing would be impossible.

We can free ourselves from a feeling of approaching fatigue, by knowing that we have within us—always immediately available—an Infinite Strength. As we allow the thought of this to enter our inner consciousness, we feel strong, vital, and equal to any emergency. "Know ye not that ye are the temple of the living God?" This power within you is the same that holds the planets in space. The power back of your word is perfect law and is fulfilled and returned to you as your *perfect strength*.

Treating Insanity

In treating one whose mind appears to be deranged, realize that there is but One Mind, which Mind is God, and is Perfect. This is the only Mind there is. It is the Mind of your patient; It is your own Mind. This Mind being a Complete, Perfect, and Indivisible Whole, cannot labor under a delusion, cannot for one moment lose Its Self-Consciousness. After you have realized this Truth about Life, know that it is also true about the one whom you are treating. His thought is perfect. If one should have a complete realization of this, knowing there is just the One Mind, there would be no doubt or confusion, and the mentality of the patient would cease to be deranged.

The practitioner must never allow himself to think of the patient as having "lost his mind." If once the consciousness of the practitioner becomes clouded by such a thought, he would be truly "the blind leading the blind." The practitioner must believe that there is but One Intelligence in the universe, and that this Intelligence is everywhere, flows in unlimited supply through every individual. Man's mentality is a point in Universal Mind, to which all things are known. In this Mind all persons are rational and poised.

TREATING LUNG TROUBLE

The spiritual idea of lung itself is universal and perfect, nothing has ever happened to it. It was, is, and ever will be—perfect. But man, through the creative medium of his thought, has caused an appearance of disease in the lung. Back of all such trouble is a consuming passion, an unexpressed emotion, a strong desire. Healing will take place to the degree that the practitioner neutralizes this belief and perceives the presence of a perfect lung.

The practitioner realizes there is a perfect body, perfect being, perfect God, perfect man, perfect expression, perfect bronchial tubes, perfect trachea, perfect lungs! The practitioner, if he would heal, must elevate his own thought. The word he speaks is law, it is power; it knows itself to be what it is. It is the law unto the case. He is now conscious that the word he speaks will neutralize and entirely destroy the false thought and condition. He says: "There is one body; this body is the Body of God, and is Perfect; It is never depleted, Its vitality is never lowered. There is no wasting away, nor burning up of substance, for substance is eternal, changeless and perfect. This Body is the body of my patient right now."

He continues until he covers what, in his own thought, appears to be the mental cause of the false condition. If he does this day after day, the patient will be relieved, though the practitioner never thinks of his patient, other than that the word of Truth is being spoken for him. He never wonders whether his word is taking effect, because he speaks into Intelligence and lets It act.

Human life is the incarnation of God in man. With every indrawn breath, we breathe in life, and with every outgoing breath, we give it forth. The lungs are constantly renewed by every respiration. With every new inspiration of thought we appropriate something of God. With every outpouring of life, expressed in faith and good deeds, we are expressing God. When we associate our breathing with the very Life and Light of God, nothing can retard the flow of life through us. A good meditation for practitioner or patient, who has any fear of lung trouble, is:

"The One Infinite Life and Substance is the only Life and Substance in existence; and this Life and this Substance is my Life now. I express through a spiritual body, which is and must continue to be, perfect. There is no wasting or destruction of any part, for that which is Eternal can never be non-existent. Any tissues that appear to be impaired are now renewed by the very Life of God, which is flowing in and through me.

"I erase from my consciousness the *belief* that the tissues of my body can be impaired, inflamed or destroyed. Joyfully, peacefully, trustingly, confidently, I give my body—every tissue, atom, and function—over to the Spirit of Life, which in Its perfection does now renew and rebuild me, even out of Itself. That Substance out of which my body is created is Spiritual, and is maintained by the all-powerful Essence of Spirit."

Vision

According to the Scriptures, mind and body must be kept pure—must be kept "single" to the good—in order that perfect, abiding sight may be attained. "The light of the body is the eye; if, therefore, thine eye be single, thy whole body shall be full of light. But if thine eye be evil, thy whole body shall be full of darkness" (Matt. 6:22, 23).

But the eyes, of themselves, cannot see. The mind within does the real seeing, the real interpreting of what the eyes look upon. The eyes can truly be called "the windows of the soul." They typify the ability of the mind to discern and understand. As the light of understanding dawns upon us, we have a habit of saying, "I see, I see," meaning that we mentally discern. *The man who clearly realizes his Oneness with all Good should have strong, clear eyesight!*

God sees, and His is the only Mind there is. It is man's Mind, and consequently he sees, whether he knows it or not. Do not fear to claim this, for it is the truth. There is no obstruction to vision, no near vision and no far vision; there is no false vision, no weak vision nor blurred vision. There is One Perfect Seeing, which is now seeing through you . . . which is now seeing through me.

When we fail to use any organ, it becomes useless. As the eyes are the organs of the soul, when we do not use our soul powers, *we lose the use of the organs through which they function!* If one does not allow the mind to look out through the eyes, the vision becomes blurred or imperfect. To regain this, one must use the inner sight.

In cases of defective sight, declare that spiritual vision is clear, and that your faith in spiritual substance is unshaken. When faith touches a certain point in our consciousness, and the light of spiritual understanding dawns upon us, we glorify the good. If we have been outwardly blind, our sight is restored. We should praise our vision. The clearness of spiritual vision should be reflected through our eyes.

Always one should be conscious of the idea of Wholeness of Life, perfect function at every point. The practitioner should know that Spiritual Substance was never destroyed at any point, on any plane of expression, and that the vision of his patient is perfect and indestructible right now. Declare daily: "Through my eyes, God sees the perfection of His Kingdom. I, too, see perfection in all creation . . . the beauty of the Omnipresent God."

Thoughts of dishonesty and suspicion make the eyes shifty. Thoughts of fear, desolation, and hopelessness make the eyes lusterless. The eyes brighten with friendliness and good cheer, when animated by the light of love, joy, faith or noble purpose.

We should be grateful for the help, if we find glasses helpful, but we must know within ourselves that we are not dependent upon them. Hold steadfastly to the thought: "I will lift up my eyes unto God, from whom comes my perfect sight." Thus we are recognizing the condition, but not acknowledging it as an entity, and we are giving to Subjective Mind a new pattern (rather the *original* pattern) for perfect eyes . . . perfect vision. "Through the prism of God's love, I recognize the Oneness of God and man. I have perfect vision right now."

CONSTIPATION

Never think a sick person is one who merely has a sick *body*. If you do, you will find yourself treating the body. Why should we not treat the body? For the simple reason that the cause of the disease is not in the body. The body is an effect and not a cause. *You must know that bodies and conditions never move, they are always moved upon.* A sick person is one who has a sick thought as well as a sick body.

Constipation is often due to a belief in limitation or burden, and is mentally helped by knowing that there is no restriction, no inaction, no limited action, no bondage, no fear, no congestion. Realize that all action is normal, harmonious and perfect.

Any thought which produces a mental tension—fear of lack, of trouble, of disease of all kinds, fear of loss of friends, or loss of position—is likely to manifest itself as constipation. Any kind of fear thought retards the free action of the life forces, thus greatly interfering with the functions of the body

In such cases a treatment for complete relaxation should be given. It is well to know: "Infinite Intelligence within me rules me, and controls and directs all of the organs of my body, so that they function perfectly according to their nature. I am an open channel for good to flow *in and through me*, freely, generously, cheerfully."

Every thought of cruelty is disturbing to the entire body. Solomon tells us that "he that is cruel, troubleth his own flesh," and every adverse thought is cruel. Thoughts of peace and good will, a recognition of the unity of all men, will produce harmony, and bring about perfect elimination in the body.

It is necessary that we release all thoughts—as well as *things*—that clutter up our lives. We are reminded that there is something resembling the Divine in the intelligence and fearlessness of the organs of our body, in the way they take that which is necessary to their sustenance and well-being, and release that which is not needed. If the organs of the body followed the average tactics of man in his acquisitive habits, if the lungs hoarded the air they take in, if the heart kept the fresh blood stored within its walls, refusing to allow it to circulate, if the stomach retained the food taken in for nourishment, what a static condition we would have! But the very reverse is true. Such perfect assimilation, elimination and circulation has never been equalled by man in anything he has invented.

"Ye shall know the truth, and the truth shall make you free." This is a promise we have all proven, in a degree. Could we but comprehend the full significance of Spiritual Substance, we should be forever freed from all congestive thoughts—selfishness, greed, undue acquisitiveness— all of which have been called *the waste products of the mind*. Understanding this, it naturally follows we should be freed from their effects.

Very often the word of healing is spoken and does not appear to operate because hindered by some obstruction. Some people are obstinate, resistant, stubborn, and they must be healed of these beliefs. The practitioner must know that there is no resistance to Truth, and no thought anywhere which can prevent the consciousness from perceiving the Truth. *Whatever the false condition is, array mental argument against it.* Turn the thought over and over, until either by reason or by chance, you hit upon the thing that is wrong. *Anyone can help the sick who can get away from the effect long enough to perceive a different cause . . . a perfect cause, back of what appears to be an imperfect effect.*

A thought of Love is always healing, and particularly so in the case of constipation. If the practitioner has a full realization that Love fulfills all the laws of life—his life and the patient's life—that there are no restrictions, no burdens, no inhibitions in Love, which is the very life within, healing will follow.

If one would take time, once a day at least, to let go of all that is not true and lay hold of Reality; let go of doubt, distrust, worry, condemnation and fear, and lay hold of Life in Its expressions of beauty, truth and wholeness, his mental congestion would be healed. Keep the mind and body open to the reception of Truth. It is the static, fixed, inflexible outlook, which produces a tendency on the part of the body and its muscles and functions to become tense and underactive. Hold steadfastly to the thought that all of life is in a state of eternal flow. Relax your thought and allow the free flow of the Life Essence, in and through you, and your body will respond to Its healing activity. Inaction will quickly disappear into its native nothingness, in the rhythm and harmony of all your bodily functions.

SKIN

The skin represents a temporary, but perfect, outward cloak, forever responsive to that deep, inner calm, that place where Life is poised in Itself. There is nothing in Spirit to break through and erupt, to congest or contaminate. Within it is perfect.

ARMS AND HANDS

The arms and hands represent man's ability to grasp ideas. To uphold his convictions of the truth. To reach out and grasp Reality. To be a partaker of the Divine Benefits.

FEET AND LEGS

The feet and legs represent man's ability to walk up-rightly. To be guided into all truth. To be led by the ever-present Mind.

FALSE GROWTHS (TUMORS, CANCER, GALLSTONES)

We must think of the subjective state of our thought as our atmosphere in the Universal Mind, for we cannot separate ourselves from the Universe. There is but One Mind and we are in It. We are in It as intelligence. It accepts our thought and acts upon it. Destructive emotions, desires or ideas, unless neutralized, will grow into some bodily condition, and may produce disease. *Disease without thought could not manifest, no matter what the disease may be.* We are surrounded by a Receptive Intelligence, which receives the impress of our thought and acts upon it.

If the thought of false growths can be erased, the manifestation can be healed. Declare: "Every plant which my Heavenly Father hath not planted, shall be rooted up." The Heavenly Father is the Reality of man and is Eternal Presence and Perfection. Dissolve the idea of false growths by knowing that there is nothing for them to feed upon. Erase the belief, in your own mentality, and you will remove it from the mentality of the patient, and thereby project healing power to his body.

In treating cancers and tumors, there should be a harmonizing of the consciousness that will cleanse the blood. Declare: "Divine Love within me, removes from my consciousness every thought unlike God (Good). In my physical body there is only room for perfection, because that thought which is sustaining and nourishing my body is aware only of perfection, nothing can come into being except from the One Creative Mind, and nothing can flourish unless there is something to nourish it. Accordingly, I know that my thought does not sustain any false growth, either consciously or unconsciously originated.

"The depression, the misunderstanding, the maladjustment, the frustration which may have taken place in my life, is now eradicated. God is the One Causation back of all manifestation, and *there could not be* cause for a development of any kind contrary or superfluous to the divine order. Therefore, there cannot remain within my body *anything* which does not express perfection. God-Life, in and through me, forever cleanses, heals, and renews every organ, and every atom in my body, after the pattern of perfection."

False mental causes are removed by a freshness of thought, sustained by an affirmative outlook of faith and trust in the perfection of life. *The only accretion which takes place in the body is that produced by the activity of Perfect Principle*, and what the body cannot use is passed freely on.

We have learned that there is only One Substance, out of which everything is made . . . cabbages and kings, hands and houses, money and men . . . consequently, any wrong condition in the human body is made from exactly the same substance from which the most perfect form is created. The pure and perfect light of Spirit dissipates and dispels every discordant form, for those things which are not implanted by Divine Spirit have no law to support them.

Whether it be cancer, fibroid tumor, a wen, a cyst, or gallstones, the practitioner must know that the Spirit indwelling his patient is perfectly and completely manifested, and that every shadow of erroneous conclusion is wiped out. False growth is neither person, place nor thing; it has no life to sustain it, cannot take root in Truth; it has no vitality, no substance and no power, and cannot be fed nor nurtured by Truth.

REMOVING THE COMPLEX

Suppose someone is constantly saying: "Everything is all wrong in the world. People are wrong, things are wrong, conditions are wrong. All is sickness and unhappiness. Nothing seems worth while." You as a practitioner must not be disturbed by this complaint. It is your business to remove this complex, for these inner emotions create outer conditions, in and through the body, and are responsible for a great deal of sickness in the world.

Treatment straightens out consciousness by clear thinking. When the inner consciousness agrees with the Truth, then—and not until then—a demonstration takes place. Specifically go over the thoughts which are wrong and use the power of your word to heal them.

Medical practice takes into consideration the thoughts back of disease, and many eminent physicians probe deeply into the "complex," the "obsession," or the "defense mechanism," disclosed by the thought of the patient, which resulted in blindness, deafness, mutism, etc.

In spiritual mind healing, we recognize that cause is never material or physical. There is only One First Cause. But it is often necessary for the practitioner to diagnose the thought of his patient; in fact, this is an important point in healing. This is psycho-analysis (from psyche, or soul). Psychoanalysis is the analysis of the soul or subjective mind. Its teaching is that within the soul, or subjective mind, all the seeds of our thoughts fall, and that most of man's physical troubles are caused by some inner conflict. The conscious mind, desiring certain things which it cannot have, sends into the subjective thought opposing desires which conflict with each other and mentally tear or bind; and as they manifest in the body, they produce disease. It is claimed that seventy per cent of all diseases are the result of suppressed emotions. These emotions are not necessarily sex emotions, but may be any suppressed desires.

It is probable that when Jesus forgave the man his sins, he realized that the man had a complex of condemnation within himself. The sense of condemnation which the race holds about itself weights it down, and it must be removed. This explains why Jesus said: "Thy sins be forgiven thee." It is feeling that hurts. It has been said: "Life is a comedy to him who *thinks*, a tragedy to him who *feels*."

We recognize that everything is in Mind and that nothing moves but Mind. That Intelligence is back of everything, acting through a thought force which is concrete, definite and real. The reason people do not realize that mental healing is possible is that they do not understand the meaning of Causation, they do not realize that Intelligence is back of all things, that there is but One Fundamental Intelligence in the Universe, and that the individual is simply a point where this One Mind manifests as person. Disease must come through Mind, in order to operate through us. There is but One Subjective Mind in the Universe, and we are always thinking into It.

The practitioner talks with his patient, explains to him the Law of Mind, teaches him the way, diagnoses his thought, points out to him that certain mental attitudes produce certain physical results, teaches him how to be harmonious in his thinking, how to be at peace, how to trust and believe in the Good. In other words, the practitioner lifts him up mentally and spiritually, and supports his thought until he can stand alone.

A practitioner must be filled with the spirit of Divine Compassion. He must have a deep, underlying sense of unity and sympathy, else he will do but little good; *but he must not have sympathy with the disease.* The only guarantee of our Divinity is in its expression through our humanity. Consequently, an enlightened soul understands the meaning of sympathy and exercises it, but not morbidly.

HEART TROUBLE

The heart is the center of Divine Love and perfect circulation. Its action is harmonious, vital, adequate and complete. There is no false action and no wrong action. The pulsations of life are steady, unceasing and perfect. "Let not your heart be troubled." Love is at the center of man's being, and the calm, continuous, pulsations of life are governed by Love.

Solomon is accredited with many words of wisdom, none of which are more appropriate just here than his admonition: "Keep thy heart with all diligence, for out of it are the issues of life" (Prov. 4:23). In the days when we had no knowledge of whether the emotions should be expressed, repressed or suppressed, the reference to the heart was hardly as significant as it is today. Now, in the light of experience, there is no question but that anything that touches the sympathetic nature of man has within it the power to build up or destroy the physical body of man. The daily record of fatalities from "heart trouble," bears evidence of this. Sudden shock, terrific loss—particularly loss of love—FEAR, all kinds of fear, are some of the thoughts which quickly manifest in the body of man as "heart trouble." The remedy for this is LOVE. "Perfect love casteth out fear"; and a Divine fearlessness, a singleness of purpose, a determination to think only God-like thoughts, should be used in treating heart trouble.

Almost every case of heart trouble can be traced to thoughts of strain and inharmony; sometimes to disappointment or disagreement with a loved one; or to a feeling of loss from financial reverses. A belief that we *can* be in a position from which God absents Himself. We reiterate, a remedy for all heart trouble is LOVE. The heart is known as the center of love, which is the healing balm for every inharmonious thought. As we recognize our Oneness with Infinite Intelligence, we are set free from uncertainty and pain. As long as we realize that our heart is a living center, through which the Love of God flows to bless eternally, not only our own lives but the lives of all whom we contact—as long as we realize this, our heart cannot be troubled.

Another thought to be handled in treating any kind of heart trouble is the thought of age. The race-suggestion carries a strong belief about the unpleasant conditions which may present themselves as one "grows old." Among these, is the physical condition termed *hardening of the arteries*, which hinders the free flow of blood to the brain. A treatment must be so formulated as to recognize that there is but One Mind, consequently, no thought of depression, fear, or suggestion of imperfection can flow through It. Man is birthless, deathless, ageless Spirit; and this should be the consciousness of our work. This leaves nothing to be born, mature, decay and die. Life cannot grow old. God—in us, and through us, *as us*—can only express according to His Own Nature, which is Perfection. Therefore, the Law of our being is the Law of perfect assimilation, elimination and circulation; and it is the law of obliteration to anything unlike Itself. A knowledge of our Oneness with the God-Life all about and within us, that this life is governed by Divine Law and Harmony within us, that our only need is to cooperate mentally with this Law of Life, will heal when we recognize Its presence and activity within us.

Some physicians now claim that the action of the heart is a reflex action, and that the dilation and contraction of the heart is controlled by sympathetic nerve centers in the spine; and while they say that *will* does not control the heartbeat, *emotions do affect the heart and sudden and unexpected grief often causes instant death*. Loving thoughts for all will remove tenseness, stimulate the heart into healthy action, and send new life to every part of the body. "Blessed are the pure in heart for they shall see God."

POISON OF ANY KIND

The treatment is similar in all cases of poison. The healing must come through a recognition that the body is pure Spirit substance. There is only One Substance, One Intelligence—God, and all the organs of the body express and manifest God or perfection. The blood of the body is the objectification of the perfect life stream, forever pure and perfect, filling every blood vessel, and circulating freely and sufficiently. There is and can be no separation from God, no belief of a life apart from God (Good), no negative thought, no thought of envy, hatred, malice or selfishness can lodge in consciousness to poison the pure Life of God, flowing in and through man.

PARALYSIS

Use the thought that Life cannot become paralyzed or inactive. Life is forever present in Its fullness. Therefore, where any form of inaction appears we should endeavor to recognize and realize the presence of Life and action. The Spirit is neither inactive nor is It too active. Its action cannot be cut off or need it be added to; where the seeming inaction is we should declare for right action. As in constipation, there is a thought of restriction back of the manifestation of paralysis; often there is a very emotional nature to deal with, and often, though not always, a lot of stubbornness and resistance to heal.

Sometimes the husband or wife, having seen the other suffering from paralysis, will resent so thoroughly the bondage of the loved one, that *further power is given to the belief*, and the same condition begins to manifest in his or her body. This person must be shown that in Mind there is perfect freedom, and that in this freedom nothing can bind him, either mentally or physically, that nothing which he ever did or thought or that anyone else did or thought, can bind him, that the very Life of God is his freedom, that this Infinite Life and Action *compels* him to act out the truth about himself on the objective plane.

When Jesus healed the paralyzed man, He first made him whole in consciousness, then told him to take up his bed and walk. This is the perfect example for us to follow in the healing of any case of paralysis. The practitioner should know, without shadow of doubt, that the very power by which the paralytic took up his bed and walked—the power by which Jesus raised *His* body—is exactly the *same* power by which paralyzed legs and arms are vitalized and made whole today. A consciousness of the One Indwelling Presence must be built up, then the patient must accept this consciousness and act upon it. *Life is an idea everywhere present in Mind, and It must be accepted as present in the organs which seem paralyzed.* The following meditation is a good one to use:

"Infinite Spirit, Complete Essence of Life, is now my life. That which is animated by Perfect Spirit or Life, must express or be like that which animates it. My thought now rests in contemplation of my real self and that clarified thought makes easy the way for the operation of the Life Essence through me.

"There is no inaction or paralysis in Mind, the Mind of God. There is no inaction or paralysis in Body, the Body of God. All manifest life is some part of the Body of God. My body is some part of the Body of God; right where the inaction appears to be, there is real life and action. The free-flowing life of Spirit is now energizing every part of my being and quickening it into life and action. The Spirit has never been paralyzed nor can It be. I feel the life of the boundless action and energy of Spirit flowing through me. I am free.

"The perfect co-ordination and functioning of the parts of my body, in their inter-related action, is in perfect rhythm and harmony. I am conscious of this perfection . . . this beauty, this perfect action . . . first, in my thought, then I recognize it in my body as the thought becomes the thing. I no longer entertain the thought of bondage. I am no longer influenced by the belief that there is, or can be, any life or action apart from God. I do not struggle. I feel my freedom flow from within me. It is complete, perfect and flowing now. I am thrilled with the Almighty force of the Universe as it courses through every part of me. It quickens every part of me into a newness of life and action. I am the power of God within me, making the physical man perfect. *I am free.*

"I know that there flows through me now the Perfect Life Essence. My body is the abiding place of this Life. The very stuff of which my body is formed is an Eternal and Perfect Substance. My body reflects the perfect motion, the rhythmic ease of Mind in action. Perfect Life is mine."

Asthma and Hay Fever

Many medical men believe that "nervous persons, and those whose work is largely mental, are most often attacked by hay fever, and that hay fever attacks only those who are predisposed to it." The general acceptance is that it is the result of an undue sensitiveness of the nostrils to the pollen of certain flowers or plants, or even the hairs of certain animals.

We should know that the claim of hay fever has no power over us, that we are inspired and directed by Infinite Mind, and that perfect discrimination and judgment are established in us. In treating oneself, declare that every day you are capable of expressing the greater possibilities which are your divine inheritance; that you are busy expressing good and have no time for any fear thoughts of asthma and hay fever.

Know that you alone are the door-keeper to the "Temple of the Holy Ghost," your body. You have the power to say what shall enter there. No false thing can enter there while you are recognizing your Oneness with Infinite Life. The pollen which you have thought irritated you is made from the very same Substance from which you are made. You are sending out only thoughts of peace, love and joy, and no irritating thought or thing can come back to annoy or obstruct the perfect functioning of every organ of your body. The passages of your mind are open only to the inflow and the outflow of good. You are sensitive only to good, dwelling in the higher altitudes of consciousness, understanding Life in Its spiritual purpose, experiencing exhilaration, vitalization, and exaltation.

It is written that the breath of God animates creation, with the living presence of a pure divinity. What breath are we breathing other than this true breath, unrestricted, flowing through channels of pure receptivity, from the Infinite Intelligence and the perfect Life of God? Let your thought dwell, not on breath nor lack of breath, *but on that which breathes*. Sense the freedom of this God-Life, flowing in and through you. You did not create the Original Substance out of which your body was formed. God Himself made your body, to be used as His Self-Expression. This channel must be perfect. With good-natured flexibility, free your thought from any sense of anxiety or strain, or indecision, or deep-seated worry and concern, knowing that you have only to keep your thought steady and clear, fixed upon the potential perfection of the Universe in which we live. When you have lifted your consciousness in this manner, use this meditation:

"My entire body is now a receptive channel for the operation of God-Life. My thought is pure, relaxed and peaceful. My breathing is not obstructed (asthma); my thought is not sensitive to any discordant or disagreeable sentiment (hay fever), as *Mind could not entertain a disagreeable sentiment*. I breathe in the eternal Life Essence. By this breath I am purified and made strong. I am freed from the belief in anything unlike Perfection."

NERVE TROUBLES

As we come to realize that thoughts are things we shall also see that different kinds of thoughts will produce different types of effects. There is but one final Truth or Reality, but It is always presenting us with varying forms of Itself. These forms are temporarily misshapen by the creative power of our own thought. For we must not forget that what we call *our thought* is really the place where we are using Creative Mind Itself. Our thought is creative, not because we will it so, but BECAUSE IT ALREADY IS SO. WE CANNOT CHANGE THIS NOR ESCAPE FROM ITS EFFECTS IN OUR LIVES.

Consequently we see that certain thoughts would depress while others would exalt. And all according to the One Law governing our lives. With this in mind, then, we understand what is meant by saying that certain thoughts should be used in treating certain cases.

Let us consider what kind of thought to use in treating nerve troubles. We do not deny that people suffer from this or any other cause. We do, however, affirm that thought may help and has the possibility of completely healing them from the trouble. The nerves certainly represent the highest form of intelligence running through the flesh. They really represent mind in the highest form it takes as it controls the human body.

The general treatment for nerve disorders should incorporate thoughts of peace, poise and power. There is no strain or struggle in the Universe. All the actions of Life are harmonious, steady, sure and quiet. Because the nerves are so responsive to thought, they react immediately to a statement of harmony. An understanding of the truth that good alone is real and true, gives us the faith essential to an establishment of a firm, unwavering mind, which is necessary if one is to have firm, steady, sensitive, quickly-responding nerves. Our thought must never waver from the premise of One Power, which is an impersonal, infinite Power for good.

We train our mind to contemplate the good, the enduring, the true. That which has caused depression, discouragement or indecision, must be neutralized by our refusal to allow it to register. Realize that the Spirit within you manifests as perfect harmony, and that every cell, atom and organ of your body is functioning according to the Divine Law. Say: "I am filled with the peace, strength, power and decision of Spirit. The life forces flow freely, peacefully, and harmoniously through every atom of my body, I am complete and perfect now. The all-powerful Mind of the Indwelling Christ in me dissolves and dissipates from my mind all belief in indecision, anxiety, depression and discouragement, for I dwell in the realm of peace."

We must heal ourselves from worry. This tension is relaxed as we gain confidence in good, in truth and in beauty. Faith must overcome fear, and strong statements of faith should be used to erase the thoughts of doubt and worry that have assailed us. "I have faith. I am faith. I abide in faith. All doubt and fear have left me. I understand why it is that I can remain in faith. I have complete confidence. I do not waver nor falter in my faith, for I know that God, the Living Spirit, is the only Presence there is or ever can be."

We should also erase the thoughts of yesterday that would rob us of today's happiness. "There is nothing arising out of the past that can disturb me. The past, the present and the future are one unbroken stream of Good. I loose all thoughts that in the past have caused anxiety. The Spirit knows no past and is not affected by the belief in any. The past is swallowed up in the victory of a perfect present, which is filled with love and protection."

Equally we must not have fear for the future. "I see that the future is bright with promise. It beckons me forward into a more complete realization of my own worth and my rightful place in the Universe. All my tomorrows will be happy and filled with harmonious occupations. I look to the future with great and pleasurable anticipation, knowing it will expand my opportunity for radiant self-expression. I love my past and my future and understand that they are but continuations of the one unbroken chain of life. There is no future to be afraid of and no past to bring discord into the present."

Such statements will tend to erase any negative stream of causation that may have been set in motion in the past. Waste no time arguing with anyone over these truths. This is true and it really works. We would better spend our time using the Law than arguing over It. Our position is to be proven by DEMONSTRATION ALONE. THIS IS THE FINAL TEST OF ALL THEORIES.

We should read, study, think and meditate upon those statements which tend to calm, to give poise and confidence, and erase all thought of fear and tension. The subjective law can only operate upon that which is given it, so we must be very careful of our patterns of thought. We live in a sea of Perfect Life and we should take time to understand and sense this in our imagination. We should think of ourselves as being surrounded by perfect life and poised in an eternal calm. We are in a sea of untroubled waters of life, from which we may freely drink. *We must do the drinking.* No one else can do this for us. We should hold out the cup of acceptance until it is filled and overflowing with the manifestations of our desires. This chalice of the heart is held up that the heavenly flow may fill it with God's abundant life.

The words of peace spoken to the nervous system will remove the tension which produces pain and inflammation of the nerves. There is neither irritation, agitation nor inflammation in God, in Spirit, in Truth, and man is the Truth. "Peace I leave with you, my peace I give unto you. . . . Let not your heart be troubled, neither let it be afraid." "I am pure Spirit. My entire nervous system is pure Spirit. I am poised in harmony, in Truth and in complete calm. My nervous system is in the Spirit within me, governing my physical body with harmony. There is no need for pain. My body is pure Spiritual Substance and as such it is perfect and harmonious."

We are poised in a sense of peace, which comes from our complete faith in God as the light, power and inspiration of our life. There will be no twitching of muscles, no uneasiness or anxiety about any outcome, if we know—whether waking or sleeping—that every step of the way God goes with us.

Blood Troubles and Skin Diseases (High Blood Pressure, Hardening of the Arteries, Eczema, Boils)

The blood stream represents the circulation of pure thought, direct from a Divine Source. The metabolism represents the intelligence within man which knows what to use, and what to cast out. This blood stream represents the spiritual flow of life, pure and perfect. The Spirit is never anaemic. We believe that the basic cause for all anaemia is a lack of the consciousness of love, and the flow of life as represented by the out-push of Spirit in joyous self-recognition. There is neither high pressure nor low pressure in this flow, since the pressure is always equalized by spiritual perfection. There is no sensitiveness, no strain, no inaction or overaction, no false action and no inadequate action. Action, being spiritual, is always perfect. This stream of life is renewed daily. It is not material, but spiritual. The blood stream is continuously renewed as it converts the idea of Spiritual Substance into material benefits. Love, harmony and peace reign supreme.

The arteries convey this blood stream, and neither harden nor soften. They are always flexible, always perfect. There is no tension nor super-tension, but always a calm flow of life forever invigorating, forever renewing, forever revitalizing, carrying to every part of the body and distributing in every part of the body, pure spiritual substance, instantly and permanently perfect. There is no inner agitation and no outward irritation.

Those of us who suffer from blood troubles and skin diseases have not proven for ourselves the promise: "Ye shall know the truth, and the truth shall make you free." Many skin diseases and blood disorders can be traced to a break in the rhythmic harmony of life. When the body is the harmonious temple of the Living God, Spirit, divine order reigns throughout. Boils, eczema, and other skin irritations, should be treated by recognizing that the blood is manifesting as pure Substance.

If one has been irritated mentally, and has not been able to adjust himself to the undesirable cause of the irritation, it is but natural that it should manifest objectively sooner or later. On the other hand, one may be unaware of the cause, it being so deeply covered in his subjective that it has not come to his outer consciousness. Criticism and inability to live with people—to adjust oneself to the many—bring about many disorders. A deep-seated resentment against persons or conditions will surely manifest itself in some disagreeable physical reaction.

The first step toward healing is one of honest self-analysis. What has been our habitual feeling toward persons around us? Have we really tried to let them live as they see fit, while claiming the same feeling for ourselves? A good treatment for this would be:

"There is no irritation, frustration, or resentment in my life. Any sense of inner agitation is now wiped away, and in its place there comes a warm sense of my oneness in essence and experience with all the good there is. The center of my being is Understanding and Intelligence. I am calm, poised and at peace with the world."

Hardening of the arteries should be treated by thoughts of love. A knowledge that body is controlled by mind and need not grow old will help eliminate *the fear* of this condition, which race-suggestion says comes to many people with what is called "old age." Treat to know that Love is stronger than any other force in the Universe, and that steadily and rhythmically the Life of God is pulsing through your body. Persistently know the truth that God's Life flows ceaselessly out through your life and back to Him, where it is renewed, purified and refreshed; and that the pulsing power of Divine Love propels it.

Suppose someone comes to you who has high blood pressure. You wish to treat to remove this sense. Your work will be recognized as effective if, after you have done your work, he can be examined and his blood pressure is found to be normal.

Take the idea of high blood pressure, or nervous pressure and all that goes with it, and transpose it for the spiritual sense that there is a divine circulation, it is the Spirit that is circulating through this person. There is nothing to inhibit It, there is nothing to accelerate It; It is always perfect circulation, there is no thought of fear or congestion. Undoubtedly the condition exists, as an experience, but as a mental practitioner, you are not dealing with objective symptoms but with thought alone.

If the circulatory system seems inadequate, then the practitioner should realize that his patient's circulation is equalized in Spirit, that Divine Life and Energy flow freely to every part of his being, cleansing, revitalizing, and restoring him to complete wholeness. There is one circulation, which is the Spirit flowing through man. There are no degenerative processes in the Spirit.

You sense this person as being Divine, the Spirit indwells him. There is no man outside of God. The more convinced a practitioner is of this, the more certain he is that there now is a divine and uninhibited circulation, and that the blood pressure is normal in the experience of the one whom he is treating—the more definite will be the results.

In every case, the mental practitioner proceeds on the assumption that *Spirit is already in his patient*. He thinks of Spirit back of the fact: the Spirit of perfect circulation, uninhibited—*that thing which must automatically eliminate everything that does not belong to that person*. Nothing can impoverish that flow; nothing can increase or diminish that pressure.

For any irregularities of the blood, the following simple meditation might be used:

"My existence is a harmonious progression, that of a son of God entering fully into conscious sonship. My career through life is a joyous, happy expression, a daily expansion into realms of life and living. My life in God is ageless, deathless, abiding. I now surrender every personal doubt, fear or hard feeling that would retard the perfect flow of life through me. There is no obstruction, no barrier in my mind, veins or affairs. I am harmonious, peaceful, free and unafraid."

Fevers

In mind healing the underlying thought in the treatment for fever is Peace. Any thought which tends to inspire, to comfort and to give peace to the mind is good. Through our knowledge of the kingdom within, we are able to claim our power and dominion.

A general treatment like the following will be found effective in allaying fever:

"At all times, I am aware of my immediate Oneness with God; and the glory of my thought makes me immune to negative experiences, even to negative suggestions. I desert fear and turn resolutely and joyously to faith, and swiftly into my experience comes the desired good. I give thanks that I am Divine and that I know my Divinity. A sacred refuge is this inner place where my thought contacts and consciously becomes one with the Indwelling Al mighty."

Obstetrics

In a treatment for child-birth, we realize that the great Law of Creation is operative. We know that no idea of God ever comes too soon or too late, but always at the correct time. We know that right action prevails.

If you are working for yourself, realize that your part is merely to accept fully the fact that the Creative Law within you *knows*; and not only knows, *but performs* every right action at the right time; that It synchronizes all impulses toward the event. It is Its nature to do so. It could not do otherwise. Let your mind dwell on the wonder of this *knowing* Intelligence, which works out the scheme of a new body, imbuing it with Its own laws of health and action, setting up the perfect working of the various systems of the body: the breathing, the circulation, the elimination, and so on. Realize that Perfection is at work, forming and projecting into the objective world that upon which Its action has been centered; that there can be no obstruction to right action on any plane of expression.

Your meditation at the moment might be:

"I am unified with Universal Law, creating, delivering, perfecting. I rest in Mind, rejoicing that I have only to accept the perfect results of this natural law. I give myself completely to this perfect Law, and am at peace. I am serene, because I know that I am in the care of Perfection in action."

Colds, Influenza and Grippe

Those who calmly announce that they are "very susceptible to changes in the weather," have accepted whole-heartedly the mental impression that the weather is a determining factor in whether or not they experience "colds." The trouble is not with the weather but in their thinking; they have not freed their consciousness from the old training that a "draft may produce pneumonia." This belief causes one to be afraid and confused. *Mental conflicts also cause confusion*, and *confusion may cause colds*. So the first step is to erase from the conscious mind all fear of drafts.

Colds have no part in your life, as the very life of God flows freely through you. Every breath you breathe bespeaks your eternal alliance with Life. We should be willing to declare our disbelief in colds and help free ourselves and others from the depleting habit of "bad colds."

A conviction that the God within sustains us now and at all times, in perfect health, will bring peace. And we should eliminate from mind the duration, symptoms, and frequency of colds, thereby removing a pattern which we no longer wish to use. We should consciously harmonize ourselves with everything and everyone about us—with people, the weather, with God and spiritual perfection.

In colds, congestion, influenza and grippe, the thought to heal is confusion. There should be a consciousness of poise, a recognition of peace; when this comes into the individual's experience, he will have fewer colds. More colds result from damp spirits than from wet feet. When we fear and resist the weather, we chill, not from the winds and rain, but from our own coldness of heart. We should claim our dominion and power in Spirit. Spirit is not subject to heat or cold.

Obesity

A normally-minded person will eat normally. If one is a glutton, it is because his mentality is filled with unexpressed longings, which he is trying to sublimate. Food is a symbol of God's love, care, and substance, and should be eaten with thanksgiving. It is a mistake to believe that either fasting or feasting can have any salutary effect in the development of the intellectual or spiritual faculties. Food does not harm man, but we dishonor God when we fear it. But there is a difference between feeding your hunger and your appetite. *It is just as disastrous to abuse God's gift by becoming gluttonous, as it is to dishonor the spiritual man by fearing food!*

To mentally free yourself from avoirdupois, declare that you are an offspring of God, that you are Spirit, that both your appetite and the assimilation of your foods are functioning in divine order, and that your body is manifesting symmetry and perfection.

TREATING KIDNEY, BLADDER AND LIVER DISTURBANCES

Mental agencies which contribute to the production of all kinds of kidney trouble are worry, anxiety, fear, and criticism. Acute attacks of nephritis, followed by death, have been caused by sudden shock and grief. The conscious knowledge that in Divine Mind we are known only as *perfection* so uplifts the thought that every mental and emotional reaction to circumstances and conditions is improved.

Diabetes:

"Since the life of God is pure and complete, and since the Life of God within me is mighty to heal, then I know that this thing which calls itself by the name of diabetes is neither person, place nor thing. I cannot be compelled to suffer from or by it. It cannot operate through me, nor be believed in by me. Whatever my blood stream needs or ought to have, it does have right now, for God is all, in all, over all, and through all, and the God Substance of my body makes me free from all claim to diabetes.

"My kidneys perform their natural function and are adjusted to their natural and spiritual perfection and operation. They are perfect because they are spiritual ideas and all that God conceived is now perfect. There is no discouragement and no condemnation operating through me. My life within me is perfect and harmonious right now and will continue to remain perfect and harmonious. I am now healed and made glad. My blood stream is pure, perfect and spiritual. I sense this, know it and understand it.

"My system, which is spiritual and perfect, contains within itself, every chemical requirement. Spirit cannot make a mistake, cannot withhold from my system anything that the system needs. There is perfect elimination and I abandon myself to the life giving force of pure Spirit."

Bladder trouble: In treating bladder trouble it is well to calm the thought. To remove any sense of inner irritation or agitation will always be of great value in removing this particular trouble. Again we should remind ourselves that there can be no real specific treatment for any particular trouble, but there is a certain way of approaching different troubles with good possibility of success. To follow the leadings of our own thought in all cases, is right, but to pay particular attention to the *specific idea* which causes the patient to suffer, is always a correct method for practice.

Purity and strength, with perfect elimination, free from any sense of condemnation, is a good central thought to work on. Remember that thoughts are things and therefore different kinds of thought give rise to different types of manifestation.

"There is no irritation, agitation or inflammation in Spirit and man is pure Spirit right now. There is perfect and divine order in every organ and function of the body. There is a discerning Intelligence which separates the false from the true. No waste substance is allowed to remain in the system. The joyous, free flow of Life and Spirit is now active through me, cleansing my mind and body from all impurities, in thought, or of the flesh. There is no worry, irritation or agitation. I am sustained in a deep inner calm. Spirit flows through me and is never obstructed by anything unlike Itself. There is no overaction, no inaction, nor is there any wrong action of Spirit within me. Its action is complete, harmonious and perfect. Everything that does not belong to Pure Spirit is washed away."

In this treatment the intention is that as a result of the statement, the bladder will be restored to its natural, perfect state.

Thoughts of greed, selfishness and jealousy cause congestion in various functions of the body, especially the kidneys. The work of the kidneys is to eliminate the poisons of the body, but when our minds are filled with thoughts of anger, hatred and resentment, we are pouring into our body *poisons in the making*. Too much of this makes a burden the kidneys are unable to carry and the upbuilding of body tissues is disturbed. But degenerative thoughts can be turned into creative, energizing, vitalizing ones. Anger can be turned into love, and the very power that has been destroying can be made to build up, not only the kidneys, but the entire body.

The *liver*, the great laboratory of the body, which abstracts certain materials from the blood, and converts them into new substances which can be used by the body for upbuilding, or eliminated when its work is done, functioning as it does with other digestive organs is an important factor in maintaining the orderly balance of the body.

When disturbances arise in the liver, it is important to erase every unpleasant experience from the memory; every hard, tense thought from the mind. Just as the liver can convert certain substances into building material for the body, so the mind—filled with the knowledge that there is but One Divine, Powerful, Vital Essence—can change inharmonious thoughts into ideas that heal, cleanse and uplift.

TREATING STOMACH AND BOWEL TROUBLES

No organ in the body is more quickly upset by a disturbed mental condition than is the stomach. Frequently people, not even familiar with the manner in which thought controls the body, are heard to remark that a certain experience has "upset my stomach."

Even those who do not habitually say grace before meals would do well to lift thought in thanksgiving—putting aside all thought of worry, distrust, and anxiety—and thereby insure a wonderful digestant, a perfect aid to assimilation.

Sometimes a constant conflict in the emotional nature because of hurt feelings will become such an irritation that it manifests as hemorrhage or stomach ulcer. Also, a deep-seated sense of discouragement and disappointment will objectify in a disturbed condition of the stomach and bowels. (Constipation is treated under a separate head.) A patient may need to be shown that super-sensitiveness is nothing more or less than an expression of selfishness, the presence of which may be unknown to him.

The very best mental remedy for stomach trouble is love and joy. Say to yourself: "The glory of my thought makes me immune to negative experiences, even to negative suggestions. The very life of God vitalizes my every organ and tissue. I now have perfect and complete faith in God as my ever-present Good. My faith fills me and elates my entire being. As my thought relaxes, all the muscles of my body relax, the Life Spirit flows through me, and my body responds perfectly to Its healing activity, and every function of my body is now brought into perfect action. The Infinite Life which is within me is now healing me, making me whole, after the pattern of an Infinite and Eternal Perfection."

Treating Insomnia

Insomnia is the result of a disturbed mental condition, either conscious or subconscious. Sometimes this arises from shock, grief, or anxiety, though often it is merely an inability to let go of the affairs of the day. Perfect trust in God within is the secret of relaxation, rest and renewal. The following is one treatment for insomnia:

"The Spirit within me is in perfect rest. The center of my being is quiet and poised. I let my inner spirit fill my whole being with peace and stillness. With this word, I now relax in body and mind. I let the Divine Tranquillity fill me.

"My mind now releases all sense of burden or strain. Nothing can hurt or disturb my spiritual self. I am free and safe. All plans and ideas can wait until later. The Divine Wisdom works through me and I am protected from mistakes. My mind is quiet, calm, and deeply still. All tension is released and the great inner peace flows out through every nerve. My body rests in the still silence of the Spirit. I bless my body and my mind, for they are good and worthy of my love.

"The great blessing of the Spirit pours through me now and protects me in all my ways. My good is around and with me so that I am secure and safe. The loving presence of Spirit is with me now and forever, so that I am divinely protected. I let go of all problems and know that Spirit is with me. The great quietness and calm of the Universal Love is within me. I am richly blessed.

"Rest permeates my mind and body with its healing presence. I do not try to make anything happen, I accept restful sleep. Restfulness pervades my room and my bed. I let the Spirit take care of the Universe and my affairs, while I release all responsibility and sleep. The all-powerful Mind of the Indwelling Christ within me dissolves all sense of wakefulness and I am at peace."

DEAFNESS

We are reminded of the words of Isaiah: "The Lord Jehovah hath opened thine ear." The ear is the physical representation of a receptive capacity of mind. An attitude of quietness and confidence, a listening attitude of: "Speak, Lord, for thy servant heareth," will open the way for the voice of Spirit to speak to the inner ear. We can so train our ears to listen to the Divine Harmony within, that we shall reproduce Its melody, rhythm and beauty in all our ways.

Hearing is a divine idea in Mind, and all divine ideas are perfect. Ideas have a service to render to the Spirit of man, and as long as man expects and accepts whole-heartedly that service, and co-operates consciously and subjectively with it, there is nothing to oppose the functioning of the physical instruments through which ideas operate.

Treat to know that your hearing is perfect, that it is God hearing through you. There is no belief in inaction that in any way can hinder this hearing, for every idea of the body is now complete and perfect and functions according to Divine Law. Be open and receptive to the Truth. Let the inner ear listen to the voice of Truth that is always speaking. Say: "I perfectly hear the voice of Good. My ears are open to the Divine Harmony. The inner ear and the outer ear are both open and receptive to the vibration of perfect harmony."

WEATHER CONDITIONS

Pure Spirit is not and cannot be governed by any weather conditions whatsoever. All weather is a manifestation of Spirit, a flowering of the Divine in sunshine, in shade, in rain and in clouds. Say:

"I am in complete unity with all. I am in complete agreement with all, and I enjoy all. There is no congestion in the weather and none in me. There is no confusion about the weather in my thought. I have no fear of any kind of weather since I know that I am at one with all. I love the clouds, the rain and the sunshine. I am one with heat and with cold. I am unified with humidity, with dryness of atmosphere, and with sunshine and shadow.

"Every atom of my body responds to this understanding that changes in weather conditions are but variations of the One Life, but different manifestations of the One God appearing to me in many forms. Each and every one of the forms I love and feel my unity with. I love the heat of the desert and the dampness of the ocean. I feel physically complete and harmonious in every climate. I do not condemn any kind of weather for all are part of myself. I am one with all. I love all and I feel comfortable in all.

"Every belief that I may ever have had that says I am afraid of weather conditions, is now vanished from my thought forever. It is no more and therefore can no longer operate. I know and feel my freedom. In this freedom I rejoice."

Thoughts about Food

Food must be a spiritual idea. It must be an idea of substance and supply. Since the food which we take into the system is fundamentally one with the body which receives it, there is no reason in Spirit why our food should harm us. We cannot expect to overeat or to eat the wrong things and have them agree with us. But there is an intelligence within us which will guide us into a proper diet. Since each is an individual, the intaking of food is an individual idea and an individual approach to Reality. Whatever our individual physical system needs to make it harmonious, Intelligence will guide us to. But we cannot expect to have our food agree with us if we are constantly condemning it.

"My food agrees with me and I agree with it. There is no condemnation in me or working through me. I understand that food is a spiritual idea of Substance and I am now in complete agreement with this idea. Everything that I eat is perfectly assimilated and perfectly eliminated. I have no trouble digesting my food, for digestion is also a spiritual idea and works in perfect harmony with all that I take into my system. My system is spiritual and harmonious with every idea that passes through it. My food is spiritual and harmonious with my system. Substance and supply for the physical body are both spiritual and cannot create any inner disturbance whatsoever."

Rheumatism

There is no bondage in the Spirit and we should endeavor to realize that the Spirit frees us from every type of bondage. As perfect love casts out all fear and frees us from the bondage of stubbornness and unbelief we should be freed from the outward picturing and manifestation of the pain and congestion which appear as rheumatism. Why should the system secrete impurities or why should there be any acidity if we are governed by Divine Intelligence as to what we should eat and by Divine Law as to how we should eliminate what does not belong to the system? It is well to remind ourselves that the system is spiritual and divinely ordained. God does not make mistakes and our muscles and joints do not need to store up waste matter which causes pain and physical distress.

To be washed clean by the Spirit should have a real meaning to us and the practitioner should believe that there is such a baptism of Spirit as this. If anyone should criticize him for such a belief he would be a poor worker in this field who ever knew that such condemnation had taken place. Of course we must expect to contradict human experience if we wish to transcend it, how else could Jesus have told the blind man to look up—He said up and not down. The worker in the field of spiritual thought must not be afraid to mentally attack any physical condition with the full assurance that he is dealing with the power that first created and as easily recreates. He does this by knowing that it is done.

Do not hesitate to know that you can heal; you can if you know that you can and not until then. Bondage and freedom are but the two possibilities of our use of the Law. Let us affirm freedom, not bondage.

"My entire system is spiritual and my physical being is now quickened into life and truth. It is cleansed and purified by the power of the word of God within me. This word which I speak is the presence, the power and the Law of God working through me.

"The energy of the pure and perfect Spirit is now cleansing me from all impurities of the flesh. My elimination is perfect. The joy of the Lord God is within and around me. I live in the sunshine of eternal truth and beauty. I love and understand life. My faith in the healing and the cleansing power of my word is complete. This word penetrates the marrow and bone of my physical being and eliminates all waste substances. My food digests perfectly. I have perfect and complete circulation of love, truth and beauty through my entire system. Love and life permeate every atom of my being. I am washed, cleansed within. I forgive all and am forgiven of all and by all. Nothing remains in my being but love. There is no pain or distress in the joints or in the muscles. My body is the body of God, the Living Spirit Almighty."

Now take the time to realize the truth of the foregoing statements. It is not so much what you say but the mental attitude you have when you say it that counts. Believe and you will be made whole, is the key thought. Perfect God, perfect man and perfect being. Conform all statements to this proposition.

HEALING INTEMPERANCE

"The Spirit within me does not long for anything. It is free, safe, and satisfied. There is no sense of insecurity or of inferiority. I am not seeking to avoid anything. I am conscious of my ability to meet every situation. There is neither depression nor discouragement in my mental outlook on life. I do not look to anything outside myself to give me pleasure, comfort or certainty. I do not long for anything and I am not afraid of anything. My whole inner being is conscious of its unity with God, of its oneness with Spirit. There is no pleasure in intemperance, nor can it offer any suggestion of happiness to me. I now see this habit for exactly what it is, an illusion, which seeks to force me to believe that there is some power outside myself which can give me either pleasure or pain. I do not anticipate such pleasure, nor is there any suggestive power in this habit which can cause me to believe that it has ever, under any circumstances whatsoever, given me pleasure. I am forever free from this thought, and from its effects. I do not will myself free from this habit, rather I perceive this habit is neither person, place nor thing. Having no law to operate, it cannot function. Having no intelligence of its own, it cannot suggest. Having no mind, it cannot will. I am now forever free from the mistaken belief that it was ever a thing of itself. I see it as forever separated from my real self, forever divorced from my imagination, thought and conviction. I am free now."

The practitioner must realize that the words he uses are the Law unto that thing whereto they are spoken. He must have a calm, unfaltering trust in his ability to reveal the real man, and in so doing, to free the physical man from the false belief. "The words that I have spoken unto you are Spirit, and are life." The practitioner must know that the false desire is exactly nothing, that it has no power over anyone, that his patient is pure Spirit and is wholly satisfied within himself. As a result of such statements there should come to the practitioner's mind a conviction that the appetite from which he is freeing his patient is entirely dissipated, that is, it ceases to be. It is not. It never existed in Spirit and can no longer appear to exist in or operate through the one whom he is healing.

SUPPLY

God is Spirit. Spirit is Substance and Substance is supply. This is the keynote to a realization of the more abundant life, to the demonstration of success in financial matters. It is right that we should be successful, for otherwise the Spirit is not expressed. The Divine cannot lack for anything, and we should not lack for anything that makes life worth while here on earth.

Everything that we do should be a success and we should be led to do those things which are constructive and worth while. To bring a realization of the Presence of the Spirit into all our acts is to prove that God is all—even in the slightest things which we undertake. Nothing is great and nothing is small to the Divine, so we should never wonder if what we are going to do will be hard or easy. God knows no hard and no easy.

A treatment after this manner should prove the law of abundance in the life of those who use such statements, and *believe in them:*

"I am surrounded by pure Spirit, by God, the Living Spirit. My thought is God thought, and it is the law unto that thing where unto it is spoken. Everything that I do shall be a success. I am led, guided and inspired by the Living Spirit of Love and of right action. I am compelled to move in the right direction and to always know what to do, *where*, and *how* to do it.

"I am surrounded by right action. I am filled with the consciousness of right action. Right action is success in all that I undertake to do. I am successful in all my undertakings, and I am compensated for all my efforts. I am surrounded by Substance, which is always taking the form of supply and always manifesting Itself to me in the form of whatever my need may be at the time.

"I always have an abundance of money and an abundance of whatever it takes to make life happy and opulent. There is a continuous movement toward me of supply, of money, of all that I need to express the fullest life, happiness and action.

"I have an inner understanding of my place in the Universe. I know that it is unique. The Divine has not incarnated in anyone else in just the same individual way that It has in me. I am unique and forever individualized. Therefore, I do not need to imitate anyone or to long for the good that belongs to another. All good is now mine and is now manifest in my experience. I do not compete with anyone, for I am and remain forever myself. This self is united with all selves, but is always an individual and a unique self.

"There is that in me which all people recognize as worth while and desirable, and everyone whom I meet loves this self of mine and recognizes its worth. I draw all toward me and those whom I can benefit and those who can benefit me are irresistibly drawn toward me. I do not strain, will or coerce. I know. The Truth makes me free from the fear of poverty or bondage, and emancipates me from the thought of limitation. I see that money, like everything else that is desirable, must be a spiritual idea, and I know that I have this idea right in my mind at this moment, I shall always have this idea of abundance. It is mine and I take it.

"The opportunity for self-expression and compensation is always open to me and I am at all times compelled to know, accept and operate upon this opportunity. I have abundance because I am abundance. 'All that the Father hath is mine.'"

A TREATMENT FOR PEACE OF MIND

We cannot be in peace until we know that the Spirit is the only cause, medium and effect in our lives. There is no past, present and future to It. Evil has no history and has never entered in to the being or the experience of Reality. The mind must come to know and to realize all these truths if it is to have real and lasting peace. A treatment such as this will be of great service in acquainting the mind with the truth of its being:

"Be still and know that I am God. I am the Christ, the Son of the Living God within me. I am the Principle of Peace within me. I am the manifestation of Love within me. My mind is poised in peace and beauty. All sense of fear or doubt is gone. I rest in calm trust and rely on the Law of Spirit to bring good into my experience.

"I contend with none, argue with none, and am filled with wonderful peace and light. There is no uncertainty about my future and no fear as a result of my past. I live in an eternal Now which is filled with good alone. Goodness and beauty follow me. Peace and joy accompany me. Happiness and wholeness fill my entire being with the realization of love and perfection.

"I am the Christ, the Son of the Living God within me. This inner mind of mine is now Divine and complete. It has no worries and no fears. It is whole, complete and satisfied. I look back over all previous experience and find that it was good, very good. I look toward the future and find that it is good, and very good. I look at the present and find that it is also good, and very good. God is in all, over all, and through all.

"I am the Christ, the Son of the Living God within me. I am the spirit of confidence. I am poised in love and reason. I am the perfect law of truth and the complete presence of beauty. . . . I am Christ, the Son of the Living God within me."

CHAPTER SIXTEEN
THE PRINCIPLES
OF SUCCESSFUL LIVING

Not Something for Nothing • *The Law Is Infinite* • *Demonstrating the Law* • *Spirit and Mental Law* • *Success and Happiness.*

NOT SOMETHING FOR NOTHING

Lessons on *prosperity* and mental control of conditions are sometimes dangerous because of the misunderstanding of this subject. Science of Mind is not a "get-rich-quick" scheme, neither does it promise something for nothing. It does, however, promise the one who will comply with its teachings that he shall be able to bring greater possibilities and happier conditions into his experience.

We do not teach that you can get what you want. If we *could* all get what we want, it might be disastrous, for it is certain that most of us would want things that would interfere with the well-being of someone else.

While we could not expect to demonstrate that which is contrary to the nature of our own existence, we not only believe but we know that it is entirely possible, through mental treatment— through right thought and belief—to greatly influence our environment, its reaction to us, the situations we meet and the conditions we contact. There is such a thing as demonstrating a control of conditions. We shall be able to prove this in such degree as we are successful in looking away from the conditions which now exist, while accepting better ones. Not only must we accept this intellectually, but our acceptance must become a subjective embodiment of which the intellect furnishes but a mental picture.

Consequently, this Science does not promise something for nothing. It does, however, tell us that if we comply with the Law, the Law complies with us. No man can demonstrate peace and cling to unhappiness. He can demonstrate resignation, and *call* it peace, but it will not be peace. No man can jump into the water and remain dry. This is contrary to law and to reason. NO PERSON WHOSE ENTIRE TIME IS SPENT IN THE CONTEMPLATION OF LIMITATION CAN DEMONSTRATE FREEDOM FROM SUCH LIMITATION! The Law Itself must be willing to give, because in so giving Life is Self-Expressed.

THE LAW IS INFINITE

The Science of Mind is based entirely upon the supposition that we are surrounded by a Universal Mind, into which we think. This Mind, in Its original state, fills all space. It fills the space that man uses in the Universe. It is *in* man, as well as outside him. As he thinks into this Universal Mind, he sets a law in motion, which is creative, and which contains within Itself a Limitless possibility.

The Law through which man operates is Infinite, but man appears to be finite; that is, he has not yet evolved to a complete understanding of himself. He is unfolding from a Limitless Potential but can bring into his experience only that which he can conceive. There is no limit to the Law, but there appears to be a limit to man's understanding of It. As his understanding unfolds, his possibilities of attainment will increase.

It is a great mistake to say: "Take what you wish, for you can have anything you like." We do not take what we *wish*, but we do attract to ourselves that which is like our thought. MAN MUST BECOME MORE IF HE WISHES TO DRAW A GREATER GOOD INTO HIS LIFE. We need not labor under the delusion that all we have to do is to say that everything is ours. This is true in Reality, but in fact it is only as true as we make it. We provide the mold for the Creative Law, and unless the mold we provide is increased, Substance cannot increase in our experience; for Mental Science does not promise anything that will do away with the necessity of complying with law.

The Law is a law of liberty, but not a law of license. It is exact and exacting, and unless we are willing to comply with Its Nature and work with It, along the lines of Its inherent being, we shall receive no great benefit. EVERY MAN MUST PAY THE PRICE FOR THAT WHICH HE RECEIVES AND THAT PRICE IS PAID IN MENTAL AND SPIRITUAL COIN.

All nature conspires to produce and manifest the freedom of the individual, that it may unloose its own energy. We may be sure God is for us—whatever our conception of God may be, whatever our conception of the relationship of Jesus, and the idea of Christ to humanity and God and our own salvation may be—this thing must act in accordance with definite Law in the Universe, and this Law says that whenever and whereever there is an adequate subjective image, which does not contradict the nature of the Universe, that image will not only *tend* to take form, but *will* take form and will manifest. This Law we did not make and we cannot change.

But this teaching should not be confused with the idea that we can show people how to get what they want, regardless. True prayer must be, "Thy will be done," but the implication relative to the *Will of God* in this prayer is not a submission to the inevitability of evil or limitation; it is a knowledge that the Will of God is *always* GOOD.

How do we know what the Will of God is? We do not, other than this: The Will of God cannot be death. Why? Because if we assume God to be the Principle of Life, the Principle of Life cannot produce death without destroying Itself. The Will of Life has only to BE Life. The Will of that which is Infinite can never be finite. Everything then should tend to expansion and multiplication in the Divine Plan. THAT is the Will of God. It has to be beauty, truth and harmony, as Troward said, as this is the true relationship of the Whole to the parts and the parts to the Whole. Therefore, we should interpret the Will of God to be everything that expresses life without hurt. This seems to be a fair, logical, sane and intelligent criterion. Anything that will enable us to express greater life, greater happiness, greater power—so long as it does not harm anyone—must be the Will of God for us. As much life as one can conceive will become a part of his experience.

A mental avenue must be provided through which the Law may operate as a law of liberty, if we are to be free. This does not mean we must please the Law, for It is impersonal and neither knows nor cares who uses It, nor for what purpose; but, because It is impersonal, It is compelled by Its very nature to return to the thinker exactly what he thinks into It. The law of mental equivalents must never be overlooked, for "Whatsoever a man soweth, that shall he also reap."

If a man is intelligent, he will naturally seek to free himself from misery and unhappiness. Theology may say that this is a selfish motivation, but it is exactly what we all are trying to do and calling it by a different name. Whether it is through the remission of sins, or the salvation of the individual soul, *every act in the life of the individual is that such an individual may express himself*. For instance, the love of a mother for her children, a man for his wife, a patriot for his country, a preacher for his religion, an artist for his art—all of these are but ways of self-fulfillment. This is legitimate self-expression.

We realize, however, that to attempt this self-expression at the expense of society or other individuals is to defeat the very purpose for which freedom exists, for back of all is a unity. Hence we find that the laws of necessity and not of theology (of which all religions and ethics and moral and social systems are but feeble lights) do ultimately compel experience into the path of true righteousness.

The criterion for any man as to what is right or wrong for him is not to be found in some other man's judgment. The criterion is: Does the thing I wish to do express more life, more happiness, more peace to myself, and at the same time harm no one? If it does, it is right. It is not selfish. But if it is done at the expense of anyone, then in such degree we are making a wrong use of the Law.

We may be quite emphatic in saying that we think the Universe exists for the expression of Spirit, and man exists for self-expression, because he is the expression of Spirit.

Man does not exist for the purpose of making an impression upon his environment. He does exist to express himself in and through his environment. There is a great difference. Man does not exist to leave a lasting impression upon his environment. Not at all. It is not necessary that we leave any impression. It is not necessary, if we should pass on tonight, that anyone should remember that we have ever lived. All that means anything is that while we live, WE LIVE, and wherever we go from here we shall keep on living.

It is quite a burden lifted when we realize that we do not have to move the world—it is going to move anyway. This realization does not lessen our duty or our social obligation. It clarifies it. It enables us to do joyously, and free from morbidity, that which we should do in the social state.

With this in mind, and believing that there is an Infinite Law of the Spirit, or Law of Life, which tends to multiply our gifts, because in so doing It multiplies Its own experience, Its own pleasure, Its own fruition; we may assume that spiritual man is already a success, is already supplied with everything that he needs. The potential of all things exists in the Universal Wholeness.

DEMONSTRATING THE LAW

The possibilities of the Law are infinite, and our possibilities of using It are limitless. There is such a thing as Universal Law and Mind, and we can use It if we comply with Its nature, work as It works. We may, or should, receive full benefit, and we will to the degree that we understand and properly use the Law. Thousands are today proving this Law, and in time all will come to realize Its truth.

We can demonstrate at the level of our ability to know. Beyond this, we cannot go. But we will constantly expand and increase in knowledge and understanding, thereby continuously growing in our ability to make use of the Law. In time, we shall be made free through It.

There is a law of unfoldment in man, which says he can advance only by going from where he is to the place where he would like to be. This is not because the Law is limited, but because It is law. As man unfolds in his mentality, the Law automatically reacts to him. The way to work is to begin right where we are and, through constantly applying ourselves to the Truth, we gradually increase in wisdom and understanding, for in this way alone will good results be obtained. If day by day we have a greater understanding and a clearer concept, if daily we are realizing more of Truth and applying It in our actions, then we are on the right path and eventually we shall be made free. It is a wonderful experiment and a great adventure to make conscious use of the Law; to feel that we can plant an idea in Mind and see it gradually take form.

The student should take time every day to see his life as he wishes it to be, to make a mental picture of his ideal. He should pass this picture over to the Law and go about his business, with a calm assurance that on the inner side of life something is taking place. There should not be any sense of hurry or worry about this, just a calm, peaceful sense of reality. Let the Law work through, and express Itself in, the experience. There should be no idea of compulsion. We do not have to *make* the Law work; it is Its nature to work. In gladness, then, we should make known our desires, and in confidence we should wait upon the Perfect Law to manifest through us.

Our part is to be ready and willing to be guided into truth and liberty. If, in the making of a demonstration, it becomes necessary to change our mode of living, then the Law will point the way and we will follow. Our correct choice will be part of the working of the Law. All doubt and fear must go and in their place must come faith and confidence, for we shall be led by the Spirit into all good.

People often say: "I don't know what to do; I don't know how to make a choice." We must realize, that there is an Intelligence within us that does know. This "guidance" is just as true in India, where people are Buddhists, as it is in America where people are Christians. It was just as true ten thousand years ago, before the advent of Christianity, as it will be ten thousand years hence.

In so far as we are going to make this thing work, *it is because we contact Universal Laws, which run through every age and race, and which answer every person.* If we can see this, we shall be able to do away with a great deal of superstition and ignorance. Let each individual immediately and directly and in his own integrity, approach the Law that Is. *There is no medium between us and the Universal Mind except our own thought. In such degree as we place a medium we have to absorb that medium before we can make a direct approach.* The Bible says, "There is no mediator between God and man except Christ." Christ means the truth about ourselves. So, if we have to make a choice and feel we do not know which or what to choose, we must be still in our own consciousness and know that the Spirit within us knows which of these ways is the right, and most constructive way, and will guide us.

When Intelligence makes a demand upon Itself, It answers Its own demand out of Its own nature and cannot help doing so! In philosophy, this idea is called Emergent Evolution. Whenever the Universe makes a demand upon Itself, out of that very demand is created its fulfillment. *But that can only be when the demand is in the nature of the Universe.*

Therefore, the person who believes that God is specializing for him is right. God is specializing for him through the Law. Such a person will realize that when he says, "There is a Divine Intelligence that knows the right answer," and accepts this statement as being true, *the answer to that problem is right then and there created in Mind*, and will be projected through his intellect whenever and wherever he is ready to receive it. *It is a new creation.*

God is forever doing new things, and when we conceive new ideas, it is an act of the Divine projecting Itself into Creation. There were no flying machines until man made them. The Spirit did not have a lot of little flying machine models put away in a cosmic cupboard somewhere. But the mind that conceived the possibility of the flying machine *is* God. The mind we use is the Mind of the Universe. This is God in man and it is only through this Mind that we understand anything. This Mind in us, responding to us, "the flight of the Alone to the Alone," of "the One to Itself," is God speaking and God answering.

St. Paul said, "We have the mind of Christ," which means that each one of us has immediate access to the Intelligence of the Universe. We give Intelligence outlet in two ways: by pure inspiration or intuition, or the more common way of bitter experience, and with most of us it is through the latter. If it were not for the divine hope in us, our experiences would be more than the human mind could digest.

Treatment is not for the purpose of making things happen; it is to provide, within ourselves, an avenue through which they may happen. The moment we think we have to treat to *compel* something, that moment we are exercising a will power, which is now up against a proposition it cannot possibly meet. Treatment is not mental coercion; it is not will power; it is not concentration. We shall never arrive at a correct method of spiritual treatment merely by learning how to concentrate for any length of time on a particular object. That is not what we are striving to arrive at. There is a mental attention which is necessary, but neither fasting nor feasting, wailing nor praising will cause us to arrive at a place of acceptance.

Treatment is not something one does to another, not something one does to an environment, nor to a situation. *It is always the thing one does to himself.* Whatever method enables him to do this is a good *method*, a good *way*. Treatment is an action in thought alone. It opens up the avenues of thought, expands the consciousness and lets Reality through. It clarifies the mentality, removes the obstructions of thought and lets in the Light. We already live in a Perfect Universe but It needs to be mentally seen and spiritually experienced before It can become a part of our everyday life.

When we treat for right action we should start with the supposition that right action already is. We do not create the right action. Something must come into the treatment which is uncompromising and absolute. Troward says that we enter the Absolute in such degree as we withdraw from the relative; and that we withdraw from the relative in such degree as we enter the Absolute. What he meant was this: in such degree as the answer and the result is contingent upon any existent circumstances . . . any existing, known fact . . . no matter how apparent, the treatment is not in the Absolute; it is in the relative and *necessarily conditioned by the contingent which is held in the mind.*

Let us take a concrete example: Suppose I am confronted with a problem and do not know the answer to it. Every known fact is against the working out of this problem. I say, "I wish to treat this situation, I wish to handle it scientifically, from the standpoint of spiritual science." *My treatment, then, must not consider the facts.* The facts are relative. The treatment must become Absolute. I wish to get it over into Mind as a complete acceptance, not of the old fact but of the new one. In such degree as this treatment partakes of the nature of Reality is it going to have power. It can have only as much power as I embody. This is the limitation of treatment, not limitation in Principle but in performance. The Thing Itself, of course, is not limited. As we have proven that Principle is not bound by precedent, we go into that realm which says: "Behold I make all things new," not carrying with us the limited belief of the reason why it cannot be. Any denial we make in treatment is simply to conduct us to a place of greater affirmation.

Spirit and Mental Law

It is impossible to divorce spiritual understanding from the proper use of mental law. The Spirit within man is God, and only to the degree that we listen to and seek to obey this Spirit shall we really succeed. At present very few people differentiate between the Spirit of the Universe and the Law of the Universe. The Spirit of God, which we think of as the Heavenly Father, is a Divine Presence, while the Law is a mechanical force.

The electrician may be a Methodist or Catholic or Buddhist. He may be a spiritual man or a materially-minded man, but electricity, being a natural law, can be used by one man as easily as by another. It will work here, there and anywhere. This does not seem strange to us, but often when we approach things which seem to be religious and spiritual, we think, "Now we are outside the realm of Law, God is good, therefore Law no longer exists." We fail to recognize with Browning that "All's love, yet all's law." We must differentiate between the Divine Presence as a Universal Spirit—a thing to be communed with—and the Universal Law, which is simply a blind Force. The Law *is* a blind Force, and lest we misuse It, *we should be very careful to follow a constructive course.* The Law is Absolute and we should trust Its impersonal action implicitly. It can do anything for us THAT WE CAN CONCEIVE OF IT DOING. It is the Law of freedom to all who believe in and obey It.

We must realize that the Universal Spirit is the Supreme Knower in the Universe. The Law can only operate on that which is known. In such degree as our knowledge partakes of Its Original Knowledge, or Nature, it has power. The highest realization we can have is a recognition of the Omnipresence of Spirit. This will set greater possibilities in motion and will, automatically, provide a better concept of life. Consequently, those people who have had the greatest sense of the Divine Presence—wherever it has been coupled with the definite knowledge of the Universal Law of Mind—have had the greatest power over that Law. This was the secret of the power of Jesus.

We should daily train our thought to recognize the Spirit in everything we do, say or think. There is no other way, to try any other way would be to make a complete failure. "Render, therefore, unto Caesar, the things which are Caesar's; and unto God the things that are God's." A constant realization of the presence of Spirit will provide a sense of Divine Companionship that no other attitude could produce. Why should we not take the highest and best? GOD IS—and we should realize this truth and make use of it. As soon as we recognize that God is, we can turn to the Law and tell It what to do.

We have no record of Jesus *asking* God to do anything, except in the Garden of Gethsemane, when He said: "O my Father, if it be possible, let this cup pass from me; nevertheless, not as I will but as thou wilt." Aside from this instance, Jesus' method of approach, during His entire ministry, was to give thanks and then command the Law to work. This is the correct manner of approach to the Spirit and the Law. Yet have we any record of another man so apparently trying to follow the Divine Will? No! When Jesus healed people and told them to get up and walk, He did not pray that they might be able to get up and walk. He exercised an authority which seemed to be the result of His communion with the Spirit, and undoubtedly it was. Practice is a definite statement in mind, a positive affirmation. It is an active, conscious, aggressive mental movement and in such degree as it embodies an idea—and there is no longer anything in our minds which denies the idea—*it will take form*, because it now becomes a part of the law and order of the Universe in which we live.

The Law is subject to Spirit and is Its servant. Man is Spirit, but until he KNOWS this, he will be only half using the Law, for he will not have a clear understanding to fall back upon. Treatment removes doubt and fear, lets in the realization of the Presence of Spirit, and is necessary while we are confronted by obstructions or obstacles. Every problem is primarily mental, and the answers to our problems will be found in Spiritual Realizations.

SUCCESS AND HAPPINESS

Success and happiness are ours when we deal with Absoluteness. This is the attitude we should have. What we need to know is the Truth. This does not mean that we need not be active; of course we shall be active, but we need not compel things to happen. Only remember we are surrounded by a Universal Subjectivity, a Subjective, Creative Consciousness, which is receptive, neutral, impersonal, always receiving the impress of our thought and which has no alternative other than to operate directly upon it, thus creating the things which we think.

Each one should realize that there is nothing in him which denies that which he desires. Our unity with good is not established while there is anything in us which denies it. People often say: "How shall I know when I know?" The very fact that one can ask this proves he does not know, for when he knows that he knows, he can prove his knowing by doing.

Thought sets definite forces in motion in Mind, relative to the individual who thinks. For instance, I am known in consciousness as Ernest Holmes, for that is my name; and every claim made for me, which I accept, operates through avenues of mind-activity and returns to me as some condition.

A good demonstration is made when Truth, gathering Its own power, lifts one out of his environment; and until that time comes, he should stay where he is, in order that he may know when he has made a demonstration. It is not a good demonstration if when we give our treatments we have to struggle just as before. Principle is Absolute, and in so far as any individual can actually induce, within consciousness, upon Principle, a definite, concrete acceptance of his desire . . . it will manifest, even though every thought on earth had to change to compel it! If it were a bit of information that was needed for the demonstration that only one person on earth knew—and that person was in the center of Africa—the information would be produced!

CHAPTER SEVENTEEN
MENTAL EQUIVALENTS

If We Know • What Do We Mean by Mental Equivalents? • The Prayer of Faith • Definite Plan • How to Demonstrate a Home • See Life Expressed • Perfect Action . . . No Mistakes.

IF WE KNOW

If we know that the Power with which we are dealing is Principle and not personality; if we know and believe that Mind is the only Actor, Cause, Effect, Substance, Intelligence, Truth and Power that there is; *if we have a real embodiment;* then we can demonstrate. If we lack, if we are poor, if we are without friends, if we are without opportunity, we should be sure to erase from our consciousness any sense of lack. We erase thought from consciousness by pouring in an opposite thought. This thought meets the other and neutralizes its effect. It rubs it out just as we rub a chalk mark off a board. We must maintain a consistent, positive, aggressive mental attitude in the Truth.

We walk by falling forward; water falls by its own weight; the planets are eternally falling through space; everything sustains itself in nature. The only reason man is limited is that he has not allowed the Divine within him to more completely express. Man's Divine Individuality compels Infinity to appear in his experience as duality *because he has believed in duality*.

WHAT DO WE MEAN BY MENTAL EQUIVALENTS?

Prayer does something to the mind of the one praying. It does not do anything to God. The Eternal Gift is always made. The Gift of God is the Nature of God, the Eternal Givingness. God cannot help making the gift, because GOD IS THE GIFT. We do not have to pray God to be God. God is God. Jesus revealed the nature of the Divine Being by his personal embodiment of the Divine Nature. He said, "As ye believe, it shall be done unto you."

The whole teaching of Jesus was based on the theory that we are surrounded by an intelligent Law, which does unto each as he believes. He implied the necessity of faith, conviction, and acceptance. That is, *it must be measured out to us according to our own measuring*. We must not only believe, we must know that our belief measures the extent and degree of our blessing. If our belief is limited only a little can come to us, because that is *as we believe*. We call this the law of mental equivalents. How much life can any man experience? As much as he can embody. There is nothing fatalistic about this. We are so constituted that we can continuously increase our embodiment. We grow in grace, as it were. We grow in power and theoretically there should be no limit to that growth. But right today we can expect to demonstrate or to have our prayers answered according to our belief and the embodiment of that belief.

Lowell said, "The gift without the giver is bare," and it is just as true that there can be no gift without a receiver. It is said, "To as many as received him, to them gave he the power." We seek to uncover the science of prayer: the essence of the Spirit embodied in it. We find that the essence of the power of prayer is faith and acceptance. In addition to the law of faith and acceptance, the law of mental equivalents must be considered. These are the two great laws with which we have to deal and we shall never get away from either. If prayer has been answered, it is not because God has been moved to answer one man and not another, but because one man more than another *has moved himself into a right relationship* with the Spirit or the Principle of Being—whichever one chooses to call It.

Faith, then, touches a Principle which responds, we may be certain of this. We should have more faith than we do rather than less, nor is it foolish to cultivate faith. ALL PRAYERS WILL BE ANSWERED WHEN WE PRAY ARIGHT. The first necessity is faith. Faith! But someone may exclaim, "This is what has always been taught, this is nothing new!" Correct, we have nothing new. We simply have a new approach to an old truth, a more intelligent, a more systematic way of consciously arriving at faith. This is what treatment is for.

Why is it that Jesus could say to the paralyzed man, "Take up thy bed and walk"? Because Jesus *knew* when he said this that the man *would* get up and walk. HE NOT ONLY BELIEVED THAT THERE WAS SOMETHING TO RESPOND TO HIM BUT HE HAD AN EQUIVALENT OF ITS RESPONSE, which is just as necessary.

The Law is Infinite and Perfect but in order to make a demonstration WE MUST HAVE A MENTAL EQUIVALENT OF THE THING WE DESIRE. A demonstration, like anything else in the objective life, is born out of a mental concept. The mind is the fashioning factor, and according to its range, vision and positiveness, will be the circumstance or experience. For example: If one sees only unloveliness in others, it is because unloveliness is a strong element in himself. The light he throws on others is generated in his own soul and he sees them as he chooses to see them. He holds constantly in his mind a mental equivalent of unloveliness and creates unlovely reactions toward himself. He is getting back what he is sending out. If a man believes himself to be a failure and that it is useless for him to try to be anything else, he carries with him the mental equivalent of failure. So he *succeeds* in being a *failure* according to law. This is his *demonstration*. Having a strong picture or mental concept, and holding to that equivalent regardless of circumstances or conditions, we must sooner or later manifest according to the concept.

It follows, then, that the range of our possibilities at the present time does not extend far beyond the range of our present concepts. As we bring ourselves to a greater vision, we induce a greater concept and thereby demonstrate more in our experience. In this way there is a continuous growth and unfoldment taking place. We do not expect to give a treatment today, for prosperity, and have a million dollars tomorrow. But little by little we can unfold our consciousness, through the acquisition of greater and still greater mental equivalents, until at last we shall be made free.

The way to proceed is to begin right where we are. It is not scientific to attempt to begin somewhere else. One who understands the systematic use of the Law will understand that *he is where he is because of what he is*, but he will *not* say, "I must remain where I am, because of what I am." Instead he will begin to disclaim what he appears to be. As his statements release wrong subjective tendencies, providing in their place a correct concept of life and Reality, he will automatically be lifted out of his condition; impelling forces sweeping everything before them, will set him free, if he trusts in Spirit and the working of the Law.

Stay with the One and never deviate from It, never leave It for a moment. Nothing else can equal this attitude. TO DESERT THE TRUTH IN THE HOUR OF NEED IS TO PROVE THAT WE DO NOT KNOW THE TRUTH. When things look the worst, that is the supreme moment to demonstrate, to ourselves, that there are no obstructions to the operation of Truth. When things look the worst is the best time to work, the most satisfying time. The person who can throw himself with a complete abandon into that Limitless Sea of Receptivity, having cut loose from all apparent moorings, is the one who will always receive the greatest reward.

The Prayer of Faith

No class of people on earth believes more in prayer than we do. Our whole theory is based not only on the belief in Spirit, but in the availability of It—Its immediate response. We even go so far as to say in everyday language: "Pray right and God cannot help responding." This is as far as anyone can go in faith. There is no confusion in the approach to Reality. It should be calm and dispassionate but filled with feeling because feeling and emotion are creative. We should combine the *letter* and the *spirit* of the Law.

Faith is the power of prayer. Now what is faith? When you analyze faith you find that it is a mental attitude against which there is no longer any contradiction in the mind that entertains it. Unfortunately, we find there is great faith *in fear*. Faith in the fear that one may lose his position; faith in the fear that one may lose material possessions; faith in the fear that one may lose his health, and so on.

If the mental attitude is in relationship to God, that is faith in God. If it is in relationship to one's ability to write a poem, that is faith in one's creative ability. FAITH IS A MENTAL ATTITUDE WHICH IS SO CONVINCED OF ITS OWN IDEA—WHICH SO COMPLETELY ACCEPTS IT—THAT ANY CONTRADICTION IS UNTHINKABLE AND IMPOSSIBLE. Before such a mental attitude can be created, there must be nothing left in the subjective state of our thought which contradicts our objective affirmation.

Faith is mental assertion elevated to the plane of realization. It is beyond the mere quibbling or mumbling of words for it identifies itself with Reality in such a manner that Reality becomes real to the believer. The Invisible becomes visible to the mind, and the unseen real.

Faith is real to the one who experiences it and cannot be denied to the mind of the one who has proven it. And what is this faith we should have? We should have faith that there is but One Mind. This Mind is both the Mind of man and the Mind of God. We use the Mind of God since there is but One Mind. This Mind is the essence of creativeness and the essence of goodness. It is available to all. It is no respecter of persons since It has already incarnated through all. It is in all and through all. Faith will not be denied, will not take no for an answer. It speaks an affirmative language. Faith knows that the universe is a Spiritual System, that man is part of this system. It knows that man's environment is also a part of this System. Because the system is perfect the condition may become perfect, and would be perfect if it were *known* to be so. Faith knows that the life of Man is God, the birthless and the deathless Reality of all Being.

Faith looks to the invisible and instead of seeing a void it fastens its gaze upon a solid reality. Faith is not hope, it is Substance. It does not look away from itself, being Substance it looks within itself. In doing this it realizes that the life of God is also the life of man. Faith affirms this and denies anything and everything that contradicts what to it is the supreme fact of existence.

Faith is essential to effective mental treatment, but this faith should be one of understanding. So faith may be said to be scientific, that is, we are now dealing with a Principle that has been defined and we know something about the way It works. We know how to use the Law governing It. Faith in this Law helps us to use our understanding with greater conviction.

Spiritual knowing is correct mental treating. Love is the impulsion of mental treatment. A consciousness of the Divine Presence in the one we are seeking to help is necessary, for we must provide different mental equivalents for healing than those which create disease.

If the manifest universe is the outward form of the thought of Spirit; if it is a result of the Self-Knowingness of God, and if we are of like nature to the Supreme Mind, then it follows that in giving mental treatment we are going through a mental process of self-knowing. Consequently, only that kind of treatment will be effective that knows it will be effective. This is the true meaning of faith for faith is not a foolish fancy, it is a dynamic fact.

The treatment will find an outward correspondence in the objective world which will exactly equal its inward conviction, when it is given, plus the necessity of its finding mental acceptance by the one for whom it is given. The more we think this over the more rational it will appear to be.

Faith in God is such a complete conviction that the Spirit will make the gift, that there is no longer any subjective contradiction. This faith can exist only in such degree as the conviction is in line with Reality. We cannot believe that any law of the Universe will ever change its own nature because we desire it to do so. AS WE COME INTO THE SPIRITUAL REALM—which is a perfectly natural and normal realm—WE HAVE TO COME INTO IT IN ITS OWN NATURE. It is a unity. There must be nothing vicious in it. Remember what Jesus said? "Therefore, if thou bring thy gift to the altar, and there rememberest that thy brother hath ought against thee, leave there thy gift before the altar and go thy way; first be reconciled to thy brother and then come and offer thy gift." Why? Because we cannot enter into peace while we are in a state of confusion. It cannot be done. We cannot manifest love when we have a mental equivalent of hate in our hearts and minds.

Definite Plan

We will say there are four men, "A," "B," "C," and "D." "A" receives $15.00 a week; "B" receives $50.00; "C" receives $75.00; and "D" receives $100.00. Suppose these four men are all without positions and each comes to a practitioner for mental treatment to obtain employment. Please do not think this is a material presentation of a spiritual truth for in the last analysis, in our philosophy, the Universe is either all matter or It is all Spirit. If it is all matter, what we formerly called matter is Spirit. If the Universe is all Spirit, what we used to call Spirit is matter. The Spiritual Universe should no longer be divided against Itself. The Bhagavad-Gita says that we shall never arrive at peace while we deal with the Pairs of Opposites. Let us not say that fifteen dollars is material and the Lord's Prayer is spiritual. Even in the Lord's Prayer, Jesus said, "Give us this day our daily bread," and He had already told them they would receive as much bread as they expected. He did not say what the size of the loaf would be.

These four men are all without positions, as we have said, and they come to a practitioner for mental treatment. The practitioner takes the thought that there is nothing but activity. He heals the belief in inactivity and declares that each one of these men is divinely active, occupied and compensated. Without question he has set a law in motion which will produce something for each of these four. We will suppose that his treatment is a good and an effective one. They accept it and consequently each finds a position. As a result probably "A" will receive $15.00 again; "B" $50.00; "C" $75.00; and "D" $100.00 per week.

"But," one might say, "the practitioner spoke the same word for each, why did they not all receive $100.00 per week?" Because the Law says that we can have only WHAT WE CAN TAKE. The practitioner's word was used for each in like manner but each could receive only his fill—only his mental capacity to comprehend. He can have more, but how is he to get it? Will a pint dipper ever hold more than a pint? One might build up the edge and rim of the dipper somewhat and make it hold more and more, so one can continuously increase his consciousness. It is just the old law that we can expand the finite but we cannot contract the Infinite.

Each man, "A," "B," "C," and "D" was full and no doubt running over when he received a position as a result of the treatment; but the positions they received, the molds which their perceptions of life had provided, were limited to the subjective remembrance already set in motion by themselves. Each attracted to himself, out of the Universal Good, that which he could comprehend. It is the old statement again that water will reach its own level by its own weight *and without effort*. So a treatment will level itself in the objective world at the level of the subjective thought and realization which projects and receives it.

This does not mean that each of the above stated men will always have to receive the same compensation, for with an enlarged consciousness each might receive more. There is nothing in the nature of finality about this because the man whose consciousness is now bringing him a smaller thing or a less important thing (we name it big and little and to us it is big or little), can if he so desires conceive the bigger thing, the more important position. The same prayer answers the big and the little.

A man does not suddenly become affluent because he sits around and thinks, "I am a multi-millionaire." But when he thinks affluently he does begin to demonstrate prosperity.

How to Demonstrate a Home

All our beautiful dreams, all our wishing and praying, for material good, will reach no higher level in our experience than our belief in the power of God and in His willingness to help us. God's willingness to help us is expressed in the existence of that Immutable Law which gives us exactly the type of objective experience for which we build a mental likeness. If we have the mental equivalent of a commodious home, roomy, light, cheery, and an income in keeping with it; if we are able to build in mind the kind of home we wish, and there is nothing in our subjective thought which denies this, then we shall be able to decide and demonstrate for ourself the kind of home we desire.

SEE LIFE EXPRESSED

One should analyze himself, saying, "Do I look at myself from a standpoint of restriction? Do I see life limited to the eternal round of getting up in the morning, eating, going to work, coming home, going to bed, sleeping, getting up again and so on?" Break the bonds of apparent necessity and see life as one continuous expression of the Infinite Self, and as this conception gradually dawns upon the inner thought, something will happen in the outer conditions to relieve the greater demands of necessity. Free yourself forever from the thought that God may be pleased by a life of sacrifice, that the world is any better because of your misery, or that righteousness is more perfectly expressed through poverty than abundance. Know that the greater abundance of every good thing which you are bringing out in your life, the more perfectly you are satisfying the Divine Urge within you. ANYTHING YOU CAN DREAM OF is not too great for you to undertake, if it hurts no man and brings happiness and good into your life. If one were doing the work he should be doing he would never become tired, because the energy which holds the universe in place is tireless. The reason we become tired is that we have cross currents of thought about our work. This arises from a belief in duality—a belief in both Good and evil.

In treating we conceive of the ultimate of the idea but never of the process. Never treat a process. We plant a seed and there is in the seed, operating through the creative soil, everything that will cause it to develop, unfold and produce a plant. *The ultimate of effect is already potential in its cause.* This is the mystical meaning of the words: "I am Alpha and Omega." Our word for the fullest expression of our life or for its smallest detail should be the alpha and omega, the beginning and the end of the thing thought of. All cause and effect are in Spirit, they are bound together in one complete whole. One is the inside, the other the outside of the same thing.

Never let anything cause you to doubt your ability to demonstrate the Truth. CONCEIVE OF YOUR WORD AS BEING THE THING. See the desire as an already accomplished fact and rest in perfect confidence, peace and certainty, never looking for results, never wondering, never becoming anxious, never being hurried nor worried. Those who do not understand this attitude may think you are inactive but remember: "To him who can perfectly practice inaction, all things are possible."

What we know about Subjective Mind proves that It is unconscious of time, knows neither time nor process. *It knows only the completion, the answer.* That is why it is written, "Before they call, I will answer." Cosmic Creation is from idea to object. It does not know anything about process; process is involved in it but not consciously. Correct practice should know that ultimate right action is now, today. If we say, "Tomorrow it is going to be," then according to the very law we are using we hold the answer in a state of FUTURITY WHICH CAN NEVER BECOME PRESENT. If a gardener holds his seed in his hand and says, "Tomorrow I am going to plant this seed," his garden will never start growing. Therefore, Jesus said: "When ye pray, believe that ye have and ye shall receive." He did not say believe and you will immediately have. He said, "Ye shall receive." He did not deny the natural law of evolution and growth. Nature operates according to a law of logical sequence.

PERFECT ACTION . . . NO MISTAKES

In mental work, we must realize that there is One Infinite Mind, which is consciously directing our destiny. Declare every day that: "No mistakes have been made, none are being made, and none *can* be made." Declare: "There is One Supreme Intelligence which governs, guides and guards, tells me what to do, when to act and how to act." Having done this in perfect faith, act with perfect assurance. Declare further: "Everything necessary to the full and complete expression of the most boundless experience of joy is mine now." Know this, see it, feel it and BE it. Do this every day for a few minutes. We should all do this until the time comes when it is no longer necessary. When that time comes we will know it because our demonstrations will have been made.

Suppose someone says, "I have made a lot of mistakes in my life, I had opportunities I did not grasp." Every man has this feeling at some time in his life. This is a direct belief that there is but one opportunity which comes to man and if he does not take it he will have no more. This is a belief in limited opportunities and it must be denied completely and specifically. It is not that we have made no mistakes, but if the belief in the necessity of mistakes stays in the consciousness, then there is bound to be a repetition. It is scientific practice to declare that there have been no mistakes in man's consciousness, that if there have been they are now wiped out. There are none in the Divine Plan, and there is no plan for man other than the Divine Plan.

If a man has had, and apparently lost, many opportunities, he must be shown that he stands at the point of limitless opportunity; that opportunity is right here today; that he sees and grasps it. It recognizes him as he recognizes it. We exist in Limitless Opportunities, which are forever seeking expression through us.

Know that there is no condemnation, for nothing can condemn unless we believe in condemnation. Destroy the thought that would place limitation or bondage upon any situation or condition. "Loose him and let him go." Talk to yourself, not to the world. There is no one to talk to but yourself for all experience takes place within. Conditions are the reflections of our meditations and nothing else. There is but One Mind, that Mind is our mind now. It never thinks confusion, knows what It wishes and how to accomplish what It desires. *It is what It desires!*

Assume a case of treatment for prosperity. Suppose one comes to you and says, "Business is bad. There is no activity." How are you going to treat him? Are you going to treat activity, business, customers, conditions or what? There is but one thing to treat, as far as the practitioner is concerned, and that is HIMSELF. The practitioner treats himself, the reason being that his patient's mind and his own mind are in the One Mind.

There is but one activity, which is perfect. Nothing has happened to it, nothing can cut it off, it is always operating. There is no belief in inactivity. What is this statement for? To neutralize the belief in inactivity. A word spoken in Mind will reach its own level in the objective world by its own weight; just as in physical science we know that water reaches its own level. You must destroy the thoughts of inactivity. Man cannot become either discouraged or afraid if he realizes that there is but One Mind which he may consciously use. The real man knows no discouragement, cannot be afraid, and has no unbelief. And he who knows of the power with which he is dealing and who plants a seed of thought in Subjectivity, knows that it will come up and bear fruit.

Bring out the idea of Substance. Make consciousness perceive that Substance is Spirit, Spirit is God, and God is all there is. Once you acquaint the consciousness with this idea, it is implanted in the Creative Power, which is externalized in your life.

Continue to declare there were no mistakes, there are none and there never will be. Say, "I represent the Truth, the whole Truth and nothing but the Truth. It is unerring, It never makes mistakes. There are no mistakes in the Divine Plan for me. There is no limitation, poverty, want nor lack. I stand in the midst of eternal opportunity, which is forever presenting me with the evidence of its full expression. I am joy, peace and happiness. I am the spirit of joy within me. I am the spirit of peace within me, of poise and of power. I am the spirit of happiness within me. I radiate Life; I am Life. There is One Life and that Life is my life now."

It is not enough to say: "There is One Life and that Life is God." We must complete this statement by saying: "That Life is my life now," because we must couple this Life with ours in order to express It. We are not *becoming* this Life, but are now in and of this Life. There is no other Life. God is not becoming: God IS. God is not growing; God is complete. God is not trying to find out something; God already knows. Evolution is not the expression of a *becoming* God, but is simply one of the ways that a God Who already IS, expresses Himself; and as such it is the logical result of involution and is eternally going on.

For the man who believes that "business is bad"; for the one who thinks he has made many mistakes and will make more; for the man who sees nothing but inactivity about him, the following meditation might be used:

"I know I am now at the threshold of all good, wisdom and Truth. All the good I can embody is now mine. I have only to open the portals of my soul and accept that which is ready to express through me.

"I expect, fully and emphatically, the answer to my prayer today. Right now do I possess this thing I so greatly desire. I remove my fear of lack and negation, for it is the only barrier which stands in the way of my experience of good. I alone can remove it, and I do remove it now.

"In this moment my good comes to me, enough and to spare, to give and to share. I can never be exhausted, my good can never be depleted, because that Source from which my good comes is inexhaustible.

"Today, in this moment, the Law responds to my thought. My word is one of affirmation, rising from the knowledge that the Good, the Enduring and the True are Eternalities in my experience. I cannot be apart from that which is my good. My good is assured me by God, the Indwelling Essence of my life."

CHAPTER EIGHTEEN
THE LAW OF ATTRACTION

Thought Atmosphere • *Attraction of Personality* • *Attracting Friends* • *Attracting Success* • *No Failures* • *No Personal Responsibility* • *The Law of Correspondence.*

THOUGHT ATMOSPHERE

Spiritual mind healing is a result of the constructive use of a mental law, which the world is gradually beginning to understand. Since we are thinking beings and cannot stop thinking, and since Creative Mind receives our thought and cannot stop creating, It must always be creating something for us. What It will make depends wholly upon what we are thinking, and what we shall attract will depend upon that on which our thoughts dwell.

Thought can attract to us that which we first mentally embody, that which has become a part of our mental make-up, a part of our inner understanding. Every person is surrounded by a thought atmosphere. This mental atmosphere is the direct result of his conscious and unconscious thought, which, in its turn, becomes the direct reason for, and cause of, that which comes into his life. Through this power we are either attracting or repelling. Like attracts like and it is also true that we may become attracted to something which is greater than our previous experience, by first embodying the atmosphere of our desire.

Taking as the starting point the idea that the essence of man's life is God, it follows that he uses the same creative process. Everything originates in the One, comes from the same Source and returns again to It. As God's thought makes worlds, and peoples them with living things, so our thought makes our world and peoples it with our experiences. By the activity of our thought, things come into our life and we are limited only because we have not known the

Truth. We have thought that outside things controlled us, when all the time we have had that within which could have changed everything and given us freedom from bondage.

Everyone automatically attracts to himself just what he is, and we may set it down that wherever we are, however intolerable the situation may be, we are just where we belong. There is no power in the universe but ourselves that can free us. Someone may help us on the road to realization, but substantiality and permanence can come only through the consciousness of our own life and thought. Man must bring himself to the place in mind where there is no misfortune, no calamity, no accident, no trouble, no confusion; where there is nothing but plenty, peace, power, Life and Truth. He should definitely, daily (using his own name) declare the Truth about himself, realizing that he is reflecting his statements into Consciousness and that they will be operated upon by It.

This is called, in mysticism, High Invocation; invoking the Divine Mind, implanting within It, seeds of thought relative to oneself. And this is why some of the teachers of olden times used to instruct their pupils to cross their hands over their chests and say: "Wonderful, wonderful, wonderful me!" definitely teaching them that as they mentally held themselves, so they would be held. "Act as though I am and I will be."

One of the ancient sayings is that "To the man who can perfectly practice inaction, all things are possible." This sounds like a contradiction until one penetrates its inner meaning, for it is only when one completely practices inaction that he arrives at the point of the true actor, for he then realizes that the act and the actor are one and the same; that cause and effect are the same; which is simply a different way of saying: "Know the truth and the truth shall make you free." To reduce the whole thing to its simplest form, whatever one reflects into Mind tends to take form.

ATTRACTION OF PERSONALITY

Every business, every place, every person, every thing has a certain mental atmosphere of its own. This atmosphere decides what is to be drawn to it. For instance, you never saw a successful man who went around with an atmosphere of failure. Successful people think about success. A successful man is filled with that subtle something which permeates everything that he does with an atmosphere of confidence and strength. The man who says of himself, "I have no personality with which to attract people," has been laboring under a delusion. He needs to be disillusioned. He must be shown that there is but One Person; this Person is manifested through every living soul. It is THE Personality. It is Complete.

The ones to whom we are most strongly attracted are not necessarily the ones who are the most beautiful physically, but are the ones from whom we receive that subtle emanation, "that something." What is *that something?* It is that which emanates from within. It is the inner recognition of Reality.

Now we know, and knowing means using the Law in a constructive way, "I and my Father are one." This is strength for the weak and life for all who believe. We can so fill ourselves with the drawing power of attraction that it will become irresistible. Nothing can hinder the man who knows that he is dealing with the One Power that creates all from Itself, moves all within Itself, and yet holds everything in its place. One with the Infinite Mind. One with the personality of God. We should let this ring through our mind each day, many times each day, until we shall never again say, "I have no personality." We have *all* Personality!

ATTRACTING FRIENDS

In turning to the Law, realize that it is a Law of Reflection. "Life is the mirror of king and slave." Emerson said: "If you want a friend, be a friend." As the idea of friendship dawns upon the consciousness, the law of attraction produces friends, for one is the picture and the other is the thing. This is the great teaching of involution and evolution, the thought involved and the result evolved. One is the treatment and the other is the demonstration. When we are dealing with Causation, we are dealing with that which has *involved within Itself* all effect, as it unfolds. We may leave it to the Law to compel right action. With this in mind let us go on to treatment.

Do we wish to attract friends? We must begin to image ideal relationships, be they social or otherwise, to sense and feel the presence of friends; to enjoy them in our mentalities, not as an illusion but as a reality, not as a dream but as an experience; to declare that their presence is now here. BUT WE MUST NEVER LOOK TO SEE IF THEY ARE HERE, BECAUSE THIS WOULD IMPLY DOUBT AND WOULD NEUTRALIZE OUR WORD. We can attract the kind of friends we wish if we specifically designate the kind, but we must never think of *certain people*, or that a particular individual must be one of the friends, for this would be hypnotic. The idea will bring the right kind of friends.

In order to have this friendship enduring, true, really worth while and a thing of beauty, we should cultivate an attitude of friendship toward everybody and everything. The one who has learned to love all people will find plenty of people who will return that love. This is not mere sentiment, and it is more than a religious attitude of mind. It is a deep, scientific fact, and one to which we should pay attention. The reason is this: As all is Mind, and *as we attract to us what we first become*, until we learn to love we are not sending out love vibrations and not until we send out those vibrations can we receive love in return.

When we find we are without friends, the thing to do is at once to send our thought out to the whole world; send it full of love and affection. Know that this thought will meet the desires of some other person who is wanting the same thing, and in some way the two will be drawn together. Think of the whole world as your friend, but you *must also be the friend of the whole world*. In this way, and with this simple practice, you will draw to you so many friends that the time will be too short to enjoy them all. Refuse to see the negative side of anyone. Refuse to let yourself misunderstand or be misunderstood. Know that everyone wants you to have the best. Affirm this wherever you go, and you will find things just as you wish them to be.

One of the first things to do, is to love everybody. If you have not done this, begin to do so at once. There is always more good than bad in people, and seeing the good tends to bring it forth. Love is the grandest healing and drawing power on earth. It is the very reason for our being, and that explains why it is that people should have something or someone to love. The life that has not loved has not lived, it is still dead. Love is the sole impulse for creation, and the man who does not have love as the greatest incentive in his life, has never developed the real creative instinct. No one can swing out into the Universal without love, for the whole Universe is based upon it.

"To him who hath loved much, much is forgiven." A man may have many shortcomings, but if he loves greatly much will be forgiven him. People are dying for real human interest, for genuine friendship, for someone to tell them they are all right. We always welcome the man who looks at the world as his friend and loves it. And it is a law that *the man who sees what he wants to see, regardless of what appears, will someday experience in the outer what he has so faithfully seen in the within*. From selfish reasons alone, if from no loftier reason, we cannot afford to find fault, to hate, or even to hold in mind *anything* against any living soul! The God of love cannot hear the prayer of the one who fails to love. In our meditation for friendship, let us make our unity with all people, with all life:

"God in me is unified with God in all. This One is now drawing into my life all love and fellowship. I am one with all people, with all things, with all life. As I listen in the silence, the voice of all humanity speaks to me and answers the love that I hold out to it.

"The great love which I now feel for the world is the Love of God, and it is felt by all and comes back to me from all. I understand all people and this understanding is reflected back to me from all. I give friendship and therefore I have friends. I help, therefore, I am helped. I uplift, therefore, I am uplifted. I am now surrounded by all love, all friendship, all companionship, all health, all happiness, all success. I AM ONE WITH LIFE. I wait in the silence while the Great Spirit bears this message to the whole world."

ATTRACTING SUCCESS

We mean by demonstration, bringing into our experience something which we had not experienced before; bringing it in as the result of conscious thought; and unless it is possible to do this, our whole science is a mistake and a delusion. Unless there is a Divine Principle, Universal Soul or Subjectivity, or Medium, which, of Itself—without any help or assistance—can produce things, and *will*, then there is nothing in this teaching. But there is a Divine Principle; and *what It does for us It must do through us*. Our part in the demonstration is to set the word in motion, thus compelling, through the Law of Subjectivity, the result or manifestation.

The subjective state of a man's thought decides what is going to happen to him in his objective experience. The subjective state of his thought is the sum total of his thinking and knowing. It is the medium between the relative and the Absolute, between the Limitless and the conditioned. Whatever is involved in it, will evolve. Therefore, when there is no longer anything in our mentality which denies our word, a demonstration will be made; nothing can stop it, for the Law is Absolute.

We should approach the Law normally and naturally and with a sense of ease. There is nothing peculiar or weird about it. It is a natural Law, working in a normal way, and must be thought of in this light. We should come to consider the Law and the Spirit as friends and think of them as such. In this way we shall gradually go from good to more good and from peace to greater peace. This is the natural unfoldment of Reality through man. We should EXPECT THE BEST, and so live that the best may become a part of our experience.

Suppose one wishes more activity in his business, more success. Every day he should see his place filled with people. See them looking at and finding pleasure in his merchandise; see them comparing prices and realizing that he is offering good values; see them delighted with the service he is giving; see them cheerful, beaming, expansive, as they enjoy the atmosphere of his place; see the uplift which the spirit of his good-will gives them. Make a mental picture of it all. We are dealing with Intelligence, and we should recognize the Power we are working with—realizing our Oneness with It—and then we should ask for what we wish and take it.

If we were treating for activity in a store we owned in Boston, we would not be treating someone in Kalamazoo for the mumps and expect that the store would demonstrate more success. WE MUST BE SPECIFIC IN WHAT WE DO, while at the same time never outlining *how* it shall be done. Remember we are dealing with Intelligence. IT IS GOING TO EVOLVE OUR CONCEPT EXACTLY AS WE INVOLVE IT. If one could take a picture of his objective circumstances and a picture of his subjective mentality, he would find them to be identical, for one is the cause of the other. One is the image and the other is the reflection of that image.

So our success in business, the activity which we generate through the operation of the Law, depends upon our ability to conceive. At all times, we are either drawing things to us or pushing them away. In the average individual, this process goes on without his knowing it, but ignorance of the law does not change its result. "What," someone will say, "do you think that I thought *failure* or wanted to fail?" Of course not. Perhaps you thought that failure *might* come, maybe you even feared it would come, or in some other way gave it entrance to your mind.

We live in Mind and It can return to us only what we think into It. No matter what we do, Law will always obtain. If we are thinking of ourselves as poor and needy, then Mind has no choice but to return what we have thought into It. "It is done unto you as you believe." Thoughts of failure, limitation or poverty are negative and must be counted out of our lives for all time. God has given us a Power and we must use It. We can do more toward saving the world by proving this law than all that charity has ever given to it.

Remember God is the silent Power behind all things, always ready to pour into our experience that which we need. We must have a receptive and positive faith in the evidence of things not seen with the physical eye but which are eternal in the heavens. All is Mind, and we must provide a receptive avenue for It, as It passes out through us into the outer expression of our affairs. If we allow the world's opinion to control our thinking, *then that will be our demonstration!* If, on the other hand, we rise superior to the world, we shall create a new pattern.

It is quite necessary, then, that the successful business man should keep his mind on thoughts of happiness, which produce cheerfulness instead of depression. He should radiate joy and should be filled with faith, hope and expectancy. These cheerful, hopeful attitudes of mind are indispensable to the one who really wants to do things in life. Declare your freedom. Know that no matter what others may say, think or do, *you are a success now*, and nothing can hinder you from accomplishing your good. All the power of the universe is with you. Feel it, know it, and then act as though it were true.

Begin to blot out, one by one, all false beliefs—all ideas that man is limited, poor or miserable. Refuse to think of failure or to doubt your own power. See only what you wish to experience and look at nothing else. We are relieved of all thought of clinging to anybody or anything. Cannot the Great Principle of Life create for us all that we need? The Universe is inexhaustible; It is limitless, knows no bounds and has no confines. We are not depending on a reed shaken by the wind, *but on the Principle of Life Itself*, for all that we have or ever shall need. It is not *some* power, or a *great* power, it is ALL POWER. All we have to do is to believe, never wavering, no matter what happens. As we do this, we shall find that things are steadily coming our way and that they are coming without that awful effort which destroys the peace of mind of the majority of the race. We know that there can be no failure in God's Mind, and this Mind is the Power on which we are depending.

No Failures

If one appears to have failed, he should realize that there are no failures in the Universe. He should completely erase the idea of failure by stating that there are no failures. If one believes that he failed last year, he will be likely to fail again this year, unless the false thought is erased. Break down everything except the recognition of the One Perfect Power, which is not contingent upon any place, person, condition, time of year, or anything but Itself. A demonstration is made when it comes straight through from the Truth. The one who wishes to make a demonstration must clear up his own subjective atmosphere, the reason being that he may be objectively making statements which his subjective thought may be denying. In this way, we often neutralize our word as fast as it is spoken.

When Jesus said: "Resist not," He meant that non-recognition of evil is the only way to avoid it. This is true according to the law of cause and effect, for what we persist in recognizing we persist in holding in place. That which we refuse to recognize, we neutralize, and it is no longer there so far as we are concerned.

So we erase any idea of failure. Now here is where it looks as if one were not telling the truth to himself, but he is declaring the truth about the Spirit that indwells him. THIS SPIRIT NEVER FAILS. Affirm this until it is a very part of your being: "This word blots out from the book of my remembrance any sense of lack, limitation, want, or fear of failure. There is no failure, no person to fail. Failure is neither person, place nor thing. It is a false thought and has no truth in it. It is a belief in lack and there is no lack. It is a belief in a limitation which does not exist."

Your word, which is one with the Infinite Life, has been spoken in calm trust. It will be taken up at once and it will be operated on. Perfect is the pattern and perfect will be the result. Your word is now establishing it forever. See this, feel it, know it. You are now encompassed by perfect life, by infinite activity, by all power, by all guidance. The Power of the Spirit is supplying you with all good, It is filling you with life and love.

Thought is very subtle and sometimes when you are making such an affirmation, arguments will rise against it. Stop at once and meet those arguments. Refuse to accept them. We speak into our words the intelligence which we are, and backed by that greater Intelligence of the Universal Mind, our word becomes a law unto the thing for which it is spoken. There goes forth from this word the Power of the Infinite.

Suppose one were treating his business and something within him should say: "There are too many people in this business," he should handle the thought of competition at once. Declare: "There is no competition and no monopoly in my experience."

Treatment is a thing of itself; it is an entity of Infinite Intelligence, Life and Action, and nothing can hinder its operation but unbelief or a lack of adequate mental equivalents. "They could not enter in because of unbelief," and because they "limited the Holy One of Israel."

Never depend upon people or say that things must come from this or that source. It makes no difference where things come from. SAY THAT THEY ARE, and let them come from where they may, and then if something occurs which points to a place for them to come from, it is correct to say: "If this is the place, then there is nothing which can hinder."

Nothing moves but Mind. God makes things through the direct act of becoming the things which He creates. This is what we do, for our thought becomes the thing thought of. The thought and the thing are one in reality. WHAT A MAN HAS AND WHAT HE IS, IS THE RESULT OF THE SUBJECTIVE STATE OF HIS THOUGHT. Keep on subjectifying thought until the balance of consciousness is on the affirmative side, and nothing can hinder it from demonstrating. This is inevitable for this is the way the Law operates. A good meditation for Opportunity is the following:

"My opportunities are unlimited. There is a Divine Urge to express. It permeates me and fills all space and all people. All of my affairs are in Its hands. To It are clearly visible the best ways, methods and means for my greater expression. I leave my affairs in the hands of this principle, and I co-operate with It.

"Today the possibilities of my experience are unlimited. The Spirit flows through me, inspiring me and sustaining that inspiration. I have ability and talent and I am busy using them. This talent is divinely sustained and marketed under a Universal plan of right action.

"Life lies open to me—rich, full, abundant. My thought, which is my key to life, opens all doors for me. I am one with Infinity, Divinity. I realize this unity. I proceed on my way as one who knows that God goes with him into an eternal day of infinite privilege. I have only to open the portals of my soul and accept that which is ready to express through me. Today I fling these portals wide; today I am the instrument through which life flows."

No Personal Responsibility

No matter how great a responsibility may rest in that which must be done, never let one moment's responsibility rest in your own thought about it, because *that to which the mind gives birth, is*, and EVERY IDEA IS BOUND TO PRODUCE AN EFFECT EXACTLY LIKE ITS CAUSE.

When we make a demonstration, we must take what goes with it. Therefore all demonstrations should be made in peace, confidence and joy, and in a realization of Divine Love and Perfection permeating everything. The reason for this is evident, for we are dealing with the

Law of cause and effect. We are not depending upon chance but upon the Law. The responsibility of setting the Law in motion is ours, but the responsibility of making It work *is inherent in Its own nature*. We must know that we are dealing with the Substance from which all things are made. Nothing moves but Mind, and we are dealing with the Mind that is the Mover, the Creator, the Cause of all that is or is to be. We should sense that back of the word which we speak is the Power of the Universe, surging to express Itself. Then speak the word consciously, knowing that it is Law.

The Law of Correspondence

The limit of our ability to demonstrate depends upon our ability to provide a mental equivalent of our desires, for the law of correspondence works from the belief to the thing. But it is within our power to provide a greater mental equivalent through the unfolding of consciousness; and this growth from within will finally lead to freedom.

What we demonstrate today, tomorrow and the next day, is not as important as the TENDENCY WHICH OUR THOUGHT IS TAKING . . . the dominant attitude of our mind. If every day things are a little better, a little happier, a little more harmonious, a little more health-giving and joyous; if each day we are expressing more life, we are going in the right direction.

And so we meditate daily upon the Universe of the All Good, the Infinite Indwelling Spirit, which we call God, the Father, Incarnate in man, trying to sense and to feel this Indwelling Good as the Active Principle of our lives. This is what the mystics call "The Man of the Heart," or "The Angel of God's Presence." This is why they taught that there are always two, for there is *what we seem to be*, and *what we really are*. As we contact this Higher Principle of our own lives—which is Perfect and Complete, needing nothing, wanting nothing, knowing everything, being happy and satisfied—and as we daily meditate upon this Indwelling God, we shall acquire a greater mental equivalent.

For those who have always dwelt on limited thoughts a very good practice is to dwell upon the magnitude of the Universe. Think how many stars there are, how many fish there are in the seas, and how many grains of sand on the beaches. Think of how big the ocean is; of the immensity of space, the bigness of everything, the grandeur of everything. Mechanically, if necessary, compel the mentality to cognize Reality. Compel the consciousness to recognize Truth through reason, if no other conviction comes.

Think, see and feel activity. Radiate Life. Feel that there is that within which is the center and circumference of the Universe. The Universe is the result of the Self-Contemplation of God. Our lives are the result of our self-contemplations, and are peopled with the personifications of our thoughts and ideas. Accept this without question for it is true.

Nothing is real to us unless we make it real. Nothing can touch us unless we let it touch us. Refuse to have the feelings hurt. Refuse to receive anyone's condemnation. In the independence of your own mentality, believe and feel that you are wonderful. This is not conceit, it is the truth. What can be more wonderful than the manifestation of the Infinite Mind? "Awake thou that sleepest, and arise from the dead, and Christ shall give thee light." "Prove me now herewith, saith the Lord of Hosts, if I will not open you the windows of heaven, and pour you out a blessing, that there shall not be room enough to receive it." "Be firm and ye shall be made firm." "Act as though I am and I will be." "Onlook thou the Deity and the Deity will onlook thee." "As thou hast believed, so be it done." "Ask and it shall be given unto you." "So shall my word be that goeth forth out of my mouth—it shall prosper."

CHAPTER NINETEEN

SUMMARY OF PART THREE:

THE PRACTICE OF SPIRITUAL MIND HEALING

In the preceding eighteen chapters of this book, the one object in mind has been to uncover mans spiritual nature and his relationship to God and the Universe. Therefore, instead of the usual recapitulation of the six chapters just concluded, we propose to make this an informal discussion of the general theme of "How to Give a Mental Treatment."

Spirituality is natural goodness. God is not a person; God is a Presence personified in us. Spirituality is not a thing; It is the atmosphere of God's Presence, goodness, truth and beauty. Religion is a life, a living. If we could forget that philosophy is profound, that religion is spiritual and life serious—all of which may be true—but if we could forget all these things, and approach Reality as normally as we go about our daily affairs, we would be better off.

If there is one thing we should learn it is that spiritual treatment must not be confused with *mental concentration*. A treatment is an active thing, if we are going to treat by a technique, by a method of procedure, if we are going to treat by a mental process. If we are going to reduce spiritual treatment to a mental science, then there is a method, a technique and a procedure in mental treatment. There is a certain mental attention we should have in giving a treatment, but this is different from the popular idea of mental concentration, as though we must hold the mind to one thought for a certain period of time.

Start with this simple proposition: The nature of God, of man and of being is perfect, harmonious, whole—Perfect God, Perfect Man, and Perfect Being—and in treatment conform your thought to this idea. Then let the treatment be a moving thing, a series of thoughts or statements followed by realization.

Gradually a conviction dawns that God is all there is, and as this conviction grows the work is done more easily, and with a greater degree of acceptance . . . a growing spiritual atmosphere comes into it. When this truth takes hold of our consciousness, and we contact what appears to be imperfect man, imperfect God, and imperfect being, we shall better know that the manifestation of imperfection has no right to exist. In actual practice, this becomes a series of statements—arguments perhaps—but a series of statements which finally culminate in the mental evidence being in favor of Perfect God, Perfect Man, and Perfect Being.

The way to learn how to treat, is to treat. At first one has the feeling in treating of wondering if anything is really happening, *until he finally realizes that this apparent nothingness with which he deals is the only ultimate something out of which tangible things could be made.*

Recent research in the field of physics has revealed that this metaphysical abstraction is the thing that physics begins with—energy and intelligence. We would add to this that intelligence may be directed by consciousness. In mental and spiritual treatment, the practitioner endeavors to enter into the consciousness of a state of unity of all life, in which unity exists past, present and future; the person for whom he is working and the unborn but potential possibility of the condition for which he works. He is dealing not with mental suggestion but with a spiritual Presence, he does not seek to force an issue, but rather permits a Creative Intelligence to perform a certain act.

We are all familiar with the idea of unity in this physical world, this physical universe: all physical form is made of one ultimate stuff, of which no one knows the nature. We are acquainted with the form. As stated above, physics has chased this form, as it were, back into a primordial unity of energy and intelligence. Perhaps this is what Emerson had in mind when he said that every fact is fluid; or what Spinoza had in mind when he said: "I do not say that mind is one thing and matter another; I say they are the same thing."

All forms are theoretically resolvable into a universal energy and substance, upon which, and through which, Intelligence operates. The Bible says: "In the beginning was the Word and the Word was with God and the Word was God; and all things were made by the Word, and without the Word was not anything made that was made." The Bible clearly speaks of the physical universe and everything in it *as though it were a word in form*; that God is Spirit; that the action of Spirit upon Itself produces creation; that man is a complement of the Universe, an incarnation of the universe, partaking of the same nature. Consequently, *his word is creative!* This should answer the question of the students who are unable to understand how thought can become a thing; how thought can influence objective life, whether it be the physical body or the physical environment.

The Bible further explains to us the uses we can make of this power of the word. It gives us the story of Adam and the Garden of Eden and the Fall to show the wrong use. Then it gives us the story of Jesus, the Christ, and His spiritual teachings, to show us the right use; and again—"As in Adam, all die, even so in Christ all are made alive." It says also that ". . . in the beginning God made man perfect, but man has sought out many inventions." It very boldly declares that death and resurrection are inventions of the human mind and not a decree of the Almighty. Referring to Adam and to Christ, the Bible says, "The first man is of the earth, earthy; the second man is the Lord from heaven." And when the disciples of Jesus asked him, "What is God's relationship to the dead?" he replied, "God is not a God of the dead but of the living, for in His sight all are alive." In other words, the Bible clearly states that we are living in a spiritual Universe, governed by mental laws; that there is an action of Consciousness, as Law, upon Substance, forever producing form, and forever withdrawing from any particular form, thus producing another; that the form changes but the Formless never.

Science tells us that all form comes from One Substance, made manifest through vibration. This further helps us to see the relationship of the Word to the formless, and teaches us the indestructibility and eternality of energy and cosmic stuff. The coal and oil we burn today passed, millions of years ago, from one form into another, and now, as they burn, are passing back into energy again. Nothing has happened to the energy except that it was temporarily imprisoned, that in its release and explosion it might produce heat and energy for utilitarian purposes. But nothing has happened to it.

The great souls gave us this spiritual consciousness five thousand years ago, but it was hard to make us believe it. They have had to remain in the background until science at last resolves the physical universe into that—not vacuum—but that substance, indefinable and indivisible, which men like Socrates announced, and upon which conclusions men like Jesus based their whole system of thought and method of procedure.

We are not denying the physical universe when we seek to explain it. Physical form is real and if it were not for form, God, or Intelligence, would not be expressed. But right here students are puzzled when we say that God does know form but not size. As Emerson said: "There is no great and no small, to the Soul that maketh all; and whence It cometh all things are, and It cometh everywhere." So far as the Law is concerned, It does not know anything about big and little. Someone will at once say: "If God knows anything, God knows big and little." God cannot know anything which is contradictory to the Divine Being. It is impossible for the Infinite to know that which is finite. The superlative cannot be the comparative.

This does not mean that God cannot know the mountain and the molehill. We have tried to make it plain that God knows form but not size. He knows both the mountain and the molehill, but not as big and little. The Infinite knows experience but not duration. *Anything that Spirit knows, is!* Because Its Being passes into becoming through Its Self-Knowing.

We believe in science, because it is organized, systematized knowledge and it is only when knowledge is organized and systematized that it can be utilized. Science is leading us surely, by its process and method, back again to the great spiritual deductions of the ages: the physical universe is One; Mind is One. I could not talk to you and you could not talk to me if your mind had a sharp cleavage, a differentiation in Reality from mine. There would be something unlike us between, and we could not converse. The very fact that we are here and can communicate with each other, establishes the Unity of Mind, and it also establishes the fact that Intelligence contacts and communicates with Itself.

Mind is individualized but never individual. This Mind which is Universal will never be any less than Universal; It will never be individual, but It will be individualized. There is a great difference. *The wave in the ocean will never be a wave by itself.* IT WILL BE THE OCEAN AS A WAVE. That is all it will be, caught up as a wave but still the ocean. Perhaps that is the concept Jesus had when he said that God delivered everything to Him, but He could do nothing except God as Him, in Him, "doeth the works."

The individualization of the Universal comes to a point in the personal, just as the human body is one with the entire physical universe. It is a different type of the same thing. So my so-called mind is not another mind, it is this Mind, but it is thinking individually. That is all. Thinking individually, it thinks differently—not necessarily better or worse, but differently.

We are individual entities in a Universe which furnishes the background and the foreground for each of us, but each is unique, different yet fundamentally alike. Why then should it seem strange—if this whole differentiation of the physical universe is but a difference of form, distinguishing objects one from another because of arrangement—that the enlightened should see back of this arrangement the Word of God?

In other words, the Cosmic Order is the Divine Mind; the Universe in which we live is a Spiritual System; we are spiritual beings but we do not know it, we do not understand it. In our ignorance we misuse our divinity without changing or destroying it. We can never change Reality, cannot destroy It nor break Its laws; but we place ourselves in such a position to It that It appears limited and unhappy and even appears to die. "By man came death, by man came also the resurrection of the dead." What is this but stating that man figured out how to die and how to be born again? God had nothing to do with it, because God "is not a God of the dead but of the living: for all live unto Him."

We are, therefore, members of the Universe, and *being members of that which unites everything, we are some part of each other!* "I am the vine and ye are the branches. . . ." Jesus' words were symbols of the Universe in which we live. Except the branch abide in the vine, it shall not bear fruit, but "if ye abide in me, and my words abide in you, ye shall ask what ye will and it shall be done unto you." Thus is the Father glorified in the Son.

Our thought, then, is creative in our world. Macrocosm—the big world—and microcosm—the little world. We reproduce the Cosmos in our individual world. The Father is greater than the Son, *yet the Father is the Son*, and *we are each other*, and *It is in all of us*. So every day we are living from this Unity, and projecting the experiences from it upon the screen of our objective lives. We have done this so long in ignorance that we appear to be bound by the outlines of the forms which our ignorance has projected. That is what Plato meant when he gave us the story of the slaves in the cave. They saw the *shadows* of bondage, and thought they were bound, while all the while the chains had no reality.

We seek a practical use of the Truth. The Spirit is the starting point of everything. There is a Presence in the Universe which we call God, Intelligence, Law, which by the very act of Its Word creates an objective form which is like Its Word. The Word becomes flesh. We are some part of this creative order and we cannot change our nature. We have to accept the truth and we should make use of it. We had better use it constructively than destructively; in happiness rather than in misery. They are made out of the same thing, but let us try to arrive at heaven instead of hell. Hell cools off when we think of heaven.

And we wish to demonstrate. What do we mean by demonstration? Nothing peculiar, nothing weird, nothing that pertains to ghost walking. To *demonstrate* means to prove, to exemplify, to manifest, to bring forth, to project into our experience something that is better than we had yesterday . . . less pain, less unhappiness, less poverty, less misery, *more good* . . . this is what is meant by a demonstration.

We would like to be happier, have greater physical health. We would like to have more of what it takes to be happy, whether it be millions or marbles. These things are nothing of themselves. It is only when we think of them as entities, within themselves, that we fall down and worship them; and then that which we should possess, possesses and obsesses us. Every great spiritual genius has taught us to this effect: If you have possessions which possess you, it is better for you to lose them that you may understand their temporary, fleeting form. No great spiritual teacher has denied the advisability of using possessions. Emerson says to cast them upon every wind of heaven, do not hold them. "Beware of holding too much good in your hand."

We would like to help ourselves and each other through using the Law of Mind. This we may do by treatment. What is a treatment? It is something the mind becomes aware of. Someone might ask, "Is it something the Spirit of God does to us?" Yes, the Spirit of God is everything, but the mind must accept, and since the mind cannot accept what it rejects, then the mind must unqualifiedly accept. This is where the trouble comes in. *We all have the spiritual power to raise the dead*, but we do not believe we have. Our mind does not *unqualifiedly accept* this. Therefore, that which we are, through disbelief, projects the form of *have-not* rather than the form of HAVE, but even in taking the form of have-not, *it demonstrates that it has what it BELIEVES*.

We enter the Absolute in such degree as we withdraw from the relative. The Bible tells us not to count our enemies. It is not easy, is it, to turn from a disease and KNOW THAT THERE IS NO DISEASE, when we know very well that it is an experience of the moment. This is not easy, but the one who can do just this, can heal. The All-Creative Wisdom does not think one thing is difficult and another easy. With God all things are possible. We must *know* this and this Power of God must be hooked up with our thought, with what we are doing. Energy unconnected does nothing, it is only when it is used, properly directed, that it accomplishes things.

We must conceive of the Spirit, God, as governing, controlling and directing man's activity. *God is not a failure.* Therefore, we must resolutely turn away from every experience which has been negative, from every experience which has been a failure, and from every experience which denies God. The mental and spiritual practitioner should deal with his field alone. He is not opposed to the medical practitioner, he does not say, "I cannot treat this man if he takes a pill." Unless the practitioner can *prove* that the man does not *need* to take a pill, the patient had better take it if it will benefit him. There is nothing weird about the application of Truth. We should not be superstitious in using the Law of Mind. But the mental practitioner should remain in his own field, which is always the field of thought.

If one is working for a person who has "high blood pressure" or "low blood pressure," after a few treatments he might have his patient go back to his physician for a physical check-up. "But," one may ask, "can I have spiritual treatment if I do this?" This is a superstitious reaction and all superstition is ignorance. If the mental and spiritual practitioner can restore normal blood pressure for his patient, a doctor who can weigh and measure it, can quickly ascertain if the work has been done. When this is understood, the closest co-operation will be brought about between physician and metaphysician. It is inevitable that the day shall come when they will understand each other. They are working in two separate fields, which at the same time have a fundamental unity in one primal principle. But the mental and spiritual practitioner works in the field of Mind alone.

Unlike the physician who must diagnose the disease and work with it, the metaphysician turns entirely away from the disease in his thought. Diseases—whether they be mumps, measles, poverty or unhappiness—all are wrong adjustments to life; this is what disease is. Lack of ease. The mental and spiritual practitioner must turn completely from the condition, as it is, and MUST CONTEMPLATE IT AS IT OUGHT TO BE . . . never as it appears to be.

And he has a technique for this, a method of procedure. He has a *way* in which he thinks. He starts with the premise that God is perfect, the Spiritual System is perfect, man is a part of this Spiritual System, therefore, the *spiritual man* is perfect. The practitioner does not deal with the material man; he says the *spiritual man* is perfect, and that disease cannot attach itself to this spiritual man. If he were dealing directly with disease, poverty or unhappiness, he would be caught in its mental vibration. We should seek to disentangle our imagination from the material man and join it with our contemplation of the spiritual man. THE SPIRITUAL MAN IS PERFECT. The spiritual man is continuously remolding and remaking the material or physical man.

In the natural processes of evolution, what we call time elapses—one day, one week, one month, one year—but in Spirit there is no time. The Spirit is Timeless. Therefore the mental and spiritual practitioner must not deal with time, he must transcend time. Not only must he transcend time, but he must resolutely turn away from *any* form of limitation. God is not limited by any form. He turns to the Formless, for out of this a new form shall come.

Let us again briefly go over what it is that one must do. He must first of all BELIEVE. The supposition is that the reader already believes or he would not be studying thus far. Why must we believe? Because God is belief. God is belief and belief is Law, and Law produces form, in substance. When Jesus explained to his disciples that they had failed to heal because of lack of faith, they protested that they did have faith *in* God. Jesus explained to them that this was insufficient; they must have the faith of God. *The faith of God* is very different from *a faith in God*. The faith of God IS God, and somewhere along the line of our spiritual evolution this transition will gradually take place, where we shall cease having a faith IN and shall have the faith OF. Always in such degree as this happens, a demonstration takes place. We must believe because God is belief; the physical Universe is built out of belief—faith, belief, acceptance, conviction.

This is only the starting point. What good is the possibility until it is used? What good is knowledge unless we make practical application of it? Therefore we must definitely speak our conviction in concrete form in Mind. A treatment should always be definite, specific, concrete. In practical treatment one does not become subjective. The creative act is always conscious. In other words, a treatment moves in thought, sets something in motion, is an active thing.

For instance, suppose we have received a request for help for a physical condition. Immediately we take the name of the person in consciousness—as every man maintains his identity in Universal Mind, just as he maintains it in the physical world—and we declare the truth about that man, the truth about the *spiritual man*, and we know that the truth about Spiritual Man is the truth about *that* man's condition right now. First, recognition; second, unification. We continue to do this until something comes into our consciousness which says "Yes." We know the work has been accomplished. This is the third step: realization. This is what a treatment is. Perhaps we would hold this consciousness a while, and we might repeat this treatment two or three times a day for a time. If we have agreed to treat the man, we should be certain to do so. At the same time, we should be careful, after the treatment has been given, that we take no responsibility of trying to make it work. The Law will work from its own energy; *how*, we do not know.

No matter what the need may be, whether we call it physical disease, poverty, unhappiness, lack of opportunity, or need for love and friendship, we should conform the words in our treatment to meet the necessity of the case. Because we are all members of one another, the word of the practitioner will rise through the consciousness of his patient into experience. There is a law in physics which says that water will reach its own level by its own weight. There is a law of metaphysics corresponding to it; consciousness will externalize at its own level, by its own recognition. We may call this faith, we may call it embodiment, we may call it whatever we will, there is something in the Universe which responds and corresponds to our mental states.

Therefore, it is imperative that we turn from the relative, because TO VIEW LIMITATION IS TO IMPRESS IT UPON THE MIND, and accentuate the state of consciousness which produced it. It is not always easy to turn from fear, from poverty and pain, and from the hurt of human existence, to that which is perfect. But whoever can do this—and will train himself to do it—will be like the man healed of blindness. He had little comprehension of *how* it had been done; he could only say: "Whereas I was blind, now I see."

BRIEF REMINDERS ON HOW TO GIVE SPIRITUAL TREATMENT

Suppose when one begins to treat a great surge of fear comes over him, arguing that he cannot give a good treatment. The thing to do is to treat this fear as a suggestion which has no power, and which, therefore, cannot convince him that he lacks the power to heal. He should say: "There is nothing in me which can doubt my ability to heal." This will neutralize the fear and free his effort.

How do we know when we have treated a patient long enough? How would one know when to stop seeing him if he were a doctor? When he is well he will need no more treatments; until this time comes, treat every day for a realization of perfection. Begin each treatment as if you had never treated the patient before, trying to realize each time that this particular treatment is going to do the work . . . perfectly.

Does it make any difference whether or not the patient is taking medicine? Not at all. If it gives him any relief, he should have it. We need all the relief we can get. The patient is healed when he no longer needs medicine. Some think they dishonor God when they take a pill. This is superstition. Discard these thoughts and give your entire attention to realizing perfection for your patient.

Healing is not accomplished through will power but by knowing the Truth. This Truth is that the Spiritual Man is already Perfect, no matter what the appearance may be. "Holding thoughts" has nothing to do with this form of treatment. If you find when you begin to give a treatment that the process gives you a headache, know that you are doing your work on the mental plane and not through spiritual realization. A treatment should leave the practitioner in better condition than before he gave it; otherwise, it is not a good treatment.

One might ask: "Is all mental disease a thought held in the conscious mind of the patient?" No, not necessarily. It may be a subconscious thought, or it may be the result of many thoughts, which brought together produce a definite result. Combinations of thought unite to produce definite effects.

Limitation and poverty are not things, but are the results of restricted ways of thinking. We are surrounded by a Subjective Intelligence, which receives the impress of our thought and acts upon it. This natural Law in the Mental World is neither good nor bad. It can only be said of It that IT IS, and that we may consciously use It. The Law is a law of reflection; for Life is a mirror, reflecting to us as conditions the images of our thinking. Whatever one thinks tends to take form and become a part of his experience. The Medium of all thought is the Universal Mind, acting as Law. Law is always impersonal, neutral, receptive and reactive.

A sense of separation from good causes us to feel restricted; while a sense of our Unity with GOOD changes the currents of Causation and brings a happier condition into the experience. Everything in the physical universe is an effect, and exists only by virtue of some invisible cause. Man's individuality enables him to make such use of the Law as he desires. He is bound, not by limitation but by limited thought. The same power which binds him will free him when he understands the Law to be one of liberty and not of bondage. The power within man can free him from all distasteful conditions if the Law governing this power is properly understood and utilized.

The Law of Mind, which is the Medium of all action, is a law of perfect balance: the objective world perfectly balances the images within the subjective world. Water will reach its own level by its own weight; and according to the same law, consciousness will externalize at its own level by its own weight. Cause and effect are but two sides of the same thing, one being an image in mind and the other its objective condition. Here is the invariable rule for knowing how to treat. We can judge the subjective concept only by its objective effect. If everything a man does leads to confusion, we should treat to know that he is poised. The Spirit is not confused over anything. If everything a man does turns out to be a failure, we must know that the

Spirit within him cannot conceive failure. What we put into the treatment will come out of it. *More* than we appear to put into it can come out of it, but not a *different* type. If I plant a watermelon seed, I will get watermelons, but I will get a number of melons, and they will have a lot of seeds which can produce more melons, so the thought is MULTIPLICITY but never DIVISION. Treatment is a definite, conscious, concrete thing. There is *intention* in a treatment and there should be a definite acceptance.

The manifest universe is a result of the Self-Contemplation of God. *Man's world of affairs is the result of his self-contemplation.* He is at first ignorant of this and so binds himself through wrong thought and action. As he reverses this thought, he reverses the condition attendant upon it. There is neither effort nor strain in knowing the Truth. Right action will be compelled through right knowing. Therefore, when we know the Truth, It will compel us to act in a correct manner.

Attraction and repulsion are mental qualities, and may be consciously utilized for definite purposes. Man, automatically and according to Law, attracts to himself a correspondence of his inner mental attitudes. Inner mental attitudes may be induced through right thinking and correct knowing. The subjective state of thought is a power always at work; it is the result of the sum total of all beliefs, consciously and unconsciously held. The subjective state of thought may be consciously changed through right mental action. The conscious thought controls the subconscious and, in its turn, the subconscious controls conditions.

Since the Law is *mental*, one must believe in It, in order to have It work affirmatively for him. But *It is always* working *according to his belief*, whether he is conscious of this truth or not. Demonstration takes place through the field of the One Universal Mind. We set the Power in motion; the Law produces the effect. We plant the seed and the Law produces the plant.

One should never allow himself to think of, or talk about, limitation or poverty. Life is a mirror and will reflect back to the thinker what he thinks into it. The more spiritual the thought, the higher its manifestation. Spiritual thought means an absolute belief in, and reliance upon, Truth. This is both natural and normal.

All is Love and yet all is Law. Love is the impelling force and Law executes the will of Love. Man is a center of God-Consciousness in the great Whole. He cannot deface his real being, but may hinder the Whole from coming into a complete expression through his life. Turning to the

One with a complete abandonment and in absolute trust, he will find that he is already saved, healed and prospered.

There is One Infinite Mind from which all things come. This Mind is through, in, and around man. It is the Only Mind there is and every time man thinks he uses It. There is One Infinite Spirit and every time man says "I am" he proclaims It. There is One Infinite Substance and every time man moves he moves in It. There is One Infinite Law and every time man thinks he sets this Law in motion. There is One Infinite God and every time man speaks to this God, he receives a direct answer. ONE! ONE! ONE! "I am God and there is none else." There is One Limitless Life, which returns to the thinker exactly what he thinks into It. One! One! One! "In all, over all, and through all." Talk, live, act, believe and know that you are a center in this One. All the Power there is, all the Presence there is, all the Love there is, all the Peace there is, all the Good there is, and the Only God there is, is Omnipresent. Consequently, the Infinite is in and through man and is in and through everything. "Act as though I am and I will be."

CHAPTER TWENTY
WHAT THE MYSTICS HAVE TAUGHT

What Is a Mystic? • *Unity* • *Individuality* • *Ultimate Salvation for All* • *Evolution* • *Cosmic Consciousness . . . Illumination.*

WHAT IS A MYSTIC?

A *mystic* is not a mysterious person but is one who has a deep, inner sense of Life and of his unity with the Whole. *Mysticism* and *psychism* are entirely different. One is *real* while the other may, or may not, be an illusion. There is nothing mysterious in the Truth, so far as It is understood, but all things seem mysterious until we understand them.

A mystic is one who intuitively perceives Truth and, without mental process, arrives at Spiritual Realization. It is from the teachings of the great mystics that the best in the philosophy of the world has come. Who was there who could have taught such men as these? By what process of mentality did they arrive at their profound conclusions? We are compelled to recognize that Spirit alone was their Teacher; they were indeed taught of God.

Our great religions have been given by a few who climbed the heights of spiritual vision and caught a fleeting glimpse of Ultimate Reality. No *living* soul could have taught them what they knew.

The great poets have been true mystics who, through their poems, have revealed the Presence of God. Men like Robert Browning, Tennyson, Wordsworth, Homer, Walt Whitman, Edward Rowland Sill, and others of like nature, have given us poetry which is immortal, because they had a spiritual sense of life.

Great spiritual philosophers are mystics. The old prophets were mystics—David, Solomon, Jesus, Plotinus, and a score of others, all had the same experience—the sense of a Living Presence. The greatest music ever composed was written by the hand of a mystic, and the highest and best in art has come from men of spiritual perception.

Man has compelled nature to do his bidding. He has harnessed electricity, caught the wind, trapped steam, and made them do his will. He has invented machines to do the work of thousands. He has belted the globe with his traffic and built up a wonderful civilization; but in few cases has he conquered his own soul. The mystic has revealed things that do not pass as ships in the night. He has revealed Eternal Verities and has plainly taught us that there is a Living Presence indwelling ALL. This constitutes the greatest intellectual and spiritual heritage of the ages. The balance of our knowledge of God must come as a direct impartation from Him. We must learn it for ourselves.

The mystic *does not read human thought*, but rather he senses the atmosphere of God. The mystics of every age have seen, sensed and taught THE SAME TRUTH! Psychic experiences, on the other hand, bear the exact opposite testimony, as they more or less contradict each other, for each psychic sees a different kind of mental picture. But the mystic experiences of the ages have revealed ONE AND THE SAME TRUTH!

A psychic sees largely through his own, or another's, subjective mentality. Consequently, his impressions are more or less colored by the vibration of his own or another's thought. He is subject to hallucinations and false impressions of every description. That is why, generally speaking, no two psychics see the same thing. Mystics have all sensed one identical Reality, and their testimony is in no way confusing, because the Spirit within them has borne witness to the same Truth.

The mystics have been perfectly normal people. They did not think of themselves as mystics, that was their language. It was natural to them—perfectly normal. They have been people like Jacob Boehme, a cobbler, pegging away at his shoes, who, looking up, saw in the geranium plant the reflection of the Cosmos—the very soul of God; like Jesus looking into the heart of nature; like Moses reading God's Law from a burning bush.

The teaching of the mystics has been that there should be *conscious courting of the Divine Presence*. There should be a conscious receptivity to It, *but a balanced one*. As one of the Apostles said, in substance, that he would rather speak ten words with his understanding than ten thousand with confusion. "God is not the author of confusion but of peace." Unlike the great psychics of the ages, who have been more or less confused, the great mystics have been intensely and pre-eminently sane people, sound people.

The philosophy of Jesus will remain sound when the belief in a material universe shall have been rolled up like a scroll and numbered with the things once thought to be real. So will be the philosophy of Buddha, Plato, Socrates, Emerson and Walt Whitman, and the philosophy we are writing about today. But the more or less unconscious disclosures of most psychics are not entirely true, even in the day in which they are given. While psychism is a most interesting field of study, we should understand it for what it is worth.

It is through the teachings of the illumined that the Spiritual Universe reveals Itself, imparting to us what we know about God. What we directly experience ourselves, and what we believe others have experienced, is all we can know about God.

Jesus taught a Power transcendent, triumphant, absolute, positive, against which lesser laws meant nothing. *By Its very Presence It heals.* The mystics did not contend or argue with people. There was nothing to argue about. THEY SAW and KNEW. They are the great revealers to man of the nature of the Universe, and the relationship of man to God.

Unity

Reason declares that that Which is Infinite cannot be divided against Itself. The Infinite *is*, therefore indivisible and consequently a Perfect Unit. "Hear, O Israel, the Lord our God is One Lord." It is also "That Whose Center is everywhere and Whose Circumference is nowhere."

All of It is present at any and every point within Itself. It is not approaching a point nor receding from it, but is always at the point. *The whole of God is present at any and every point within God.* It was to this Indwelling Spirit that Jesus prayed, for God is within man as well as throughout all creation. It is "That thread of the All-Sustaining beauty which runs through all and doth all unite." "His lines have gone out into all places." "There is no place where God is not."

This concept enabled Job to say, "In my flesh shall I see God." All life is bound together by One common Law of Love, and Love is the Self-Givingness of Spirit. It was the realization of this One Presence which illumined the saints and sages of the past. "I and the Father are One." "The Father that dwelleth in me, He doeth the works." We must come to sense this marvelous Presence, for this is the secret of successful metaphysical work: God in all and through all.

All manifestation of Life is from an invisible to a visible plane, through a silent, effortless process of spiritual realization. WE MUST UNIFY IN OUR OWN MENTALITIES WITH PURE SPIRIT. To each of us, individually, God or Spirit is the Supreme Personality of the Universe— the Supreme Personality of that which we, ourselves, are. It is only as the relationship of the individual to the Deity becomes enlarged that one has a consciousness of power.

In treatment there should always be a recognition of the absolute Unity of God and man: the Oneness, Inseparability, Indivisibility, Changelessness. God as the big circle and man as the little circle. Man is in God and God is man, just as a drop of water is in the ocean, while the ocean is the drop of water. This is the recognition which Jesus had when he said, "I and the Father are

One." There is a perfect Union, and to the degree that we are conscious of this Union, we incorporate this consciousness in our word; and our word has just as much power as we put into it, no more and no less.

Within this Infinite Mind each individual exists, *not as a separated but as a separate entity*. We are a point in Universal Consciousness, which is God, and God is our Life, Spirit, Mind and Intelligence. We are not separated from Life, neither is It separated from us, but we are separate entities in It—individualized centers of God Consciousness.

We came from Life and are in Life, so we are One with Life; and we know that Instinctive Life within—which has brought us to the point of self-recognition—still knows in us the reason for all things, the purpose underlying all things; and we know that there is nothing in us of fear, doubt or confusion which can hinder the flow of Reality to the point of our recognition. We are guided daily by Divine Intelligence into paths of peace, wherein the soul recognizes its Source and meets It in joyful union, in complete At-One-ment.

The power of Jesus is understood when we study His method of procedure. Consider His raising of Lazarus from the dead. Standing at the tomb, He gave thanks; this was recognition. He next said: "I know that thou hearest me always;" this was unification. Then He said: "Lazarus, come forth"; this was command. The method is perfect and we shall do well to follow it. This method can be used in all treatment. First, realize that Divine Power is; then unify with It; and then speak the word as "one having authority," for the Law is "the servant of the Eternal Spirit throughout all the ages."

Jesus prayed that all might come to see the Unity of Life. "That they may be One even as we are One," was His prayer as He neared the completion of His great work—the prayer that enabled those closest to Him to understand the Unity of Spirit, in which man clearly recognizes his Oneness with his Creator and with all Creation. All mystics have sensed that we live in One Life: "In Him we live and move and have our being."

The Unity of Good is a revelation of the greatest importance, for it teaches us that we are One with the Whole and One with each other. The Fatherhood of God and the actual Brotherhood of Man will be made apparent on earth to the degree that man realizes true Unity.

INDIVIDUALITY

The higher the sense of Truth, the greater will be the realization of the uniqueness of individual character and personality. The real Self is God-given and cannot be denied. *It is the place where God comes to a point of Individualized and Personified Expression.* "I am the light of the world."

Individuality means self-choice, volition, conscious mind, personified Spirit, complete freedom and a Power to back up that freedom. There could not be a mechanical or an unspontaneous individuality. Individuality must be created in the image of Perfection *and let alone to make this stupendous discovery for itself*; it emerges from the Universal. Psychology teaches the personification of this individuality, which is true as far as it goes, but metaphysics universalizes it by unifying it with the Whole. There is a Universal nature of Man, inherent within him, which causes the manifestation of his personality. The Spirit of God.

We have now discovered a unity with the Whole on the three sides of life, or from all three modes of expression. We are one with the body of the physical world; One with the Creative Law of the Universe in the mental world; and One with the Spirit of God in the conscious world.

Could we ask or hope for more? Would it be possible for more to be given? We could not ask for more and no greater freedom *could* be given. From now on we shall expand, grow and express only to the degree that we consciously cooperate with the Whole.

All of the great mystics have taught practically the same thing. They have all agreed that the soul is on the pathway of experience, that is, of self-discovery; that it is on its way back to its Father's House; and that every soul will ultimately reach its heavenly home.

They have taught the Divinity of Man. "I have said, Ye are Gods; and all of you are children of the Most High." They have told us that man's destiny is Divine and sure; and that creation is complete and perfect *now*. The great mystics have all agreed that man's life is his to do with as he chooses, but that when he turns to the One, he will always receive inspiration from on High.

They have told us of the marvelous relationship which exists between God and man, and of a close Union that cannot be broken; the greatest of the mystics have consciously walked with God and talked with Him, just as we talk with each other. It is difficult to realize how this can be. It is hard to understand how a Being, so Universal as God must be, can talk with man. Here alone, the mystic sense reveals the greater truth and knows that, infinite as is the Divine Being, IT IS STILL PERSONAL TO ALL WHO BELIEVE IN ITS PRESENCE! It is entirely possible for a man to talk with the Spirit, for the Spirit is within him, and He who made the ears, can hear.

Since we see that *personality* is what one does with his *individuality*, we should turn within (as have all those great souls who have blessed the world with their presence), we should turn within and FIND GOD. It should seem natural to turn to the Great Power back of everything; it should seem normal to believe in this Power; and we should have a sense of a Real Presence when we do turn toward the One and Only Power in the entire Universe.

This method is by far the most effective. It gives a sense of power that nothing else can and in this way proves that it is a Reality. It would be a wonderful experiment if the world would try to solve all of its problems through the power of Spirit. Indeed the time will come when everyone will . . . "From the highest . . . to the lowest."

Undoubtedly the power of Jesus lay in His recognition of the Infinite Person as a Responsive, Conscious, Living Reality; while, on the other hand, He recognized the Law as an arbitrary force which was compelled to obey His will. He combined the personal and the impersonal attributes of Life into a perfect Whole. THE INFINITE IS PERSONAL TO EVERY SOUL WHO BELIEVES IN THE INFINITE. It is a mistake to so abstract the Principle that we forget the Living Presence. It is the combination of the two which makes work effective. A sense of real completion can come only to that soul that realizes its Unity with the Great Whole. Man will never be satisfied until his whole being responds to this thought, and then, indeed, will "God go forth again into Creation." "To as many as believed, gave He the power."

Ultimate Salvation for All

The mystics have taught that there is but One Ultimate Reality; and that this Ultimate Reality is *here* NOW, if we could but see It. The great mystics have been illumined. They have seen through the veil of matter and perceived the Spiritual Universe. They have taught that the Kingdom of God is now present, and NEEDS BUT TO BE REALIZED! And they have apparently sensed that this Kingdom is within.

One of the most illuminating things which mysticism has revealed is that *evil is not an ultimate reality*, it is simply an experience of the soul on its journey toward Reality. Evil is not an entity, but an experience on the pathway of self-unfoldment. It is not a thing of itself but simply a misuse of power. It will disappear when we stop looking at, or indulging in, it. We cannot stop believing in it as long as we indulge in it, so the mystic has always taught the race to turn from evil and do good.

Furthermore, the mystics have taught the ultimate salvation of all people and the immortality of every soul. Indeed, they have taught that IMMORTALITY IS HERE AND NOW, IF WE WOULD BUT AWAKE TO THE FACT. "Beloved, now are we the sons of God." *Since each soul is some part of the Whole, it is impossible that any soul can be lost!* "God is not the God of the dead but of the living." Damnation has been as foreign to the thought of the mystic as any concept of evil must be to the Mind of God.

The great mystics taught that *man should have no burdens*, and would have none if he turned to the "ONE." "Come unto me all ye that labor and are heavy laden and I will give you rest." As Jesus knew that it would be impossible for all men to come to Him as a Personality, He must have meant that we should come into His understanding of Life and Reality. Some day we shall learn to lay our burdens on the altar of Love, that they may be consumed by the fire of faith in the Living Spirit. Man would have no burdens if he kept this "High Watch toward The One"— if he always turned to God.

In mental healing, the spiritual practitioner should sense everyone as a Divine Being, thus causing an awakening of the Divinity which is latent in all people. This spiritual awakening should never be divorced from the mental act, which is to awaken the mind to the realization of Spirit. The Universe is *now* a spiritual system. The problem of evil does not enter into this contemplation. This does not mean that we can keep on doing evil. It is a personal and not a Cosmic problem and disappears when we no longer contemplate it.

Our individualized Universe is forever complete, yet forever completing Itself, in order that every experience may teach us to transcend some previous one, in ever ascending cycles, upward bound. This is the true meaning of misfortune or vicissitude or suffering, which is never a thing in itself. Our recognition of Truth is Its pronouncement of Itself, and when a man says "I am," it is God proclaiming His own Being. Emerson said he was often conscious of Jove nodding to Jove from behind our backs.

For a practical application, suppose one is treating a person who is low in vitality. The practitioner must recognize not *low vitality* but Real Vitality, recognizing the I-Am-ness, the All-Powerfulness, God. IN SUCH DEGREE AS WE CONTEMPLATE THE SPIRIT OF LIVINGNESS, IT BECOMES MANIFEST. A clear idea of livingness personifies itself as physical vitality. *Thus our recognition of It becomes Its recognition of us at the level of our recognition of It.*

There is a great difference in our reaction when we believe that evil is an entity and when we understand that we merely have the *possibility* of experiencing it. The Universe does not demand suffering! Suffering is man-made, through ignorance. It will continue until man learns how to make it negative in his experience. Someday we shall decide that we have had enough suffering.

There *cannot* be a Law in the Universe which demands evil, lack, limitation, and the experience of unhappiness, to provide shades to magnify Its glory. Therefore, the mystics have taught that evil has only the power to destroy itself; that it is not God-ordained. From the viewpoint of Reality, it is an illusion, but they have not denied it as an experience. It is an experience all have had. The great have not failed to recognize the *appearance* of evil, but they have separated the appearance from the reality. They have done away with evil as a cosmic entity—NO DEVIL, NO HELL, NO TORMENT, NO DAMNATION outside of one's own state of thought, NO PUNISHMENT outside of that self-inflicted, through ignorance; and NO SALVATION OUTSIDE OF CONSCIOUS CO-OPERATION WITH THE INFINITE. *Heaven and Hell are states of consciousness.*

EVOLUTION

The Universe, both visible and invisible, is a Spiritual System. Man is a part of this Spiritual Order, so indivisibly united with It that the entire Cosmos is (or may be) reflected in his mind! Evolution is the awakening of the soul to a recognition of its unity with the Whole. Material evolution is an *effect*, not a *cause*. This reverses the popular belief, declaring that *evolution is the result* of intelligence, rather than intelligence being the result of evolution!

The aim of evolution is to produce a man, who as the point of his objective thought may completely manifest the whole idea of life, may bring Unity to the point of particularization, finding nothing in the Law to oppose It. The man Jesus became the Christ through a complete realization of the Unity of Spirit and the Absoluteness of His word. His physical and spiritual faculties, His objective and subjective mind, were completely poised and perfectly balanced.

It is evident if this realization took place in any other individual, *his* word would be manifested likewise. Because behind the word is Universal Soul, Omnipotent Law. The Spirit is Limitless, but can only be to us what we believe It to be. Why must we believe It is? Because, UNTIL WE BELIEVE THAT IT IS, WE ARE BELIEVING THAT IT IS NOT! It is all a matter of belief, *but belief is scientifically induced into a subjective state, through conscious endeavor.*

To repeat: The aim of evolution is to produce a man who, at the objective point of his own self-determination, may completely manifest the inner life of the Spirit. Even the Spirit does not seek to control us, It lets us alone to discover ourselves. The most precious thing a man possesses is his own individuality; indeed, this is the only thing he really has, or is. For one instant to allow any outside influence to enter or control this individuality is a crime against his real self.

In the Bible we read: "Beloved, now are we the sons of God, and it doth not yet appear what we shall be, but we know that when He shall appear we shall be like Him, for we shall see Him as He is." Even though this process of evolution is still taking place—has not stopped and perhaps never will stop because we shall forever unfold—even in this state of incompletion, "NOW are we the sons of God." As we more completely evolve, we shall see the Christ appear and "when He shall appear, we shall be like Him, for we shall see Him as He is," being transformed from glory to glory, by reason of that Divine Urge within each one of us. Even now the Divine Reality is accomplished in Infinite Mind. Within each one of us is an indestructible, an eternal, God-intended man, a perfect Being . . . our perfect being.

Always the idea of perfected man must have been in the Divine Mind; involved within the *cause* is its *effect*. And in the Mind of the Eternal, man must be perfect. God is perfect Mind and cannot conceive imperfect ideas, hence the idea of man as held in the Mind of God, *must be a perfect idea*. The perfect man is the only man God knows!

Man, being an individual, may do as he wills with himself—as Browning said, he may desecrate but he can never lose his life. The Spirit ever has a witness within us and the God-intended man already knows that he is One with the Whole; that Nature is comprised of One ultimate Power, using many instruments and having many avenues of expression. The time has come in our evolution when we should awaken to the recognition that behind each one stands the Eternal Mind—that each has complete access to It; that each may come to It for inspiration and revelation—and that surrounding all is a Divine Law obeying the dictates of this Eternal Mind.

Evolution is a principle which, though invisible, finds manifestation in every form of life. It is the logical or necessary outcome of Universal Intelligence of Spirit; *but evolution is an effect of Intelligence and not its cause*. Evolution can only follow involution. Involution is the idea, while evolution is the unfoldment of the idea. INVOLUTION PRECEDES EVOLUTION AND EVOLUTION FOLLOWS WITH MECHANICAL PRECISION, PROPELLED BY AN IMMUTABLE LAW . . . the Law of Cause and Effect.

God is Universal Intelligence or Spirit. The only way Intelligence can move is by an interior movement. God must move within God, if God is ALL. He moves within and upon Himself. It is evident that the movement back of the objective world must be a subjective movement— a movement of consciousness. It is necessary, then, that whatever movement takes place, it MUST take place within and upon the One; and it follows that whatever is created, is created out of this One.

God moves upon God. This is the starting point of Creation. *Every time one conceives an idea, it is God expressing Himself.* He is eternally knowing, and eternally known, through everyone. It is God's nature to know and there is an emotional craving, or desire for expression, inherent in the Universe. There is a Universal Law obeying the Will of Spirit. This is the Law through which that which is involved, evolves. We, as conscious Spirit, set a Universal Law in motion which makes *things* from *ideas*. The Spirit INVOLVES, the Law EVOLVES. The Law does not know that It is evolving; it is Its nature to evolve and this nature is mechanical.

Evolution, then, is not a thing in itself; it is an effect. Behind all objective form, there is a subjective likeness which exactly balances and is the prototype of the form. The thing involved perfectly balances the thing evolving from it. *Evolution is the time and the process through which Spirit unfolds!* In so far as any individual understands this mental Law, he is able to use it. We must learn *how* It works and comply with the *way* It works. Always, It is an obedient servant. As a man sows, so also shall he reap. Involution and evolution, the thought and the thing, the Word and the Law, the purpose and the execution . . . this is the sequence.

While there is liberty in the evolving principle, it is always in accord with certain fundamental laws of necessity. It seems as though behind evolution there is an irresistible pressure, compelling more, better, higher and greater things. For instance, if we study the evolution of locomotion, from the rising of man from the clod, we see him riding upon a horse, in a cart, in a wagon, and so on to the automobile and the airplane. What is this but the evolution of locomotion, the unfolding through man's mind of the possibility of travel? If we watch the evolution of travel by water, we find the same thing from the raft to modern ships.

What is the inevitable end of locomotion? Could it be other than that *we shall ultimately do away with every visible means of transportation? When we shall have unified with Omnipresence, we shall be omnipresent.*

When we shall have arrived at a sufficient understanding, our thought will take us where we wish to be. When we know enough, we shall be able to pass on to another plane and come back again, if we wish to do so. When we know enough to multiply the loaves and fishes, we shall do so. When we know enough to walk on the water, we shall be able to do that and it will all be in accordance with natural law in a spiritual world.

Cosmic Consciousness . . . Illumination

Dr. Bucke defines Cosmic Consciousness as: "One's consciousness of his unity with the Whole." The mystic intuitively perceives Truth, and often without any process of reasoning—immediately is aware, with what Swedenborg called a sort of "interior awareness," a spiritual sense.

There can and does descend into our minds—embody and personify in our person—a Divinity, a Unity, the Spirit of God, the direct incarnation of the Original Thing, in us—the mystical presentation of Christ.

Dean Inge, perhaps the best thinker in the Anglican Church of today, tells us that Plotinus had seven distinct periods of *cosmic consciousness*, in which state he was so completely unified with the Universe that he became One with It. His spiritual philosophy was a result of these experiences. Plotinus, you will recall, was one of the greatest of the Neo-Platonic Philosophers.

Dr. Bucke, the author of that most rational book, "Cosmic Consciousness," cites many instances of known and authentic records of people who have had definite Cosmic experiences. In his scientific approach to this subject, he calls attention to the necessity of distinguishing between psychic revelations and Cosmic Consciousness.

Reports of the experiences of most psychics are contradictory. While on the other hand, the experiences of those who have entered into Cosmic Consciousness—over a period of thousands of years—tell us an identical story, once we get the key to their language—*all* tell the same story of Reality. The psychic may or may not be true; the spiritual is always true. The psychic realm is the realm of the subconscious, or relative first cause. The spiritual is the realm of First Cause. Therefore, we may read Buddha, Jesus, Plato, Socrates, Aristotle, Swedenborg, Emerson, Whitman, Browning or any of the other great mystics, no matter in what age they have lived, and we shall find the same Ultimate. By reading the writings of most psychics, we enter confusion; therefore, we must understand clearly this vital difference between psychism and mysticism. One may or may not be true; the other is always true.

The intelligence in an animal which directs its actions and tells it where to go to find food and shelter, we call instinct. It is really Omniscience in the animal. The same quality, more highly developed, makes a conscious appearance in man and is what we call *intuition*. Intuition is God in man, revealing to him the Realities of Being; and just as instinct guides the animal, so would intuition guide man, if he would allow it to do so.

Here again we must be careful not to mistake a psychic impression for an intuitive one. *Psychic impressions may control; intuition remains in the background and waits for recognition.* "Behold I stand at the door and knock."

All arbitrary control of man must have stopped as soon as he came to a point of self-knowingness. From this point, he must discover himself; but intuition, which is nothing less than God in man, silently awaits his recognition and co-operation. The Spirit is always with us if we would but sense Its Presence. Mystics have felt this wonderful Power working from within; and have responded to It; and as certain evidence that they were not laboring under delusions, THEY HAVE ALL SENSED THE SAME THING. Had the impressions been psychic only, each would have seen and sensed a *different* thing, for each would merely have been seeing through the darkness of his own subjective mentality.

Cosmic Consciousness is not a mystery, it is the Self-Knowingness of God through man. The more complete the operation of that Power, *the more complete is man's conscious mentality*, for the illumined do not become less, but more, *themselves*. The greater the consciousness of God, the more complete must be the realization of the True Self—the Divine Reality.

Illumination will come as man more and more realizes his Unity with the Whole, and as he constantly endeavors to let the Truth operate through him. But since the Whole is at the point of the Inner Mentality, it will be here alone that he will contact It. "Speak to Him, thou, for He hears." Always in such degree as one has spiritual sense, he realizes universality in his own soul. The great mystics have had that sense and have felt the possibility of an immediate communion with the Universal Spirit. This essence has run through all theologies and has been the cause of much of their vitality. Theology with all its weakness has been stronger in its strength than it has been weak in its weakness, because the vital elements in it have been greater than the devitalizing ones. It would not have lived unless this were true.

The only God man knows is the God of his own Inner Life; he can know no other. To assume that man can know a God outside himself is to assume that he can know something of which he cannot be conscious. This does not mean that man is God; it means that the only God that man knows is within, and the only life man has is from within. God is not external but is Indwelling, at the very center of man's life. This is why Jesus said that the Kingdom of Heaven is within and why He prayed: "Our Father which art in Heaven."

The great mystics like Jesus have taught that as we enter into the One, the One enters into us and *becomes us* and *is us*. They have taught the "Mystical Marriage," the union of the soul of man with the Soul of God, and the Unity of all Life. The great mystics while sensing this Unity—the Universality of all things—have also sensed the individualization of Being and the individuality of Man as a Divine Reality. Tagore, in seeking to explain this, says that the individual is immersed in, but not lost in, Nirvana, and he uses the illustration . . . "as an arrow is lost in its mark," still remaining an arrow. The mysticism of Buddha did not teach the annihilation of the soul, but the eternality of an ever-expanding principle of the soul.

The highest mental practice is to listen to this Inner Voice and to declare Its Presence. The greater a man's consciousness of this Indwelling I AM, the more fully he will live. This will never lead to illusion, but will always lead to Reality. All great souls have known this and have constantly striven to let the Mind of God express through their mentalities. "The Father that dwelleth in me, He doeth the works." This was the declaration of the great Master, and it should be ours also; not a limited sense of life but a limitless one.

It is impossible to put into words or into print what a mystic sometimes sees, and it is as difficult to believe—to realize that it is so—as it is to put it into words. But there is a certain inner sense which, at times, sees Reality in a flash which illuminates the whole being with a great flood of light. This, too, might seem an illusion unless the testimony were complete, but *every* mystic has had this experience . . . some in a greater degree than others. Jesus was the greatest of all the mystics and, once at least, after a period of illumination, his face was so bright that his followers could not look upon it. All mystics have seen this Cosmic Light. This is why it is said they were illumined. They have all had the same experience, whether it was Moses coming down from the mountain, Jesus after the resurrection, Saul on his return to Damascus, Emerson walking across the Common in Concord—where suddenly he became conscious of this light—or Whitman who refers to it as that which "stuck its forked tongue" into his being as he lay on the grass, or whether it was Edward Carpenter who, after leaving Whitman and looking up, thought all of New York City was in flames. This light the great artists have sensed so completely that they have depicted it as a halo around the heads of saints, an atmosphere of light.

Bucke points out that the illumination of all mystics has been accompanied by a great light. He feels that Emerson walked on the verge of this light for many years—and more continuously than most people—but did not have quite as definite an experience of its fullness as some others; but that he had what we might term a greater continuation of what we shall call a *lesser* light.

It is interesting that LIGHT should come with an expansion of consciousness. "The light shines in the darkness and the darkness comprehendeth it not." We all, in varying degrees, enter into this sense—into this illumination—all people have sensed that Truth is Light. If a spiritual treatment could be seen (and a spiritual treatment merely means the mind unifying with Good) it would be seen as a pathway of light. This light is not created. It is not a psychological explosion; it is something which pre-exists. It is useless to try to visualize it or to make it appear. It is not a trick of concentration. "The Kingdom of Heaven cometh not by observation."

In moments of deepest realization, the great mystics have sensed that One Life flows through all, and that all are some part of that Life. They have also seen Substance, a fine, white, brilliant stuff, forever falling into everything; a Substance indestructible and eternal. It is at such times of complete realization that they have been blinded by the LIGHT of which we have been speaking.

Remember, all of this takes place in a perfectly normal state of mind and has nothing whatever to do with the psychic state. It is not an illusion but a reality; and it is during these periods that real revelations come. Perhaps a good illustration would be to suppose a large group of people in a room together, but unaware of each other's presence; each is busy with his own personal affairs, suddenly the room is illuminated for a second and they all see each other. Afterwards they try to tell what they saw. In flashes of illumination, the inspired have seen *into the very center of Reality*, and have brought back with them a picture of what they saw and felt. Briefly, these have been their conclusions: they have been firmly convinced of immortality . . . immortality NOW, not to be achieved at some future date; individuality, God as personal to the individual; the inevitable overcoming of all evil by good.

Therefore, they have taught that in such degree as one's concept of God is sufficient, evil disappears. How are we going to make this practical, other than feeling this in our meditation for practical work, for healing, for demonstration? This is what we mean by a method, a procedure, a technique and a realization: that accompanying the method and technique should always come as much of the realization as we can generate at that time. In the method and the technique, something is said. This is a moving thing, but when we reach that other place—illumination—nothing is said . . . something is FELT.

CHAPTER TWENTY-ONE
SOME PHASES OF
THE SUBJECTIVE LIFE

The Subjective Mind • Race-Suggestion • Subjective Mind and Inspiration • Mental Atmospheres • Tuning in on Thought • Streams of Consciousness • The Spirit of Prophecy.

THE SUBJECTIVE MIND

We have already seen that what we call the soul is really the subjective part of us. We wish to look a little further into some of the phenomena of the soul.

We do not have two minds, but we do have a dual aspect of mentality in what we call the objective and subjective states of consciousness. The objective mind is that part of the mentality which functions consciously. It is the part of us which is self-knowing and without it we would not be self-conscious entities. Our conscious mind is the place where we consciously live and are aware that we are living. This is Spirit.

Our subjective mind is our mental emanation in Universal Subjectivity. It is our individual use of mental law. We certainly do not wish to deviate from that which psychology teaches about the mind of man in its conscious, subconscious, or subjective states. We merely wish to add this: *the reason we have a subjective mind is that Subjectivity existed in the Universe prior to our use of It; and where we use It, It forms around us a subjective personification of ourselves, which is a result of the action and the reaction of our thought.*

The subjective mind is the seat of memory and contains a remembrance of everything that has ever happened to the outer man. It also contains the family and race characteristics. It retains these memories, in a certain sense, as mental pictures. The subjective mind might be

536

compared to a picture gallery, upon whose walls are hung the pictures of all the people whom the individual has ever known, and all the incidents which he has ever experienced.

RACE-SUGGESTION

Race-suggestion is a very real thing, and each individual carries around with him (and has written into his mentality) many impressions which he never consciously thought of or experienced. When we realize that the individual's subjectivity is his use of the One Subjective Mind, we shall see that a subjective unity is maintained between all people, and that individual mentalities who are in sympathetic vibration with each other, more or less mingle and receive suggestions from each other. This is the meaning of mental influence, which is indeed a very real thing.

Just as each person, place or thing has a subjective atmosphere or remembrance, so each town, city or nation has its individual atmosphere. Some towns are bustling with life and action, while others seem dead. Some are filled with a spirit of culture, while others are filled with a spirit of commerce. This is the result of the mentalities of those who live in such places. Just as a city has its atmosphere, so does an entire nation. The combined thought of those who inhabit a nation creates a national consciousness which we speak of as the *psychology* of that people.

Subjective Mind, being Universal, the history of the race is written in the mental atmosphere of the globe on which we live. That is, everything which has ever happened on this planet has left its imprint on the walls of time; and could we walk down their corridors and read the writings, we should be reading the race history. This should seem simple when we realize that the vibrations of the human voice can be preserved on the receptive phonograph disc, or the sound film, and reproduced at will. If we were to impress one of these discs, or a strip of the sound film, and lay it away for years (properly protecting it) it would still reproduce these vibrations. It is not difficult, then, to understand how the walls of time may be hung with the pictures of human events, and how one who sees these pictures may read race history. There is a tendency, on the part of all of us, to reproduce the accumulated subjective experiences of the human race.

SUBJECTIVE MIND AND INSPIRATION

Since the individual subjective mind is the storehouse of memory, it retains all that the eye has seen, the ear heard, or the mentality conceived. Since it contains much that the outer man never consciously knew, and is the receptacle of much of the race knowledge through unconscious communication, it must (and does) have a knowledge that far surpasses the objective faculties.

Realizing that the subjective draws to itself everything that it is in sympathy with, we see that anyone who is sympathetically inclined toward the race, or vibrates to the race-thought, might pick up the entire race-emotion and experience and—if he were able to bring it to the surface—could consciously depict it. Many of the world's orators, actors and writers have been able to do this, which explains why some of them have been so erratic, for they have been more or less controlled by the emotions which they have contacted.

Anyone contacting the subjective side of the race-mentality, with the ability to bring it to the surface, *will have at his disposal an emotional knowledge that many lifetimes of hard study could not accumulate*. But IF ONE HAD TO SURRENDER HIS INDIVIDUALITY IN THE PROCESS, HE WOULD BETTER REMAIN IGNORANT.

There is, of course, a much deeper seat of knowledge than the subjective mind, which is the Spirit; direct contact with the Spirit is Illumination.

MENTAL ATMOSPHERES

Each person has a mental atmosphere which is the result of all that he has thought, said and done, and consciously or unconsciously perceived. The mental atmosphere is very real, and is that subtle influence which constitutes the power of personal attraction, for personal attraction has but little to do with looks. It goes much deeper and is almost entirely subjective. This will explain our likes and dislikes for those with whom we come in daily contact. We meet some only to turn away without a word, while others we are at once drawn toward, and without any apparent reason. This is the result of their mental atmosphere or thought vibration. No matter what the lips may be saying, the inner thought outspeaks them, and the unspoken word often carries more weight than the spoken.

TUNING IN ON THOUGHT

Thought-transference, or telepathy, is such a commonly known fact that it is not our purpose to do other than discuss it briefly. However, there are some facts which might be overlooked unless we give them careful attention. The main fact to emphasize is that mental telepathy would not be possible, *unless there were a medium through which it could operate*. This medium is Universal Mind, and it is through this medium, or avenue, that all thought-transference, or mental telepathy, takes place.

Telepathy is the act of reading subjective thought, or of receiving conscious thought from another without audible words being spoken. But there must be a mental *tuning in,* so to speak, just as there must be in radio. We are surrounded by all sorts of vibrations and if we wish to catch any of them distinctly, we must tune in. Even then, there is a great deal of interference and we do not always get the messages clearly. We often get the wrong ones, and sometimes many of the vibrations come together and seem to be nothing but a lot of noises, without any particular reason for being. It is only when the instrument is properly adjusted to some individual vibration that a clear message may be received.

This is true of mental telepathy, which is the transmission of thought; the receiver must tune in. *It does not follow, however, that the sender knows that this is taking place*, any more than a radio speaker knows how many are tuning in to hear his address. In other words, one might pick up thoughts just as he picks up radio messages. Some have the ability to tune in on thought and read it more or less accurately. These people we call *psychics*, but all people are really psychic, since all have a soul or subjective mind. What we really mean is that a psychic, or medium, is one who has the ability to objectify that which is subjective—to bring to the surface of conscious thought that which lies below the threshold of the outer mind. The *medium* reads the book of remembrance and it is marvelous how far-reaching this book may be. Whatever may have happened at any time on this plane remains within its subjective atmosphere as a memory picture of the experiences of those who have lived here. These pictures, or vibrations, may be clearly discerned by those who can read them.

Since the Universal Subjectivity is a Unity it follows that all of these pictures exist at any and every point within It. Consequently, we may contact at the point of our own subjective mind (which is a point in Universal Subjective Mind) every incident which has ever transpired on this planet. We might even see a picture which was enacted two thousand years ago in some Roman arena, for the atmosphere contains such pictures.

Each person in his *objective* state is a distinct and individualized center in Universal Mind, but in his *subjective* state (in his stream of consciousness, or at his rate of vibration) each is Universal, because of the Indivisibility of Mind. Wherever and whenever any individual contacts another upon the *subjective* side of life, if he is a psychic (if he objectifies subjectivity) he may see a thought form of that person, but *it does not necessarily follow that he would really be seeing the person.*

We need not be astonished when a psychic gives us the complete history of our family, even to reciting the things that engaged the attention of our ancestors while they were on earth. The psychic is merely reading from the subjective remembrance.

STREAMS OF CONSCIOUSNESS

Each being an individual entity in Mind is known by the name he bears, and by the vibration which he emanates; for while we are all in One Mind or Spirit, each has a separate and individualized personality.

According to the Unity of Mind, thought is everywhere present, and so long as it persists it will remain present. What is known in one place, may be known in all places. Time, space and obstructions are unknown to Mind and thought. It follows, that anyone tuning into our thought, will enter into our stream of consciousness, no matter where we are and no matter where he may be. If we still persist after the body shall have suffered physical death (and we are convinced that we shall) this law must still hold good, for past and present are one and the same in Mind. Time is only the measure of an experience, and space, of itself, is not apart from, but is *in*, Mind.

A psychic can enter the stream of thought of anyone whose vibration he can mentally contact, be that person in the flesh or out of it; and since we are all psychic—all having a soul element—we are all doubtless communicating with each other to the degree that we sympathetically vibrate toward each other. We do not all have the ability to *objectify* psychic impressions, and ordinarily they never come to the surface. However, they are there just the same. This is why we often feel uneasy in the presence of certain people, or when we mentally contact some condition and are aware of a disturbed inner feeling, without any apparent reason.

There are many normal psychics who can, while in a perfectly objective state, read people's thoughts and perform many other wonderful feats of the mind. This is normal and no harm can come from it. It is, indeed, one of Nature's ways of working and is most interesting. Any psychic power which can be used while in a normal state of mind is harmless and helpful; by this we mean one that can be used while one is in a conscious state.

THE SPIRIT OF PROPHECY

We have explained how it is that the psychic vision can look into the past and see what has transpired—by reason of the fact that it is dealing with a field in which there is no past, no present and no future, but merely a continuation of being. Because this is so, any incident which has transpired in the past is an active thing in the present, unless the vibration is neutralized, when it no longer has existence anywhere.

Just as it is true, apparently, that the incidents of the past continually rehearse themselves in the same manner that a picture hanging on the wall for the next ten thousand years (if nothing happens to it) will look just as it does now, so anyone contacting a previous incident, clairvoyantly, will see it as though it were now transpiring . . . not past. This is the way in which clairvoyant vision operates. The continuation of the past, through the present, into the future, is a movement of causation passing from cause to effect; and because the movement is first set in motion in a field of Mind which is purely subjective, *both cause and effect will exist at any point during the sequence of this movement*. The clairvoyant vision, then, contacting it at any point—even before the final outcome—will see the final outcome.

There is nothing fatalistic about this. A thing can appear to be fatalistic without necessarily being so. This we should understand, because the human mind in its ignorance has created great psychic laws for itself. Therefore, if one has been told anything in the way of a prophecy which is negative, it should be directly refuted, because that negation exists in the realm of subjective causation . . . not spiritual causation.

To repeat this in a clearer way, perhaps: Subjective Mind can deduce only; It has no power of initiative or self-choice, and is compelled by Its very nature to retain all the suggestions which It receives. The best illustration of this is in the creative soil, in which the gardener plants his seed. The soil does not argue nor deny, but goes to work on the seed and begins to create a plant which will represent the type of manifestation inherent, as idea, in the seed; from a cucumber seed, we get cucumbers, and from a cabbage seed, we get cabbages. Always the law maintains the individuality of the seed as it creates the plant; never does it contradict the right of the seed to be what it really is. Involved within the seed is the idea of the plant, as are also those lesser ideas which are to act as a medium between the seed and the plant. Involved within the seed are both cause and effect, but the seed must first be placed within the creative soil if we wish to see the plant. In the creative soil (or in the seed) *the full and perfect idea of the plant must exist as a completed thing, else it could never be brought into manifestation*. The idea of the full-grown plant must exist somewhere in the seed and soil, if it is ever going to materialize.

This teaches us a lesson in subjectivity. Thoughts going into the subjective are like seeds; they act through the creative medium of Mind and must have, within themselves, the full power to develop and to express; but how could they express unless they were already known to Mind? THEY COULD NOT, so Mind must view the thought as already completed in the thing; and *Mind must also contain the avenue through which the idea is to be expressed*. EVERY THOUGHT SETS THE FULFILLMENT OF ITS DESIRE IN MOTION IN MIND, AND MIND SEES THE THING AS ALREADY DONE!

Mental *tendencies* set in motion cast their shadows before, and a psychic often sees the complete manifestation of an idea before it has had time to materialize in the objective world. This is what constitutes the average spirit of prophecy, for prophecy is the reading of subjective tendencies and seeing them as already accomplished facts. The subjective mind can deduce only, but its power of logic and sequence appears to be perfect.

For illustration, suppose there is a window one mile distant; I am throwing a ball at this window and the ball is halfway to it, going at the rate of one mile a minute. Now you come into the picture, see the ball, measure the distance, compute the speed with which the ball is passing through the air and say: "The ball is halfway to the window, it is travelling at the rate of one mile a minute and in just one half a minute the window is going to be broken by the ball passing through it." Let us suppose that you are the only one who sees the ball, for the rest are looking at the window, and in half a minute it is broken. How did you prophesy that the window would be broken? *By drawing a logical conclusion from an already established premise.*

A similar thing takes place when a psychic exercises the spirit of prophecy, because he is getting his own subjective contact with the condition and simply interpreting what comes to him; but this is the logical, deductive, conclusive power of his subjective thought—seeing a thing completed, by first seeing a tendency set in motion and computing the time it will take to complete it. There are but few, however, who possess any reliable spirit of prophecy.

CHAPTER TWENTY-TWO
FINDING THE CHRIST

Who Is Christ? • God . . . Infinite Personality • The Indivisible Whole • The Triumphant Christ.

WHO IS CHRIST?

Who is Christ? The Son, begotten of the *only* Father—*not* the "only begotten Son of God." The mystical conception of Christ means the Universality of Sonship, *embodied in any individual who recognizes this Sonship.*

Eckhart, one of the great mystics of the Middle Ages, said: "God never begot but *one* Son, but the Eternal is forever begetting the only begotten." This conveys the same sense as our New Testament statement "world without end." This world forms and disintegrates, as the body does, but creation goes on forever. Therefore, the Eternal is forever begetting that which is the realization of Its own perfection. It is an eternal process; It is the Son of God, and the Son of God is Christ.

Christ means the Universal Idea of Sonship, of which each is a member. That is why we are spoken of as members of that One Body; and why we are told to have that Mind in us "which was also in Christ Jesus." Each partakes of the Christ nature, to the degree that the Christ is revealed through him, and to that degree he becomes the Christ. We should turn to that Living Presence within, which is the Father in heaven, recognize It as the One and Only Power in the Universe, unify with It; declare our word to be the presence, power and activity of this One. We should speak the word with belief in its power, because the Law is the servant of the Spirit.

If we could stand aside and let this One Perfect Life flow through us, *we could not help healing people!* This is the highest form of healing. We have gone through many abstract processes of reasoning and have found out what the Law is and how It works. Now we can forget all about the Law and know there is nothing but the Word—the Law will be working automatically. We must forget everything else and let our word be spoken with a deep inner realization of love, beauty, peace, poise, power, and of the great Presence of Life *at the point of our own consciousness*.

There is a place in the mentality—in the heights of its greatest realizations—where it throws itself with complete abandonment into the very center of the Universe. There is a point in the supreme moment of realization where the individual merges with the Universe, but not to the loss of his individuality; where a sense of the Oneness of all Life so enters his being that there is no sense of otherness. It is here that the mentality performs seeming miracles, *because there is nothing to hinder the Whole from coming through*. We can do this only by providing the mental equivalents of Life, by dwelling and meditating upon the immensity of Life and the fact that, as vast, as immense, as limitless as It is, the whole of It is brought to the point of our own consciousness.

We comprehend the Infinite only to the degree that It expresses Itself through us, becoming to us that which we believe It to be. So we daily practice in our meditations the realization of Life: "Infinite, indwelling Spirit *within me*, Almighty God *within me*, Real Substance *within me*, that which is Truth *within me*." Jesus said: "I am the way, the truth, and the life: no man cometh unto the Father but by me."

How true this is! We cannot come unto the Father Which art in Heaven except through our own nature. Right here, through our own nature, is the gateway and the path which leads to illumination, to realization, to inspiration, to the intuitive perception of everything. The highest faculty in man is intuition and it comes to a point sometimes where, with no process of reasoning at all, he instantly knows.

Christ is the embodiment of divine Sonship which has come, with varying degrees of power, to all people in all ages and to every person in some degree. Christ is a Universal Presence.

We do believe that in the unique personage of Jesus, this Christ was more fully orbed than in anyone of whom we have record. We do believe that in the person of Jesus more of God was manifest. We also believe that Christ comes alike to each and all. There is no one particular man predestined to become the Christ. We must understand the Christ is not a person, but a Principle. It was impossible for Jesus not to have become the Christ, as the human gave way to the Divine, as the man gave way to God, as the flesh gave way to Spirit, as the will of division gave way to the will of unity—Jesus the man became a living embodiment of the Christ.

If we can look upon Jesus from this viewpoint, we shall be able to study his life as a living example. What is more inspiring than to contemplate the consciousness of a man who has the faith to stand in front of a paralyzed man and tell him to get up and walk, *and to know very well that he is going to get up and walk*; or to stand in front of the tomb of a dead man and tell him to come forth! Such an example as this is worth something, but if the whole performance were enacted in the mind of a man *entirely unique and different from us*, then it would mean no more to us than studying the biography of hundreds of other men. Fortunately, we do not have to contemplate Jesus as being "unique and different," for the Bible makes it more than plain that he was a man like as we are.

As the human gives way to the Divine, in all people, they become the Christ. In the case of Jesus, there was such a surrendering of an isolated will, that a greater incarnation of the Divine actually took place. The mystic Christ comes from the bosom of the Unseen Father, proclaiming the love of God through His own love of humanity.

Asleep in the heart of Cosmic Love,
Unborn . . . Universal . . . Potential,
The Christ Child lay
And the great Mother Soul,
Brooding over her unborn child,
Conceived it in the stillness
Of her Universal Nature,
Imparting to it her own being.

Born into time and experience,
Unnoticed, unseen, yet alive and aware,
The Christ Child incarnated in human form,
Taking the likeness of men and women,
Yet giving no sign of Its presence,
Waiting with utmost patience and love
The revelation that should disclose Itself
And proclaim the reign of peace.

Many ages passed and vanished
In the long yesterdays of time,
And still the Christ Child waited.
Nations appeared and disappeared;
Toil—famine—pestilence and want,
Hunger—cold—heat—and thirst,
War—hatred—blood—and ruin,
And still the seed of Perfection—unrevealed.

But the Universal Wholeness
Cannot be forever subjected,
Nor Cosmic Love be kept from human form,
That which was given must be revealed.
The seed of Perfection must burst.
The shoots of heavenly planting
Must break the cords that bind,
Fanning the human into a blaze Divine.

And so the long appointed day arrived,
A voice from out the stillness
Spoke: "This is my Beloved Son—
Let the earth be still in his presence,
Let the beasts of the field . . . the birds of the air
And all living creatures, be still.
Let the hosts of heaven sing praises,
And let deep cry unto deep."

Then spoke the child:
"I am come to bring peace.
I am the child of joy, and
To all who will, I give life.
I am formed of happiness.
I am come from the eternal stillness.
Quietness and confidence are mine.
In the heart of the Father I have lived forever.

"Oh! Nations and all people,
Look unto me and be saved.
Behold my face, shining as the sun,
And my feet, shod with righteousness.
In my left hand are riches and honor
And in my right, peace forevermore,
All that I am—all that I have—
I give."

Christ . . . the Idea of Universal Sonship . . . the entire creation, both visible and invisible. There is One Father of all. This One Father, conceiving within Himself, gives birth to all the Divine ideas. The sum-total of all these ideas constitutes the Mystic Christ. Jesus understood his own nature. He knew that as the human embodies the Divine, it manifests the Christ Nature. Jesus never thought of himself as different from others. His whole teaching was that what he did, others could do. He located God and the Kingdom of Heaven within himself. He had plunged beneath the material surface of creation and found its Spiritual Cause. This Cause he called God or the Father.

It is now nearly two thousand years since this wonderful man labored in the vineyard of human endeavor, pointing a way to Eternal Reality. Centuries have passed; nations have risen, only to decline and fall. Science has solved many problems. Invention has harnessed subtle forces, and our land is filled with institutions of learning—but the world is looking for another great teacher, one who will again show it the way. Never before was there such an inquiry into the hidden meaning of things . . . never such a searching after God and Reality. It seems as though all people are engaged in this search, and that no one can be satisfied until he has made the great discovery for himself; but to how few has come the real Truth—the realization that God is indwelling in the soul and spirit of man! And yet this realization is what gave Jesus his wonderful power—this, and a correct knowledge of spiritual Law in the mental world.

GOD . . . INFINITE PERSONALITY

God, or Spirit, is Supreme, Infinite, Limitless Personality. And we should think of the Divine Being as such—as completely responsive to everything that we do. There should come to us a sense of communion, a spontaneous sense of an Irresistible Union. If we had this, we would demonstrate instantaneously!

An evolved soul is always a worshipper of God. He worships God in everything; for God *is* in everything. God not only is *in everything, but He is more than everything He is in!* "Ye are the light of the world." That is God in us. All that we are is God, yet God is more than all we are. The nearer consciousness comes to this Truth, the more Cosmic sweep it has, the more power it has.

The realization that God is personal to all who are receptive to the Divine influx, enables one to communicate with the Spirit, receiving a direct answer from It. This Jesus was able to do. He was able to balance the personal and the impersonal attributes of being, for the Law is only a natural force, while the Spirit is always Self-Knowing. In studying the life and teachings of Jesus, the most unique character of history, we discover a few simple ideas underlying his philosophy, the embodiment of which enabled him to become the Christ.

Fundamental to his concept of life was his belief in a Universal Spirit, which he called God, or the Heavenly Father. This Heavenly Father was an Intelligence, to which he consciously talked and from which, undoubtedly, he received a definite reply. Jesus located God in his own soul. So complete was this realization that he was unable to find a place where the being of Jesus began and the Being of God left off, or where the Being of God began and Jesus ceased to be.

This Jesus discovered and taught: that whatever is true of Man, of the *reality* of his nature, is the Divine Presence within him. Coupled with this dynamic realization, with this enlightening concept of Deity—of placing God at the center of his own being—was the realization of an absolute Law, obeying his will, *when this will was in harmony with the Spirit of Truth.* This concept of God and man, and the relationship between them, places the philosophy of Jesus in a different category from that of other teachers. Christ is the image of God, the likeness of the Father, the Son of the Universe, the Man that Spirit conceives. Christ is not limited to any person, nor does He appear in only one age. He is as eternal as God. He is God's Idea of Himself, His own Self-Knowingness. For Christ to be found in us is to put off the old man, with all his mistakes and doubts, and put on the new man, who is always certain that he is beloved of the Father. The Christ always comes with power and might, awakened by the still, small voice of Truth.

The Indivisible Whole

Our conscious intelligence is as much of Life as we understand. We have stopped looking for the Spirit, because we have found It. It is what you are and It is what I am; we could not be anything else if we tried. The thing that we look *with* is the thing we have been looking *for.* That is why it is written: "I have said, ye are gods; and all of you are children of the most High." (Psalms 82:6) We have stopped looking for the Law. We have found It. In the Universe, we call It Universal Subjectivity or Soul. In our own experience, we call It the subjective state of our thought, which is our individual use of Universal Law. We have found the Law and demonstrated It. We find that both the Law and the Spirit are Limitless. What is it we need for greater freedom? Nothing but a greater realization of what we already know.

We should never hesitate to say that we know the Truth, because we do, for the realization of the Unity of God and man *is* the Truth. We simply need a greater realization of this. How are we to get it? Only by penetrating deeper and yet deeper into our own Divine Nature—pushing further and further back into the Infinite. *Where* are we to do this? THERE IS NO PLACE EXCEPT WITHIN THAT WE CAN DO IT. *Who* is to do it for us? NO ONE. No one can. Others can treat us; they can set the Law in motion for us and help us to become prosperous.

This is both good and helpful, but the evolution of the individual—the unfoldment of personality, the enlightenment of the soul, the illumination of the spirit—can come only to the degree that the individual himself purposes to let Life operate through him. "Let this Mind be in you which was also in Christ Jesus" (Phil. 2:5). This is the Mind of God—the only Mind—the Supreme Intelligence of the Universe.

The answer to every question is within man, because man is within Spirit, and Spirit is an Indivisible Whole! The solution to every problem is within man; the healing of all disease is within man; the forgiveness of all sin is within man; the raising of the dead is within man; Heaven is within man. This is why Jesus prayed to this indwelling "I am" and said: "Our Father which art in Heaven," and again he said: "The Kingdom of Heaven is *within you*."

Each of us, then, represents the Whole. How should we feel toward the Whole? In the old order we thought of the Whole as sort of a mandatory Power, an autocratic Government, an arbitrary God, sending some to heaven and some to hell, and all "for His glory." Now we are more enlightened and we realize that there *could be no such Divine* Being. We have meditated upon the vastness of the Universe as Law, and we have said, "God is Law. There is a Divine Principle which is God."

In the new order of thought, we are likely to fall into as great an error as in the old thought, unless we go much deeper than thinking of God as merely Principle. GOD IS MORE THAN LAW OR PRINCIPLE. God is the Infinite Spirit, the Limitless Conscious Life of the Universe; the One Infinite Person, within whom all people live . . . The One Indivisible Whole.

HOLY, HOLY, HOLY,
Inner Presence, Great and Mighty,
Inner Light that shines divinely,
Inner Life that lives completely,
Inner Joy that smiles serenely,
Inner Peace that flows so deeply,
Inner Calm, untroubled, happy,
Inner Love, that gives so freely,
Inner Truth, that never fails me,
Inner Power that holds securely,
Inner Eye, that sees so clearly,
Inner Ear, that hears Him always,
Inner Voice, that speaks supremely,
Inner Good, that binds me to Thee,

HOLY, HOLY, HOLY——
Lord, God within me.

We must not look afar to see the Christ, for He is ever near at hand. He is always within us. To the individual, there can never be any power, truth or life, unless he is able to realize or recognize it. Jesus stands alone as a man who knew himself and was cognizant of his relationship to the Perfect Whole. In the ecstasy of self-realization, he proclaimed the Truth to be working through him.

Thou art the center and circumference of my life,
The beginningless and endless part of me,
The eternal Reality of me;
The everlasting Power within me;
The eternal Good working through me;
The infinite Love impelling me;
The limitless Peace and Calm within me;
The Perfect Life, living through and in me;
The Joy of the Soul and the Light of the Spirit, illumining me.
O Lord, God, Eternal and forever Blessed, Thou art my whole being!

Jesus spent much of his time communing with his own soul, for it is through our inner thought that we contact God. To this remarkable man, out of the silence of his own soul, came a direct revelation of his Sonship, his Oneness with God. Back of the conflict of ideas; back of the din of external life and action; back, back in the innermost recesses of uplifted thought and silent contemplation, there is a Voice ever proclaiming: "This is my Beloved Son." Seldom does this voice penetrate the outer world of human experience, seldom does anyone allow it to perfectly express through him. We must learn to listen for this voice. Call it conscience, intuition, or what we will, it is there. No man need go unguided through life, for all are divine at the center and all are Images of the Most High!

Sweet song of the Silence, forever singing in my heart!
Words cannot express, the tongue cannot tell;
Only the heart knows the songs which were never sung, the music which was never written.
I have heard that great Harmony and felt that great Presence.
I have listened to the Silence; and in the deep places of Life, I have stood naked and
    receptive to Thy songs and they have entered my soul.
I am lost in the mighty depths of Thy inner calm and peace.

As the external Jesus gave way to the Divine, the human took on the Christ Spirit and became the Voice of God to humanity. How wonderfully he did this, constitutes the history of Christianity, and much of the enlightenment of modern civilization. And yet it would be a grave mistake to suppose that he was different from other men. He was a man who knew himself and his direct relationship to the Whole. This was the secret of his success.

To think of Jesus as being different from other men is to misunderstand his mission and purpose in life. He was a way-shower, and *proved his way to be a correct one!* His method was direct, dynamic, and powerful, yet extremely easy and simple to comprehend. He believed in God *in himself*, as Power and Reality. Believing in God within, he was compelled to believe in himself.

To the illumined, has ever come self-realization and I-AM-NESS. Who could proclaim himself to be the way, the truth, and the life, unless he had understood that God indwelt his own soul? The Christ Spirit comes to all alike, proclaiming Itself as the Son of God, even unto the humble *in spirit*. Proud of his divinity, yet humble before the greatness of the Whole, Jesus spoke from the heights of spiritual perception, proclaiming the deathless reality of the individual life, the continuity of the individual soul, the unity of Universal Spirit within all men. This was the Christ speaking, the Son begotten of the only Father—the Son of God. Humble in his humanity, compassionate in his tenderness, understanding the frailties of the human mind, he let the Great Spirit speak through him, in words of love and sympathy. He proclaimed his divinity through his humanity and taught that all men are brothers. No man ever lived who valued the human soul more than Jesus, for he knew it to be the personification of God.

> *I AM, what more can I say? I am, it is enough!*
> *Because Thou Art, I am!*
> *From out of the deeps of me, I AM!*
> *In and around me, I am! Over and through me, I am!*
> *O Inner Being, Eternal and Blessed, Complete and Perfect!*
> *Birthless and Changeless and Deathless, I AM! I AM! and evermore shall be.*

The mystic Christ comes from the bosom of the Unseen Father, proclaiming the love of God through His own love of humanity. To know God is to love, for without love there is no knowledge of God. As the Christ awakens, the divine spark—shot from central fires of the Universal Flame—is able to warm other souls by the radiance of its own self-unfoldment.

We give only what we have. The only shadow we cast is of ourselves; this shadow lengthens as we realize the Great Presence in which we live, move and have our being. Who would entertain the Christ, *must invite Him!* He does not come unbidden, nor sit at any man's table an unwelcome guest; neither does the Divine Presence force Itself upon any. He stands at the door and knocks; WE MUST OPEN IF WE ARE TO RECEIVE. But how can we receive unless we first believe? We must believe that Christ indwells our own lives and stimulates all of our actions, for without Him we can do nothing. To realize within oneself a divine Presence, a perfect Person, is to recognize the Christ. No man ever walks life's road alone; there is ever Another who walks with him; this is his inner Self, the undying Reality, which his personality but poorly emulates. Let us learn to be still and let the Truth speak through us; to be still and know that the inner light shines.

Be still, O Soul, and know. Look unto the One and be illumined.
Rejoice and be glad, for thy Spirit lights the way.
Lift up thine eyes and behold Him, for He is fair to look upon.
Listen for His voice, for He will tell thee of marvelous things.
Receive Him, for in His presence there is peace.
Embrace Him, for He is thy Lover.
Let Him tarry with thee, that thou mayest not be lonely.
Take council from Him, for He is wise.
Learn from Him, for He knows.
Be still in His presence and rejoice in His Love forevermore.

THE TRIUMPHANT CHRIST

The Christ knows that His individuality is indestructible; that He is an eternal Being, living forever in the bosom of the Father. The Christ triumphs over death and the grave, breaking through the tomb of human limitation into the dawn of eternal expansion. The Christ rises from the ashes of human hopes, pointing the way to a greater realization of life. The Christ IS ALWAYS TRIUMPHANT, IS EVER A VICTOR, IS NEVER DEFEATED, NEEDS NO CHAMPION! The Christ places His hand in the outstretched hand of the Universe, and walks unafraid through life.

Through the long night watches, His hand clasps mine.
At the break of dawn, His hand clasps mine.
In the daytime of work and endeavor,
From Eternity to Eternity, His hand clasps mine.

When time shall have passed,
When Eternities shall be strewn about like falling petals,
And Space and Worlds shall be swallowed up in everlasting blessedness,
His hand will clasp mine!

We are never left without a witness of the Eternal, and in our greatest moments—in those flash-like visions of mystic grandeur—we know that we are made of eternal stuff, fashioned after a Divine Pattern.

CHAPTER TWENTY-THREE

IMMORTALITY

The Meaning of Immortality • *Where Did Man Come from and Why?* • *What Is the Body?* • *Shall We Have a Body Hereafter?* • *The Ether of Science* • *Is There Spirit Communication?* • *What of Reward and Punishment?* • *Shall We Rest in the Hereafter?* • *Personal Convictions of Life Eternal.*

The Meaning of Immortality

To most of us, *immortality* means that we shall persist after the experience of physical death, retaining a full recognition of ourselves, and having the ability to recognize others. If our full capacities go with us beyond the grave, we must be able to think consciously, to will, to know and to be known, to communicate and to receive communications. We must be able to see and be seen, to understand and to be understood. In fact, if one is really to continue as a self-conscious personality beyond this life, he can do so only if he maintains a continuous stream of the same consciousness and self-knowingness that he now possesses.

Personal identity of course postulates memory, which binds into one sequence the old life and the new. This means that man must carry with him—after the experience of physical death—a complete remembrance, for it is to this alone that we must look for the link which binds one event to another, making life a continuous stream of self-conscious expression. To suppose that man can forget, and still maintain a self-conscious identity, is to suppose that one could cut off his entire past without destroying the logical sequence of personality. Remembrance alone guarantees personality. Where is this faculty? Cut a man into the smallest bits, analyze and dissect every atom of his physical being, and you will never find memory. There is something about the personality which not only performs its functions, but also remembers what it has done, and which can anticipate future events. What is it? It is the thing we are talking about, the non-physical faculty of perception, the thing that knows . . . The Knower. *Individuality* might remain without remembrance, but not so with *personality* for what we are is the result of what we have been, the result of what has gone before.

We are not content with the thought that immortality is merely the result of one's life and work, which he has left behind; for instance, that he immortalizes himself in his offspring—we still ask "What of the man?" Man, then, if he is to have an immortality worthy of the name, must continue as he now is beyond the grave. DEATH CANNOT ROB HIM OF ANYTHING IF HE BE IMMORTAL!

Where Did Man Come from and Why?

To inquire *why* Life itself is, is useless, for Life is self-existent, and all of the science, wit and art of man can never fathom that which is self-existent. "I am that I am." Since we are, we must have evolved from, or become manifested in, that which is. Our physiological and psychological reactions, are reactions to something which has an actual existence, intelligence and consciousness. Our actions and reactions can be analyzed. The invisible Life Principle incarnated in us *cannot be analyzed*. Any attempt to do so is futile.

Facts admit of proof, Life announces Itself. We know that we are; even a flat denial of our existence would constitute a bold affirmation of its reality. If we were to push our history back to some *beginning*, we should still be compelled to make the simple statement that man is. If man's life is of God, then it comes from a Source that had no beginning, so the question as to WHY he is, must forever remain unanswered. God could not tell *why* God is! To suppose that Life could give an excuse or reason for being would be to suppose an absurdity. Life IS, and right at this point all inquiry into Truth starts, and from this point alone must this inquiry continue.

We are not so much interested, however, in *why* we are, as in *what* we are. That we are some part of Life, no one can deny and keep faith with reason.

What Is the Body?

When man first awakened to self-consciousness, he had a body with a definite form, showing that Instinctive Life—which is God—had already clothed Itself with the form of flesh. Body or form is the necessary outcome of self-knowingness. In order to know, there must be something to be known. Some kind of a body (or expression) always was and always will be, if consciousness is to remain true to its own nature.

Body is a concrete manifestation, existing in time and space, for the purpose of furnishing a vehicle through which Life may express Itself. The physical Universe is the Body of God; it is a manifestation in form of the Mind of God. It is that Creation which—while It may have beginnings and ends—of Itself neither begins nor ends. The manifestation of Spirit is necessary, if Spirit is to come into Self-Realization—hence, Body.

We say that body is composed of matter, but what is matter? Science tells us that matter is an aggregation of small particles arranged in some kind of form. We are also told that matter is in a continuous state of flow. Strange as it may seem, we do not have the same physical bodies that we had a few months ago, they have completely changed. New particles have taken the place of the old, and the only reason that they have taken the same form is that something *within* has provided the same mold. Our bodies are like a river, forever flowing. The Indwelling Spirit alone maintains the identity.

SHALL WE HAVE A BODY HEREAFTER?

Through introspection, I know that I am; and by observation I note that when death comes, this I Am appears no longer to be. The body lies cold, inert, lifeless; its warmth, color and responsiveness have fled. Is it possible for one observing this process to doubt that something tangible and real has left this plane? When the body is given back to the native elements from which it sprang, the knowing, willing and thinking factors that constitute human personality and an individualized stream of consciousness have departed.

The table has four legs, yet it does not walk; the ear does not hear; nor does the tongue wag *unless there is someone to wag it*. The brain does not think, if the brain were endowed with power from on high, it would think on forever; isolate it and it will not think. It is the thinker using the brain, who thinks. There is also one using the power of vision, looking through the windows of the eyes, who sees.

The soul needs a physical body here, else it would not have evolved one. But when by reason of disease, decay or accident the physical body is no longer an adequate instrument through which the soul may function, it lays the present body aside and continues to function through a more subtle one.

When we pass from this plane, shall we become *spirits* or shall we have tangible bodies? *Form is necessary to self-expression.* We reiterate, there can be no consciousness without something of which to be conscious. It is one of the first laws of consciousness to clothe itself in form. The soul clothes itself in form here, and if it continues to live after the passing of the physical body, it is reasonable to conclude that it will still need and have a body. *If the soul can create and sustain a body here, there is no reason to deny its ability to create and sustain one hereafter!* We are *spirits* now as much as we ever shall be. The laws of Mind and Spirit do not change with the passing of the physical body. But the question might be asked, "From what substance would the soul create a new body?" The new idea of ether supplies a theory to fit this need.

THE ETHER OF SCIENCE

Science is rapidly proving that there is much more in the Universe than we can see with the naked eye. We are now being taught that ether is more solid than matter. We know that the ether penetrates everything; it is in our bodies, at the center of the earth, and throughout all space. This means that within our present bodies there is a substance more solid than the body which we see. This idea is very far-reaching, for it shows that we might have a body within the physical one, which could be as real as the one of which we are accustomed to think. If Instinctive Man has molded the outer body in form, why should It not mold the inner one into definite form? There is every reason to suppose that It does and no reason to suppose the opposite. In all probability, there is a body within a body to infinity.

We do not depart from reason when we assume this, for while we say that two bodies cannot occupy the same space simultaneously, we must remember that we are talking about only one plane of expression; and the plane upon which we are now living with its form of matter is probably but one of innumerable planes, each having its own *matter* with its corresponding form. The new idea of matter and ether has proved that form can lie within form without interference, for it has been shown conclusively that there is a substance which can occupy the same space which our body does. Once this theory is accepted, it enables us to better understand the saying, "There are celestial bodies and bodies terrestrial." . . . "There is a natural body and there is a spiritual body." No doubt, as time goes on, it will be proved that there is something still finer than the ether. This may go on to infinity. There is every reason to suppose that we have a body within a body to infinity, and it is our belief that we do have.

The "resurrection body," then, will not be snatched from some Cosmic Shelf, as the soul soars aloft. It is already *within* and we may be certain that it will be a fit instrument for the future unfoldment of the soul. If this is true, and if remembrance links events together, in a continuous stream of consciousness and form, then *the future body will resemble this one*, except that it will be free from disease, old age, or whatever hinders a more complete flow of the Spirit.

It would seem, then, that we have a spiritual body now, and need not die to receive one. We now remember the past, and have outlived many physical bodies during this life. So it looks as if we were already immortal and need not die to take on immortality. If there are many planes of Life and consciousness, as we firmly believe, perhaps we only die from one plane to another. This thought makes a strong appeal and seems reasonable.

Some think that death robs us of the objective faculties, and that we pass out in a purely subjective state, but personally we are unable to follow the logic of such an assumption. To suppose that the objective faculties die with the brain, is to suppose that the brain thinks and reasons. This is proved to be false through the experience of death itself, for if the *brain* could think, it would think on and on forever. No, it is not the *brain that thinks*. The *thinker* thinks through the brain perhaps, but of itself the physical brain has no power to think or feel. Detach the brain and it will not formulate ideas nor work out plans. THE *THINKER* ALONE CAN THINK!

It is not merely pleasing and satisfactory to suppose that we pass from this life to the next, in full and complete retention of our faculties: it is logical. Jesus revealed himself to his followers after his resurrection, *to show them that death is but a passing to a higher sphere of life and action.* TO KNOW THAT WE MAINTAIN AN IDENTITY INDEPENDENT OF THE PHYSICAL BODY IS PROOF ENOUGH OF IMMORTALITY. This, together with the fact that remembrance maintains a constant stream of recollection; and the realization that mentality can operate independently of the body—performing all of its normal functions without the aid of the body—and that the new theory of matter and ether furnishes proof of the possibility of a body within a body to infinity, and that the inner man is constantly forming matter into the shape of a body; all of these evidences should prove to us that *we are not going to attain immortality*, but that WE ARE NOW IMMORTAL! Our contention is not that dead men live again, *but that a living man never dies.*

Is There Spirit Communication?

It would be interesting to know whether the spirits of the supposed dead cause certain physical manifestations experienced by many people. One thing is certain, these manifestations are either caused by those who are supposed to be dead, or they are produced by those now in the flesh. This is self-evident. Since they occur, *something* must make them happen. Whether the manifestations are caused by the so-called dead or by the living, *the agency used is either a mental body or the direct power of thought operating upon objects.*

More than forty years ago (and but little new has been discovered since in this field) Hudson, in his "Law of Psychic Phenomena," carefully goes through an elaborate process of reasoning— the result of years of painstaking investigation—and completely proves that *all of the manifestations do take place.* He then goes through an extensive, and to him conclusive, argument to show that they ARE NOT CAUSED BY SPIRITS, declaring that *we have no reason to suppose the presence of an UNKNOWN agency when we know there is one present who could be producing the phenomena.*

Scientific research in the realm of the psyche, the subjective soul life, has taught us many valuable lessons; and has demonstrated beyond question of doubt that there are people who, while in a certain state of consciousness, are able to see without the agency of the physical eye, hear without the agency of the physical ear, and communicate without the tongue. Indeed, every faculty of the senses has been duplicated in the mind alone. It would take volumes to enumerate the data compiled by able and scientific minds in furnishing evidence for these facts, and they may be accepted as authentic. This evidence leads us to suppose that the soul can operate independently of the physical instrument. A careful examination of these facts, together with years of personal and immediate experience, will remove all doubts. Those who have carefully investigated do not question this evidence.

Why has Nature provided us with such subtle powers unless She foreknew our need of them sometime, somewhere? Nature is not foolish; She does nothing without an ample reason, leaves no gaps and provides for all emergencies. In everyday living, the etheric and subtle qualities of the soul are not needed. It seems logical to infer that in providing for the continuity of life and the triumphant progression of the soul, Nature has endowed us with duplicate senses that we may be able to reproduce our entire life, with all of its action and reaction, on another plane.

Now, if our reasoning power is correct, and it is proved that physical manifestations take place *through some power which is mental*, and if it is proved that those who have passed on *might* still be near us, then we cannot see where the argument against spirit agencies could be considered perfect. We are inclined to feel that the very facts in the case *prove that at least some of these manifestations could be produced by either the living or the so-called dead*; and such we believe to be the case.

There are thousands of cases on record where people have penetrated the veil of flesh and seen into the beyond. If we cannot believe the experiences of so many, how can we believe in any experience at all? Of course, there is a large field for deception, and it is not probable that all alleged communications are real, but to state positively that they are all illusions is to throw the lie in the face of human thought and say that it *never* sees clearly. There is certainly more argument and evidence in favor of the theory of the possibility of spirit communication than against it, and so far as we are concerned, we are entirely convinced of the reality of this evidence.

If spirits really exist, and if we all live in One Mind; and if mentality can communicate with mentality without the aid of the physical instrument, *then spirit communication must be possible!* Since we know that the above stated facts are true, we have no alternative other than to accept the conclusive evidence and to realize that, *while it may be difficult to communicate with the departed, yet it has been done.*

It is evident that any such communication MUST BE MENTAL. It would be thought-transference, or mental telepathy, at best. Now, if the supposed entity knows that we wish to communicate with it, and if it is consciously present trying to communicate with us, then it must—by the power of its thought—cause its message to come up through our subjectivity to an objective state of recognition. Consequently, how very difficult to receive a coherent message! For instance, suppose one tries to *think* a lecture to an audience, how much would that audience be likely to receive? Yet this is exactly what would happen, UNDER THE VERY BEST CONDITIONS, if the departed were trying to impress our thought, and we knew that they might do so and we were trying to receive it! I believe that they do seek to communicate with us and that they often succeed—perhaps more often than we realize—but I repeat, "How difficult it must be!"

Whether or not the spirits are present is uncertain. Just because a psychic *sees the picture* of a certain person around or near us, does not mean the person is actually there; for the pictures of all our friends are always in our mental atmospheres. It is imperative that we make this distinction, as people sometimes become unbalanced, from accepting *as real and actual* that which is only a picture . . . only a mental impression. It is quite absurd to suppose that *at any time we wish*, we can call anyone whom we ever knew and have him talk with us. We are unable to do so here, and the psychological and metaphysical laws are the same on every plane. TO SUPPOSE THAT WE CAN COMPEL THE ATTENTION OF ANYONE OUT OF THE FLESH, ANY MORE THAN ONE IN IT, IS AN ABSURDITY, and if we could, what would we hope to gain? *People out of the flesh know no more than they did when in the body.*

However, I believe that we often do communicate with the subjectivity of those who are departed, whether they know we are doing so or not; but the messages that come in our present state of evolution are very incoherent. I believe that an unconscious communication goes on, more or less, all the time and that those people whom we have greatly loved are still conscious of us. We might feel only a vague sense of their presence, much as did the niece in "The Return of Peter Grimm." She felt, you will recall, a vague sense of her uncle; that he was trying to impress her with his thought and desire; she felt a blind groping, and that is probably as clearly as we should be able to receive most messages.

We all have psychic capacities but they should never be forced, for it is only when the subjective comes to the surface while we are in a perfectly normal state, that a normal psychic power is produced. To lose the self-consciousness, in order to let the subjective come through, is never good or right and furthermore is likely to be destructive. The psychic capacity is normal only to the extent that it can be used while in a self-conscious state. Many people are annoyed by their psychic powers—constantly seeing things the average person does not see, continually getting impressions. These people are very near to subjectivity and it bothers them. They can easily be healed and should be.

There is, however, a normal psychic capacity, and some are able to discern mental causes with perfect ease. Jesus was such a one. He was able to tell the woman she had been married five times, and that the man with whom she was then living was not her husband. He read that out of her thought, but he did it while in an objective state, for he was able to consciously and objectively exercise his *subjective* faculties. This is perfectly normal, but to let go of the volitional and choosing faculties—which alone constitute individuality—and become immersed in subjectivity, is very dangerous.

It is a crime against individuality to allow the conscious faculties to become submerged. We should control the subjective and not let it control us. The teaching of *the illusion of mind* sprang up because men of wisdom perceived that people might mistake the shadow for the reality; the form for real substance; the hollow voice for revelation, and thereby be misled. This is why they warned against these things, and against having *familiar spirits*, and they were right. Never let any voices speak to you unless you are in control of the situation. NEVER ADMIT ANY MENTAL IMPRESSIONS OR IMAGES THAT YOU DO NOT WISH TO RECEIVE, OR THAT YOU CANNOT RECEIVE CONSCIOUSLY Say: "There is no power, in the flesh or out of it, but the One, which can enter my consciousness. Anything that obeys the One, conforms to the One, believes only in the One, and comes only through the consciousness of the One, is perfectly welcome but ANYTHING OTHER THAN THAT CANNOT COME."

The only value that an understanding of psychic phenomena can have—and the only reason for introducing any discussion of it in this book—is that without a comprehension of it, we do not understand the complete workings of the mind. We do not understand the experiences which people often have, and in a consistent philosophy which deals with Mind, *the lack of an understanding of psychic phenomena would be inexcusable!* For anyone in this day to say that powers of clairvoyance, telepathy, etc. are not exercised, is to admit his own ignorance.

These things do happen, and are continually happening in more and more instances. The thing to do is not to deny what happens, but to find a logical and scientific explanation of it. It is our business to explain all mental action—in so far as at present it is explainable—and so we must find an answer which will cover the law of psychic phenomena. MIND, with the laws governing It, is the whole answer, for each plane reproduces the one next to it; and psychic phenomena are but reproductions of man's physical capacities on the mental plane. "What is true on one plane, is true on all."

WHAT OF REWARD AND PUNISHMENT?

What of *reward* and *punishment?* Shall we be rewarded for our virtues and punished for our short-comings? Can we think of reward and punishment from any other viewpoint than that sin is a mistake and punishment a consequence, that virtue and righteousness must find their corresponding effects in our experience? God neither punishes nor rewards. Such a concept of God would create an anthropomorphic dualism, a house divided against itself. Such a house cannot stand. Life is a blessing or a curse, according to the use we make of it. In the long run, no one judges us but ourselves and no one condemns us but ourselves. We believe in a law that governs all things and all people. If we make mistakes, we suffer. We are our own reward and our own punishment.

Some suffer, some are happy, some unhappy, according to the way they contact life. No one judges us but ourselves. No one gives to us but ourselves and no one robs us but ourselves. We need not fear either God or the devil. There is no devil, and God is Love. The problem of good and evil will never enter the mind which is at peace with itself. When we make mistakes, we suffer the consequences. When by reason of enlightenment and understanding, we correct such mistakes, we no longer suffer from them. Understanding alone constitutes true salvation, either here or hereafter.

We need fear nothing in the Universe. We need not be afraid of God. We may be certain that all will arrive at the final goal, that not one will be missing. Every man is an incarnation of God. The soul can no more be lost than God could be lost. We should neither be disturbed by the wailing of prophets, nor the anathemas of theology. We cannot believe that because we have subscribed to some creed, we have thereby purchased a seat in heaven, nor can we believe in any vindictive or malicious power in the universe, which damns us because we have erred through human ignorance. We believe in God and that He is Good. What more can life demand of us than that we do the best that we can and try to improve? If we have done this, we have done well and all will be right with our souls both here and hereafter. This leaves us free to work out our own salvation—not with fear *or* even with trembling—but with peace and in quiet confidence.

SHALL WE REST IN THE HEREAFTER?

The questions might arise in our minds, "*Where* shall we go when we die?" "Shall we engage in activity or shall we be inactive?" These are natural questions. Where shall we take this marvelous mind and subtle body? If today is the logical continuance of yesterday, then all of the tomorrows which stretch down the vista of eternity, will be a continuity of experiences and remembrance. We shall keep on keeping on. We shall continue in our own individual stream of consciousness but forever and ever expanding. Not less but ever more: more and still more ourselves.

Our place hereafter will be what we have made it. We certainly cannot take anything with us but our character. If we have lived in accordance with the law of harmony, we shall continue to live after this Divine Law. If we have lived any other way, we shall continue to live that way until we wake up to the facts of Being.

When we came into this life, we were met by loving friends who cared for us until we were able to care for ourselves. Judging the future by the past, we can believe that when we enter the larger life, there will be loving hands to greet us and loving friends to care for us until we become accustomed to our new surroundings. Nature provides for herself there as well as here. We confidently expect to meet friends who are on the other side, and to know and be known. We cannot believe otherwise. We should not look forward to a hereafter without activity; but to a place where our work will be done in greater harmony with the Divine Law, because of greater understanding. A place where there was nothing to do, would be eternal boredom.

With this understanding of eternity, should we not be able to view our passing in a different light? The experience loses its sting, the grave its victory, when we realize the eternity of our own being. Nature will not let us stay in any one place too long. She will let us stay just long enough to gather the experience necessary to the unfolding and advancement of the soul. This is a wise provision, for should we stay here too long, we would become too set, too rigid, too inflexible. Nature demands the change in order that we may advance. When the change comes, we should welcome it with a smile on the lips and a song in the heart.

Personal Convictions of Life Eternal

I believe in the continuation of the personal life beyond the grave, in the continuity of the individual stream of consciousness with a full recollection of itself and the ability to know and to make itself known. I wish to feel, when the experience of physical death shall occur, that that which I really am will continue to live beyond the grave. I wish to feel that I shall again meet those friends whose lives and influences have made my life happy while on earth. If I could not believe this, I would believe nothing in life; life would have no meaning and death could not be untimely, unless it were long delayed. If personality does not persist beyond the grave, then death would be an event to be devoutly longed for and sought after.

I believe that certain experiences have given us ample evidence to substantiate the claim of immortality. I know that my own experience justifies a complete acceptance in my mind of my own and other people's immortality. Is there any one who, standing at the bier of a loved one, can possibly feel that the real end has come? It is useless to say that their influence lives after them. That is true, of course, but we hope for more than this; WE WISH TO FEEL THAT *THEY* STILL LIVE! How anyone can feel otherwise seems unthinkable. I want to live and keep on living and to know that I am I; and unless immortality means this, death means the cutting off of all conscious life, contact or recognition, and it could then be truly said of the personality that it dies with the grave.

Poets have sung of the eternality of the soul, while the saints and sages of the ages have assured us that man is an immortal being. It is recorded that Jesus rose from the dead and made Himself known to his immediate followers. The faith of countless millions of the Christian Religion has been based, to a great extent, on its teachings of immortality. The philosophy of Christianity can be traced largely to Greek thought and ideals, but the Christian Religion itself rests its greatest hope on the assurance that a man rose from the dead and passed from this plane to the next, retaining and carrying with him into the beyond those qualities and attributes which constitute that personal stream of consciousness known as an individual.

But I cannot base my hopes of immortality on the revelation of anyone but myself. So far as I am concerned, nothing can exist to me unless I am aware of it. While I believe in other men's revelations, I am sure only of my own. I look upon the belief in immortality neither as a vague dream, nor a forlorn hope, but as a *proven fact*. One cannot doubt that which he knows to be so, and why should he deny the evidence of his senses, his reason and his personal experiences, in one field more than in another? Immortality, or the continuation of personal existence beyond this life, *has been so completely demonstrated to me* that it would be unthinkable for me to assume an opposite position, even for the purpose of debate. Here, within myself, is something that knows. Here is something that knows that it IS, and knows that life itself moves with a tide as irresistible as the recurring seasons.

I do not believe in the return of the soul to another life on this plane. The spiral of life is upward. Evolution carries us forward, not backward. Eternal and progressive expansion is its law and there are no breaks in its continuity. It seems to me that our evolution is the result of an unfolding consciousness of that which already is, and needs but to be realized to become a fact of everyday life. I can believe in planes beyond this one without number, in eternal progress. I cannot believe that nature is limited to one sphere of action.

The average man *desires* to live beyond the grave. In most instances where this desire is lacking, we find those whose experiences in this world have been so negative that their greatest hope is for utter oblivion, a complete nothingness. The average man desires an eternal progress, an everlasting expansion, a complete reconciliation between this life, the grave and everlasting existence. Even the best men feel that their lives here have been marred by incompleteness. Nine out of ten people believe in some type of immortality, which demonstrates that people not only *wish* to believe, but that—in the face of all difficulties, disappointments and disillusionments—THEY ACTUALLY DO BELIEVE!

It is human to grieve over the loss of dear ones. We love them and cannot help missing them, but a true realization of the immortality and continuity of the individual soul will rob our grief of hopelessness. We shall realize that they are in God's keeping and they are safe. We shall know that loving friends have met them, and that their life still flows on with the currents of eternity. We shall feel that we have not lost them, they have only gone before. So we shall view eternity from the higher standpoint, as a continuity of time, forever and ever expanding, until time, as we now experience it, shall be no more. Realizing this, we shall see in everyone a budding genius, a becoming God, an unfolding soul, an eternal destiny.

Time heals all wounds, adjusts conditions, explains facts; and time alone satisfies the expanding soul, reconciling the visible with the invisible. We are born of eternal day, and the Spiritual Sun shall never set upon the glory of the soul, for it is the coming forth of God into self-expression. We must give ourselves time to work out all problems. If we do not work them out here, we shall hereafter. There will be time enough in eternity to prove everything. Every man is an incarnation of eternity, a manifestation in the finite, of that Infinite which, Emerson tells us, "lies stretched in smiling repose."

With all these facts confronting us, we should learn to trust life. There is no power in the universe which wishes anyone ill. Life is good and God is Good. Why not accept this and begin to live? No man need prepare to meet his God, he is meeting Him every day and each hour in the day. He meets Him in the rising sun, in the flowing stream, in the budding rose, in the joy of friendship and love, and in the silence of his own soul.

When we meet each other, do we not feel that subtle Presence which flows through all things and gives light and color to our everyday experiences? In our own souls, in the silent processes of thought and understanding, do we not sense another Presence? There is something Divine about us which we have overlooked. There is more to us than we realize. Man is an eternal destiny, a forever-expanding principle of conscious intelligence . . . the ocean in the drop of water, the sun in its rays. Man, the real man, is birthless, deathless, changeless; and God, as man, in man, IS man! The highest God and the innermost God is One and the same God.

And so we prepare not to die, but to live. The thought of death should slip from our consciousness altogether; and when this great event of the soul takes place, it should be beautiful, sublime . . . a glorious experience. As the eagle, freed from its cage, soars to its native heights, so the soul, freed from the home of heavy flesh, will rise and return unto its Father's house, naked and unafraid.

When death shall come
And the spirit, freed, shall mount the air,
And wander afar in that great no-where,
It shall go as it came,
Freed from sorrow, sin and shame;
And naked and bare, through the upper air
Shall go alone to that great no-where.
Hinder not its onward way,
Grieve not o'er its form of clay,
For the spirit, freed now from clod,
Shall go alone to meet its God.

CHAPTER TWENTY-FOUR
GENERAL SUMMARY

The Mind of man is some part of the Mind of God, therefore it contains within itself unlimited possibility of expansion and self-expression.

The conscious mind of man is self-knowing, self-assertive; it has volition, will, choice and may accept or reject. It is the only part of man's mind which can think independently of conditions.

The sub-conscious mind of man is simply the Law of Mind in action. It is not a thing of itself but is the medium for all thought action. It is the medium by which man may call into temporary being whatever he needs or enjoys on the pathway of his experience.

The Mind of God is Infinite. The mind of man is some part of this Infinite, Creative Mind of God. Therefore the mind of man is as infinite as is man's capacity to understand his true relationship to God or Spirit. The mind of man is continuously unfolding into a greater recognition of its real plan in the creative order of the Universe. It does not yet comprehend its own power or scope but it does know how, in some measure, to consciously co-operate with the Infinite.

Spirit is really the only Mind there is. It is Eternal. It never began nor will It ever cease to be. It is complete and perfect, happy and whole, satisfied and at peace with Itself. The Spirit is the only Conscious Intelligence in the Universe. Therefore It is the only Directive Intelligence in the Universe.

Because the mind of man is the Mind of God in man, the mind of man is conscious and directive. It is to man what God is to the Universe.

God is Spirit. That is, without parts. A Universal Unity and Wholeness. God is Mind. The self-knowing Mind of God is the Spirit of God and at the same time the Spirit of man. Mind in its self-knowing state is Spirit. The Mind of God and the Mind of man is the same Mind. The conscious mind of man is part of the Self-Knowingness of the Mind of God. The conscious mind of man is the Self-Knowingness of Spirit operating through the thought of man. Hence its creativeness.

The conscious mind of man is that part of, or unity with, the Supreme Spirit which enables man to be an individual unit, separate in identity without becoming separated from, the Whole Spirit of God, the Whole Mind of God. Without this conscious mind of man in an individualized state God, or the Spirit, would have no independent offspring, therefore God would not be completely expressed. The Eternal has placed Himself at the center of man's being in order that man may function individually. The discovery of this, the greatest truth about man, is the greatest discovery of the ages.

It is this Divine Self-Knowingness in man which distinguishes him from all other creation. It belongs to man alone. It appears full-orbed in man alone. Man alone is able to consciously work out his own destiny, to determine what manner of life he shall lead. For it is written that God created him but little lower than the angels and crowned him with glory and honor.

The subjective mind of man is part of the Universal Subjective Mind of God. It is the place where every man individualizes himself on the subjective side of life. It is his use of the Law of Cause and Effect. It is his use of the Law of Karma. It is the Law of the Whole, now individualized as a law of the apparent part. It may produce either freedom or bondage according to the way that it is used. Man's use of the Universal Law makes it appear as though his subjective mind were an entity of itself. It never is, however, and this is one of the main points we should remember. It is not separated from the Universal, but is, in a certain sense, the property of the individual in the Universal. God and man are One, but God is greater than man. The Whole is greater than Its parts.

The Universal Subjectivity is Mind in an abstract and formless state. That is, it is a potential energy and a latent power, which means that It is unformed, but always ready to take form. It is Mind and Substance in an unformed or uncreated state of being. It is ready to become molded into any or all forms. It is unexpressed Power, Substance and Creativeness. It is unexpressed

Mind. It waits to be called into form or expression. It exists in its original state, invisible but potential with all possible form. A creative, universal energy waiting to be used, to be operated upon. Willing, but having no volition of Its own. Ready, but having no initiative. Formless, but ready to take form.

Mind in Its subjective state is Universal. Mind in Its subjective state cannot act until It is set in motion by mind in a conscious state. Therefore Universal Subjective Mind is a doer and not a self-conscious knower. It knows how to do but It does not have any conscious knowledge that It is doing. Man calls It forth into expression.

In Universal Mind is contained the essence of everything that ever was, is or shall be. The seen and the unseen are in It and governed by It. It is the sole and only Creative Agency in the universe and all other apparent creative agencies are *It* working in different ways. Things exist in the Universal Mind as ideas. Ideas take form and become things in the concrete or the visible world. Thought calls things forth from the universal into expression.

The correct understanding that Mind in Its unformed state can be called forth into individual use is the key to all proper mental and spiritual work from a practical viewpoint. To know that we are surrounded by such a creativeness is not enough, however, we must use this knowledge for definite purposes if we expect to make conscious use of the law for personal self-expression. In this limitless Medium the potential of all our desires exists in an unformed state. The Unformed is ready to take form, but having no intention of Its own, because It is not self-knowing, form must be imposed upon It. Form is imposed upon It by the self-knowing mind of God and of man. Man in the little world. God in the Great World.

The invisible essence of Mind is Substance. That is, an unformed stuff, an energy. It is energy plus intelligence. Intelligence is conscious energy working upon unformed substance in accord with law. When man makes a demand upon himself or upon the Universe which flows through the self, he is making a demand upon Original Mind and Original Energy. Thus his demand causes Original Mind and Energy to produce certain specific things for him. Thus is a new creation produced by the same Creative Force or Energy that produces all things. The Mind that man uses to conceive new ideas is the Original Mind of God. There are not two minds but One. The Universal and the individual are one in Essence. Any apparent difference is in degree only.

No form is permanent. All forms return into the Formless. The Formless is Eternal. All form is temporary. There is an eternal play of Life upon Itself. This is necessary in order that Mind may be expressed. Man is an expression of Original Mind and he can call temporary forms into being if he wills to. Indeed he cannot stop doing this and thereby hangs the tale of good and evil.

Through our own individualized subjective mind we contact the Law of the Universe and make use of the Mind of God. Our conscious mind is limited, but the Subjective part of us, being Universal, is without limit. This Limitless Medium we may use for whatsoever purpose we will. If we use It for destructive purposes we shall bring destruction upon ourselves. The Universe is fool proof. But there is no liability in using any creative power if we use it constructively.

We can tap the reservoirs of the Universal Mind through the use of our own thought. We can use this power for the healing of the physical body or for the changing and the control of conditions around us, the reason being that both body and affairs are fluent. They are Mind held in form.

Man's mind is the Mind of God functioning at the level of man's understanding of his place in the Universe. Man contacts the Mind of God at the center of his own being. It is useless to seek elsewhere. "The Highest God and the innermost God is One God." Through the medium of Mind man unifies with the Universe and contacts a Power that can do anything for him that he is able to conceive of Its doing. Of course, this Power will never deny Its own Nature.

This Law of Mind is man's access to the Original Creative Genius of the Universe, and has no intention for us other than the intention that we give It. The Will of Spirit is already imposed upon It to do all those things which we call the automatic processes of nature, whether in our physical bodies or in the physical body of the Universe.

The Spirit has already ordained that nature shall be perfect. It would be impossible for Spirit to ordain anything else since, in order to be at all, It must be perfect in Its nature. God is Will and Representation. A perfect cause must produce a perfect effect. The normal functions of life are harmonious but we interfere with these in our ignorance and thus bring discord into temporary being. In the life process of automatic functioning both in our bodies and throughout the universe as a whole the laws of being are set and immutable. While in the use that we make of the Law of cause and effect in our individual experience we are responsible. We are given, or by the necessity of our nature have, the power and the necessity of using the Law as though It existed solely for us. It goes in the direction—in our mental affairs—that we give It.

It can have no other direction for us and know no other. But, of course, in the Great Whole, the Universe is not run on the scale of man's ignorance. Knowledge alone can free man from an ignorant and self-imposed bondage.

But so far as man is concerned, outside of the automatic and necessary functions of Universal Mind, man is free to do as he wills and the Universal Mind, as Law, can know about the individual only what he knows about himself. The cosmic engine is started but man guides it in his own life. It goes for him in the direction in which it is driven. This driving is not by force but by agreement, unification and acquiescence. We must believe. On this hangs all the law and the prophets. Heaven and hell are tied up in man's beliefs. It is the law of his life.

The engine of the Subjective Mind must be guided. It is neither person, place nor thing of Itself. It is Subjective to the desire of man, consequently It has for him only the power he decrees It to have.

Because thought is made of the stuff that forms the universe into definite creation the Law is charged with the power that we give It. No more and no less. It responds by correspondence. It is a mirror and a perfect one. It molds our ideas and beliefs into visible form and casts them back multiplied. It does not know that It is doing this, but It knows how to do it. This is one of the great enigmas of the universe.

The nature of Reality is such that Universal Mind has unlimited power but so far as man is concerned It has only the power which he gives to It. He gives It power when he says, "I am weak, sick or unhappy." It says for him what he first says for himself. And since, for countless ages, man has believed that which is not true of God, his body and environment reflect this limited concept of the Universe. This Law is a force in nature to be used and brought under conscious control of the spirit of man which is his conscious mind. Man's conscious mind is the consciousness of God in him.

Mind as Law is helpless without direction. It has nowhere to go and nothing to do of Itself. IT MUST BE DIRECTED OR IT WILL DO NOTHING OF PERMANENT WORTH FOR MAN. Mind as Law is an abstraction, merely a possibility. Man is a concrete knower; he is the consciousness of Spirit, individualized, the personality of God multiplied. Spiritual man is One with Spiritual God. Spirit operates through man as self-knowingness and this makes man distinct and different from all other creations so far as mentality is concerned. Mind as Law is unconscious Intelligence and lives only through man. It is his to command, his servant. It has no desire of Its own. Man is Its desire, will and purpose.

While Mind as Law is always subjective to man's desire, we must not forget that It has Infinite Intelligence within Itself. It is Mind in the abstract and in the unformed. It is Mind in an unthought state, so to speak. It takes concrete form from desires and mental images impressed upon It. It resides within us for the purpose of being used and It should be used definitely and with conscious knowledge that It is being used for specific purposes. It will do for us whatever we wish It to do provided we first create the thought mold.

God as Conscious Mind is Spirit. God as Subjective Mind is Law. God as Conscious Mind is Self-Knowing but the Law of God's Mind, like all other laws of nature, is given us to be used.

The Law of Mind obeys the orders that are given It whether we are conscious or unconscious that such orders are being given. Being entirely sensitive to our thought and by its very nature absolutely receptive as well as intelligent and responsive to it—and at the same time being creative—it is easy to see what a tremendous power we have at our conscious disposal.

The Universal Mind in Its subjective state is what we mean by the Law of Mind. The subjective Medium is limitless and can do anything that we may wish It to do. It must obey the conscious thought since It has no power to reason other than deductively. This is why conscious thought has power. Power and energy are phases of mind acting as law. Mind in all its phases is some part of God. Man is some part of God and since God or Spirit is a complete and a perfect Unit then man's mind is simply the place where he individualizes God.

The only concentration necessary in the best use of Mind is specific mental attention and complete mental acceptance. Always remember that you are not dealing with a reluctant Force but with a completely receptive one which, by Its very nature, is compelled to receive the images of your thought. It has no other choice and can conceive no other. You make up Its mind for It.

Acceptance and realization. These words are fraught with the greatest meaning to the one who wishes to consciously use the creative power of thought for definite purposes. Acceptance and realization are mental qualities and may be consciously generated.

When we treat we should be specific. "Whatsoever things we desire" when we pray we should "believe that we have them." If we wish money we should ask for, or mentally accept, money.

If we wish a home we should ask for, or mentally accept, a home. We can put as much detail into our mental work as we desire. Sometimes to do so will be of great service in gaining a complete mental acceptance of our desires. This is the whole secret, a complete mental acceptance and embodiment of our desires.

Our mental acceptances should be filled with conviction, warmth, color and imagination. The creative power responds to feeling more quickly than to any other mental attitude. Therefore we should try to feel the reality of what we are doing when we give a treatment. This reality is felt as we become more and more convinced that Spirit responds to us.

We should grow into the understanding that Spirit responds to us and becomes more conscious of Its Presence within us. It is the very breath of our breath . . . the imagination back of our word. It is the creative power in our thought and the law and energy that executes that thought. "God is all in all, over all and through all." There can be no greater or more complete Allness. This Allness is within us, or we may say that within is the only place we can contact It. It is necessary to understand this else sometimes we shall be trying to reach outside and this is impossible.

If one were to make a complete mental picture of himself as he would like to be, filling in all the details of his desire and trying to accept the whole thing as a present reality, he would soon demonstrate that the control of affairs is from within out and not from without; the cause being that whatever exists as a mental picture in Mind must tend to, and finally does take form if the picture is really believed in and embodied.

We should be careful to distinguish day dreaming and wistful wishing from really dynamic and creative treatment. When we treat we do not wish, we KNOW. We do not dream, we STATE. We do not hope, we ACCEPT. We do not pray, we ANNOUNCE. We do not expect something is going to happen, we BELIEVE THAT IT HAS ALREADY HAPPENED.

We should think clearly and allow the image of our thoughts to sink into a subjective state. We do not crowd them down, we let them sink into this inner receptivity with power and with conviction. Our individual subjective mind is our place in the Universal Creative Law and immediately connects us with limitless power and energy.

There is a vast difference between "holding thoughts" and holding things in thought. One is the attempt at an impossible coercion; the other is a mental acceptance. To hold thoughts, as though we were forcing issues, does no good and utilizes but a fraction of the creative power at our disposal. To hold in thought, as though we were LETTING something happen, is to use the greater power . . . the greatest power of all.

Conscious thought is the starting point of every new creation. Trained thought is far more powerful than untrained since the admission that thought is power gives it added power. This is one of the great secrets of Mental Science. Conscious thought is the starting point. The Subjective Law knows only to obey. It can do nothing else. It has no will of Its own. We impress our will upon It. We do not will, as though we were using an arbitrary force, we impress It. We should be careful to differentiate between these two attitudes of mind.

The idea of a successful life will create success. This idea will find objective form in the outer world of the one who holds to it with conviction. It must first become established in the conscious mind. It will then transmit itself into a subjective embodiment and when this happens success will become habitual.

If one does not know exactly what he wishes to do he should treat himself for general success in whatever he attempts to do. He must treat himself for guidance into the knowledge of that which would be best for him to do, remembering that the Inner Mind knows infinitely more than the intellect. It knows how to take ideas and form objective circumstances around them. Naturally the sooner we know just what we wish to do the quicker we shall create mental images that are definite and the Creative Mind can more quickly set to work to carry out our plans for us.

The objective mind alone may consciously decide what is to happen. All subjective decisions are merely conclusions built on already accepted premises, ideas or thought patterns. The conscious mind may change these thought patterns and thereby cause a different flow of energy and intelligence toward the objective of its desire. The Spirit alone has the power of real self-expression and true volition. This is why we call the conscious part of mind, the Spirit of man; the conscious Mind of the Universe, the Spirit of God.

Remember that when you use your subjective mind you are using the Creative Power of the Universe. For the two are really one. There is but One Mind, whether It be individual or Universal. Remember also that Mind in its conscious state is Spirit, whether we think of It as in man or in God, that is, whether we think of It as individual or Universal. Mind in its unconscious or subjective state is the Law of cause and effect. The Law of cause and effect of Itself is not an entity but is the way that we use the great Law of all life. From this viewpoint any particular effect may be changed by altering our thought relationship to the fundamental Law which gives rise to lesser causes and effects. This we cannot do while we look only to that which is limited or already in form. We DEAL WITH THE FORMLESS.

We must consciously know that we can use creative power. The more complete such acceptance on our part, the more completely we shall be able to use this power for definite purposes. We should develop a conscious conviction of our ability to know and to understand the way that the mind works. We shall not be able to do this while we listen to those who deny us, or themselves, the privileges we wish to enjoy. No one ever yet found a living soul in a dead body or learned that affirmations of life and health will become beneficial by denying any power to them.

If, at times, we doubt our ability to use the law, we should again remind ourselves that it is not I but the Spirit of the Father in me who doeth the work. This will straighten our thought and place us again on the road of faith and understanding. WE MUST BELIEVE. WE MUST LEARN HOW TO BELIEVE. WE SHOULD TREAT OURSELVES UNTIL WE DO BELIEVE. No one ever started at the top. Let us be happy to begin right where we are and grow.

We attract to ourselves the objective form of our subjective embodiments. Law knows how to make things out of ideas. We do not consciously know how It does this; nor do we know how corned beef and cabbage are turned into flesh and bone, but they are and we have been so accustomed to the thought that they are, that we have implicit faith that they will continue to be. Should we doubt this phenomenon we should be thought queer. When we believe in the Law of Mind in the same way we shall be surprised at the results we shall receive.

Thoughts of lack, poverty and limitation contain within themselves the conditions necessary to produce lack, poverty and limitation. Remember that we are not dealing with two powers, but with one, ever presenting Itself in varying guises. "To the pure thou wilt show thyself pure; to the froward thou wilt show thyself froward." It will become to us what we are to It. The Law knows us only as we first know ourselves. We make up Its mind because Its mind is subjective. The Spirit controls the Law. This is the great mystery, the limitless wonder of the universe— that, which out of nothing, can make something. But Its nothing is really the Substance of every something.

Because all people have believed in lack a law of human thought has been made which binds the race. Limitation is the result of an ignorant use of the Law. Every advance in any science proves this to be true. The real Law is one of freedom. By that freedom we bind ourselves until we learn how to change the thought and by so doing to change the limitation into freedom. The two are merely a different use of the One Law.

Limitation is a condensation of the idea of want. Mind accepts this idea as though it were true and then makes it true in our experience. It is not always easy to see this nor is it easy to rise above it, but it can be done and we should begin at once to control our thought patterns in such a way that they will produce plenty instead of lack.

The Law of Mind is not selective. That is, It is receptive without caring what It receives. It is creative without caring what It creates. It knows how to do without consciously knowing that It is doing or what It is doing. It seems strange that the first thing to realize is that there could be such a Law in the universe. But on second thought we find that all natural laws are of a like character, no natural law is ever selective of itself. This is why we must realize that the Spirit Itself is more than any or all laws as we understand them. Conscious mind controls the Law of Mind. The Law of Mind is sensitive but not conscious from the standpoint of having any selective quality. Selectivity is the office of the conscious mind while creativeness is the office of the Inner Mind.

Thoughts of lack manifest as limitation. Thoughts of abundance manifest as success and happiness. Failure and success are but two ends of one stick. All conditions and every circumstance is of the nature of effects and can in no way limit Mind unless we take them as a fresh starting point for a creative pattern. The thought that any given condition is a thing of itself tends to make it appear to be a thing of itself. Reverse the thought and the condition tends to become reversed.

The Law can know no conditions as such. It knows form but not size. Outline is real but limitation is unreal to Mind. In the Absolute nothing depends on anything but ideas. Ideas are form, condition, circumstance, cause and effect, and everything that happens between cause and effect. This is what a treatment is. It is a thing of itself if we know that it is. It is what we know it to be.

"Fear not, little flock, it is your Father's good pleasure to give you the kingdom." Fear is the great enemy of man. But fear is a mental attitude and as such can be converted into something else. Fear is the reverse mental attitude to faith, and is a result of the lack of faith. Fear brings limitation and lack in its wake and destroys the happiness and possibility of a greater degree of livingness to those who suffer from it.

Fear blocks the more complete givingness of the Spirit to Its highest form of manifestation on this planet, which is mankind. Fear arises from that mental attitude which limits the possibility and the willingness of Spirit to give us the good we so greatly desire. There is nothing wrong in the desire for self-expression. God is more completely expressed through the man who lives largely than through the one who lives meagerly.

Fear is a belief in limitation, a denial that the Divine is the Center and the Source of all good. We must do all in our power to overcome it. "Perfect love casts out fear"; that is, confidence overcomes the depression of doubt. Mental depression can produce physical and financial depression. The psychology of economic cycles proves this. In the midst of plenty humanity lives in want, because of fear. To overcome fear is the greatest adventure of the mind of man.

We should contact a larger field of faith. This is done by understanding that God is the giver and the sustainer of human life and expression. God is all there is. He is Substance and Supply. We must learn to accept this. If it is God's pleasure to give us the Kingdom then it should be our privilege to accept the gift.

The Spirit has not withheld good from us, but ignorance of the true law of supply has caused us to have fear. "They could not enter in because of their unbelief and because they limited the Holy One of Israel." We should endeavor to stop limiting God. All things are given unto us but we shall have to do the taking. God gives in the abstract, we receive in the concrete. The gift of Heaven is forever made. The receiving of this gift is an eternal process of forever expanding the finite.

Since we cannot contract the Absolute we shall have to expand the relative. The Infinite will not be, or become, less than Itself. We are of Its nature. We did not make our own being. All we can do is to accept that the being which we are is some part of the Divine. To know this is to overcome fear. Whether this fear is of lack, pain, sickness or death, it is always a belief that there is something other than Life or that Life withholds pleasure, peace, success and Heaven from us.

Love alone can overcome fear because love surrenders itself to the object of its adoration. The soul must make a complete surrender of itself to the Spirit. That is, the Law must come under subjection to the Spirit. The will of the Spirit is peace, clear thinking and happiness, It could have no other will.

Should we learn to contemplate those things which are desirable and to forget the rest, we would soon overcome fear through faith. Both are mental. Let us learn to reverse the thoughts of fear and transmute them into faith.

Since Spirit is present in Its entirety at all times and in all places it follows, that all of Spirit is wherever we center our attention. And since Spirit is both receptivity and creative responsiveness it follows that wherever we center our attention its image must concentrate substance into the form of such attention. This is fundamental to our concept of mental and spiritual treatment. For it is not by external power nor through objective might that our work is to be done, but through the Spirit and the Law. The Spirit guides and the Law executes. That which we can take is given us.

Pure Spirit exists at the center of all form. Of Itself, It is formless but It is ever giving birth to form. The forms come and go but *It* goes on forever. We are some part of It. If pure Spirit is at the center of everything and is always responding to our thought there is no limit to Its manifestation for us except the limitations that we set.

If it is difficult to see this, realize that our subjective self is the immediate connection between the Absolute and the relative. It is our share of the Law and immediately connects us with the Creativeness of the Whole. The Absolute is in relationship to Itself alone. It is not circumscribed by any form but remains independent of all forms. It can as easily create a new form for us as to perpetuate an old one.

Mind is the realm of causes. Conditions are in the realm of effects. Effects flow from causes and not from themselves. Thought is the instrument of Mind. New thoughts create new conditions. We must learn to think in the Absolute. This means to think independently of any given or experienced effect. "Judge not according to appearances." This thought strikes away the shackles of bondage and finds a new cause at work.

Just as we can conceive of some definite idea, then go on to the conception of another, so we can treat for as many conditions as we can clearly conceive.

We cannot account for the seen without having faith in the unseen. All advance in science or any other branch of learning must follow this rule if it is to accomplish anything. To believe in

Life is to believe in the invisible. As science postulates some etheric movement at the center of all objective form, so we start with the premise that this initial movement starts as Pure Intelligence, independent of any form but ready to take form. All form is temporary even though it lasts for countless millions of years. That is, any given form comes and goes in a process of time for any given time is temporary.

We have arrived at the conclusion that Spirit or the Mind of God is all Causation. Then Spirit or Mind is also all effect. Cause and effect are but two ends of one Unity. The physical end is visible, the spiritual invisible, but may be inwardly perceived and outwardly experienced.

Spirit, then, is all there is at this very hour and all creation is spiritual. The Universe is a Spiritual System impregnated with Divine Ideas and peopled with Spiritual Forms. The ideas of God are perfect laws on their way to producing complete and perfect effects. The Universe is alive, conscious, awake and aware. It is love and life. It is law and order. It is a Cosmos.

Mind is forever conscious of Itself and of what It does. Its consciousness is Its law. Its consciousness is perfect and Its laws are perfect. Mind cannot be conscious of anything but Itself, since It is all. Spirit is conscious of man since man exists and since God must be conscious of all that is. Therefore man is, because God is conscious of him. And God's consciousness of man must be complete and perfect. Generic man must be held in the Mind of God as a complete and perfect manifestation of the Divine.

Mind is all-inclusive and all-pervading. Mind is also self-governing and self-propelling. Spirit is conscious of love as It is conscious of life. It is inspired by love and Its government is one of love. Thus love is the fulfilling of the perfect law. Law is the outcome of love and love is the outpusher through law. Love and law go hand in hand to produce a complete and perfect manifestation.

Man's consciousness of God constitutes his real and immortal self. There is really only one man viewed from the Universal sense, but in this one, or "grand man" as it has been called, there are innumerable persons. Each is in direct relationship to the Whole. Each is an image of God but God is not lessened by being represented in innumerable forms and through limitless numbers of mentalities any more than the figure five would become exhausted by being used by innumerable mathematicians.

Our consciousness of God is our real self and at the same time it is both personal and impersonal. It is personal in that it is personified through us and it is impersonal in that we are all using a universal power. When we know that we are using such a power all doubt as to our ability to use it will vanish and our words will be spoken with spontaneous reliance on Truth.

In spiritual healing the practitioner deals with thought alone. He is not dealing with a sick body or a sick man. There is no one to be healed in the Truth and we must think in the Truth if we expect to heal. There is no material body to be healed and no material man to suffer pain or anguish. Disease is neither person, place nor thing to the one who wishes to heal. The practitioner must try to become conscious of perfection alone and nothing else. In whose mind is he to become conscious of perfection? In the only person's mind he can ever be conscious of anything, in his own mind. The first man to be healed is the practitioner.

Here in his own mind he meets the belief in the necessity of sickness or discord. He repudiates this belief and explains to himself what the real truth is. He is conscious, as his explanation goes on, that he is meeting and neutralizing false claims held to be true about his patient. Knowing that they are false, he resolves them into thoughts and heals the thought. The whole process is one of thought and realization and could not be anything else.

The practitioner works within his own mind until he is mentally satisfied, until the whole reaction in his thought causes him to understand that his patient is now healed. This healing is really the action of Spirit upon the mind of the healer, the active Principle of truth, goodness and harmony.

Since the Divine must hold us as some part of Its eternal perfection, we are fulfilling our destiny when we think of ourselves as already Divine and perfect. To contemplate that Divine Life which is at the very center of everyman's life—this is the very essence of mental healing.

This is what we mean by realization. Words carry the mind forward to a place in thought where realization begins. At this point the most effective work is done. It is an inward feeling, a silent sense of Divine Reality. Troward tells us that the Divine Spirit is the limitless potential of human life. Which means that the human is really Divine but will ever evolve into newer and better states of conscious being.

In practice we state clearly in words what these ideas mean to us and then we relate these statements to some needed experience or to some desired good which we have not been experiencing. After using whatever words will bring conviction to our thought we pause and try to realize the presence of the All Power from which every special good comes. This is adding the Spirit to the letter of the Law. However we should never forget that both the letter and the Spirit are necessary in our work. The letter molds while the Spirit creates. The thought is a mold, conviction is the molten substance poured into this mold. One is not complete without the other and many people make the mistake of using only one of these essential states of consciousness.

When we live in obedience to the Power which is over us we shall be able to consciously direct the lesser conditions that are around us. Adam was permitted to name all creation and man was supposed to exercise an authority over all that is below him. This means his whole physical environment, of course. But this power was abused and the experience of lack, sickness and limitation fell upon humanity. Adam symbolizes everyman's experience. The allegory of Eden is the story of human evolution.

Wherever the image of thought is set, there the Power to create resides. "God if thou seest God, Dust if thou seest dust." Can we see good where evil appears to be? Then we can remove the evil. When we bring a lamp into a darkened room, where does the darkness go? The darkness neither came nor did it go, anywhere. It never was a thing of itself, merely a condition. And we have power over conditions.

The light is greater than the darkness nor has the darkness any power over the light. The darkness is the great denial of the light but it really did not deny the light for where the light was the darkness was not. By merely bringing in the light the darkness vanished into its native nothingness. This is the power of Reality over seeming opposition or apparent separation.

The relationship between the individual and the Universal Mind is one of reflection. That is, what we image for ourselves, It images for us. Then it follows that the very law which creates bondage could as easily create freedom. The Divine intends freedom for us but the very fact that we have creative thought, and that we are real individuals, presupposes the use of our creativeness in more than one way.

We can sit in the shade or move into the sunshine. Sitting in the shadow we may not really believe that there is any sunshine. But the sun would be there all the time and all the time we are in bondage the real freedom exists. It is there but we must awake to it. The Law of Mind as quickly creates one form as another for us and we must allow the patterns of our thought to become molded from the highest sense of Reality we possess.

By giving our complete attention to any one idea we automatically embody it. We attract to ourselves the objective likeness of this embodiment. The thought becomes a thing. The mental state takes on form, color and temporary reality. We outwardly experience our states of consciousness. But since the apparent without is merely a reflection of the within, which is its cause, what we most need to do is to start with the simple proposition of the creative power of thought and from this inner recognition know that circumstances are formed and held in place.

If we believe in suffering we shall suffer. Life responds to us in the way we approach It. We should choose that which we wish to embody and by constant attention to it take on all its characteristics. Let us choose to be identified with power, with love and beauty, with peace and happiness. Let us identify ourselves with abundance and with success.

The objective form to which we give our attention is created from the very attention which we give to it. The objective is but the reflection of the subjective state of thought. Life is a blackboard upon which we consciously or unconsciously write those messages which govern us. We hold the chalk and the eraser in our hand but are ignorant of this fact. What we now experience we need not continue to experience but the hand which holds the eraser must do its neutralizing work. "I will blot out their transgressions and remember them no longer against them" was written by one who saw the board, the chalk and the eraser. Life is a motion picture of subjective causes. What is the screen and are the figures real? Yes and no. Real as figures but not self-created, not self-perpetuating. Happy is the one who holds the projecting machine firmly in his conscious thought and who knows how to make conscious use of it.

The will of God is always toward that which expresses life and happiness. To suppose that the will of God could be in opposition to the advancement of our lives would be to think of Spirit as being self-destructive. It is always seeking self-expression through us and will never deny us anything. The Law says that if our desires are destructive we shall suffer from them until the lesson is learned. And what is this lesson? It is simply that the Universe is One and never two. It refuses to operate against Itself. It is fool proof.

The Spirit cannot be, or become, antagonistic toward us. It is always flowing into us and ever expressing Itself through us. This self-expression of God is also the self-expression of man for the two are One. The "I AM" is both individual and universal. All individuality merges into universality. All forms are rooted in one common creative Mind and the Spirit of God is the Spirit of man.

To practice the Presence of God is to awaken within us the Christ Consciousness. Christ is God in the soul of man. The resurrection is the death of the belief that we are separated from

God. For death is to the illusion alone and not to Reality. God did not die. What happened was that man awoke to Life. The awakening must be on the part of man since God already is Life.

To practice the Presence of the Divine in others is to practice mental healing for it is a recognition of this Divine Presence which heals. All the words used in the process of healing are for the purpose of building up the realization that "I Am is in the midst of thee."

In mental treatment we should feel as though the whole power of the universe were running through the words we speak. The words must become "Spirit and Life" if they are to overshadow the thoughts and actions that have brought about a discordant condition. As much conviction as we have, *that* we may use.

The conviction that heals is that God is all in all and that there is no material cause or effect. The practitioner treats, not a patient nor a disease; he seeks to heal the thought of its mistaken idea that causation is independent of good. To do this he must contradict what appears to be so. He would be an ineffective worker in this field who judged the possibilities of his work by observing outside happenings.

Effective treatment must be independent of any existing circumstance whatsoever else it will not enter the realm of an Unconditioned Causation. It will have fallen to the level of those secondary causes which seek to perpetuate themselves in human experience. To rise above the contemplation of conditions is to enter that field of Causation which makes all things new in our experience. From this viewpoint there is no hard and no easy case to handle. All cases represent but different phases of human belief and one would yield to the Truth as quickly as another if we were sure of our spiritual position.

Thoughts are more than things, they are the cause of things. Things have no independent existence since there can be nothing external to some comprehending mind. Our work is done in Mind alone and our entire equipment is thought and a knowledge of the Power which it utilizes. This Power is superior to the intellect in Its creativeness.

Only when we put our very best into our spiritual work will it satisfy us. A spiritual power is released through true thinking that is as much a law as is chemical affinity. There is no deliverance of the real self without mental conviction. To have faith in God is to follow this faith through by having faith in the self. The real self is God and as such is to be implicitly trusted.

The spark which burns at the center of our own soul is caught from the living and eternal flame of the Spirit.

But the letter without the Spirit does not quicken the flesh into newness of action. It is cold and unresponsive. Feeling is at the center of the Universe and reflected through man's consciousness sheds its glow wherever the thought travels. Law governs its action and God Himself fulfills its promises.

There must come a time in our experience when we speak the conviction that is within us. This conviction of the Spiritual Universe in which we live is real and powerful. The light cannot be borrowed from another. Each has been furnished with a divine torch whose wick burns from the oil of the eternal and ever renewing substance of faith in oneself and in others.

No good can come to us unless it make its advent through the center of God Consciousness which we are. The hope of destiny is latent in the slumbering thought and genius lies buried until the attention is winged with love and reason. To help those in need is indeed a great privilege. But the blind cannot lead the blind. We must awake to the realization that a Divine Partnership has already been formed between the seen and the invisible.

Unless there were a unifying Principle of life existing as One all-embracing Mind, in which everyone lives and everything subsists, then we could not recognize each other. Indeed we could not be conscious of living in the same world. This Mind in which we live is at all times independent of any individual action on our part. We are in It and It flows through us, but It is always more than we are.

Our own presence and our consciousness of the presence of the physical world around us implies the necessity of a Universal Intelligence which co-ordinates everything into one complete Unity. This means that there must be a universal standard of Reality which we do not set, but which we may discover. One of the first discoveries we make is that living in a mechanical world we are still spontaneous individualities.

The physical universe is always mechanical. The Spirit is always spontaneous but because the Spirit is a Unity, It can never do anything that would contradict Its own nature.

Into this world we project an idea of ourselves as personalities. Since this action is spontaneous, but at the same time subject to the reaction of the mechanics of the Universe, we may or may not be reflecting freedom, happiness and apparent wholeness into the Law. Personality is bound, in its objective form only, to mechanical laws. This is necessary else there could be no self-expression. The way personality uses these mechanical laws, whether consciously or unconsciously, depends upon a realization of its right relationship to God, man and the Universe.

The chief characteristic of the subjective Law is that It is sensitive, creative and can reason only from a deductive viewpoint. Being the very essence of sensitiveness It is compelled to receive the slightest impression of thought; being creative, It is compelled to act upon this thought; and being deductive, It cannot argue back or deny any use of It that may be made.

If someone should ask whether or not God has any intention for him the answer would be that the only intention God could have, if man is an individual, would be to let the individual alone to discover himself. In this discovery of the self man impresses the Law (which is sensitive, creative and can deduce only) with the images of his own belief about himself, and the Law creates a form around these images.

Other than the instinctive and automatic actions of the physical body, the Law knows about us only that which we know about ourselves. Therefore it makes all the difference in the world what we are impressing upon the Law as being true about ourselves. For if we think poverty and lack we are certainly creating them and causing them to be projected into our experience. If, on the other hand, we think abundance, then the Law will as easily and as willingly create abundance for us. It is all so simple that it seems unbelievable. But for the average person who has no knowledge of this Law, his only use of It will be a reflection of what the consensus of human opinion believes must take place in the life of the majority of individuals who may happen to be living at any time on this earth. The savage thinks after the mode of his tribe and the more civilized thinks after the mold of racial belief.

To assert our individuality is to rise above the law of averages into that more highly specialized use of the Law which brings freedom rather than bondage, joy in the place of grief and wholeness instead of sickness. We cannot do this unless we are first willing to "judge not according to appearances." In this judging "not according to appearances" we are impressing the Law with a new idea of ourselves . . . a less limited idea; and we are learning to think independently of any existing circumstances. This is what is meant by entering the Absolute.

We may be sure that the whole aim of evolution is to produce innumerable selves which are all consciously centered in the Universal Self. The individual "I" is a complement to the universal "I AM." And any method that would seek to erase or to obliterate this individual "I" must be based upon a false philosophy. But "the Father is greater than I." This must never be overlooked for all further evolution of the individual will depend upon his conscious co-operation with the Law and with the Spirit; the Spirit is greater than any particular use of the Law of cause and effect.

If we believe that as isolated personalities we are able to heal through mental and spiritual methods we shall be likely to fall into the error that it is human will that accomplishes the desired good. And perhaps our human will power will some day tell us that it no longer has the strength to keep on working, that it is tired or that it no longer has the inspiration to continue. It is evident that we must not allow ourselves to think this way if we wish to accomplish anything worth while.

If we are swayed by the opinions of others or by the belief that we are not yet ready to help others, then we are falling under the illusion that we are using an isolated power and do not understand that which really heals is the knowledge that the spiritual man is already complete and perfect.

The practitioner knows that the spiritual man needs no healing but that this has not yet become revealed to the mind. What the healer does is to mentally uncover and reveal the Truth of Being, which is that God is in and through every man, and that this Indwelling Presence is already Perfect. We separate the belief from the believer and reveal that which needs no healing. Thought is sifted and that which does not belong to the real man must be discarded. Whatever is of a discordant nature does not belong to the Truth of our Being. We really heal the thought. The Spirit of man needs no healing for the Spirit of man is God.

Ignorance stays with us until the day of enlightenment, until our vision toward the Spirit broadens and casts out the image of a no longer useful littleness. What we now experience we may cease experiencing if we have the will and the imagination to set our vision in an opposite direction and hold it there. It is the office of the imagination to set the vision. The will should hold it in place until the creative genius of the inner life transforms the image of limitation and transmutes it into liberty under law.

"With right glance and with right speech man superintendeth the animate and the inanimate," rightly said the ancient whose knowledge of unseen Principle gave him power over his objective world. But this is more than a saying. It is a truth and should become a part of our everyday practice. That is, we should daily practice correct thinking. We should decide what we wish to have happen in our lives. We should be sure that it implies no hurt for anyone and then we should be certain that we now have this desire, whatever it may be.

A mystic is one who intuitively perceives Truth and who without conscious mental process arrives at Spiritual Realization. The mystics include the great prophets, the inspired writers, the illumined souls of all ages. What we have received from them constitutes the greatest intellectual and spiritual heritage of the ages.

All the mystics have recognized the absolute unity of God and man. Within the Infinite Mind each individual exists, not as a separated, but as a separate and distinct entity. We are a point in Universal Consciousness, which is God. We are not separated from Life, neither is It separated from us, but we are separate entities in It, individualized centers of God Consciousness.

True mystics have not denied the reality of individuality. They have all agreed that the soul is on the pathway of experience, of self-discovery; on the way to its Father's House. They have told us of the marvelous relationship which exists between God and man . . . of a close Union which cannot be broken.

Since we see that personality is what one does with his individuality, we should turn within, as have all the great mystics who have blessed the world with their presence—we should turn within and FIND GOD; and we should have a sense of a Real Presence when we do turn toward the One and Only Presence in the entire Universe.

One of the most illuminating truths which mysticism has revealed is that there is no ultimate reality to evil. NO DEVIL, NO DAMNATION OUTSIDE OF ONE'S STATE OF THOUGHT, NO PUNISHMENT OUTSIDE OF THAT SELF-INFLICTED THROUGH IGNORANCE, and no salvation outside of conscious co-operation with the Infinite. Consequently, they have taught that the answer to every problem is in man's own consciousness.

It is one thing to say that God is unfolding through His idea of Himself, but quite another thing to say that He is gradually becoming conscious of Himself. An "unfolding" God implies a forever-out-pouring Spirit and a forever-manifesting Deity. Evolution is the time and the process through which an idea unfolds to a higher state of manifestation; and since ideas are Divine Realities, evolution will go on forever. But evolution is an *effect* of Intelligence and not its *cause*. Evolution follows involution.

All emerge from that One Whose Being is ever present and Whose Life, robed in numberless forms, is manifest throughout all Creation. Creation is the logical result of the outpush of Life into self-expression. It is the coming forth of Spirit into manifestation. The One encompasses and flows through All, spilling Itself into numberless forms, and personalities. These forms and personalities, propelled by the Cosmic Urge which brings them into being, have, within themselves, an impulse planted by the Divine; and since the Divine is Limitless and Perfect, It must and ultimately will bring all creation into a state of perfect manifestation.

By Cosmic Consciousness, we mean "One's consciousness of his unity with the Whole." This is not a mystery, however, but the Self-Knowingness of God through man. Illumination will come as man more and more realizes his Unity with the whole, and as he constantly endeavors to let the Truth operate through him.

The great mystics like Jesus have taught that as we consciously enter into the One, the One enters into, and becomes us. While sensing this Unity, they have also sensed the individualization of Being and the individuality of man as a Divine Reality.

In flashes of illumination, the inspired have seen into the very center of Reality. They have been convinced of immortality *now*; of God as personal to the individual; of the inevitable overcoming of all evil by good. In such degree as we become conscious of God, evil disappears.

Man is Universal on the subjective side of life, and in this way is connected with the subjectivity of all with whom he is in harmonious vibration. Mental suggestion operates through the subjective mind, and a silent influence is always going on through this avenue in the form of race-suggestion. A silent communication takes place at all times between friends, on the subjective side of life; when it comes to the surface, when one receives a clear impression of thought without the use of words, it is called mental telepathy.

Telepathy, which is the act of reading subjective thought, takes place through the medium of Universal Subjectivity. In order to mentally receive a message, and bring it to the surface, one must be in tune with the vibration of that message. Since the whole field of subjectivity is Universal, it follows that everything which has ever been thought, said or done, is retained in the race-thought; and since this field is a unity, all of the vibrations are ever-present and may be contacted at the point of anyone's mentality. In his objective state, man is separate and distinct, but on the subjective side of life he is Universal.

Each maintains a stream of consciousness in the One Mind, and anyone contacting this stream may objectify it. Because of the Universality of the Medium, the individual stream of consciousness is always omnipresent, whether the one from whom it emanated be in the flesh or out of it. Time and space are unknown in Mind . . . the past and the present are one. Everyone who has ever lived has left behind a mental picture of himself. These pictures are often seen when one is in a subjective state. This does not mean that we really see the person; what we see, generally, is the picture.

The mystical conception of Christ is an idea of the Universality of Sonship, embodied in any individual who recognizes this Sonship. We comprehend the Infinite only to the degree that It expresses Itself through us, becoming to us that which we believe It to be. We cannot come unto the "Father Which Art in Heaven" except through our own spiritual nature. As the human gives way to the Divine in a person he becomes the Christ. There is One Father of All. This One Father, conceiving within Himself, gives birth to all the Divine ideas. The sum-total of all these ideas constitutes the Mystic Christ. This profound truth Jesus discovered and taught: that whatever is true of man, of the reality of his nature, is the Divine Presence within him. The answer to every question is within man, because man is within Spirit, and Spirit is an Indivisible Whole. Jesus stands alone as a man who knew himself and realized his relationship to the Perfect Whole. As the external Jesus gave way to the Divine, the human took on the Christ Spirit and became the Voice of God to humanity. The Christ is always triumphant, is ever a victor, is never defeated, needs no champion.

FINAL CONCLUSION

In conclusion, what the world needs is spiritual conviction, followed by spiritual experience. I would rather see a student of this Science prove its Principle than to have him repeat all the words of wisdom that have ever been uttered. It is far easier to teach the Truth than it is to practice It.

But the practice of Truth is personal to each, and in the long run no one can live our life for us. To each is given what he needs and the gifts of heaven come alike to all. How we shall use these gifts is all that matters! To hold one's thought steadfastly to the constructive, to that which endures, and to the Truth, may not be easy in a rapidly changing world, but to the one who makes the attempt much is guaranteed.

The essence of spiritual mind healing—and of all true religious philosophy—is an inner realization of the Presence of Perfection within and around about. It is the hope of heaven, the Voice of God proclaiming: "I am that which thou art; thou art that which I am."

PART FIVE

TEACHINGS

From the New Testament

(Quotations from the Scofield Reference Edition)

FROM THE
TEACHING OF JESUS

(It is intentional that the pronoun referring to the man Jesus is not capitalized in this book.)

WHY JESUS HAD SUCH POWER

In this book, no attempt is made to discuss *all* the sayings of Jesus. He lived in a world of spiritual realization far beyond that of which the average man has any understanding. As spiritual things must be spiritually discerned, so the full meaning of his sayings can never be clear to us until we have attained a consciousness equal to his. But in the record of his sayings there is much which bears witness to our own belief, and, no doubt, could we penetrate the meaning of his teaching, we should have a perfect explanation of our own philosophy.

Jesus discerned spiritual truth. Why or how we do not know, nor does it make any difference. The world has not produced another like him and, until it does, he must receive a unique place in the history of human character.

MAN SHALL NOT LIVE BY BREAD ALONE (MATT. 4:4)

What did Jesus teach? "It is written that man shall not live by bread alone, but by every word that proceedeth out of the mouth of God."

Who eats of bread alone, will continually hunger. To the physical benefits of the human board must be added the spiritual strength of divine wisdom.

The Meek Shall Inherit the Earth (Matt. 5:5)

"The meek shall inherit the earth." This is a teaching of nonresistance. War lords and plunderers of human possessions have come and gone. Kingdoms have risen only to crumble in dust and become numbered with past events. Passion and lust for power have strewn the earth with destruction. It would seem as though *the meek* had lost out in the titanic struggle for temporal supremacy.

In the midst of this drama of human existence, Jesus declared that the meek shall inherit the earth. Let us inquire if his teaching is a true one. Do we teach our children to follow the steps of a Caesar and a Napoleon? Or do we tell them the story of Jesus or Buddha? The cross is mightier than the crown and we teach our children that LOVE MASTERS EVERYTHING! The meek shall inherit the earth. To whom have our artists turned for inspiration and that quickening power which enables them to depict the ideal? Not to the war lords, nor even the captains of industry, but *to the meek*.

What characteristics are set before us as being worthy? Have not faith and belief in the divine Goodness been the theme of our greatest singers? Who could write a beautiful story about hell? But *heaven* and *love* have inspired thousands to the uplifting of humanity. Jesus was right when he said that the meek shall inherit the earth. *They have done so and will continue to do so!*

They That Hunger Shall Be Fed (Matt. 5:6)

They who hunger and thirst after righteousness shall be filled. Is there anyone who does not have a soul hunger? Does not the spirit of man thirst after knowledge and understanding, yearn for Truth and Reality, as blind men yearn for light? And his hunger can only be satisfied with spiritual food, as manna from heaven.

Let us inquire into this teaching and see if it be an illusion. Turn to the history of those who have been spiritually-minded, and the question is answered. They have not received a stone when they asked for bread. All who have been hungry have been fed; their hunger has been blessed, in that it has led them to that only food—that heavenly manna—which has sustained, strengthened and up-held them, while the rest of the world (with thirst unsatisfied and appetite unappeased) has eagerly inquired from what store they bought their goods. They who hunger and thirst after Reality are always fed, and directly by the hand of God Himself.

THE MERCIFUL SHALL OBTAIN MERCY (MATT. 5:7)

"Blessed are the merciful; for they shall obtain mercy." Again we are confronted with an apparent contradiction. Do the merciful always obtain mercy? From casual observation, it would seem otherwise. But are not many of our observations based on a finite outlook, from a limited concept? Can we estimate life from the range of *one* human experience? If life begins with the cradle and ends with the grave, then are all our hopes, not only forlorn, but useless. It is only when the "eye views the world as one vast plain, one boundless reach of sky," that it sees truly.

The perspective of reality is lost when we view life from the range of a short experience. Jesus saw beyond the veil and estimated life from the great perspective—the long run of the adventure of the soul. He knew that the law of cause and effect takes care of all, and that the "Mills of God" will grind the chaff of unreality from the wheat of the Spirit. What matter if these mills do not do all of their grinding while we are clothed in flesh! Did not Jesus know another life which to him was as real as this one? Can we expect, in this world, to receive full compensation for all our work? Of course not. We are building on an eternal foundation, one that time cannot alter nor experience destroy.

A true estimate of real values cannot be built on the shifting sands of time alone. In the long run, *the merciful will obtain mercy!* In the long run, we shall reap as we have sown!

THE PURE IN HEART SHALL SEE GOD (MATT. 5:8)

"The pure in heart shall see God." Can we ever see God? Is there any news of Heaven other than that which comes through our own thought, or through the thought of another? *Who thinks purity sees it*, and is beholding God. The face of "The Ancient of Days" onlooks eternity, and the upward glance ever sees this reality in all things. The pure in heart not only *shall* see God, but *do* see Him.

The peacemakers are called the children of God. We never associate warriors with the Divine Kingdom. Struggle and strife are outside the Kingdom; they cannot enter in because of their confusion. Only peace can enter the gates of Reality and sit at the table of love. The Divine Host serves not His bounty to confusion, but distributes His gifts to those who enter His gates with peace in their minds and love in their hearts.

"Ye are the light of the world." Man is the candle of the Lord. How important then that this light be kept trimmed and burning with the oil of pure Spirit, through the wick of peace and joy. In this way do we glorify that Indwelling God who is the Heavenly Father and the Cosmic Mother of all.

THE ALTAR OF FAITH (MATT. 5:23)

Again, Jesus tells us that our gifts, brought to the altar of life, are unacceptable while there is aught between us and our fellowman. Here is a hard saying. We cannot always please our fellowmen. Human experience has taught that this is impossible. What attitude, then, are we to assume? This: whether we please or whether we displease, we need have no personal animosity toward others. The altar of faith is approached through peace and goodwill toward all. The Divine Ear is attuned to harmony and cannot be approached through discord.

When we agree with our adversaries quickly they will disappear, for there can be no reality to us unless we recognize it. But if we recognize that which is false, by our acceptance of it, we shall be delivered to the judgment whereby we ourselves have judged. The utmost farthing must be paid, until we no longer indulge in evil doing.

Jesus tells us to resist not evil, to love our enemies, and to do good to them who would do us evil, for this is to manifest the spirit of love, which is God. God loves all alike and causes His rain to fall and His sun to shine alike upon all. In arms which are all inclusive, Divine Love encompasses everything.

THE FATHER WHO SEETH IN SECRET (MATT. 6:4)

We are not to give our alms before men to be seen of them, but to do good for the pure love of good. Here Jesus is teaching the lesson of sincerity. Men will come and men will go, friend and foe alike may fall away, but *always the soul shall be thrown back* upon itself. The Indwelling Spirit who lives in the secret place of our lives, will ever be with us. And this Father who seeth in secret will reward us openly. Here, again, is a suggestion of the Law of Cause and Effect, about which Jesus so often spoke.

Our prayers are to be made to God in the secret place of our own being. They are not to be shouted aloud for the ears of men. The soul must enter this secret place, naked and alone. This is how the One returns to the One.

THE SECRET OF PRAYER (MATT. 6:6)

The secret of prayer and its power in the outward life depends upon an unconditioned faith in, and reliance upon this inner Presence. We must enter the closet. That is, we are to shut out all else and enter the Presence of Spirit, in quietness and confidence—believing. Prayer has power, not through repetition, but by belief and acceptance. Prayer is to be simple, direct and receiving. We are to believe that God indwells our own life, that this Divine Presence is sufficient for all needs. We are to believe that God will provide for and bless us abundantly. And when we enter this secret place, we are to leave all else behind; all hate, animosity and vindictiveness, for only in so doing can we enter.

HOW GOD FORGIVES (MATT. 6:14, 15)

We are told that God will forgive us *after* we have forgiven others. This is a direct statement and one that we should ponder deeply. Can God forgive until we have forgiven? If God can work for us only by working through us, then this statement of Jesus stands true, and is really a statement of the law of cause and effect. We cannot afford to hold personal animosities or enmities against the world or individual members of society. All such thoughts are outside the law and cannot be taken into the heavenly consciousness. Love alone can beget love. People do not gather roses from thistles.

The Father who seest in secret will reward us openly. Shall we not learn to enter the "secret place of the Most High," within our own soul, in gladness? We are to fast without outward sign, but with the inner mind open and receptive to the Good alone. Our treasure is already in heaven, and our thought can take us to this treasure only when it is in accord with divine harmony and perfect love.

THE SINGLE EYE (MATT. 6:22)

If our eye is single, we shall be filled with light. That is, when we perceive the Unity of Good, we shall perceive it in its entirety, an undivided whole. But if our eye be filled with evil, we shall remain in darkness. We must cleave to the good, and trust absolutely in the Law of God to bring about any desired end. Spirit will mold our purposes when we allow It to do so. As we learn to depend more and more upon the perfect Law, we shall find that the outward things which are necessary to our good, will be provided. We shall be cared for as the lilies of the field, which live directly upon the Divine bounty. And yet they toil not nor do they spin.

THE DIVINE BOUNTY (MATT. 6:26)

As God cares for the birds, who do not gather into barns, so shall we be cared for if we trust and do not doubt. But we are to *seek* the Kingdom first. Jesus bade us to completely trust in God for everything and in every instance. He had a complete reliance upon God. Dare we say that such a confidence will be misplaced? Have we ever tried it? Until we have tried and failed, we are not in position to contradict this theory. Those who have implicitly relied upon this theory are proving the principle to be definite, and one upon which an absolute reliance may be placed.

Have no fear of tomorrow; enjoy today. Refuse to carry the corpse of a mistaken yesterday. What untold misery is suffered through the burdens imposed by our yesterdays and the bitter prospects of our tomorrows! The good of the present day is too often sandwiched between these two impossible situations. The day in which we live is sufficient. We are to live today as though God were in His Heaven, while all is well with our souls.

Jesus made the greatest claim upon God, of anyone who ever lived. He demanded a complete and unreserved trust in the goodness and loving kindness of the Creator. And harking down the ages—since he lived and taught his marvelous philosophy to mankind—those who have followed his teachings have been justified in their faith.

Judge Not, That Ye Be Not Judged (Matt. 7:1)

"Judge not that ye be not judged, for with what judgment ye judge ye shall be judged, and with what measure ye mete, it shall be measured to you again." This statement could come only from one who had a deep insight into the universal law of Cause and Effect, which balances everything, and sees that in the long run, everyone receives his just due. This law Emerson called the "High Chancellor of God." The law of cause and effect is the law of perfect balance, of logical sequence and of inevitable consequence. Whatever a man sows, he must reap.

The law of cause and effect is immutable, and every man's action produces an effect in his life, which he must ultimately experience, unless he transcends the law already set in motion. Such a concept supposes that we are surrounded by a Universal Law, which is entirely impartial, and which returns to the thinker the logical effect of his actions. Man, being a free agent in this law—whether consciously or in ignorance—is continually setting it in motion to some definite end. Therefore it is true, unalterably true, that *he must reap as he has sown!*

This means that life must return to us the manifestation of our motives, thoughts and desires—whether these motives, thoughts and desires were intended for ourselves or others. It means that the thought of judgment, criticism and condemnation must, in time, operate against the one who sets it in motion! It is doubtless necessary to the well-being of society that our civil laws be enforced, else in our present state of evolution, there would be no protection from those who seek to destroy society; but personal condemnation can be entirely eliminated.

Ultimately we shall see that the Universe rests on the shoulders of Love; that God is Love; and that all the errors of man are the result of ignorance of his own true nature. The happy outlook on life is always constructive; the understanding heart is filled with sympathy and helpfulness toward all. An evolved soul judges no one, condemns no one, but realizes that all are on the road of experience, seeking the same goal, and that each must ultimately find his home in Heaven.

In the long run, nothing judges us but the immutable Law of Cause and Effect. Whoever deserves punishment will receive it, and whoever merits reward will find that it is brought by the hand of the Almighty and delivered to him. There is a direct law responding to condemnation and a direct law responding to praise and appreciation. It is, of course, the same law used in different ways.

There is a Law, common to all people, which responds to every man's belief in life, at the level of that belief. No man can be happy who lives in a continuous state of condemnation of people, conditions and things. We must learn to praise and not condemn.

Religious Morbidities

Those who have made a study of soul analysis are aware that poisonous secretions in the body are often the result of religious morbidities. The time has come to break the bondage of these false impressions. We are free souls, free spirits, and because this is true, our thought has creative power, and since it has this power, we must carefully choose what we are to think, for everything moves in circles.

We do not say there is no evil experience. We say, evil is not an entity, but a misuse of a power, which of itself is good. We shall never know the nature of good by dissecting the nature of evil.

Thought Retards or Quickens

Everything our thought rests upon is either retarded or quickened by the power of that thought. Everyone is a law unto himself, under the great law of cause and effect governing all things.

When we constructively praise and creatively bless, life abounds with love, peace and joy. Let goodness shine forth. Let us learn to see that everyone is an evolving Christ. Let us so live and think that we may retire at night in peace, knowing that no harm can come to the soul; that we may rise in the morning renewed in body and in mind, with a brighter outlook, a happier expectation and a clearer joy, looking upon all with love, condemning none and blessing even those who seek to injure us. Let us learn to be perfect, even as that Divine Being, residing in the heart of all and overshadowing Eternity, must also be perfect.

Self-Healing Must Come First of All

If we think we can guide our brother aright, while our own feet still walk in darkness, we are mistaken. We must first clarify our own vision, then we shall become as lights, lighting the way for others. But can we teach a lesson we have not learned? Can we give that which we do not possess? To suppose so is hypocrisy, a thing to be shunned. Jesus tears the mantle of unreality from the shoulders of hypocrisy, winnowing from the soul of sham and shallowness its last shred of illusion. We cannot see Reality until our eyes are open; until the light of eternal Truth has struck deeply into our own souls.

Scientific Prayer (Matt. 7:7)

We now come to a definite teaching regarding prayer. We shall receive that for which we ask. It shall be opened to us when we knock and we shall find that for which we are searching. This teaching implies the definiteness of spiritual and mental work. God is Intelligent Mind and Spirit, and there is a direct response from this Universal Intelligence to our intelligence. If we ask for bread, we shall not receive a stone. But we are told we must ask *believing*, if we are to receive.

Here again we are meeting the Law of Cause and Effect in the teachings of Jesus. Prayer is a mental, as well as a spiritual, function of intelligence. It is a certain manner of approach to the Spirit, a conscious act of the mind, a concrete experience of the knowing faculty. Prayer should be direct and specific, and should always be accompanied by a positive receptivity God cannot answer prayers which have no meaning. The answer to prayer is in the prayer when it is uttered or thought. We do not "pray aright" when we are in opposition to the fundamental harmony. The whole teaching of Jesus, relative to prayer, is that God will answer when we pray aright. Jesus points to the fact that if we, being human and consequently limited, know how to give good gifts to our children, how much more will God give good gifts to those who ask; and he explicitly tells us to ask directly for what we want.

God and Creation

We are to know the Truth by its fruits. The certain estimate of reality is ever evidenced by its worth in actual living. We are not to separate life from living nor God from His creation. One is the Cause, the other is the effect. The invisible things of God are manifested through the visible, and unless the invisible thought and desire of man is in line with Truth, his acts will fall into error. While we are told not to judge, we are clearly warned not to fall under the illusion of accepting the false for the true.

ENTERING THE KINGDOM OF REALITY (MATT. 7:21)

It is not everyone who says: "Lord, Lord," who enters the kingdom of harmony; *only those who do the will of love can enter*. The temple of Truth is approached by the pure in heart, and entered by those who serve but one master, which is Truth.

In no way can this passage (from Matt. 7) be misconstrued to mean, or even to suggest, anything like the theological hell. Jesus never taught the popular concept of hell. He was laying down a philosophy of life for time, as well as for eternity. He knew that eternity must be made up of different times. To suppose an eternity without the element of time, is to suppose an impossibility, for it means to suppose an unexpressed existence.

The wise man builds his house on the solid rock of Truth, and not on the shifting sands of instability. He measures causes by effects and estimates Reality by that which is real and enduring. The foolish man, living only in sense perception, has no measure for Reality and builds his home on false opinion and erroneous concept; the vicissitudes of fortune upset his frail building, the storms of experience tear the walls apart, while the edifice falls about him in ruins. Truth alone endures to Eternal Day.

THE HEALING OF THE CENTURION'S SERVANT (MATT. 8:5–14)

In Matthew Eight, we have a beautiful story in the life of Jesus, which shows his great compassion and love for humanity: the healing of the centurion's servant. Note that the centurion would not allow Jesus to come to his house, but asked him to speak the word only.

The centurion, being a man in authority on the physical plane, recognized that Jesus exercised like authority on the mental and spiritual planes. Without this recognition, he would not have known that Jesus could heal his servant by the power of his word. "Speak the word only, and my servant shall be healed." It is no wonder that Jesus marveled at this faith. And how quickly was this faith answered by an affirmative response from a heart of love and a mind of understanding. "Go thy way; and as thou hast believed, so be it done unto thee."

How simple the words, yet how fraught with meaning! What majesty and what might! From whence came the power of this spoken word? Is it not necessary to suppose that the word of man—when spoken in compliance with the law of Truth—is also all-powerful? We cannot believe that Jesus had an occult power not possessed by other men. To think this would be superstition. We certainly cannot suppose that he was especially endowed with power from on high, for this would be to believe in a partial God. There is but one logical explanation of the power of Jesus: *He believed what he taught, and so completely lived his teachings, that he was able to demonstrate them.* But we should remember that his will was ever in accord with the Divine Mind.

JESUS FORGIVES A MAN AND HEALS HIM (MATT. 9:5, 6)

Now some of the scribes who heard Jesus tell the sick man that his sins were forgiven said he blasphemed God in attempting to forgive sins. But Jesus—reading their thoughts and knowing what was in their minds—asked them if it were easier to forgive or to heal. "For whether is easier to say, Thy sins be forgiven thee; or to say, Arise and walk?" In order to prove his position, he healed the man, saying: "Arise, take up thy bed, and go unto thine house."

This incident has to do with a great psychological law. If one labors under a great burden of past mistakes, he devitalizes his body and if the condemnation is great enough—it might render the body incapable of moving. Jesus, seeing that the sick man was laboring under a load of condemnation, told him that his sins were forgiven. This removed the weight from the man's consciousness, making it possible for him to receive the healing word.

Would Jesus have forgiven the man if he had thought that God held anything against him? Certainly not. He knew that the Eternal Heart is one of love, and that God forgives from the foundation of the universe. Indeed, he knew that the Divine Mind is too pure to behold evil and knows nothing about sin.

GOD KNOWS NO EVIL

Why should it disturb anyone to be told that God knows nothing of his sin, nothing of his want, nothing of his lack of any kind? *The tragedy would be if God did know.* If God knew sin, He would be a sinner, for *what the Infinite Mind knows must BE!* Sin or mistakes are outside the province of Reality. Jesus knew this. He also knew that while man labors under the sense of condemnation, the burden of his thought weighs him to the dust. Being able to read thought, he knew just what step to take in relieving the burden of this man's mind, before telling him to arise and walk.

We shall do well to remember this lesson. How often we condemn when we should forgive, how often censure when we might praise! What untold grief of heart might be relieved by words of cheer and forgiveness. Especially should this lesson be remembered in the training of children, for they so readily respond to the thought of others. Remembering that the Spirit holds no evil toward man, and that God is Love, we should emulate this divine lesson and forgive all, that our hearts may be free from the burden of our own condemnation.

New Cloth and Old Garments (Matt. 9:16, 17)

In saying that "no man puts a piece of new cloth on an old garment or new wine into old bottles," Jesus was teaching a lesson in religious development. We are continuously living a new life, and when the old and the new do not fit nicely together, the old—being no longer able to contain the new—should be discarded. Continually we must expect new revelations of old truths. We should never lose sight of the fact that the soul is on the pathway of an endless and ever-expanding experience, and that only by expansion can it evolve. This does not mean that we should cast away any good the old has to offer, but that we convert it into a greater good. Accepting the lessons and experiences of the past, and taking the best from everything, we should press boldly forward, looking ever for the Truth, and ever ascending higher and higher into the heavens of reality.

There is no limit to the possibility inherent in all men. Let the timid soul put its complete trust in good and press bravely on.

Thy Faith Hath Made Thee Whole (Matt. 9:20, 21)

"And behold, a woman which was diseased with an issue of blood twelve years, came behind him and touched the hem of his garment; for she said within herself, If I may but touch his garment, I shall be whole."

It is said that Jesus was aware of her presence and turned to her with the words, "Thy faith hath made thee whole." This is a lesson in impersonal healing, showing that the spiritually-minded are surrounded by an atmosphere of Reality the very presence of which heals. Again, we find Jesus emphasizing the teaching—that it is done unto us as we believe. "And the woman was made whole from that hour."

In healing the blind men, Jesus asked them if they believed that he was able to restore their vision, and upon their acceptance of his ability to do so, he said, "According to your faith be it unto you." Again he was showing the necessity of faith and belief, as supreme requisites in the demonstration of spiritual power.

The Law of Circulation (Matt. 10:8)

"Freely ye have received, freely give." When the law of circulation is retarded, stagnation results. It is only as we allow the Divine current to flow through us on and out, that we really express life. The law of giving and receiving is definite. Emerson tells us to beware of holding too much good in our hands.

Because of the unity underlying all life, no man lives entirely unto himself, but through himself, he lives unto the whole, which whole embodies all other lives. Therefore, "he that findeth his life shall lose it; and he that loseth his life, shall find it."

When a man's thought rests entirely upon himself, he becomes abnormal and unhappy; but when he gives himself with enthusiasm to any legitimate purpose, losing himself in the thing which he is doing, he becomes normal and happy. Only as much life enters into us as we can conceive, and we conceive of life—in the larger sense—only when there is complete abandonment to it. Let the one who is sad, depressed, or unhappy find some altruistic purpose into which he may pour his whole being and he will find a new inflow of life of which he has never dreamed.

Whom Shall We Try to Help? (Matt. 10:12, 13)

But Jesus was wise in the ways of the world, as well as in heavenly wisdom, and he counselled his followers against attempting to help people, when they wished no help. He said, "And when ye come into a house, salute it. And if the house be worthy, let your peace come upon it: but if it be not worthy, let your peace return to you."

This is a lesson which sincere students of Truth often discover to their great chagrin. People do not always receive their message, and when this happens there should be no controversy, no argument, and no sense of disturbance; but, abiding in the conviction of the ultimate acceptance of truth by all, they should let their peace return unto themselves and go calmly on their way, undisturbed, unprejudiced, non-combative, but certain of themselves . . . certain of the Truth upon which they stand. If, however, they are called upon to defend their faith, they should remember that the Spirit, indwelling their lives, will put into their mouths the very words which they should speak; the great teacher said: "For it is not ye that speak, but the Spirit of your Father which speaketh in you" (Matt. 10:20). Never forget that there is an indwelling Spirit which *knows*.

Nothing Can Be Hidden (Luke 12:2)

In saying, "there is nothing covered, that shall not be revealed; and hid, that shall not be known," Jesus was referring to the Mind that knows; to the all-seeing eye, from which nothing is concealed. The Cosmic Ear hears everything, the Eternal Mind knows all things, and the Law of cause and effect brings everything to pass in due time.

A MAN'S FOES (MATT. 10:36)

"And a man's foes shall be they of his own household." There are no enemies external to our own mind. This is one of the most difficult problems to understand, and—simple as it sounds— it penetrates the depths of creative causation. *Nothing can happen to us unless it happens through us.* That which we refuse to accept, *to us* cannot be, and that which to us *is*, cannot help becoming a reality in our lives. But someone will say, "I did not conceive of this evil which came upon me; it was not in my mind." The question then arises, "Can any particular evil be real to one, if he refuses to entertain it in his thought?" The answer must forever be, *it cannot.* This is one of those "hard sayings" which it is difficult to understand, but the principle involved is plain.

If we can divorce our lives from the thought of evil—from receptivity to it—if we can bring our mentality to a place where it no longer conceives evil, then evil cannot exist for us. The proof of this doctrine remains for individual conviction, through experience, but it is well worth trying.

THE REWARD OF TRUE VISIONING (MATT. 10:41)

"He that receiveth a prophet in the name of a prophet, shall receive a prophet's reward; and he that receiveth a righteous man, in the name of a righteous man, shall receive a righteous man's reward." There comes to each the logical and exact result of his own receptivity. To each, life brings the reward of his own visioning; to the pure, all is pure. To the righteous, all is righteous, and to the good, all is good. The reward of merit is an objective outcome of merit itself and not a thing superimposed by any Divine Mandate. Each man is rewarded not for virtue but *through* virtue.

WISDOM IS JUSTIFIED OF HER CHILDREN (MATT. 11:18, 19)

"Wisdom is justified of her children." Jesus had been questioning his hearers about John the Baptist. "For John came neither eating nor drinking, and they say, He hath a devil. The Son of man came eating and drinking, and they say, Behold a man gluttonous, and a wine-bibber, a friend of publicans and sinners. But, wisdom is justified of her children."

This shows that the world ever finds some flaw in human character. If a man *fasts*, he is possessed of peculiar ideas; and if he *feasts*, he is a materialist and a glutton. But Jesus would have us understand that virtue consists neither in eating nor drinking, nor yet in abstaining from eating and drinking. "Wisdom is justified of her children." A man may desire to fast, and be wise, or he may desire to feast and still be wise. VIRTUE IS INDEPENDENT OF ANY MATE-RIAL FORM WHICH IT MAY TAKE. The children of wisdom look to the inner, and not to the outer, for justification. Wisdom knows neither publican nor sinner, but is conscious only of herself, though she may dress in many garments.

If one believes that virtue consists in fasting, then virtue appears to him through fasting; but to him who finds no virtue in fasting, *feasting* may appear to be a greater virtue. We are over-concerned with non-essentials, straining at gnats, while swallowing mountains of superstition.

THE CHILD-LIKE FAITH (MATT. 18:3, 4, 5)

Jesus tells us that the child-like mind is more receptive to Truth than the over-intellectual who demand too rational an explanation of those truths which must be accepted on faith alone. What man can explain why he lives? The self-evident fact of living is the only explanation possible or necessary. In the whole life, and through the entire teaching, of this marvelous man, we find a child-like faith in the universe and an implicit trust in the goodness of God. Judging his work by its results, and its influence on succeeding ages, we are compelled to accept the fact that "Wisdom is justified of her children."

THE REAL FATHER AND SON (MATT. 11:27)

"And no man knoweth the Son, but the Father; neither knoweth any man the Father, save the Son, and he to whomsoever the Son will reveal him."

What reasonable explanation can we find to this passage, unless we look for some hidden meaning behind these words of the great teacher? God alone knows the real Son, forever hidden in the bosom of the Father. To God, this idea of sonship must be pure, complete and perfect; divine, holy and indestructible. With our present limited vision, we neither see nor know the *real* Son, but the Father within knows and understands. "Neither knoweth any man the Father, save the Son, and he to whomsoever the Son will reveal him." God is revealed through the Son, and the Son reveals himself to other sons when he realizes that God is his life. This implies a direct relationship between God and man.

If one would know God, he must penetrate deeply into his own nature, for here alone can he find Him. If he would reveal God to his fellowmen, he must do so by living such a God-like life, that the Divine Essence flows through him to others. The only way to know God is to be like Him; and while this may seem discouraging in our present state of evolution, we should remember that we have but started on an eternal ladder which ever spirals upward.

When Jesus said to come to him and find rest ("Come unto me all ye that labour and are heavy laden and I will give you rest . . .") did he mean that we should, or could, come unto his personality? Of course not. Jesus knew that his human personality would soon be dissolved in his divine individuality. He knew that he was soon to leave this world and go on to a deeper realization of life, truth and beauty.

It is evident, then, that he was referring to his understanding of life, when he told all who are weary to come unto him and find rest. Had he not already explained that God indwells every soul? He was inviting people to penetrate more deeply into their own natures, if they would find peace and comfort. This has ever been the lesson taught by the illumined that we find God only within ourselves, and God can work *for* us only by working *through* us. God reveals Himself directly through the Son. The Son reveals God, when he realizes that God is already within him. This understanding would not produce an undue conceit, nor would it set man in the temple of God *as* God; but it would place a true estimate of value on the life of man.

The Power at the Heart of God

Peace is the power at the heart of God. It is through the revelation of the self, to the self, that one understands life; that he approaches the power which is at the heart of God. This comes through a recognition of the unity of the individual, with the Spirit *back of, in*, and *through all*.

The problem of philosophy is to unite the Infinite with the finite; to join the abstract with the concrete; to find a meeting place between the Absolute and the relative; to unify with First Cause. The same problem confronts religion and is, indeed, its whole purpose: to unify man with God. This is also true of science, but from a different angle. Science seeks to join causes with effects, and by so doing make practical use of its knowledge. Science is really spiritual, while philosophy leads to true religion. Science is the handmaid of religion and philosophy.

The Great Search

The world seeks a solution of its great riddle—the apparent separation between God and man; between life and what it does; between the invisible and the visible; between the Father and the Son—and until this riddle is solved, there can be no peace.

Peace is an inner calm, obtained through man's knowledge of what he believes and why. Without knowledge, there is no lasting peace. Nothing can bring peace but the revelation of the individual to himself, and a recognition of his direct relationship to the Universe. He must know that he is an eternal being on the pathway of life, with certainty behind him, certainty before him, and certainty accompanying him all the way.

Peace is brought about through a conscious unity of the personal man with the inner principle of his life—that underlying current, flowing from a divine center, pressing ever outward into expression. But this can never come by proxy. We can hire others to work for us, to care for our physical needs, but *no one can live for us. This we must do for ourselves.*

THE NEED OF SPIRITUAL EXPERIENCE

We need spiritual experience, a first-hand knowledge of life and Reality. There is no medium between God and man, nothing between life and living, between heaven and hell, but an idea. But an idea has no real value until it becomes an experience.

In conversation, we assume great knowledge of religion and philosophy, but how much do we really experience? We can *know* only that which we experience. All great religions have taught truth, but it means nothing to us unless it becomes our truth.

We need spiritual experience. We shall never know peace until we embody it, we shall never know Truth until we become Truth, and we cannot know God unless we sense Him within our own being. The Spirit is ever giving, but we must take. What life does for us must be done through us.

Spiritual experience is deep, calm and self-assertive; it is the result of actually realizing that Presence which binds all together in one complete Whole. This experience comes in the stillness of the Soul, when the outer voice is quiet, when the tempest of human strife is abated; it is a quickening of the inner man to an eternal reality.

Spiritual experience is a fact. Spirituality may be defined as an atmosphere of good, the realization of God. It cannot—and does not—borrow its light from another, no matter how great or noble that other may be. It springs from within, coming from that never-failing fountain of life, which quenches every thirst, whose Source is in eternity; the well-spring of self-existence. It is a revelation of the self to the self, putting one back on the track of his own self-dependence on Spirit, his own at-one-ment with Reality.

THE CAUSE OF HUMAN TROUBLES

The integrity of the universe cannot be questioned nor doubted. The Spirit *must be, and is, perfect*. That which is back of everything must be good, must be complete, must be love and harmony. When we are out of harmony with some special good, it is because we are off the track along that particular line of the activity of Spirit.

But how are we to regain the lost Paradise? Only through soul culture and by careful self-analysis. What is my viewpoint of life? This is a question each should ask himself. What do I feel my relationship to the great Whole to be? What do I believe about the Cause back of all? From whence come discouragement, fear, doubt and calamity? They *cannot* proceed from the eternal Source—that perfect fount of life—the inexhaustible One. Therefore, they must come from my own consciousness. They cannot be born of the Truth. The Truth is God, and God is free, happy, peaceful and ever poised in His own Being. I must set myself right with the universe. I must find the way back to the central fire, if I am to be warmed. I must find the Source, if I am to be supplied. *I must be like God, if I wish to realize His Spirit in my life!*

A change of consciousness does not come by simply willing or wishing. It is not easy to hold the mental attention to an ideal, while the human experience is discordant, but—it is possible. Knowing the Truth is not a process of self-hypnosis, but one of a gradual unfoldment of the inner self.

How to Approach the Spirit

If we wish to come to the Spirit for the healing of our wounds, let us come in peace and with spontaneous joy, for the Spirit is joy; let us come with thanksgiving also, for a thankful heart is in harmony with life. But we must come in quiet confidence, with an open and receptive mind, a believing heart, naturally, sanely and expectantly. In this way, we are entering the portals of Reality, clad in garments of righteousness.

We often think what we require is money, friends and physical healing. After *these things*, do those, who are outside a knowledge of the Law, seek; and they do well, for we need all these things. But *they are the effects of right relationships to life*. All people need some form of healing. Most people are unhappy, few have any realization of permanent peace. We seek fragments, when the whole is at hand. How illogical to think that anything can rise higher than its source. The Universe is a perfect, undivided whole, and healing can take place only when one is unified with It. How can anyone, then, be healed in part? Let us seek wholeness above all else.

If we would come to the Universal Wholeness, we must approach it through the law of its own nature. This means that we must give our undivided attention to the spiritual unit back of all things. Since all else is included within this unit, we find our *particular* good only through unity with life. This conscious unity makes our mind receptive to completion, since Life Itself is complete. This perception is always an inner light, for the individual can use only such knowledge as he inwardly possesses. In reality, we know God or Truth, only as we ourselves embody God or Truth. AND SINCE IT IS IMPOSSIBLE TO EMBODY ANYTHING OUTSIDE OUR-SELVES, THIS KNOWLEDGE MUST BE AN INNER LIGHT. The Truth Itself is Infinite, but we only embody the Infinite in degree. To the degree that we do embody Reality, we become poised and powerful.

THE PURPOSE OF THE SCIENCE OF MIND

The whole purpose of the Science of Mind is to reconcile the apparent separation of the spiritual world, *which must be Perfect*, with the material world, which appears imperfect. The Spiritual world is the CAUSE of the material; we are spiritual beings governed by mental law. ONLY THAT WORLD CAN APPEAR TO US WHICH WE MENTALLY PERCEIVE. Man's experience is the logical outcome of his inner vision; his horizon is limited to the confines of his own consciousness. Wherever this consciousness lacks a true perspective, its outward expression will lack proper harmony. This is why we are taught to be transformed by the renewing of our minds. Since no one lives by proxy, but each unto himself, every individual must make the test in his own soul.

AND JESUS KNEW THEIR THOUGHTS (MATT. 12:25)

"And Jesus knew their thoughts. . . ." That is, he had an extended vision which enabled him to know what others were thinking. He had healed a man possessed of unclean thoughts, and the priests had reasoned within themselves that his power to do this was of the "evil one."

Jesus, understanding what was in their minds, told them that a house divided against itself cannot stand; and that if he cast out evil by the power of evil, then evil would be a house divided against itself. "But," he said, "if I cast out devils by the Spirit of God, then the kingdom of God is come unto you."

We cannot do good while we continue to do evil, nor can we heal evil except by the power of good. To all sincere students of Spiritual Science, this lesson is a guide post, pointing to the fact that the thought of good must ever overcome any thought that is less than good. By the presence of good, evil is cast out, just as by the presence of light, the darkness disappears.

GOOD THOUGHTS AND A GOOD HARVEST (MATT. 7:17, 18)

A good tree produces good fruit, so good thoughts bear a harvest of good deeds, while evil consumes itself in the flame of its own fire. If a man's life produces good deeds, then the man is himself good; and this, no matter what his particular religious belief may or may not be.

The mouth speaks from the heart. It is impossible for a man to conceal himself. In every act, word, or gesture, he stands revealed as he is, and not as he would have himself appear to be. From the universe, nothing is or can be hidden; the very walls have ears and the mirror of life cannot help reflecting back to us that which we really are.

Jesus plainly tells us that we are held accountable for the very words which we speak. No man ever lived who placed a greater power in the word. By our words we are justified or condemned. The word may be considered to be the complete thought and act of man. There must be a thought before there can be an act, and a thinker before there can be any thought. The thinker condemns or justifies himself through his thought.

The Father-Mother God (Matt. 12:47, 48)

It is related that while Jesus was talking, he was told that his mother and brethren waited to speak with him. "But he answering said unto him that told him, Who is my mother? and who are my brethren?" He then told them that whoever does the will of God is his mother, sister and brother. We are not to suppose, by this, that he did not care for his earthly parents or friends. He was explaining that anyone who lives in harmony with the Truth, automatically becomes the brother, the sister or the mother of all.

This is a lesson in the brotherhood of man. God is the Androgynous Principle, the Father and Mother of all. Our earthly parents symbolize this heavenly parentage. Jesus was a consciously cosmic soul, who recognized his unity with all. He knew that love must become universal before it can reach its maturity. Hence he said that all who live in harmony with the Truth are brothers in it.

To Him Who Hath Shall Be Given (Matt. 13:12)

"Whosoever hath, to him shall be given, and he shall have more abundance; but whosoever hath not, from him shall be taken away even that he hath."

This certainly sounds like a very hard saying, and is most discouraging to one who has not fathomed the depths of its meaning. We appear to have little enough, and to have this little withdrawn from our small possessions seems more than we can bear. And for us to feel that those *who already have*, are to receive more, sounds unfair.

Let us examine this saying in the light of an understanding of the law of cause and effect, that subtle reality which lies hidden in the creative power of man's mind. Unless one conceives of himself as possessing good things, he will not possess them. From the objective world of such a one, even that which he has will be taken away. This is but another way of stating the law of cause and effect, that immutable principle, which governs all things.

The Concept of a Successful Man

Could we see the mentality of a successful man, we should find the imprint of success written in bold letters across the doorway of his consciousness. The successful man is sure of himself, sure of what he is doing, certain of the outcome of his undertakings. As much gathers more, as like attracts like, so success breeds greater success, and conviction is attended by certainty. The whole teaching of Jesus is to have faith and to believe. He placed a greater value on faith and belief than any individual who has ever taught spiritual truth. We are to believe in ourselves because we have first penetrated the invisible Cause back of the real self. We are to have absolute faith in our work, because we have positive conviction of the inner power which enables us to do this work.

But to those who believe only in failure, the law comes in corresponding measure, measuring back to them the logical outcome of their beliefs. The habitual failure bears, across the threshold of his thought, an image of his inability to attain. The old law says that what little he has shall be withdrawn until he has learned the lesson of life and action.

Each should train himself—and do so consciously—to conceive of himself as a success. Sailing on that boundless sea of livingness, upon whose bosom we are all carried forward, we should go from success to greater success. All thoughts of failure or depression must be erased from the mentality, and positive thoughts of achievement should take their place. Have faith in God, in life, and in your fellowman. KNOW THAT RIGHT IS MIGHT. Get some degree of real conviction and stay with it. The Cosmic Mind is neither wishy-washy nor willy-nilly. It is positive, certain of Itself and sure of the outcome.

The Seeing Eye (Matt. 13:16)

"Blessed are your eyes, for they see; and your ears, for they hear." What is it the eye should see and the ear hear? Do not all people's eyes see and their ears hear? No. But few, indeed, when looking, see, or listening, hear.

We are to see that Spirit creates all things by the power of Its own word, and that we are spiritual beings. We are to hear that inner voice of Truth, which is ever proclaiming the freedom of all life, the eternal unity of God with man. It is useless for those who have never experienced this inner seeing or hearing to deny its reality. A man might as well say there is no meadow because he has never seen one. The world needs spiritual experience, as it needs bread and butter. Men need spiritual convictions as they need meat and drink. And with spiritual convictions come all else. To those who have, shall be given.

THE KINGDOM AND THE MUSTARD SEED (MATT. 13:31, 32)

"The kingdom of heaven is like a grain of mustard seed." From a knowledge of mental action, we know that a *constructive idea*, planted or buried in the subjective mind, tends to grow into a real condition. Jesus could not have chosen a more comprehensive way to illustrate his point.

THE KINGDOM IS LIKE LEAVEN (MATT. 13:33)

"The kingdom of heaven is like leaven." We know that thoughts planted in mind have the power to chemicalize opposing ideas, and leaven the whole lump of subjectivity. In this way, ideas gradually permeate the mind and influence all thought and action. If the idea is of heaven, it will certainly bring about a heavenly state.

THE PEARL OF GREAT PRICE (MATT. 13:45, 46)

The kingdom of heaven is likened unto a pearl of great price, for which a man will sell all that he has, that he may possess it. This, perhaps, best explains the way of the illumined. To them, the kingdom of heaven has meant everything, and has been above all else. We find them going away by themselves that they may more completely enjoy this inner realization of their relationship to the Whole. A divine companionship has ever attended such, on the pathway of human experience. The description of the things they have seen, felt and heard, constitutes some of the most valuable lessons the world has ever learned.

The only news we have of Heaven has come through the consciousness of men, and to those few who have penetrated the veil of illusion and entered the realms of deeper reality, we owe a debt that cannot be paid in any other terms than those of appreciation and thanksgiving.

That the illumined have had experiences which the average man cannot conceive of, is certain; and that anyone who wills to know Truth may know it, is evident to all who make the attempt. But let us not forget that spiritual experiences are normal, natural and rational. The illumined have always had rational intellects and well-balanced mentalities.

No experience is salutary, unless it be gained while in a normal state of mind. Too great a warning cannot be given against any attempt to break through the veil, when in any other but a perfectly normal mental state.

Jesus lived in the spiritual world just as normally as we live in the material, and just as consciously. And what is the spiritual world? And where is it? It is right here, could we but see it. Behind everything material, stands the spiritual, supporting it, and without which there could be no material.

THAT WHICH DEFILES (MATT. 15:18, 19, 20)

Not what we eat or drink, but what we think, defiles. The issues of life are from within. If a man is clean in his mind, then is he clean indeed. We must keep the mental house free from any thought which contradicts the truth of being.

Life is what consciousness makes it. This is a great realization. Experience may appear to disclaim this fact, but the principle involved is an immutable one, and cannot be shaken any more than the integrity of the universe can be violated.

Let each resolve to be true to himself, true to his inner light, true to the Truth as he understands It. When every man learns to speak the Truth, a complete salvation will come to the world. If one thinks impurity, then his acts will be impure. If his thought dwells on purity and Truth, then his acts—reflecting his mind—will make him pure and true.

Every plant which is not of God's planting shall be rooted up. In the long run, everything that does not belong to the Heavenly Kingdom will be destroyed. Truth alone can endure.

WHEN THE BLIND LEAD THE BLIND (MATT. 15:14)

"If the blind lead the blind, both shall fall into the ditch." We must be careful what kind of thought we are following. We must test all ideas to see whether they are of the Truth. It is a mistake to accept every man's philosophy simply because it sounds plausible. We are to be on guard against accepting that which is not true. And let us remember this: the Truth is simple, direct and always self-evident.

False ideas heaped upon false ideas make bad matters worse. The whole confusion of the world arises from fundamental errors of thought. Chief among these errors—and the father to a greater part of the others—is a belief in duality. The belief in duality supposes that evil is equal to good: that a suppositional devil divides, with Good, the kingdom of Truth. Such things cannot be. Remember the teachings of Moses, that "God is One." If, on the other hand, we accept that evil has a power equal to good, then we must fall into the ditch of our own confusion.

To believe in the good alone, may seem fallacious to many, but he who thus believes will find his path lighted by a torch which flickers not, nor fails.

WHO WOULD SAVE HIS LIFE SHALL LOSE IT
(BASED ON MATT. 16:24–27)

This is another of those mystical sayings of Jesus which must be carefully considered before accepting it. Does God demand that we give up everything if we are to enter the Kingdom of

Heaven? Of course not! To suppose that God wills us to be limited is to contradict the Divine Nature. God's only will is to Be, and for all to Be, for God can conceive of man only as part of Himself.

It must be, then, that what we are to lose is the sense of living apart from Life. We find ourselves in the Divine Idea, immersed in the Infinite Godhead, one with the Perfect Whole. But should we think that we, of ourselves, without this relationship rightly established, can be, or can express, *then we cut the cord that binds us to the main power line and lose what little power we have.*

We are powerful only as we unite with Power. We are weak when we desert this Power. Not because God is jealous, but because this is the way things work. The idea of a false renunciation—of the giving up of all pleasure and benefits in this life—is not even suggested in the teachings of Jesus. Self-effacement, the neglect of the body, the belief that we must be unhappy and poor in order to serve the Truth, all these are immature ideas which deny the divine birthright of the soul, the incarnated Spirit of the Most High within us.

When we are willing to lose a personal sense of responsibility; when we let go of the thought of isolation and claim a real unity with God, then we lose the personal and find the Universal. But remember, as the greater always includes the lesser, so the Universal always includes the personal, which is a personification of Itself.

Man is to lose the small estimate of himself, the isolated person, and is to find the greater reality, the incarnated and real ego. The image of the Father cannot be defaced nor can all the wit or the sham of man really obliterate this image. The Eternal Light is God, and this Light illumines the pathway of the personal when there are no obstructions.

Who leans on the Truth, throwing all—with an undivided attention—on the scales of Reality, will find them balanced rightly, through the great law of compensation, which weighs and measures everything exactly as it is.

FASTING AND PRAYER (MATT. 17:21)

We are not to suppose that the physical act of fasting, or the metaphysical act of prayer, can move the throne of grace to a kindness which is otherwise withheld. God plays no favorites and the Law of the Universe cannot reverse Its own nature. Fasting and prayer often do bring our thought closer to Reality, not because of the fasting or the prayer, but because they open up greater fields of receptivity in our minds.

If one wishes to embody an ideal and is willing to give up all else to attain it, *then he is fasting and praying!* He is sublimating an old idea with a new and a better one. If he is willing to abstain from the old and cling to the new, then he is giving greater reality to the new, and in this way contacting the Law from a more affirmative angle.

A steadfast determination to attain some purpose, the letting go of all that opposes it, a complete reliance upon the Law of Good, and an unqualified trust in Spirit—this is true fasting and real prayer.

The scientist, in profound thought and meditation before his problem—deserting all to solve it—is praying a true prayer to the principle of his science. The poet, waiting in the silence of his own soul for inspiration, is praying that he may invoke the spirit of poetry to his listening ear. The sculptor, chiselling at his marble, contemplating the beauty to be brought forth, prays to his god of art; and the farmer, kneeling beside his cabbage patch, trusts in the natural Law of Good to bring his seed to harvest.

We live in a fasting and praying world, but often we do not read the signs aright. We are too used to the outward sign to realize its inward significance. The world is much better than it knows or feels itself to be.

HEALING THE LUNATIC (MATT. 17:14–19)

What majesty and might do we see in the calm words of Jesus! "Bring him hither to me." No doubt is here, no sense of approaching failure, no lack of trust in the perfect Law which governs all. "And Jesus rebuked the devil; and he departed out of him."

Surely this lesson should teach us that evil is but an obsession and—from the standpoint of eternal Reality—a complete illusion. Could we cast out evil from our thought if evil were a real entity or had actual power? The answer is self-evident, we could not. Evil flees before Reality and to the mind which knows it, evil is not.

AS LITTLE CHILDREN (MATT. 18:3)

We must become as little children. How we long for a return of that simple trust in life which children have; in their minds there are no doubts—they have not yet been told that they are sinners, destitute of divine guidance and spiritual life. The life of the child is lived in natural goodness. God is natural goodness. The prison walls of false experience soon build themselves into barriers, shutting out the light, and the child grows into a man, often losing his sense of that inner Guide, leading his footsteps aright.

We must return the way we came. As little children, who know that life is good and to be trusted, we are to approach our problems *as though they were not.* Approaching them in this manner, they will vanish.

Let not the materialist deny us this right, nor the unbelieving cast any reflection of his blindness before our eyes. There is a wisdom and power not of the flesh, which springs perennially from the inner life—all-powerful and all-wise.

WHATSOEVER YE SHALL BIND ON EARTH (MATT. 18:18)

Next we come to a passage difficult to understand and one which has caused confusion in many minds. "Whatsoever ye shall bind on earth shall be bound in heaven; and whatsoever ye shall loose on earth shall be loosed in heaven."

A superficial reading of this passage might lead one to suppose that this earth provides the last chance for the salvation of the soul. But this is not the meaning of the text which implies that the experience of death cannot change all. As a man has lived on earth, so he will continue to live after death. If he has been pure, he will continue to be pure. If he has been otherwise, he will continue to be otherwise.

False experience will continue until the lesson is learned, until the soul turns from that which hurts to its greater good. The spirit of man is of like nature to the Spirit of God, and it is impossible for the Spirit of God to remain in darkness. The next life is a logical continuation of this one and could not be otherwise.

DIVINE FORGIVENESS (MATT. 18:21, 22)

In the next passage, Jesus clearly explains the meaning of *divine forgiveness*. He says that we should forgive until seventy times seven. This is but another way of saying that forgiveness is eternal and ever available. What a load is dropped from the shoulders of personal responsibility, when we realize that the Eternal Mind holds naught against anyone! But, to those who feel that this is unfair, it will be a hard saying. "What," says one, "are not my virtues to be rewarded above those who have none?" O, foolish one and blind, what do you know about virtue? Has your life always been beyond reproach? Have you never fallen short of the divine calling? Who are you to point the finger of scorn at your brother? The man who feels self-righteousness rise from his petty virtues, lives a life of self-delusion.

Know this: Virtue does not know that it is virtuous, and could it know, it would immediately become vicious. Virtue is sweet as the morning dew, soft as the evening star, and brilliant as the noonday sun. Could the dew tell why it is sweet, the star say why its light is soft, or the sun say why it shines? When we learn to put away our petty virtues with our petty vices, then shall we see clearly—not what either virtue or vice is—but what Truth is!

The mind which condemns, understands not the truth of being, and the heart which would shut the door of its bosom to one who is mistaken, strangles its own life, closing its eyes to a greater vision. The biggest life is the one which includes the most.

Not that we foster vice or place a premium upon wrong-doing, but that we understand the frailties of human nature and learn to overlook much. To him who loves much, much is forgiven.

A Formula for Effective Prayer (Matt. 21:21, 22)

THE THINGS WE NEED, WE ARE TO ASK FOR—and WE ARE TO BELIEVE THAT WE RECEIVE THEM! This plumbs the very depths of the metaphysical and psychological law of our being, and explains the possibility of an answer to our prayers.

When we pray we are to believe that we have. We are surrounded by a universal law which is creative. It moves from the thought to the thing. Unless there is first an image, it cannot move, for there would be nothing for it to move toward. Prayer, which is a mental act, must accept its own answer as an image in mind, before the divine energies can play upon it and make it productive.

As we must plant a seed before we can reap a harvest, so we must believe before our prayers can be answered. Prayer should reach a point of acceptance, an unqualified and undisputed place of agreement. Let us take the mental images of our desires to the bosom of the Creative Life, and here make them known by impressing them upon It with positive belief. If we do this, our prayers will be answered.

But let us remember that true prayer is always universal. There can be no good to us alone, only as that good is for all. This does not mean that we are to refrain from asking what we desire, but that we should wish only for that which is good. For instance, it is good to have a home; it is good for all people to have homes while here on earth; it is right to ask for one, but it would not be right to ask for one belonging to another.

If we wish to pray for a home, we should take the idea of a house with us into the silence and meditate upon its actual being. We should believe that we have and own a home, but we should leave the idea free to fulfill itself, without any definite choosing of how, where, why, or when. In this way, we pray aright and when we so pray, we pray effectively.

God wills us to have everything. As we express life, we fulfill God's law of abundance, but we do this only as we realize that there is good enough to go around—only as we know that all of God's gifts are given as freely and fully as the air and the sunshine . . . alike to all.

The Two Great Commandments (Matt. 22:36–41)

The two great commandments are to love God and our brother man. On these hang all the law and the prophets. Love is a complete unity with life, and we cannot enter this state unless we are in unity with all that lives, for all life is One. To love God alone is not enough, for this would exclude our fellowman. To love our fellowman alone is not sufficient, for this would be too limited a concept of God.

When we realize that God and man are One and not two, we shall love both. We shall love man as an expression of God, and God as the Life Principle in all.

From this teaching, we are not to suppose that we are to love that in each other which does not savor of right, we are to love the right alone. We are to look for God in each other and love this God, forgetting all else. But would this compel us to accept from people that which is not good? Of course not! It is not necessary for one to make a doormat of himself in proving that God is love, for this would be like suffering for righteousness' sake, which is always a mistake.

We should be wise in the ways of the world, as well as imbued with Divine wisdom. We are not to mistake a counterfeit for the real, nor accept every man's doctrine lest we disagree. The Truth is positive but non-combative; It is sure of Itself, but never argumentative. It loves sincerity and abhors deceit. Above all else, the Truth is wise, It represents the All-seeing Eye, from which nothing can be hidden. The student of Truth will receive all that comes in the name of the Lord, that is, all that is of the Truth; all else will fall by its own weight.

History Proves the Reality of Truth (Matt. 26:52)

As we glance over the pages of history, this saying of Jesus stands sure and true: ". . . for all they that take the sword shall perish with the sword." Those nations who have risen by the sword have fallen among the ruins of their own false hopes. History has proven that strife begets strife, that the way of the transgressor is hard.

In international strife, all nations are beaten, in so far as they have taken up the sword in hate, avarice or lust. We do not recognize this apparent power which lasts for a day, for it is but a false gesture, defeating its own purpose as falseness ever must.

Jesus speaking from the viewpoint of Eternal Truth, said that all who take the sword shall perish with it. THOSE WHO HAVE GIVEN THE BEST TO THE WORLD HAVE ALWAYS BEEN BEST REMEMBERED BY IT, AND MOST LOVED THROUGHOUT THE AGES. If we attempt to measure existence from this short span of life, it would not be explained, and we should find no real answer to life itself. Hate begets hate and strife produces strife. Love alone overcomes all and justifies the eternity of her dominion.

GOD TURNS TO US AS WE TURN TO HIM (LUKE 15)

The parable of the Prodigal Son constitutes one of the greatest spiritual lessons in the history of religious education. It is an attempt, on the part of the Great Teacher, to show that God turns to us as we turn to Him; that there is a reciprocal action between the Universal and the individual mind; that the Spirit is ready to help us whenever we turn to It.

The greatest lesson we have to learn is the unity of Love and Law; the necessity of law in shaping a divine individuality and the necessity of experience in awakening to this divine individuality.

God is Love and God is Law; the Love of God is omnipresent and the Law of God is omnipresent. The Love of God is the Divine givingness: the eternal outpouring of Spirit through Its creation. The Law of God is the Law of Cause and Effect, which says that we can have only what we take. Since this taking is a mental and spiritual (as well as physical) act, *we can take only that to which we are receptive.* Jesus taught that it is done unto us as we really believe. "The thought is ever father to the act."

THE TWO SONS

In presenting the parable of the Prodigal Son to his listeners, Jesus began by saying that the Father (which is the Universal Spirit) had two sons, meaning that, as the son of God, man has the right of self-choice. This carries with it the possibility of an apparent duality (but, of course, not a real one) and the possibility of experiencing good and evil. Moses referred to the same thing when he said that he had set a blessing and a curse before the Children of Israel, and they must *choose* whom they would serve. The two sons referred to in this story, allegorically denote the two states of consciousness necessary to real individuality. Man is a conscious, self-knowing mind, equipped with volition and choice; he is an individual and can do as he chooses.

GOD DOES NOT ARGUE (LUKE 15:11–32)

"A certain man had two sons: And the younger of them said to his father, Father, give me the portion of goods that falleth to me. And he divided unto them his living."

When the younger son asked for his portion of good, God did not argue with him; did not try to dissuade him; did not suggest that he was using bad judgment. God never argues. To argue is to suppose an opposite and God has no opposite. We argue to arrive at a correct conclusion. God is already the correct conclusion of all things, therefore, He does not need to argue. Plotinus tells us that Nature never argues, that It contemplates Itself; that Its contemplation creates a *form*, through which It may become expressed. Undoubtedly, this is the whole meaning and process of Creation.

"And he divided unto them his living." There was no argument. God did not tell the son that it would be far better for him to remain at home. He did not say that he might come to want and suffer, perhaps starve. He did not tell him anything: "He divided unto them his living." The Universe gives us what we ask; experience alone will teach us what is best to have. "He divided unto them his living." No clearer statement of individuality could possibly be inferred than this. The son received exactly what he asked for; no more, and certainly no less. The cup of his acceptance was filled from the universal horn of plenty; he could do with it as he chose.

THE FAR COUNTRY

"And not many days after, the younger son gathered all together, and took his journey into a far country, and there wasted his substance with riotous living."

When the son had received his share of goods, he went into a "far country." We are all in this "far country," for it symbolizes the descent of the soul, or the outer rim of spiritual existence. It does not mean a place, but rather a state of consciousness. If God is omnipresent, we cannot escape the Divine Presence, so this "far country" means a state of consciousness which has separated itself from the eternal good. The "true meaning," I believe, of the "far country" would be a *conscious* separation from God, an isolated state, one in which there appears to be no remembrance of God as an actual, living, and ever-present Reality; one where man feels himself to be separated and entirely apart from the Eternal Good.

This "far country" has as real a meaning today as it had in the hills of Galilee, nearly two thousand years ago, for all of us have come from heaven and nearly all feel the isolation of this seeming apartness from the Eternal Good. Indeed, the whole endeavor of mankind is to return to the Father's House.

WHY WE ARE IN WANT

"And there wasted his substance with riotous living. And when he had spent all, there arose a mighty famine in that land; and he began to be in want."

When one separates himself from the Divine Fire, he becomes an isolated spark. We are strong only when united with Life. As soon as our consciousness is detached from spiritual wholeness, we can no longer draw from that inexhaustible reservoir of eternal existence, so we become exhausted—there is nothing to fall back upon.

Life is one perfect Wholeness. The Universe is a Unit. God is One. IT IS IMPOSSIBLE FOR MAN TO FEEL SEPARATED FROM THE SPIRIT WITHOUT FEELING LOST AND IN WANT. This is why Jesus said he could do nothing of himself, but could work only as the currents of divinity ran through his personal mentality. That subtle something which runs through all things and which we call "*the Thing Itself*," that *energy* without which nothing can be energized, that *Life* without which nothing can live, that *Power* without which nothing can move, and that *Spirit* without which nothing can be—IS GOD. It is only as we live in conscious union with the Spirit, and consciously let It work through us that we really live.

The Fallen Man

So, the prodigal son "began to be in want. And he went and joined himself to a citizen of that country; and he sent him into his fields to feed swine."

The symbolism here is most interesting, for it perfectly depicts the state of humanity while in the "far country." The "citizen" referred to means the attempt, on the part of man, to find some cause outside of Spirit. Man seeks to league himself with material forces alone, not realizing that there can be nothing outside the Unity. Most of us seek the cause in the effect and unknowingly put the cart before the horse, not realizing that the flower is already in the seed, and that effects must follow causes. There can be no true alliance apart from life and no good apart from a unity with the Whole. "And he sent him into his fields to feed swine." Jesus was a Jew. The Jews did not consider the meat of the swine lawful to eat; consequently he used this term to show how completely the prodigal son had fallen from his high estate—he must even be compelled to feed the despised swine. This demonstrated that his state of being was so low that it would be impossible for it to be any worse. It had reached the outer rim of reality.

No One Gives to Us but Ourselves

"And he fain would have filled his belly with the husks that the swine did eat; and no man gave unto him."

How true this is; no one can give unto us but ourselves and no one can rob us but ourselves. "There are no gods to say us nay, for we are the life we live." In our greatest extremity, in the moment of great need and dire distress, who can help or serve us? All of our troubles come from an isolated sense of being; *we alone* can return to the "Father's House."

The question might be asked, "Where was God and why did He not come to the rescue of His beloved son? Did He not care—was He heedless about His son's welfare? Why did God allow such a thing to happen?" There is only one answer to all questions of this nature: God is always God, and man can always do as he pleases. He would not be an individual unless this were possible. The Father is never conscious of incompletion. The Father's House is always open, the latch string ever hanging out, the door always ajar, but man must enter, if he wishes to abide within.

Harmony can never become discord. The truth can never produce a lie. God can never be less than God. Could God enter into a field of strife, *then* He would not be God. God cannot enter the pig pen. We cannot contract the Infinite, but we can expand the finite. "And no man gave unto him." It is always thus.

THE GREAT AWAKENING

"And when he came to himself, he said, How many hired servants of my father's have bread enough, and to spare, and I perish with hunger!"

"And when he came to himself." This is the great awakening, the moment in which we now live; in this moment we are asking this question of ourselves! Is there not plenty in the universe? Why do we want? In this divine awakening, there seems to be an inner witness who remembers that we came from a heavenly state. There seems to be an answer from that great within which says the Father's House is filled with peace, power and plenty. The Universe is not limited. It is abundant, lavish, extravagant. Nothing can be taken from, nor added to, It. Creation is the play of Life upon Itself.

We know, by intuition, that there is something beyond what we have so far consciously experienced in this world. Poets have sung of it and there are moments, in the lives of all, when the veil seems thin between and we almost enter into the heavenly estate. This is the meaning of coming to one's self. We are still in the awakening state, we have not yet consciously entered the state of perfect wholeness. We know that such a state is a reality, and that we shall yet attain this reality. Nothing can dislodge this inner and intuitive perception from our mentality; we know it as certainly as we know that we live. This is God in us knowing Himself. We are awakening to the realization that the Universe is perfect and complete. It gives. It is love. It is good and wills *only good* to all alike.

Self-Condemnation

The prodigal said, "I will arise and go to my father, and will say unto him, Father, I have sinned against heaven and before thee, And am no more worthy to be called thy son: make me as one of thy hired servants."

This represents a theological state of mind which is quite common to all of us; one of self-condemnation and personal distrust; it is morbid and detrimental to our welfare; a theological state of introspective morbidity, which might be classed as one of our worst mental diseases. Self-condemnation is always destructive and should never be indulged in by anyone, it is always a mistake. There is no question but that all of us have done that which is not for the best. From this viewpoint, all have been sinners, because all have fallen short of the Divine Calling. If we have sinned, it is because we have been ignorant of our true nature and because experience was necessary to bring us to ourselves.

And the Father Saw Him Afar Off

"And he arose, and came to his father. But when he was yet a great way off, his father saw him, and had compassion, and ran, and fell on his neck, and kissed him."

This is the most perfect lesson ever taught by the Great Teacher. "When he was yet a great way off, his father saw him, and ran and fell on his neck and kissed him." This means that God turns to us as we turn to Him. A more beautiful thought could not be given than this! There is always a reciprocal action between the Universal and the individual mind. As we look at God, God looks at us. Is it not true that when we look at God, God is looking through us at Himself? God comes to us as we come to Him. "It is done unto us as we believe." "Act as though I am and I will be."

God Does Not Condemn

"And the son said unto him, Father, I have sinned against heaven and in thy sight, and am no more worthy to be called thy son.

"But the father said to his servants, Bring forth the best robe, and put it on him; and put a ring on his hand, and shoes on his feet.

"And bring hither the fatted calf, and kill it; and let us eat, and be merry: For this my son was dead, and is alive again; he was lost, and is found. And they began to be merry."

The great lesson to learn here is that God never reproaches and never condemns. God did not say to the returning son, "You miserable sinner, you are no more worthy to be called my son." He did not say, "I will see what I can do about saving your lost soul. I will spill the blood of my most precious son in hopes that by this atonement your life may be made eternal." He did not say, "You are a worm of the dust and I will grind you under my feet in order that you may know that I am God and the supreme power of the universe." No, GOD DID NOT SAY ANY OF THESE ATROCIOUS THINGS! What the Father did say was, "Bring forth quickly the best robe, and put it on him: and put a ring on his hand and shoes on his feet." Here Jesus is showing that God is Love and knows nothing about hate.

God Knows No Sin

Perhaps the most significant thing in this paragraph is the fact that *God did not answer his son when he talked about being a sinner.* The Father talked about something else. This is one of the most wonderful lessons in the whole story. God does not know evil and therefore cannot talk about, or conceive it in any form. God does not even hear us, could not hear us, when we talk about sin or evil. If He could hear it, He would be conscious of it; if He could be *conscious* of it, He would not be wholly good. If God could know evil, then evil would be an eternal reality. But God is sinless and perfect and *nothing can reflect itself in the Divine, save a perfect image.* If God could know sin, He would be a sinner. It is enough to know that this cannot be.

The Best Robe

Now, the "best robe" was a seamless garment and typifies a state of complete unity, as does the ring. The robe is seamless and the ring is without beginning or end. It begins everywhere and ends nowhere. It is like Eternity and Eternal Reality. It perfectly describes the Divine Nature. "The fatted calf" represents the abundance of God's love and providence.

The Father's House Always Open

And so the son found everything in the Father's House just as he had left it. Nothing had changed and he was made welcome to all the divine stores. But *he had to return* to find joy and peace forevermore. How wonderful is Reality! While we may have seemed to be away from it, it has ever remained the same and is ever ready to reveal itself to us. All we have to do is to go half way; that is, turn to it and it will turn to us. The Truth known is instantly demonstrated; *for the Truth is Changeless Reality and cannot come and go.* No matter how long we may have been away from Reality in our thought, It is always here, ready to spring forth, full-orbed, into expression. No matter how long a room may have been darkened, the entrance of light instantly illuminates it. What becomes of the darkness when the light enters? Where did it come from and where does it go?

It is difficult to comprehend such an infinite possibility as an instantaneous reconciliation with the universe; we demonstrate this only in degrees, because our consciousness is not yet fitted to perceive the wholeness of complete perfection.

THE STAY-AT-HOME SON

"Now his elder son was in the field: and as he came and drew nigh to the house, he heard music and dancing.

"And he called one of the servants, and asked what these things meant. And he said unto him, Thy brother is come; and thy father hath killed the fatted calf, because he hath received him safe and sound.

"And he was angry and would not go in: therefore came his father out, and intreated him.

"And he answering said to his father, Lo, these many years do I serve thee . . . and yet thou never gavest me a kid, that I might make merry with my friends. . . .

"And he said unto him, Son, thou art ever with me, and all that I have is thine."

How human the stay-at-home son was, and what a theological attitude he took in regard to his younger brother! He had not entered himself and he was not willing that anyone else should enter. His real attitude was that God should condemn everything that he, himself, did not like or believe. He was puffed up with self-righteousness and personal conceit, filled with petty vanity, and fuming with anger over his brother's welcome home. I expect that we meet him in ourselves nearly every day—in our personal experiences with other people—in our intolerant attitude and uncharitableness toward others who do not think as we think. But God knows as little about self-righteousness as He knows about evil, for both are false; therefore, He said unto the elder son, "Thou art ever with me, and all that I have is thine." This implies that the elder son had missed the mark as well as the younger, for he had been living in the midst of plenty and had not recognized it. He needed but to have asked and he would have received all that the father had. Both sons were foolish but it is a question which was the more completely deluded.

THE APPLICATION OF THE STORY

But to bring this story down to our own experience—for it is a lesson for everyone for all time—we live in the midst of eternal good, but it can only be to us what we believe it to be. We are at the mouth of the river, but we must let down our own buckets if we wish them to be filled with the pure waters of Reality.

We are surrounded by a Spirit of living Intelligence, and eternal givingness, love, goodness and power, that wishes to express Itself through us. There is a Divine Urge within, ever pushing us forward to the goal. We are also surrounded by an immutable Law of cause and effect, and because of our divine individuality and the necessity of experience in order to come to a realization of what, and who, we are, we are subject to the causes which we have set in motion. All is love and yet all is law. Both love and law are perfect and we, as individuals, can experience only what we really believe and act upon.

GOD CAN ONLY GIVE US WHAT WE TAKE

God cannot give us anything unless we are in a mental condition to receive the gift. The Law cannot do anything *for* us unless It does it *through* us. Belief is absolutely necessary to right demonstration.

We are on the path of experience, just waking to the real fact of our true being; as we awake, we find we are surrounded by many false conditions, but there is something within which remembers the *real* state. If one will sit in quiet contemplation of good, as an inner experience, he will experience the good which he contemplates. He can do this only as he turns from that which is evil and dwells on the good alone. The Universe will not be divided.

THE UNIVERSE HOLDS NOTHING AGAINST US

The Universe holds nothing against us. No matter how many mistakes we have made, we are still perfect beings within, and the within may become the without, if we will carefully train ourselves to listen to the inner voice of truth which speaks to us in our moments of quietness and solitude.

There is nothing in the Universe that wishes evil to anyone. Indeed, it is only as we experience good that God is expressed through us. The more completely we realize good, happiness and success, the more perfectly do we express God and the more of God do we become, that is, the more does God become personified through us.

As the prodigal returns to his father's house, so must we return, not with a morbid mind, but consciously and definitely, with direct intent and a complete concentration of purpose. The journey back should be fraught with happiness and joyful expectation for we shall be met with a smile from the Universe and shall be folded in the arms of love forever.

THE ETERNAL COMPLETION

Substance and supply exist eternally in the Father's House; health, happiness and success are native to the Heavenly Home, and God Himself shall be our Host. More we could not ask, more could not be given than that which has been given from the foundations of the Universe.

Discord, misery, and unhappiness are the result of a misuse of our true nature, the result of ignorance. Ignorance of the law excuses no one from its effects; but knowledge clothes us in the seamless robe, while wisdom puts the ring of completion on our finger and understanding feeds us with the fat of the land.

No one who has tried this has failed; it would be impossible to do so. If any have thought they have failed, let them realize that somewhere *they* have fallen short of the divine calling. The Truth cannot fail, for it is God, the Absolute and Unconditioned One, who is the Truth.

Let us no longer fight the old; let us no longer remember that we were once on the outer rim; let us forget the past and live in the eternal present of God's happy smile. Today is good; tomorrow will be even better, and that vista of tomorrows that stretches down the bright eternities of an endless future will all be good, for the nature of Reality cannot change.

THE NEW BIRTH (JOHN 3:3–9)

"Except a man be born again, he cannot see the kingdom of God." Jesus is referring to the heavenly birth, which means being born into the knowledge of Truth. He refers to this as being born of water and Spirit.

The symbol of water is used to express the idea of a complete immersion in Spirit. As water flows in and around, so we are immersed in an everlasting Spirit which flows around, in and through us. To be immersed in water symbolizes our recognition that we are surrounded by pure Spirit. It is the outward sign of an inner conviction. But water alone cannot make us completely clean or whole. We must be born of the Spirit, for "that which is born of the Spirit is Spirit."

Man partakes of the Divine nature and the Divine nature is man. The recognition of this is being born of the Spirit. But we cannot be born of the Spirit unless we do the will of the Spirit and the will of the Spirit is goodness, peace, mercy, justice and truth. It is conscious union with God.

The new birth comes not by observation nor by loud proclamation, but through an inner sense of reality. We cannot tell where this comes from, if we look to outward things, as it proceeds from the innermost parts of our own being.

HEAVEN (JOHN 3:13)

"And no man hath ascended up to heaven, but he that came down from heaven, even the Son of man which is in heaven." Here is another of those hidden meanings which places Jesus among the great mystics. He says that no man can go to heaven unless he came from heaven, and that he can neither go to, nor come from, heaven *unless he is already there!*

This is in line with the idea that the Truth knows neither yesterday, today nor tomorrow. It knows sequence but not time. Only that can return to heaven which was born in heaven, and since heaven is not a place, but a state of consciousness, the return must be a recognition that heaven is already within. The son of man, who is also the son of God, is already in heaven and knows it not.

THE SON OF MAN (JOHN 3:14)

As Moses lifted up the serpent in the wilderness, so Jesus tells us must the son of man also be lifted up. By looking on and believing in this son, we are saved. Jesus could not have been referring to his own personality, for he knew that this would soon be taken from the sight of humanity. We must look for a deeper meaning.

We must be lifted up, that is we must realize our Divine nature and relationship to the Truth of God. This relationship is one of complete unity. The cross represents the tree of life and may also be thought of as the tree of unity.

When Moses lifted up the serpent, those who looked upon it were healed. This understanding produced a consciousness of unity, which had healing power. The Life Principle is either looked upon as material or spiritual. When looked upon as material, it casts us from the Garden of Eden—the garden of the soul. The Life Principle viewed only as *matter* is death, but viewed as life and unity, It becomes life everlasting. Moses elevated the Life Principle and Jesus did the same. The son of man must be *lifted up*, even as Moses lifted up the Life Principle, symbolized by the serpent.

We are reminded here of another symbol, one used in the Old Testament, that of the serpent which cast Adam and Eve out of the Garden of Eden. The serpent meant the outer rim of spiritual existence—the Life Principle viewed from an isolated and materialistic basis. The worship of material existence, apart from God, cast Adam and Eve from the Garden of Perfection. The attempt to live in *effects*, apart from true Cause, always does this.

The story of the Fall, taken literally, would be ridiculous to the point of absurdity; hence it is necessary to look for a deeper meaning. The writer was trying to teach a Cosmic lesson . . . the lesson of right and wrong. The Garden of Eden typifies life in its pure essence. Adam means man in general, generic man. Man exists in pure Life and has all of Its agencies at his command. This is the meaning of his being told to till the soil and enjoy the fruits of his labor.

The Tree of Life is our *real being*, and the tree of the knowledge of good and evil means the possibility of dual choice—that is, we can choose even that which is not for our best good. Man is warned not to eat of the fruit of this tree, for it is destructive.

Eve, the woman in the case, was made from a rib of Adam. This story suggests the dual nature of man as a psychological being. The woman is made from the man. She must have been in him else she could not have been made out of him, and the story clearly states that she was taken from his being.

Adam and Eve are potential in all of us. The serpent represents the Life Principle, viewed from a material basis, which beguiles us in this way: he says that evil is as real as good; that the devil has equal power with God; that negation equals positive goodness, and that the Universe is dual in Its Nature. From the acceptance of this argument, we experience both good and evil. And should we come full-orbed into individuality, without having learned the lesson of unity, we should live forever in a state of bondage. This is the meaning of God saying, "He shall become as one of us and live forever." The eternal Mind does not wish us to live forever in bondage, and this is what would happen unless we first learn the lesson of right and wrong.

And so that part of us which can be fooled eats of the fruit of dual experience and in so doing reveals its own nakedness. The native state of man is one of purity, peace and perfection, and it is only when we compare these with impurity, distress and imperfection, that we are revealed as naked. Emerson tells us that virtue does not know it is virtuous. It is only when virtue tastes of impurities that it becomes naked and must hide from itself.

The Voice of God, "walking in the garden in the cool of the day," means the introspective and meditative part of us, which in its moments of pure intuition and reason, sees the illusion of a life apart from God or Good. Error is ever a coward before Truth, and cannot hide itself from Reality, which sees through everything, encompasses all and penetrates even the prison walls of the mind with Its clear effulgence.

The conversation between God and Adam and Eve, in the Garden of Eden, represents the arguments that go on in our own minds, when we try to realize the truth. These arguments are familiar to all. The expulsion from the Garden is a necessary and logical outcome of tasting of dual experience. If *we believe in both good and evil, we must experience both*.

But, lest we should become discouraged, we remember that Moses lifted up the serpent in the wilderness and those who looked upon it were healed. The serpent means the Life Principle. Viewed from a material basis alone, it casts us from a perfect state. Lifted up, that is, viewed from a true meaning of the Unity of God, it heals. Here is the choice again, only stated in different words. The difference is not in the thing itself, but in the way we look at it.

The son of man is every man who ever lived or ever will live. Our life is from Spirit, not from matter. This viewpoint is the truth and truth alone makes free. We come into everlasting life as we elevate this inner principle to a sense of the unity of man with God. Each must lift himself to the cross of the Tree of Life, thus unifying himself with Reality. The concept is glorious and the reward certain. The revelation of the self to the self—this is the great lesson of lessons.

When We Are Strong (John 5:19)

"The Son can do nothing of himself." We are strong only as we are in unity with good, which is God. But the Father showeth the Son, that is, it is revealed to us, through the innermost parts of our being, that there is a complete unity, a perfect wholeness. As this concept of unity takes place, it brings with it great authority. The Father quickens the Son, the Son quickens whom he will.

Here is a lesson in the practical application of the Science of Mind. As the subjective state of thought becomes unified with goodness and love, it automatically reflects these in whatsoever direction the thought goes. *The tendency of this inner thought sets the tendency of the outward life.*

Let us make this plain. IF ONE IS NOT ATTRACTING GOOD INTO HIS LIFE, THERE IS SOMETHING WRONG WITH HIS UNCONSCIOUS THINKING. The subjective state of his thought is wrong. As the subjective state of his thought constitutes the sum total of his belief, it is his habitual *attitude* toward life and living. This inner thought content is the sole medium between the Absolute and the relative, between causes and conditions.

When this inner thought is clarified, that is, when it knows the truth, it will reinstate the outer man in peace, poise, health and happiness. This inner thought becomes clarified as we unify with good; *this* is the inner quickening. Following this is the outer quickening—the outward sign of the inner belief.

The Word of Power (John 5:26)

As the Father has life, so the son has life. Again we have the teaching that there is but One Life, Mind or Spirit. This Life is now our life, and manifests through us as we believe in It. When our word is spoken in this consciousness of life, power and action, then our word IS life, power and action.

THE WORD HAS POWER ONLY AS IT IS ONE WITH POWER. The word is a mold which decides what form the thought is to take as it assumes shape and becomes a part of our conditions. Mental treatment is for the purpose of forming the word into such shapes and designs as are desirable for experience.

The word gives form to the unformed. The greater the consciousness behind the word, the more power it will have. Just words, without conviction, have no power, and *just conviction without words*, will never stir up latent energy. There must be a combination of the two to make a complete thing.

We are surrounded by a spiritual consciousness and a mental law. From combinations of these two, all things are made. We unify with the spiritual consciousness as we become aware of it, we speak it into form as we believe in the power of our own word. In treatment, there should be first a realization of power, then a spoken word. One generates, the other distributes.

The Meat Which Perisheth (John 6:27)

"Labour not for the meat which perisheth." Jesus knew that we need food to eat while in the flesh, so he could not be referring to literal food, but rather to that inner substance which is spiritual.

Starvation takes place on more than one plane. More people are starved spiritually and intellectually than physically. A full stomach will never appease an appetite for learning, nor can a loaf of bread satisfy the inner craving for reality. The *whole being* needs to be fed—bread and meat for the body, knowledge and wisdom for the soul, atmosphere and consciousness for the Spirit.

We live on three planes at the same time. To attempt to desert any one of these, to the cost of the others, is abnormal. To live only on the physical plane is to become a brute. To live on the intellectual plane alone, might produce a learned and a scientific man, but he would lack true perception. To live only on the spiritual plane, might cause one to become a dreamer without any practical way of making his dreams come true.

The Three Planes of Life

Man is a threefold principle of life and action; he is spirit, soul and body. From the Spirit he receives inspiration and guidance; in the soul he finds a perfect Law of life; and through the body he proves that he is a real individualization of the Invisible Principle.

Man's mind should swing from inspiration to action, from contemplation to accomplishment, from prayer to performance. This would be a well-balanced existence. The Spirit fires the soul with energy and understanding; the soul, which is the subjective mentality, vitalizes the body and animates all that we do.

No greater mistake could be made than to think we must separate life from what it does. We must unify and not divide. The Spirit must go forth into creation through law and action. Life must enter living, and God must flow through man, if there is to be a real representation of the Divine through the human.

Let us feel that our purposes are animated and inspired from on high and then let us go forth and make our dream come true in human experience. With an invisible Intelligence to guide, and an immutable Law to direct, let us take our place in any legitimate activity, and thus cause our dreams to come to full fruition.

The Light of the World (John 8:12)

"I am the light of the world." Jesus was not referring to his human personality, but to the Principle inherent in generic man. They who follow this inner Principle shall have the light of life; for this Principle is life.

"I Am" has a dual meaning. It is both individual and universal. God was revealed to Moses as the great "I AM," the Universal Cause, the Causeless or Self-existent One. Moses taught that "I AM" is the First Principle of all life, and the Law of cause and effect running through everything. The whole teaching of Moses is based upon the perception of this "First Principle."

Jesus said that he came, not to destroy the law of Moses, but to fulfill it. How could he fulfill it except by teaching the relationship of the universal "I Am" to the individual "I"? In all the sayings of Jesus, we find this thought brought out: that God is Universal Spirit and man is His image and likeness . . . an individualization of His eternity. Therefore, when we understand our own "I" we shall walk in that light which lights the world unto the perfect "I AM."

We can consider this from another viewpoint. Man is the only self-knowing mind of which we are conscious. A self-knowing mind, of course, is one that is conscious of what it knows. Man, the only self-conscious being in this world, must be the light of the world. To know this and to understand why it is so, is to know *that* Truth which alone can make free. Truth is eternal and eternity is timeless, hence, if one knows the Truth, he will never see death. Death has nothing to do with life everlasting, and is but an impatient gesture of the soul, wishing to rid itself of a body no longer useful.

LOVE (JOHN 13:34, 35)

Love is the central flame of the universe, nay, the very fire itself. It is written that God is Love, and that we are His expressed likeness, the image of the Eternal Being. Love is self-givingness through creation, the impartation of the Divine through the human.

Love is an essence, an atmosphere, which defies analysis, as does Life Itself. It is that which IS and cannot be explained: it is common to all people, to all animal life, and evident in the response of plants to those who love them. Love reigns supreme over all.

The essence of love, while elusive, pervades everything, fires the heart, stimulates the emotions, renews the soul and proclaims the Spirit. Only love knows love, and love knows only love. Words cannot express its depths or meaning. A universal sense alone bears witness to the divine fact: God is Love and Love is God.

LET NOT YOUR HEART BE TROUBLED (JOHN 14:1)

"Let not your heart be troubled; ye believe in God, believe also in me." His disciples were depressed, having an instinctive sense that Jesus was about to depart from them. They were filled with sadness. It was on the eve of his betrayal that he spoke these words, "Let not your heart be troubled," with that calm certainty which has ever been given to the believing. He was not afraid. He had already plumbed the depths of human existence and penetrated into the beyond. He knew that he was an immortal being.

Our hearts are troubled over many things and our mental burdens often become unbearable. It seems, at times, as though a cup of bitterness were being held to unwilling lips, with the demand that they drink. Jesus, standing at the threshold of his greatest experience, foreknew that he would turn apparent defeat into glorious victory. From the calm depths of an undisturbed soul, he spoke words of comfort to those of lesser understanding.

He told them to believe in God, and because of their belief in God, to believe also in him. Again he is referring to the individual "I" as the outward manifestation of the Universal "I AM." *We are to believe in ourselves because we believe in God. The two are ONE.* We are to know that passing events cannot hinder the onward march of the soul. The temporal imperfection of the human cannot dim the eternal integrity of the Divine.

IN MY FATHER'S HOUSE ARE MANY MANSIONS (JOHN 14:2)

"In my father's house are many mansions." This world, with all its wonders, is not the only one that we shall inhabit. There are many others and we shall inhabit each in time. If this life were the only life, Jesus would have told his followers so. He held out no false promises, never deceived. He spoke only the Truth.

"I go to prepare a place for you." What more beautiful thought than that those who go before shall be there when we arrive! There is no doubt, only an expansion of the soul, an enlargement of the experience. But Thomas, who was a disciple, said that he did not know where Jesus was going nor did he know the way. Jesus answered, "I am the way, the truth and the life." Again he is referring to the individual "I" the son of the eternal "I AM." This son is the way to the Father. We approach Reality through our own natures and through no other source. "No man cometh unto the Father but by me." God is within and it is here that we meet Him. The inward gaze alone can reveal the Father.

WHO SEES THE SON SEES THE FATHER (JOHN 14:9)

"He that hath seen me hath seen the Father." Many think, from this statement, that Jesus was claiming to be God, but such was not the case. God is the invisible Life Essence of all that is, the Intelligent Energy running through all. This Life we *feel* but do not see. We see only what It does, never the Thing Itself.

Life manifests Itself through the individual. Therefore, when one manifests goodness and purity, he is revealing the Father. This is what Jesus meant when he said, "He that hath seen me hath seen the Father."

He said that his words were the words of God. As all forms of energy return again into their source, so the word of Truth is the word of God, no matter who speaks it, or when it is spoken. Man reveals, but does not absorb, the Divine Nature.

"He that believeth on me, the works that I do shall he do also." It could not be otherwise. The nature of Reality was not exhausted in the man Jesus, but made manifest through his life and works. We are to do likewise, and what we ask in the name (which is our own name) believing in the Father which is God, and in the son, which is ourselves, we shall receive. In this way, the Father is glorified in the Son.

THE HOLY COMFORTER (JOHN 14:16)

We are told that The Holy Comforter, the Spirit of Truth, will make all things known to us, for He is with us and in us. No more comprehensive statement could be made. The Spirit of Truth is in all people—not unto Jesus alone—but unto all alike . . . again the revelation of the self to the self; a divine awakening to the eternal Reality inhabiting eternity and finding its abiding place in time, through our own natures.

As the Holy Comforter comes, He makes all things known to us. Intuition is the speech of this Comforter. "I am in my Father, and ye in me, and I in you." The eternal Father begets the eternal Son. This Son is generic, all are members of this Universal Sonship, all are members of the one Tree of Life, from which every individual shoot springs. The Trinity is a Unity.

And that peace which comes from the innermost recesses of the Spirit is left with us: a peace which the world cannot take away, for it springs from the bosom of the Father of light, love, life and wisdom.

ABIDING IN THE ONE (JOHN 15:7)

"If ye abide in me and my words abide in you, ye shall ask what ye will, and it shall be done unto you."

It is impossible for humanity to *literally* abide in the man Jesus, so we must look for a figurative meaning in these words. He is speaking of the spirit of his teachings; and the whole *spirit* of his teachings is to the effect that man is an individualized center of God-Consciousness. The spirit of man is the Spirit of God, for God is One.

When we abide in the One, we *cannot* ask amiss, but must ask for that which is right and good. Consequently, our prayers to the One will be answered. But let us remember that prayer is answered according to law, and this law is one of liberty and never one of license. True liberty comes only through true harmony; true harmony only through true unity; and true unity can come only through the conscious realization that we are one with God or Good.

Jesus implies a power which can and will work for those who harmonize with, and believe in it. But we must first *abide* in the Spirit of Truth. And what is the Spirit of Truth other than that we live in conscious unity with good and do harm to no one? Goodness is natural, while evil is abnormal.

To trust in the law of good is to constantly believe that we are surrounded by a Power which can and will cast all fear from our minds, free us from all bondage, and set us safe and satisfied in a new order of living.

THAT YE BEAR MUCH FRUIT (JOHN 15:8)

"Herein is my Father glorified, that ye bear much fruit." When we express a greater living-ness, then Life is more completely expressing Itself through us. A barren tree does not express the principle of abundance and production, so a life barren of good does not fully express the divine ideal.

Evolution has brought man to a point of self-expression and it can do no more for him until he consciously co-operates with it. Its law is one of growth and unfoldment. God goes forth anew into creation whenever anyone discovers a new truth or increases knowledge about an old one. Each is a center of the All, and each has access to the All, through his own nature.

Jesus refers to his joy on the eve of his greatest lesson to mankind. That joy which is full and complete. That joy which no man can take away: the joy of a sense of completion. He was about to lay down his earthly life, as the greatest object lesson ever taught. And what was this lesson? That LOVE knows no bounds and that the Eternal Goodness gives Itself to all. God as man, in man, is man.

OTHER TEACHINGS
FROM THE NEW TESTAMENT

THE LAW OF CORRESPONDENTS (ROMANS 1:20)

This teaching incorporates the great law of correspondents. The spiritual world contains an image of the physical; the physical is a counterpart of the spiritual. A true estimate of the outward symbol points to the spiritual reality behind it.

We understand the unseen by correctly viewing the seen. The outward effect must partake of its inward nature. The physical universe is the result of an inner Intelligence, working through Law. Behind form is idea. The Formless creates form, through the creative power of Its own Mind and Spirit.

Behind every effect there is a cause, and if this cause is a spiritual idea—which it must be—then it follows that should the spiritual idea be discerned, *the physical effect would be like it*. The entire possibility of demonstrating the Law of Good depends upon this proposition. The idea is father to the fact. Ideas are real, having the power within themselves to be made manifest.

The whole teaching of the Bible is to the effect that God is Universal Spirit, and Universal Creation. He creates by the power of His Word. This Word is the law of His Being. Man reproduces the Divine Nature on the scale of the individual. He also uses creative power which works through the law of his word. From this he cannot escape, he need only to use this power constructively and all will be well. If he uses the creative power of his thought destructively, then it will destroy.

In the Science of Mind, we learn that persistent, constructive thought is the greatest power known and the most effective. If the visible effect in our lives is not what it should be, if we are unhappy, sick and poverty stricken, we know the remedy. The Truth is always the remedy, and the Truth *is* that the law of liberty is the only real law. When we reverse the process of thought, the effect will be reversed.

There Is No Condemnation (Romans 8:1)

"There is therefore now no condemnation to them . . . who walk . . . after the Spirit." As it is impossible for us to be in another man, and as it is necessary that each live his own life, within the One Life, it follows that the writer was not referring to personality but to a universal Principle.

We are in Christ when we are in the Truth; we are in the Truth when we live in harmony with It. There is no mystery about this. It is common sense. The law of the Spirit makes us free from sin and death. The law of the Spirit is freedom, and knows no bondage. When we enter the Spirit, we come under Its law of freedom.

"To be spiritually minded is life and peace." Who does not long for life and peace? These are contained in the Spirit, which is the center and circumference of all. The carnal mind is not subject to the law of God because it is a limited concept of Truth. The carnal mind symbolizes anything that disbelieves in the supremacy of Good; it is a belief in isolation, a sense of separation from good.

The Spirit That Raised Jesus (Romans 8:11)

The Spirit that raised Jesus dwells in all. This Spirit quickens our mortal bodies when we let It. Here is a lesson in mental and spiritual healing. As the Truth dawns upon the subjective state of our thought, it stimulates it into newness of action. Everything works from within out. The body is a reflection of the soul and when the soul, which is the subjective state of thought, is illumined by the Spirit, it quickens the mortal part of us and heals the body. The mortal is always an effect, a creature of time but a necessary one, for without it we could not function as objective individuals.

The Spirit of Adoption (Romans 8:15)

We have not received a spirit of bondage but one of adoption. This is a mystical and beautiful saying. It implies that we are adopted by the Supreme Spirit as Its own offspring. How could it be otherwise, since we are made of the same stuff as the central fire? There is no fear in the

Spirit, and there will be none in us when we realize who and what we are. God wishes us well and knows only that we are now free and perfect. This is the spirit of freedom whereby we are all born free.

Joint Heirs with Christ (Romans 8:16, 17)

The inner Spirit, which is God, bears witness to the divine fact that we are the sons of God, the children of the Most High. As sons of God, we are heirs to the heaven of reality; joint heirs with Christ. This means that we are all one in Christ as we are one in God. Christ typifies the Universal Son, of which each is an individual member.

Our expectation looks for a more complete manifestation of our own inner divinity. Evolution will bring this about, as it does all things. We are an unfolding Principle of life, Truth, perfect law and action. We wait for a more complete unfolding of our inner life. It is already within, the perfect way and the eternal Truth. We wait for the unfolding of ourselves, through the law inherent within our real nature.

The Inner Light (Romans 8:21)

The creature shall be delivered from bondage. As the inner light dawns, it delivers the outer life from bondage. This is in line with the teaching that everything is from within out. When the *soul* knows freedom, the *law* will free the body, and the outer life will express health, happiness and success.

All things work for our good. Even that which we call evil is salutary, leading us to the Way, the Truth and the Life. Suffering should teach us a lesson which would cause us to refrain from making more mistakes; it carries a blessing with it *when we learn how to garner knowledge from experience.*

Predestination (Romans 8:29)

"For whom he did foreknow, he also did predestinate." God foreknows His own perfection and the perfection of His entire creation, so it is foreknown and predetermined by the Divine Mind that all shall be sons of God. Man cannot forever keep himself from his birthright; all will eventually be saved from themselves—as there can be no such thing as eternal damnation. To believe in such an absurd doctrine is worse than ignorance. Emerson tells us that there is no sin but ignorance. God knows only perfection; when we know as God knows, our troubles will be rolled up like a scroll and numbered with past illusions.

GOD'S WILL FOR HIS CREATION (ROMANS 8:31)

"If God be for us, who can be against us?" If God is all there is and the universe is One, *then there is no power, presence or law against the Truth!* One with the Truth is a totality. If our whole endeavor is to be, and to do, that which is constructive, then we are with God and we may be sure He is ever with us. God knows no outside. *He is ever inside. The outer rim of Reality is exactly at the center of Itself.*

NOTHING can keep us from the love of God. What a comfort! What joy to know that all is well with the soul! What untold sufferings we have had because of our doubts and fears! And we are told not to be afraid, for it is the Father's good pleasure to give us the Kingdom. Man alone has tried to rob us of our birthright—the glorious liberty of the Sons of the Most High.

Let us honor God more and man less. Let us seek within for the cause; it can be found in no other place. There is nothing that can keep us from this inner vision of the Eternal Reality.

THE RENEWING OF YOUR MIND (ROMANS 12:2)

"Be ye transformed by the renewing of your mind." Today we know what this means. The renewing of the mind is a scientific act. As the conscious thought pours truth into the subjective channels of creative energy, the body is automatically renewed; this is mental healing. Mental healing is a conscious act, as well as an established fact, in the experience of many people. Instead of the old concepts of disease and failure, we are to inject those of liberty, freedom, health, harmony and success.

Mental healing is subject to the exact laws of Mind and Spirit, and is accomplished by correct knowing. This knowing is a mental attitude toward the Truth. It is the *Truth* which makes free and it is the *mind* which knows the Truth.

The body is healed as the inner mind is transformed; as the old and false images of thought are renewed by images of Truth and Life. The process through which this renewing takes place is a conscious one, and may be practiced by anyone who understands the principle involved.

BLESS AND CURSE NOT (ROMANS 12:14)

"Bless and curse not." Here is the whole law and prophets. We are to overcome evil with good. Evil lasts but for a day, while goodness shines to eternity and loving kindness is the very nature of Deity. As the darkness has no power over light, so evil is overcome with good.

"Vengeance is mine; I will repay, saith the Lord." This is a statement of the law of cause and effect. God does not avenge, but the law of cause and effect exacts the uttermost farthing. We need not worry how things are coming out; the law takes care of everything and returns to each exactly what is his due.

THE GREAT AWAKENING (ROMANS 13:11)

"Now it is high time to awake out of sleep." The belief in a life apart from Good is a dream from which we must awake, if we are to taste the waters of Reality, which flow from the Source of Life.

As one awakes from a nightmare, so the mentality awakes from the dream of a living death to a realization of eternal life. We cast off the works of darkness when we realize that evil is not an entity but a fraud. The armor of light is the Truth, the very knowing of which makes free.

This awakening is a process of evolution, a little here and a little there, until the whole eye is opened and we see that life is neither separate from God nor different from Good. Life is God, and Good is the only power there is, or can be.

To awaken oneself is to be healed, made prosperous, happy and satisfied; to be made every whit whole, to be complete as we were intended to be. God is a God of the living and not of the dead. He sees and knows only perfection and completion; happiness and satisfaction. When we shall think of ourselves as *God* knows us, then complete salvation will come to us.

THE LAW OF GOD IS ONE OF LIBERTY (II COR. 3:17)

The law of God is one of liberty and not one of bondage. The Spirit of the Lord is everywhere. Freedom and liberty are also everywhere if we could but see them. Freedom, like Truth, is self-existent and self-propelling. The Spirit, Truth, and Freedom are co-existent with one another.

Whenever we are conscious of God, or pure Spirit, we are made free. This is proven in mental and spiritual healing; when we are conscious of *perfect life*, the body is healed. We must become unconscious of the imperfect and conscious of the perfect alone. Since our ideas of perfection are limited to our present understanding, we do not yet manifest perfection. With a greater unfoldment of Reality through our consciousness, we shall evolve a more perfect body.

In the demonstration of abundance, we seek to realize the liberty of the Sons of God—the freedom whereby God proves His absoluteness. This is done, not by meditation upon limitation, but by contemplating plenty, abundance, success, prosperity and happiness.

It is unscientific to dwell upon lack, for it will create the undesired condition. It *is* scientific to meditate on plenty, to bring the mind to a point of conceiving an eternal flow of life, truth and energy through us . . . *and through everything that we do, say or think!*

How to Demonstrate Liberty

To demonstrate liberty, drop all negative thoughts from the mind. Do not dwell upon adversity but think plenty into everything, for there is power in the word. Meditate on the things you are doing as being already done—complete and perfect.

Try to sense the Infinite Life around and within you. This Life is already fully expressed and complete. This Life is your life *now* and the life of all that you do, say or think. Meditate upon this Life until your whole being flows into It and becomes one with It.

Now you are ready to prove your principle by allowing this Life to flow through the thing that you are working on or for. Do not will or try to compel things to happen. Things happen by an immutable law and *you do not need to energize the Essence of Being;* It is already big with power. All you need do is to realize this fact, and then let it be done unto you, or unto that for which you are working. L-E-T is a big word and an important one. By taking thought, you do not add one cubit to Reality, but you do *allow* (let) Reality to manifest in the things you are doing.

As the power of your meditation is centered on what you are doing, life flows through that thing, animating it with real power and action, which culminates in the desired result. The Spirit of God is loosed in your work. Where this Spirit is, there is liberty.

Mental Expansion (II Cor. 3:18)

"But we all, with open face beholding as in a glass the glory of the Lord, are changed into the same image from glory to glory, even as by the Spirit of the Lord."

As our thought is opened and we behold the image of eternity within ourselves, we are changed by this image into a newness of Life. This is accomplished by the Spirit of God.

The subjective state of thought is the creative medium within us, which fact psychology has proven beyond any question of doubt. Emerson tells us that we are inlets and might become outlets to the Divine Nature. We are already *inlets*, but we must *consciously become outlets*. A great mystic tells us that the upper part of the soul is merged with God and the lower part with time and conditions. Plotinus says that when the soul looks to God alone for its inspiration, its work is done better—even though its back is turned to its work. And Jesus tells us to seek the Kingdom of God first and that all else will be added unto us.

Now the image of God is imprinted upon each one of us and all reflect the Divine Glory to some degree. Indeed we are part of the Divine Glory. When our thought is turned from limitation to the greater glory, we then reflect that glory.

When the subjective state of our thought receives its images from Reality, it, in turn, reflects this Reality into all that we do. Gradually, as this process takes place, the outer man becomes changed, and as his concepts become enlarged, so his conditions and physique take on a newness of life.

And this change in the outer is brought about by the Spirit of God. The Spirit of God—being the One and Only Presence in the Universe—brings about events and re-molds conditions after Its own likeness.

THE ASCENDING SCALE OF LIFE (II COR. 3:7–12)

We are changed from glory to glory. This implies that the divine scale is ever ascending. There is no end to the Divine Nature and therefore no end to the possibility of our expressing It. BUT WE MUST BEHOLD IT, we must look steadfastly into this Reality, if we are to image It in our own minds.

Here is no forlorn outlook, no limited concept! All that God has, or IS, belongs to us and is ours to make use of. We are not to separate Life from living, but unite the two into a perfect One. . . . The Thing and the way It works; the glory, and the image of the glory in common affairs of everyday life. Nor hath eye seen nor can tongue tell the greater possibility of any soul. Only God has revealed this through His Son. And this Son is each one of us, from the apparent least to the apparent greatest.

The world is saturated with Divinity, immersed in Reality, and filled with possibility. We must take this divine possibility and mold it into a present actuality in everyday experience. This is the way to freedom, the pathway to peace and happiness.

THE DIVINE IDEAS (II COR. 4:8, 9)

Even in our troubles we are not cast down, and though we appear to be deserted, we are not destroyed. All our experiences are working to the end that we learn the lesson of life and return to the Father's House as freed souls.

We should not despise apparent failures—the temporary chagrins of life—for they are salutary, leading the soul to the inner Christ, the Way, the Truth, and the Life. When the experience is complete, the lesson will be learned and we shall enter the paradise of contentment.

We do not look at the things which are seen as being eternal. Behind the visible and changeable is the changeless Reality, the Eternal One, working in time and space for the expression of Itself. The Divine Ideas stand back of all human thought, seeking admittance through the doorway of the mind.

If we look at love long enough, we shall become lovely, for this is the way of love. God is

Love. If we gaze longingly at joy, it will make its home with us, and we shall enter its portals and be happy. If we seek the Divine in men, we shall find it, and be entertaining angels unawares.

God's ideas and attributes are eternal and cannot change. In change, is the Changeless. In time, is the Eternal and Timeless. In *things*, the Creator manifests His power and glory forevermore.

IMMORTAL CLOTHING (II COR. 5:1–10)

This body, in which we seem to live, is not the eternal body. We have a body not made with hands, eternal in the heavens. As our thought reaches up and on to that greater truth, we are clothed upon from heaven. That is, we more perfectly pattern the Divine and consequently more completely manifest the Eternal.

We do not wish to be unclothed but clothed upon. This is an interesting concept, for it implies that immortality clothes itself in definite forms, more beautiful than those which now appear.

We are to know no man after the flesh, but even Christ after the Spirit. Thus are we swallowed up of life. Death is overcome, not by dwelling upon it, but by contemplating eternal life. It is the belief of the writer that should one become completely unconscious of death and all fear of it, one would never know that he died, even though he went through the experience of passing from this life to the next. Death would be swallowed up of life.

It seems probable that when the last enemy is overcome, we shall pass from one experience to another at will; that the soul will clothe itself in a body on whatever plane it finds itself—a body which will express the soul on that plane. We are to know no man after the flesh but after the Spirit.

THE INNER MAN (EPH. 3:16)

"To be strengthened with might by his Spirit in the inner man." The *inner man* is Christ, and Christ is the son of God. The inner man is revealed by what he does. As we do not see God, so we do not see the real man. We never see causes, only effects; but the effect loudly affirms the nature of its cause.

The Spirit of God dwells in the inner man with power and might. The outer man reflects this Spirit in so far as the intellect allows it to come forth into expression.

When Christ dwells in us in love, which is unity, we are able to understand the things that the saints have understood. *Saint* simply means an unusually wise and good man—all saints have been human beings just as we are, for God makes all people alike. The universe plays no favorites.

To be filled with the fullness of God is to manifest our true nature, which is Christ, the Son of God—"the power that worketh in us." This power is the power of God, and if we admitted no other, we should ever be satisfied, happy, prosperous, well and complete.

THE ENDLESS CREATION (EPH. 3:20, 21)

"World without end." This refers to the endless creation of the Almighty. Particular worlds will always begin and end, as do cabbages and kings; but creation itself—the necessity of God's manifesting Himself in time and in space—will never end. If creation could end, then God would end. As this is unthinkable, it follows that "world without end," or worlds without end, are necessary to the expression of Spirit.

THE UNITY OF LIFE (EPH. 4:1–7)

The unity of the Spirit is kept through the bonds of peace. Other than peace suggests confusion and separation. The Spirit is a perfect unit and we harmonize with this unity when we maintain a state of peace in our minds.

"There is one body and one Spirit." The entire creation is this body—the Body of God, who is One Spirit. Within this one Body are all bodies; that is, within the one creation—which is the product of the One Spirit—are all bodies.

We have learned that all material forms come from one ultimate substance. Any special body is some manifestation of this original stuff. The original substance takes many forms; multiplicity, or many, within unity, or the One.

"One Lord, one faith, one baptism." One Lord, who is the indwelling Christ, generic man or the universal Son. There is but one faith, for faith is an affirmative mental attitude toward the universe; and one baptism, which is the realization that we are in the One Spirit.

"One God and Father of all, who is above all, and through all, and in you all." It would be impossible to make a clearer statement of Truth: One Life behind all that lives! One, One, One . . . never two. The unity of all life. To learn this is to know a secret of the ages.

Here is a mystical saying: God is in all, through all, and above all, which means that we *partake* of the One Life . . . It is *all of us* . . . but we are not all of this Life. No man can exhaust the Divine Nature, but all live by, in, and through It. It is in us but also above us; It is in us but also below us; It is in us but also around us—It is what we are but infinitely more than we are! We shall ever ascend into a greater expression of this One, but we can never completely encompass It. This is a glorious concept, and one which fills us with wonder at the majesty of our own being—forever hid with Christ in God.

THE RENEWING OF THE MIND (EPH. 4:23, 24)

We are told to be renewed in mind by the Spirit and to put on the new man, which is created in true holiness. The Science of Mind teaches how to accomplish this. The mind is the creative factor within us, and when the mind takes its pattern after the Spirit, it automatically renews the outer man after true holiness or wholeness.

Whatever the mind holds to and firmly believes in, forms a new pattern of thought within its creative mold, as whatever thought is held in the mind tends to take outward form in new creations. This is the secret—and the whole secret—of the creative law of mind.

BE STRONG IN THE LORD (EPH. 6:10)

"Be strong in the Lord and in the power of his might." To be strong in the Lord is to be sure of ourselves, *because we are sure of the Principle of Life which manifests Itself through us.*

We wrestle not against outward things but against inward ideas and beliefs. The power of darkness is the power of false belief and superstition. If a man can change his inner concept, his whole life will be changed. All *cause* is from within, all effect is forever without.

WICKEDNESS IN HIGH PLACES (EPH. 6:12)

Wickedness in high places means an inverted use of the law of righteousness, the misuse of the powers of the mind. The mental law is neutral, plastic, receptive and creative. There is a right and a wrong use of this law, just as there is a right and a wrong use of any other law.

THE ARMOR OF GOD (EPH. 6:13–18)

The armor of God is faith in the good, the enduring and the true. Against such, there is no law. That is, against Truth, nothing can stand. The armor of God suggests protection to those who believe in and trust the law of Good. With this armor—knit together by that thread of unity running through all, strong with the strength of the Almighty, burnished with clear vision and true estimates of life and Reality—we are safe. We abide under the shadow of the everlasting Truth. With Moses, we can say, "underneath are the everlasting arms."

The breastplate of righteousness covers and gives sanctuary to the heart of hearts, the innermost soul of man. The feet, shod with the gospel of peace, can travel and not become weary. With Solomon we are happy when we find Wisdom, for "Her ways are ways of pleasantness and all her paths are peace."

And we take also "the shield of faith, wherewith ye shall be able to quench all the fiery darts of the wicked." The positive thought of Truth is a shield against which nothing unlike Itself can stand. In the Science of Mind, we learn that no thought of negation can enter a mind already filled with peace and faith. The suggestion of limitations, fear and doubt cannot find entrance to that mental home where God is enthroned as the Supreme Guest.

And the sword of the Spirit is the word of Truth. This has also been called a two-edged sword, cleaving the false from the true, cutting its way across the path of confusion, uprooting the thistles and briars, clearing the way for Truth and beauty to flourish in the home of the soul.

The Word of God is not a battle hymn of righteousness, but a paean of praise, a psalm of beauty and a song of joy. "If God be for us, who can be against us?"

The Mind That Jesus Used (Phil. 2:5, 6, 13)

We are to let the mind be in us which was in Christ Jesus. Note carefully the manner in which the expression is used. *The mind which was in Christ Jesus.* This means the Mind of God. Not our personal mind—marvelous as this is with its different ramifications—but the mind which Jesus used: the Divine Mind of the Creator and Ruler of the universe.

To *have the same mind that Jesus used*, implies a power which is available to all and may be used by all. The mind which was in Christ Jesus was the Mind of Truth; hence, he became the *way*. But we are also to become the *way*, and this can be accomplished only when we use the same mind that he used, which is the Mind of God.

We have the Mind of Christ in such degree as we trust implicitly in the Universe, and no longer do those things which contradict the fundamental goodness. From this Mind, proceeds the perfect Law, which is the Law of Liberty.

This Mind is God working in and through us. God can work *for* us only by working *through* us. Consequently, there is no other name under heaven whereby a man may be saved—not the *name* of Jesus, but *the Mind of Christ*. The individual is thrown back upon himself and upon the Universe. Every man has the Mind of Christ, if he will admit it, *but he can use this Mind only when he is in harmony with Life!* Nature always guards herself against any undue approaches and the righteous alone may enter the portals of Truth.

A Pattern for Thought (Phil. 4:8, 13)

We are to *think on those things which are of good report*. That is, we are to think on those things which are of the Truth. If we do this, we can accomplish because of our own inner mind, which is Christ. This Mind is the Creator of the heavens and the earth and all they that dwell therein.

And God will supply all our needs. This is a beautiful thought: that we are fed from the table of the Universe, Whose board is ever spread with blessedness and peace; Whose loving-kindness has never been fathomed; Whose grace and truth are the cornerstones of Reality. WE ARE TO BE FED, CLOTHED, AND SUPPLIED IN EVERY NEED, STRAIGHT FROM THE CENTER AND SOURCE OF ALL. More than this, we could not ask. Greater, could not be given. Lowell tells us that "Heaven alone is given away," and all is ours for the asking. Shall not this asking, then, include all righteousness and truth?

REJOICE EVERMORE (I THESS. 5:15–23)

We are to rejoice evermore. There is no sadness in the Spirit. It is happy and free, for It knows neither depression nor confusion, and we belong to It, are in and of It. We are to rejoice evermore.

CONSTANT PRAYER

"Pray without ceasing." This means to be always on the affirmative side of life. To pray without ceasing is to doubt never, but to always trust in the Law of Good. This inner communion is essential to the soul and natural to the mind. It is a constant recognition of our relationship to that Presence in which we live and move and have our being.

"In everything gives thanks." An attitude of gratitude is most salutary, and bespeaks the realization that we are *now* in heaven. How we love to do for those who co-operate with, and are grateful for, our small endeavors! Gratitude is one of the chief graces of human existence and is crowned in heaven with a consciousness of unity.

QUENCH NOT THE SPIRIT

"Quench not the Spirit." We are not to be ashamed of our trust in God, nor are we to deny the Inner Light that lights every man's reason to the ultimate reason of all. Spiritual emotion is common to all people, and is one of the ways through which the Spirit works. When this emotion is blocked, it hinders the currents of life from flowing and the result is stagnation. In psychology, we learn that congested emotions are disastrous to health. If this is true of the physical emotions, how much more must it be true of those higher emotions which are altogether spiritual!

What is true on one plane is true on all. There are ascending scales of being, and each reproduces from the lowest to the highest, each plane partaking of the nature of the Whole, since all are in, and of It. If physical emotions unexpressed, can congest the subjective thought, producing mental and physical confusion—and they can—it follows that unexpressed spiritual emotions can congest the soul and hinder a more complete flow of life through the individual. This is in accordance with Law.

If the artist suppressed all spiritual emotion, he would never be a great artist. In art, we call this emotion temperament; in oratory, we call it inspiration; and in purely spiritual things, we call it Illumination. Somewhere the soul must stand naked to the Truth, if it is to receive It in all Its fullness. There must be an outlet as well as an inlet, if there is to be a continual flow. "Quench not the Spirit," but let the intellect decide to what the emotions are to respond. This is the secret of a well-balanced life.

"Prove all things, hold fast to that which is good." We are not to be afraid of strange ideas or doctrines, but are to prove them and accept only that which is true. We are to analyze, dissect and investigate until we know the Truth and then hold fast to It. In this way, all advance must come, whether in science, philosophy, religion or anything else.

Ask in Faith, Believing (James 1:5—18)

If we lack wisdom, we are to come to the Source of all knowledge and we shall receive it. But how are we to ask? In faith, believing. A double-minded man gets nowhere. How true this is! GOD CAN GIVE US ONLY WHAT WE TAKE, and since the taking is a mental act, WE CAN TAKE ONLY WHAT WE BELIEVE WE ALREADY HAVE! This is in accord with the teachings of Jesus: that when we pray, we must believe we already have the answer to our prayer.

Anything that is not of faith is sin, or a mistake, as we are told in another passage of this book of wisdom. Faith in God and in ourselves should be *consciously generated*. All trouble comes from disbelief in the Universe, followed by wrong acts, which are the result of disbelief and ignorance of the Law of Good, which is a Law of Liberty.

The lesson is simple enough. When we ask for anything, we are to believe that we have it, but *we are to ask for that which is in unity with life*. This unity includes health, happiness and success. These are native to the atmosphere of God and to the atmosphere of the inner man, which is Christ. Let us dislodge doubt, fear and unbelief and trust implicitly in Good.

Evil Is Created by Man (James 1:13)

Very emphatically the writer tells us that God never tempts any man. He says that God cannot be tempted and that all temptation is from our own minds. It could not be stated more plainly. Evil is *man created*, while God—the Eternal Goodness—knows nothing about it. He is too pure to behold evil and cannot look upon it. Evil is the direct and suppositional opposite to good, and has no reality behind it, or actual law to come to its support. GOD TEMPTS NO MAN. It is a mistake to say that God tries us to see if we are fit to enter the kingdom of heaven. God tries no man.

We make our own mistakes, suffer from our own foolishness, and we must also make our own return journey into righteousness. God was, is and will remain, the Essence of Life, Truth and Purity. Let us enter this Essence in belief and be freed from our unbelief and human mistakes.

All goodness and every good gift cometh from the Father of light. Darkness has no father, but is an illegitimate child of superstition and unbelief, having no parentage in Reality. The Universe is not divided against Itself. The good teacher said, "A house divided against itself cannot stand."

There is no shadow of turning in the Truth. It is just what It is, and there can be nothing either added to or taken from It. It is One and never two. We enter the One through a consciousness of unity with It.

DOERS OF THE WORD (JAMES 1:22, 27)

"Be ye doers of the word, and not hearers only, deceiving your own selves." This should teach us not to make idle talk about our understanding. What we *know*, we can *do*. What we cannot *do*, we only *suppose* . . . we only think we know. Unused knowledge is suppositional and unreal; it is an assumption and as such, never produced anything. Not everyone who says Lord, Lord, but those who *do* the will of Truth, enter in.

But we deceive ourselves when we boast about our understanding, and are unable to prove that we possess any! A silent *conviction* is worth more than the loudest proclamation from the housetops of those who shout affirmations to the great nowhere. An ounce of conviction is worth many pounds of affirmation.

Pure religion manifests itself through acts of kindness and mercy. It is not arrogant—claiming a front seat in heaven—but is humble before the great Whole. It unifies with all humanity and finds no great difference between saint and sinner. Such a religion as this, the world of today needs, for it is sick of pretense and would like a practical demonstration of a belief in God, made manifest through good works.

THE LAW IS NO RESPECTER OF PERSONS (JAMES 2:1–11)

James speaks of being *convinced of the law as transgressors*. He does not say that God is convinced we are transgressors, but that the law is convinced. This passage is filled with meaning. God is natural Goodness, Eternal Freedom, and pure Loving-kindness. But the Law is a cold, hard fact, returning to each the result of his own acts, be they false or true. The Law is a neutral, but an intelligent, force—a doer and not a knower. All law is of the same nature.

When we do wrong, the law punishes. When we do right, it rewards. Everything is according to law and order; this is the only way the universe could function. If our thought is of God, or Good, we shall be using the Law in the right way. When our thoughts and acts are opposed to God, or Good, we transgress and are punished. "There is no sin but a mistake and no punishment but a consequence." In like manner, Emerson tells us "there is no sin but ignorance," and this is true, for if we knew the Truth, we should not misuse the law.

The law is no respecter of persons and will bring good or evil to any, according to his use or misuse of it. It will be a law of freedom to the righteous and one of bondage to those who misuse it. *We cannot escape from the creative power of our thought and there is no use in trying to do so.* All we need to do is to use the law from the right motive, then we shall be made free.

The Prayer of Faith (James 5:15)

The prayer of faith is an unconditional belief in both the ability and the desire of Spirit to hear and answer. The prayer of faith heals the sick through the law which says that whatever images of thought are held in the subjective side of mind will tend to appear in the body, or in the body of affairs.

When the prayer of faith penetrates the subjective thought and neutralizes false images, then the sick are raised into health. Even God cannot heal the sick, unless this psychological change takes place in the inner creative thought. All is love but all is law: one balances the other. Law cannot, and will not, depart from its nature.

When we pray, believing, we erase false ideas from our inner thought, then the Spirit can make the gift of health. When we admit the light, it comes in, since there is no way it could enter except through a receptive mind.

If we could give up our diseases—offer them on the altar of faith to the Giver of all life—we would be healed. It is not easy to release our troubles; we are prone to linger with them. But, by effectual and fervent prayer, we gradually loose false thought into its native nothingness. God is perfect life, and when we enter His light, we are healed.

The Confession of Mistakes (James 5:16)

James tells us to confess our faults. This thought suggests one of the great psychological truths of the inner nature. Psychoanalysis—which is the analysis of the soul or subjective mind—is a scientific method for the erasure of false beliefs. It is often forgiveness of sins, done in a scientific manner.

Our minds are burdened with many things. Often our religions—which should automatically balance our mentalities—suppress them, and create morbidness on the subjective side of thought. This happens when we feel condemned for our mistakes. The Bible tells us that God will blot out these mistakes and remember them no more against us forever. This is complete removal and erasure of all mistakes. How could it be different? God is of pure eye and perfect mind; He is perfect Spirit. When we enter this Spirit and bare our souls to Its great light, we loose our troubles and are healed.

The confession of sins, or mistakes, helps us to let go of troubles, and to feel that the Universe holds nothing against us. Sin means making mistakes, and while we continue to make them, we continue to perpetuate their dire results. We should come daily to the Spirit of Goodness for a complete washing away of all mistakes, fears and troubles.

The man who feels that his mistakes can be blotted out, is in a better psychological position, than the one who thinks God will not forgive. We should learn to let go of our mistakes and remember them no longer against ourselves. Nothing is gained by holding to past errors. The best thing to do is to let go of and forget them altogether.

It is scientific to consciously let go all our troubles. It is most unwise to hold them. Some will say that it is right that we should suffer for our past errors. It is right that we should suffer; we already have done so and will continue to do so until we pay the last farthing. BUT THE LAST FARTHING IS PAID WHEN WE LET GO AND TRUST IN THE LAW OF GOOD.

It is impossible for a sane person to believe that God delights in condemning or damning anyone. God is natural Goodness and eternal Loving-kindness, and holds nothing against anyone.

We suffer so long as we make mistakes. We are healed when we come to the Spirit for that cleansing which takes away the mistakes of the world, converting them into great lessons, ever pointing the way to Truth and beauty; to life, health, happiness and success.

It is scientific for one to consciously let go of his troubles and errors, feeling that they no longer affect him. He has learned the lesson that false ideas do not pay and is willing and glad to turn from all that hurts to the Great Light. And the Spirit, because of Its nature of Wholeness, is ever ready to take him in Its embrace and make him whole again.

NOW ARE WE THE SONS OF GOD (I JOHN 3:1–4)

The world does not know the son of God. Material sense cannot recognize the spiritual. Spiritual things must be spiritually understood. God's love is complete in us, in that we are His sons—the sons of freedom and not of bondage.

"Now are we the sons of God." Not in the hereafter, but in the Now, are we just what we are and what we must be—because of our true natures. "Now are we the Sons of God." The birth of the soul into the light of Spirit is an awakening to the realization that God has been with us all the time. "Now are we the sons of God." Today is the day of complete salvation, not tomorrow or the day after, but NOW.

It does not now completely appear what we really are, for now we see only in part, but when He shall appear we shall recognize Him, for we shall see Him in His true light. This "He" means ourselves—*the Christ in us*, our hope and assurance of eternal glory. We shall be like Him. We have inwardly been like Him all the time, but when He shall appear, we shall see Him as He is; that is, we shall know, even as we also are known—we shall know ourselves.

"We shall see him as he is." Not as He now appears, for He is hidden in the innermost recesses of our nature. We shall see Him with the spiritual eye that dims not; with a clear sight that penetrates all suppositional opposites and announces the ever-present Reality. We shall see ourselves as we really are, forever held in the bosom of the Universe—the Sons of God.

Who doeth right, is right, even as He is right. This again reveals us to ourselves. This is the great revelation: the revelation of the self to the self. But before this can take place, we must have consciously come into our birthright. We must have returned to the Father's House. This return is a conscious act on our part.

When we do right, we are right, and when we are right, we are like Him, for then we shall see Him. This refers to the Christ indwelling every soul. The Son of God in all His beauty and strength.

Even if our hearts condemn us, we know that the Spirit, which gave the heart, is greater than Its gift. God is greater than all human mistakes and in God alone is there peace and happiness. God is natural Goodness and eternal Loving-kindness.

"Who is born of love is born of God, for God is Love." Without love, nothing can be accomplished. With love, all things are possible. And when we love, our prayers are answered and the gift of heaven is made. The gift of heaven is Life and not death; Love and not hate; Peace and not confusion.

And we enter into this paradise through the gateway of love toward one another and toward God. Love is greater than all else and covers a multitude of mistakes. Love overcomes everything and neutralizes all that is unlike itself. Love is God.

PART SIX

MEDITATIONS

MEDITATIONS FOR SELF-HELP AND HEALING

In these short meditations I have tried to set forth some ideas which my experiences in mental healing have given me. I have found that a few brief statements, mentally affirmed, followed by a silent meditation, have been most effective in the healing work.

Most of these meditations have been written in the first person in order that those using them may be able to do so just as they are written.

It is not claimed that there is any occult power in the words, but that words similar to these are effective in inducing a greater realization of life.

First, decide which meditation you wish to use; then become quiet and composed. Then carefully read the meditation several times, phrase by phrase, endeavoring to realize the meaning of the words and trying to enter into the atmosphere of the thought. After having done this, meditate upon the words, following that meditation until you feel a sense of realization.

COME, AND LET ME HEAL YOU

Come and I will heal you.

The inner power of Life within me is God,
and God has all power.

I will heal and help all who come to me.

I know that the realization of Life and Love
within me heals all who come into Its
presence.

I silently bless all who enter my atmosphere.

It is not I, but the Father Who dwelleth in
me, He doeth the works.

I heal all who come near me.

. .

HE IS MIGHTY WITHIN ME TO HEAL

God within me is mighty to heal.

He healeth me of all my diseases and
removes all fear from me.

My God within is now healing me of all
sickness and pain and is bringing
comfort to my soul.

God is my life; I cannot be sick.

I hear the voice of Truth telling me to arise
and walk, for I am healed.

I am healed.

. .

I DO NOT INHERIT DISEASE

There is no inherited tendency to disease
nor ill health.

I am born of Pure Spirit.

False ideas cannot be transmitted from one
to another, and I am free from race-
suggestion.

My Life is from Above, and I remember that
I was always Perfect and Complete.

An Inner Light shines forth and frees me
from the bonds of false belief.

I came from the Spirit.

. .

NO CONGESTION

There is no congestion nor stoppage of
action.

Life, flowing through me, is Perfect and
Clear;

It cannot be stopped, retarded nor hindered.

I feel the One Life flowing through me now.

It eliminates all impure secretions and
cleanses my thought from any suggestion
of false deposits in the flesh.

I am Clean, Pure and Perfect, and my Word
eliminates all else.

There is no congestion.

. .

NO FALSE GROWTH

"Every plant which my Heavenly Father hath
not planted, shall be rooted up."

There is no false growth and nothing for
one to feed on. I am free from all
thought of, or belief in, anything false
or fearsome.

I cast out all fear and with it all manifestation
of fear.

A false idea is neither person, place nor
thing, and has no one to believe in nor
experience it.

I am now One with The Perfect Life of
Complete Wholeness.

My Word casts out all fear.

. .

NO WEARINESS

There is no weariness.

Mind and Spirit do not become tired nor
weary, and I am Mind and Spirit.

The flesh cannot become weary, since it has
no mind of its own.

I am free from all illusions of weariness.

My whole being responds to the thought
of Life.

I am alive with the Great Vitality of the
Spirit.

I am alive with Spirit.

. .

PERFECT HEARING

My hearing is perfect.

It is God in me hearing His own voice.

I hear That Voice, and no belief in inaction
can hinder that hearing.

There are no impaired organs.

Every idea of the body is now complete and
perfect and functions according to the
Divine Law.

I open my ears to hear.

I am receptive to Truth and can understand it.

Open my ears that I may hear.

. .

PERFECT VISION

There is One Vision and One perfect seeing.

My eyes are open and I behold Perfect Life.

No suggestion of imperfect vision can enter
my thought.

I perceive that all people can see, and that
the One, looking through all, sees and is
not limited in vision.

I am one with a complete understanding
of Truth.

I do open my eyes and I do see.

This Word operates even through me and
manifests through my eyes NOW.

Open my eyes that I may see.

. .

THE ALL-SEEING EYE

The Eye of the Spirit cannot be dimmed, neither can It be limited in Its ability to see.

My eyes are the Vision of my Indwelling
Lord; they are the Windows of my Inner
Spirit and are always open to the Vision
of Truth.

I see with the Vision of the Spirit, and this
sight cannot be weakened nor lost; it is
forever effective.

My word which I now speak is the Law of Perfect Sight, my eyes are opened and I see.

Spirit sees through me.

. .

THE HEALING OF THE FLESH

My flesh is the Manifestation of the Spirit in
my body.
It is kept perfect through the Law of God.
"In my flesh shall I see God."
The mantle of flesh is perfect and complete
here and now.
It is one with the Body of God, and cannot
be sick, nor suffer.

My flesh is Perfect.

• •
•

THERE IS NO PAIN

There is no pain nor inflammation.
All fear is swept away in the realization
of Truth.
I am free from every belief in pain.
The Spirit cannot pain, and I am Pure Spirit.

I am free from all pain.

• •
•

HAPPINESS AND COMPLETION

I am happy and complete, today and forever.
Within me is that which is Perfect and
Complete.
It is the Spirit of all Life, Truth and Action.
I am happy in the certain knowledge of this
Inner Light.
I cannot be sad nor sorry, but must radiate
Joy and Life,
For Life is within me now.

I am happy and complete.

• •
•

HERE AND NOW

Perfection is already accomplished.
I am that Perfect Life here and now.
Today I express the Limitless Life of the
All Good.
Today I manifest my Completion in every
part of me.
Today I am saved.

Here and now I am healed.

• •
•

MAJESTIC CALM

The Inner Mind is still.
The Soul reflects the Most High.
The Spirit of man is God.
In the great calm of the All Good,
I rest in peace and security.
My life is now reflecting the Perfect Whole.
I am Peace; I am calm
I am security and complete satisfaction.
I am One with God.

I am filled with peace.

• •
•

NO LOSS

There is no loss.
Nothing can be lost, misplaced nor
forgotten.
There was never any loss nor confusion.

Creation is Perfect and Complete, within the One are all things, and all are known to the One.

I am now in complete harmony with the Whole and I cannot lose nor misplace anything.

I am constantly finding more and more Good.

I know that there is no loss.

• •
•

OH, FOR A TONGUE TO EXPRESS

Oh, for a tongue to express the Wonders which the Thought reveals!

Oh, for some Word to comprehend the boundless idea!

Would that some Voice were sweet enough to sound the harmony of Life.

But Within, in that vast realm of thought where the Soul meets God, the Spirit knows.

I will listen for that Voice and It will tell me of Life, of Love and Unity.

Speak to me, Spirit.

• •
•

O SOUL OF MINE, LOOK OUT AND SEE

O Soul of mine, look out and see; look up and know Thy freedom.

Be not cast down nor dismayed; be uplifted within me and exult, for Thy Salvation has come.

Behold the wonders of the Great Whole and the marvels of the Universe.

Look out and see Thy good. It is not afar off, but is at hand.

Prepare Thyself to accept and believe; to know and live.

Let Life enter and live through Thee, Soul of mine, and rejoice that Thou hast vision so fair and so complete.

Rejoice that the Perfect Whole is so completely reflected through Thee.

My light has come.

• •
•

SEEING THE PERFECT

My eyes behold the complete and perfect in all Creation,

"In all, over all and through all."

I see the perfect; there is nothing else to see, and no suggestion of otherness can enter my thought.

I know only the perfect and the complete.

I am perfect and whole, now.

I see the Good.

• •
•

THE CIRCLE IS COMPLETE

The Circle of Love is complete.

It comprehends all, includes all, and binds all together with cords of Everlasting Unity.

I cannot depart from Its Presence nor wander from Its care.

My Love is complete within me.

The Love of God binds me to Itself, and will not let me go.

I shall make a home for you, O my wonderful Love, and we shall journey through
life hand in hand.
I shall sit in your Presence and learn the
wondrous things You will tell me;
For You are God.

Love sits within me.

∴

THE THINGS THAT ARE

The things that are, were and evermore
shall be.
Time, chance and change begone from my
thought!
The Changeless is here to stay, and the
Timeless cannot cease from Being.
The things that are shall remain, though
heaven and earth should pass away.
I rest secure and safe within the Life of
Endless Perfection and Completion.
My whole Being responds to the Realization
of the Complete Whole.

I am that which Is.

∴

A SONG OF HOPE

My Life is in Thee, O Inner Presence.
I look upon Thee and hope springs forth into
realization.
O Hope within me, undying evidence of
Good,
Thou dost completely hold me in Thy loving
embrace,

And from this fond caress assurance shall be
born, and confidence and love.

My hope is in Thee.

∴

BE STILL AND KNOW

"Be still and know that I am God."
I am still in Thy Presence.
I am quiet and peaceful, for I put my trust
in Thee.
A great stillness steals over me and a great
calm quiets my whole being, as I realize
Thy Presence.
The heart knows of Thee, O Most High
within.
It is still in Thy Presence, and it puts its
whole confidence in Thee alone.

In Thy Presence I am still.

∴

CAST ASIDE ALL DOUBT

Cast aside all doubt, O Soul of mine, and be
unafraid, for Thy power is from On High.
He Who sitteth in the heavens shall be Thy
champion;
Thou need not fear; Come forth, O Spirit,
from within and express Thyself through
me and let not my doubts hinder Thy
approach.
My faith shall go forth to meet Thee, and my
confidence shall embrace Thee.
My waiting thought shall bid Thee welcome
to my house of Love,

And Joy shall accompany us through the ages
yet to come.

I lay aside all fear and doubt.

DIVINE COMPANIONSHIP

I have an Inner Friend who walks and talks
with me daily.
He is not afar off, but is within me, a con-
stant companion.
I shall never become lonely, for my Friend is
always near.
I have but to speak and He answers.
Before ever my lips spoke He told me of
His love.
O my kind Friend, how dear to me is Thy
presence.

The Spirit within me is my Friend.

HIS EYE IS ON THE SPARROW

"His eye is on the sparrow and I know He
watches me."
This is a blessed thought, for it means that
we cannot wander from His Presence,
nor depart from His care.
Always He will watch over us and
comfort us.
Forever we shall sit in His house and
ceaselessly He will care for us.
The All-Seeing Eye cannot overlook any
one, and all, all shall be kept in
His care.

All are kept in His care.

HOPE CANNOT DIE

Hope cannot die. Eternal Hope is forever
warm and fresh within me; the deathless Hope built upon the rock of sure
knowledge.
O Hope Sublime, O Life Supreme, behold I
come to Thee as a tired child, and Thou
dost rekindle within me the fires of Faith.
Strong, swift and sure, Faith springs forth
into action and my entire Being rises to
meet the Dawn.

Hope, Faith and Love are in me.

I AM NOT ALONE

I am not alone, for a Presence goes with me
and daily accompanies me on my travels.
Always I shall find this Divine Companion
with me.
He will not desert nor allow me to go alone.
He will always be with me and near me, and
will always provide for every want.

My life is hid with Christ in God.

I WENT INTO A MOUNTAIN

I have discovered a Secret Place within,
where the thought goes into a mountain
high above the din of the world.

I have found in this mountain a Place of
   Peace and rest,
A Place of joy and comfort to the heart.
I have found that the Secret Place of God is
   within my own Soul.

   I will listen for Thy Voice.

. .
.

THE JOY OF THE SOUL

My Soul within me rejoices at the realization
   of Life.
I am made glad as I behold my inner Light;
I cannot be sad nor depressed, for the All
   Good has claimed me as Its own.
O Soul within me, rejoice and become glad,
   for Thy Light has come and Thy Day of
   Salvation is at hand.
Be still within me and behold Him Who
   sitteth On High.

   I rejoice in my Life within me.

. .
.

FREEDOM FROM SIN

I am free from belief in sin; there is neither
   sin nor sinner.
There is no judgment against anyone.
God does not condemn and man cannot.
All fear of sin is removed from me; all belief
   in punishment is gone from me.
I live by the One Power, and no thought can
   enter to disturb me.

   There is neither sin nor sinner.

. .
.

FREE FROM SENSITIVENESS

My feelings cannot be hurt.
No one wishes to harm me, and there is
   nothing in me that can believe in any
   separation from the All Good.
I perceive that I am free from all people, and
   I cannot be harmed nor mistreated.
I have such a sense of unity with all that the
   circle is complete and perfect.
I love my friends and they love me, and that
   love is in, and of, God, and cannot be
   marred nor hindered.

   I am filled with joy and love, forever.

. .
.

I KEEP THE PROMISE

I shall keep the promise that I have made to
   myself.
I shall never again tell myself that I am poor,
   sick, weak nor unhappy.
I shall not lie to myself any more, but
   shall daily speak the truth to my inner
   Soul, telling It that It is wonderful and
   marvelous; that It is One with the Great
   Cause of all Life, Truth, Power and
   Action.
I shall whisper these things into my Soul
   until it breaks forth into songs of joy
   with the realization of Its Limitless
   possibilities.

   I shall assure my Soul.

. .
.

LOVE GLEAMS THROUGH THE MIST

Through the mist of human fear love gleams
and points the way to freedom.
I now decree and declare that I am free
from all sense of bondage.
I am made perfect and whole through
knowledge of the Real Life within me.
No illusions can enter my thought.
I know that there is One Power, and I know
that this Power now protects me from
all harm.
As Perfect Love casts out all fear, so my fear
flees before the knowledge of Truth.

I am not afraid.

. .
.

NO BONDAGE

There is no bondage nor limitation.
Every part of me moves in perfect harmony
and freedom.
I cannot be tied, bound nor made
inactive, for
I am Free Spirit, and the Power of my Life is
from on High.
There is no inaction nor false action,
And I am now completely Free.

I am free.

. .
.

NO CONDEMNATION

There is no condemnation in me nor
operating through me.
I am free from the belief or thought of men.

I walk my own way, immune to all suggestion of condemnation.
Only those thoughts can enter my mentality
which I allow to enter.
I do not, and cannot, receive adverse
thoughts.
Only those thoughts which are helpful and
life-giving can find entrance to my house.

There is no condemnation.

. .
.

NO FALSE HABIT

There are no vicious nor false habits.
Every desire of my thought and heart is
satisfied in the Truth.
I do not long for anything nor feel the lack
of anything.
I am complete within myself; I am perfect
within myself; I am happy and satisfied
within myself.
I am One with All Life within me.

I am free.

. .
.

NO HYPNOTISM NOR FALSE SUGGESTION

There is no hypnotism nor false suggestion.
I represent the One Mind which cannot act
against Itself nor can It act against me.
I am immune to all suggestion and cannot
receive false thoughts, nor harbor them.
I am surrounded with a circle of Love and
Protection.
Asleep or awake, I am free from false
thoughts.

I see the nothingness of all belief in, or fear
of, otherness; and I know that The One
and Only Mind, alone, can act.

Only the Good can enter.

. .

NO MISTAKES

There are no mistakes; none have ever been
made and none ever will be made.
Nothing ever happened in the past to hinder
or hurt.
There is no past, and I know, and can see,
that there is no belief in any past to rise
against me.
I live in the Now, free from any yesterdays or
tomorrows.
Now, I am Happy, Free and Complete.

There are no mistakes.

. .

THERE ARE NO RESPONSIBILITIES

The Spirit has no responsibilities.
The Spirit knows no want nor fear.
It is complete within Itself, and lives by
virtue of Its own Being.
I am Spirit and cannot take on the fears of
the world.
My ways are made straight before me.
The pathway of Life is an endless road of
Eternal Satisfaction and Perfect Joy.
My Life within me is Complete and Perfect,
and has no cares nor burdens.
It is Free Spirit and cannot be bound.
I rejoice in that Freedom.

I rejoice in freedom.

. .

THE TIME HAS COME

The time has come, the hour has struck.
The power from within has come forth and
is expressing through my word.
I do not have to wait; today is the time.
Today I enter into all Truth; today I am
completely healed.
Today I enter into my inheritance.

Today the Truth has made me free.

. .

WITHIN THY LAW IS FREEDOM

O, My Soul within me, Great is Thy Presence
Within Thy Law is freedom to all who will
believe.
I believe in Thy Law and I love Thy precepts.
I know that Thy Law is perfect and It is a
delight to my Soul,
for It is illumined with Thy Words of Power.
Thy Law is complete freedom to me, and to
all for whom it shall be spoken.
I speak the Word of freedom to all, and all
shall receive it.

I am free in Thy Law.

. .

BEAUTY

I behold the Beautiful and the Pleasant.
My eyes see only that which is beautiful to
look upon.

I will not see anything else nor believe in anything else.
I know that beauty has entered into my life, and will always remain there.

I see only the beautiful.

• •
•

FRIENDSHIP OF THE SPIRIT AND OF MAN

The Friendship of the Spirit and of man is mine now and forever.
Even now I see the countless numbers of friends coming and going around me.
I enter into this friendship and this companionship with gladness and rejoicing.

I receive my friends.

• •
•

I SERVE

I serve the world.
I wait upon the Lord within all men;
I call forth glory from On High through the minds of all people.
I obey the will of Him Who inhabits Eternity.
I do the works of Him Who dwelleth among the heavens.
My Lord within commands and I obey.

I do good to all people

• •
•

I SHALL NOT DOUBT NOR FEAR

I shall not doubt nor fear, for my salvation is from On High, and the day of its appearing is now at hand.

I shall not doubt nor fear, for my whole being responds to the realization of Life within and around me.
I shall not fear, for the Hosts of Heaven are waiting upon me, and the Law of the Universe is my Salvation.

I shall not fear.

• •
•

I WAS TOLD TO LIVE

By some inner mystic Presence,
I was told to live and to love, to laugh and to be glad.
I was told to be still and know of the One Almighty Power, in and through all.
I was told to let that Power work through and in me.
I believed that voice and I received my Good.

I am healed—The joy of Life.

• •
•

LAW

I meditate upon the Law of God.
It is a Perfect Law and is now working for me and in and through me.
"The Law of the Lord is perfect."
I speak into that Law and it is done unto me.

Thy Law is in my heart.

• •
•

LOVE

The Love of the All Good is within me and through me.

That Love goes out to meet all who come
into my atmosphere.
It radiates to all and is flowing through all.
My Love within me is Perfect.

Thy Love within me is Perfect.

. .
.

LOVE DISSOLVES ALL FEAR

Greater than fear is Love.
Love dissolves all fear, casts out all doubt and
sets the captive free.
Love, like the River of Life, flows through
me and refreshes me with its eternal
blessings.
Love cannot be afraid; it is fearless and
strong, and is mighty in its works.
It can accomplish all things through the Inner
Light of that faith in the All Good,
Which fills my very Being with a Powerful
Presence.

Love casts out all fear.

. .
.

MY AFFAIRS

My affairs are in the hands of Him
Who guides the planets in their course,
And Who causes the Sun to shine.
Divine Understanding attends me on the Way,
And I shall not be hindered in my work.
My affairs are controlled by Perfect
Intelligence,
And cannot be hindered from expression.
I know that all that I do is done from the
One Motive:

To express Life; and Life will be
expressed
In and through me. I cannot hinder it.

I am controlled by Intelligence.

. .
.

MY BUSINESS

My business is directed by Divine
Intelligence.
The All-Knowing Mind knows what to do
and how to do it.
I do not hinder, but let It operate in my
affairs.
It prospers and directs me and controls
my life.
My affairs are managed by Love, and
directed by
Wisdom, and they cannot fail to prosper and
expand.

My affairs are in His hands.

. .
.

MY PROFESSION

My profession is the Activity of the Great
Mind working through me.
As such It is a Divine Activity and is
constantly in touch with Reality.
I am inspired in my work from On High
with lofty ideals,
And my thought is illumined by the
All-Knowing One.

I am inspired.

. .
.

NO DELAYS

There are no delays in the Divine Plan
for me.
Nothing can hinder the operation of this Law
unto my Life and Action.
Obstructions are removed from my path,
and I now enter into the realization and
manifestation of complete fulfillment.
I do not have to wait, for the Law waits upon
me at every turn in Life's road.

Now it is done unto me.

• •
•

NO MISREPRESENTATIONS

No one can misdirect; none can mislead me.
I am free from the belief in all lies and
untruths;
I know and speak only the Truth, and the
Truth alone can be spoken to me.
I know the false and can understand
the Real.
I cannot be fooled nor misled; I am guided
by Truth alone.

There is no lie nor liar.

• •
•

NO OBSTRUCTIONS

There are no obstructions to Life's Path; no
hindrance to man's endeavors.
Let my Word be the Law of elimination to all
thought of hindrance or delay,
And let the thing that I speak come forth
into manifestation at once.

I behold it and see that it is even now done,
complete and perfect.

I receive now.

• •
•

NO OVER-ACTION NOR INACTION

There is no over-action nor inaction in
Divine Law, for everything moves
according to perfect harmony.
Every idea of my body functions in accor-
dance with this Law of Perfect Life.
I now perceive that the action within me is
perfect, complete and harmonious.
Peace be unto every part of me, and perfect
Life to every member of my body.
I act in accordance with Divine Law.

I am Perfect Life throughout my whole Being.

• •
•

ONE WITH PERFECT ACTION

I am One with Perfect Action. Everything
that I do, say or think is quickened into
action through this right understanding
and this correct knowing.
The harmonious action of the Great Whole
operates through me now and at all times.
I am carried along by this Right Action and
am compelled to do the right thing at the
right time.
There is nothing in me that can hinder this
action from flowing through me.

The action of God is the only action.

• •
•

PEACE, POISE AND POWER

Peace, Poise and Power are within me, for
they are the witnesses of the Inner Spirit
of all Truth, Love and Wisdom.

I am at peace within me, and all about re-
sponds to that Great Calm of the Inner
Soul which knows its rightful place in the
All Good.

Power is born from within me and passes
into my experience without effort or
labor.

I rest in Security and Peace, for the Inner
Light shines forth and illumines the way.

I rest in Thee.

. .
.

STILLNESS AND RECEPTIVITY

I am still and receptive to Life.

I let Life flow through me into all that I do,
say or think.

I shall let my Life be what it is, and shall not
worry nor complain.

I am now entered into the Secret Place of
the Soul where complete quiet reigns
supreme and where God talks to me.

I receive.

. .
.

THANKSGIVING AND PRAISE

I will give thanks to my Inner Life for all Its
Marvelous Wonders, and for all Its Wonderful Works.

I will sing and be glad, for I know that I am
hidden with Truth in a Perfect Life.

The fullness of Joy is mine.

. .
.

THE INNER LIGHT

The Light of Heaven shines through me and
illumines my path.

The Light Eternal is my guide and my
protection.

In that Light there is no darkness at all.

It is a Perfect Light shining from the altar
of a perfect Love.

O Light and Love within me, Thou art
welcome.

Light shines through me and illumines the Way.

. .
.

THE NIGHT IS FILLED WITH PEACE

I wrap myself in the mantle of Love and fall
asleep, filled with Peace.

Through the long night Peace remains with
me, and at the breaking of the new day I
shall still be filled with Life and Love.

I shall go forth into the new day confident
and happy.

I rest in Thee.

. .
.

THE SEAL OF APPROVAL

The Seal of Approval is upon me, and I am
not condemned by the thought or the act
of man.

I will fear no evil, for I know that the Great
    Judge of all controls my every act.
Let every fear of man be removed from
    me and let the Silence of my soul bear
    witness to the Truth.

God approves of me.

∴

THE SECRET WAY

There is a Secret Way of the Soul which all
    may know.
It is the Way of Peace and Love.
This Secret Way leads into places of joy
And into the house of good.
It is the Way of the Spirit, and all may enter
    who will.
I tread the Secret Way of good, the Path of
    Peace,
And I enter into "The Secret Place of The
    Most High."

The Secret Place of The Most High is within me.

∴

THE SHINING PATH

The Pathway of Life shines before me unto
    the Perfect Day.
I walk the pathway of the Soul to the Gate of
    Good.
I enter into the fulfillment of my desires.
Nothing need be added to and nothing can
    be taken from the All Good which is
    forever expressing Itself in me.

Daily shall I receive Its great blessings and
    my Soul shall rejoice forevermore.

I am now entered into my good.

∴

THE THINGS I NEED COME TO ME

Whatever I need comes to me from the
    All Good.
Divine Intelligence working through me
    always knows just what
I need and always supplies it when I need it.
    This Law is unfailing and sure, and cannot
    be broken. I receive my Good daily as I
    go along the pathway of Life, and
I cannot be robbed of my birthright to
    freedom and happiness.

I receive my Good.

∴

THE WAY IS MADE CLEAR BEFORE ME

The Way is made clear before me; I do not
    falter nor fall.
The Way of the Spirit is my Way, and I am
    compelled to walk in it.
My feet are kept on the Path of Perfect Life.
The Way is prepared before me, and that Way
    is a Path of Peace, of Fulfillment and Joy.
The Way is bright with the light of Love and
    Kindness.
The Way I tread is a pleasant and a happy one.

I see the Way and I walk in It.

∴

AS LOVE ENTERS, FEAR DEPARTS

As Love enters, fear vanishes.

I am so filled with Love that no fear can
enter my thought.

I am not afraid, for I know that a Perfect Intelligence guards and governs my every act.

Perfect Love casteth out all fear.

I am unafraid, and strong in my faith in that
inner Presence that keeps me from
all harm.

Perfect Love casteth out all fear.

. .
.

INFINITE LIFE WITHIN

Infinite Life within me, which is God, guard
Thou my feet and keep Thou my way.

Let me not stray from Thee, but compel me
to do Thy will.

I am guarded and governed by an Infinite
Intelligence and an Omnipotent Power.

No mistakes can be made and none ever have
been made.

An unerring judgment operates through me
and I am led by the

Spirit of Truth into all Good and into all
Peace and Happiness.

Infinite Life is within me.

. .
.

MY FEET SHALL NOT FALTER

My feet shall not falter, for they are kept
upon the path of Life through the Power
of the Eternal Spirit.

This Spirit is my spirit now.

Guide Thou my feet; compel my way; direct
my paths and keep me in Thy Presence.

My feet are guarded and I am guided into
The All Good.

He guides my feet.

. .
.

NO HARM SHALL BEFALL YOU

No harm shall befall you, my friend, for a
Divine Presence attends your way and
guards you into The All Good.

Loving kindness awaits you at every turn of
Life's road.

Guidance is yours along the pathway of
experience,

And an Infallible Power protects you.

God, Himself, and no other is your Keeper.

I proclaim this for you.

. .
.

POWER TO LIVE

I have the power to live the life of good.

My power is from On High, it cannot be
taken from me;

It will not leave me desolate.

Power flows through me and is in me, and

I can now feel and sense it.

The Power to live is in me and it cannot
desert me.

It is my power and is continually present.

I am the power to live.

. .
.

THE CIRCLE OF LOVE

A circle of love is drawn around me and
  mine, and all.
No harm can enter that Sacred Circle, for it
  is the Love of God.
It is a complete protection from all evil.
"I will fear no evil, for Thou art with me."
There is no evil and no harm.
I am free from all sense of fear.

Love surrounds and protects me.

• •
•

THE CIRCLE OF PROTECTION

I draw around me a circle of love and
  protection.
No harm can enter nor find place within that
  charmed circle of life and love, for it represents God's Loving Care and Eternal
  Watchfulness.
I will rest within me now, and I will speak
  comfort to my Soul and tell It of all the
  wonders of Its life, safe from the din of
  strife and fear.

I am protected from On High.

• •
•

THE POWER WITHIN BLESSES ALL

The Power within me is blessing all mankind, and is forever healing all with
  whom I come in contact.
The Power within me is God, and It must bless
  and help and heal all who come near It.

Silently the work goes on, and silently all are
  being helped by this Inner Power which is
  operating through me.
I will give thanks that my Power within is
  silently blessing and helping every one
  to whom my thought reaches.

The Life within me blesses all mankind.

• •
•

THE QUICK ANSWER

My answer comes quickly and surely back to
  me from On High.
My answer will not fail me, for the Law of
  the Universe is the Power through which
  it comes.
I shall not doubt nor fear, for the answer is
  swift and certain.

My answer comes.

• •
•

A SONG OF JOY

There is a Song upon my lips today; it sings
  of the glad heart and the happy ways
  of Life.
I will listen to my song, for it carols to me
  the glad tidings of Great Joy, of Love
  and Life.
It tells me of the Wondrous Journey of the
  Soul and the Boundless Life in which my
  life is hid.

I am filled with joy.

• •
•

BORN OF ETERNAL DAY

Child of All Good, you are born of
 Eternal Day.

There is no evening of the Soul, for it shall
 live forever.

It is Deathless and Perfect, Complete and
 One with the Everlasting.

No thought of tomorrow can disturb the
 calm of him who knows that Life is one
 Eternal Day.

No fear can enter where Love reigns, and
 Reason keeps faith with Hope.

The thoughts of the tomorrows and the
 yesterdays are swallowed up in the great
 realization of the Perfect Here and the
 Complete Now.

Today I completely accept my wholeness.

. .
.

I ARISE AND GO FORTH

I arise and go forth into the Dawn of the
 New Day, filled with faith and assurance
 in the All Good.

I arise, I arise, I sing with joy!

I proclaim the One Life: "In all and
 through all."

I arise, I arise, I shout with gladness that is
 within me.

I declare this day to be Complete, Perfect
 and Eternal.

I respond to Life.

. .
.

INSPIRATION

Come, Thou Great and Infinite Mind and
 inspire me to do great deeds.

Acquaint me with Thy knowledge and in Thy
 wisdom make me wise.

I would be taught of Thee, Inner Light, and
 inspired by Thy presence.

I will listen for Thy Voice and it will tell me
 of great things to be done.

I will walk in Thy Paths and they will lead
 me into All Good.

I will be inspired from On High.

O Wonderful Presence, flooding me, filling
 me with Thy Light, Thou dost inspire me!

I feel the inspiration of Spirit.

. .
.

THE DAWN HAS COME

Out of the darkness of the long night the
 Dawn has come.

I rise to meet the new day, filled with
 confidence and strength.

I arise and go forth into the dawn, inspired and
 refreshed by the Living Spirit within me.

O Day, you shall never die; the sun shall
 never set upon your perfect glory.

For the Lamp of the Soul has been re-kindled
 with the oil of Faith,

And Love has cleansed the windows of Life
 with the spirit of gladness.

They shall nevermore grow dim with fear,
 for Perfect Love casteth out all fear.

I am renewed in strength through knowing
 Good.

My light has come.

. .
.

COMPLETE CONFIDENCE

My confidence in the All Good is complete.
My faith in the Power of Spirit is supreme.
I have no doubts nor uncertainties.
I know that my Good is at hand, and
I realize that no fear can hinder
That Good from making Its appearance in
    my life and affairs.
I know that my Life and Good are complete.
Evil cannot touch nor hinder my work.
I rest in security, for
THE ONE MIND IS MY COMPLETE
REFUGE AND STRENGTH.

I am serene and confident.

. .
.

DRAWING THE GOOD

I draw my Good to me as I travel along
    the Way of Life, and nothing can keep It
    from me.
My Good will always follow me.
I accept the Good and rejoice that it is with me.

I accept the Good.

. .
.

I FEAR NO EVIL

"I will fear no evil, for Thou art with me."
I will not be afraid, for the All Good is
    constantly with me and is always near at
    hand to guide and comfort.

There is no evil in the Truth, and no
    power of darkness to hinder the Light
    from shining.
I will not be afraid, for there is One
    within Who protects and keeps me
    from all harm.

I fear no evil.

. .
.

I HAVE KNOWN, ALWAYS

I have always known the Truth, and no fear
    can keep my inner knowledge from me.
My wisdom from within comes forth into
    daily expression.
Knowledge from On High is given to me,
    and I shall always be led of the Spirit.

I know the Truth.

. .
.

I MEET MY GOOD

Today I meet my Good; it knows me and
    will not let me depart from it.
My Good is at hand, and I cannot be robbed
    of it.
Good is forever expressing itself to me
    and mine.
I can even now see and hear and feel the All
    Good in and around me.
It presses itself against me, and fills me with
    a great surge of Life.

My Good is at hand.

. .
.

MY ATMOSPHERE

My atmosphere is attracting the Good; it is
constantly on the alert to see and know the
Good, and to bring it into my experience.

There is that within me that calls forth
abundance and happiness from Life. I
am surrounded with an atmosphere of
Peace, Poise and Power.

All who come in contact with that great
Calm of my Life are made strong and
confident, are healed and blessed.

"Bless the Lord, O my Soul, and all that is
within me, bless His Holy Name."

I am hid with Christ in God.

. .
.

MY GOOD IS COMPLETE

My Good is complete; it is finished; it is now
here and is conscious of me and of mine.

I do not have to wait for my Good; it is at
hand and ever ready to spring forth and
express itself to me.

I accept my Good and gladly acknowledge it
to be my daily companion.

My Good is mine now, and I can see it and
feel it and know it.

Today I claim my Good.

. .
.

MY OWN SHALL COME TO ME

From far and near my own shall come to
me. Even now it is coming to me and I
receive it.

My own is now manifesting itself to me, and
I see and know its presence. My own
shall know and respond to me.

My own cannot be kept from me, neither
can I keep my good away from me. I
receive my good NOW.

My own shall find me. No matter where I
go, it will follow and claim me.

I cannot hide myself from my own.

My own shall come to me, even though I
deny it; for there is nothing in me that
can hinder it from entering and taking
possession of my Soul.

My own is now expressed.

. .
.

MY SOUL REFLECTS THY LIFE

My Soul reflects Thy Life and rejoices in the
happy thought that it looks on Thee
alone.

O Soul of mine, look out and up and on; and
reflect to me the wondrous Life of The
All Good.

Look thou upon The One, and be saved.

Behold thou His Face forevermore.

My Soul reflects Thy Life.

. .
.

SORROW FLEES FROM ME

As the Great Joy of Life comes into my
Soul, flooding me with Its wondrous
light, all sorrow and sadness flee
from me.

I shall not grieve, for nothing is lost nor
gone from me.
My own cannot be kept from me.
My own knows me and will follow me
wherever I go.
I am filled with the Joy of living and the
Great Peace that comes to all who
believe.

I am made glad forevermore.

. .
.

SUBSTANCE AND SUPPLY

The Substance of the Spirit is my Daily
Supply.
I cannot be without my Good.
I can see that the constant stream of
Life, flowing to me, brings into my
experience all that makes Life happy
and worthwhile.
I rest in security, knowing that Infinite Good
is within and is expressing through me.

I receive my good.

. .
.

THE EVER AND THE ALL

Life always was and evermore shall be,
"World without end."
All the Power there is, is mine now.
All the Life, Truth and Love of the Universe
is now and forever
Flowing through my Soul.
The All Good cannot change.
I shall always have access to my Eternal God
within me.

I am Changeless Life within me.

. .
.

THE HOUSE OF LOVE

I dwell in the house of Love;
My dwelling place is filled with peace and
eternal calm.
Love attends me in my home of the Soul, and
Joy awaits upon me in the "Secret Place of
the Most High."
My house is built for me by the hand of
Love, and
I shall never leave this Home of the Spirit,
for it is always present.
I shall abide in this home forevermore.

My house is a house of love.

. .
.

ARISE, MY SPIRIT

Arise, my Spirit, arise and shine.
Let Thy light illumine my path, and let Thy
wisdom direct my way.
Compel my will to do Thy bidding, and
command my Soul to look to Thee.
I will follow Thee, my Spirit, and learn
of Thee.
I will sit in the Silence and listen and
watch, and
I will see Thy light and hear Thy voice.
I will follow Thee and will not depart
from Thee,
For in Thee alone is Peace.

Arise and shine.

. .
.

COMMAND MY SOUL

Spirit within me, command my Soul to do
Thy bidding;
Compel me to follow the course of Truth
and Wisdom.
Control my inward thoughts and my
outward ways,
And make me to understand Thy Laws.
Command my Soul to turn to Thee for
guidance and light;
To turn to Thee for wisdom and knowledge.
Let the paths of my Life be made straight
and sure;
Let the Journey of my Soul find its
completion in Thee.

Command my Soul to do Thy bidding.

. .
.

DESPAIR GIVES WAY TO JOY

Despair gives way to joy at the thought of
Thee, Indwelling Good.
I cannot be sad when I think of Thee.
My sorrow is turned to gladness and my
shame to rejoicing.
My tears are wiped away and the sunlight of
the Spirit shines through the clouds of
depression and lights the way to Heaven.

Thy Joy has made me glad.

. .
.

FREE SPIRIT WITHIN ME

Free Spirit within me, Unbound and Perfect,
teach me Thy ways and make known to
me Thy Limitless Completion.
O Spirit of Life, control my every action and
thought.
Compel me to follow Thy light that I too
may be free and complete.
I will follow Thy footsteps and learn of Thee
all the wondrous secrets of Life.
I will follow Thy Light into the Perfect Day.

Free Spirit within me.

. .
.

FULLNESS OF LIGHT

The Light of Life is full within me and
around me.
It shines forth into the Perfect Day.
O Light within, lighting my path to peace,
I adore and love You and I let You shine.
Go forth and bless all who come to You,
Light within.
My Light radiates to all and through all.

My Light has come.

. .
.

HE WHO INHABITS ETERNITY

He Who inhabits Eternity keeps watch over
me and mine.
"He Who neither slumbers nor sleeps"
forever keeps watch over all.

I will rest in the assurance of Love and
Protection.
O Thou Great Overshadowing Presence,
I am conscious of Thy care; I am aware of
Thy loving kindness.
I rest in Thee.

Be still and know.

. .

I LISTEN

I will listen for Thy voice, Inner Presence.
It will guide me and acquaint me with all
knowledge.
Thy voice is sweet and tender; it is always
kind and gentle.
O Lover of my Soul, how I adore Thee!
How I love Thee!
How I love Thy voice; it thrills me with
gladness and joy.
It fills me with peace and calm, and it
soothes me.
It quiets me and gives me wonderful rest.
I listen, O Divine Speaker, I listen to Thee
alone.

I listen for Thy voice.

. .

JOY HAS COME TO LIVE WITH ME

Joy has come to live with me. How can I
be sad?
I do so love Thy presence, which is joy
within me.

It makes me glad and I sing, for I am so filled
with Thy Spirit that I cannot be depressed
nor unhappy.
I am filled with the joy of the Spirit, and I
overflow with the gladness of life.
Thou art a Happy Companion to travel with
me through Life;
Wonderful Joy, Thou art so radiant and
beaming,
It is impossible to be sad in Thy presence.
I shall give myself to Thee and remain with
Thee, for Thou art complete and satisfying.
I find fulfillment in Thee, and joy
forevermore.

I am filled with the Spirit of Joy.

. .

MY THOUGHT IS IN THEE

My thought is in Thee, Inner Light.
My words are from Thee, Inner Wisdom.
My understanding is of Thee, Inner God.
I cannot be hid from Thee, my inspiration
and my life.

My thought is in Thee.

. .

O LOVE DIVINE

O Love Divine within me, I am overpowered
by Thy Presence.
I am speechless, for words cannot utter the
things that Thou hast revealed to me.
Why dost Thou love me so, and why clasp
me so close to Thy Eternal Heart?

O Blessed Presence, I know, for Thou hast
claimed me as Thine own.
I shall nevermore walk apart from Thee.

The love of God is within me.

. .

PEACE STEALS THROUGH THE SOUL

Peace steals through the waiting Soul, and
the comfort of the Spirit comes into the
stillness of the heart.
Peace, like an ocean of Infinite Life, reflects
itself through me and calms every turbu-
lent feeling.
I am at peace and rest in the knowledge of
the All Good which is at hand.

I rest in peace.

. .

STAND FORTH AND SPEAK

Stand forth and speak, Spirit within me.
Proclaim Thy presence, announce Thy
course.
Declare through me Thy wondrous
works and
Let the children of men hear Thy voice.
Behold, He maketh all things new.
The Spirit within speaks words of Truth and
Life to all.
The Spirit within me is God.

I speak the Truth.

. .

SUBTLE ESSENCE OF SPIRIT WITHIN ME

Subtle Essence of Spirit within me, flowing
through me;
Elixir of Life in my veins purifying me with
Thy marvelous Life,
I let Thy Spirit cleanse me from all false
thought and idea;
I let Thy Life flow through me in a complete
and Perfect Whole.

I feel the presence of Spirit within me.

. .

THE EVERLASTING ARMS

His Arms enfold me, His Strength upholds me,
His Presence fills me with Life and Joy.
I shall nevermore be sad nor depressed, for I
know that I do not walk Life's path alone.
There is One Who goes with me and tells
me all the things that I should know.
There is a Presence with me guiding me into
the Perfect Way.

I rejoice in knowing that I am not alone.

. .

THE MANTLE OF LOVE

Like a cloak His Love is wrapped around me.
Like a warm garment, It shelters me
from the storms of life.
I feel and know that an Almighty Love envel-
ops me in Its close embrace.
O Love Divine, My Love, how wonderful
Thou art. I am open to receive Thy great
blessing.

Love envelops me.

. .
.

THE VOICE OF TRUTH

The Voice of Truth speaks to me and
through me.

The Voice of Truth guides me and keeps me
on the Path of the Perfect Day.

I will listen to the Inner Voice and It will tell
me what to do in the hour of need.

I shall be told everything that I ought to
know when the time of need arrives, and
I shall not be misled.

The Voice of Truth cannot lie, but always
speaks to me from On High.

Nothing enters but This Voice, for it is the
Voice of God.

God speaks to me.

. .
.

THE WITNESS OF TRUTH

There is a Witness within me who knows the
Truth and who will not let me enter into
falsehood.

My Inner Guide keeps me on the Pathway of
Life and directs me at all times to that
which is right and best.

I shall never be without this witness of the
Spirit, for I believe in It and accept It as
the Great Companion of the Soul.

The spirit within me is perfect now.

. .
.

THROUGH THE LONG NIGHT WATCHES

Through the long night watches Thou hast
been with me.

In the dark places of human ignorance Thy
hand hath guided me,

Thy light hath lighted the pathway of
desolation to a land of plenty.

I have perceived Thee from afar, and my
soul hath yearned to Thee, O Thou
Mighty One!

The Spirit within me hath urged me on to
the goal, and I have not been misled.

I have been guided and guarded through the
long journey, and Thy Presence hath been
made known to me.

I awake from the dream and reënter the
house of my Lord clothed with Peace and
robed in colors of Light.

The Spirit of Truth watches over me.

. .
.

THY STRENGTH IS SUFFICIENT

O Spirit of man and God within me, Thy
Power is great, and Thy Knowledge goes
beyond the range of human experience.

Thy Wisdom excels that of all else, and
beside Thee there is none other. In
Thy Strength do I daily walk and live;
In Thy Presence do I always rest in peace
and joy.

Spirit within me and without, Powerful
Thou art, and Great; Wonderful is
Thy Might, and Complete is Thy
Understanding.

I let Thy Mighty Strength flow through me,
And out into all the paths of my human
endeavors.

Life from within expresses through me.

. .

WAITING ON THEE

In waiting on Thee there is fullness of Life.
I wait on Thee, my Inner Lord; I listen for
Thy voice.
I hear Thy word; I do Thy will; again I wait
on Thee.
And listening, I hear Thee say: "Be perfect,
be complete; live, love, be glad."

Sit thou in the stillness and let thy Lord speak.

. .

WHOSE RIGHT IT IS TO COME

He has come Whose right it is.
He has made His home within me, and will
nevermore depart from me.
I shall walk no more alone, for One walks
with me
Who knows the path of Life, and Whose feet
will never falter nor fail.
My Inner Light shines through the mist of
human beliefs
And frees me from the bondage of fear and
limitation.
I shall walk with You, my Friend, and shall
learn of You the ways of Life and Freedom.
We shall travel together from this day, and
none can part us,

For we are united in the perfect bonds of an
everlasting unity.

I walk with Thee.

. .

I CONTROL MY MENTAL HOUSEHOLD

I conquer my mental household and cast out
all fear and doubt.
Let my Word cast out all sense of fear and
doubt and let my thoughts be lifted unto
Him Who lives Within.
My Word has dissolved all fear within me,
and has cast out all doubt.
My Word shall guard my thought and make
me receive only that which is Good and
Perfect.

I control my life.

. .

MY WORD COMES BACK TO ME

My word comes back to me laden with the
fruits of its own speech.
My word is the Law unto my Life, and the
Law unto everything that I speak.
O Word, go forth and heal and bless all
humanity.
Tell them of their Divine Birthright.
Tell the stranger that he is not alone, but
that One goes with him Who knows
and cares.
Tell the sick that they are healed and the
poor that they cannot want,
Tell the unhappy of the joy of the Soul, and

break the bonds of those who are in
prison.

My word shall come back to me
blessed of God and man.

. .

MY WORD SHALL BEAR FRUIT

The Word of my mouth shall bear fruit.

It shall accomplish and prosper, and shall not
return unto me void.

My Word is the law unto the thing
whereunto it is sent, and it cannot
come back empty-handed.

I send out my Word and it is the law unto
my life.

My Word is the Law unto the thing
whereunto it is spoken, and will
become fulfilled in the right way and
at the right time.

My Word is complete and perfect, and is the
Presence and the Power of the One Mind
that is in and through all.

I speak the Word and know that it will
accomplish.

I wait in perfect confidence for the Word to
fulfill itself in my life.

My Word Is Law.

. .

O MAN, SPEAK FORTH THY WORD

O man, speak forth thy word and be not
afraid.

Did you not know? have you not heard?

His Divinity is planted within thee, and thy
word is one with all power.

The Spirit of the Most High is thy Spirit, and
the Word of God is thy word.

Thy freedom is hid within thee, and thy
inner light shall illumine thy way.

Speak man, and be free! Announce and
proclaim thy works!

Let thy word go forth with power, and thy
Spirit shall conquer all.

Spirit within me, speak.

. .

THE POWER OF THE WORD

The Word is a mighty Power, and that Word
is in me and through me now.

My Word is one with the All Good and cannot fail to accomplish the desired ends.

My Word goes forth with Power unto
everything that I do, say or think.

The Word is my Power by day and by night.

I will speak that Word and trust in the great
Law of Life to fulfill it.

I speak the word in full confidence.

. .

THE WORD OF POWER

My Word is a Word of Power, for I know
that it is the Word of the Great God
within me.

My Word shall accomplish and prosper, and
shall do good unto all who call upon
my name.

My Word is a tower of strength and cannot
be denied.
It is complete and perfect here and now.
My Word is the Word of God.

My word is the word of God.

. .
.

THE UNASSAILABLE TRUTH AND THE
IRRESISTIBLE WORD

The Truth within me is unassailable, and the
Power of the Word is irresistible.
I can even now feel that my Word has gone
forth with Power and Reality, and that it
will accomplish that purpose for which
it was created.
Limitless is its Power and wonderful are
its works.
It can be nothing less than the Almighty
working in and through me.
I will let this Word of the Spirit go forth
from my mouth, and heal and bless
the world.
It shall be as a strong tower unto all who call
upon it.
The Truth is Complete and Perfect, and is
within me now.

My Word is complete and perfect, now.

. .
.

I BEHOLD IN THEE HIS IMAGE

I behold in thee His Image.
In thee, my friend, I see God, and through
you I feel His presence.
I see in the hand that gives, His hand;

And in the voice that speaks of Love, I hear
Him speak.
For His lines have gone out into all places,
And from the highest to the lowest, all, all
partake of His nature.
"For He is all in all, over all and through all."

I perceive that God is in all people.

. .
.

I SEE NO EVIL

I see no evil; I behold only the good.
I have seen the drunkard lying in the gutter,
and the saint kneeling in ecstasy before
the high altar of his faith; but I have found
no difference.
I have perceived that each, in his own
tongue, is seeking to express the
One Life.
I will not separate and divide; I cannot
condemn nor censure, for I know that
there is but One in All.
I know that all came from the One, and all
will return to the One.
I know that all are now in the One, and that
each is seeking to express the One.

I know and love all.

. .
.

I SHALL NEVER DIE

I shall never die, for the Spirit within me is
God and cannot change.
My life is hid within the Universe of
Love and Light, and that Light shall live
forever.

Go, fear of death and change; begone
    from my thought, fear of death and
    uncertainty.
That which is cannot become that which is
    not; and that which I am can never
    change.
The Spirit of Eternity is enthroned within
    me, and the Life of Endless Ages flows
    through my being.
From Eternity to Eternity my Life flows
    along its way of peace and harmony.
Time brings but more glory to crown me
    with its pleasures.

My life is forever.

LOVE TO THE WORLD

My Love goes out to every one in the world;
I do not exclude anything, for I love all
    Nature and everything that is.
My Love warms and lightens everything that
    it touches, and it goes out into all places.
The Love flowing through me is a Power to
    all who come into contact with it, and all
    feel and know that I love.
Love within me is Complete and Perfect.

Love within me is Complete.

MY LIFE IS ONE WITH GOD

My life is in God; it cannot be hurt nor hin-
    dered in its expression.
God lives and expresses through me; His
    work is complete and perfect in me now.

I know His life to be my life, and I know that
    my life is complete and perfect.

My Life is in God.

NO MISUNDERSTANDINGS

There are no misunderstandings.
All is made clear between the ideas of Good.
No false sense of separation can come
    between people, nor disturb the
    realization of the Unity of All Life.
I perceive that I am one with all people, and
    all are One with me.
There is no separation.

There is no separation.

THE DIVINE PLAN FOR ME

The Divine Plan for me is Perfect. I am held
    in the Mind of God as a Complete and
    Perfect Expression of Life and Truth.
No power can hinder nor mar this Inner
    Image of Reality, for It is God-given and
    God-kept.

God gave and God will keep.

THE PERSONALITY OF GOD

The Great Personality of God is my Person-
    ality; the Limitless Knowingness of The
    Spirit is my Knowingness, and the One
    Mind is my mind.

All, All live in One Infinite Being, and each
manifests the One Who is formed
through and in all.

Man is the Personality of God in manifestation and cannot be left without the Inner
Witness of the Spirit.

I now realize that the Infinite Personalness of
the Spirit is my Personality, and I rejoice
to know the Truth about myself.

God is my Personality.

• •
•

THE RADIATION OF LIFE

The life of God within me radiates and
shines forth from me in a constant
stream of Light to all.

The One Life flowing through me is Life to
all who come near.

The One Power operating through me is
flowing into everything that I contact.

Life radiates from me.

• •
•

UNITY

Today I realize that I am One with the All
Good; my God and I are One.

I cannot be hid from His face.

I behold Thee, O Most High, enthroned in
my temple of flesh.

Thy secret place is within me. I feel Thy
presence,

I hear Thy voice, I rejoice in Thy Light.

Today my body responds to the Divine Be-
hest: "Be perfect."

I know of my perfection and wholeness; I am
complete and perfect now.

Let every thought of disease flee from me,
and let Thy Light shine.

O Light Eternal, O Light of my Life, I
come into Thy presence with joy and
thanksgiving.

So be it.

• •
•

WITHIN THEE IS FULLNESS OF LIFE

Within Thee is fullness of Life.

Within Thee is complete Joy and everlasting
Peace.

Within Thee is all.

Thou art in me as I am in Thee, and we are
all in all.

My Life is full and complete within me, and
that Life I give to all men freely;

And from all I receive again that which I
have given, For it is One in All.

I am One with the fullness of All life.

• •
•

I AM COMPLETE IN THEE

Almighty God, Everlasting Good, Eternal
Spirit, Maker of all things and Keeper of
my Life, Thou art All.

Infinite Presence within, in Whom all live;
Joy Supreme, flooding all with gladness, I
adore Thee.

Eternal Peace, undisturbed and quiet, I feel
Thy calm.

O Thou Who dost inhabit Eternity and dost dwell within all Creation, Who Dost live through all things and in all people, hear Thou my prayer. I would enter Thy gates with joy and live at peace in Thy House.

I would find a resting place in Thee, and in Thy presence live.

Make me to do Thy will and from Thy wisdom teach me the ways of Truth.

Compel me to follow Thee and let me not pursue the paths of my own counsel.

O Eternal and Blessed Presence, illumine my mind and command my will that my Soul may be refreshed and that my life may be renewed.

As deep cries unto deep, so my thought cries unto Thee and Thou dost answer.

I am renewed and refreshed; my whole being responds to Thy love, and I am complete in Thee.

All my ways are guarded and guided, and I shall live with Thee eternally.

O Lover of my Soul and Keeper of my Spirit, none can separate us, for we are One.

So shall Thy Wisdom guide me, Thy Presence dwell within me, Thy Love keep me and Thy Life envelop me now and forevermore.

I rest in Thee.

MEDITATIONS, CONCLUDED

The following meditations are

printed just as they were given

in class and group work.

MEDITATIONS

A Treatment for Alcoholism or Other Drug Addiction

There is but one Universal Life, God or Spirit. This Universal Life is a principle of perfect harmony and right action. It is an omnipresent and self-knowing principle, whole and complete within Itself. It is forever calm and peaceful. It is, therefore, a principle of complete satisfaction which knows no unsatisfied desire. The only appetite or desire of Infinite Mind is for the complete manifestation of Its own constructive contemplation.

My life is a part of this Universal Life; Its peace, calm and satisfaction are manifesting in and through me *now* in absolute perfection. My spirit, being one with Universal Spirit, has nothing to desire or long for—save the natural expression of peace, poise and complete satisfaction. That subjective race-thought, which speaks to me as limitation or a desire for abnormal stimulation, has no answering or recognizing voice within me. I turn from all such inharmonious thoughts toward the reality of my oneness with Universal Life (the Father) realizing here in the formless Realm of Reality, the complete satisfaction of knowingness, the sense of calm well-being, wisdom and understanding. Here within the Realm of Reality (the Kingdom of God) I sense the truth of my complete mastery over all *things*. My body is that concept of Universal Mind which is composed of the Creator's perfect ideas (God's body). Within the form, which is commonly termed the human body, is nothing which can speak to me, demanding anything whatsoever. I dwell within the Realm of the Universal and declare that the calm and complete satisfaction of the Self-Knowing God is expressing in and through me, unhindered and unopposed.

I go forth with a complete sense of mastery in the realm of form (my earth experience) unafraid, happy and joyous in my expression of all that is desirable and constructive; knowing that all destructive desires and inharmonious thoughts disappear and dissolve into the nothingness from which they came, having no power to perpetuate themselves, since they are neither person, place nor thing.

I Do Know the Truth and I Am Free

A TREATMENT TO HEAL CONFUSION OR DISCORD

I know there is a Spirit in me which unfolds Itself to me; and I know that this Spirit—or Infinite Wisdom and Divine Love and Perfect Law—enlightens my consciousness and awakens within me, within the personal, the knowledge of Its meaning, the realization of Its Presence, and the power of Its Law. I am conscious that this Universal IT is an ever-present Being to me and to every man, because where the Universe personifies, It becomes personal. Therefore, there is within me an immediate Presence, the Infinite of the finite self, all-knowing, all-wise, and forever perfect. It is this Real Me that I seek to vision in my thought, that I seek to embody in my consciousness. It is that ME that cannot be sick, knows no lack, has no limitation, never suffered want, and cannot experience fear.

The Spirit of Infinite Peace is my spirit now. The Presence of That which is perfect is within me, in every function, in every organ, every attribute and every atom. In each cell, there vibrates the perfect Divine Wholeness.

And this comprehension, this application to myself, this knowingness, reveals me to myself and heals the apparent confusion and discomfort, because WHERE THAT PERFECT CIRCULATION IS *KNOWN*, IT IS ESTABLISHED! Where that perfect efficiency is known, it is demonstrated. THE TRUTH KNOWN IS IMMEDIATELY MANIFEST, and I am now conscious of my own wholeness, my own depth of being, the spiritual me, the Divine Self.

And now I know that my Divine Self is not separated from the self that appears; that the Universal Self is made manifest because the Word is made flesh and dwells in the midst of my physical me. The Word becomes activity and surrounds me with a harmonious activity—with happy action and perfect reaction. The Word becomes Light and guides me into all good. The Word becomes beauty and surrounds me with beauty. The Word, which is Substance, becomes supply and brings to me everything I need, because "The Word was with God and the Word was God," and the Word is God.

This consciousness of Wholeness, this recognition of the Self, obliterates every belief of confusion and discord from my life.

I Accept the Fullness of My Own Divine Well-Being

Within myself is that which is perfect, that which is complete, that which is divine; that which was never born and cannot die; that which lives, which is God—the Eternal Reality. Within myself is peace, poise, power, wholeness and happiness. All the power that there is and all the presence that there is, and all the life that there is, is God—the Living Spirit Almighty—and this Divine and Living Spirit is within me. It is Wholeness. It is never weary. It is never tired. It is Life. It is complete Peace. It is never afraid; It is never confused. It is always poised and peaceful. It is always in a state of perfect equilibrium.

This is the truth about *myself*; there is no other self. Every image of fear is erased from my mind, every sense of confusion leaves my thought. My mind now entertains and reflects the Divine into everything which I do, say and think—into my body, into my affairs. That Divine within me is Wholeness, and my mind reflects this Wholeness into every organ, every function, every action, every reaction of my physical being, renewing it after the Perfect Pattern—the Christ within me. Universal Substance reflects Itself, into my mind, into daily supply, so that everything I need each day is supplied. *Before the need, is the thing, and with the apparent need it is met.* There is Something within me which goes before me and prepares the way wherever I go—making straight the way, making perfect the way, making immediate and instant, and permanent and harmonious, every situation. Consequently, my mind reflects the fullness of that Divine Substance, which heals every sense of lack in my life. Peace, poise, power, perfection, Living Spirit within me, is me, myself.

I Accept the Fullness of My Own Divine Well-Being

The Gifts of God Are Mine Today

It is the Father's good pleasure to give me the Kingdom of Heaven, or harmony and abundance. Today He opens to me the blessings of His infinite and eternal treasure, inviting me to dip deeply into it. As I believe in my heart, so it is done unto me in all things. As I ask, so do I receive, a full measure unto my faith, pressed down and running over.

These and other Divine promises and assurances sing in me; the Still Small Voice reminds me that all that the Father hath is mine. This day I listen deeply to that Still, Small Voice and believe Its promises.

I fear nothing—neither lack, limitation, disappointment nor distress of any kind, for is not the Father always with me? What caused the appearance of lack in my life? Simply my fear, or my belief that the Father could forsake me. I do not believe that now, and it no longer matters to me what is the appearance of today, or what has gone before. Today is new, and I am newly awakened in it, and I believe with dauntless faith that my good, in full measure, comes to me from God today.

I now believe that it is, indeed, the Father's good pleasure to give me of His bounty. I know that He gives as I ask, without question or limit, and I am ready to receive.

The Gifts of God Are Mine Today

ABUNDANCE IS MY INHERITANCE

Abundance is mine. I cannot be deprived of my supply. The trees do not lack for leaves, nor do the flowers fail to bloom. Am I not as important as they? "Consider the lilies of the field, they toil not neither do they spin, yet . . . Solomon in all his glory was not arrayed as one of these."

I look at the lavish wastefulness of Nature and know that God intended me to be as abundantly supplied, with everything that makes for beauty, well-being, progressive living and happiness. I, myself, am to blame when these "fruits of the Spirit" fail to appear.

Since I know the Truth of my being, I will no longer hinder or retard my good from coming to me. I will expect and accept all that I need to make life happy and worth while; for I am a child of the Spirit, and every attribute of It—every attribute of Good—is my inheritance.

Nothing but lack of faith can keep my good from me, for I am one with the Universal Essence of Life, or Spirit, and Its Substance will manifest in my experience *as I believe*. No longer will I go for my good, carrying only a dipper to be filled. This day, as I turn to the Father within, I bring "all the empty vessels" knowing they will be filled, and my abundance will become manifest.

Abundance Is My Inheritance

MY VIBRATION ATTRACTS FRIENDS TO ME

I am never alone, never lonely, for I have as companions and friends those people who are drawn to me by the ever-active and immutable Law of Attraction. I *desire* to be loved, therefore, I allow myself to love greatly, to feel warmly inclined toward people; to be interested in them and helpful on their behalf. I give as I wish to receive. It is not enough that I *profess* to love people. I must really love people, more dearly than I have ever loved before, because all men are my brothers.

I do not outline who shall be my friends and companions, for there is no desire to coerce, compel or suggest to anyone. The Law of Attraction brings into contact and relationship with me all those people in whose company I find the greatest profit and enjoyment and to whom I may give the most.

I am happy and radiant, for I enjoy at all times perfect companionship. I trust implicitly the Law of Attraction to bring into my environment and atmosphere friends and loved ones, and establish for me a community of interest and helpfulness. As I love and co-operate with my fellowman, so does he love me and give his co-operation to me. I am happy in all of my companionships and relationships, because they are worked out perfectly by the Law, and the Law is motivated to work for me BY MY LOVE FOR PEOPLE.

My Loving Thought of Others Attracts Friends to Me

Peace Is the Power at the Heart of God

My peace is found at the heart of God. The heart of God, for me, is found at the very center of my being. It does not matter how closely the confusion of the outer world presses against me, I am not even disturbed by the confusion in my immediate environment. I know that the only way to counteract confusion is to bring peace into play. "Peace I leave with you, my peace I give unto you; not as the world giveth, give I unto you." These words of assurance stay with me, and I hear them re-echoing in the depths of my being.

I surrender all of my fears—those nameless fears which have beset me for such a long time, dulling my pleasure and clouding with misery and apprehension all of my days. I am now through with fear. What, indeed, is there for a divine and immortal being to fear. Certainly *not people*, for as I am a divine and immortal being, so is every man, and every man is my brother. I recognize the one Life Principle, working in and through and inspiring the motives of everyone I contact.

I do not fear sickness, disease or death, because the eternal and perfect Life animates my body and goes always about Its perfect work, healing and renewing that body. I am not afraid of want or lack, for the one infinite Essence supplies me with everything I need all of the time. There is nothing for me to fear, for I am an inseparable part of God. I live in Him; He lives in me; and I draw upon His perfect peace.

My Peace Is Found at the Heart of God

GOD RESTORES ME TO PERFECT HEALTH

The Spirit within me is God, that Spirit is perfect. That Spirit is divine, whole, happy, complete. Spirit of Infinite Peace is within me, and that Peace—poised in perfect life, complete in perfect happiness—that Spirit within me is God and is Whole. That Wholeness is perfect now.

God is an immediate Presence and an immediate Experience in my mind and soul, and I am conscious of this Perfect Presence, this Divine Wisdom, this Eternal Wholeness. Now I recognize that the Principle of Life is in me and around me and operates through me; that It has no want, has no fear, has no doubt, has no limitation. There is that within me which guides me into opulence, into success, into harmony and love and beauty and friendship, and It does this in peace, in joy and in certainty. I *let* that Divine within me—using whatever method It may— restore me to perfect health, perfect happiness and harmony and bring into my experience everything that is good, that is perfect, that is true and successful.

I am not only *one* with this Spirit, *but this Spirit is all that I am*. It is my whole being, and this Divine Wisdom is in my thought, causing me to act and move intelligently, to make right choices and to follow right pursuits. There are no problems in this Divine Wisdom. Therefore, the road is made straight before me; every obstacle is removed and I am led—irresistibly led— to the Absolute, certain goal of Good, of accomplishment, of success.

God Restores Me to Perfect Health

I ALLOW MYSELF TO DIP DEEPLY INTO MY DIVINE NATURE

This meditation is built from the idea that each one of us has within himself a deeper nature, and, of course, this deeper nature, being an eternal unity with God, or with the Living Spirit, is more than man; it is where the being of man, or the nature of man, merges into the Being of God. So, as we dip deeply into our Divine Natures, let us realize that entering the Secret Presence of this Tabernacle of God, we will, like the Pilgrims of old, have to shed that which does not belong to the Kingdom of Good. We have to deliberately drop that which would hurt. We cannot enter this Gate of Good with a sword in our hands.

So we let go of everything and turn to that Divine Depth within our own nature, wherein the Spirit of God—the Spirit of Love and the Spirit of Peace—dwells with calm serenity. We withdraw into that place within us which has never been hurt, nor has ever been sick, has always and forever lived in divine and eternal peace . . . the Kingdom of God, which is Good. And this Inner Kingdom within is all-peace, all-power and all-perfection. We drop all hate, all fear, all animosity, all resentment. We cast out of our consciousness every doubt and every sense of uncertainty. We know that we are entering into that atmosphere of Wholeness, of happiness and completion where there is no fear, no doubt, no uncertainty, no lack, no want. Here is wholeness, perfection, peace, power, beauty, love, supply and life. We know that the abundance of this life is showered upon us; that we are guided and guarded into right action, into right decision; daily, hourly, minutely, the Principle of Intelligence directs us, the Presence of Love warms us, the Peace of God covers us. And we are led into the pathway of this peace, into the knowledge of this perfection.

We are conscious of the Indwelling God, and we are conscious that the Indwelling God is filling (instantly renewing) our bodies, absolutely eliminating from us whatever there is that does not belong; co-ordinating every function, every organ, every action and reaction (the circulation, the assimilation, the elimination), making it perfect. The Life Principle of every part of our being is perfect and harmonious and now functions perfectly in us. The whole order of discord is changed into the natural order of harmony and wholeness, and we *let* that Divine Power be *exactly what It is* in us. We are no longer afraid, for love casts out fear. Our faith destroys all fear. We awake from the dream of fear to the vision of Reality, where there is no shadow of which to be afraid. We awake from the dream of lack and want and unhappiness to the knowledge of harmony, of abundance and of peace.

I Allow Myself to Dip Deeply into My Divine Nature

PERFECT INTELLIGENCE DIRECTS MY THOUGHT

We now let go of everything and enter into a state of peace. We know the Spirit within us is God, the Living Spirit Almighty . . . that God Who is Infinite, Perfect and Complete, never needed anything, never had any trouble, *never could* destroy; the God Who never operated against Himself, Who never condemned Himself—the Spirit that fashions each of us from His own perfect Being. "All in all, we know Thee, God, omnipresent, full and free; one with every pathway trod, our immortal destiny."

That Infinite Wholeness is perfect peace within us. That Infinite Intelligence is working through us and our affairs; our thought is inspired, guided, governed and directed by Divine Wisdom. That Infinite Wholeness is the circulation of ideas, of intelligence, wisdom, truth and life. It is the elimination of every conception of confusion. It is the assimilation of that which is whole, happy, perfect. The Divine Intelligence is the government of our affairs. Each has within himself this guide to truth, to reason, to beauty, to right action, to certainty and to peace.

Perfect Intelligence Directs My Thought

I Am Not Bound by Any Mistake

Let us now let go of everything and enter into the consciousness of that which we believe. The Spirit within each one of us is God, and It is perfect, It is love, reason, life, truth and beauty. It is limitless and perfect and complete and whole. It knows no lack and no limitation.

There is nothing we have done, said or thought which rises up against us, which has power over us or which limits us; there is no memory of fear, no condemnation for previous mistakes. With the desire to free ourselves from the further indulgence in the mistake, the effect of the previous mistake is wiped out, just as light dissipates the darkness. The Universe holds nothing against us; It can hold nothing against us, because It can know nothing unlike Itself. Therefore, It only knows us as Perfection. There has never been an occurrence for which we have to suffer! Consequently, every apparent shortcoming—which could be traced to some mental or spiritual infringement of the Law—is not only removed *but the effect is healed!*

That means there is no history to our case. All of its history is this minute wiped out in the knowledge that today the perfect Law—the Law of Freedom—is the only Law there is in our experience. We enter into that freedom with joy, free from every sense of sadness and burden. We enter into it with laughter, with lightness. It is something which lifts us above the heaviness of morbidity and lack and limitation, into that rarer atmosphere where our opinions do not collide, and we enter into it with peace, free from fear.

We know that Infinite Wholeness is in us and through us and around us now, and we are conscious that we are renewed this moment, instantly and perfectly, after the image of Perfection. We are today guided into right action in every exercise of our affairs. Since there is no great and no small to the Infinite, all that seems of little consequence in our lives has the Divine Guidance just as perfectly and completely as that which we think of as being tremendously important. We are guided into the knowledge of happiness, of certainty, of wholeness and of freedom; and we know that there is that subtle Essence of the Spirit, which emanates from us at all times, healing everything It contacts.

I Am Not Bound by Any Mistake

My Ideal Merges into the Real

We now let go of everything and enter into the contemplation of peace and good and truth and beauty. We are conscious that God is All there is, there is nothing else. We are certain that the Spirit of Reality is our spirit, flows into our spirit and through our spirit. And we are conscious that Love does guide and direct, lead, maintain and sustain. We know that each one of us is a center of this Divine Life, in this Perfect Peace, this Complete Happiness, and this Absolute Wholeness; and we know that this Perfection—which is the center of our very being—is projected into every atom of our being.

We know that the Law of this Being is perfect and there is no obstruction to Its operation. We know that the Principle within us guides us, not only into the way of Truth, but in the way and the performance of that knowledge. WHATEVER IS FOR OUR BENEFIT IS ALREADY PROVIDED. It is all one thing. It is all One Presence, operating through One fundamental Law, therefore, everything necessary to our well-being (whether we think of it as spiritual, mental or physical), everything necessary to remove any belief in obstruction and the inflow and out-push of that Spirit, is brought into our experience. All good, all substance, all supply, all activity, all opportunity for self-expression is ours now!

My Ideal Merges into the Real

I Represent the Principle of Perfection

In each human being, the Whole is represented, and the entire knowledge of wisdom, of health, and the perfection of every act, manifests—is represented—and it is through this Inner Divine Voice, the Divine Nature within us, that we are able to perceive and trust, and come into conscious contact with, this Divine Principle. In the sight of this Within, we are perfect. We must try to see ourselves as God sees us, free and filled with vitality and sufficiency for every occasion.

It is not enough to confess that God is the only Power there is. It is only when this consciousness of power is hooked to the dynamo of the mind that there is generated, through the imagination, an embodiment of that which is able to loose it in any direction it sees fit. It is not enough merely to say that there is One Mind and that Mind is God. To this we must add: "That Mind is my mind now." That completes the thought, makes possible a loosing of the Divine Intelligence through our own imagination.

Let us not forget that, in treatment, we must sense the embodiment of that which we wish to experience. The statements which are made in the treatment are for the purpose of delivering to the imagination, in a certain form, THAT WHICH WAS TRUE BEFORE WE MADE THE STATEMENTS. The whole problem is not one of *creation*, but one of *direction*, and there is no direction unless there is first an embodiment. Let us try this in our meditation. We know that we reflect the Divine Perfection and that there is an intuition within us which guides us. We know that all the power there is and all the presence there is, is this perfect Spirit, this Divine Reality, which is around us and through us and in us. Now, each turning directly to his own thought, says:

699

"The Spirit within me, which is God, the Living Spirit Almighty, is Perfection. It is Wholeness; It is Peace. It is Divine Guidance, Perfect Peace, Complete Wholeness, Absolute Perfection, and right now, this moment, this Spirit governs every act of my life. It surrounds me with Light, in which there is no darkness, no gloom, no heaviness and no fear. In this Light, I live and move and have my being. And this Light dispels all darkness and casts out all fear.

"This Divine Wisdom within me guides every act, directs everything in my life, toward happiness, toward peace, toward power; and being the Spirit of Love, It surrounds me with beauty, with friendship and with joy. Being the Giver of Life, every day I receive that which is perfect, abundant, happy, joyful and free. Being that Divine Thing which individualizes in me, It is entirely individual, personal and unique. I am the expression of my own complete self, and there is no barrier or bar to that self-expression. Being the Spirit of Substance, that Spirit within me is the Father of Supply, and It brings to me everything necessary to my unfoldment, and keeps me in the wisdom through which It governs me, now and forever."

I Represent the Principle of Perfection

I Take the Christ Way to Fulfillment

When Jesus said, "No man cometh unto the Father but by me," of course, he meant the I AM. This I AM, then, means the inner Reality of every man's nature, and when we stop to figure it out, how can we come unto God, the Living Spirit, except through the avenues of our own consciousness, which is the only approach to God we could possibly have? It is another way of saying that the only way we shall ever approach Reality is by uncovering the Divinity already latent within our own consciousness, in our own soul, in the center of our own being.

Every man is Divine and the *Christ Way* is the way of the unfoldment of his Divinity through his humanity; the uncovering of his spiritual individuality and the use that his personal man, or his personality, makes of it. Meditation is for the purpose of consciously recognizing man's Divinity and uncovering it. In order to come into the Christ Way, into the consciousness of our own Divinity, we lay aside every fear or doubt or worry, and we enter into the silent, peaceful contemplation that the Spirit of the Living God is within us—all the Power there is, all the Presence there is, and all the Life there is, is right here. Each one turns to himself, knowing that:

"The Spirit within me is God, that Spirit is perfect, and because that Spirit is perfect, my knowledge of that Spirit destroys every doubt, every fear, casts out all uncertainty and all unbelief, and fills me with a knowledge of my own perfection. There is that within me which is perfect, Divine, happy and whole and harmonious. There is that within me that has never been afraid, never been limited, and it is this Christ Nature within me that I now recognize and speak into manifestation through my being; that the Spirit within me, which is perfect, shall remove every consciousness of disease, shall stimulate activity and recognize perfect circulation of these Divine ideas, and establish within me, not only the knowledge of that Divine Perfection which I really am, but shall establish in my physical being a manifestation of that knowledge of Reality, or the realization of that Presence, and whatever there might be within me, which does not belong, is now eliminated, cast out and destroyed.

"Divine Guidance IS, and that Perfect Intelligence is now governing the activity of my life into the fulfillment of joy, into the fulfillment of love, of unity, of happiness and success, now and at all times."

I Take the Christ Way to Fulfillment

The Eternal Cycles of Life in Motion Fulfill My Faith

This is another way of saying that something happens when a man believes. Faith is operated upon by some principle which is a government of Law and Order, and which has within Itself the power to execute Itself. Prayer is not to ask God to be God. There is a Supreme Intelligence in the Universe, we cannot tell It anything; what little we know, we have drawn from It. There is an Absolute Spirit around us, It does not need our existence. It has already surrendered Itself to us but we have not yet surrendered ourselves to It. That is what prayer—or treatment—is for. We do not pray the Principle of Peace to desist from confusion, but we seek that Peace that it shall enter into our confused souls. Therefore, prayer or meditation is for the purpose of becoming receptive to the Divine Influx, which already owns everything, knows everything, governs all things, and creates what we need—if we but permit it to—in Its own Nature, which is goodness, truth and beauty. Each turns to the within in something after this fashion:

We let go of everything, drop every fear from our minds, drop all confusion from our thought, and enter into the inner secret communion with that great Reality, which is our Universal Self—God—in Whom we live and move and have our being. We are conscious that this Divine Presence overshadows and indwells. It is both *without* this physical, mental being and *within* this physical, mental being. Therefore, It is the spiritual Reality of this being, the I AM, which is Universal, Eternal, and Perfect.

Now this Spirit is our Spirit. It is our life from which we now draw full, complete and perfect being. This Divine Intelligence does govern us intelligently; It does direct us consciously, accurately, unerringly. We surrender to It every fear, every sense of uncertainty of the future, every thought of any morbidity of the past. We surrender all confusion and doubt, and we know that this Divine Influx removes every mental obstruction to peace; It removes every sense of condemnation and judgment, and we enter into the fulfillment of Its perfection now. We believe if there is any part of our physical being which needs healing, It heals it; that that Power within us and around us which creates, can recreate, can make whole now. We believe if there is any conflict in our mental being, it can be removed, because the Spirit is higher than the mind and more than the body, and we are dealing with that Spirit which, animating the mind with Divine Intelligence, produces an influx of spiritual life in the body, healing, without effort, both mind and body. We relinquish, we let go, those things which bother us mentally or hurt us physically. We know that the Divine Presence is the Eternal Healer, because It is the everlasting Giver of life. And we know the Intelligence which created the Universe and projected it in form and governs it with perfect Law—that Divine Being directs our movements intelligently, coherently, constructively, certainly, bringing to each that which he calls success and prosperity, happiness, fulfillment of life, action. And we know that that Divine Being, governing everything out of Its own Nature, works without effort—Birthless and Deathless and Tireless, It moves through us to perfect ends, now.

The Eternal Cycles of Life in Motion Fulfill My Faith

SPIRIT
ABSOLUTE
FIRST CAUSE——GOD
THE GREAT I AM
CONSCIOUS MIND
PURPOSEFULNESS
SELF-PROPELLING

ONLY——ALL
KNOWING NO OTHER
FATHER-MOTHER GOD
UNCONDITIONED ONE
UNITY——MACROCOSM
THE GREAT HOUSE
MASCULINE
ACTIVE

SELF-EXISTENCE
VOLITION——LIFE——TRUTH
POWER——CHOICE——WILL
FREE SPIRIT
PEACE——POISE
THE WORD
PERFECT LOGOS

PERSONALNESS
CONSCIOUS IDEA
CHANGELESS
OMNISCIENCE
OMNIPOTENCE
OMNIPRESENCE
REASON DEDUCTIVE ONLY

SOUL
CREATIVE MEDIUM
SUBJECTIVE——UNCHOOSING
SUBCONSCIOUS MIND
IMMATERIAL
ILLUSION OF MIND
IMPERSONAL
FEMININE
NEUTRAL
PLASTIC
MAYA

BLIND FORCE——LAW
NOT KNOWING——ONLY DOING
MEDIUM OF THOUGHT,
POWER AND ACTION
CINEMA PICTURES
REASON——DEDUCTIVE ONLY
PASSIVE AND RECEPTIVE

KARMIC LAW
KNOWN AS
THE SERVANT OF THE
ETERNAL SPIRIT
THROUGHOUT
THE AGES

REFLECTION
ILLUSION OF MATTER
MULTIPLICITY——MANY

BODY
EFFECT
FORM
OBJECTIVE
CONDITIONS
RESULTS
TIME
SPACE
THINGS

RELATIVE MIRROR
EMANATION

METAPHYSICAL CHART NO. I.

This chart, which is called the Universal Chart, shows the Universe as a Trinity of Being. The upper section designates those attributes of Spirit which are Self-Conscious. The middle section shows the subconscious aspect of Law; and the lower section shows the effect of Spirit working through the medium of Universal Mind. Read and carefully study the full explanation and meaning of the words used in this chart as found in the glossary.

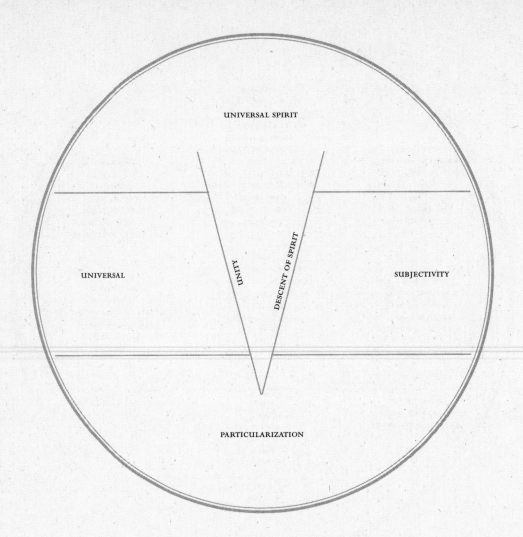

METAPHYSICAL CHART NO. II-A.

This chart shows, first, the Universal Spirit; then the Universal Soul or Subjectivity, which is the medium of all thought, power and action; then the particularization or manifestation of Spirit.

The point drawn down through the center symbolizes the descent of Spirit into matter, or form. It is necessary that Spirit be manifested in order to express Itself. The word "Unity" on the descending line shows that all come from the One. Man reënacts the whole Universal Life, and his nature is identical with Spirit. What is true of the Whole is true of any one of Its undivided parts. Man comes to a point of individualization in the Whole and is subject to the Law of the Whole.

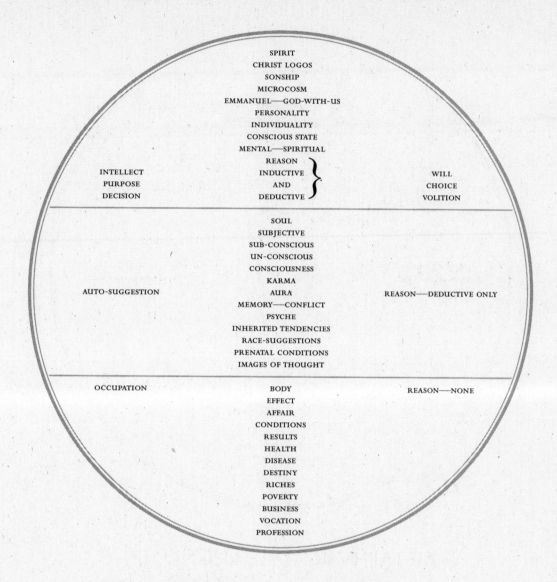

METAPHYSICAL CHART NO. II-B.

This chart shows how man reënacts the Whole and is subject to the law of his own being. If the meaning of this chart is carefully studied it will be made plain that man thinks consciously and that his conscious thought becomes the law of his life. The upper section stands for the Self-Conscious man; the middle section stands for the subconscious man; and the lower section stands for the man as he appears in the flesh and in the conditions of his life.

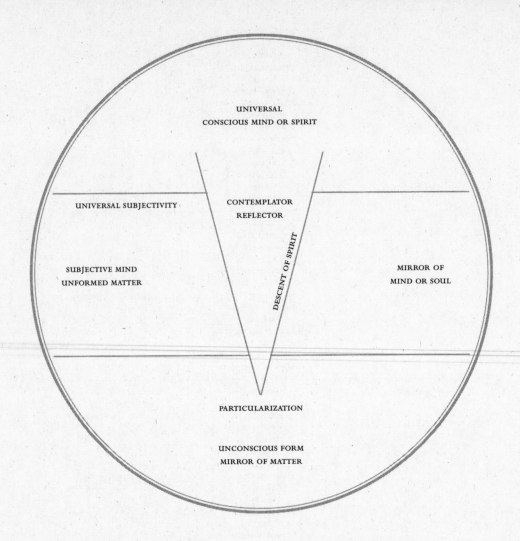

METAPHYSICAL CHART NO. III.

The upper section of this chart shows how the conscious mind, or spirit of man, reflects or contemplates itself, through the medium of soul or subjectivity, into form or matter. The middle section represents the World-Soul or Subjectivity; the Mirror of Mind and unformed matter; the Servant of the Spirit; the lower section shows the result of self-contemplation as it takes form in the world of matter. Read and carefully study the metaphysical meanings of the words used in the glossary.

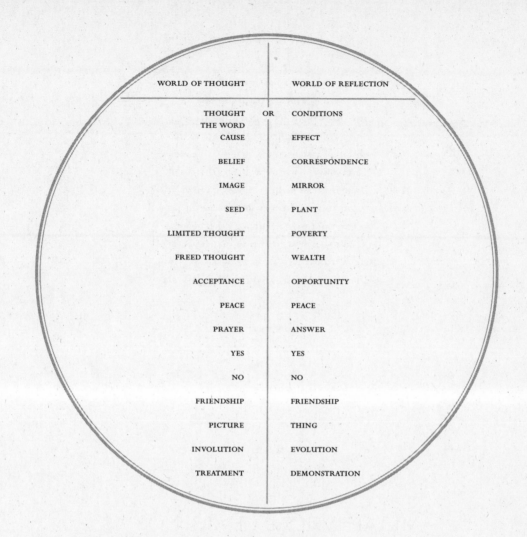

WORLD OF THOUGHT		WORLD OF REFLECTION
THOUGHT	OR	CONDITIONS
THE WORD		
CAUSE		EFFECT
BELIEF		CORRESPONDENCE
IMAGE		MIRROR
SEED		PLANT
LIMITED THOUGHT		POVERTY
FREED THOUGHT		WEALTH
ACCEPTANCE		OPPORTUNITY
PEACE		PEACE
PRAYER		ANSWER
YES		YES
NO		NO
FRIENDSHIP		FRIENDSHIP
PICTURE		THING
INVOLUTION		EVOLUTION
TREATMENT		DEMONSTRATION

METAPHYSICAL CHART NO. IV.

HOW IDEAS MANIFEST AS THINGS

This chart is divided into two sides, representing the world of thought and the world of reflections. It represents the law of cause and effect. The world of thought is the world of ideas, while the world of reflections means the results of thought. The world of reflections is entirely a world of effects and is, of itself, unconscious and unknowing. Consider everything on the left side of this chart to be thoughts or ideas; and consider everything on the right side to be the automatic results of the law as it works out into effects. By using this chart in conjunction with the explanations already given, it will be plain just how the law of cause and effect works from the idea to the thing.

THE TRIUNE UNITY

THE INDIVISIBLE WHOLE——

WITHIN WHICH IS ALL OF ITS PARTS

THE ABSOLUTE WITHIN WHICH IS THE RELATIVE

THE UNCREATED WITHIN WHICH IS THE CREATED

THE CHANGELESS WITHIN WHICH IS ALL CHANGE

THE FORMLESS WITHIN WHICH IS ALL FORM

THE LIMITLESS WITHIN WHICH IS ALL SPACE

THE TIMELESS WITHIN WHICH IS ALL TIME

THE UNIVERSAL WITHIN WHICH IS THE INDIVIDUAL

THE ONE PERSON WITHIN WHOM ARE ALL PEOPLE

SOURCE AND CENTER OF ALL LIFE POWER AND ACTION

TRUTH, LOVE, MIND, SPIRIT, THE EVER, AND THE ALL

<u>GOD</u>

Our father
which art
in
Heaven

THE
SON

PERSONALITY....INDIVIDUALITY

<u>M A N</u>

METAPHYSICAL CHART NO. V.

This is the Mystic's chart and shows how the Universal becomes the Particularization of Itself through man. Man comes to a point in the Universal, or God, and is the Idea of God as man. The Father is represented as the Whole just back of, or above, or within, man. This is the Indwelling God to Whom we pray and with Whom we talk. The mystic has the ability to consciously talk to God and to consciously receive a direct answer from the Spirit. In this chart it is shown that the Absolute contains the relative, within Itself, but is not limited by the relative. We must remember that the relative does not limit, but expresses, the Absolute. All change takes place within the Changeless. All form subsists within the Formless. All conditions obtain within that which is Limitless; and Creation is eternally going on within that which is Uncreated. All are activities of the One Mind and Spirit of God. All people come to a point of individuality within that which is Universal.

SPIRIT OR CONSCIOUS MIND

ONE AND ONLY KNOWING

POWER IN GOD OR MAN

THE PSYCHIC SEA——SUBJECTIVE

FALSE OR TRUE——MIRROR OF MIND

MEDIUM OF ALL PSYCHIC PHENOMENA

THOUGHT FORMS OR MENTAL PICTURES

OBJECTIVE

ILLUSION OF MATTER

FALSE OR TRUE

MIRROR OF MATTER

METAPHYSICAL CHART NO. VI.

This is the psychic's chart and should be carefully considered, as it shows that the Spirit, or Conscious Mind, operates through a mental field, or law, which is a world of reflections. Thought is first reflected into Mind and then into matter. Read again the meaning of the conscious and the subconscious aspects of being. The world of Subjectivity is the Psychic Sea and the Medium of all subjective action. From the standpoint of man's thoughts it may be false or true, according to the way in which he thinks. It is the picture gallery of the soul, both from the universal and the individual sense. The illusion of matter means that the false mental pictures will produce a false form in the world of objectivity. Mind is not an illusion, but might contain false pictures which would be illusions; matter is not an illusion but may take on false conditions. We must learn to separate the false from the true.

Glossary

It is not claimed that the definitions in this glossary will, in every case, keep faith with regular dictionary definitions; but they do give the metaphysical meaning of the words as they are used in this textbook.

A glossary, in its wider sense, may be not merely a partial dictionary, but a running commentary, explaining more fully the words used by the author. In this case, it is the belief (and the deliberate intent) of the writer that a thorough study of this glossary, *in conjunction with the four chapters of the "Introduction" to this book*, will provide a workable knowledge of the Science of Mind, as well as stimulate a desire for the more complete knowledge embodied in the text of the book.

ABSOLUTE—The Unconditioned—that which nothing can limit; that which forever transcends any conceivable limitation or determination. Unconditioned perfection. Self-Existent, Self-Sufficient. Often used as a synonym for God. Truth is absolute and remains unaffected by the opinions, desires or beliefs of men.

ACCUMULATED CONSCIOUSNESS—The sum-total of all that one has ever said, thought, done or seen, consciously or unconsciously.

ACTIVE PRINCIPLE OF LIFE—The Self-Conscious Spirit. The Self-Existent Intelligence in the Universe which reveals Itself in all Its creation.

AFFIRMATION—To affirm anything is to state that it is so, and to maintain this as being true in the face of all evidence to the contrary. Human thought can only affirm, for even at the moment of denial, it is affirming the presence of that which it denies! Repeating an affirmation is leading the mind to that state of consciousness where it accepts that which it wishes to believe.

ALL-ONLY OR ALL GOOD—This refers to God or Spirit: All the Substance, Life, Power, Love, Beauty, Intelligence in the Universe, both manifest and unmanifest.

ALPHA—That which is first. The beginning.

ANDROGYNOUS—Having the characteristics of both sexes. In connection with Deity, it is expressed as "Father-Mother God." Coleridge conveyed the idea as "The truth is, a great mind must be androgynous."

ANTICHRIST—A wrong use of the Law. The spirit of Antichrist is the spirit of one who, understanding the Law, uses It for destructive purposes.

APPARITION—Thought forms which sometimes are seen by people while experiencing great mental stress. An unexpected or spectral appearance. Sometimes used synonymously with the word "ghost."

APPEARANCE—The word "appearance" is used in this textbook to distinguish *that which seems to be,* from that which *actually is.* Negative thinking may produce conditions which *appear* to be true, but these results have no power, no reality, except as given power BY OUR BELIEVING THAT THE APPEARANCE IS THE ACTUALITY. Disease, discord, and limitation have no spiritual prototypes. They are false manifestations which have objectified in the body or in the affairs of human life.

ASSURANCE—In reality, *assurance* is having "the mind which was in Christ Jesus." It is consciousness of our Oneness with All Good.

ATMOSPHERE (MENTAL)—An influence, or condition, surrounding a place, person or thing. A person whose atmosphere is one of love and cheerfulness will always attract friends. In the same way, places are permeated with the thoughts of the people who inhabit them, and this mental atmosphere of a place or thing may easily be felt by one contacting it.

ATONEMENT—The theological idea back of the word "atonement" is that of expiation and amends. The sense in which we use it is that of complete harmony: at-one-ment.

ATTRIBUTE (OF GOD)—We frequently speak of "the attributes of God." By this, we mean the being, essence, nature of; that which is inherent in. "That which the mind perceives as constituting the essence of substance."

AURA—The mental atmosphere surrounding a person.

AUTOMATIC INDIVIDUALITY—There is no such thing. The world should cease asking, "Why did God not *make* man good?" If there had been a way by which the Divine Creative Process could have compelled man to appear on the scene of experience, with all of his freedom, then this would have been done. The only way God can evolve an individual, spontaneous and free, is to let it alone and allow it to awaken to itself. See definition of *individuality.* A mechanical or automatic individuality is a contradiction of terms, an impossibility.

AUTOSUGGESTION—Suggestion may come from many sources, but autosuggestion means when one makes suggestions to himself, either consciously or unconsciously. Autosuggestion is frequently the result of an expectant belief.

BEING—That which exists actually or potentially. Generally used as conscious existence. When capitalized—Being, it refers to the Divine Being, God. There is but one Source of being—God—and we are connected with It at all times.

BELIEF—Conviction or feeling of the truth of a proposition or condition. *Belief* may go no farther than intellectual assent while faith embodies a trust and confidence. "Belief admits of all degrees, from the slightest suspicion to the fullest assurance."

BIBLE—The sacred book, or books, of any race or people. When we merely refer to "the Bible," the reference is to our Christian Bible. Any other Bible is identified by name . . . as the "Koran," the Mohammedan Bible, etc.

BLESSING—Constructive thought directed toward anyone or any condition. You *bless* a man when you recognize the divinity in him. You *bless* a man's business when you think correctly about that business.

BODY—The outward form. The entire manifestation of Spirit, both visible and invisible, is the Body of God. Within this One Body of God is included all lesser bodies. This One Body, coupled with the Intelligence running through It, is called the Son, or the Second Person of the Trinity. This, of course, includes man, both visible and invisible. It also includes every gradation of consciousness, from the simple to the complex, from a cell to an archangel. It is the entire manifestation of Spirit on any and all planes. Body is the definite outline of flesh, containing all of the ideas which go to make the complete physical instrument.

BODY OF GOD—See explanation above. The manifest creation in its entirety.

CAUSE . . . CAUSATION . . . FIRST CAUSE—Cause is that which occasions or produces an effect. The reason, motive or occasion. Causation, too, is the act or agency by which an effect is produced. FIRST CAUSE always means that from which everything comes. The Cause of all that is made manifest on any plane. That Which comes first. The first in any creative series. The Life back of things.

CENTER OF GOD-CONSCIOUSNESS—Man's self-knowing mind is his perception of Reality. IT IS HIS UNITY WITH THE WHOLE, OR GOD, ON THE CONSCIOUS SIDE OF LIFE, and is an absolute guarantee that he is a Center of God-Consciousness in the vast Whole. He is God, expressing through him, as himself.

CHANGELESS, THE—This refers to the One that cannot change by reason of the fact that being All, there is nothing for It to change into but Itself. The One Cause back of all never changes, but It constantly creates forms; and so we perceive a changing form within that which is Changeless.

CHANNEL—A channel is that through which anything passes. We speak of man being a "channel for good." We mean that good passes through him. The Divine Urge of Life must be expressed; and as It pushes out into expression through man's life, man becomes the channel for the outflow of Divine Wisdom: a channel for all that God is.

CHRIST, THE— The Word of God manifest in and through man. In a liberal sense, the Christ means the Entire Manifestation of God and is, therefore, the Second Person of the Trinity. Christ is Universal Idea, and each one "puts on the Christ" to the degree that he surrenders a limited sense of Life to the Divine Realization of wholeness and unity with Good, Spirit, God.

CHRIST WITHIN—Christ in man means the idea of Sonship, the Perfect Man as He must be held in the Mind of God. Christ within each and all.

CLAIRAUDIENCE—The ability to perceive sounds without the ear. Generally associated with the idea of spiritualism, though it is a faculty, or ability, that may be exercised in a perfectly normal state. Extra sensory perception.

CLAIRVOYANCE—The ability to see mentally. Seeing without the physical eyes. The ability to perceive things out of the range of ordinary eye-sight. Extra sensory perception.

COALESCE—To unite in one body or product. Growing together. Mingling.

COETERNAL—Always existing. Uncreated. Without beginning and without end. Law, Spirit, Substance are coeternal.

COEXISTENT—That which exists with. Contemporary existence.

COMMUNION—Unity . . . agreement. Interchange of thoughts and purposes . . . concord, participation. We turn to the Father within, knowing He will guide us. This is communion. Mental or spiritual contact.

COMPENSATION—Recompense, reward, remuneration, balance. The law of balance in the mental world, cause and effect. As you sow you reap.

COMPLEX—An involved or twisted way of thinking. The root word of *complex* means to entwine. So in mental work when we speak of a complex we refer to an attitude of mind, the result of two or more entangled states of consciousness; usually on the emotional side of life, always a mental state, subjectified.

CONCEIVE—To take into one's mind. Conceive suggests the idea of grasping something, as a thought. To apprehend by reason or imagination.

CONCENTRATION—Concentration is bringing to a focus. We weed out the undesirable thoughts that the remaining thoughts may have more power. Someone has compared it to the manner of using electricity. A huge stream flowing slowly is measured as voltage in electricity, but when this same stream, through an apparatus termed the *coil*, is reduced to fine intensity, it is called amperage. Concentration does for the mind what the coil does for the electricity. A particular thought is strengthened in power and intensity by the removal of unrelated thoughts, which would otherwise dissipate the energy.

CONCEPT . . . CONCEPTION—The term "conception" is used to indicate the act of conceiving. Throughout this textbook the word "concept" is used as idea. The embodiment of an idea. An inner mental likeness of some desired good.

CONCRETE CAUSE—Definite idea.

CONDITION—That which follows cause; the effect of law.

CONFLICT—In the study of psycho-analysis, which means the analysis of the soul, we learn that the subjective side of thought (being the seat of memory) often retains thoughts and suppressed emotions which more or less tear or bind. This is what is meant by inner conflict. A struggle, a mental opposition, generally unconscious or subconscious.

CONSCIOUS IDEA—No two ideas are alike. The Creative Mind of the Universe, being Infinite, conceives a limitless number of things and each thing, therefore, is separate and distinct in the great Whole. Just as the atoms of science are cemented by ether, so each idea of Divine Mind is united in One Spirit. No two things are alike; no two roses are alike; no two people are alike. All come from One Life; all are in One Life and live by It; but each forever maintains its identity in the Perfect Whole.

CONSCIOUS MIND—The Self-knowing Mind in God or in man. The Intelligence in the Universe which reveals Itself in all Its creation. It is impossible for us to conceive of Universal Consciousness, but we glimpse it through our use of "the One Mind common to all individual men."

CONSCIOUSNESS—Mental awareness. Consciousness is both objective and subjective. Objective consciousness is a state of conscious awareness, equipped with will, decision, and discrimination. Its reasoning is both inductive and deductive, therefore it has self-choice. The subjective consciousness is entirely a reaction to this objective volition. It is creative but not discriminative. It is, of course, conscious, but it is not self-conscious. It is conscious in the same sense that the soil is conscious of the seed. It knows how to produce a plant, but it is not conscious that it is producing it. It has no reflective, deductive, or discriminating factors. It is compelled by its very nature to accept and create. When we speak of mind in its self-conscious state we mean Spirit, whether we think of it in God or man. When we speak of consciousness in a subjective state, we refer to the mental medium, the Universal Subjectivity, which is also the subjectivity of man. In referring to the subjective state, the Bible uses the word "soul," the psychoanalyst uses the term "the unconscious," the psychologist, "subjective" or "subjective consciousness." All have the same meaning.

CONTAGION . . . CONTAGIOUS—Communication of any thought or influence, as the *contagion of enthusiasm*. Exciting similar emotion or conduct in others. The *contagion of fear*.

CONTEMPLATE—To know within the self. To design, propose, meditate. In its deeper meaning, to become one with. Emerson said that the mind which contemplates God, becomes God.

CONTROLLING CONDITIONS—Man's affairs are controlled by thought working through the avenue of the One Mind. Conditions are the result of causes . . . another term for effect. Conditions are always effects. Conditions being always the externalization of thought, it follows that they can be controlled by changing the thought—by thinking constructively.

CONVICTION—The act of convincing or compelling the admission of a truth.

CORRESPONDENCE, THE LAW OF—The law of correspondence works from the belief to the thing. If we believe we shall have only a little good, only a little good will come into our experience. The demonstration we make *corresponds* with our ability to provide a mental equivalent of our desire.

COSMIC CONCEPTION—The Divine Mind giving birth to Its Idea.

COSMIC CONSCIOUSNESS—Perception of the Whole. Supreme, intuitive knowledge of the divine order, beyond and above the intellectual faculty of comprehension.

COSMIC MIND—The Mind of God.

COSMIC STUFF—Undifferentiated Substance. Pure Spiritual Substance from which all things are made.

COSMIC PURPOSE—The ideas of Spirit propelling themselves into outer expression. The desire of Spirit executing Itself.

COSMIC URGE—The desire of Spirit to express Itself.

COSMOS—The Universal World, visible and invisible. Any self-inclusive system, characterized by order and harmony.

CREATION—The giving of form to the Substance of Mind. Creation always was and always will be. To be conscious is to create, because Spirit has to be conscious, and therefore must have something of which to be conscious. Creation is God making something out of Himself, or Itself, by becoming the thing He creates. The thought of God, coming into expression must go on forever. We must understand that *Creation* does not mean making something out of nothing, but means the passing of Substance into form, through a Law which is set in motion by the Word of Spirit. There could not be a time when the activity of Spirit would cease. The whole action of Spirit must be within Itself, upon the Law (which is also within Itself) and upon the Universal Stuff, or matter, which is also within Itself. The three must in reality be One; hence, "The Trinity."

CREATIVE MEDIUM—From the Universal sense, it is the World-Soul; and from the individual sense, it is the subjective state of a man's thought. Like the creative soil in which seeds are planted and from which plant life grows, the Soul of the Universe is the Creative Medium, into which the Word of Spirit falls, and from which Creation arises. We must be careful not to think of Soul and Spirit as separate, for they are really two parts, or aspects, of the same Reality, being Self-Existent and Coeternal, each with the other.

CREATIVE MIND—The Universal Soul or Subjectivity. The Feminine Principle of the Universal Life.

CREATIVE SERIES—Any particular and concrete manifestation of Spirit.

CREATOR—God. The immutable, inexorable, unchangeable Principle back of, and responsible for, all existence. The impersonal, Father-Mother God. The Limitless . . . The Whole.

DEATH—"God is not a God of the dead, but of the living, for in His sight, all are alive." The Spirit is both birthless and deathless. The Principle of Life cannot know death. The experience of dying is but the laying off of an old garment, and the donning of a new one. "There are bodies celestial and bodies terrestrial, there is a material body and a spiritual body." This spiritual body is the resurrection body.

DECISION—Firmness, steadfastness, resolve . . . determination.

DEDUCTIVE REASONING—Deductive reasoning is that process of reasoning which follows an already established premise. Inductive reasoning is an inquiry into truth; a process of analysis. God, therefore, could only reason deductively. That which is Infinite does not have to *inquire* into Truth. The conscious mind of man can reason both inductively and deductively. It can reason from the Whole to the part or from the part to the Whole. That which is subjective can reason deductively only.

DEITY—God.

DEMAND—To make a demand upon the Universe, merely means to request, claim, or to accept some good which heretofore we have not been experiencing. When we speak of making a demand upon the Universe, we do not mean coercion, will power, or even mental concentration. We mean the recognition and acceptance of some definite and specific good. The power already exists to create, but it is personal to us only when we first recognize it, unify with it, and comply with its law. Be certain that you are not attempting to force or will anything to happen. "We do not have to struggle, we do not have to strive. We only have to know."

DEMONSTRATE . . . DEMONSTRABLE . . . DEMONSTRATION—Through the mental and spiritual activity of thought, directed toward a definite end, we bring about a greater good, a more abundant life, a better condition than existed before. This is called demonstration. We can demonstrate at the level of our ability to *know*. The treatment which leads to the demonstration is not for the purpose of *making something happen*, but is to provide an avenue, within ourselves, through which things may happen. Spiritual demonstration is manifestation of Reality.

DENIAL—The mental act of knowing that any negative condition need not be. Denial clears the way for a realization of Truth; it is a wiping out of wrong reasoning. It is a clearing of the ground, a dredging of the mental channels, preparatory to the building of positive, constructive affirmation. Do not stop with the denial. That is only the preliminary step; deny the false and affirm the Real. The need of denial ceases as thought rises to real spiritual perception.

DESIRE—Half-hearted wishing must not be confused with desire. Our wishing is always capricious; we long for one thing today and tomorrow our attention is directed elsewhere. Desire is that *something* which impels us to reach out and take our own. This is the Divine Urge, which operating as Law produces energy. And energy must find an outlet. This is why *suppressed desire* often produces discord and discomfort. "Desire for anything is the thing itself in incipiency." This means that legitimate desire is the voice of Spirit in you, trying to indicate that the thing you desire is already on its way to you. "Before they call, will I answer."

DESTINY—The result of what a man thinks. Effect, which has been decreed according to perfect law . . . cause and effect.

DEVIL—Any thought of duality. Anything that would deny the Oneness and Allness of Good. Any idea which dilutes Truth. The only devil we shall ever know will be that which appears as the result of our negative thinking. The personification of any belief in evil.

DIAGNOSIS—In medical terms, to make a diagnosis is to recognize the presence of disease from its signs or symptoms. In metaphysics, it may mean judgment based on critical perception or scrutiny . . . perception of motives and character. Unearthing mental causes.

DIMENSION—Measure in a single line, as length, breadth, depth, etc., usually plural, indicating measurable parts. Metaphysically, dimension is the relative extent of consciousness at which we have arrived on our journey. We begin with instinct and travel all the way to intuition.

DISCARNATE—Stripped of flesh. Disembodied of the physical life. One who has passed on.

DISEASE—Disease is an impersonal thought force operating through people which does not belong to them at all. While in every case disease is an effect and must first have a subjective cause, nine times out of ten it is not conscious in the thought of the person who has it. Man is fundamentally perfect. Our whole premise is Perfect God, Perfect Man, Perfect Being. On this alone do we base all our argument.

DIVINE COMPANIONSHIP—Man re-enacts the Divine Nature, and makes use of the same Laws that God uses. We find in man the same androgynous nature that we find in God. This nature we call his objective and subjective faculties. His objective mentality impregnates his subjective with ideas; and in its turn the subjective, gathering force and energy, projects these ideas into forms. We are like God, we are God as us, so we experience Divine Companionship. We walk and talk with the Father within. We have but to speak and He answers.

DIVINE IDEAL—Divine Ideas are the ideas of God. The Divine Ideal is the perfect image held forever in the Mind of God. The Perfect Body, the Spiritual Body, is the fulfillment of the Divine Ideal and is the Real Man which all of us hope to manifest. This is the pattern by which we try to bring out perfection in our lives. In each one of us there exists the Divine Image of ultimate perfection, for God indwells everything which He creates.

DIVINE INFLUX—The continuous inpouring of God's blessings. When we open our minds to the influx of Divine Wisdom we are allowing our lives to be guided by the Infinite. We are keeping our consciousness open to the Divine Influx.

DIVINE MIND—There is no such thing as *your* mind, *my* mind, *his* mind, and God's Mind. There is just Mind in which we all live and move and have our being. We think of Conscious Mind and Spirit as One and the Same. That which we call our subjective mind is, in reality, our identity in Infinite Mind . . . our center in the Universal Subjective Mind. Divine Mind is the One Mind. The Spirit within us is the Divine Mind. "Mortal mind" and "carnal mind" are terms used to describe that mind which gathers its information through the physical senses. Divine Mind is the Real Mind.

DIVINE NATURE—The true nature of all things.

DIVINE PRINCIPLE—Spiritual Causation, operating through Universal Law. Such is the power of right thinking that it cancels and erases everything unlike itself. Place no limit on Principle. It answers every question, solves every problem, is the solution to every difficulty. We are limited, not by Principle, but by our ability to see perfection. One who understands the use of Divine Principle never tries to suggest or personally influence another.

DIVINE PROTECTION—The Power of the Absolute lives forever within us and delivers us forever from anything and everything unlike Good. Divine Protection is omnipresent.

DIVINE SCIENCE—The facts known about mental and spiritual law. Organized, orderly arranged, knowledge of the operation of the Laws of Infinite Mind; the study of the Creator and His Creation.

DIVINE URGE—The inner desire to express life. The desire to do and accomplish more, to be more completely happy, prosperous and well, is right. It is part of that eternally progressive spirit of unfoldment, and we should surrender the entire situation to the working of Intelligence, with the conviction that Intelligence will use us as a perfect channel.

DOGMA—Certain fixed, or set beliefs are signified by *doctrines, creeds, dogmas*. Doctrine usually refers to something which is taught; and creed is a more or less brief outline of what has been determined by the leaders in interpreting their particular religion. Dogma goes beyond this into the arrogant assertion of doctrine, even to the point of indicating its authority to state what others shall think and believe.

DOUBT—There is no room for doubt in a treatment. Realize that you treat with your understanding, through the Law. Meditate upon the spiritual significance of the statements you make, until you induce within consciousness a definite concept of an already established fact, even though the fact may not have become objectified.

DREAM WORLD—This reference applies to the world of thoughts which are unexpressed.

DUALITY—The belief in duality has robbed theology of power and has polluted philosophy with untruths; it has divided science against itself, and has made countless thousands go through life with saddened hearts. Duality has been believed in since time immemorial, and, indeed, is still believed in by many. By duality, we mean a belief in more than One Power back of all things.

In theology, the belief in duality has given rise to the idea of a God and a devil—each with equal power to impose upon man a blessing or a curse—and men have worshiped a devil just as truly as they ever worshiped God. Even today this monstrous thought is robbing men of their birthright to happiness and a sense of security. But the time has now come for a clearer understanding of the Nature of Deity. That there is a God, no one can deny; that there could be a God of vengeance and hate—having all the characteristics of a huge man in a terrible rage—no person can well believe and keep his sanity. True philosophy in all ages has perceived that the Power back of all things must be One Power; and the clearer the thought of Unity, the greater has been the philosophy. In science, the belief in duality created Spirit and matter . . . a dual universe. This is rapidly disappearing now as science recognizes that all matter is in a state of constant flow. True philosophy and true science will someday meet on a common basis and recognize that the Infinite must be One. Whatever change takes place, must take place within the One, but the One must be Changeless. If the eye is "single" to the good, if the vision remains steadfast, we become one with it.

DYNAMIC—Full of power; characterized by action, potency, forcefulness.

EFFECT—That which follows cause. Effect is that which did not make itself, but which must have a power back of it causing it to be. All manifestation is effect and all effect is subject to its cause. The Creator is greater than His Creation. Everything which we see, touch, taste, feel, hear or sense with the physical senses is an effect. "Things which are seen are not made of things which do appear." This means that what we see comes from what we do not see. If all cause is existent in Spirit, and if the Law which executes the Will of the Spirit is subjective, and if the body is only an effect, it follows that both cause and effect are spiritual.

EGO—The I Am of the Bible, the Christ, the perfect idea of God. In metaphysical terms, the Ego refers to the Real Consciousness of man. In psychology it carries a slight variation of interpretation, implying an organization or system of mental states. In this textbook we frequently use it merely to convey the thought of the inner man . . . the real self.

EMANATE—To flow forth from. To originate.

EMMANUEL—"God-with-us." The Christ in every one.

EMERGENT EVOLUTION—That type of evolution which takes place from the *necessity* of the condition. When we needed fingers, we grew them.

EMOTION—Mental energy set in motion through feeling. Any of the feelings of joy, grief, fear, hate, love, awe, reverence. "Emotion is consciousness attendant upon other forms of consciousness (as perception or ideation) to which it gives their feeling tone." In the well-balanced person, emotion is controlled by the intellect, but in many people there is conflict between the emotion and the intellect. Emotion uncontrolled produces chaos; unexpressed it produces confusion, conflict, and complexes, for energy will have an outlet. Bottled up, it creates a pressure that is the cause of much damage to the physical man.

ENERGY—Energy is a divine and unfailing attribute and consequently there is never any lack of it. Always the word carries the idea of strength, vigor, potency, vitality. In metaphysics it may sometimes be used synonymously with Life, Spirit . . . Divine Energy. Aristotle used the word to convey the realized state of potentialities, as opposed to their unrealized state. Physics deals with various kinds of energy . . . mechanical, electric, thermal, chemical, etc., etc. Often in this textbook it may mean inherent power.

Thought is creative energy, shaping the undifferentiated Substance into form. There is a form of mental energy, defined as "the ability to move objects without physical contact." This is called Telekinetic energy.

ENTHUSIASM—An exaltation of soul. A lively manifestation of zeal. A keen interest in people and things at home and abroad; it has been called "The Fortune-Teller of Life." Enthusiasm is compelling, and sweeps everything before it. The root word from which we get *enthusiasm* actually means "inspired" and one truly filled with enthusiasm is like one inspired, as if possessed with a divine power . . . which one actually is. We become enthused in the consciousness that we are God-sustained and filled with God-power. Such consciousness makes our enthusiasm irresistible.

ENTITY . . . ENTITIES—Anything which actually exists, visible or invisible. Being, essence, existence. *Disease is not an entity*.

EQUIVALENT—Alike in significance and value. To make a demonstration we have to have a mental equivalent of our desire. The Eternal Gift is always made. It is meted out to us according to our own measure. If we believe a little, we only receive a little. This we call the Law of Mental Equivalents. As much as we can embody. The reservoir of God is available. If we use only a one-inch pipe (believing we shall do well to barely eke out an existence) the stream of spiritual substance will trickle through in a tiny stream. We can choose the twelve-inch pipe, if we can believe, and allow the pure spiritual substance to flow through to us, "pressed down and running over." It all depends on how great a consciousness of God we can embody . . . how great our mental equivalent.

ERROR—Error means incorrect thinking. It means thinking based upon the belief in some power or presence opposed to good.

ESOTERIC AND EXOTERIC—Esoteric refers to the inner teachings; the mysterious and hidden philosophies and hidden truths of the ages. It refers to that part of the teachings which have been kept from the multitude. Exoteric means the revealed teachings which have been given to the multitude. The parables of Jesus were esoteric teachings. Any teaching whose meaning is hidden is esoteric. It has the same significance as occult; means inner, hidden, only partially revealed, while exoteric means outer, completely revealed. That which was once completely occult and esoteric is today revealed, and we have but little use for the word, since any attempt to conceal the truth would be ridiculous.

ETERNAL—Having no element of time. Without beginning, without end. Also may imply a state or quality other than time. As *eternal bliss, eternal glory*. Immortal, imperishable, uninterrupted, boundless. One of the appellations of God.

ETHER—A universal medium which is supposed to be the last known analysis of matter; it interspheres all things and all space. The fine particles of matter, or electrons, are supposed to be cemented together by the ether. Ether seems to be, to the material world, what mind is to the mental world . . . a universal medium. If the present theory of ether is true, it means that we now have, within our present bodies, a substance more solid than the one we now see. There is every reason to suppose that we have a body within a body to infinity.

EVIL—That which seems destructive. Evil is an experience of the soul on its journey toward the realization of Reality. Evil will remain a problem as long as we believe in it. Of itself, it is neither person, place nor thing, and will disappear in the exact proportion that we cease using destructive methods. As long as we make mistakes, just so long we shall be automatically punished.

EVOLUTION—The passing of Spirit into form. All emerge from that One Whose Being is ever present and Whose Life, robed in numberless forms, is manifest throughout all creation. Creation is the logical result of the outpush of Life into self-expression. It is the coming forth of Spirit into manifestation. The unfoldment of First Cause is what we call evolution. Since the idea is still in an unfolding state, it appears as though we lived in an imperfect universe. Evolution is the time and the process through which an idea unfolds to a higher state of manifestation; and since ideas are Divine Realities, evolution will go on forever.

EXTERNAL . . . EXTERNALIZATION . . . EXTERNALIZE—Our living is the externalization of the ideas and beliefs to which we have given our acceptance. External means related to the outside, outwardly perceptible. To externalize is to make manifest. The externalization is that which is objectified.

FACULTY—"Any mode of bodily or mental behavior regarded as implying a natural endowment or acquired power; the faculties of seeing, hearing, feeling, etc." Personality. Executive ability, efficiency.

FAILURE—A deficiency, a lack of performance, want of success. Sometimes the death of the old that the new may become manifest. Weakness, imperfection, a falling short. A recognition of this is the first step toward progress.

FAITH—"Faith is the substance of things hoped for, the evidence of things not seen." Faith is a mental attitude, so inwardly embodied that the mind can no longer deny it. Faith is complete when it is both a conscious and subjective acceptance. Faith may be consciously generated. In spiritual terminology, faith means a belief in the presence of an invisible principle and law which directly and specifically responds to us. "Thy faith has made thee whole."

FALL, THE—The story of the Fall in the Old Testament is a symbolic presentation of the evolution of Man, and his spiritual awakening. Taken literally, this story would be ridiculous. The writer was attempting to teach a cosmic lesson. The Garden of Eden typifies life in its pure essence. The Tree of Life is our real being, and the tree which bore the fruit of the knowledge of good and evil, refers to our Divine Intelligence, carrying with it, as it must, the possibility of self-choice, without which possibility we could not be individuals, but would be automatons. We may choose even that which is not best for us, therefore man was warned not to eat from the fruit of this tree. Adam typifies our objective faculties and Eve typifies the subjective. Adam and Eve are potential in all of us. The serpent represents the Life Principle viewed from a material basis and beguiles us in this way; he says that evil is as real as good; that the devil has equal power with God; that negation equals positive goodness, and that the universe is dual in its nature. From the acceptance of this argument we experience both good and evil. And should we come full-orbed into individuality without having learned the lesson of unity, we should live forever in a state of bondage. This is the meaning of God saying, "He shall become as one of us and live forever." The Eternal Mind does not wish us to live forever in bondage and this is what would happen unless we first learn the lesson of right and wrong.

And so that part of us which can be fooled eats of the fruit of dual experience and in so doing, reveals its own nakedness. The native state of man is one of purity, peace and perfection, and it is only when he can compare these with impurity, distress and imperfection, that he is revealed as naked. Emerson tells us that virtue does not know it is virtuous. It is only when virtue tastes of impurities that it becomes naked and must hide from itself.

The voice of God, walking in the Garden in the cool of the day, means the introspective and meditative part of us, which, in its moments of pure intuition and reason, sees the illusion of a life apart from God or Good.

Error is ever a coward before Truth, and cannot hide itself from Reality, which sees through everything, encompasses all and penetrates even the prison walls of the mind with Its clear effulgence.

The conversation between God, and Adam and Eve in the Garden of Eden, represents the arguments that go on in our own minds, when we try to realize the truth. These arguments are familiar to all and need not be enumerated.

The expulsion from the Garden is a necessary and logical outcome of tasting of dual experience. If we believe in both good and evil, we must experience each.

FAMILIAR SPIRITS—This refers to the control of consciousness through the instrument of some invisible agency, sometimes supposed to be discarnate spirits. Psychic contacts.

FATE—An arranged or predetermined life or event. Foreordination. If one believes in fate, he must be healed of this thought for there is no such thing. There is One Perfect Power, forever operating, and never contingent upon any place, person, time of year or anything but Itself.

FATHER-MOTHER GOD—The Masculine and Feminine Principles of Being, as included in the Androgynous One, or First Cause. God as the Universal Parent Mind and Spirit.

FEAR—"Perfect love casteth out fear." "Fear not, little flock, it is your Father's good pleasure to give you the kingdom." Fear is the antithesis of Faith. It is the negation of confidence. Like Faith, fear may be conscious or subjective, and if it is to be eliminated, it must be removed both consciously and subjectively.

FEMININE PRINCIPLE—The Universal Soul. In man, the subjective or subconscious intelligence. The Universal Medium, or Soul, has been called the "Womb of Nature" and the "Holy Mother," because It is receptive to the Spirit, and is impregnated with Divine Ideas. It gives birth to the Ideas of the Spirit, and is, therefore, the Feminine Principle of Nature.

FIRST CAUSE—That which is the cause of all things. The Uncreated, from which all Creation springs. The Cause of all that is manifest on *any* plane. That which comes first. The first in any creative series. The First Cause is both Masculine and Feminine in Its Nature, and includes the Intermediate Principle of Creative Activity.

FORCE—Some of the early philosophers referred to the Soul, or Creative Medium, as a "Blind force, not knowing, only doing." This we know to be true of all law. Law knows only to do, it has no conscious volition of its own. Thought *force* is the movement of consciousness which sets law in operation. The movement of consciousness upon itself creates a motion or vibration in Intelligence, upon Substance, the force of which is equal to the reality of the thought set in motion. *Force*, used as a verb, means to compel.

FORM—Any definite outline in time and space. Forms may be visible or invisible. In all probability, all space is filled with many kinds of forms. Form is the result of a definite idea. Form is real as form, but is not self-conscious; it is subjective to the power that created it. Forms come and go, but the Power back of them remains forever and is Changeless. Form is temporary but Mind is Eternal. It is necessary that Spirit should manifest in *some kind of form*, in order that It may come into Self-expression through Self-realization. This is the meaning of that Creation which is eternally going on. Form is always effect … never cause. Unconscious Form, or Mirror of Matter, means that the material world reflects the forms of thought which the Soul holds before it. This depicts the Creative Process and sequence:

First in the chain of Causation is the Word, and this Word is conscious of Itself; next comes the action of Law, reflecting the Word. (This Law is subjective and obeys the Word, reflecting It into form or matter, being at first unformed, or a Universal Undifferentiated Substance.) It then takes form, through the power of the Word acting upon It, on the subjective side of life. Soul and Substance are both subjective to the Spirit; form, or matter in form, has no volition.

FORMLESS—God as Spirit. Mind as Law. Substance in an unformed state. The unformed is forever taking form. No particular form can be permanent.

FORMLESS SUBSTANCE—The ultimate Stuff from which all forms are created, universally present, in an unformed state, and acted upon by conscious and subconscious intelligence. It is the nature of Soul to give form to the ideas with which It is impregnated; hence, Soul contains Substance within Itself.

FREE SPIRIT—That which cannot be bound. It is free to do as It chooses, but cannot, of course, do anything which denies Its own Nature.

FREEDOM—Real freedom means that man is created in the image of perfection and let alone and allowed to make the discovery for himself. Freedom of will means the ability to do, say and think as one wishes; to express life as one personally desires. "Ye shall know the truth, and the truth shall set you free," Jesus taught. The understanding of Truth—Infinite Principle—is the emancipator. We are bound by our very freedom; our free will binds us. The Universe, being deductive only, cannot refuse us anything. The very force that makes us sick can heal us. As man realizes his Oneness with Creative Mind, he is released from the bondage of false thinking. He sees, too, that freedom means liberty but not license.

GARDEN OF EDEN—The Garden of Eden typifies man's original state of perfection before he began to have experience. The Tree of Knowledge means the Life Principle, which can be used both ways. It bore the fruit of knowledge of both kinds of experience, good and evil, freedom and limitation. Man must choose which kind of fruit he will eat. The serpent typifies the Life Principle, viewed from the materialistic viewpoint; it casts man from his perfect state through his belief in duality and separation. Man chose to depart from Good, and man alone must choose to return to It. God lets him alone, for he is a free agent and may do as he wills with himself. When a man decides to return to his Father's House, he will find his Father is still there. God's creation is perfect and we must awake to this fact and know that we are now in the Kingdom of Heaven.

GENERIC—Characteristic of; a universal judgment; pertaining to, or having the rank of, a genus, as a *generic name, a generic description, a generic quality*.

GHOST—The mental form of any person, in the flesh or out of it. An apparition, a disembodied human spirit. Any faint, shadowy semblance.

GOD—The First Cause, the Great I Am, the Unborn One, the Uncreated, the Absolute or Unconditioned, the One and Only. Spirit, or the Creative Energy which is the cause of all visible things. Love, Wisdom, Intelligence, Power, Substance, Mind. The Truth which is real, the Principle which is dependable.

GOD-CONSCIOUSNESS—Man's self-knowing mind is his Unity with the Whole, his perception of Reality. This Unity with God, on the conscious side of life, is the guarantee that man is a Center of God-Consciousness, that he is some part of the Consciousness of God.

GRACE—Grace is the givingness of Spirit to Its Creation and is not a special law, but a specialized one. In other words, Grace is, but we need to recognize it. It is not something God imposed upon us, but is the logical result of the correct acceptance of life and of a correct relationship to the Spirit. We are saved by Grace to the extent that we believe in, accept, and seek to embody the Law of Good; for the Law of Good is ever a Law of Liberty and never one of limitation. Limitation is not a thing, not an entity, but a belief. Freedom is a Divine Reality.

GREAT ACTOR—The Spirit.

GREAT DISCOVERY, THE—The greatest discovery ever made was the discovery of the creative power of thought, because upon this hinges man's entire evolution. The ability to affirm, to say "I am," to be conscious of one's relationship to the Universe, is not only a guarantee that man Is, and is some part of the Universe, it is itself a proclamation of the Universe, since the only knowledge of God we can have must come through the consciousness of man. The consciousness of man is an extension of the consciousness of God.

GREAT HOUSE, THE—Another way of saying the Universal.

HABIT—Any act which has become a part of the subconscious mentality. Habits are formed by first consciously thinking, and then unconsciously acting. What one thinks today will tomorrow be part of his memory; and since memory is active, what he thinks today as a conscious thought will tomorrow be a submerged *but active thought* . . . habit.

HALO—The emanation that appears around the head. The halo which artists have portrayed around the heads of saints is real, and not merely an idea of the artist. A mental and spiritual emanation.

HAPPINESS—A state of well-being or enjoyment of good of any kind. The general term applies to the enjoyment, or pleasurable satisfaction, attendant upon welfare of any kind. In metaphysics, it means a state of inner peace, a consciousness of the Goodness of God and the beneficent attitude of the Universe, a realization that joy can come to every man. It has a definite effect on mind, body and affairs. A state of permanent joy. It is never the will of God, or Universal Harmony, that any man should be unhappy. We have a right to any happiness of which we can conceive, provided that happiness hurts no one, and is in keeping with the nature of progressive Life.

HARMONY—Concord or agreement in facts, opinions, manners, interests, etc. The secret of all progress is getting into a right relationship with the Universal. "In tune with the Infinite." In tune with Infinite Order is harmony. Contacting Infinite Intelligence, recognizing the Father within, accepting the underlying laws of Creation and moving in Its mighty rhythm, is harmony. Such harmony adjusts our affairs and enriches our lives.

HEALING—Mental healing means Mind healing. To heal means to make whole. We seek to heal men's mentalities, knowing that to the degree in which we are successful, we shall also be healing their bodies. Belief in duality has made man sick and the understanding of Unity will heal him. God stands to us for the One Life in which we all live. MENTAL TREATMENT IS A DIRECT STATEMENT IN MIND OF WHAT WE WISH TO HAVE DONE AND A REALIZATION THAT IT IS DONE. Healing is the result of clear thinking and logical reasoning, which presents itself to consciousness and is acted upon by it. Realize that you are a Divine Idea and that your word is the law unto the thing unto which it is spoken. The whole idea of healing, when understood, is the substitution of Truth for sense-testimony. This restores man to a condition of wholeness.

HEAVEN—A state of happiness. Heaven is within, it revolves about us; it is the result of that atmosphere of conviction which our thought awakens within us. The Kingdom of Heaven is unformed, unlimited, unconditioned. Heaven is not a place, a locality, "with streets of gold and gates of pearl." It is the real state of Being. We do not *make* it real, for it is eternal Reality. If we abide in the Father and He abides in us, in harmony, in power, in peace, in wisdom; and our thought is friendly, happy, confident and open, our Kingdom of Heaven is a good *place* in which to live.

HELL—A discordant state of being. A belief in duality. A sense of separation from God. A belief that our good is *always to be*, and never is. Hell is not a location.

HIGH INVOCATION—Invoking the Divine Mind; implanting within It seeds of thought relative to oneself.

HOLY GHOST—The third Person of the Trinity. The Servant of the Spirit. Used in the sense of the World—Soul or Universal Subjectivity.

HUMANITY—Mankind; human beings collectively; the human race. The multiplied expression of God as people. The many who live in the One.

HUMILITY—True humility does not mean self-abasement, but is rather that attitude which Emerson tells us is willing to get its "bloated nothingness out of the way of the Divine Circuits." It is an intelligent recognition that the whole is greater than any one of its parts. "Stand still and watch the sure salvation of the Lord."

HYPNOTISM—The mental control of another.

I AM—The "I Am" is both individual and universal, that is, the individual "I" is part of the Universal "I Am." The "I Am consciousness" means that part of thought, both conscious and subjective, which not only affirms its unity with God, but which also understands the meaning of its affirmation.

IDEA—An idea is a mental concept. Any object of the mind existing in apprehension, conception, or thought. A theme. The Ideas of God are the Divine Realizations of His Own Being. The real Ideas are eternal. No two ideas are alike. The Creative Mind of the Universe, being Infinite, thinks of a limitless number of things, and each thing is, therefore, separate and distinct in the great Whole. Just as the atoms of science are cemented together by the ether, so each idea of Divine Mind is united in One Spirit. No two things are alike; no two people are alike. All come from One Life; all are in One Life and live by It, but each forever maintains its identity in the Perfect Whole.

ILLUMINATION—Inspiration reaching a Cosmic state. A direct contact with Reality or God. A complete intuitive perception. It is the Self-Knowingness of God through man. Illumination comes as man more and more realizes his Unity with the Whole, but since the Whole is at the point of the Inner Mentality, it will be here alone that he will contact It. "Speak to Him, thou, for He hears." The only God man can ever know is the God of his own Inner Life.

ILLUSION—The ancients taught an illusion of mind and an illusion of the material universe. The illusion of mind they called Maya, the great "feminine illusion," which does not refer to woman, but to the subjective universe, which contains many images which are false, the results of man's erroneous conclusions. This does not mean that the subjective world of itself is an illusion, but it might present us with an illusion unless we were careful to discriminate between the false and the true. Jesus said, "Judge not according to appearances." Even the physical universe is not what it seems to be. As a matter of fact, neither the physical nor the subjective universe are things of themselves. As Plotinus said, "Nature is the great no-thing, yet it is not exactly nothing," since Its business is to receive the forms of thought which the Spirit lets fall into It. The illusion is never in the thing, but in the way we look at it.

IMAGE—The mental likeness of anything. The soul or subjective mind, contains all of our thoughts as mental images or pictures.

IMAGINATION AND WILL—Coué announced a great truth when he said that imagination is superior to the will; but he did not explain the philosophy behind this truth. Will is an assumption, pure and simple. We do not will to live; we live because we have life and cannot help living. We did not make Life and we cannot change It, but we can use It, and the use of Life is through the imagination; because this faculty has, at its roots, the very well-spring of life and action. Imagination carries with it feeling and conviction, which means life and action. It awakens within us all the inner forces of nature and stirs into action latent powers which otherwise would never come to the surface. Will power may be necessary in its place, as a directive agency, but as a creative agency, it is non-existent. To feel that we have to *will* something to happen casts doubt into the face of Creation, and pre-supposes that Life is not Self-Existent and Self-Propelling. Imagination taps the very roots of Being and utilizes the same Power that brought the world forth from chaos. "The worlds were framed by the Word of God." Imagination is the power of the word, while will is the directive agency, denoting the purpose for which the word is spoken. Man reproduces the power to create, and in his own life, controls his destiny through the activity of his word. This word cannot be *willed*, but it can be *imagined or imaged* forth into expression.

IMMANENT—Remaining or operating within the subject considered; neither derived from, nor passing, without; indwelling; inherent. Contrasted with the word *transcendent*, which means reaching beyond, surpassing. We recognize that *God is both immanent and transcendent*, which means that He is in us as us, but infinitely more than all that we are.

IMMATERIAL—The word actually means not consisting of matter. The Soul is immaterial as we think of matter, but It might be termed *the matter of Spirit*, the substance of Spirit. As all matter in the physical world finally resolves itself into the ether from which it came, so we may think of the Substance of Soul as we think about the ether and realize that every thing in form finally becomes Soul Stuff again.

IMMORTALITY—The Deathless Principle of Being in all people. For a study of this subject, see Chapter Twenty-three.

IMPERSONAL—Not belonging to any particular person or persons. The Creative Medium is Impersonal, having no personality of Its own. It neither knows nor cares who uses It, but is always ready to work for any or all alike. It is very important that we remember this. The Creative Mind is impersonal receptivity, in that It receives all seeds of thought.

INCARNATION . . . INCARNATE—The Spirit of God in all Creation. To incarnate is to embody, to enshrine, to give form to. Any concrete or actual form exemplifying a principle.

INDIVIDUALITY—The Real Idea of man, as distinguished from the outer personality. Each one is a separate entity in Mind and no two are alike. Each is an individualized center of God-Consciousness. We are born with our individuality. Our personality is the use we make of our Divine Individuality.

INDUCE—The act of planting seeds of thought in Creative Mind.

INDUCTIVE REASONING—Reasoning from effect to cause. Deductive reasoning is that process of reasoning which follows an already established premise. It is from whole to part. Inductive reasoning is an analysis, an inquiry into Truth, so it follows that God can only reason *deductively*, since He does not have to inquire into that which is true.

INDWELLING CHRIST—Generic man, manifesting through the individual. The idea of Divine Sonship. The Real Man. As much of this Reality appears as we allow to express through us. Read Chapter Twenty-two for complete elaboration.

INDWELLING EGO—The *Spirit* of man, as differentiated from his soul or subjective mentality. The Real Man, which is the conscious part of him.

INDWELLING GOD—The Real Man is as much of God as he is able to embody. The Divine Spark, Birthless and Deathless. As we *recognize* His indwelling, the wisdom, the love, the power of God Himself are ours to use.

INFINITE—That which is beyond human comprehension. The Infinite is God.

INHERENT LIFE—Real life as distinguished from latent life. Inalienable, inseparable; involved in the essential character of anything; inbred, inwrought, essential. Connected with us as a permanent attribute. Our inherent life, our indwelling God, assures us all the life and health, peace, joy and abundance that we can desire or conceive of.

INHERITED TENDENCIES—The subjective, being the seat of memory, contains the race characteristics and tendencies. We do not inherit disease but we do inherit tendencies. This is the way that family and race traits are handed down.

INNER SIGHT—The spiritual capacity of knowing the Truth. It is a mental quality which brings the mentality to a comprehension of Reality.

INSANITY—A temporary or permanent control of the conscious mind by the unconscious or subjective. This control may be complete or in degrees. Psychologists find it difficult to distinguish between sanity and insanity, since we are all insane in such degree as we entertain wrong conclusions about life; but in its broader sense, insanity means a temporary or permanent loss of the objective faculties. The throne of reason is usurped, while the subjective, emotional reaction to life controls the thought. The real mind, of course, cannot be deranged, and a complete mental treatment for insanity is to know there is but One Mind, which is now functioning, and perfectly functioning, in the individual who appears to be insane.

INSPIRATION—From the human side, inspiration means contact with the subconscious of the individual or the race. From the Divine, it means contact with the Universal Spirit.

INSTINCT—That quality in an animal which directs its action and tells it where to go to find food and shelter, we call instinct. It is really Omniscience in the animal. The same quality in man we call intuition.

INSTINCTIVE LIFE—The One in everything.

INSTINCTIVE MAN—The Spiritual Man.

INTELLECT—Mental quality of analysis. That part of the mentality concerned with the acquisition and retention of knowledge, as distinguished from the emotions and the will. Emotion uncontrolled produces chaos; unexpressed it produces confusion. When we combine thought with feeling, intellect with emotion, and add to this a recognition of the Father within, we have a power which is irresistible.

INTUITION—Intuition is God in man, revealing to him the Realities of Being. Just as instinct guides the animal, so would intuition guide man, if he would allow it to operate through him. The ability to know without any process of reasoning. God knows only intuitively.

INVOLUTION—Invoking the Law. Setting the Law in motion. Giving a mental and spiritual treatment. Planting the seed of thought in the Creative Mind of the Universe. Involution precedes evolution and evolution follows involution with mathematical certainty. We deal with the Creative Principle of involution and evolution. Involution is the creation of the concept. Evolution is the time or process it takes for the concept to become manifest. Involution is a conscious act. Evolution is purely mechanical.

JEALOUSY—The result of an inferiority complex and sensitive nature.

JESUS—The name of a man. Distinguished from the Christ. The man Jesus became the embodiment of the Christ, as the human gave way to the Divine Idea of Sonship. See Chapter Twenty-two for further elaboration.

JOY—The emotion excited by the expectancy of good. Gladness, delight, exultation.

JUDGMENT—"Judge not that ye be not judged, for with what judgment ye judge, ye shall be judged." Judgment is merely the law of cause and effect operating. The Universe holds nothing against anyone. "He sendeth rain on the just and on the unjust." We are judged by our own acts. Punishment and reward are automatic reactions of the law. Anna Besant said, "Karma is the law that binds the ignorant and frees the wise." If we would wish our judgment to be good, happy, and constructive, then we must make a like use of the law.

KARMA—The subjective law of tendency set in motion by the individual. The mental law acting through him. Karmic Law is the use that man makes of his mentality. Karma is not Kismet, for Kismet means "fate," and Karma simply means "the mental tendency." Karma is both individual and collective. We do not recognize Karma as *inevitable* retribution. Since we know that all life is an *effect* . . . of which mind is the cause . . . we know that at any time we can change our thinking and set in motion new laws which shall govern our lives. When peace, harmony and love rule in our thinking, we know they will register in our lives as effect, bringing health, happiness and prosperity; any previous Karma, different from that, will be set at naught.

KINGDOM—"The kingdom of heaven" is not a place; it is "within" in our deepest thought. It is the Reality of our individual awareness and it is the Reality of Universal Mind. It is the recognition of our Oneness with the Divine. It is the Perfect Design which is God's idea of

Creation, and can only be discerned spiritually. It is the *real* of everything. The *kingdom* of God is the *consciousness* of God. As we think the thoughts of God, we shall have a newer, diviner life in our body and in our affairs. We shall have entered the Kingdom.

KISMET—Destiny, fate.

KNOWLEDGE—The word "knowledge" as used throughout this textbook means that which will bear the test in the light of Truth. Real knowledge is the conscious awareness of the indwelling Father, the certainty that God abides at the center of our being, as perfect health, complete joy, power, wisdom, and goodness, and ready to come forth into manifestation at our bidding. This knowledge is the secret of all power. Ordinarily, in a general sense, the word *knowledge* merely means the sum-total of facts the mind has perceived and believed. Metaphysically speaking, we *can* only know that which is *true*. If we *believe* that which is false, it may seem to operate as Truth, because "It is done unto us as we believe."

KNOWING NO OTHER—The Spirit could know nothing outside Itself. It is the Center and Circumference of everything that exists. It has no enemies, no differences, no otherness, no apartness, no separation from Itself; is Undivided, Complete and Perfect within Itself. It has no opposites and no opposition. It knows only of Its own ability to do; and, since It is All, It cannot be hindered in any way, shape or manner. It is not possible to conceive of such a complete Life and Power; but we do catch glimpses in moments of real inspiration when we realize, to a degree, that God is All.

LACK AND LIMITATION—These are synonymous terms and indicate that something is missing in our lives. We believe we are without health, wealth, friends or opportunities. Money is an objective representation, a symbol, of an eternal substance WHICH FOREVER FLOWS and which is forever manifesting itself in the visible world. We should endeavor to know that there is an Intelligence guiding our affairs, and that this Intelligence is perfect, that the law of this Intelligence is immutable. As we withdraw our attention from the limited world of *effect*, and dwell unwaveringly on the Limitless Good, we shall have destroyed the only reason whereby lack and limitation could manifest in our lives. We enter the Absolute in such proportion as we withdraw from the limited.

LATENT LIFE—Life that depends upon reality. Distinguished from inherent life.

LAW—Mind in action. The Creative Medium of Spirit is the great Mental Law of the Universe. It is the Law of the Spirit. It is the Universal Law of Mind. The Laws of Mind and Spirit must be understood if they are to be consciously used for definite purposes. There is no limit to the Law, but there appears to be a limit to man's understanding of it. The thing that makes us sick is the thing which heals us. We need not look for a law of sickness and a law of health. There is only One Law. Our misuse of this makes it appear that there are many laws. Whatever we think, believe in, feel, visualize, vision, image, read, talk about, in fact, all processes which affect or impress us at all, are going into the subjective state of our thought, which is our individualized use of Universal Mind. The Law is a blind force, and whatever goes into the subjective state of our thought tends to return again as some condition. See the Chapter on "Control of Conditions" for further elaboration, on Law of Attraction, Law of Correspondence, Karmic Law, etc.

LEVITATION—Where a body, or object, is lifted without the aid of any physical medium.

LIBIDO—The emotional urge within life which causes all expression.

LIFE—The animating Principle of Being . . . that Inner Something that makes everything live. Life and Power are necessary attributes of a Limitless Being, and go hand in hand to complete a Perfect Being. Life is That Which Lives, and Power is the Energy with which It operates. Considering Life and Power as a combined unity of Causation, we see that they constitute the underlying basis of all manifestation, visible and invisible. In the objective world, Life is the Power that binds everything together. It appears that Life manifests on different levels. In the mineral world, it seems to be unconscious, yet chemical affinity is a manifestation of Life, as the attraction of Itself to Itself. In plant life, It manifests as a power to express in one spot, but without volition to move about. This does not indicate that Spirit is limited, but merely one of the ways that It works. In the animal world, we see different degrees of Life's manifestation, from the first cell life up to man. For instance, a dog is more intelligent than a fish, yet each has the power to move about. In man, Life expresses in terms of Volition and Self-Will; It is manifesting at the level of Self-Consciousness. While the Spirit, of Itself, must always know Itself, we are perfectly justified in saying that It manifests on different levels, proving It is limitless. If It had to manifest on one level only, then It would be limited. When Spirit manifests in a purely mechanical way, we say It is Unconscious Life; when It manifests in the animal world, we speak of it as simple consciousness; when It manifests in and through man, we say that It is in a Self-Conscious State. As this Self-Conscious State of man's mentality reaches a larger world of realization, and comprehends something of Its Unity with the Whole, we say that It is in a Cosmic State. Thus we know of four different levels upon which Spirit manifests: Unconscious State, Simple Consciousness, Self-Consciousness, and Cosmic Consciousness. All are but different ways through which the One Power operates. Life, then, is that quality of Being, running through all, which enables anything to be what It is.

LIGHT—In flashes of illumination, the inspired have seen INTO THE VERY CENTER OF REALITY, and have brought back with them a distinct impression of what they have seen and felt. A glimpse of this Reality illumines the whole being with a flood of light. Every mystic has had this experience. Jesus was the greatest of all mystics; and once, at least, after a period of illumination, his face was so bright his followers could not look upon it. In moments of deepest realization, the great mystics have sensed that One Life flows through ALL; and that all are some part of that Life. They have also seen Substance, a fine, white, brilliant Stuff, forever falling into everything; a Substance indestructible and eternal. At times, the realization has been so complete that they have been actually blinded by the light. Light was the first great revelation of Divine Creative Energy that called all living things into being . . . "Let there be light and there was light." There is healing light in the rays of the sun, which we term a *physical light;* there is healing power in the wonderful high-powered lamps, but how much greater is the healing power which Jesus recognized in himself and in others! "I am the light of the world; he that followeth me shall not walk in darkness, but shall have the light of life." ". . . I have set thee to be a light . . ." "He that loveth his brother abideth in the light." ". . . the sons of God, without rebuke . . . ye shine as lights in the world."

LIMIT . . . LIMITLESS—In this study of the Mind, we are dealing with that which is without limit. "Limitless" is used to indicate Spirit, God.

LOGIC—Reasoning which keeps faith with itself. The science of the laws of thought.

LOGOS—The Word of God manifest in and through man. "The Divine Creative Word." An emanation of the Divine Consciousness to the receptive mind, and may be called the source of illumination. It has been called "the universal source of light and reason." "The Word was with God and the Word *was* God." It is Spirit; It is Power. It is the same Power by which we create. "Thou shalt also decree a thing, and it shall be established unto thee."

LOVE—Love is the self-givingness of the Spirit through the desire of Life to express Itself in terms of creation. Emerson tells us that Love is a synonym for God. We are also told in the New Testament that "He that loveth not, knoweth not God; for God is love." Love is free from condemnation, even as it is free from fear. Love is a cosmic force whose sweep is irresistible.

LORD—Another term for the Indwelling God. "And the Lord shall guide thee continually . . ." My Lord is the Christ within my own soul.

MACROCOSM—The Universal World. It is another word for the Whole.

MAN—The objectification of God in human form. The idea of God manifested in the flesh. The Sonship of the Father. Generic man is the Type, and the personal man is the concrete expression of the Type. The highest expression of God on this planet.

MANIA—An irresistible desire controlling personal action . . . a desire too strong to be controlled. We speak of one having a mania for certain things; that is, he has subjectified so much desire along some particular line that he becomes controlled by the very power which he has set in motion. This shows how very careful we should be to control our thinking, never allowing the mentality to conceive ideas which we do not wish to see manifest.

MANIFESTATION—To manifest, means to show forth or to make evident. Everything we see—plants, animal, man, every visible thing—is a manifestation of God, differing only in degree, and *every manifestation contains, in essence, the whole*, as one drop of ocean water is as perfect, in essence, as the entire body. We are not all of God, of course, but the Reality within us is God. As we make conscious use of the Law, planting an idea in Mind and watching it come forth into form, into objectivity, we are producing a manifestation.

MASCULINE PRINCIPLE—The Assertive Principle of Being. The Self-Conscious, Self-Propelling Power of Spirit. The Projective Principle of Life, impregnating the Universal Soul with Its ideas and concepts. The Self-Assertive Spirit in either God or man.

MATERIAL MAN—The objective man, not opposed to Spirit, but the logical outcome of the Self-Knowing Mind.

MATERIALISM—Materialism does not exist in spiritual vision, for matter, to it, is soul-substance in manifestation. The old idea of a solid, static universe is gone, and science gives us instead a dynamic, fluidic energy, everywhere present.

MATTER—Any form which substance takes in the world of sense and objectivity. The illusion of matter refers to false forms. Science tells us that matter is an aggregation of small particles, arranged in some kind of form; and that matter is in a continuous state of flow. Our bodies are like a river, forever flowing; the Indwelling Spirit alone maintains the identity. We are now learning that ether is more solid than matter.

MAYA—World of mental illusion.

MECHANICAL—Proceeding automatically; done as if by a machine.

MEDITATION—The general acceptance of the term meditation is contemplation or continuous thought. We mean to convey something more—the recognition of the Father within, the certainty of our Oneness with the Whole, the immediate availability of the Power and Wisdom resulting from this Oneness. Such communion with God brings harmony into our lives and affairs; establishes the law of health and prosperity, and makes us a light to all who cross our pathway.

MEDIUM—A middle or intermediate thing; that which lies between; a substance through which a force acts or an effect is transmitted. The Universal Medium, or Soul, is receptive to the Spirit, and is impregnated with the Divine Ideas. This Creative Medium is neutral. The Creative Medium of Spirit is the great Mental Law of the Universe. It is the One Medium through which all Law and all Power operate. That which we term *our* subjective mind is the medium through which we contact the Universal Mind.

A person whom we call a *medium* is one who objectifies subjectivity.

MEEKNESS—Means that quality of Sonship which so consciously recognizes its Oneness with the Whole that it can effectively practice non-resistance; not only that but forgives with the completeness that gives an actual good in return for an evil given. Such was the meekness of Jesus.

MEMORY—Thoughts today dropped by our conscious mind into subjective mind, tomorrow become memory. The subjective retention of ideas. The soul, or subjective mind, is the seat of memory, and retains within itself everything that the individual has ever said, thought, seen, heard, felt, read or been told; and indeed everything that has ever happened to him. It also contains race memory.

MENTAL ATMOSPHERE—The mental emanation of anything, any person or any place. Everything has some kind of a mental atmosphere.

MENTAL ATTITUDE—An attitude means a position assumed, or studied, as indicating action, feeling or mood. Our mental attitude, then, is the general tendency of our mind . . . the *tendency* our thought takes, as a whole.

MENTAL CORRESPONDENTS—The inner image in mind which balances the outer objectification of itself. Every objective thing has an inner mental correspondent.

MENTAL EQUIVALENT—Having a subjective idea of the desired experience. As we bring ourselves to a greater vision than the range of our present concepts, we can then induce a greater concept and thereby demonstrate more in our experience.

MENTAL IMAGE—Subjective likeness.

MENTAL INFLUENCE—As we recognize our Oneness with the Whole, we are consciously opening our thought to the highest influence from every direction. We should never allow ourselves to be influenced by anything we do not consciously allow to enter our thought. A mental influence which would attempt to plant in our subjective mind a thought which would come up from within and cause us to do things we would not otherwise do, is hypnotic. The statement that ONLY THE ONE MIND CONTROLS will protect us from any and all wrong mental influences.

MENTAL LAW—Universal Subjectivity is the avenue through which God operates as Law . . . the law of mental action. The Mental Medium must be thought of as the Mental Law.

MENTAL MEDIUM—This definition is tied up with the one just preceding it. It has been proven that thought operates in such a manner as to make it possible to convey mental impressions from one person to another, showing that there is a mental medium between all people. This leads us to the conclusion that we are surrounded by a Universal Mind, which is the Medium of the communication of our thoughts.

MENTAL PLANE—JUST BETWEEN THE Spiritual and the physical. The three planes intersphere each other.

MENTAL SCIENCE—The Science of Mind and Spirit. A systematic knowledge of the laws governing the Mental and Spiritual World.

MENTAL TREATMENT—The act, the art, and science of inducing thought in Mind, which thought operated upon by Law, becomes a manifest condition.

MENTALITY—An individual use of Universal Mind. There is One Mind, but within this One Mind are many mentalities.

MESMERISM—The influence of personality.

METAPHYSICS . . . METAPHYSICAL—The scientists of today are closer than ever before to agreeing with the metaphysician that God is Creative Intelligence, or Mind, everywhere present in the Universe, and manifesting through every created thing. Metaphysics is more than a speculative philosophy. It is the Science of Being. William James considered it an unusually obstinate attempt to think clearly and consistently. Metaphysics may be termed that which is beyond the known laws of physics.

METAPHYSICAL PRINCIPLE—The Universal Creative Mind. As Spirit, it is conscious; as Law, it is subjective.

METHODS OF TREATMENT—While several methods of treatment are used, there are but two distinct methods; one is called argumentative and the other realization. The argumentative is one in which the practitioner argues with himself about his patient, to bring himself to the point of a complete affirmation. The argument is entirely within his own mind. The method of realization is where the practitioner realizes within himself—without any argument—the perfect state of his patient. In either case, treatment is for the purpose of inducing an inner realization of perfection in the mentality of the practitioner, which inner realization, acting through Mind, operates in the patient.

MICROCOSM—The individual world, as distinguished from the Universal.

MIND—No one has ever seen Mind or Spirit. The only proof we have of Mind is that we can think, but we are perfectly justified in believing that we have a mind. Actually, there is no such thing as *your* mind and *my* mind, *his* mind, *her* mind, and *God's* Mind. There is just Mind, in which we live, move and have our being. Mind is both conscious and subconscious. Conscious Mind is Spirit, either in God or man. Unconscious Mind is the law of conscious Mind acting and is, therefore, subconscious or subjective. Mind is potential energy, while thought is the dynamic force which produces the activity for manifestation. The One Mind is all of Truth. Our mind, that point in God-Consciousness which we call *our mind*, is as much of Truth as we will allow to flow through and bless us.

MIRROR OF MATTER—The physical universe.

MIRROR OF MIND—The subjective world, reflecting the images of thought which are projected into it by the conscious mind. The term is used because the Subjective Side of life acts like a mirror: It reflects the forms of thought that are given It.

MISTAKES—God makes no mistakes. All mistakes rest in the experience of man. "There is no sin, but a mistake, and no punishment but a consequence." We must declare that no mistakes have been made, none are being made, and none are going to be made. If mistakes have been made we must neutralize their effect by the direct declaration that they no longer have power over us.

MISUNDERSTANDING—A misinterpretation, a disagreement. Can we not see by now, what fundamental error brings about this condition? Could it be other than a lack of realization of the Unity of all life? Recognize that there is but One Mind; see God in each, and the trouble will be healed.

MONEY—The symbol of God's Substance; the idea of Spiritual Supply objectified. As God is Spirit, and man is God's creation, Spirit is man's Substance; but Spirit is All, so money is an expression of Substance.

MORTAL MIND—It is what the Bible terms the "carnal mind." It is a belief in duality. Actually, there is but the One Mind, the Divine Mind, and that is the Mind we use.

MYSTICISM . . . MYSTICS—A mystic is one who senses the Divine Presence. Some people confuse *mysticism* with *psychism*, and it is important that we make a clear distinction. A mystic is one who intuitively senses Reality. The highest and best that we have in civilization—music, art, religion, philosophy, poetry, science, etc.—is the result of the mystic sense which has been perceived by a few in each age. The psychic capacity, at best, deals only with human thought; only reads subjective pictures and tendencies. A mystic does not read human thought but senses the Thought of God. For complete information on this, read the chapter "The Completed Whole."

MULTIPLICITY . . . MANY—From One come many. All come from the One, and all live in, and by, the One. From Unity comes multiplicity, but multiplicity does not contradict Unity. It is like the soil: we grow many plants from one soil, but the Unity of the soil is never disturbed. So the One Mind, working through the Creative Medium of the Universe, produces many things.

NATURAL MAN—Instinctive or Spiritual Man.

NATURE OF GOD—We have already discovered that the Nature of God is "Triune"—Spirit, Soul, and Body . . . Father, Son and Holy Ghost . . . or The Thing, How It Works, and What It Does. There is an entire chapter devoted to this.

NAZARENE—Because Jesus came from Nazareth, he was frequently referred to as "the Nazarene," yet this same Nazarene was the most complete manifestation of the One Mind who has ever lived.

NECESSITY—That which makes an act or an event unavoidable. Irresistible force; something indispensable.

NEGATIVE . . . NEGATION—A negative thought is any thought which is untrue. The belief in duality is the father of most negative thinking. A negation is the act of denying; a declaration that something is not. Negative thinking denies the Truth of Being.

NEUTRAL—Not caring which way it works. All laws are neutral.

NEUTRALIZING THOUGHT—The act of mentally erasing thought images.

NONRESISTANCE—Fighting any adverse condition only increases its power over us, because we are making a *reality* of it. Someone has said that "the language of resistance is pain, but nonresistance finds the harmony of the universe and swings into its motion, going with the stream of power which nourishes and protects." Resistance is the offspring of fear and ignorance; nonresistance is the offspring of love.

NORMAL . . . NORMALCY . . . NORMAL STATE—The word normal means natural, without affectation or pretense. *Normalcy* is the state or fact of being normal. A normal state, a normal condition of mind, would be a complete balance between the objective and subjective states of consciousness.

OASIS—A green spot in a sandy desert. A refuge.

OBJECTIVE . . . OBJECTIFIED—"That which is external to the mind" is the general definition; we mean rather that which is visually externalized. Thought has power to objectify itself.

OBJECTIFICATION—The act of objectifying. The effect.

OBJECTIVE MIND—The conscious mind.

OBJECTIVE PLANE—The outer world of expression.

OBJECTIVE SIDE OF THOUGHT—The conscious side of thinking.

OBLIGATION—Any duty imposed by law, promise or contract.

OBSCURE—To darken, to hide, to make less intelligible. Misty.

OBSESSION—To come under the influence of persons, ideas, ambitions, fears, etc. Any thought influence from any source whatsoever which seeks to usurp the throne of reason and self-choice.

OBSTRUCTION—To obstruct is to impede, to hinder, to stop operation.

OBSTRUCTION TO THOUGHT—It must be apparent that there can be no obstruction to thought. Time, space and obstructions are unknown to Mind and thought. Anyone tuning in our stream of consciousness, our thought, will be one with it, no matter where they may be.

OCCULT—Hidden, concealed.

OCCUPATION—The thing our thought causes us to do. Same as *vocation*.

ODIUM—Abhorrence, antipathy, reproach. Stigma.

OLD AGE—Life cannot grow old. When we recognize there is but One Mind, and that no thought can flow through It of depression, fear or decay, no suggestion of imperfection; when our consciousness is that Man is Birthless, Deathless, Ageless Spirit, we will no longer grow old. Scientists have proven now that no part of the physical body is more than a few months old.

OMNIPOTENCE—The All-Powerful One. God.

OMNISCIENCE—The All-Knowing, All-Perceiving Mind of God.

OMNIPRESENCE—The Constant Presence of the Undivided Whole. Read again the chapter on Unity. Omnipresence is everywhere present.

OMNISCIENT INSTINCTIVE I AM—God in man and things.

ONE, THE—Means God.

ONE MIND—We have covered this under *Mind*.

ONLY-ALL—Beside Which there is none other. That Which has within Itself all that really is. The Life of everything and the Love through everything. The One Presence and the One Infinite Person Whom we call God or Spirit. Within this One all live.

OPPORTUNITY—Fit or suitable time; a chance. There can be no lack of opportunity; to believe in lack would be to limit God. In the unseen, the supply for every want awaits demand. "Desire for anything is the thing itself in incipiency." Life is open, rich and full. As we realize our unity with the Divine, our thought opens all doors to us; Undifferentiated Spirit flows through us, inspires us, and sustains that inspiration through to manifestation. Opportunities are unlimited.

ORDER—A condition in which everything is so arranged as to play its proper part; methodical or established system.

ORIGINAL . . . ORIGINALITY . . . ORIGIN—The *origin* is that from which anything springs, the primal cause. The source, the root, the commencement. Original means not copied, imitated, reproduced or translated. The first. Originality is being able to create without a pattern. Thinking for oneself. Read Emerson's Essay on "Self-Reliance."

OUTLINING—It is not our business to outline, to say how our good shall come. Our work is to specifically set the Law in motion. A right attitude is one which believes there is but One Mind and that this Mind knows exactly what to do, and how to do it, and that It does it at the bidding of our spoken word; that It opens the best channels, using the right agencies, human and divine, for the accomplishment of our desire. We should speak our word and believe that after it is spoken, it gathers unto itself whatever is necessary to its fulfillment. The Law does the rest.

PARENT . . . PARENT MIND—Parent is one who brings forth; a begetter; a source. The Parent Mind is God.

PARTICULARIZATION—Concrete forms produced by the Spirit.

PASSIVE AND RECEPTIVE—Means neutral and feminine.

PASSIVE ACTIVITY—To be passive and also to be active means to be non-resident to those vibrations which are inimical to our peace, while at the same time we declare for the condition we desire. This is different from *enduring* a condition. While in the midst of things one seems unable to change to his liking, he must practice knowing, with all the God Mind within him, that the condition he desires is present in its fullness. It is present in his consciousness, complete and perfect. A person who is actively conscious that the invisible perfection is present—while being to all appearance in the midst of imperfection—is practicing *activity*, while being *passive* to the imperfection. Emerson must have meant this when he said: "I see action to be good, when the need is, and sitting still to be also good." In our mind we may sit still in undesirable conditions and at the same time be very active in creating desirable conditions.

PASSIVE RECEPTIVITY—Willing to receive any and all forms of thought.

PATENT—That which is obvious.

PEACE—A state of inner calm. An inner calm so complete that nothing can disturb it. The Peace which comes only from the knowledge that It is All. Fathomless Peace is meant by the Peace of the Spirit. This is the peace to which Jesus referred when he said, "Peace I leave with you, my peace I give unto you." The Infinite is always at peace because there is nothing to disturb It. A realization of our Oneness with Omnipresence brings peace, the peace which is accompanied by a consciousness of power.

PERCEPT . . . PERCEIVE . . . PERCEPTION—Percept is an external object perceived by the mind. It is distinguished from a concept, which is an inner idea. To perceive is to see, used in connection with the act of seeing with the physical eye; also used to convey comprehension by the mind.

PERFECTION—The real state of being; complete so that nothing is wanting. Ideal faultlessness; the divine attribute of complete excellence. The only way a treatment can possibly be effective is for the practitioner to see *only perfection* in his patient, regardless of appearances.

PERSONAL ... PERSONALIZED—*Personal*, relating to an individual, his character, his conduct, his motives, his affairs, etc. *Personalize* is to make personal; to relate to the individual.

PERSONALITY—That which constitutes distinction of person. Personality is the result of man's experience; it is the sum-total of all he has said, done, felt, thought, hoped for and believed in; it is the result of his reactions to the events of life. Factors to be considered in the development of personality are heredity, race-suggestion, environment, child training, education, autosuggestion, and, indeed, anything and everything that impinges upon consciousness. Therefore, we are what we are largely because of the nature of our accumulated consciousness. Personality is the objective evidence of individuality. Our Personality is the use we make of our Divine Individuality. Just as a fine architect uses only the best materials, and plans most carefully how to construct his building, so should we, in the building of personality, choose most carefully the kind of materials we wish to use. Each one builds according to the pattern of his own desires.

PERSONALNESS—We do not think of God as a tremendous Person, but we do think of the Spirit as the Infinite Personalness in and through all Life. Infinite Self-Knowingness is the Abstract Essence of all personality. To think of God simply as an Infinite Principle would be to resolve the Divine Being into an Infinite IT, a cold, impersonal Law, containing no warmth or color, and certainly no responsiveness. Such a concept of God would rob man of his Divine Birthright and throw him, empty-handed, into an abyss of Law and Action, without motive or direction. No worse state of mentality could be imagined than one in which man thought of God simply as Principle. The very fact that man comes from the Universe in a self-conscious state, proves that behind all manifestation there is a Power that knows Itself; and a Power that knows Itself must be Personal. It is not, of course, limited. It must be Infinite. As wonderful as the concept may be, God is Personal to all who believe in Him. God is responsive to all who approach Him, and God is the Element of Personalness back of all personality. We could not be conscious beings unless there were a First-Consciousness in the universe.

PHENOMENA—The plural of phenomenon. That which strikes one as strange, unusual and unaccountable.

PSYCHIC PHENOMENA—Phenomena of the soul or subjective mentality. Whether psychic phenomena are caused by the agency of spirits, or by some inner power of our own mentality, that they are caused by mind power is apparent; for they are not caused by what we call physical force at all, but by some finer power than we, at present, understand. Some power, independent of the body, can see, hear, feel, smell, touch and taste without the aid of the physical instrument. Some power of intelligence within us can travel, communicate, project itself, recognize and be recognized, without the aid of the physical instrument. Such things, we call psychic phenomena, but there must be a natural and normal reason for all this. We do not yet understand psychic laws to any great extent.

PHILOSOPHY—A man's idea of life. Philosophy has been defined as the science of things divine and human. Practical wisdom. Philosophy has always transcended science, for philosophy deals with causes while science deals with effects. Many things which philosophy has taught for thousands of years are today being demonstrated by science.

PITY (SELF-PITY)—Self-pity can destroy the last vestige of happiness for anyone. It is folly for us, knowing that we are Divine, to fashion chains of self-pity which keep us from coming into the full and glorious expression of life. We should pour ourselves forth in greater love (whenever we begin to feel sorry for ourselves) and seek every possible avenue for expressing love, looking not to the results, but knowing all the while that love is its own healing. We are one with the eternal good of the Universe and have no reason to ever feel sorry for ourselves!

PLANES—Different rates of vibration. When we speak of "different planes" of existence, we are not indicating places, localities. We are recognizing certain levels or stages of thought . . . planes of consciousness. As our minds expand, as our awareness increases, we advance from one plane to another, from the animal consciousness to the Cosmic Consciousness.

PLASTIC—Easily molded.

POISE—Mental balance. Poise is that perfect balance which maintains everything in its proper place, without effort. It is the law of equilibrium without which nothing could be maintained. It is the law of balance that must exist in the Infinite Mind, since there is nothing to disturb It. Poise, or balance, is the law back of what we term the "Law of Compensation." It is Life perfectly balancing Itself. Self-Existent Life alone could produce complete poise. We cannot fathom the full meaning of poise as it exists in Spirit; but we can understand that it means an Eternal power, unruffled by conflicting emotions, always sure of Itself, unhurried and certain. The activity of the mind may be so perfectly adjusted, so perfectly poised, that it will give the impression of suspended motion.

POOR—See *Poverty*.

POSITIVE AND NEGATIVE THOUGHT—Positive and negative thinking are merely two ways of using the same mind through the power of self-choice. Positive thinking is direct and affirmative, sure of itself and moving straight toward its objective. Light is a positive principle, as it were, and when set in operation, the negative condition of darkness is instantly overcome. The statements of Jesus were always positive.

POTENTIAL—Inherent possibility.

POVERTY—An impoverished thought. A belief in lack or limitation. A lack of the knowledge that substance and supply are spiritual. A result of the inability to perceive that prosperity is ever-present. A denial of good. A limited sense of the Universe.

POWER—The energy by which everything lives. The Creative Medium of Spirit is the great Mental Law of the Universe. The Universal Law of Mind. It is the one Medium through which all Law and all Power operate. And man's creative power is marvelous; for every time he thinks, he sets the Law in motion. As his thought sets the Law in motion, he is specializing It for some definite purpose. This should give to all a sense of freedom and a realization that there is neither competition nor monopoly. It leaves each to work out his own salvation, not with fear and trembling, but with a calm sense of peace and assurance. Man may transmute as much of the Infinite Energy into degrees of power as he chooses to use.

PRACTICE . . . PRACTITIONER—A practitioner is one who practices mental and spiritual healing; and demonstrates for other than physical healing. The practitioner knows within himself the truth about his patient; and that self-knowingness rises into the consciousness of the patient. We treat man, not as a patient, not as a physical body, not as a diseased condition; neither do we treat the disease as belonging to him; we do not think of the disease as being connected with him nor a part of him. The practitioner realizes that man is born of Spirit and not of matter. Spirit is Changeless, Perfect and Complete. He realizes this until he sees his patient as a living embodiment of Perfection. (See chapter on Healing.)

PRAISE—Praise is expressed appreciation and commendation. Applause, laudation, honor. All of creation responds to praise. It is said even vegetation grows best for those who praise it; animal trainers would never succeed without praise; children need approbation to stimulate and inspire them. It is even necessary that we praise our own ability. Through an inherent law of Mind, we increase whatever we praise. Praise yourself from weakness to strength, from ignorance to intelligence, from poverty into abundance!

PRAYER—Refer to chapter on Prayer.

PRECEPT—A law, a mandate, a rule, a principle.

PRENATAL—Conditions before human birth.

PRESENCE, THE—"The Presence" is God. To meditate upon the Presence of God is to indraw the Universe into one's own soul. God is not a person but a Principle personified in each of us. Spirituality is the atmosphere of this Principle. Religion is Its outward form.

PRIMORDIAL—First in order; original; a first principle or element. For "primordial substance" see *Substance*.

PRINCIPLE—The Science of Mind is the study of the Principle of Being. The source or cause from which a thing results; a truth which is unchangeable. We first understand a principle and then relate it to our problem for a final test.

PROBLEM—A question proposed for solution. A matter stated for examination or proof. The "problem of evil" will be a problem as long as we believe in it.

PROCESS—"Process" denotes a progressive action, or a series of acts or steps, to make or produce something. There is no "process of healing" though there may be a process *in* healing.

PROPHECY . . . PROPHET—To prophesy is to tell of something that is to take place in the future. The one who makes this prophecy is called a prophet.

PROSPERITY—Prosperity is the out-picturing of substance in our affairs. Everything in the Universe is for us. Nothing is against us. We must know that everywhere we go we meet friendship, love, human interest, and helpfulness. Life is ever giving of Itself. We must receive, utilize, and extend the gift. Success and prosperity are spiritual attributes belonging to all people, but not necessarily used by all people.

PROTOTYPE—The original idea of any form.

PSYCHE—Soul or subjective.

PSYCHIC—A psychic is one who is able to consciously function in the subjective; able to see that which is pictured in the subjective, whether it be something which occurred in past ages or something at the moment. It might be either. A psychic power should always be under control of the conscious mind; it is not a normal, or balanced condition, to allow the subjective to control the conscious mind. When a psychic power is under the control of the conscious mind, it affords a wonderful storehouse of knowledge. All people are psychic, but all people are not mediums. A medium is one who objectifies the psychic sense.

PSYCHO-ANALYSIS—A systematic analysis of the subjective thought. It is a mental diagnosis. It is based upon the theory that Nature is perfect and when let alone will flow through man in a perfect state of health. The purpose of the analysis is to uncover the complex and heal the conflict, through removing it. It takes into account every experience the individual has ever had, paying much attention to his early training, and more especially to his emotional reactions to life. In the hands of those who thoroughly understand the principle by which it works, recognizing its limitations as well as its beneficial effects, it is prolific of good. But, in the thought of this writer, it is a thing without a soul, a skeleton without flesh. It lacks the warmth, the fire, the reality of spiritual realization. It is useless to remove a complex unless at the same time we place in its stead a realization of what life means. We must not tear down without building up. The proper analysis of the soul (the subjective) *coupled with real spiritual recognition*, will do wonders, however, and is well worth while.

PSYCHOLOGY—Study of the workings of the human mind. The science of mental actions and reactions.

PSYCHOMETRY—Reading from the soul side of things. Psychometry is a clairvoyant state, wherein the operator is able to read from the soul or subjective side of things. This reading is referred to as being able to "psychometrize." Everything has its mental atmosphere, which is the result of the thoughts surrounding it. To psychometrize means to read from this mental atmosphere and tell what it radiates.

PSYCHIC PHENOMENA—This is covered under the title of "Phenomena."

PSYCHIC WORLD—The world of subjectivity.

PUNISHMENT—There is no sin but a mistake and no punishment but an inevitable consequence. Wrong doing must be punished, for the law of cause and effect must be eternally operative. Right doing must be rewarded for the same reason. We do not say that man cannot sin; that he does not sin and that, therefore, there will be no punishment. What we do say is that MAN DOES MAKE MISTAKES AND HE IS THEREBY AUTOMATICALLY PUNISHED. He will continue to be punished until he finds the way. This does not mean that there is an evil power in the Universe. There is only One Power and that is God. But it does mean that there is an immutable Law of cause and effect running through everything and no human being can escape its operation. Sin is its own punishment and righteousness is its own reward!

PURPOSE—Determination with incentive.

PURPOSEFULNESS—When we speak of the purposefulness of Spirit, we mean that conscious mind has the ability to know what it wishes to express, and *the power to express it*. Dean Inge says that there can be no such thing as an "Infinite Purpose" because this would be a contradiction of the meaning of the word *purpose*. This is probably true; in fact it seems self-evident, but *it does not follow that there could be no such thing as an element of purposefulness running through the Eternal Mind!* Indeed, the evidence of this quality of being is so complete in the Universe that we cannot deny it. The evolution of creation on this planet alone would presuppose some kind of a purposefulness. The word *purposefulness* might be defined, in general terms, as the very antithesis of aimlessness; it is the spirit of significance, of importance, a commingling of desire and determination; an inner recognition of the Divine Urge.

RACE-MIND—The race-mind is the subjective thought of the race.

RACE-SUGGESTION—Human beliefs operating through the mentality of the individual. The tendency to reproduce what the race has thought and experienced. This race-suggestion is a prolific source of disease. These accumulated subjective tendencies of the human race are operative through any person who is receptive to them.

RACE-THOUGHT—This is another way of expressing race-suggestion. The way to protect oneself from it is by knowing that it cannot operate through him; by knowing that he cannot be affected by *suggestion*.

RADIATE—To illuminate, to brighten, to irradiate, to enlighten intellectually or spiritually.

REACTION—Reciprocal, or return, action or influence. Heightened activity and overaction, succeeding depression or shock. An action induced by vital resistance to some other action. So when we speak of the Law of Action and Reaction, it is simply the law of cause and effect.

REALITY—The truth about anything. Reality actually means that which is indestructible, incapable of decay. Reality is unchanging and everlasting. The self we see is what man has thought about himself, the form he has molded by his thought. The Real Self is Perfection, for God could not know anything unlike Himself. Our Sonship is Reality—Christ abiding in us. The Kingdom of God within is Reality. Reality, as concerning man, is that God in man, as man, is man.

REALIZATION—We should turn to that Living Presence within, Which is the Father in Heaven, recognize It as the One and Only Power in the Universe, unify with It; declare our word to be the presence, power and activity of that One, and speak the word as if we believed it, because the Law is the servant of the Spirit. If we could stand aside and let the One Perfect Life flow through us, we could not help healing people; we could not help having a perfect realization of perfection. The word *realization*, at any time, means an impression of reality on the mind; a clear apprehension; an acceptance by the mind that a thought or condition is actual. In this textbook, when we speak of "a perfect realization," we are referring to a realization of our Oneness with Good. There is a point in the supreme moment of realization, where the individual merges with the Universe, but not to the loss of his individuality; where a sense of the Oneness of all Life so enters his being that there is no sense of otherness. It is here that the mentality performs seeming miracles, because there is nothing to hinder the Whole from coming through. As immense and limitless as Life is, the Whole of It is brought to the point of our consciousness. We comprehend the Infinite only to the degree that It expresses Itself through us, becoming to us that which we believe It to be. Right here in our own nature is the path that gradually leads to realization. Subjective comprehension of Truth.

REANIMATE—To invigorate.

REASON—The mental ability to analyze, determine and form an opinion. The human mind can reason both inductively and deductively. The Divine Mind can reason only deductively. This must be apparent. Since inductive reasoning is an analysis, which is always an inquiry into truth and God IS TRUTH, it follows that God can reason only deductively. That which is Infinite does not have to *inquire* into the truth. So it follows that there can be no inductive reasoning in either the Spirit or the Soul of the Universe. There can be no inductive reasoning in Spirit, because It knows all things; there can be no inductive reasoning in the Soul of the Universe, because It is the Creative Medium and *if It could reason inductively, It could reject certain thoughts because It could analyze!* Soul or subjectivity can never reject; it is bound by its own nature to accept. Deductive reasoning is that process of reasoning which follows an already established premise. It is from the whole to a part. Spirit simply announces Itself to be That which It is. If we were to ascribe to It any reasoning power, we should be compelled to say that It reasons deductively only, or from the Whole to the part.

RECEPTIVITY—The power or capacity of receiving impressions. The quality of being able to absorb, hold, or contain . . . capacity. The Spirit can only give us what we can take, and since the taking is a mental process it is necessary for us to accept the fact that the SPIRIT HAS ALREADY PROVIDED EVERYTHING. We can increase our receptivity by treating ourselves something after this manner: "There is that within me which knows, understands, accepts, believes, recognizes and embodies. I know and I know that I know. I believe and am conscious that I believe. I am confident of the power of my own word, and have implicit reliance upon the truth. I expect the Truth to operate." In this manner, one becomes more and more conscious of a Divine Presence, Power and Law responding to his word. Thus one consciously builds up his receptivity of Truth.

RECOMPENSE—To give in return.

RECONCILE . . . RECONCILIATION—To cause to be friendly again. To adjust. The removal of any inconsistencies, any inharmonies.

RE-ENACT—To repeat an action which has previously taken place.

REFLECT . . . REFLECTION—To reflect is to throw, or turn back, thoughts upon anything; to consider mentally; to think seriously. Reflection is an image given back. Any state in which the mind considers its own conduct.

REGENERATE—To give new life or vigor.

REGRET—To feel dissatisfaction or grief on account of something, which has been done or which has been left undone. A looking back with longing . . . perhaps reproach.

REINCARNATION—Rebirth in the flesh. To *incarnate* means to give actual form to, to embody in some living type. *Re-incarnate* merely means to incarnate again. The theory of reincarnation believed in by many, is that we live again on this earth (after the experience of death) in a different form.

RELATIVE—That which depends upon something else.

RELATIVITY AND ABSOLUTENESS—Absolute is defined as "free from restrictions, unlimited, unconditioned." "The Unlimited and Perfect Being, God." Relativity is defined as "existence only as an object of, or in relation to, a thinking mind." "A condition of dependence." The Absolute, being Unconditioned, is Infinite and All; It is that Which Is, or the Truth. It is axiomatic that the Truth, being All, cannot be separated, limited or divided; It must be Changeless, Complete, Perfect and Uncreated. *Relativity* is not a thing of itself, but only that which functions within the Absolute and depends upon It.

We wish to affirm relativity without destroying Absoluteness. This can be done only by realizing that the relative is not a thing apart from, but is an experience IN, the All-Comprehending Mind. The relative does not contradict the Absolute, but affirms It; and *the relative alone guarantees that there is an Absolute*. The Absolute is Cause, the relative is effect. To suppose that there could be an Absolute without a relative, would be to suppose that there could be an unexpressed God or First Cause. This is unthinkable and impossible. The Consciousness of God must be expressed, hence the relative. Time, space, outline, form, change, movement, action and reaction, manifestation and creation, all are relative, but all are real—not apart from, but within the Absolute. Relativity subsists within existence, and inherent Life is potential and latent with limitless possibilities. The relative and the Absolute do not contradict each other.

RELIGION—A man's idea of God, or of gods.

REMISSION—Forgiveness of sins; release.

REPRESSION—The energy set in motion through the creative urge within man is the dynamic power of Mind, and unless it becomes expressed, it will congest within the mentality. Inhibited action produces inner conflicts, which mentally tear and bind; and as they manifest in physical correspondents, they produce nervous disorders. It is claimed that a large percentage of diseases is caused by the suppression of some form of emotion—any desire that remains unexpressed. Things will stand just so much pressure and no more; when a limit is reached an explosion will follow, unless some avenue of expression is provided. All irritation and agitation are mental in their cause, and a sense of calm and peace alone can heal them.

Fear is an intense emotion, and if bottled up, secretes poison in the system. Anger, malice, vindictiveness and kindred emotions are but subtle forms of fear, arising from a sense of inferiority. All these emotions must be swept off the board if one is to gain peace, calm and poise—the union of which alone can give power.

If we were completely expressed, we would never become sick or unhappy. The average person goes through life expressed only in part and always with a sense of incompletion and dissatisfaction. Something must be done to make the individual complete, if he is to remain normal and happy and really alive. When an emotion conflicts with the will, and becomes suppressed or repressed, it returns to its subjective state, *but remains active*. It may remain in a subjective state for years, but eventually, unless neutralized, it will manifest. Let one go for years with some unexpressed longing, and he will have created such a desire that it will have become irresistible in its inclination toward expression.

People often become seething caldrons within because of inhibited action. Energy must have an outlet. The solution of the problem of desire is to transmit any destructive tendency into some form of action which is constructive. However, an intellectual form of expression alone will not do this, for only those things to which we can give the complete self will solve the problem. Love is the givingness of self to the object of its adoration. We should all have something that *we love to do*, something that will completely express the self, something that will loose the energies of Life into action and transmute the power into creative work. We should learn to love all people, not just some people.

This does not exclude the great human relationships which mean so much to all of us; but it does take the sting out of life, and does free the individual to love all, adore some, and find happiness everywhere. I can imagine someone saying, "This is too impersonal a teaching." It is not impersonal at all; this does not mean that we care less for people; indeed, we shall find that for the first time in life, we really care, but the sting will have gone. Refuse to have the feelings hurt. Refuse yourself the pleasure and morbidity of sensitiveness. Come out of the emotional intoxication and be YOURSELF. Never allow the thought to become depressed or morbid. Engage in some form of activity that will express the better self. Do not attempt to draw life from others; live the life that God gave you; it is ample and complete. Live, love and laugh! Let the heart be glad and free; rejoice in the thought of life and be happy. Realize God, in and through all, and unify with the Whole. Why take fragments when the Whole is here for the asking?

RESENTMENT—Anger, displeasure, indignation, hatred, ill-will, pique.

RESIST . . . RESISTANCE—To resist is to obstruct, hinder, check, thwart, counteract, oppose. Resistance is the act of striving against.

RESOLVE—To determine, to conclude, to become of an opinion.

RESPONSIBILITY—The word *responsible* means involving a degree of accountability. Liable. And responsibility . . . that for which anyone is responsible. We repeatedly state that we assume no responsibility to *make a treatment work*. We assume full responsibility for *giving* the treatment. It is the Law which makes it work. We do not create the power by which the treatment does its work. We merely set that power in operation. Therefore, we should not become more anxious over a cancer than over a headache.

RESULTS—What happens as a necessary result of the law of cause and effect. Results follow mathematically. Conditions.

RESURRECTION—Rising from a belief in death. A restoring or a renewal. We recognize that life is an unfoldment and must necessarily culminate in a victory over death. Jesus made it plain that we should do "even greater things." He taught us that the Kingdom of Heaven is not reached through the gateway of death but by overcoming our limited beliefs while here . . . by recognizing the Father within. For further elaboration of the subject of *resurrection*, we refer you to the chapter on Immortality.

REVELATION—Becoming consciously aware of hidden things. Since the mind that man uses is the same Mind that God uses, the One and Only Mind, the avenues of revelation can never be closed. But no man can receive the revelation for another. I cannot buy your revelation and you cannot buy mine. Remember when Simon wished to buy from Peter the power which spiritual understanding gives? "But Peter said unto him, Thy money perish with thee, because thou hast thought that the gift of God may be purchased with money. Thou hast neither part nor lot in this matter; for thy heart is not right in the sight of God." Nor does this *revelation* come any more for begging and beseeching than it does for buying. It is "the gift of God." Eventually we shall know that the priceless revelation of "*my* Lord and *my* God" comes only when we turn to the Father within, Who has been there all the time awaiting our recognition . . . waiting to give us our revelation.

REWARD—The only reward we shall ever receive is that which is the inevitable consequence of the law of cause and effect.

RICHES—Ideas of abundance; result of the consciousness of supply.

RITUAL . . . RELIGIOUS CEREMONIAL . . . RITUALISM—Emphasizing such things as altar lights, eucharistic vestments, the eastward position, wafer bread, the mixed chalice, incense, etc.

ROSEMARY—An emblem of fidelity, or constancy . . . for remembrance.

RUT—A groove; a regular course; a fixed direction. All of us occasionally find ourselves in a mental rut. We need to pick ourselves up and reaffirm our position in Divine Mind; we need to see ourselves surrounded by everything that makes life worth while, and know that Truth is not bound by any existing conditions.

SACRIFICE—To suffer to be lost for the sake of obtaining something else. To make an offering.

SAGE—One versed in spiritual truths.

SAINT—A holy man.

SALVATION—Salvation is not a thing, not an end, but a Way. The way of salvation is through man's unity with the Whole. Grace is the givingness of Spirit to Its Creation.

SAVIOR—Jesus stands forth from the pages of human history as the greatest figure of all time. His teachings contain the greatest lesson ever given to the human race; and his life and works, while on earth, provide the grandest example that was ever given to man. In this philosophy, no attempt is made to rob Jesus of his greatness or to refute his teachings. Indeed, it is based upon the words and the works of this, the most remarkable personality that ever graced our planet with his presence; and, until a greater figure appears, Jesus will still remain the great Wayshower to mankind. Let us not waste time, then, in theological discussions which lead nowhere; but, following his example, let us do the works which he did. "The works that I do shall ye do also; and greater works than these shall ye do; because I go unto my father."

SCIENCE—Knowledge of laws and principles; organized knowledge. The results of science and the revelations of religion are growing closer and closer together.

SCRIPTURES . . . SCRIPTURAL—Any sacred literature.

SEER—A prophet. One gifted with spiritual insight. One who sees into causes.

SELF-ANALYSIS—To analyze anything is to resolve it into its constituent parts or elements. Self-analysis is the act of analyzing oneself. Look into your own past and find out what you are afraid of and convince the mentality that there is nothing to fear. Look the world squarely in the face; sift the mentality to its depths, removing every obstruction that inhibits the free flow of those great spiritual realizations which we have talked about from time to time in this textbook.

SELF-CHOICE—This term implies that we have the ability to make selection of one or more things. That is what individuality is: self-choice with the ability to choose backed with the power to externalize that choice. To be an individual, a man had to be created with self-choice.

SELF-CONFIDENCE—A belief in one's own ability.

SELF-CONSCIOUSNESS—Personally conscious. Distinguished from Cosmic Consciousness, which is a consciousness of the Unity with the Whole.

SELF-EXISTENT—Living by virtue of its own being. Spirit is Self-Existent.

SELF-KNOWING MIND—The conscious mind.

SELF-PROPELLING—Having power within itself. Spirit is Self-Propelling.

SELF-REALIZATION—A consciousness of the self.

SELF-RECOGNITION—An awareness of one's Divinity.

SEQUENCE—The order in which events are connected or related. Simple succession.

"SERVANT OF THE SPIRIT THROUGHOUT THE AGES"—The Universal Soul, being the Creative Principle of Nature, and the Law of the Spirit, has been called "The Holy Ghost" or "The Servant of the Eternal Spirit throughout the ages."

SERVICE—Service is the keynote to success and implies constructive work; also, loyalty to your work and to all concerned in it.

SILENCE—This word is used oftener and perhaps less understood than any one word in the terminology of the metaphysician. There is no place we must go for *the silence*; there is no particular posture we must assume; there is no formula we must repeat. We enter this "inner tabernacle" by whatever route we may. Some people live in such conscious unity with Good that *instantly* they can turn within and direct the avenues they wish the Good to take. Others need to approach by prayer, by singing, by reading a verse from the Bible, by repeating an inspirational poem. If we know that God is forever right where we are, we shall not be *reaching out* in every direction for Him. We enter the inner chamber of our mind and close the door on all discord and confusion, and commune with our God, our spiritual consciousness; Our Father within. Our eyes do not see visions and our ears do not hear sounds. The Silence is our communion with Spirit; our awareness of our Unity with Good, our understanding that "the Father within, he doeth the work."

SIMPLE CONSCIOUSNESS—The consciousness of the animal.

SIN—We have tried to show that there is no sin but a mistake and no punishment but a consequence. The Law of cause and effect. Sin is merely missing the mark. God does not punish sin. As we correct our mistakes, we forgive our own sins.

SINCERE—Being in reality what it appears to be. Sound, true, honest; free from hypocrisy or dissimulation; straightforward.

SONSHIP—We are all Sons of God and all partake of the Divine Nature.

SOUL—The Creative Medium of Spirit; the subjective side of life; the Mirror of Mind, for It reflects the forms of thought which are given It. Man's soul life re-enacts the Soul Life of the Universe. Soul is subjective because it takes the thought of conscious mind and acts upon it. Its nature is subjective and It cannot analyze or reject; It can only carry out the orders given It. Infinite in Its power and ability to do, but not knowing that It does.

SOUL OF THE UNIVERSE—The Universal Creative Medium.

SPACE—Space, like time, is not a thing of itself, but is only the outline of form. It is a relative distance within the Absolute. Space, also, is necessary to the expression of Spirit; for without it no definite form could be produced. We must not be confused over the ideas of time and space, as they are not things of themselves. They are entirely relative but none the less necessary. Space is the distance between two specific forms. The Cosmic World.

SPECIALIZE—To bring into concrete form.

SPIRIT—God, within Whom all spirits exist. The Self-Knowing One. The Conscious Universe. The Absolute. Spirit in man is that part of him which enables him to know himself. That which he really is. We do not see the spirit of man any more than we see the Spirit of God. We see what man does; but we do not see the doer.

We treat of Spirit as the Active and the only Self-Conscious Principle. We define Spirit as the First Cause or God; the Universal I AM. The Spirit is Self-Propelling, It is All; It is Self-Existent and has all life within Itself. It is the Word and the Word is volition. It is Will because It chooses. It is Free Spirit because It knows nothing outside Itself, and nothing different from Itself. Spirit is the Father-Mother-God because It is the Principle of Unity back of all things. Spirit is all Life, Truth, Love, Being, Cause and Effect, and is the only Power in the Universe that knows Itself.

SPIRIT OF MAN—God in man.

SPIRIT OF THE UNIVERSE—The Self-Knowing Mind of God.

SPIRITS—Personalities.

SPIRITUAL—The Atmosphere of God.

SPIRITUAL CONSCIOUSNESS—The realization of the Divine Presence.

SPIRITUAL MAN—Man in a conscious state.

SPIRITUAL REALIZATION—The realization of the Divine Presence.

STAGNATE—To become dull or inactive.

STRAIN—Tension; excessive stress.

STREAM OF CONSCIOUSNESS—The automatic, mental emanation of the subjective state of thought.

SUBJECTIVE—Beneath the threshold of consciousness. The inner side. Subconscious.

SUBJECTIVE ACTIVITY—The inner action of the automatic law.

SUBJECTIVE CAUSATION—The mental law set in motion.

SUBJECTIVE SIDE OF LIFE—The inner side of life, as law.

SUBJECTIVE STATE OF THOUGHT—The sum-total of all one's thinking, both conscious and unconscious.

SUBJECTIVE TENDENCY—The subjective trend of thought.

SUBJECTIVE TO SPIRIT—The Law is subjective to the Spirit.

SUBJECTIVITY OF THE UNIVERSE—The Universal Soul or Mental Law.

SUBLIMATE—To transmute energy into another form of action.

SUBSIST—To live by virtue of Spirit.

SUBSTANCE—The formless back of all forms. The *Primordial Substance* is the ultimate formless Stuff, from which all things come.

SUCCESS—The favorable termination of anything attempted.

SUGGESTION—Receiving the thoughts of another. Suggestion accepts the ideas of others and believes in them. It may be conscious or unconscious.

SUPERNATURAL—That which is considered above or beyond natural law or order. Miraculous, superhuman, preternatural.

Preternatural exceeds in some way that which is natural, ordinary or explicable, *without being felt as supernatural. Superhuman*, many times used as the equivalent to supernatural, is often used in hyperbole of what, though merely human, far exceeds ordinary standards, as when we speak of someone putting forth "superhuman effort" in the accomplishment of something. In metaphysics, we learn that much of what has been termed *supernatural*, is divinely natural; is the working out of natural law. It is only termed miraculous when we do not know the law back of, and governing, it. The supernatural simply means over and beyond or above that which is natural—not a violation of nature's laws but a transcendence of them.

Supply—Supply is the general term used to cover every conceivable need. The verb supply means merely to provide for, contribute to, accommodate with. *Supply*, the noun, as we use it so often through this textbook is synonymous with substance. And we have already learned that God is the substance of all things, and this Substance is Itself the *supply of* every demand that can be made. In political economy we learn that supply is the amount of a commodity available for a demand. In the Science of Mind, we learn that the supply of *every good* awaits our demand: "All that the Father hath." Somewhere there is already provided a lavish abundance for every want—a supply equal to any claim that can be made upon it—BUT THE DEMAND MUST BE MADE! "As you believe." Each has the power to demand his share of the gift God has provided of health, wealth and power. Each is supplied AS he believes.

Symbol—A mental impression denoting spiritual or mental truth. Most Hebrew scholars regard the Bible as an allegory, recording the spiritual advancement of the Jewish people. Jesus certainly thought it worth while to present some of his most important teachings in the form of parables. To him, everything in the natural world was a symbol of some spiritual truth . . . a representation of how the Cosmic Plan was working out in the unfoldment of man.

Tact—Tact actually implies delicate and sensitive perception, sympathetic understanding, particularly with reference to that which is fit, graceful or considerate under certain circumstances. A discerning sense of what is right, proper, or judicious.

Talmud—The body of Jewish civil and canonical law not in the Pentateuch.

Taoism—One of the principal religions of China, founded by Laotse, Chinese philosopher, in the sixth century B.C.

Telekinetic Energy—Telekinetic energy is defined as "the ability to move ponderous objects without physical contact." This form of energy is displayed in that class of mental phenomena which cause objects to move without any physical agency, and is, therefore, caused by some form of *mental energy*, or by some agency other than physical.

Telepathy—Thought transference. This is so well known that it is only necessary to emphasize one fact: mental telepathy would not be possible unless there were a Medium through which it could operate. This medium is Universal Mind.

Tendency—Proclivity, inclination, bent, bias, leaning in a certain direction. *Tenor*, on the other hand, suggests rather the *prevailing* course, or continuity, of the thing itself.

Thanksgiving—It has been said that "the prayer of thanksgiving is the prayer of appropriation." This was the manner in which Jesus prayed when he raised Lazarus from the tomb: "Father, I thank thee. . . ." Recognition, unification, and realization are the three steps in prayer or treatment. When we speak the words of thanksgiving to the God within, knowing "before they ask will I answer," there is something in this attitude of thanksgiving that carries us beyond the field of doubt into one of perfect faith and acceptance, receptivity . . . realization. Appreciation, gratitude and thanksgiving—the motive power which attracts and magnifies the hidden potentialities of life.

THE ONLY—The One Power . . . God.

THEOLOGY—That which treats of the nature of God. That which men have thought about God and formulated into creeds and doctrines and given to the world as reliable principles by which men should live. Theology often concerns itself more with the forms of worship than the spirit which inspires it, dealing with doctrines rather than life. Let us not be disturbed by any dogmatic announcements but rather seek our own spiritual illumination. Theology may concern itself with how Jesus was born; let us concern ourselves with the truths he taught.

THEORY—A general principle offered to explain some phenomena, and rendered more or less plausible by evidence in the facts.

THEOSOPHY—The "Theosophical Society" in America was founded in 1875. Among its declared aims was "To form a nucleus of a universal brotherhood of humanity, without distinction of race, creed or color." It embodied some Buddhistic and some Brahmanistic theories. In its modern teaching, it embraces the laws of Karma, Causation, and Reincarnation. It holds up lofty ideals on the Immanence of God and the Solidarity of Life. Those who have studied our textbook will know that we agree that we are *immortal now*; we stress the Immanence of God, but we interpret the teachings of Jesus as plainly instructing that the Law of Karma (Cause and Effect) can be changed at any moment through a knowledge of, and the application of, the principle of the Science of Mind.

THINGS—All *things* are thoughts made manifest. Nothing exists in the universe, whether it be rock, tree, or human being, that was not first idea; that did not first exist in Universal Mind as a perfect concept.

THOUGHT—The movement of consciousness. It works through Law but that Law is consciously set in motion. See chapter on this.

THOUGHT FORMS—All thought has definite form on the subjective side of life.

TIME—"Sequence of events in a Unitary Whole." An excellent definition given by Dean Inge, for of course, time is not a thing of itself. It is simply a measure of experience in eternity. Time does not contradict Eternity, but allows It to become expressed in terms of definite experience. Time is necessary since it allows experience to take place within the One, but time is never a thing of itself. It is impossible to measure time; for yesterday is gone and tomorrow has not come, and today is rapidly slipping past. If we were to attempt to put a finger on any period of time, it would be gone before we could point to it. But, illusive as time is, it is necessary to experience.

TRANCE—A subjective state. A state in which conscious, voluntary movement is suspended.

TRANSCENDENT—That which is of superlative quality. Reaching beyond. Surpassing.

TRANSITION—Passage from one stage, or plane, or state to another.

TRANSMUTE . . . TRANSMUTATION—To change from one nature, form or substance into another. To transform.

TREATMENT—Treatment is the art, the act, and the science of consciously inducing thought within the Universal Subjectivity, for the purpose of demonstrating that we are surrounded by a Creative Medium which responds to us through a law of correspondence. In its more simple meaning, treatment is the time, process and method necessary to the changing of our thought. Treatment is clearing the thought of negation, of doubt and fear, and causing it to perceive the ever-presence of God.

TRINITY—The threefold Universe. A trinity of being appears to run through all Nature and all Life. For instance, there is electricity, the way it works, and what it does. There is the seed, the creative medium of the soil, and the plant. But through the Trinity of God and man, there runs a Self-Conscious Spirit, and this is what distinguishes man from the brute. Man duplicates the Trinity of God in spirit, soul and body. We are One with all matter in the physical world; One with the Creative Law of the Universe in the Mental World; and One with the Spirit of God in the Conscious World. Man as the little circle, God as the Big Circle. We are a point in Universal Consciousness, which is God; and God is our Life, Spirit, Mind and Intelligence. We are not separated from Life, neither is It separated from us; but we are separate entities in It—Individualized Centers of God Consciousness.

TRIUNE UNITY—The Trinity.

TRUTH—That which is. It is the Reason, Cause and Power in and through everything. It is Birthless, Deathless, Changeless, Complete, Perfect, Whole, Self-Existent, Causeless, Almighty, God, Spirit, Law, Mind, Intelligence, and anything and everything that implies Reality. By a process of axiomatic reasoning, we arrive at the conclusion that Spirit knows nothing outside Itself. The Truth is that which Is; and being that which Is, It must be Infinite and All. Being Infinite or All, the Truth can have nothing outside Itself, other than Itself, or unlike Itself, by which to divide Itself; consequently, the Spirit is Indivisible, Changeless and Complete within Itself. Itself is all that is—both Cause and Effect, the Alpha and the Omega.

ULTIMATE—The word means the last; final; most remote in space or time; the extreme; arrived at as the last result; incapable of further analysis, division or separation; conclusive. The *ultimate* of *effect* is already potential in *cause*. We should conceive of our word as being *the thing*, the beginning and the end of the thing thought of, the cause and the effect—and both are in Spirit, the Ultimate. There is no ultimate evil, for the ultimate of everything is God—Spirit. Consequently, *there is ultimate salvation for all*. Since each soul is some part of the Whole, it is impossible that any soul can be lost.

UNCHOOSING—By this we mean not able to choose. The Soul, unlike Spirit, has no choice of Its own. Being subjective, It is bound to receive but cannot choose. We must always bear in mind that Soul simply reflects the images that the Spirit casts into It.

UNCONSCIOUS—Not known or apprehended by consciousness. The Soul is subconscious, but certainly not *unconscious*.

UNCONSCIOUS MEMORY—Subjective memory.

UNCONSCIOUS THOUGHT—Unconscious subjective thought. A man does not always *think about* the particular disease he finds himself experiencing, but his subjective mind may have been entertaining certain combinations of thought which logically produced certain diseases. If he were angry much of the time, poison would be secreted in his system and there would be a tendency to manifest as some disease. The manifestation of itself might be a disease he had never heard of and he would say, "How could my thought have anything to do with such a disease when I never even heard the name of it?" Yet it is not difficult to see how *his thought had been the causation back of the disease.*

UNITY—The Oneness of God and man. The enlightened in every age have taught that back of all things there is One Unseen Cause. There is no record of any great thinker who has taught duality. This teaching of Unity . . . "The Lord our God is One God . . ." is the chief cornerstone of the Sacred Scriptures of the East, as well as our own Sacred Writings. It is the mainspring of the teachings of modern philosophies, such as Unity Teachings, the New Thought Movement, the Occult Teachings, the Esoteric or Inner Teachings, of our own Religious Science, and even much that is taught under the name of Psychology. Science has found nothing to contradict this teaching, and it never will, for the teaching is self-evident. An entire chapter in the textbook is available for the further elucidation of this subject. The word *Unity,* we might explain here, signifies the union of parts, a result of many drawn together into one perfect harmonious whole . . . Oneness . . . One Life, of which we are a part; One Intelligence, which we use; One Substance, which is brought into manifold manifestation; One Principle, as Jesus taught: "That they may all be one, even as Thou, Father, art in me and I in Thee, and they also in us."

UNIVERSE—The Cosmic World. In the entire universe, One Power Alone really acts, the Power of the Word of God. If the Universe were not Perfect It could not exist for a single moment. It is self-evident, then, that everything in It must be perfect. The student of Truth must realize and maintain that he lives in a Perfect Universe, among perfect people. "Perfect God, Perfect Man, Perfect Being." This is our premise. Thus the soul acquaints itself with God and is at peace.

UNIVERSAL LAW—Divine Creative Principle.

UNIVERSAL MIND—The Creative Medium of Spirit.

UNIVERSAL POWER—This is the entire Power of God. How can an individual use this? Just as an individual, who is only part of the Whole, can breathe the wholeness of the air and partake of the wholeness of the sunshine. Just as the mathematician, who is not the principle of mathematics but who is in unity with it, has access to the totality of numbers. Just so we individualize the Universal Power. We can have and use as much as we wish . . . "As we believe."

UNIVERSAL SOUL—The Universal Subjectivity.

UNIVERSAL SPIRIT—The Conscious Mind of God . . . the Universe of conscious mind and self-determination. In Chart Number III, this is clearly shown. The Universal Subjectivity means the Creative Medium of the Spirit. *Particularization* means the world of matter and forms. The *descent of Spirit* means the passing of Spirit into form—the particularization of Spirit into many things. The point drawn from the top of the chart to the bottom of the section, symbolizes the Unity of all Life. Spirit passes through Law into form. Multiplicity comes from Unity, but never contradicts Oneness. The many are within the One.

Man's life partakes of the Divine Nature, and this chart may be used in the individual or the Universal sense. Our conscious mind is some part of the One Conscious Mind of the Whole. The Complete Nature of God is reflected in man, and he uses the same law that God uses; for there is but One Law, as there is but One Spirit. Both God and man use the same Creative Medium or Universal Subjectivity. It is the *law* of all thought and action. THINGS COME FROM ONE SOURCE THROUGH ONE COMMON LAW AND ONE COMMON CREATIVE MEDIUM. We think of our lives as One with the Whole, on all three planes of expression. We are one with the Conscious Mind, one with the Creative Law, and in our bodies we are one with all matter.

No matter what we are treating or for what purpose, THE MEDIUM OF ALL THOUGHT IS THE UNIVERSAL LAW! It particularizes Itself through the power of the word that is spoken into It. The word alone is conscious. The Law is automatic and the form is without self-determination. Universal Spirit means the universe of conscious mind and self-determination.

UNIVERSAL SUBJECTIVITY—The Creative Medium or the Universal Mind. See further description above under head of *Universal Spirit.*

URGE—To urge is to push, drive, impel; to ply with motives, arguments, persuasion, or importunity; to insist upon; to present in an earnest manner. An urge, then, it is apparent, is a stronger emotion than a half-hearted wish. We refer constantly to "the Divine Urge." How can we distinguish this from a human impulse? Is there any difference? How are we to know whether our ends are entirely selfish or whether we are really merging with the greater good of the Whole? Although the Universal Urge works through the individual, It never loses sight of Its own Cosmic Purpose. We must, therefore, ask ourselves whether only selfish ends will be attained by the fulfillment of our desires, or will it benefit all, at least hurt no one. The Divine Urge is altruistic, serving the many through Its least expression. It deals with spiritual factors, such as love and service for their own sake; It is true to Itself on every plane of expression.

VIBRATION . . . VIBRATE—Vibration is Law in execution. To vibrate may mean to fluctuate, to waver. A moving or swinging to and fro. We speak of being in vibration to one thought and then another; we mean being in harmony with one thought and then another, switching from one to another. The vibration of a book is the mental atmosphere of that book; it is what we "read between the lines" as well as on the lines. We speak of the high vibration of a room, particularly a room used for spiritual and mental treatment, and we mean the spiritual consciousness which has been engendered there. All phenomena are determined by their rate of vibration. From what we term *inanimate* to man—the highest of God's creations—all are made of the One and Only Substance. The difference in the form is determined by the vibration. Water, ice and vapor are all the same substance, differing only in rate of vibration. The highest vibration which man experiences is from Love.

VICTORY—A gaining of the superiority in *any* struggle. To the metaphysician, every victory is won in the silence of his own soul; by turning to "the Father within."

VISION—The ability to see. People who close up all their avenues of receptivity, who are not open to new ideas, who refuse to recognize beauty, who *refuse* to SEE—frequently find themselves losing the power to use their physical eyes. "Spiritual blindness" is a misnomer for *actually* there is no obstruction to vision; there is no near vision and no far vision; there is no weak vision and no blurred vision. There is only One Perfect Seeing, which sees in and through us. GOD SEES AND HIS IS THE ONLY MIND THERE IS. It is our Mind; consequently, man sees, whether he knows it or not. Perfect identification of the self with that Mind in which Substance and Idea are One will forever insure perfect vision.

VISUALIZE . . . VISUALIZATION—The art of mentally projecting a thought form into the Universal Creative Medium. *Visualizing* means mentally seeing the things that you wish to have or to do. When you mentally see the things you desire—and see them clearly—you are presenting Universal Mind with images of thought; and, like the creative soil of the ground, It at once tends to project them into form. If the thought image is clear, it provides a good mold; if it is imperfect the mold is a poor one. This does not mean one must set his mind or hold thoughts; it simply means that he must think clearly.

There are practitioners who use the method of visualization almost entirely, and this is the manner in which they work. They decide definitely what they wish to image into Mind. They become quiet and begin to see the complete outcome of their desire in mental pictures, in every detail. If it is a house they wish, they know the exact type of house. In the silence of their thought, they mentally see themselves in this house, living in it, entertaining their friends in it, etc., and they mentally go from room to room, stopping to admire some picture or some piece of furniture. Mentally, they make this house just as real as possible. They enter it, sit down in it, etc., and they say, "I am now living in this house." They have set the word in motion, through the Law, which will bring this house into realization, unless they definitely neutralize the thought. They continue this every day until the house appears. The method is the same, whether it be a house or a dress, a position or a husband. This is one way, and is good if we know no better. It is good as far as it goes and there are people to whom this seems an excellent approach. Our only comment about it is that it is a form of limitation.

If we meant to purchase gloves, it is not likely we would approach the clerk with a picture of gloves; we would state the kind of gloves we desired, kid or fabric, and the latest style. If we showed a picture only, the clerk might answer that they carried nothing of that kind, and we would never be shown all the lovely new styles with which their cases were filled. When we learn to read and write, we no longer draw pictures to indicate our needs. Since we recognize our Oneness with Substance, since we know that desire is the thing itself in incipiency—supply and demand are one—we know that we need only turn over to Intelligence our highest conceptions of beauty as we make our demand for a home, and there will be delivered to us something much finer than it was possible for us to picture.

VITALITY AND ENERGY—Energy is a divine and unfailing attribute, and therefore is never depleted, limited, or destroyed. Vitality means that on which life depends, but vitality in man comes from, and is of, God. The vitality of God is Self-Existent, Self-Propelling. As I become conscious of my Oneness with Good, I am filled with enthusiasm, and a sense of energy and vitality. God is the Indwelling Power of my life. As I open myself to the inner, vital Life, and merge myself with Its flow, I find myself energized and vitalized.

VOCATION—The thing our thought causes us to do.

VOLITION—The power to act independently. The power of conscious choice. There is but the one volitional factor in the Universe, and this is Spirit, or the Self-Knowing Mind. The Spirit cannot stop knowing.

WHOLE—When we speak of "the Whole," we are speaking of God. Man's self-knowing mind is his perception of Reality. It is his Unity with the Whole, or God, on the conscious side of life, and is an absolute guarantee that he is a Center of God-Consciousness in the Vast Whole.

WILL—Will means decision coming into execution. To will is to determine by an act of choice. Volition, choice and will must be attributes of Spirit. They mean practically the same thing. We must be careful, however, not to think of these qualities of Spirit in terms of human or limited thought. When we choose, we make a selection, which means there are two or more things to choose from; but when Spirit chooses, It simply announces. The Spirit does not have to *will* to make things happen; things happen because it is the will of Spirit that they should be. *This will*, then, is simply the execution of a purpose; and since Spirit is Absolute, there can be nothing to deny Its Will. Choice, volition, and will are necessary and real attributes of Self-Existent Power; for without them there would be no channel through which the Ideas of God could be expressed. In man these qualities—volition, choice, and will—are limited, but in God they are limitless.

WORD—The Word means, of course, the ability of Spirit to declare Itself into manifestation, into form. The Word of God means the Self-Contemplation of the Spirit. The Manifest Universe, as we see It, as well as the Invisible Universe that must also exist, is the result of the Self-Contemplation of God. "He spake and it was done." "The word was with God and the word was God."

Index

See the Contents pages for chapter headings and lists of meditations.
Such words as are not found in the Index are located in the Glossaries.

A

Abiding in the One, 636
Ability, Definition of, 228
About the Study of Life, Nothing
    Supernatural, 301
Absolute
    Causation, 365
    Intelligence, 59, 339
Absoluteness
    dealing with, 142
    and Relativity, 217
Abundance, 309, 694
Acquiring Faith, The
    Technique of, 406
Act of Incarnation, The, 392
Action
    Law Is Mind in, 51, 93, 381
    No Mistakes, Perfect, 149, 154,
      497
    of Spirit within Itself, The, 74, 352,
      363
Action
    perfect, 151, 497

power and, 51, 75, 99, 385
    and reaction, the law of, 91
Active, Definition of, 47
Active, Not Passive, Treatment, 325
Activity, Treating for, 152
Activity of the One Mind, 393
Actor, Mind is the, 110
Adoption, The Spirit of, 639
Affairs, Definition of, 79
Affirmation, The supreme, 243
Against Us, The Universe Holds
    Nothing, 627
Age, No, 127
Agitation and Fear, Irritation, 233
Aim of evolution, The, 86, 195
All Knowledge, Contains, 323
All-Only, Definition of, 712
All Principles Are as Intangible, 328
All Thought Is Creative, 313
Allness of truth, 57
Allowed to Choose, We Are, 433
Altar of Faith, The, 586
Always Open, The Father's House, 625
Always a Power, 403

Analysis
    psycho-, 130
    self-, 238, 749
And Jesus Knew Their Thoughts, 610
And the Father Saw Him Afar Off, 624
Answer
    is in man, The, 170
    Prayer is its own, 142, 402
Antichrist, Christ and, 84, 244
Apologies, No, 177
Apparitions, 197, 215
Appearance is the reality, Back
    of the, 122
Application of the Story, The, 627
Approach, The Mental, 403
Approach the Spirit, How to, 609
Argue, God Does Not, 620
Argument in treatment, 131
Armor of God, The, 647
Arms and Hands, 459
As Little Children, 616
Ascending Scale of Life, The, 644
Ask in Faith, Believing, 650
Asthma and Hay Fever, 464

Atmospheres
    Mental, 89, 183, 286, 538, 712,
       716, 734
    Thought, 500
    Unpleasant, 191
Atmosphere of Our Thinking,
    The, 394
Atmosphere of places, The, 184
Atonement, The, 238
    our part in, 242
    vicarious, 240
Attracting Friends, 141
Attracting Success, 504
Attraction
    The Law of, 83, 141, 285, 500, 695
    of personality, 148, 501
Aura
    Definition of, 78, 281, 712
    The human, 191, 214
Auto-suggestion, Definition of, 79
Available to All, 405
Awakening, An, 35
Awakening, The Great, 623, 642

B

Basis for Mental Healing, The, 392
Basis of thought, A new, 24
Bear Much Fruit, That Ye, 636
Beginning, The, 337
Being, The Trinity of, 32, 356
Belief
    in duality, Results of, 34
    law of, 90
Believe, How Much Can We, 318
Believing, Ask in Faith, 650
Be Strong in the Lord, 647
Best Robe, The, 625
Beyond Your Understanding,
    Do Not Try to Go, 112, 449
Bible, Treatment Not
    Explained in, 411
Bind on Earth, Whatsoever
    Ye Shall, 617
Birth, The New, 628
Black magic, 208, 215

Bladder Trouble, 472
Bless and Curse Not, 623
Blind force, Soul as, 40
Blind Lead the Blind, When the, 614
Blood Troubles and Skin Diseases, 467
Bodily perfection, Meditations on,
    247
Body
    Definition of, 51
    Form Within the Formless, 364
    Hereafter, 556
    Man awakes with a, 207
    The Objective Man Is, 374
    The resurrection, 208
    Spirit, Soul and, 38, 40
    That Which Changes, 363
    unconscious without the thinker,
      The, 22
    the unity of all, 73
    What Is the, 207, 555
    Without Mind Has No Volition,
      80, 434
Boils, 467
Bondage
    Freedom or, 369
    There Is No, 254, 476
Book, The vibration of a, 190
Bounty, The Divine, 597
Brain does not think, The, 22
Bread Alone, Man Shall Not Live by,
    593
Brief Reminders on How to Give a
    Spiritual Treatment, 517
Bring Thought into Line with Reality,
    330
Burden, Freedom from, 161
Business
    Definition of, 89
    A Practitioner's, 413

C

Capacities, Normal psychic, 195
Causation
    Absolute, 365
    Definition of, 282

Cause
    of Evolution, Intelligence Is the, 531
    Evolution Is Effect Only, and
      Involution Always, 531
    of Human Troubles, The, 608
    Perfect Effect Is Produced by
      Perfect, 221
    True Thought Deals with First, 334
Cause and effect, 56, 364
    Definition of First Cause, 42, 284,
      713
    cause of psychic phenomena, 202
Causes and conditions, 150, 425
    of psychic manifestations, 209
Center of God-Consciousness,
    Man a, 71, 158, 378, 519
Chance, Nothing happens by, 68
Changeless, The, 55, 339, 351
    Definition of, 48
Changeless Reality, 97, 426, 625
Changeless Spirit, The, 58
Changes, That Which, 363
Character, high, Definition of, 228
Charm
    Definition of, 228
    How to create personal, 183
Child-Like Faith, The, 606
Children
    As Little, 616
    Treating, 127
    Wisdom is Justified of Her,
      605, 606
Choice
    Definition of, 77, 749
    Individuality and, 73
Choose, We Are Allowed to, 433
Choosing Thought, 96
Christ
    Joint Heirs with, 640
    The Triumphant, 552
Christ, The, 173
    and Antichrist, 84, 244
    Logos, Definition of, 77
Cinema pictures, Definition of, 51
Circulation, The Law of, 603
Clairaudience, 196, 282, 714

Clairvoyance, 196, 214, 282, 714

Clear Thinking, Healing Is, 113, 438

Cloth and Old Garments, New, 603

Clothing, Immortal, 645

Colds, Influenza and Grippe, 471

Comforter, The Holy, 635

Commandments, The Two Great, 618

Communication

    mental, 210

    spirit, 210

    Subjective, 181

Communication, Is There Spirit, 558

Companionship, Meditations on

    Divine, 251, 663

Completeness, Meditations on, 249

Completion, The Eternal, 628

Complex, Removing the, 460

Compromises, God Never, 429

Concentration, 224, 282

Concept of a Successful Man, The, 612

Concepts Limit Us, Only Our

    Own, 435

Condemn, God Does Not, 624

Condemnation

    Self, 624

    There Is No, 639

Condition, Turn Entirely from

    the, 427

Conditions, Causes and, 150, 425

    Definition of Conditions, 52, 79

    necessary for best results in psychic

        work, 187, 214

    prenatal, 79, 287, 705, 742

Confession of Mistakes, The, 652

Conflict

    Definition of, 78, 715

    of desire, 234

Confusion, No, 405

Congestion, 126

Conscious

    and unconscious thought, 23, 442,

        500

    idea, Definition of, 48

    mind, Definition of, 42, 282

    mind in God and man, 32, 282,

        715

Conscious Thought, Disease Is Not

    Always Due to, 111, 438

Consciousness

    Cosmic, 45, 164, 182, 532

    Definition of, 78

    Streams of, 189, 289, 751

Constant Prayer, 649

Constipation, 457

    Healing, 125

Contains All Knowledge, 323

Control, emotional, Definition of,

    229

Conversation Be in Heaven,

    Let Your, 331

Conviction, 407

Convictions of Life Eternal,

    Personal, 563

Correspondence, The Law of, 155,

    285, 508, 697, 754

Correspondents, The Law of, 638

Cosmic Consciousness, Illumination

    and, 164, 213

Country, The Far, 621

Create, How Can Spirit, 359

Created by Man, Evil Is, 650

Creation

    eternal, 39

    Forms of spirit or, 38

    God's Will for His, 641

    Meaning of, 38

    The voice of God in, 36

Creation, God and, 600

    In the Beginning, 337

    The Endless, 646

    The Story of, 338

Creative

    medium, Definition of, 49, 282, 716

    medium, Thought and, 89

    order, sequence of, 224

    power, Man's marvelous, 224

Creative, All Thought Is, 313

Creative Principle, How We Use, 358

Crystal gazing, 198, 215

Curse, modern, 198

Curse Not, Bless and, 641

Cycle of necessity and Karmic law, 91

D

Dead, Ghosts and phantasms

    of the, 197

Deafness, 475

Deals with First Cause, True

    Thought, 334

Deals Only with Thought, Mental

    Practice, 425

Decision, Definition of, 78, 717

Deductive reasoning, 54, 68, 282,

    360, 717, 729, 745

Deductively, The Soul

    Reasons, 360

Deep Inquiry, A, 36, 340

Defiles, That Which, 614

Definite, Mental Work Is, 324

Definite Plan, 145, 494

Definition of Spirit, The, 350

Demonstrate

    a Home, How to, 146, 495

    Liberty, How to, 643

Demonstrating the Law, 484

Demonstration, 95, 148, 467, 717

    or bringing things to pass, 136

    Let Us Not Fool Ourselves

        about, 417

    our part in, 137, 141

    by proof, 154

    When and What Is a, 416

Depend upon Principle, 116

Describing the Infinite, 339

Desire, 232, 235, 283, 717

    The conflict of, 234

Destructive Use of the Law, 482

Diabetes, 472

Difference Between Prayer and

    Treatment, The, 399

Different Methods of Treatment, 414

Difficulty, The great, 36

Discovery

    greatest of all time, Mind, 21,

        344

    first great, 20, 344

    greatest ever made, 74, 725

    of laws, 345

Discovery (*cont.*)
 of race-thought, the, 25
 that thought reached others, 25
Disease
 Definition of, 89, 718
 is impersonal, 109, 437
 is mental, 113, 115
 not always due to conscious
  thought, 111, 438
 not an entity, 126
Disposal, Limitless Power at Man's,
 312
Disturbances
 Kidney, Bladder and Liver, 472
 Stomach and Bowel, 473
Divine Bounty, The, 597
Divine companionship, 136, 488,
 613, 718
 Meditations on, 251, 252, 663
 nature, Man re-enacts the, 300
Divine Forgiveness, 617
Divine Ideas, The, 331, 342, 644,
 718, 723, 734
Divine Mental Picture, A, 57, 367
Divine Nature Is in Every Man, 315
Do Not Try to Go Beyond Your
 Understanding, 112, 449
Doers of the Word, 651
Does Not Argue, God, 620
Done unto Us, It Is, 393
Doubt
 Remove, 129
 How to remove, 115
Doubts, Have no, 112
Dress, Definition of, 229
Duality
 and science, 35
 in philosophy, 35
 Results of belief in, 34
 in theology, 34

E

Earth
 The Meek Shall Inherit the, 594
 Whatsoever Ye Shall Bind on, 617

Ectoplasm, Theory of, 201
Eczema, 467
Eden, The Garden of, 284
Effect
 Cause and, 56, 364
 of Intelligence, Evolution
  Is an, 531
 A Perfect Cause Must Produce a
  Perfect, 221
Effect, Cause and, 56, 364
 Definition of First Cause, 284, 713
Effective Prayer, A Formula for, 618
Embodiment, If We Have a Real,
 143, 490
Emmanuel—God-with-us, Definition
 of, 77, 283, 720
Emotion
 and intellect, 234
 of sex, The, 234
Emotions, Congested, 233, 649
Endless Creation, The, 646
Energy, Telekinetic, 201, 289, 752
Entering the Kingdom of Reality, 601
Enthusiasm, Definition of, 228, 721
Entity
 Disease not an, 126
 Soul Never an, 360
 Subjectivity Never an, 360
Equivalents, Mental, 151, 490
Essential to Happiness, Prayer Is, 401
Eternal, Personal Convictions of
 Life, 563
Eternal Completion, The, 628
Ether
 Mind and, 359
 of Science, The, 207, 557
Evil
 God Knows No, 602
 Good Only, Not Good and, 319
 Is Created by Man, 650
 No ultimate, 161, 754
 The problem of, 64, 106, 218, 371
Evolution, 244, 283, 529, 722
 The aim of, 86, 195
 Further, 169
Expansion, Mental, 643

Expectancy of Good, Fill the Mind
 with the, 331
Experience, Man's, 66
Experience, The Need of Spiritual, 608
Experiment, A wonderful, 69
Explained in the Bible, Treatment Is
 Not, 411
Expressed, See Life, 148, 486
Eye
 The Seeing, 612
 The Single, 197

F

Facts, Many are waking up to the, 69
Factors necessary for dynamic
 personality, 227
Failures, No, 153, 506
Faith, 403, 503, 722
 The Altar of, 586
 Always a Power, 403
 Available to All, 405
 Based on Knowledge, 404
 Believing, Ask in, 670
 The Child-Like, 606
 Conviction As Leading to, 407
 Hath Made Thee Whole, Thy, 603
 Knows, 493
 Looks to the Invisible, 493
 The Mental Approach to, 403
 Mental Assertion Elevated to
  Realization, 503
 Misplaced, 404
 Must Not Be Lukewarm in Our, 406
 The Negative Use of, 404
 No Confusion in Healing by, 405
 The Prayer of, 492, 652
 The Technique of Acquiring, 406
 Understanding, 404
 Vitalizing, 406
Fall, The meaning of the, 219
Fallen Man, The, 622
False Growths (Tumors, Cancer,
 Gallstones) 126, 459
Far Country, The, 621
Fasting and Prayer, 615

Fate, 147, 723

Father
Who Sees the Son Sees the, 635
Who Seeth in Secret, The, 586

Father-Mother God, 54, 350, 611
Definition of, 46, 283, 723

Father and Son, The Real, 606

Father's House Always Open,
The, 625

Father's House Are Many Mansions,
In My, 634

Fatigued, Why People Become, 453

Favorites, The Universe Never
Plays, 310

Fear, Irritation, Agitation and, 233

Fear, No, 129

Fed, They That Hunger Shall Be, 594

Feet and Legs, 459

Female, Male and, 236

Feminine, Definition of, 50, 283, 723

Fevers, 470

Fill the Mind with the Expectancy of
Good, 331

First Cause
Definition of, 42, 284, 713
True Thought Deals Directly
with, 334

First Great Discovery, The, 20, 344

Foes, A Man's, 605

Food, Thoughts about, 476

Fool Ourselves, Let Us Not, 417

Force, Explanation of Soul as
blind, 51, 54, 348, 384, 724

Force, Thought, 95, 494, 724

Forgiveness, Divine, 617
Jesus Forgives a Man and Heals
Him, 602

Form
Definition of, 52, 284, 724
The idea must take, 121
or mirror of matter, 104, 724

Form Within the Formless, 364
Body is, 364

Formless and the formed, 73

Forms, 57
of Spirit, or creation, 38

Formula for Effective Prayer, A, 618

Free Spirit, Definition of, 45, 724

Freedom
or Bondage, 369
Implies Possibility of Suffering, 370
Evil Is the Misuse of the
Law of, 64, 371
Is Not Mysterious, The Road to,
313

Freedom
from burden, 161
The meaning of, 63
We are bound by our own, 93

Freedom to Do, Say and Think, 63,
706

Friends, Attracting, 141, 502

Fruit, That Ye Bear Much, 636

G

Garden of Eden, The, 219, 725

Garments, New Cloth and Old, 603

General Summary of Four Sections of
Science of Mind, 573

Genuineness, Need for simplicity,
humility and, 229

Ghosts and phantasms of the dead, 197
sometimes can speak, 197

Give Us What We Take, God Can
Only, 627

Given, To Him Who Hath Shall
Be, 611

Gives to Us but Ourselves,
No One, 622

God
Man reënacts the nature of,
67, 368
within, Meditations on the spirit
of, 269
Universal Mind, or Spirit, Is 316
Worship of, 33

God Can Only Give Us What We
Take, 627

God-Consciousness, Man a
center of, 71

God and Creation, 600

God
Does Not Argue, 620
Does Not Condemn, 624
Does Not Punish, 750
Does Not Punish the
Mathematician, 329
Forgives, How, 597
Infinite Personality, 171, 547
in Creation, The Voice of, 36, 340
in the Beginning, 337
Is One of Liberty, The Law of, 642
Knows No Evil, 602
Knows No Sin, 642
Man Re-Enacts the Nature of,
67, 368
Never Compromises, 429
Now Are We the Sons of, 640
One with, 71, 315, 378, 397
The Armor of, 677
The Father-Mother, 54, 350, 611
The "Personalness" of, 355
The Power at the Heart of, 607, 695
The Pure in Heart Shall See, 595
The Thought of, 39, 341
The Threefold Nature of, 32, 349
The Voice of, 36, 340
The Word of, 341

God
in creation, The voice of, 36, 340
Definition of, 171, 725
Father-Mother, Definition of, 46,
283, 723
Infinite Personality, 171, 547
as Law, the word of, 31
The law of, 25, 37, 68, 238
and man, 67
and man, Conscious mind in, 32
The personality of, 242, 571, 685
The thought of, 39, 160, 341
The threefold nature of, 32
The word of, 31, 37, 39, 45, 46,
77, 285, 341

God Turns to Us As We Turn
to Him, 620, 624

God-with-us, Emmanuel, Definition
of, 77, 283, 720

Gods, Many, 33, 61, 385

God's Will for His Creation, 641

Good, Fill the Mind with the
  Expectancy of, 331

Good, Hold to the, 172

Good Harvest, Good Thoughts
  and a, 610

Good manners, Definition of, 228

Good Only, Not Good and Evil, 319

Good Thoughts and a Good
  Harvest, 610

Governing Prayer, Laws, 400

Grace, Salvation and, 220

Great Awakening, The, 623, 642

Great Commandments, The Two, 618

Great Discovery, The First, 20, 344

Great "I AM," Definition of the, 42

Great Price, The Pearl of, 613

Great Question "Why," The, 21

Great Search, The, 607

Greatest Discovery of All Time . . .
  Mind, The, 21, 344

Grippe, Colds and Influenza, 471

Growths, 136

Growths, False, 459

H

Habit, 192, 284, 725

Habits
  Are Acquired and Treated, How, 451
  are formed, How, 93
  are healed, How, 119

Halo, 191, 284, 726

Hand, Grasping objects without
  the, 200

Hands, Arms and, 459

Happiness, Prayer Is Essential to, 401

Happiness, Success and, 488

Happy, Learning to Trust Will Make
  Us, 314

Hardening of the Arteries, 462, 467

Harmony of life, Meditations on
  the, 256

Harvest, Good Thoughts and
  Good, 610

Hath Shall Be Given, To Him
  Who, 611

Hay Fever, Asthma and, 464

Headache, 118, 453

Heal, How to, 110, 128, 438

Healed, What Can Be, 120, 448

Healing
  The Basis of Mental, 133
  of the Centurion's Servant,
    The, 601
  Definite work in, 152
  by Faith, No Confusion in, 405
  Intemperance, 488
  Is Clear Thinking, 113, 439
  the Lunatic, 616
  The Medium of, 116, 442
  Must Come First of All, Self-, 600
  Not Limited by Principle, 107
  Spiritual Mind, 391, 435, 500, 590
  What We Understand about, 101,
    430

Heals Him, Jesus Forgives a Man
  and, 602

Health
  Definition of, 79, 229
  Function of, 473, 474

Heart Be Troubled, Let Not
  Your, 634

Heart of God, The Power at the, 607,
  695

Heart Shall See God, The Pure in,
  595

Heart Trouble, 461

Heaven, 284, 726
  Let Your Conversation Be in, 331

Heirs with Christ, Joint, 640

Help, Whom Shall We Try to, 604

Hereafter
  Personal Convictions of Life, 563
  Shall We Have a Body, 556
  Shall We Rest in the, 562

Hidden, Nothing Can Be, 604

Hidden Within, The Seed of
  Perfection Is, 317

High Blood Pressure, 467, 469

High Places, Wickedness in, 647

History of the individual, Reading
  the, 188

History Proves the Reality of
  Truth, 619

Holy Comforter, The, 635

Home, How to Demonstrate a, 146,
  495

Hope a Subtle Illusion, 326

House, The Great, Definition of, 47

House Are Many Mansions, In My
  Father's, 634

House Is Always Open,
  The Father's, 625

How Can Spirit Create, 359

How God Forgives, 597

How Habits Are Acquired and
  Treated, 451

How Laws Are Discovered, 29, 345

How Much Can We Believe, 318

How to Approach the Spirit, 609

How to Demonstrate a Home, 146,
  495

How to Demonstrate Liberty, 643

How to Give Treatment, Not
  Explained in the Bible, 411

How to Heal, 110, 128, 438

How to Use It, 328

How We Understand Its Operation,
  353

How We Use the Creative Principle,
  358

Hudson's Theory, 200

Human Aura, The, 191

Human Troubles, The Cause of, 608

Humility, 229, 727

Humor, Sense of, 228

Hunger Shall Be Fed, They That, 594

I

"I AM," Definition of the Great, 42

Idea
  Definition of conscious, 48
  must take form, The, 121

Ideas, The Divine, 183, 644, 718

Ideas, We deal with, 111

Ideation, Spiritual Mind Healing, 419

If We Have a Real Embodiment, 143, 490

If We Know, 490

Illumination, 184, 727

Illumination and cosmic consciousness, 164, 532

Illusion, Hope a Subtle, 326

Illusion
of matter, Definition of, 53
of Mind, Definition of, 50, 284

Images of thought, Definition of, 79

Imagination and Will, 221, 728

Immanent power, Meditations on, 262

Immaterial, Definition of, 49, 728

Immortal Clothing, 645

Immortality, 57, 215, 366, 572
The meaning of, 206, 284, 572, 728
Psychic phenomena and, 177, 206

Impersonal
Definition of, 50, 728
Disease Is, 109, 437
The Universe, 321

Impressions, Where Do We Get Our Mental, 346

In the Beginning, God, 337

In My Father's House Are Many Mansions, 634

Incarnation, The Act of, 392

Incarnation of Spirit, The, 64

Incentive, Definition of, 229

Incurable to Spirit, No Disease Is, 108, 446

Individual
Reading the history of the, 188
What the mystics have taught about the, 163

Individuality, 60, 106
and choice, 73
Definition of, 77, 285, 728
means self-choice, 73
Realization of, 162
what it really means, 63

Indivisible Whole, The, 122, 168, 521

Inducing Thought, 97, 395

Inductive reasoning, 54, 68, 360
Definition of, 285, 729

Infinite, Describing the, 339

Infinite, The law is, 134, 329, 482

Infinite is personal to all, The, 173

Infinite Personality or God, 171, 547

Influence and obsession, Personal, 193

Influenza and Grippe, Colds, 471

Information, Receiving, 152

Inherit the Earth, The Meek Shall, 594

Inherited tendencies, Definition of, 79, 729

Inner Light, The, 260, 549, 640, 670

Inner Man, The, 645

Inner powers cause for thought, 202
sense awakens, The, 21

Inquiry, A Deep, 36, 340

Insanity, 194, 285, 729
Healing of, 128
Treating, 454

Insomnia, 474

Inspiration, 285, 729
Meditations on, 264
Subjective mind and, 182

Instinct and intuition, 164

Instinctive man, 19, 285, 729

Intangible, All Principles Are as, 328

Intellect
Definition of, 78, 285, 730
Emotion and, 234

Intelligence
Absolute, 59, 357
Creative, of the Universe, 309
Subjective, 357

Intemperance, Healing, 488

Intuition, Instinct and, 164

Intuition Is Spirit Knowing Itself, 373

Inventor, Helping an, 144

Invisible, We Must Trust the, 332

Irritation, Agitation and Fear, 233

Is There Spirit Communication, 558

It, How to Use, 328

It Does, What, 320

It Is Done unto Us, 393

It Works, The Way, 316

Its Nature, 351

Its Operation, How We Understand, 353

Itself, The Action of Spirit Within, 74, 352, 363

Itself, Spirit Knows, 37, 341, 352

Itself, The Thing, 309, 315

J

Jesus, Joint Heirs with, 640

Jesus, Lessons from the Teaching of, 593

Jesus, mind of, 648

Jesus, The Power of, 165

Jesus, The Spirit That Raised, 484

Jesus, Why saints have seen, 190

Jesus Forgives a Man and Heals Him, 602

Jesus Had Such Power, Why, 593

Jesus Knew Their Thoughts, And, 610

Jesus
Careful preparation of, 240
as a Saviour, 242

Joint Heirs with Jesus, 640

Judge Not, That Ye Be Not Judged, 598

Justified of Her Children, Wisdom Is, 605

K

Karma, Definition of, 78, 285, 730

Karmic law, 55, 78, 81, 95, 348
The cycle of necessity and, 91
Definition of, 51

Kidney Trouble, Treating, 472

Kingdom Is Like Leaven, The, 613

Kingdom and the Mustard Seed, The, 613

Kingdom of Reality, Entering the, 601

Knew Their Thoughts, And Jesus, 610

Knowing No Other, Definition of, 46, 731

Knowledge, Contains All, 323

Known, The Secret Already, 325
Knows Itself, Spirit, 37, 341
Knows No Evil, God, 602
Knows No Sin, God, 642

L

Law, 92
    Demonstrating the, 484
    Is Infinite, The, 134, 482
    Is No Respecter of Persons,
        The, 329, 651
    Love Rules Through, 322
    Mind in Action Is, 51, 93, 381
Law
    of Attraction, The, 285, 500, 694
    of Circulation, The, 603
    of Correspondence, The, 155, 285,
        508, 697, 754
    of Correspondents, The, 638
    of God Is One of Liberty, The, 642
    Oneness with All, 94, 382
    Spirit and Mental, 135, 487
    The Destructive Use of the, 382
Law
    Definition of, 51, 285, 731
    is Infinite, The, 134, 482
    is Mind in action, 93, 381
    Karmic, 51, 55, 91, 95, 730
    Mental, 31, 135, 312, 348, 487,
        735, 751
    of action and reaction, 91, 744
    of belief, A, 90
    of correspondence, The, 155, 285,
        508, 697, 754
    of God, 25, 37, 68, 238
    of Mind, The, 24, 157, 567, 570,
        572
    of reflection, 140, 156, 502
    Oneness with all, 94, 382
    Only one, 86, 114
    Servant of the Word, 37
    Spirit and Mental, 135, 487
    Subjective, 89, 380, 450
    The cycle of necessity and
        Karmic, 91

The possibilities of the, 135
The word of God as, 31
Unity with, 71
We are dealing with, 90, 382
Laws
    Governing Prayer, 400
    how discovered, 29, 345
    Mental, 348
    Mental and spiritual, 67
Lead the Blind, When the Blind, 614
Learned All It Can/Should Through
    Suffering, The World Has, 63,
    241, 369
Learning to Trust Will Make Us
    Happy, 314
Leaven, The Kingdom Is Like, 613
Legs, Feet and, 459
Lesson of Nature's Laws, The, 66
Lessons from the Teaching of
    Jesus, 593
Let Not Your Heart Be Troubled, 634
Let Us Not Fool Ourselves, 417
Let Your Conversation Be in
    Heaven, 331
Levitation, 201, 285, 732
Liberty, The Law of God Is
    One of, 642
Life
    Ascending Scale of, 644
    Definition of, 44, 285, 732
    expressed, See, 148, 496
    Meditations on the
        harmony of, 256
    Never Limit Your View of, 428
    Nothing Supernatural about the
        Study of, 311
    Shall Lose It, Who Would
        Save His, 614
    Self-existent, 243
    The Three Planes of, 632
    The Unity of, 648
Life Eternal, Personal
    Convictions of, 563
Life Expressed, See, 148, 496
Light of the World, The, 633
Light, The great, 162

Light, The Inner, 260, 549, 640, 670
Like Leaven, The Kingdom Is, 613
Limit on Principle, Place No, 97, 428
Limit to Thought, No, 327
Limit Your View of Life, Never, 428
Limitations, We Set Our Own, 397
Limitless Medium, 82, 375, 570
Limitless Power at Man's
    Disposal, 312
Limit Us, Only Our Own
    Concepts, 435
Little Children, As, 616
Live by Bread Alone, Man
    Shall Not, 593
Liver Trouble, 472
Logos
    Definition of, 77, 285, 733
    The perfect, 46
Look Only at What You Want, 144,
    427
Lord, Be Strong in the, 647
Lose It, Who Would Save His Life
    Shall, 614
Love, 106, 158, 235, 238, 322, 519,
    545, 620, 634
    Definition of, 228, 285, 733
    Sex not necessary to the expression
        of, 235
    The true meaning of, 235
Love Rules Through Law, 322
Lunatic, Healing the, 616
Lung trouble, Healing, 123
Lung Trouble, Treating, 455

M

Macrocosm, Definition of, 47, 285,
    733
Magic, Black, 198
Magnetism, Definition of, 295
Male and female, 236
Man
    The Concept of a Successful, 612
    The Divine Nature Is in Every, 315
    Evil Is Created by, 650
    The Fallen, 622

The Inner, 645

The Son of, 629

Where from and Why, 206, 555

Man a center of God-consciousness, 71, 713, 725, 728, 758

and his manifestation, Medium between, 137

awakes with a body, 207

born perfect, 109

come from and why, Where did, 206, 555

comes through subjectivity, 108

Conscious mind in God and, 32

God and, 32

is identified in mind, 85

Nature waits on, 67

reënacts the nature of God, 67, 368

The answer is in, 170

Threefold nature of, 32, 349

to the universe of spirit, The relation of, 66

Man forgiven and healed by Jesus, 602

Man and God, What We Believe about, 335

Man Re-Enacts God, 106, 434

Re-Enacts the Nature of God, 67, 361

Man Shall Not Live by Bread Alone, 593

Mania, 202, 214, 286, 733

Manifestation, Medium between man and his, 137

Causes of psychic, 209

Manners, Definition of good, 228

Man's

creative power marvelous, 224

experience, 66

nature, What psychology teaches about, 70

whole trouble, 239

unity with the whole, 70

Man's Disposal, Limitless Power at, 312

Man's Foes, A, 605

Man's Relationship to the Spiritual Universe, 368

Man's Self-recognition, Nature Waits on, 20, 343

Mansions, In My Father's House Are Many, 634

Many, Multiplicity, Definition of, 53, 286, 737

Masculine, Definition of, 47, 286, 733

Mathematician, God Does Not Punish the, 329

Matter

Definition of, 734

illusion of, 53, 161, 691, 734

last stages of, 72

Resolved into a Universal Ether, 72, 375

subjective mind and unformed, 104

unconscious form or mirror of, 104, 286, 724, 736

Maya, Definition of, 51, 286, 358, 734

Meaning

of the Fall, The, 219

of Freedom, The, 63

of Immortality, The, 206, 554

of love, The true, 235

Meat Which Perisheth, The, 632

Meditation, 175, 734

Medium

A universal, 26

between man and his manifestation, 137

creative, 49, 282, 716

Limitless, 82, 375, 570

of all thought, power and action, 51

of healing, The, 116, 442

Thought and the creative, 89

through all, Mental, 30

Soul the Creative, 288, 750

Universal Subjectivity Is Limitless, 82

Medium of Healing, The, 116, 442

Meek Shall Inherit the Earth, The, 594

Memory, 128, 345

Definition of, 78, 286, 734

Seat of, 181

Suggestion becomes, 30

Mental

atmospheres, 183, 538

Communication must be, 210

Definition of, 77

Disease is, 115

equivalents, 151, 490, 721

influence, General theory of obsession and, 194

law, 31, 348; Spirit and, 135, 437

medium through all, 30

pictures, 187; many, 191

and spiritual laws, 67

state do we go out, In what, 208

treatment is real, 107

Mental Approach, The, 403

Mental Atmospheres, 89, 183, 286, 538, 712, 716, 734

Mental Equivalents, What Do We Mean by, 490

Mental Expansion, 643

Mental Healing, The Basis for, 392

Mental Impressions, Where Do We Get Our, 346

Mental Law, Spirit and, 135, 487

Mental Laws, 348

Mental Picture, A Divine, 367

Mental Practice Deals Only with Thought, 425

Mental Work Is Definite, 324

Mental World, Treatment Is a Spiritual Entity in the, 332

Mentality, Projecting the, 198

Merciful Shall Obtain Mercy, The, 595

Mercy, The Merciful Shall Obtain, 595

Messages, Deep telepathic, 188

Metaphysics, 238, 286, 735

Metaphysics and Physics, 353

Method, The Scientific, 322

Methods of Treatment, 87, 414, 735

Microcosm, Definition of, 77, 286, 736

Mind
of history, The, 185
Only one, 59, 354
or Soul, Mirror of, 104, 286, 736
or Spirit, conscious, 42, 104, 282, 715
Proof of, 29
subconscious, 49, 356
Subjective, 71, 78, 81, 83, 104, 116, 180, 356, 373
the greatest discovery of all time, 21, 344
The law of, 24, 61, 157, 385, 570, 572
The race, 185, 240, 744
The self-knowing, 76, 188, 715, 749
Universal, 25, 134, 289, 755
We argue in, 92
Wrong use of, 92
Mind
Activity of the One, 393
and Ether, 359
and Inspiration, Subjective, 182, 537
Healing, A Recognition of the Power of, 419
Healing, Spiritual, 391, 437
in Action, Law Is, 93, 381
Only One, 59, 354
or Spirit, Is God, Universal, 316
That Jesus Used, The, 648
The Greatest Discovery of All Time, 21, 344
The Renewing of the, 641, 647
The Science of, 28, 29, 134, 311, 316, 346, 610
The Subjective, 180, 182, 373, 536
with the Expectancy of God, Fill the, 331
Mind
and Inspiration, Subjective, 182, 537
and unformed matter, subjective, 104
at work, Unconscious, 24
Definition of conscious, 42, 282

Definition of illusion of, 50, 284
in action, Law is, 93, 381
in God and man, Conscious, 32, 282, 715
is the actor, 110
Minds, Only Two Names, There Are Not Two, 311
Mirror
of matter, Unconscious form or the, 104, 286, 724, 736
of Mind, or Soul, 104
of the subjective, The, 225
Misplaced Faith, 404
Mistakes
The Confession of, 652
No, 149, 154, 497
Perfect Action, No, 497
Misunderstanding, Healing a, 147
Morbidities, Religious, 599
Mother-Father God, Definition of, 46, 283, 723
Multiplicity, Many
Definition of, 53, 286, 737
Unity and, 56, 365
Mustard Seed, The Kingdom and the, 613
Mysterious, The Road to Freedom Is Not, 313
Mystery in Truth, No, 326
Mystic, Definition of, 286, 523
Mysticism and the psychic sense, True, 160
Mystics have taught, What the, 160, 523; about the individual, 163

N

Names, There Are Not Two Minds, Only Two, 311
Nature, Its, 351
Nature
of God, Man reënacts the, 67, 361
of God, The Threefold, 32, 349
waits on man, 67
waits on man's self-recognition, 20, 343

What psychology teaches about man's, 70
Nature Is in Every Man, Divine, 315
Need of Spiritual Experience, The, 608
Nerve Troubles, 465
Nervousness, 131
Never Limit Your View of Life, 428
Never Plays Favorites, The Universe, 310
New Birth, The, 628
New Cloth and Old Garments, 603
No Confusion, 405
No Failures, 153, 506
No Limit to Thought, 327
No Mystery in Truth, 326
No One Gives to Us But Ourselves, 622
No Personal Responsibility, 143, 507
No Sensation in Treatments, 114, 441
Normal state, 194, 737
Normalcy, 162, 737
Not Something for Nothing, 481
Nothing Can Be Hidden, 604
Nothing Can Hinder the Operation of the Law, 259
Nothing Supernatural about the Study of Life, 311
Now Are We the Sons of God, 653

O

Obesity, 471
Objective
Definition of, 52
The subjective obeys the, 71
Obsession, 193, 287, 738
of discarnate spirits, 193
and mental influence, General theory of, 194
personal influence and, 193
Obstetrics, 470
Obstructions to thought, No, 190
Obtain Mercy, The Merciful Shall, 597
Occupation, Definition of, 79, 738
Old Garments, New Cloth and, 603

Omnipotence, Definition of, 48, 738
Omniscience, Definition of, 48, 738
One, Abiding in the, 636
One with God, 71, 397
One Mind
 Activity of the, 393
 Only, 59, 354
Oneness with All Law, 94, 382
Only-All, Definition of, 48, 738
Only One Mind, 59, 354
Only Our Own Concepts Limit
 Us, 435
Open, The Father's House Always,
 625
Operation, How We Understand Its,
 353
Opinion, Our Estimate of
 Reality, 373
Opportunity, 153, 507, 738
Order, The sequence of the creative,
 224
Originality, 228, 738
Ourselves, Let Us Not Fool, 417
Own Answer, Prayer Is Its, 142, 402
Own Limitations, We Set Our, 397

P

Pain
 Healing, 118
 Treating, 452
Paralysis, 126, 463
Part in demonstration, Our, 141
Passive and receptive, Definition of,
 51, 738
Passive Treatment, 325
Pattern for Thought, A, 648
Peace, Definition of, 45, 287, 739
Peace of Mind, Treatment for, 480
Pearl of Great Price, The, 613
People Become Fatigued, Why, 453
People get tired, Why, 120
Perfect Action, No Mistakes, 497
Perfect Cause and a Perfect
 Effect, 221, 426, 570
Perfect Universe, The, 221, 426,

Perfection
 Definition, 287, 739
 Meditations on bodily, 247
 Seeing, 123, 444
Perfection Is Hidden Within, The Seed
 of, 317
Perisheth, The Meat Which, 632
Personal
 charm, how to create, 183
 influence and obsession, 193
 readings, 188
Personal Convictions of Life
 Eternal, 563
Personal Responsibility, No, 143, 507
Personality
 Attraction of, 148, 501
 Definition of, 78, 287, 740
 Factors necessary for a
  dynamic, 227
 of God, 242, 571, 685
 God—Infinite, 171
Personalness, Definition of, 47, 740
"Personalness" of God, The, 355
Persons, The Law Is No
 Respecter of, 329, 651
Phantasms of the dead, Ghosts
 and, 197
Phenomena, The cause of psychic, 740
Philosophy
 Duality in, 35
 leads man's thought, 36
Physics, Metaphysics and, 371
Picture, A Divine Mental, 57, 367
Pictures (cinema)
 Definition of, 51
 Mental, 187, 191
Place No Limit on Principle, 97, 428
Places
 The atmosphere of, 184
 Wickedness in High, 647
Plan, Definite, 145, 494
Planes of Life, The Three, 632
Plastic, Soul as, 51, 55, 287, 741
Plays Favorites, The Universe
 Never, 310
Poise, Definition of, 45, 287, 741

Poison of Any Kind, 463
Poor, Why Are People, 26
Possibilities of the law, 135
Poverty, Definition of, 79, 287, 741
Power
 Always a, 403
 at the Heart of God, The, 607, 695
 at Man's Disposal, Limitless, 312
 of the Word, The, 127, 275, 444
 The Word of, 631
 Why Jesus Had Such, 593
 Within, The, 397
Power
 and action, Medium of all
  thought, 51
 Definition of, 44, 287, 741
 of Jesus, The, 165
 Man's marvelous creative, 224
 Meditations on immanent, 262
 must be controlled, The
  psychic, 194
 should not be forced, The
  psychic, 211
 and strength, Definition of, 228
 of the word, 127, 462; Meditations
  on the, 275
Powers
 Abnormal psychic, 195
 cause for thought, Inner, 202
Practice, Deals Only with Thought,
 Mental, 425
Practice, The highest, 165
Practice of Spiritual Mind
 Healing, 510
Practitioner
 The Business of the, 88, 118, 424,
  453
 Definition of, 287, 742
 The First Requisite, 412
 What one does, 86, 122
 What one must know, 113, 122
 Who Is a, 96, 113, 133, 412
Prayer, 399, 742
 Constant, 649
 of Faith, The, 492, 652
 Fasting and, 615

Prayer (cont.)

A Formula for Effective, 618

Is Essential to Happiness, 401

Is Its Own Answer, 124

Laws Governing, 400

Scientific, 600

The Secret of, 596

and Treatment, 399

Prayer is its own answer, 142, 402

Predestination, 640

Prenatal conditions,

Definition of, 79, 287, 742

Preparation, Jesus' careful, 240

Price, The Pearl of Great, 613

Principle

Depend on, 116

Healing power not limited by, 107

How We Use the Creative, 358

Place no limit on, 97, 428

of Prosperity, The, 142

Re-stated, The, 324

Principles Are as Intangible, All, 328

Problem of evil, The, 64, 106, 218,
371

Profession, Definition of, 79

Projecting the mentality, 198

Proof

Demonstration by, 154

of Mind, 29

Prophecy, The Spirit of, 202, 540

Prosperity, The principle of, 142

Proves the Reality of Truth,
History, 619

Psyche, Definition of, 78, 287, 743

Psychic

best results in psychic work, 187,
214

capacities, normal, 195, 211, 561

manifestations, What causes, 209

phenomena, The cause of, 202

phenomena and immortality, 177,
208

power must be controlled, the,
194; should not be forced, 211

powers, Abnormal, 195

sense, True mysticism and the, 160

Psycho-analysis, 130, 237, 288, 743

Psychology teaches about man's
nature, What, 70

Psychometry, 186, 188, 214, 743

Punish, God Does Not, 329, 750

Punishment

Sin and, 64, 239, 329

and Reward, 371, 730

What of Reward and, 562

Pure in Heart Shall See God, The, 595

Purpose, Definition of, 78, 744

Purpose of Science of Mind, The, 610

Purpose of Treatment, The, 409

Purposefulness, Definition of, 42, 744

Q

Quench Not the Spirit, 649

Quickens or Retards, Thought, 599

R

Race-Mind, The, 185, 744

Race-Suggestion, 109, 537

Definition of, 79, 288, 744

Race-Thought, Discovery of, 25

Raised Jesus, The Spirit That, 639

Rappings, 201

Reaction, The law of action and, 91,
744

Reading Thought, 31, 347

Readings, Personal, 188

Real Father and Son, The, 606

Reality

Back of the appearance is the, 122

Bring Thought into Line with, 330

Changeless, 97, 426, 625

of Truth, History Proves the, 619

Realization, 174, 288, 744

of individuality, 162

Reason

deductive only, 48, 51, 79, 226

Inductive and Deductive, 68, 77

The two ways to, 68

Reasons Deductively, The Soul, 360

Receptive, and passive, 51, 739

Re-Enacts the Nature of God, Man,
67, 368

Reflection

Definition of, 53, 746

Law of, 140, 156, 502

Rejoice Evermore, 649

Relation of man to the universe of
spirit, The, 66

Relativity, Absoluteness and, 217

Religious Morbidities, 599

Reminders on How to Give a
Spiritual Treatment, Brief, 517

Removing the Complex, 460

Renewing of Your Mind, The, 641,
647

Repeating Treatments, 117, 452

Repression and Sublimation, 231

Requisite for Practitioners, The
First, 412

Respecter of Persons, The Law Is
No, 651

Responsibility, No Personal, 143,
420, 507

Re-stated, The Principle, 324

Rest in the Hereafter, Shall We, 562

Result of Our Own Thinking,
The, 380

Results

Definition of, 52, 79, 748

in psychic work, Conditions
necessary for best, 187, 214

of belief in duality, 34

Resurrection body, The, 208, 557

Retards, Thought Quickens or, 599

Reward

and Punishment, What of, 562

of True Visioning, The, 605

Righteousness and, 64

Rheumatism, 476

Riches, Definition of, 79, 288, 748

Riddle of Simplicity, A, 321

Righteousness and Reward, 64

Road to Freedom Is Not Mysterious,
The, 313

Robe, The Best, 625

Rules through Law, Love, 322

S

Saints have seen Jesus, Why, 190
Salvation
    and grace, 220
    of all, Ultimate, 161, 528, 754
Save His Life Shall Lose It, Who
    Would, 614
Saviour, Jesus as a, 242
Saw Him Afar Off, The Father, 624
Scale of Life, The Ascending, 644
Schoolroom, Handling a, 155
Science, 28, 60, 345, 512
    Definition of, 288, 749
    Duality and, 35
    The "ether" of, 207, 557
Science of Ether, The, 207, 557
Science of Mind, The, 29, 134
    How to Use, 328
    The Purpose of, 610
    The Thing Itself, 309
    The Way It Works, 316
    What It Does, 320
Scientific Method, The, 322
Scientific Prayer, 600
Search, The Great, 607
Seat of memory, 181
Secret, The Father Who Seeth in, 596
Secret Already Known, The, 325
Secret of Prayer, The, 596
See God, The Pure in Heart Shall,
    429
See Life Expressed, 148, 486
Seed, The Kingdom and the
    Mustard, 613
Seed of Perfection, The, 317
Seed of thought, The, 119
Seeing Eye, The, 612
Seeing Perfection, 123, 444
Sees the Son Sees the Father,
    Who, 635
Seeth in Secret, The Father Who, 596
Self-analysis, 238, 749
Self-choice, Individuality means, 63,
    73, 526
Self-Condemnation, 624

Self-confidence, Definition of, 228,
    749
Self-existent
    Definition of, 43, 288, 749
    Life, 243
Self-Healing Must Come First
    of All, 600
Self-knowing mind, The, 58, 70, 288,
    749
Self-propelling, Definition of, 43,
    288, 749
Self-Recognition, Nature Waits on
    Man's, 20, 60, 343
Sensation in Treatments, No, 114,
    441
Sense of humor, 228
Sequence of the creative order,
    The, 224
Servant, The Healing of the
    Centurion's, 601
Servant of the Spirit throughout the
    Ages, 51, 54, 312
Servant of the Word, Law as, 37
Service, Definition of, 228, 749
Set Our Own Limitations, We, 397
Sex
    becomes destructive, When, 235
    emotion of, 234
    not necessary to the expression of
        love, 235
    spirit of, 231
Shall We Have a Body Hereafter, 556
Shall We Rest in the Hereafter, 562
Simplicity, A Riddle of, 321
Simplicity and genuineness, suitable
    humility, 229
Simplified, The Story of Creation,
    338
Sin, God Knows No, 625
Sin and punishment, 64, 239
Sincerity, Definition of, 228
Single Eye, The, 197
Skin, 458
Skin Diseases, Blood Troubles and, 467
Smelling where there is nothing to
    smell, 200

Son, The Real Father and, 606
Son, The Stay-at-Home, 626
Son of Man, The, 629
Son Sees the Father, Who Sees
    the, 635
Sons, The Two, 620
Sons of God, Now Are We the,
    653
Sonship, Definition of, 77, 288,
    750
Soul, 81, 356
    as blind force, 40
    Definition of, 49, 78, 86, 288, 750
    as immaterial, 49, 728
    Mirror of mind or, 104
    as neutral, 50
    as plastic, 51
    as unchoosing, 49, 754
Soul and Body, Spirit, 371
    Never an Entity, 360
Soul of Man
    the Creative Medium, 50, 104
    One with the Soul of the
        Universe, 80, 372
    Reasons Deductively, The, 360
    the Seat of Memory, 181
Space, Definition of, 53, 288, 750
Spirit
    communication, 210, 558
    Definition of, 42, 77, 288, 750
    Definition of conscious
        mind or, 42, 282
    Definition of Free, 45, 724
    Definition of Universal, 104, 290,
        755
    is expressed, The, 232
    knows itself, 37, 341
    of God within, Meditations on the,
        269
    of prophecy, The, 202, 540
    of sex, The, 231
    or creation, Forms of, 38
    The givingness of, 241
    The incarnation of, 64
    The relation of man to the universe
        of, 66

Spirit

Communication, Is There, 558

Create, How Can, 359

How to Approach the, 618

Is God, Universal Mind or, 316

Its Nature, 351

and Mental Law, 135, 487

Spirit

of Adoption, The, 639

the Changeless, 55, 426

Knowing Itself Is Intuition, 373

Knows Itself, 37, 341

No Disease Is Incurable to, 447

not affected by apparent condition, 426, 466

of Prophecy, The, 202, 540

Quench Not the, 649

Soul and Body, 371

That Raised Jesus, The, 639

the Whole of, 81, 372

within Itself, The Action of, 56, 352

Spirit Works for Us by Working Through Us, 317

Spirits, We do not control, 211

Spiritual

Definition of, 77, 289, 751

laws, Mental and, 135, 487

Spiritual Entity in the Mental World, Treatment Is a, 332

Spiritual Experience, The Need of, 608

Mind Healing, 391, 437

Spiritual Treatment

Brief Reminders on How to Give a, 517

Mental Treatment and, 756

Spirituality, Definition of, 229

Stages of matter, The last, 72

Stammering, 131

State

mental, we go out in, 208

Normal, 194, 737

of trance, The, 195

Stay-at-Home Son, The, 626

Stomach and Bowel Troubles, Treating, 473

Story, The Application of the, 627

Story of Creation Simplified, The, 338

Stream of thought, Entering the, 601

Streams of Consciousness, 189, 289, 751

Strength, Definition of power and, 228

Strong, When We Are, 631

Strong in the Lord, Be, 647

Study of Life, Nothing Supernatural about the, 311

Subconscious mind, Definition of, 49

Subjective

communication, 181

Definition of, 49, 78, 751

law, 89, 380

mind, 180, 536; and inspiration, 182, 537; and unformed matter, 104; builder of the body, 23, 29, 30, 162; not unconscious, 92; seat of memory, 181

mirror of the, 225

obeys the objective, 71

Subjective Intelligence, 357

Subjective Law

The Divine Creative Medium, 89, 380

The Potential of All Things, 484, 569

Subjective Mind, the, 180, 536

Subjective Mind and Inspiration, 182, 537

Subjectivity

lesson in, 203

Never an Entity, 360

The Operation of Law, 504

Suggestion and, 181

Sublimation, Repression and, 231

Subtle Illusion, Hope a, 326

Success

Attracting, 504

Definition of, 228, 751

and Happiness, 488

Successful Man, The Concept of a, 612

Suffering All It Can/Should, The World Has Learned Through, 63, 241, 369

Suggestion, Race, 109, 537

Suggestion

Auto, 79

becomes memory, 30

and subjectivity, 181

Suggestions for Treatments, 447

Summary of Nature of Being, 384

Summary of Spiritual Mind Healing, 419, 510

Ideation, 419

Practice, 510

Supernatural about the Study of Life, Nothing, 311

Supply, 478, 752

T

Table tipping, 201, 215

Tact, Definition of, 228, 752

Take, God Can Only Give Us What We, 627

Teaching of Jesus, Lessons from, 593

Technique of Acquiring Faith, The, 406

Telekinetic energy, 201, 289, 752

Telepathic messages, Deep, 188

Telepathy, 196, 289, 539, 752

does not explain everything, 210

Tendencies, Inherited, 79, 354, 729

Tenderness, Definition of, 228

That Which Changes, 363

That Which Defiles, 614

That Ye Bear Much Fruit, 636

The Act of Incarnation, 392

The Action of Spirit Within Itself, 74, 352, 363

The Altar of Faith, 596

The Application of the Story, 627

The Armor of God, 647

The Ascending Scale of Life, 644

The Atmosphere of Our Thinking, 394

The Basis for Mental Healing, 392

The Beginning, 337

The Best Robe, 625

The Brotherhood of Man, 162, 526, 611

The Cause of Human Troubles, 608

The Child-Like Faith, 606

The Concept of a Successful Man, 612

The Confession of Mistakes, 652

The Definition of Spirit, 350

The Destructive Use of the Law, 482

The Divine Bounty, 597

The Divine Ideas, 331, 342, 644, 718, 723, 734

The Endless Creation, 646

The Eternal Completion, 628

The Ether of Science, 207, 557

The Fallen Man, 622

The Far Country, 621

The Father-Mother God, 46, 54, 283, 350, 611, 723

The Father Who Seeth in Secret, 586

The Father's House Always Open, 625

The First Great Discovery, 20, 344

The First Requisite, 412

The Great Awakening, 623, 642

The Great Search, 607

The Greatest Discovery of All Time . . . Mind, 21, 344

The Healing of the Centurion's Servant, 601

The Holy Comforter, 635

The Indivisible Whole, 122, 168, 521

The Inner Light, 260, 549, 640, 670

The Inner Man, 645

The Kingdom Is Like Leaven, 613

The Kingdom and the Mustard Seed, 613

The Law of Circulation, 603

The Law of Correspondence, 155, 285, 508, 697, 754

The Law of Correspondents, 638

The Law of God Is One of Liberty, 642

The Law Is Infinite, 134, 482

The Law Is No Respecter of Persons, 329, 651

The Light of the World, 633

The Meaning of Immortality, 206, 554

The Meat Which Perisheth, 476

The Medium of Healing, 116, 442

The Meek Shall Inherit the Earth, 594

The Mental Approach, 403

The Merciful Shall Obtain Mercy, 595

The Mind That Jesus Used, 648

The Need of Spiritual Experience, 608

The New Birth, 628

The Operation of Law, 504

The Pearl of Great Price, 613

The Perfect Universe, 221, 426

The "Personalness" of God, 355

The Power at the Heart of God, 607, 695

The Power Within, 397

The Power of the Word, 127, 275, 444

The Prayer of Faith, 492, 652

The Principle Re-stated, 324

The Pure in Heart Shall See God, 595

The Purpose of the Science of Mind, 610

The Purpose of Treatment, 409

The Real Father and Son, 606

The Renewing of the Mind, 647

The Renewing of Your Mind, 641

The Result of Our Own Thinking, 380

The Reward of True Visioning, 605

The Road to Freedom Is Not Mysterious, 313

The Science of Mind, 29, 134

The Scientific Method, 322

The Secret Already Known, 325

The Secret of Prayer, 596

The Seed of Perfection Is Hidden Within, 317

The Seeing Eye, 612

The Single Eye, 197

The Son of Man, 629

The Soul Reasons Deductively, 360

The Spirit of Adoption, 639

The Spirit of Prophecy, 205, 540

The Spirit That Raised Jesus, 639

The Stay-at-Home Son, 626

The Story of Creation Simplified, 338

The Subjective Mind, 180, 536

The Technique of Acquiring Faith, 406

The Thing Itself, 309, 315, 334

The Thought of God . . . The Word of God, 341

The Three Planes of Life, 632

The Threefold Nature of God, 32, 349

The Two Great Commandments, 618

The Two Sons, 620

The Triumphant Christ, 552

The Unity of Life, 80, 161, 646

The Universe Holds Nothing Against Us, 627

The Universe Impersonal, 321

The Universe Never Plays Favorites, 310

The Voice of God in Creation, 36, 340

The Way It Works, 316

The Way of Treatment, 410

The Word of Power, 631

The World Has Learned All It Can/ Should Through Suffering, 63, 241, 369

Theology, Duality in, 34

Theory
  Hudson's, 200
  of ectoplasm, 201

There Are Not Two Minds, Only Two Names, 311

There Is No Condemnation, 639

They That Hunger Shall Be Fed, 594

Things
  Definition of, 53, 753
  Thoughts are, 101, 396
  into thoughts, Resolve, 121
  Time will prove all, 202

Think correctly, Man realizes he must, 27

Thinker
  Body unconscious without the, 22
  We do not see the, 22
Thinking
  The Atmosphere of Our, 396
  Each is the logical result of his
    own, 89
  Healing is clear, 113, 439
  The Result of Our Own, 380
  in treatment, 112
Thoroughness, Definition of, 228
Thought
  Choosing, 96
  Conditions are controlled by, 26
  and the creative medium, 89
  Deals Directly with First Cause,
    True, 334
  Definition of images of, 79
  Disease not always due to
    conscious, 11, 438
  does, What right, 118
  Entering the stream of, 601
  force, 95, 494, 724
  Inducing, 97, 395
  Inner powers cause for, 202
  new basis of, 24
  No obstructions to, 190
  of God, The, 39, 341
  Philosophy leads man's, 36
  power and action, Medium
    of all, 51
  reached others, Another great
    discovery, 25
  Reading, 31, 347
  The conscious and the
    unconscious, 23, 442, 500
  The seed of, 119
Thought, Tuning in on, 186, 538
Thought, A Pattern for, 648
Thought Atmosphere, 500
Thought Back of Mind Healing,
  The, 726
Thought, Each of Us Is Today the
  Result of His, 89
Thought
  Force, 95, 396

Inducing, 97, 395
into Line with Reality, Bring, 330
Is Creative, All, 313
Mental Practice Deals Only
  with, 425
Thought
  of God, The, 39, 341
  No Limit to, 327
  Reading, 31, 347
  Retards or Quickens, 599
  Tuning in on, 186, 538
Thoughts
  Are Things, 144
  Deal only with, 425
  about Food, 476
  go, Where our, 29
  and a Good Harvest, Good, 610
  Interesting, 202
  And Jesus Knew Their, 610
  Resolve things into, 111
  We do not send out, 124
Threefold nature of God, 32, 349
Threefold nature of man, 32, 349
Throat trouble, 126
Thy Faith Hath Made Thee
  Whole, 603
Time
  Definition of, 52, 753
  has come to know the Truth,
    The, 69
  will prove all things, 202
Times, The Greatest Discovery
  of All, 21, 344
To Him Who Hath Shall Be
  Given, 611
Trance, The state of, 195, 289, 753
Treated, How Habits Are Acquired
  and, 451
Treating
  Arms and Hands, 459
  Asthma and Hay Fever, 464
  Blood Troubles, 467
  Boils, 467
  Cancer, 459
  Child-Birth, 470
  Children, 443

Colds, Influenza and Grippe, 471
the Complex, 117, 460
Constipation, 457
Deafness, 475
Diabetes, 472
Eczema, 467
False Growths, 126, 459
Feet and Legs, 459
Fevers, 470
Gallstones, 459
Hardening of the Arteries, 462, 467
Headache, 118, 453
Heart Trouble, 461
High Blood Pressure, 467
Insanity, 128, 454
Insomnia, 474
Intemperance, 488
Kidney, Bladder and Liver
  Disturbances, 472
Lung Trouble, 123, 455
Nerve Troubles, 465
Obesity, 471
Obstetrics, 470
Pain, 452
Paralysis, 126, 463
Poison of Any Kind, 463
Rheumatism, 476
Skin Diseases, 467
Stomach and Bowel Troubles, 473
Tumors, 459
Vision, 125, 456
Weather Conditions, 475
Treating for activity, 152
  Guidance in, 128
Treatment
  Argument in, 131
  of children, 443
  Explanation of, 137, 146, 289,
    409, 753
  is real, Mental, 107
  Methods of, 87, 414, 717
  Thinking in, 112
Treatment
  for Fatigue, 435, 454
  for Peace of Mind, 480
  No Sensation in, 114, 441

Treatment
Not Explained in the Bible, 411
Prayer and, 399
The Purpose of, 409
Repeating, 117, 129, 452
Suggestions for, 447
The Way of, 409
What It Is, 409
Treatment
Active, Not Passive, 325
Brief Reminders on How to Give a
Spiritual, 517
Different Methods of, 414
as a Spiritual Entity in the Mental
World, 332
Treatments
No sensation in, 114, 441
Repeating, 117, 129, 452
Trinity of Being, 32, 346, 349
Triumphant Christ, The, 552
Trouble, Man's whole, 239
Troubled, Let Not Your
Heart Be, 634
Troubles, The Cause of Human, 608
True Thought Deals Directly with
First Cause, 334
True Visioning, The Reward of, 605
Trust the Invisible, We Must, 332
Trust Will Make Us Happy,
Learning to, 314
Truth
Allness of, 57
Definition of, 45, 289, 754
demonstrates itself, The, 115
History Proves the Reality of, 619
is known, The, 170
No Mystery in, 326
The time has come to know
the, 69
Tuning in on Thought, 186, 538
Turn Entirely from the
Condition, 427
Turning within, 166
Turns to Us As We Turn to Him,
God, 620, 624
Two ways to reason, The, 68

U

Ultimate, 754
Look to the, 149
evil, No, 161, 754
salvation of all, 161, 528
Unchoosing, Soul as, 49, 754
Unconscious
Definition of, 78, 754
mind at work, 24
thought, The conscious and the, 23
Understand about Healing,
What We, 101, 430
Understand Its Operations,
How We, 353
Understanding, 198
Do Not Try to Go Beyond
Your, 112, 449
Faith, 404
Unity
of all, 161
of all body, The, 73
complete, 74, 584
Definition of, 46, 755
with Law, 71
Meditations on, 277
and multiplicity, 56, 375
with the Whole, Man's, 70, 220
Unity, 33, 46, 74
how can we reconcile suffering and
lack with, 379
Modern science teaches, 379
of Life, The, 80, 161, 646
One with the Law of the
Whole, 71, 315, 378
Universe
Holds Nothing Against Us,
The, 627
Impersonal, The, 321
Man's Relationship to the, 368
Never Plays Favorites, The, 310
The Perfect, 221, 426
Man One with the Soul of the,
80, 372
Universal
medium, 26, 31

mind, 25, 289, 755
spirit, Definition of, 104,
290, 755
Universal Mind, or Spirit, Is God,
316
Universal Subjectivity Limitless
Medium, 82, 375
Universe
is alive, The, 40
The perfect, 221, 426
of spirit, The relation of man to
the, 66
Us, It Is Done unto, 193
Use It, How to, 328
Use of the Law, The Destructive, 382
Use the Creative Principle,
How We, 358
Use of mind, The wrong, 92, 133
Used, The Mind That Jesus, 648

V

Vibration of a book, The, 190
View of Life, Never Limit Your, 428
Viewpoints, Different, 65
Vision, 125, 456
Visioning, The Reward of True, 623
Visualize, How to, 223
Vitalizing Faith, 406
Vocation, Definition of, 79, 758
Voice
Definition of, 229
of God in creation, The, 36, 340
Voices, Independent, 197
Volition, 58, 342
Definition of, 77, 758

W

Waits on Man's Self-Recognition,
Nature, 20, 343
Want, Look Only at What You, 144,
427
Want, Why We Are in, 621
Way It Works, The, 316
Way of Treatment, The, 410

Ways of reasoning, Two, 54

We Are Allowed to Choose, 433

We Must Trust the Invisible, 332

We Set Our Own Limitations, 397

Weather Conditions, 475

What Can Be Healed, 120, 448

What Do We Mean by Mental
Equivalents, 490

What Is the Body, 207, 555

What Is a Demonstration, When
and, 416

What Is Incurable, 108, 446

What Is a Mystic, 523

What Is a Practitioner, 96, 113, 133,
412

What It Does, 320

What It Is, Treatment, 409

What of Reward and
Punishment, 562

What You Want, Look Only at, 144

What We Understand about
Healing, 101, 430

Whatsoever Ye Shall Bind on
Earth, 617

When the Blind Lead the Blind, 614

When We Are Strong, 631

When and What Is a
Demonstration, 416

Where Did Man Come from and
Why, 206, 555

Where Do We Get Our Mental
Impressions, 346

Who Is Christ, 543

Who Is a Practitioner, 96, 113, 133,
412

Who Sees the Son Sees the
Father, 635

Who Would Save His Life Shall Lose
It, 614

Whole, The Indivisible, 122, 168, 521

Whole, Man's unity with the, 70

Whole, Thy Faith Hath Made
Thee, 603

Wholesomeness, Definition of, 228

Whom Shall We Try to Help, 604

Why Jesus Had Such Power, 593

Why People Become Fatigued, 453

Why We Are in Want, 621

Wickedness in High Places, 647

Will
Definition of, 43, 77, 758
Imagination and, 221, 728

Will for His creation, God's, 641

Wisdom Is Justified of Her
Children, 605

Within, The Power, 397

Within, Turning, 166

Word
Alone Is Conscious, The, 39
Definition, 45, 290, 758

of God, The, 37, 77, 341, 714,
733, 755, 758; as Law, 31
Law as servant of the, 37
Meditations on the power
of the, 275
Power of the, 127, 444

Word
Doers of the, 651
of God, The Thought of God,
The, 341
of Power, The, 631
The Power of the, 127, 275,
444
The Starting Point of All Creation,
46

Words used in Universal Chart,
Metaphysical meaning of
the, 42, 77, 104, 180

Work in healing, Definite, 117

Works, The Way It, 316

Works for Us by Working Through
Us, Spirit, 317

World, The Light of the, 633

World Has Learned All It Can/Should
Through Suffering, The, 63, 241,
369

Worship of God, 32

Writing
Automatic, 199
Independent, 199

DISCOVER THE WORLD OF ERNEST HOLMES

The Landmark Guide to Spiritual Living

The Science of Mind: The Definitive Edition

A Philosophy, a Faith, a Way of Life

978-0-87477-865-6 (hardcover)

978-0-87477-921-9 (paperback)

The Science of Mind: The Complete Edition

Features the original 1926 and expanded 1938

editions—published together for the first time

978-1-58542-842-7 (paperback)

A Treasury of Inspiration and Guidance

A New Design for Living

978-1-58542-814-4

Love and Law

978-1-58542-302-6

The Hidden Power of the Bible

978-1-58542-511-2

The Essential Ernest Holmes

978-1-58542-181-7

365 Science of Mind

978-1-58542-609-6

Prayer

978-1-58542-605-8

Simple Guides for Ideas in Action

Creative Mind 978-1-58542-606-5

The Art of Life 978-1-58542-613-3

Creative Mind and Success 978-1-58542-608-9

This Thing Called You 978-1-58542-607-2

Discover a Richer Life 978-1-58542-812-0

Living Without Fear 978-1-58542-813-7

Think Your Troubles Away 978-1-58542-841-0

It's Up to You 978-1-58542-840-3

Coming Soon

Questions and Answers on the Science of Mind

TARCHER
PENGUIN

For more information:
www.penguin.com
www.tarcherbooks.com
www.scienceofmind.com